CRIME & PUNISHMENT IN THE LONE STAR STATE

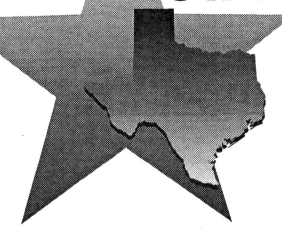

Mark A. Stallo
Keith N. Haley
Collin County Community College

McGraw-Hill, Inc.
Primis Custom Publishing

New York   St. Louis   San Francisco   Auckland   Bogotá
Caracas   Lisbon   London   Madrid   Mexico   Milan   Montreal
New Delhi   Paris   San Juan   Singapore   Sydney   Tokyo   Toronto

McGraw·Hill

A Division of The McGraw·Hill Companies

**CRIME AND PUNISHMENT
IN THE LONE STAR STATE**

Copyright © 1997 by The McGraw-Hill Companies, Inc. All rights reserved. Printed in the United States of America. Except as permitted under the United States Copyright Act of 1976, no part of this publication may be reproduced or distributed in any form or by any means, or stored in a data base retrieval system, without prior written permission of the publisher.

McGraw-Hill's Primis Custom Publishing consists of products that are produced from camera-ready copy. Peer review, class testing, and accuracy are primarily the responsibility of the author(s).

6 7 8 9 QSRQSR 9 8 7 6

ISBN-13: 978-0-07-303313-6
ISBN-10: 0-07-303313-8

Editor: Judith A. Wetherington
Cover Design: Jessica L. Weber
Printer/Binder: Quebecor Printing Dubuque

ABOUT THE AUTHORS

Mark Stallo is president of the International Association of Crime Analysts, a non-profit organization which strives to improve information sharing, training, and professionalism in the analytic field. He is also a Sergeant for the Dallas Police Department. He is assigned to the Computer/Crime Analysis Unit and has been employed by the City of Dallas for over 17 years. Among his assignments at the police department are Central, Northeast, and Southwest Patrol Divisions, Police Personnel (Recruiting), Planning and Research and Crime Analysis.

He has received a B. S. from the University of Cincinnati, in Criminal Justice, 1979. He also received a M. S. from the University of Texas at Dallas (UTD), in Management and Administrative Science, in 1985, and a Master of Public Affairs (MPA) from UTD in 1995. He has lectured for a number of agencies and organizations and has taught at the Collin County Community College.

Keith Haley is currently the Dean and Professor in the School of Criminal Justice at Tiffin University in Ohio. Mr. Haley was most recently the Coordinator of the Criminal Justice Program at Collin County Community College in Texas and has served as the Executive Director of the Ohio Peace Officer Training Council that state's law enforcement standards and training commission; Chairman of the Criminal Justice Department at the University of Cincinnati which offers B.S., M.S., and Ph.D. degrees in criminal justice; police officer in Dayton, Ohio; Community School Director in Springfield, Ohio; Director of the Criminal Justice Program at Redlands Community College in Oklahoma; an electronics repairman and NCO in the Marines. Haley holds the following degrees: B.S. in Education from Wright State University; M.S. in Criminal Justice from Michigan State University. Haley has written several books, many articles and papers, and has served as a consultant to many public service, business, and industrial organizations.

TABLE OF CONTENTS

CRIME AND CRIMINALS

The Killer Cadets	1
Crime in Texas: 1996	14
Crossing	22
McDuff was Free to Kill	31
The Public Hell of Bob Carreiro	43
Family Violence Intervention: Attitudes of Texas Officers	52
Merchant of Death	60
CRITICAL THOUGHT AND ANALYSIS WORKSHEET	65

CRIMINAL INVESTIGATION

See No Evil	69
Sweet Song of Justice	89
The Last Ride of the Polo Shirt Bandit	96
Gang Rape	107
The Texas Rangers Revisited: Old Themes and New Viewpoints	117
The Twilight of the Texas Rangers	132
The Death Beat	144
CRITICAL THOUGHT AND ANALYSIS WORKSHEET	155

PROSECUTION AND JUDGMENT

Rush to Justice	159
The High Times of Gerry Goldstein	163
Does DaRoyce Mosley Deserve to Die?	172
Crime and Punishment in Dallas	183
CRITICAL THOUGHT AND ANALYSIS WORKSHEET	189

CORRECTIONS AND PUNISHMENT

Who Determines who Will Die? Execution Laws show a Wide Variance	193
Death Row Granny	198
Prison Guards and Snitches	213
A Guard in Gangland	226

Judicial Reform and Prison Control:
    The Impact of *Ruiz vs Estelle* on a Texas Penitentiary   237
Private Prisons in Texas: The New Penology for Profit   257
The Great Texas Prison Mess   271
Capital Punishment 1995   283
CRITICAL THOUGHT AND ANALYSIS WORKSHEET   299

ISSUES IN CRIMINAL JUSTICE

Market of Death, Market of Fun:
    Anatomy and Analysis of a Gun Show   303
Ice-T, No Sugar: Law Enforcement and Political Reactions
    To the Gangster Rap "COP KILLER"   319
Black Before Blue   336
The Rookie   346
Regulation of Sexually Oriented Businesses   357
Crime Analysis: The Administrative Function   368
Mapping Software and Its Value to Law Enforcement   381
CRITICAL THOUGHT AND ANALYSIS WORKSHEET   387

INTRODUCTION

Today crime has everyone's attention. Far too many stories come forth from friends, media broadcasts, and personal experiences about how people's lives are forever altered by the misguided and evil actions of others. We are still lacking solid solutions to the crime problem, but experts and laymen alike persist in their attempts to find answers. Many of the most strident efforts to fight crime in America are found in Texas.

As criminal justice academicians we strive to teach both theory and practice, but find that we often fall short in exciting students about the stunning reality of crime, criminal behavior, and the operations of our system of justice. <u>Crime and Punishment in the Lone Star State</u> attempts to correct that oversight. The book is divided into five sections: Crime and Punishment; Criminal Investigations; Prosecution and Judgment; Corrections and Punishment; and Issues in Criminal Justice. You will find in these sections stories that will bring shock, dismay, compassion, quandary, and perhaps even anger about the treatment of the victims of crime, the agents of justice, and even the suspected and convicted criminals.

We hope you enjoy the book and learn something that you didn't know.

Crime and Punishment in the Lone Star State will satisfy students and professors in a number of ways:

1. Provide detailed stories and cases about Texas, the state where we live and study;

2. Give instructors an extra learning resource which they can utilize in one or all of the following courses: Crime in America; Introduction to Criminal Justice; Criminal Investigation; or in more specialized police, court, and corrections courses;

3. Eliminate the need in many cases of having to put articles of local interest on reserve in the library;

4. Infuse local reality into an existing course in the criminal justice curriculum;

5. Give students an opportunity to apply textbook theories and explanations to crimes, cases, criminals, and problems which mean the most to them, those in their own state and localities;

6. Allow students to use and develop their critical thinking and analysis skills by completing the Critical Thought and Analysis exercises at the end of each article;

7. Allow students and instructors to practice their discussion skills by using the Criminal Justice Discussion Methods list included in the Appendix;

8. Explore the rich heritage, exuberance, and spirit of Texas and its people as they contend with the problems of crime and criminal justice, perhaps our most pressing social issue.

We leave you with the same wish a kindly table server in a good restaurant would offer, "enjoy", but also "think" for there is much here to contemplate.

Crime and Criminals

THE KILLER CADETS

They were young. They were smart. They were successful. They were in love, and they were cold-blooded murderers. Why did they do it?

By Skip Hollandsworth

THEY PROBABLY FIRST SAW EACH OTHER at a cross-country meet in the early autumn of 1995 -- two high school girls from neighboring small towns, competing in the two-mile run. There is no evidence that they said hello. Nor did they shake hands, as athletes sometimes do before the start of a race. Why should they have? It is doubtful the two girls even knew one another's names. Adrianne Jones was a clear complexioned, sun-kissed blonde, the kind of girl one boy described as "not just good looking, but I *mean, good looking."* Diane Zamora, thinner and not as tall, was mesmerizing in a different way – her hair was a dark circle around her face, her eyes dark as well, her eyebrows like slim shadows against her skin. "When she looked at you," another boy would later say, "it was hard for you to stop staring back."

There was no reason for you to imagine that they had anything in common beyond cross-country. They were just pretty teenagers in the full bloom of youth. What Adrianne and Diane did not know about each other was that they were both drawn to the same boy – a lean, muscular high school senior named David Graham, who was described as "the perfect guy" by one classmate and "a brilliant student" by another. David was the kind of young man any parent would admire. He made straight A's. He said "yes, sir" and "yes, ma'am" when talking to adults. "His life was so unblemished," and one woman who knew him, "that he didn't so much as throw a spitwad in school."

At the time, David had chosen to be with Diane, who was called "the disciplined one" of the family by her mother because she would start studying for school before six o'clock each weekday morning. But David could not deny that there was something intriguing and somewhat seductive, about Adrianne, who was called "bubble butt" by her mother because her bottom moved in sexy little circles when she walked. He found himself spending more time with her, talking to her, staring at her hazel eyes.

The two girls lined up for the Cross-country race, waiting for the starters gun. It would not be long before they would meet again.

I thought long and hard about how to carry out the crime, I was stupid, but I was in love.
 -- From the killer's confession

IN THE EARLY MORNING HOURS OF DECEMBER 4, 1995, A FARMER driving along a desolate county road saw the body of a teenage girl on the ground behind a barbed-wire fence. At first, he thought he was looking at road kill. The girl's face was nearly unrecognizable. One bullet hole was in her left cheek, another in her forehead. She had been hit so hard on the left side, of her head that the part of the skull above her ear was caved in like a pumpkin. She was wearing flannel shorts and a gray T-shirt that read, "UIL Region I Cross Country Regionals 1995." Within hours, police officers identified her as Adrianne Jones, a sixteen-year-old high school sophomore from the town of Mansfield, southeast of Fort Worth.

A former farming community built around a grain elevator, home to an old indoor rodeo arena and some cheery antique stores along Main Street, Mansfield was one of the last places in the Dallas-Fort Worth corridor that still felt like a small town. In 1984, looking for a safe, place to raise his family, Bill Jones moved his wife, Linda, and his three children -- Adrianne and two younger brothers -- to Mansfield from the Dallas area. He found a modest neighborhood where the homes were clustered together, the yards were like little green squares, and the echoey souvenir of children at play drifted down the streets. Jones, who made his living repairing heavy construction equipment, was a no-nonsense, bearded man who kept his heavy brown work boots on when he arrived home at the end of the day, wearing them even when he sat in his easy chair. He also was determined to keep a tight rein on his children -- especially Adrianne, who was known as AJ. "I truly felt that if we had some rules that kept her away from teenage temptations," Jones said. "we'd be okay." It was only that autumn that he had allowed Adrianne to stay out past nine o'clock on weekends. If she told him she was going to a movie or to Six Flags Over Texas in nearby Arlington with friends, he would often make her produce a ticket stub when she came home to prove where she had been. He had nailed her bedroom windows shut so she couldn't sneak out of the house at night.

It could hardly be said that Adrianne was a rebel. She took advanced honors courses, studied at least two hours a night, and was a good athlete. After she hurt her knee playing for the girls soccer team, she decided to join the girls' cross-country team to get in better shape, and she became so good in the two-mile run that she helped the team qualify for the November regional meet in Lubbock. "Her school spirit was just so awesome," said Carla Hays, an editor for the school newspaper, the *Mansfield Uproar,* bestowing upon Adrianne one of the greatest compliments a high school girl could receive. "I could see her becoming a cheerleader someday." She also managed to work twenty hours a week at Golden Fried Chicken, a local fast-food restaurant. "She was my superstar employee," said the restaurant manager, Tina Dollar. "I made her the cashier at the drive-through window because she knew how to put a smile on everyone's face. She wore a hat with a smiley face drawn on the visor, and after taking an order, she'd say funny things to the customers like, 'Okay, drive forward to the ninety-ninth window to get your food!'"

Adrianne thrived on attention, especially when it came from the teenage boys around town. One of Adrianne's closest friends, Tracy Bumpass, called her "a big flirt." Linda Jones, a chatty blonde who worked during the day as a massage therapist in a Mansfield hair salon, said her daughter would spend two hours putting on makeup just to make it look like she wasn't wearing any: "When I asked her why she went to such trouble to put her makeup on before she went out of the house, she said, 'Mom, you never know who you might meet.'"

And there were plenty of high school guys who wanted to meet her. They'd slowly cruise by the Joneses' house. A few of the courageous ones would pull into the driveway to talk to Adrianne, who would be waiting for them in the front yard, casting quick glances toward the front door to see if her father was watching them. "I'm sure lots of guys really liked Adrianne," said Sydney Jones, a friend and former soccer teammate. "She was the kind of girl who would say hi to you in the hallway at school even if you didn't know her."

It was precisely Adrianne's popularity that was going to make the investigation into her murder so difficult. (Because Adrianne's body had been found in the outskirts of the Dallas suburb Grand Prairie, detectives from that city's police department -- Dennis Clay and Dennis Meyer -- and their boss, deputy police chief Brad Geary, were put in charge of the case.) Adults who are murdered rarely have more than a couple of dozen people close to them. But a high school student crosses paths with hundreds of other students every day. And it quickly became clear to the detectives that Adrianne knew her killer, or killers. There was no sign at the crime scene that she had struggled. There were no marks that her hands or legs been restrained. Nor was there any indication that someone had broken into her house or had gone through her window to abduct her. Furthermore, an autopsy found no evidence that Adrianne had been sexually assaulted, which meant that this was not the act of a rapist. Adrianne's death, the cops realized, was more like an execution, the result of some colossal fury. As one investigator would later say, "It takes a cold-blooded person to shoot a pretty young girl in the face from two to four feet away. That girl was mangled, and it was sickening to look at."

Never did I imagine the heartache it would cause my school, my friend, Adrianne's family or even my community.

IT WAS A STORY THAT WOULD EVENTUALLY SEND SHOCK WAVES across the entire country: a terrifying. macabre tale that would have people everywhere asking what had to happened to the best and brightest of America's youth. At the start, however, Adrianne Jones's murder was just another killing in a small town. Because so much local media attention was then focused on the kidnapping and brutal murder of a little the girl named Amber Hagerman in Arlington. Adrianne's death barely made the front pages of the Dallas and Fort Worth newspapers. In a society long accustomed to driveby shootings and metal detectors at school entrances, dead teenagers didn't warrant the press that they once did.

But within Mansfield itself, the news had residents reeling. High school administrators set up special rooms for students to meet with counselors. A tree was planted in memory of Adrianne next to the junior varsity soccer field, more than 150 of her classmates joined hands around the tree and shouted, "Unity! Strength! Courage!" Some residents wore ribbons in her memory, and a small cross made from two branches wrapped with red electrical wire was placed where, her body had been discovered. After the family held a private funeral for Adrianne at the Methodist church, Linda Jones agreed to allow the cross-country and soccer teams to come to the church for a second memorial service. On the altar was a glamorous color photo of Adrianne, taken a few weeks earlier, that Linda planned to give her for Christmas. "Try to remember the things about Adrianne," she said in a spontaneous eulogy, trying to bolster the spirits of the students. "Do you remember the way she walked with that bubble butt of hers?" Nearly crazed with grief, Linda consulted psychics to try to find out what had happened to Adrianne. She made sure to wear some item of her daughter's almost every day either a piece of clothing or her shoes or her makeup. At night, she and Bill left the light on in Adrianne's bedroom, as if hoping their daughter would find her way back home. Kids drove past the house, staring through the open curtains, able to see Adrianne's vanity, where she had put on her makeup, her stereo, and her bookcase, which still held a couple of her Stephen King novels. Among the nearly 2,500 students at Mansfield High, it didn't take long for the rumors to start flying. "A lot of us had this weird feeling that the killer was walking the halls with us," said April Grossman, a friend of Adrianne's who also ran cross-country and played on the soccer team. "Those of us who were really close to Adrianne were scared because we thought she might have been killed because of something she knew. And we thought, will the killer come after us thinking that Adrianne had told us the secret?"

Some kids said they had heard that Adrianne used to slip out of the house to attend all-night "rave" parties as far away as Denton (an hours drive north of Mansfield). Maybe, they whispered, someone she had met at a rave wanted to kill her. Others said they had heard she knew drug dealers. There, was so much gossip about the boys Adrianne had been with that Linda went so far as to tell one reporter that her daughter was no "sleep-around." There was even a preposterous story that a close girlfriend of Adrianne's had wanted to kill her because Adrianne had told that girl's mother about getting drunk at a party. "About the only thing we didn't hear," Bill said, "was that Adrianne had been abducted by aliens.

Still, for the investigators in the case – who had come to include the Mansfield police, a Texas Ranger, and extra Grand Prairie detectives -- Adrianne's murder had all the makings of a high school whodunit. Although Texas Education Agency had named Mansfield High a mentor school (a distinction given only to the best high schools in the state), the teenagers there where like teenagers anywhere their lives often driven by insecurities, inchoate yearnings, and a provincial restlessness. Wavering in that territory that lies between childhood and adulthood, the students tried on and discarded different selves as quickly as they went through blue jeans, always searching for the perfect fit. It was here that they confronted raw new emotions, like their own budding sexuality, and here that they first attempted to make their way through such moral dilemmas as whether to "do it" or not.

Sitting outside the high school in their unmarked cars, watching students troop in and out, the detectives prepared themselves to enter the humid realm of adolescence. They talked to school officials about the students who had a knack for minor trouble. They asked other kids if they knew anyone who was jealous of or angry at Adrianne. Within days, they had compiled a long list of kids they wanted to talk to.

Bill and Linda Jones had told the police that on the night of Adrianne's death, they had reluctantly allowed her to talk on the phone past her usual ten o'clock cut-off time. Her new boyfriend, Tracy Smith, had been out of town that weekend with his parents, and he didn't call until ten-thirty. Bill and Linda didn't know Tracy that well. He was a large kid who was built like a lineman on a college football team, and he went to high school in the nearby town of Venus. Apparently, he and Adrianne had met just a couple of months earlier at the Golden Fried Chicken. Bill told Adrianne she could talk to Tracy but only for a few minutes.

During that call, Linda heard her daughter say, "Hold on, there's someone on the other line." Adrianne punched the call-waiting button and spoke quietly for a minute, then clicked back over and finish her conversation with Tracy.

"Who was that who called in?" Linda later asked.

According to Linda, Adrianne replied, "Oh, that was David from cross-country, and he's upset about something."

After talking with Tracy, Adrianne went to her room. At ten forty-five, Linda Jones saw that Adrianne was still awake, ironing her pants for school the next day. She seemed "sort of antsy," Linda said. Linda told her to turn off the lights and go to bed.

Sometime after midnight, one of Adrianne's younger brothers heard the constrained tumble of a slow-moving engine outside the house. When he looked out the window, he saw what he thought was a pickup truck driving away

The next morning, Adrianne was nowhere to be found, and Linda and Bill thought she might have risen early to go running. But when they discovered her running shoes in her bedroom, they got anxious. Linda called Lee Ann Burke, the cross-country coach at Mansfield High, and asked, "Who is someone named David on the cross-country team?

"Well, there's David Graham," Burke replied.

"Adrianne's missing," Linda said, "and I think he called her last night."

Burke was baffled. She didn't even know David and Adrianne were friends. David, a senior, was a decent cross-country athlete, but he was best known around the school for his position as battalion commander of the school's Junior ROTC program. Burke sent April Grossman to David's second-period math class to ask him if he had called Adrianne the previous night. David stared at April as if she were not making sense. "Did I talk to Adrianne? No. Why would I?"

As their investigation began, the detectives did conduct a perfunctory interview with David Graham, but they were so certain he was not involved that they didn't even try to give him a polygraph test. For one thing, David's name was not among the thirty or so listed in Adrianne's personal phone book. Nor did the detectives hear his name mentioned by any of Adrianne's friends when they asked who might have had a close relationship with her. In fact, Tracy Bumpass said that Adrianne told her all of her "deepest, darkest secrets," but not once had she ever talked about David.

Besides, David had supposedly been seen with tears in his eyes at the memorial service, seemingly stunned like everyone else that Adrianne was gone. Few students considered themselves good friends with David -- "We all knew him, but we really didn't know him, you know?" said Kenny Grant, whose locker was next to David's throughout high school -- and he certainly was not part of the school's most popular crowd. Still, he intrigued other kids. With his military buzz haircut and ramrod posture, he seemed to be a throwback to a different era. The youngest of four children, David lived with his father, Jerry Graham, a retired Mansfield elementary school principal. He was divorced from David's mother, Janice, a former teacher who lived in Houston. At the age of seven, after seeing his first air show, David told his father he wanted to become an Air Force pilot, and he never wavered from his dream. Although ROTC students at Mansfield High were usually the subjects of jokes -- "We thought of all of them in their green uniforms as sort of geeky," one girl said -- it was clear that David was going places. He was a National Merit commended student (just below the rank of National Merit semifinalist), and Congressman Martin Frost had agreed to support his application to enroll the next fall in the U. S. Air Force Academy in Colorado Springs. "Some of the more sarcastic guys in school would address him as Colonel Graham," said Jennifer Skinner, who sat near David in a government class his senior year. "But you could tell they sort of said it out of respect." Added another classmate, David Brennan, "He could fall asleep during class and then wake up and still answer the teachers questions."

David Graham might have seemed tailor-made for the military -- when he and others in the ROTC squadron presented the colors before the football games, he stood so perfectly still that people tended to watch him instead of the flag -- but he never came across as one of those overly aggressive GI Joe types. He quit the football team after his freshman year because, it was said, he didn't have the necessary ferocity to make it in Texas high school football. What's more, girls liked him for his courtly manners. Angel Lockhardt, who was on the girls' cross-country team, said David gave her rides home a few times after cross-country practice, "and he always acted like a gentleman."

Plenty of girls would have dated David -- "He was one of the last cool guys on earth," a girl who served with David in the Mansfield High ROTC would later tell a reporter -- but what few of them knew was that he already had a girlfriend. Her name was Diane Zamora, and she was a high school senior in the nearby town of Crowley. She was just as smart as David, and she was equally determined to get into one of the U.S. military academies. She was a member of the student council, the Key Club, the National Honor Society, and the Masters of the Universe, a science organization. She played flute in the marching band, and like David, she ran on her high school's cross-country team. "When you looked at the two of them together," one of Diane's relatives said, "you just knew that a great future lay before them."

The plan was to (and this is not easy for me to confess) break her young neck and sink her to the bottom of lake ...

THE FIRST MAJOR SUSPECT TO EMERGE in Adrianne's murder was a Mansfield teenager, Tara (not her real name), who lived in a trailer park and already had something of a reputation around town. A year before, she thought her boyfriend had had a sexual encounter with one of Adrianne's closest girlfriends. According to police records, Tara attacked the girl with a baseball bat, hitting her over the head, breaking her cheekbone, and leaving her with a concussion. Tara also shot and wounded her boyfriend. A restraining order was filed against Tara to keep her out of school and away from the girl she had attacked. At the hearing, Adrianne testified for her friend. Tara, in turn, allegedly told Adrianne, "I'll get you for this." Some students were convinced Tara was the killer. She fit their picture of what a killer would be: a surly, aimless individual far removed from the mainstream of suburban teenage life who had already shown her willingness to use a gun and a bat.

But the police discovered that Tara had a solid alibi, and she passed a polygraph test. Although Bill and Linda told the police they were suspicious of Adrianne's boyfriend, Tracy Smith -- Linda said he had never tried to contact the family after Adrianne's killing -- he too passed a polygraph.

Tracy did, however, give the police another clue. He said that Adrianne had told him that it was someone named Bryan who had clicked through on the phone that night. She had never mentioned David. She had said that "Bryan" was depressed and wanted to meet her that night to talk.

The detectives then learned that a Mansfield teenager named Bryan McMillen worked at an Eckerd's near a Subway sandwich shop where Adrianne once worked. According to Adrianne's friends and family, Bryan had become infatuated with Adrianne and often dropped by the Subway to see her. "He began to bother her so much that when she saw him coming, she started ducking her head behind the counter," Linda Jones said.

The investigators' suspicions were heightened when they discovered that the seventeen-year-old Bryan took four kinds of medication to battle symptoms of clinical depression. They asked him to come to the police station for an interview. According to an affidavit, Bryan first said he didn't know an Adrianne Jones. Then he admitted that he did. A detective asked him if he had talked to Adrianne the night she was murdered. Bryan said he could have talked to her, but he didn't remember. He had been drinking that night for the first time in six months, he said, and had become intoxicated. When asked why he had been drinking, Bryan said he had gotten upset because all of his friends had found girlfriends, but he hadn't. He told detectives he felt like the "odd man out."

It wasn't hard for the police to put this scenario together: a lonely boy, unable to get the beautiful blonde from the high school to pay attention to him, devising a way to meet her late at night, then losing control. The detectives bored in, asking Bryan if he had gone to Adrianne's house that night. Bryan said he might have. He said it was also possible he could have taken her somewhere. He just didn't remember, he said.

A week later, in the pre-dawn hours of December 15, 1995, police officers armed with guns and a search warrant arrived at Bryan's house. He was arrested for murder, and his pickup truck was impounded. This time, the story made the front pages of the newspapers, but several of Bryan's friends defended him, saying that he was a gentle, slightly baffled kid who would never resort to violence. Bryan's father insisted that the night of the murder, Bryan come home never left the house.

Finally, after Bryan had spent Christmas and New Year's Eve in jail, a lead prosecutor in the district attorney's office arranged for a polygraph. "He not only passed," the prosecutor said, "he passed with flying colors."

Bryan's release triggered more rumors, but no other suspects emerged. Because Adrianne's brother had said that he had seen a pickup truck, the police ran computer checks to find any student who owned one. It never occurred to anyone that the vehicle her brother had seen might not have been involved in the murder. Nor, apparently, did anyone guess that Adrianne had told Tracy about a "Bryan" to keep him from learning about her relationship with someone else. Only months later would Tina Dollar, the manager at the Golden Fried Chicken, remember that Adrianne had once pulled a small photo of a boy out of her wallet and showed it to her.

"His name is David," Adrianne had said.

... [Her] beautiful eyes have always played the strings of my heart effortlessly. I couldn't imagine life without her, not for a second did I want to lose her.

DAVID GRAHAM AND DIANE ZAMORA first met about four years before Adrianne Jones's murder, when their parents began dropping them off at a small airfield south of Fort Worth. They went there for weekly meetings of the Civil Air Patrol, an Air Force auxiliary organization that teaches the basics of the military life and leads search-and-rescue missions for downed aircraft. But there was no romance between them in their younger years. Despite her good looks, Diane was careful around guys. She did have a boyfriend during her sophomore year in high school, but the relationship was not particularly heated. When the two went out for dinner on Valentine's Day, Diane asked to be taken home at eight-thirty because she needed to study. "She kept telling us she wanted to focus on her studies and her goals instead of on guys," said her aunt Sylvia Gonzalez. "And she always made it a point to tell us she was never going to lose her virginity unless she got married. When two of her cousins got pregnant in high school, she said she couldn't believe how stupid they were. She swore that nothing like that would happen to her."

In the world of high school sexual skirmishing, Diane firmly put herself into the camp of "good girls." A girl who goes too far, she would often say to her family, gets called a slut. When she realized during her sophomore year that her boyfriend was bent on having sex with her, she dumped him.

Diane's father, Carlos, a kind, soft-spoken man, was an electrician; her mother, Gloria, was a registered nurse. The family was deeply religious. Gloria was the daughter of a minister who led a nondenominational Spanish-speaking church on the south side of Fort Worth. Gloria, her five sisters, and their families never missed Sunday services, and after church, the entire Zamora clan would gather for lunch at a cafeteria. Diane was the eldest of the Zamora's four children, and the most driven. When she was nine years old, she announced to her family that she wanted to become an astronaut. She sent off for NASA brochures, and by high school she was keeping a spiral note book containing a list of achievements she had to accomplish to get a college scholarship. She knew exactly what her grade point average and SAT Scores needed to be. She carried a knapsack full of schoolbooks everywhere in case she got stranded and had some time to fill.

At Crowley High School, Diane was not one of the social girls who gathered between periods in the school's chalky-smelling hallways to swap gossip. While she was not considered unfriendly, she was known around school as someone who kept to herself. "She didn't have a whole lot to say," one student said. She preferred associating with the smart kids at school -- "homework buddies," she called them -- and she was determined to become an academic star. Late in her junior year, when she posed for her high school graduation picture, she asked that she be allowed to wear the special tassel for being in the top 10 percent of her senior class-even though she had no idea at that time whether she would achieve that honor. Diane said she wanted to have the photograph as a way to keep her motivated.

Diane did end up in the top 10 percent of her senior class. Gloria Zamora told her friends that the reason Diane worked so diligently was because she knew her parents could not afford to send her to a good college. When her father got laid off from work, Diane watched Gloria take on two nursing jobs a day and then sell Mary Kay cosmetics on the side to help pay the family's bills. At one point, the electricity was cut off in their small house for more than a week. Diane studied by candlelight. But even with her ambition, Diane was still a teenager, filled with the same impulses and longings as any other girl her age. While she kept Civil Air Patrol military fatigues in her closet, she also had a collection of teddy bears on her bed. She took an after-school job at Fast Forward, a store oriented to teenage girls, because she liked the discount she could get on hip clothes. She listened to both contemporary Christian music and popular groups like Pearl Jam. "Diane was a really sweet girl," said one former neighbor, Dale Roger. "But I thought she was a little naive and sheltered from the outside world. She was really a virgin in life, You know? She hadn't really experienced anything. She didn't know all the things that could happen between people."

And then, in August 1995, just before the start of her senior year, her life changed. She told her parents that she had fallen for a boy: David Graham. He was just like her, she said breathlessly. It was not only that they had known as children what they wanted to do with their lives. They both loved calculus, physics, and government, and they talked on the phone late into the night about their homework. Their feelings, well known to any adolescent, were a mixture of adoration and total possessiveness. When they were together, they never stopped touching. Diane would put her arm around his waist, sliding one finger into a belt loop, and David would encircle her with his arms. "He always had both arms around her, like he was afraid she was going somewhere," said Diane's aunt Sylvia. "The two of them looked like they were wrapped up in one another."

It was not difficult for David and Diane to be swept away by the romantic grandeur of their relationship. By then, they were the stars of the Civil Air Patrol -- David was a cadet-colonel in the CAPs youth division, the highest accolade given, and Diane was the wing secretary -- and they saw themselves as the top guns of the twenty-first century. David saw himself becoming a great fighter pilot, Diane a famous astronaut. Abandoning her plans to study physics at an academically elite major university, Diane applied to the Air Force Academy, where David was set on going. After she learned that the deadline had passed for applications, she applied to the U.S. Naval Academy with the intention of transferring her commission after graduation from the Navy to the Air Force so she could be stationed with David.

Diane's family knew that David's personality was a little different. He had a collection of hunting rifles, which he once brought over to their house. When he came to church with Diane, he wore his combat boots, pants, and a T-shirt, and he kept his arms closely around her through the service. He once showed up at the Zamoras' house with a couple of his ROTC buddies from Mansfield. For entertainment, David took them out to the front yard and ordered them to march back and forth. "Diane was laughing, thinking it was funny," said Sylvia, "but I think the rest of us wondered a little when David said; 'I can get these guys to do whatever I want.'"

Still, no one could say that David was ever impolite around Diane or her family. On weeknights he drove the eighteen miles from Mansfield to Crowley and quietly sat in the Zamoras' living room to do homework with her. When her parents couldn't afford a pair of $100 combat boots for Diane, David bought them. After Diane had a serious wreck driving David's pickup truck, requiring pins to be put into her left hand, David spent entire nights at the hospital with her. "Unlike that other boyfriend of hers who just wanted to go all the way," said a relative, "David genuinely cared for Diane. I don't think Diane had ever had that kind of attention."

That September, about a month after they started dating, they told Diane's parents that they were engaged. David had sold a couple of his hunting rifles to make a down payment for an engagement ring. They were going to get married, they said, on August 13, 2000, after they graduated from their military academies. They already had the wedding planned. They were going to charter a bus to carry their relatives in Texas to the famous Cadet Chapel on the Air Force Academy's campus. There, David would wear his uniform, Diane a white wedding dress, and at the end of the ceremony, they would walk under crossed swords held by other cadets.

Not long after they announced their engagement, her family confirmed, Diane lost her virginity to David -- an act that had a dramatic impact on her life. "After it was over, she was real confused by what had happened," one relative said. "I know she felt guilty because she had wanted to wait. But once she went through with it, she became more committed than ever to David. I remember her saying, 'If I can't be Mrs. David Graham, then I will die as Miss Diane Zamora.'"

Indeed, they were hopelessly in love, focused as laser beams on each other. In that classic teenage way, they developed their own secret love code. She called him Tiger (the Mansfield High School mascot was a tiger), and he called her Kittens. And they ended many of their telephone conversations with the words. "Greenish brown female sheep."

Greenish brown is the color olive. A female sheep is a ewe. Olive ewe. I love you.

When this precious relationship we had was damaged by my thoughtless actions, the only thing that could satisfy her womanly vengeance was the life of the one that had, for an instant, taken her place.

ON THE FIRST WEEKEND IN NOVEMBER, David traveled to Lubbock with other members of the Mansfield High cross-country team for the regional meet. Both the boys' and girls' squads had qualified, and the school provided them a large van for the trip. One of the students who went on that trip was Adrianne Jones.

In many ways, Adrianne was Diane Zamora's polar opposite, an ebullient girl who knew how to charm guys and get them to look twice at her. When she posed for one studio portrait, she made sure to show some cleavage. Although she wasn't overtly promiscuous in a way that would make her an outcast among the more popular girls, she was far from sexually naive. Diane, on the other hand, rarely put on makeup for school, and except for David, she thought most high school guys were immature.

It is not known if anything happened between Adrianne and David in Lubbock. No one can remember whether they sat next to one another on the van or stayed up late talking at the motel. Some of Adrianne's friends think she would have kept her distance from David. As one friend pointed out, Adrianne had her standards: She would never sleep with another girl's boyfriend.

But something did happen when they returned to Mansfield. For whatever reason -- perhaps Adrianne looked at David on that van and saw the kind of guy that even her father would like -- she asked him to give her a ride home. They didn't go straight to her house. Adrianne surprised him by asking him to take some turns that he knew were out of the way. They ended up behind an elementary school, where David parked the car, and he and Adrianne had sex -- a brief but truly fatal entanglement.

Apparently they told no one. Their encounter seemed to have been an impulsive, one-night fling. But a month later, late in the evening, a friend of David's who lived in the nearby town of Burleson heard a tapping at his window. David and Diane, their clothes bloodied, came through the window, According to the friend, David begged him to ask no questions. But the friend noticed that both David and Diane were upset. They lay on the floor and held each other. It was the same night Adrianne Jones disappeared from her home and was murdered.

But the friend never reported the incident to the police, and soon David and Diane were back to their old ways. Using his father's credit card, David bought Diane and Gloria leather coats as Christmas presents. He got Diane's engagement ring out of layaway so she could begin to wear it. On Valentines Day, he gave her a teddy bear and flowers.

Diane's family could not help but wonder about the relationship as it progressed. David and Diane seemed so absorbed in one another's lives ... *so obsessed.* "No matter what we were talking about, Diane brought up David's name. She was always talking about David this or David that," said Diane's cousin Ronnie Gonzalez. One night when they were apart and David didn't call, Diane tearfully begged her mother to call his house to see if anything terrible had happened to him. David was no different. He came over every afternoon to stay so late that he would fall asleep on the couch. His father would call, demanding that he come home, but David would dawdle for hours before leaving. Whenever Diane would go to a school function at night, David would phone every hour from his home until she got back.

That spring, they learned within days of each other that they had been accepted to their academies -- David to the Air Force, Diane to the Navy. At special ceremonies at their high schools, they were presented with their academy acceptance letters. The Mansfield students gave a long ovation to David, who had Diane at his side. "I know this sounds strange to say now," recalled Becki Strosnider, the former editor of the *Mansfield Uproar,* "but we thought it was so cool that he had followed his dream." For her part, Gloria was so proud of what her daughter had done that she called the Hispanic-oriented La Estrella section of the *Fort Worth Star-Telegram* and suggested a story. When the reporter, Rosanna Ruiz, spoke with David and Diane, she asked them if they were being realistic about being married in the year 2000, considering they would be so far apart. But the two insisted that they would stay in touch daily through e-mail. "I was surprised at how adamant they were," Ruiz recalled. "They said they were certain the marriage was going to happen and that there were not going to be any outs. Then they stopped and looked at one another."

In the summer of 1996, after nearly three hundred interviews, detectives put the case on what they called slow-down mode, Bill and Linda Jones sank deeper into despair. Bill had to restrain himself to keep from interrogating every teenager he saw in town. Linda would get into her car at night and drive to the site where Adrianne was found hoping she might come across the killer. Some students continued to see counselors about Adrianne's death. April Grossman painted a portrait of Adrianne in art class to honor her. She showed it to David, who sat behind April in government. He looked at it, and then said, "You did a good job, April."

We realized it was either her or us. . . I just pointed and shot.

ONLY 1,239 YOUNG PEOPLE WERE accepted out of the 8,730 who applied to enter the Air Force Academy for the fall 1996 semester. Of the nearly 10,000 who applied to the U.S. Naval Academy in Annapolis, Maryland, only 1,212 were accepted, 200 of those being women. Just by getting into their academies, David Graham and Diane Zamora had become part of a select group of American teenagers. To stay there, however, they had to survive grueling summer boot camps designed to eradicate their civilian habits and teach them the exacting discipline of military life. For the freshmen at the academies -- known as plebes at the Naval Academy and Doolies at the Air Force Academy -- the six-week summer sessions were humid days of nonstop marching, push-ups, running, and taking orders. Upperclassmen belittled them every time they made a mistake. At meals, the freshmen were required to keep their eyes focused on their plates at all times except when questioned by a superior. They had to be prepared to answer a barrage of questions and recite long passages about academy rules from memory. The system was unnerving and often demoralizing, and it was not unusual to see a cadet or midshipman resign his or her commission before the summer was over.

By all indications, David successfully completed his Basic Cadet Training in Colorado Springs. According to relatives who read them, Diane's letters home indicated that she was capably enduring "plebe summer" in Annapolis. She wrote in detail about her daily schedule, from the ninety minute calisthenics sessions at six in the morning to the evening drill period in which they marched with M16 rifles. She wrote that she was going to church again at the Naval Chapel and that she had joined the glee club.

But her squad leader, Jay Guild, a good looking plebe from suburban Chicago, said Diane was not physically keeping up with the other plebes and seemed emotionally distracted. "She liked to talk about David," Jay said. "She missed him a lot. She often talked about him very strangely, as if she didn't trust him but she still wanted to be with him. It was very odd."

Jay said Diane went on "crying fits" when David wouldn't answer her e-mail. She told him she suspected David was cheating on her with a female cadet at the Air Force Academy. Apart from David for the first time since they had begun dating, Diane became plagued with jealousy, and she decided, in turn, to make David jealous. According to one source, Diane stopped sending David e-mail for several days, telling him that her computer had broken. A few weeks into the plebe summer, Jay added, Diane told him that she was considering breaking up with David, and she suggested that the two of them become boyfriend and girlfriend. She then sent David an e-mail telling him that Jay had kissed her.

David and Diane, who once had found such security in their all-consuming devotion, seemed to be whirling out of control. When David heard about Diane and Jay, he attempted to contact Navy officials to inform them that Jay was sexually harassing Diane. He sent threatening e-mail to Jay, demanding that he have nothing more to do with Diane. One person close to the investigation said that David wrote, Diane letters begging her not to deceive him. In the letters, David would write such lines as, "Remember what binds us together."

It was clear that Jay was captivated by Diane. When Diane's parents and Jay's mother arrived in Annapolis for Parents' Weekend on August 9, they were told that Jay and Diane had been reprimanded by upperclassmen for fraternizing. He had been seen sitting on the edge of her bed at night at Bancroft Hall, the coed dormitory where all the midshipmen lived. The truth was that Gloria was relieved to hear the news about Jay and Diane. "I got the very strong feeling that Diane's parents felt the relationship between Diane and David had become an unhealthy one," said Jay's mother, Cheryl Guild. At one point in the weekend, Diane and her parents went to lunch with Jay and his mother. During that lunch, Diane got up to call David. Cheryl could see Diane across the room, talking on the phone, and she noticed the girl was physically shaking. Gloria leaned toward Cheryl and said, "I wish Diane had met Jay first."

Jay said that at one point in the summer, Diane told him that she and David had a secret "that we'll take to the grave." He asked Diane if David had ever cheated on her before. "She said yes, and I said, 'What did you do about it?' She told me that she had asked David to kill the other girl."

Stunned, Jay listened as Diane told him that she had watched David kill a girl named Adrianne. She never said she had participated. "All she said is that she told him to do it and she saw him do it," Jay said.

Although the Academy's strict honor code, known as the Brigade of Midshipmen Honor Concept, states that a midshipman must immediately report another midshipman who lies, cheats, or breaks the law in any way, Jay told no one and would eventually be asked to resign from the Academy because of his silence. "I didn't want to believe it," he said. "I thought maybe she was trying to get attention."

But in late August, Diane told the story again, this time to her two roommates, Mandy Gotch and Jennifer McKearney. They were having a late-night conversation. and one of the girls mentioned how Diane and David seemed so in love. According to sources at the Naval Academy, one roommate said to Diane, "You two sound like you would do anything for each other."

Diane replied, "Yes."

"Even kill for one another?" the roommate asked.

Diane paused. "We, have," she said. Then she told them the story about Adrianne whether out of guilt or pride, no one is sure. Initially, the two roommates were skeptical about what they had heard, but the next day, they nervously told a Navy chaplain about the conversation. The chaplain contact Navy attorney at the Academy, who then began calling police departments in the Dallas-Fort Worth area to ask if they had an unsolved murder of a teenage girl. On August 29, he contacted the Grand Prairie Police Department. The next morning, detectives were on a flight to Annapolis.

I wanted it to be a dream . . . . I wanted to be able to drive Adrianne back home, to go to sleep, and to wake up back on December 3, free to make my decisions all over again.

THEY PULLED HER OUT OF THE FIRST pep rally, of the season for Navy's football team, the first night when the plebes were allowed to mingle with upperclassmen and feel a part of the Academy. Across the Yard came the sound of pounding drums and cheering midshipmen as Diane was escorted down a long hallway in the administration building and then was led into a room where several detectives and Navy officials waited.

She admitted to nothing. She said only that she had been insecure throughout plebe summer, and she thought such a tale about murder would make her look tougher in the eyes of other plebes.

The cops weren't buying it, what could they do? They had no evidence against her. Navy officials told her they were temporarily suspending her and sending her home until the matter was straightened out. They gave her an airplane ticket that took her from Baltimore to Atlanta and then on to Dallas. When Diane reached Atlanta, however, she changed planes and flew to Colorado Springs, where she went to see David.

No one knows what was said between them. But the two did have their photographs taken by a friend of David's. David was wearing his Air Force uniform, Diane her all-white Naval outfit. In that one moment they looked at the camera with a nearly desperate look, as if they knew that this was their last time together -- that the fairy tale was over.

When the detectives arrived in Colorado Springs, David insisted that he couldn't imagine why Diane would tell such a blatantly false story. But the cops told him they had found his friend in Burleson and had heard the story of the bloody clothing. Then the Air Force officers told the young cadet that he had a duty to reveal the truth. Finally, David broke. He sat down at a word processor and typed a four-and-a half-page confession (reprinted in part in the *Dallas Morning News*) that one forensic psychologist would later equate with a Danielle Steel novel. David wrote that for a month after his evening with Adrianne, he was tormented by "guilt and shame." The "perfect and pure" relationship between him and Diane, he added, had been defiled by "the one girl [who] had stolen from us our purity." Eventually, he told Diane about his tryst. "For at least an hour she screamed sobs that I wouldn't have thought possible, It wasn't just jealousy. For Diane, she had been betrayed, deceived and forgotten." He then said Diane gave him an ultimatum: kill Adrianne. David agreed. "I didn't have any harsh feelings for Adrianne," he wrote, "but no one could stand between me and Diane."

And so, David admitted, was he called Adrianne on the night of December 3, 1995 and said he wanted to see her. He picked her up in a Mazda Protege owned by Diane's parents. Diane was hiding in the hatchback. They drove out to a secluded country road, and Adrianne reclined the passengers seat, no doubt hoping for another romantic interlude. According to David's confession, while he held Adrianne, Diane raised up from her hiding place and hit her in the head with a dumbbell that belonged to David. Adrianne, however, did not die. "I realized too late that all those quick, painless snaps seen in the movies were just your usual Hollywood stunts," David wrote. "Adrianne somehow crawled through the window and, to our horror, ran off. I was panicky, and just grabbed the Makarov 9mm to follow. To our relief (at the time) she was too injured from the head wounds to go far. She ran into a nearby field and collapsed.... In that short instant, I knew I couldn't leave the key witness to our crime alive. I just pointed and shot.... I fired again and ran to the car. Diane and I drove off. The first things out of our mouths were, 'I love you.'" And then Diane said, her thirst for revenge suddenly slaked, "We shouldn't have done that, David."

The police recovered the handgun along with several dumbbells from the attic of the Graham's home. They also confronted Diane, who by then was back in Texas. She stared at the officers. Then she quietly went to the station to give her own confession. She was put in a solitary cell on a separate floor from David -- she looked like a harmless teenage girl in a sleeveless shirt and blue jeans. Every day, she did push-ups and sit-ups in her cell. She asked her mother for history and government textbooks so she could continue her studies. She said little, to the guards or to her fellow female inmates, except for one prisoner who regularly cried because she missed her children. Diane sang her a contemporary Christian song she had memorized back in high school titled "Faith."

In Mansfield, as everywhere else, the question on everyone's mind was, Why? It was one thing, residents said, to read about urban gang kids shooting it out over rivalry, but how did the culture of the streets -- where loyalty and vengeance are valued above life and law -- infect upstanding small-town kids? There were the usual discussions about teenagers' values being shaped more by shabby movie violence and the angry lyrics of their favorite singers than they were by moral lessons from their parents.

Other citizens were shocked to learn that more than one of David's friends had suspected that David was involved in Adrianne's murder, yet never said anything to the police. It was as if the most important thing among these teenagers was not "narcing" on a friend.

After the initial wave of national publicity over the arrests, Anna Barrett, a reporter for the *Mansfield News-Mirror,* began looking for positive stories to write about the high school to help the community's morale. "But something has changed in this town," site said. "You can feel it." Indeed, within a month after the arrests, a junior at Mansfield High was shot in the face with a shotgun and killed. A girl who had been on the cross-country team hanged herself because of personal problems. As for Bill and Linda Jones, they changed their phone number to avoid the calls from reporters, television shows, and movie producers. One producer, explaining why David and Diane's story would be a great miniseries, said in an interview, "It's a modern-day *Romeo and Juliet* only they kill someone else instead of each other."

What remained unfathomable was how David and Diane could convince themselves that only death could eliminate the one blot on their perfect teenage love affair. How could they imagine that sexual betrayal was a far worse crime, than murder? It seems clear that David convinced Diane that Adrianne was a seductress who lured him behind the elementary school. According to one police source, Diane told her roommates at the Naval Academy that just before she hit Adrianne in the head, she looked at her and said, "I know who you are! I know what you've done!"

Perhaps a trial will provide the definitive answer to why they did it. The, district attorney's office has not determined whether it will seek the death penalty for the two eighteen-year-olds. There is an outside chance that David's attorney, Dan Cogdell of Houston, will get David's confession thrown out of court because he had allegedly been confined to his quarters at the Air Force Academy for more than thirty hours before the police took the confession. If a judge rules that the confession is admissible, however, then it is possible that Cogdell and John Linebarger, a prominent Fort Worth defense attorney who has been hired by Diane's family, will try to position their clients to point fingers at each other. "If I think attacking the Zamora girl is the appropriate line of defense, I will do it," said Cogdell, who added that he believes David wrote his confession to cover for Diane. A couple of investigators agree with him, believing that Diane had a Lady Macbeth, liked control over David's life, coaxing and taunting him into letting his impulses and desires overcome his scruples. But others suggest that David, who brought guns and violence, sex and betrayal into Diane's sweet and studious life, exercised his spell over her by enlisting her as a partner in murder -- using death to bind them together for life. There is even a third theory that David, wanting to prove that he cared nothing for Adrianne, took one shot, and Diane, consumed with fury, took the other.

Still, it is difficult to imagine that David and Diane will someday turn into adversaries in court. When David was being escorted to the county jail in Fort Worth, a television reporter asked if he had anything to say to Diane. David looked at the camera and said, "I love you." As for Diane, one afternoon she motioned toward a guard and asked if she would pass on a message to David.

"What is it?" the guard asked.

Diane paused. "Tell him, 'Greenish brown female sheep.'"

CRIME IN TEXAS: 1996

By
Texas Department of Public Safety

Crime in Texas 1996 Overview

FOR MORE INFORMATION:

- Mike Cox, Laureen Chernow and Sherri Deatherage Green
  DPS Public Information Office
  Phone 512/424-2080

- Uniform Crime Reporting Section
  PO Box 4143
  Austin, TX 78765
  Phone 512/424-2091

**Uniform Crime Reporting
Crime Records Service
Texas Department of Public Safety
Dudley M. Thomas, Director**

AUSTIN—The number of violent crimes reported in Texas decreased in 1996, but a rise in the number of property crimes accounted for an overall crime increase of 2.6 percent compared with 1995, according to crime statistics released by the Department of Public Safety.

"Except for a slight (.2 percent) increase in the number of aggravated assaults reported, all categories of violent crime were down nearly one percent (.8 percent) last year," DPS Director Col. Dudley M. Thomas said. "Though Texans were statistically safer last year, they were slightly more likely to lose their property to thieves and burglars."

Property crime, which includes burglary, theft, and motor vehicle theft rose 3 percent in 1996, according to DPS Uniform Crime Reporting records.

Despite the overall 2.6 percent increase in the number of crimes reported, the crime rate—the number of crimes reported per 100,000 population—was up by only .4 percent. The violent crime rate was 644.2 in 1996 compared to 663.7 the year before, a decrease of 2.9 percent. The property crime rate was 5064.1, up .9 percent from 5020.8 in 1995.

The decrease in violent crime in 1996 clearly was fueled by a 12.9 percent drop in the number of murders reported in the state. Robbery was down 2.6 percent and rape down by 1.8 percent. Even though aggravated assault was up .2 percent, the rate of all violent crimes was down, including the rate for aggravated assault.

"While the number of crimes was up last year, so was the number of arrests made by Texas law enforcement officers," Thomas said. "Overall arrests were up 1.4 percent and arrests for drug law violations were up 4.5 percent."

The Texas UCR program also collects information on hate crimes in the state. In 1996, 350 incidents of hate crime involving 494 offenders and 348 victims were reported to the DPS by Texas law enforcement agencies.

In addition, DPS also collects information on Family Violence incidents. During 1996 there were 178,389 incidents of family violence reported. These incidents included 190,945 victims with 187,005 offenders.

Statistical Crime Analysis
Index Crimes

To track variations in crime, UCR summarizes crime information as the Crime Index. The seven crimes that make up the Crime Index are murder, rape, robbery, aggravated assault, burglary, larceny-theft, and motor vehicle theft. For each of these crimes, UCR collects reports of crimes, while for non-Index Crimes the program tracks only reports of actual arrests.

Index Crime Volume

The total estimated number of Index Crimes reported for 1996 was 1,091,878. This volume of crime represents an increase of 2.6 percent when compared to 1995.

Index Crime Rate

The crime rate reported by UCR is defined as the number of crimes committed per 100,000 population. This mechanism allows comparisons between periods of time to be made without being affected by population swings. For 1996, the Texas Index Crime Rate was 5,708.3 crimes per 100,000 population. This rate increased .4 percent compared to 1995. The crime rate is based on the 1996 Texas population of 19,128,000.

Property Value

- The value of property stolen during the commission of Index Crimes in 1996 was more than $1.3 billion.
- The value of stolen property recovered by Texas law enforcement agencies in 1996 was more than $547 million.

Texas Crime Volume by Offense

Offense Type	Offense	1996	1995	Percent Change
Violent Crime	Murder	1,476	1,694	−12.9%
	Rape	8,374	8,526	− 1.8%
	Robbery	32,796	33,666	− 2.6%
	Aggravated Assault	80,572	80,377	+ 0.2%
	Violent Crime Total	**123,218**	**124,263**	**− 0.8%**
Property Crime	Burglary	204,335	202,637	+ 0.8%
	Theft	659,397	632,523	+ 4.2%
	Motor Vehicle Theft	104,928	104,939	− 0.01%
	Property Crime Total	**968,660**	**940,099**	**+ 3.0%**
	INDEX CRIME TOTAL	**1,091,878**	**1,064,362**	**+ 2.6%**

Texas Crime Rate by Offense

Offense Type	Offense	1996	1995	Percent Change
Violent Crime	Murder	7.7	9.0	−14.4%
	Rape	43.8	45.5	− 3.7%
	Robbery	171.5	179.8	− 4.6%
	Aggravated Assault	421.2	429.3	− 1.9%
	Violent Crime Total	**644.2**	**663.7**	**− 2.9%**
Property Crime	Burglary	1,068.3	1,082.2	− 1.3%
	Theft	3,447.3	3,378.1	+ 2.0%
	Motor Vehicle Theft	548.6	560.5	− 2.1%
	Property Crime Total	**5,064.1**	**5,020.8**	**+ 0.9%**
	INDEX CRIME TOTAL	**5,708.3**	**5,684.5**	**+ 0.4%**

Arson

In 1996, reported arson offenses increased 6.4 percent from 1995. Property damage from arson was reported at over $133 million in 1996.
- 10,108 arsons were reported in 1996.
- 9,498 arsons were reported in 1995.

Texas Peace Officers Killed or Assaulted

- Three Texas law enforcement officers were killed feloniously in the line of duty due to criminal action during 1996.
- Two Texas law enforcement officers were killed in duty-related accidents during 1996.
- There was a 8.7 percent increase in the number of assaults on Texas officers in 1996 when compared to 1995.
  - 5,194 Texas officers were assaulted in 1996.
  - 4,777 Texas officers were assaulted in 1995.

The UCR Program

In an effort to quantify the increases and decreases in the number of crimes committed in Texas, the Uniform Crime Reporting program (UCR) collects reports of crimes and arrests from Texas law enforcement agencies. This information is printed in *Crime in Texas* and in periodic special news releases.

Data Estimation

Although the Texas UCR program enjoys a high rate of participation among Texas' law enforcement community, not every agency reports its crime information. To provide data that is comparable to other years, it is necessary to estimate the information for non-reporting agencies. In 1996, the 926 agencies whose statistics are presented here cover 99.9 percent of Texas' population.

Texas Arrest Totals

Arrests	1996	1995	Percent Change
Murder	1,303	1,437	− 9.3%
Aggravated Assault	25,575	26,426	− 3.2%
Motor Vehicle Theft	11,316	11,742	− 3.6%
Driving Under the Influence	85,359	88,372	− 3.4%
Drunkenness	184,373	190,544	− 3.2%
Drug Offenses: Drug Possession	80,379	76,172	+ 5.5%
Drug Offenses: Drug Sale & Manufacturing	9,509	9,827	− 3.2%
Drug Offenses: **Total Drug Offenses**	**89,888**	**85,999**	**+ 4.5%**
Weapons; Carrying-Possessing	15,708	18,701	−16.0%
STATE TOTAL ARRESTS	**1,124,861**	**1,109,747**	**+ 1.4%**

Texas Arrest Totals — 1986-1996

Year	Juveniles	Percent Change	Adults	Percent Change
1996	186,103	+ 1.7	938,758	+ 1.3
1995	182,956	+ 2.4	926,791	− 1.7
1994	178,677	+15.6	942,481	+ 3.1
1993	154,524	+11.5	914,404	+ 2.2
1992	138,620	+ 3.8	894,739	+ 2.9
1991	133,569	+ 7.6	869,512	− 0.7
1990	124,135	+12.0	875,805	+10.3
1989	110,854	+ 8.1	794,312	+ 5.5
1988	102,561	− 4.5	752,698	− 1.8
1987	107,411	− 2.2	766,143	− 4.2
1986	109,858	+ 1.7	799,947	+ 0.4

Hate Crime

The Texas Hate Crimes Act defines hate crimes as crimes motivated by prejudice and hatred including incidents for which statistics are kept under the federal Hate Crimes Statistics Act. The federal law defines hate crimes as crimes that manifest evidence of prejudice based on race, religion, sexual orientation, or ethnicity.

The Texas Hate Crimes Act directed every law enforcement agency within Texas to report bias offenses to the Department of Public Safety.

Volume

The total number of reported Texas hate crime incidents in 1996 was 350. This represents an increase of 7.7 percent when compared to 1995. These incidents involved 348 victims, 494 offenders, and resulted in a total of 366 offenses.

Hate Crime

	1996	1995	% Change
Reported Incidents	350	325	+ 7.7%
Reported Victims	348	316	+10.1%
Reported Offenders	494	447	+10.5%
Reported Offenses	366	345	+ 6.1%

Bias Motivation

The largest percentage of hate crime reports were racial in nature. The second most commonly reported bias motivation was sexual orientation. The third most common bias motivation was ethnic/national origin, and the fourth most common form of hate crime was religious.

Hate Crime Bias Motivation

Bias Nature	Group %	Bias Type	Volume	% of Total
Racial	67.8%	Anti-White	44	12.0%
		Anti-Black	190	51.9%
		Anti-Am. Indian/Alaskan Native	0	0.0%
		Anti-Asian/Pacific Islander	6	1.6%
		Multi Racial Group	8	2.2%
Sexual Orientation	17.2%	Anti-Male Homosexual	45	12.3%
		Anti-Female Homosexual	13	3.6%
		Anti-Homosexual (Male & Female)	3	0.8%
		Anti-Heterosexual	0	0.0%
		Anti-Bisexual	2	0.6%
Ethnicity National Origin	12.3%	Anti-Arab	3	0.8%
		Anti-Hispanic	36	9.8%
		Anti-Other Ethnic/National Origin	6	1.6%
Religious	2.7%	Anti-Jewish	8	2.2%
		Anti-Catholic	0	0.0%
		Anti-Protestant	0	0.0%
		Anti-Islamic (Moslem)	2	0.6%
		Anti-Other Religion	0	0.0%
		Anti-Multi-Religious Group	0	0.0%
		Anti-Atheist/Agnostic	0	0.0%
Total	100.0%	Total	366	100.0%

Location

Residences and homes were the most frequently occurring locations of bias crimes during 1996. The second most common locations were highways, roads, streets and alleys, and the third most common were parking lots and garages.

Hate Crime Location

Location	Volume	%
Air/Bus/Train Terminal	3	0.8%
Bank/Savings and Loan	1	0.3%
Bar/Night Club	6	1.6%
Church/Synagogue/Temple	5	1.4%
Commercial/Office Building	5	1.4%
Construction Site	0	0.0%
Convenience Store	8	2.2%
Department/Discount Store	2	0.5%
Drug Store/Doctor's Office/Hospital	1	0.3%
Field/Woods	6	1.6%
Government/Public Building	3	0.8%
Grocery/Supermarket	3	0.8%
Highway/Road/Street/Alley	74	20.2%
Hotel/Motel	1	0.3%
Jail/Prison	2	0.5%
Lake/Waterway	1	0.3%
Liquor Store	0	0.0%
Parking Lot/Garage	45	12.3%
Rental Storage Facility	0	0.0%
Residence/Home	137	37.5%
Restaurant	16	4.4%
School/College	27	7.4%
Service/Gas Station	3	0.8%
Specialty Store	0	0.0%
Other/Unknown	17	4.6%
TOTAL	366	100.0%

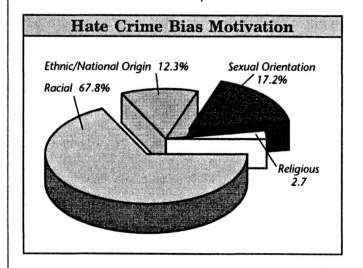

Hate Crime Bias Motivation: Racial 67.8%, Ethnic/National Origin 12.3%, Sexual Orientation 17.2%, Religious 2.7

Offenders

In 1996, 494 offenders were involved in incidents of hate crimes. Hate crime incidents can be perpetrated by multiple offenders, the following chart displays the suspected offenders' race totaling to 350.

Hate Crime Offenders by Incident		
Suspected Offenders' Races	Number	%
White	211	60.3%
Black	51	14.6%
American Indian/Alaskan Native	0	0.0%
Asian/Pacific Islander	4	1.1%
Multi-Racial Group	5	1.4%
Unknown	79	22.6%
TOTAL	**350**	**100.0%**

Victims

Information on the victims of hate crimes is limited to victim type. While the bias motivation information identifies the offender's bias, the victim may not actually belong to the group the offender sought to harm. For this reason, information on the victims' group membership is not recorded.

Victim type, in the hate crime data collection program, is listed as: individual, business, financial institution, government, religious organization, society/public, other and unknown. Of the victim types, individuals were the main hate crime target.

Hate Crime Victim Type by Offense		
Victim Type	Number	%
Individual	271	74.0%
Business	3	0.8%
Financial Institution	0	0.0%
Government	1	0.3%
Religious Organization	2	0.5%
Society/Public	9	2.5%
Other	79	21.6%
Unknown	1	0.3%
TOTAL	**366**	**100.0%**

Offenses

Offenses in the hate crime data collection program are defined in accordance with federal Uniform Crime Reporting definitions and do not necessarily conform to Texas state definitions. Complete offense definitions are available in the *Crime in Texas* annual publication or from UCR upon request.

Hate crime offense information falls into the eight index crimes—murder, rape, robbery, aggravated assault, burglary, larceny-theft, motor vehicle theft, and arson—plus simple assault, intimidation, and vandalism. Of these offense categories, aggravated assault, simple assault, intimidation and vandalism accounted for 94 percent of all bias crime offenses in 1996.

Hate Crime Offenses		
Offense	Volume	%
Murder	0	0.0%
Rape	1	0.3%
Robbery	8	2.2%
Aggravated Assault	63	17.2%
Burglary	6	1.6%
Larceny-Theft	2	0.5%
Motor Vehicle Theft	0	0.0%
Arson	4	1.1%
Simple Assault	97	26.5%
Intimidation	102	27.9%
Vandalism	83	22.7%
TOTAL	**366**	**100.0%**

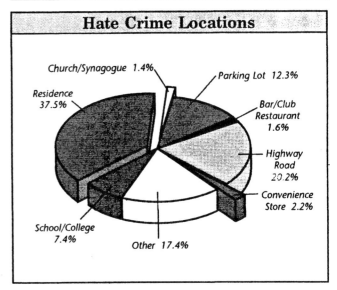

Hate Crime Locations: Residence 37.5%, Church/Synagogue 1.4%, Parking Lot 12.3%, Bar/Club Restaurant 1.6%, Highway Road 20.2%, Convenience Store 2.2%, Other 17.4%, School/College 7.4%

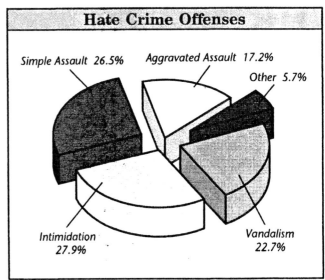

Hate Crime Offenses: Simple Assault 26.5%, Aggravated Assault 17.2%, Other 5.7%, Vandalism 22.7%, Intimidation 27.9%

Family Violence

The Texas Family Code defines family violence as an act by a member of a family or household against another member that is intended to result in physical harm, bodily injury, assault, or a threat that reasonably places the member in fear of imminent physical harm. The law excludes the reasonable discipline of a child. By definition 'Family' includes individuals related by consanguinity (blood) or affinity, marriage or former marriage, biological parents of the same child, foster children, foster parents, and members or former members of the same household (including roommates).

Family Violence

	1996	1995	% Change
Reported Incidents	178,389	172,476	+3.4%
Reported Victims	190,945	184,926	+3.3%
Reported Offenders	187,005	181,246	+3.2%

Victim's Relationship

Relationship Type	Group %	Relationship of Offender	Percent of Total
Marital	58.35%	Husband	5.43%
		Wife	28.00%
		Common-Law Husband	2.96%
		Common-Law Wife	17.83%
		Ex-Husband	0.73%
		Ex-Wife	3.40%
Parental/Child	15.06%	Father	1.77%
		Mother	4.73%
		Son	2.41%
		Daughter	3.36%
		Stepfather	0.69%
		Stepmother	0.27%
		Step-Son	0.82%
		Step-Daughter	0.99%
		Foster Parent	0.01%
		Foster Child	0.01%
Other Family	26.59%	Grandfather	0.09%
		Grandmother	0.27%
		Grandson	0.10%
		Granddaughter	0.18%
		Brother	2.57%
		Sister	3.45%
		Step-Brother	0.11%
		Step-Sister	0.99%
		Male Roommate	2.21%
		Female Roommate	8.02%
		Male In-Law	1.02%
		Female In-Law	1.42%
		Other Male Family Member	1.84%
		Other Female Fam. Member	3.91%
		Unknown Relationship-Male	0.11%
		Unk. Relationship-Female	0.30%

Offenders

In 1996, a reported 187,005 offenders were involved in incidents of family violence.

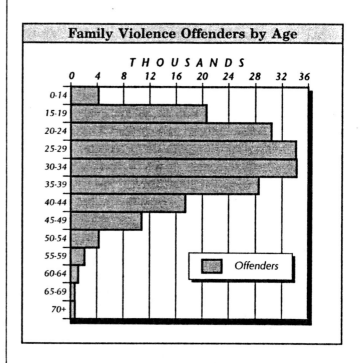

Victims

Incidents of family violence in 1996 involved a reported 190,945 victims.

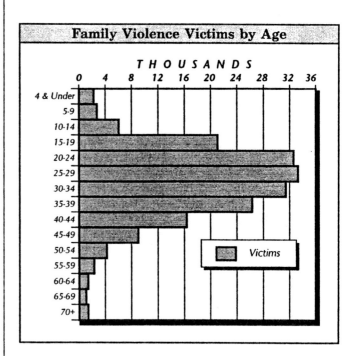

Officers

Potential assaults on peace officers are a serious problem inherent to police intervention and investigation of family violence. In 1996, during the course of reported family violence incidents, 813 Texas law officers were assaulted. By contrast, during this same period 5,194 assaults were made on law officers during all types of police activity.

Offenses

Family violence offense information falls into six general categories: assaults, homicides, kidnapping/abductions, robberies, forcible sex offenses, and nonforcible sex offenses. Of the six main categories, assaults accounted for 98 percent of all offenses.

Type	Group%	Offense	%
Assaults:	97.92%	Aggravated Assault	16.38%
		Simple Assault	70.10%
		Intimidation	11.44%
Homicides:	0.15%	Murder & Nonnegligent Manslaughter	0.14%
		Negligent Manslaughter	0.008%
		Justifiable Homicide	0.002%
Kidnapping Abduction:	0.15%	Kidnapping/Abduction	0.15%
Robbery	0.14%	Robbery	0.14%
Forcible Sex Offenses:	1.53%	Forcible Rape	0.55%
		Forcible Sodomy	0.20%
		Sexual Assault with Object	0.06%
		Forcible Fondling	0.72%
Non-forcible Sex Offenses	0.11%	Incest	0.06%
		Statutory Rape	0.05%

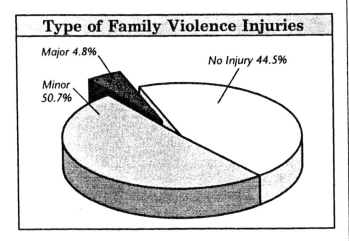

Injuries

Considering the injuries sustained by victims of family violence, it should be noted that the police officer who responds to the disturbance call determines the extent of injuries. Therefore, all injuries are considered to be apparent injuries at the time of the report. If later medical attention indicates that the injuries were more or less severe than noted by the responding officer, this information is not included in the family violence report. The majority of reported injuries (51 percent) were minor; in 44 percent of family violence reports 'no injury' was recorded. Major injuries were reported in 5 percent of the cases.

Of the apparent major injuries, severe lacerations were the most common at 32 percent, possible internal injuries were reported in 30 percent of the reports, and apparent broken bones were noted in 14 percent of the cases.

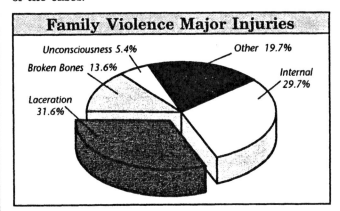

Weapons

The most common weapon involved in family violence cases was physical force through the use of hands, feet, and fists (strong-arm), which accounts for 74 percent of the incidents. The Texas Family Violence law considers the use of threats and intimidation to be serious enough to report and, thus, 12 percent of the reports were listed as involving no weapons. Knives or cutting instruments (4 percent), blunt objects (3 percent), firearms (2 percent) and other (6 percent) account for the remaining cases. Considered as other weapons were motor vehicles, poison, explosives, fire, drugs, unknown, and miscellaneous weapons.

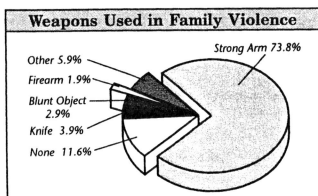

Crime in Texas Cities 50,000 to 100,000 Population
1996 vs 1995

Agency	Year	Murder	Rape	Robbery	Aggravated Assault	Burglary	Larceny Theft	Motor Vehicle Theft	Total	% Change
Baytown PD	1996	6	25	91	206	595	2,736	504	4,163	+ 4.2%
	1995	6	33	112	238	668	2,513	425	3,995	
Bryan PD	1996	6	43	83	371	915	2,799	303	4,520	+ 5.8%
	1995	4	50	69	354	763	2,799	234	4,273	
Carrollton PD	1996	1	15	65	268	659	2,425	348	3,781	- 1.1%
	1995	2	28	68	209	709	2,424	384	3,824	
College Station PD	1996	0	24	32	75	391	2,206	105	2,833	+ 6.7%
	1995	1	29	45	75	313	2,107	85	2,655	
Denton PD	1996	3	35	83	257	583	2,646	210	3,817	- 5.1%
	1995	1	45	53	279	640	2,823	180	4,021	
Galveston PD	1996	11	62	265	755	911	3,380	682	6,066	- 8.9%
	1995	15	55	356	941	1,234	3,337	722	6,660	
Harlingen PD	1996	0	1	54	263	1,045	2,962	216	4,541	- 4.3%
	1995	1	2	52	312	951	3,152	304	4,744	
Killeen PD	1996	2	82	142	253	932	3,616	263	5,290	+ 8.4%
	1995	3	75	175	193	949	3,204	279	4,878	
Lewisville PD	1996	0	22	46	71	548	2,588	271	3,546	+ 4.2%
	1995	5	16	53	91	516	2,426	296	3,403	
Longview PD	1996	8	69	176	268	994	4,020	584	6,119	+10.7%
	1995	2	78	163	268	1,041	3,482	493	5,527	
McAllen PD	1996	5	23	148	370	1,475	7,730	946	10,697	-15.0%
	1995	5	29	145	504	1,762	9,193	953	12,591	
N. Richland Hills PD	1996	1	12	36	80	457	1,613	211	2,410	+ 3.0%
	1995	1	17	49	91	364	1,646	172	2,340	
Odessa PD	1996	14	35	128	928	1,198	4,136	309	6,748	- 0.2%
	1995	4	37	113	971	1,269	4,034	331	6,759	
Port Arthur PD	1996	5	21	153	450	1,067	1,952	477	4,125	- 2.7%
	1995	13	11	147	544	1,286	1,920	317	4,238	
Richardson PD	1996	4	20	67	162	594	2,724	197	3,768	- 1.7%
	1995	1	14	87	130	574	2,777	252	3,835	
San Angelo PD	1996	2	37	39	375	739	3,923	160	5,275	+ 7.6%
	1995	3	26	31	341	739	3,624	138	4,902	
Temple PD	1996	1	12	80	200	553	2,556	223	3,625	+14.4%
	1995	5	72	61	133	523	2,153	223	3,170	
Tyler PD	1996	9	54	191	376	952	4,466	357	6,405	-11.4%
	1995	7	47	166	485	1,169	4,928	427	7,229	
Victoria PD	1996	2	29	60	506	748	2,394	173	3,912	-13.8%
	1995	4	30	55	527	956	2,724	241	4,537	

Crime in Texas Cities Over 100,000 Population
1996 vs 1995

Agency	Year	Murder	Rape	Robbery	Aggravated Assault	Burglary	Larceny Theft	Motor Vehicle Theft	Total	% Change
Abilene PD	1996	7	66	126	399	1,120	4,008	245	5,971	− 1.3%
	1995	5	80	131	480	1,044	4,095	214	6,049	
Amarillo PD	1996	11	71	334	1,012	2,116	9,857	687	14,088	+ 6.0%
	1995	16	84	242	1,038	2,419	8,883	611	13,293	
Arlington PD	1996	17	156	618	1,687	3,395	13,165	2,274	21,312	+ 4.5%
	1995	9	154	521	1,892	3,224	12,306	2,298	20,404	
Austin PD	1996	41	270	1,376	2,135	7,575	27,187	3,695	42,279	− 0.7%
	1995	46	308	1,336	2,360	7,521	27,434	3,581	42,586	
Beaumont PD	1996	15	203	420	614	1,958	6,362	737	10,309	− 7.8%
	1995	14	189	420	607	1,749	7,414	788	11,181	
Brownsville PD	1996	11	22	231	887	1,328	6,911	477	9,867	+17.4%
	1995	7	26	204	580	1,264	5,793	534	8,408	
Corpus Christi PD	1996	18	276	485	2,241	3,773	22,006	1,668	30,467	+ 4.1%
	1995	31	216	504	2,013	3,785	21,271	1,454	29,274	
Dallas PD	1996	217	740	6,122	9,201	17,960	49,018	17,143	100,401	+ 1.8%
	1995	276	852	5,899	8,942	16,705	49,068	16,882	98,624	
El Paso PD	1996	30	245	1,195	3,668	3,942	31,694	4,360	45,134	+ 8.3%
	1995	37	242	1,076	3,593	3,828	29,034	3,882	41,692	
Ft. Worth PD	1996	68	319	1,692	2,905	7,917	21,481	4,520	38,902	− 1.9%
	1995	108	332	1,965	2,939	7,334	22,128	4,861	39,667	
Garland PD	1996	14	63	210	490	1,786	6,150	849	9,562	−16.3%
	1995	7	102	271	580	2,146	7,244	1,068	11,418	
Grand Prairie PD	1996	3	50	147	956	1,068	3,734	924	6,882	+ 6.7%
	1995	12	28	140	515	1,065	3,714	974	6,448	
Houston PD	1996	261	1,002	8,276	12,917	25,402	65,080	22,391	135,329	+ 2.8%
	1995	316	837	9,222	11,885	24,830	61,976	22,536	131,602	
Irving PD	1996	8	65	202	529	1,480	6,342	857	9,483	− 3.1%
	1995	5	56	213	557	1,344	6,723	889	9,787	
Laredo PD	1996	11	27	242	760	1,672	7,477	1,051	11,240	+10.7%
	1995	14	22	174	897	1,628	6,529	886	10,150	
Lubbock PD	1996	15	126	276	1,649	2,456	7,472	954	12,948	− 3.4%
	1995	18	122	297	1,467	2,441	8,086	974	13,405	
Mesquite PD	1996	3	8	64	363	564	4,781	669	6,452	−11.5%
	1995	1	20	89	491	825	5,195	672	7,293	
Midland PD	1996	4	58	80	235	1,030	3,273	286	4,966	+ 2.6%
	1995	8	68	88	309	1,004	3,074	287	4,838	
Pasadena PD	1996	9	63	189	642	1,408	3,983	984	7,278	+ 6.7%
	1995	15	63	176	801	1,225	3,661	880	6,821	
Plano PD	1996	0	49	97	423	1,443	5,918	388	8,318	+ 8.7%
	1995	4	38	92	513	1,345	5,282	380	7,654	
San Antonio PD	1996	115	637	2,350	1,637	13,685	60,488	8,796	87,708	+ 9.7%
	1995	142	658	2,345	2,033	13,961	52,370	8,422	79,931	
Waco PD	1996	14	92	386	860	2,092	6,832	1,277	11,553	+14.8%
	1995	16	131	457	904	1,900	5,553	1,103	10,064	
Wichita Falls PD	1996	9	81	152	636	1,020	4,436	370	6,704	− 4.4%
	1995	8	90	211	552	1,183	4,601	366	7,011	

CROSSING

*Most of the drugs in this country come across the border at El Paso,
and federal drug agents know who is behind the massive smuggling operation.
What they don't know is how to stop him.*

THE PUBLISHER OF A JUÁREZ NEWSPAPER answered a knock at his door one evening and found two strangers standing on his doorstep. "We have come here on behalf of a friend." One of them said in Spanish. "He would like to pay you a substantial sum of money every month, and in exchange, you will let him review every article you intend to publish about Amado Carrillo Fuentes."

The publisher tried to conceal his fear. "No." he said. "I can't agree to that sort of thing."

The two strangers looked at each other. One of them said. "Well, then, since you can't do that, let's try another arrangement. Either you will let our friend pay you a substantial sum of money every month in exchange for which you will not publish anything about Amado Carrillo Fuentes, or you will be killed."

The men on the doorstep then said, "*Buenas noches,*" and departed into the Juárez night, leaving the publisher to ponder the two options. Overnight, a third choice occurred to him. He resolved to sell his newspaper.

This story about the notorious Mexican drug trafficker Amado Carrillo Fuentes was told to me by a knowledgeable American source. When I told it to two members of the Juárez media one morning in October, they exchanged knowing looks. Earlier in the year, said one of them; a photographer from the publisher's paper had taken pictures of Carrillo's compound near the Juárez racetrack. An interested party later contacted the paper. His message was succinct: "Pesos or bullets?" The photographs never made it into print.

"Here in Juárez," the other added, "no one mentions his name in the press. Television, radio, newspaper -- it's the same editorial policy."

The three of us were having this conversation over coffee at Sanborn's, a fashionable restaurant on the Paseo Triunfo de la República frequented by politicians, journalists, and industrialists. Three months before, it was widely rumored that Amado Carrillo Fuentes had made an appearance in this very restaurant, accompanied by several body guards, a few members of the heroin-smuggling Herrera family, and a man who happened to be a Mexican police official. Though it was a rare sighting of the elusive drug lord, there could be no doubt that Carrillo intended to be seen. "It was a demonstration of his strength to dine in public with the official" one of the members of the Juárez media told me. "He was reminding everyone who was really in charge of the Juárez *plaza*."

Reminders of Carrillo's power have usually come in other forms, ranging in degrees of subtlety -- from the Boeing 727's bearing tons of Colombian cocaine that land on his rural Chihuahuan airstrips in the dead of night, to the bodies strewn across the southern outskirts of Juárez every time Carrillo's drugs fail to reach their destination. Both with pesos and with bullets, the so-called Lord of the Skies has emerged as the most dominant drug trafficker in Mexico. More cocaine enters the U.S. through his organization than any other, in addition to the substantial quantities of methamphetamine and black tar heroin his underlings ferry across the border. By no coincidence, today more drugs are smuggled through the El Paso-Juárez corridor -- consisting of four pedestrian and vehicular bridges linking Mexico to Texas and the U.S. – than anywhere else in America. Thanks to Amado Carrillo Fuentes, El Paso is well on its way to becoming a Little Miami, a city whose prosperity is dependent upon the drug trade. And, thanks to Carrillo, Juárez has become a city held hostage, where two hundred to four hundred people have been murdered over the past three years as a result of the drug trade.

None of this has occurred by accident. In his ascendancy, the fortyish Lord of the Skies benefited from luck and opportunity, apprenticeships and family relations, the misfortunes of his peers and the good sense to learn from their mistakes. As a result, Carrillo is untouchable, his incalculable wealth and his equally innumerable crimes scarcely blinked at by the Mexican government and its law enforcement officials -- while on the other side of the border, just a couple of miles from the warehouses that store his drugs, American federal agents gnash their teeth and wait for Carrillo to commit some fatal error. It is like waiting for a bridge to collapse.

THE HISTORY OF EL PASO-JUÁREZ AS THE DRUG SMUGGLER'S preferred port of entry begins around 1983, when a Colombian operative showed up in Juárez and established residence there. By the time the man departed in 1985, he had built an elaborate network by which the infamous Medellin drug cartel could fly its Colombian cocaine into the interior of Mexico and have the drugs driven north into the United States by Mexican traffickers, who would then deliver the goods at a designated site to Colombian distributors, who would disperse the cocaine throughout the biggest cities in America.

American law enforcement officials knew nothing about the Colombian operative or his operation until some time after September 28, 1989. On that day, the Drug Enforcement Administration received a tip that led agents to a warehouse in Sylmar, California, a suburb of Los Angeles. After obtaining a warrant, DEA agents entered the warehouse. What they discovered was more than $12 million in cash stuffed in boxes and bags on the floor of the warehouse, along with a staggering quantity of boxed cocaine: 21.38 tons, with a street value of $6.5 billion. It was, and still is, the largest cocaine seizure in American history.

Four men were initially spotted around the warehouse, were arrested and then interrogated at the DEA headquarters in Los Angeles. The suspects were surprisingly forthcoming -- until a Colombian American woman burst into the interrogation room and declared, "I represent all four of these men and wish to speak with them privately." After the attorney left the building, the four suspects told DEA agents that they had nothing further to say. But by then, a key fact had already been divulged: All 21.38 tons had entered the U.S. through the El Paso-Juárez corridor.

"The Sylmar bust was our wake-up call," says Phil Jordan, who at the time was the DEA's special agent in command of the Dallas District and now is the director of the El Paso intelligence Center, which gathers and analyzes all law enforcement data pertaining to international drug trafficking. Until that point, the feds had almost no clue that the Colombians had set their sights on Juárez. Traditionally, drugs had moved into the U.S. via New York City, until crackdowns in the sixties and seventies inspired the drug lords to ship their products through Caribbean waters and into Miami. The federal government responded in 1982 with stepped up interdiction along the Florida coastline. Multi-ton seizures compelled politicians to proclaim that America was winning the War on Drug. Yet, federal agents knew otherwise. Inland seizures proved that massive quantities of marijuana, cocaine, and heroin were still finding away to cross the border. But where was the corridor?

Common sense would have given them the answer. Mexico. After all, Mexicans had mastered the art of smuggling contraband guns to tequila, over the course of the past two centuries. The savvy, the manpower and some of the tools of the trade -- including police corruption -- were already in place for the Colombians to exploit. Furthermore, A cargo traveling across Mexico wouldn't have to sit in the water until conditions were favorable along the coastline. The drugs could be flown into the Mexican interior, far afield of U.S. radar detectors, and then driven to the edge of the border. The drugs could sit there, indefinitely warehoused, until the time was right to join the procession of vehicles that crossed the international bridges.

And which bridges? Federal anti-drug agencies guessed the Tijuana Ports of entry. But despite the heavy trafficking from Baja California into the U.S., clogging up the Tijuana corridor wasn't going to arrest the influx of illegal drugs by any means. For as any geography textbook would have told them, the most heavily populated metropolitan area on any international border *in the entire world* is El Paso-Juárez. And as and map would have shown the, a vehicle that crosses the Bridge of the Americas into El Paso is, in a matter of minutes, on Interstate 10 – bound westward for California, eastward for Florida, and within an hour's drive of I-25 north. An Architect in the employ of traffickers could not have designed two more accommodating sister cities. A tractor-trailer could receive five tons of cocaine at a Chihuahuan airstrip, drive anonymously through the cramped international checkpoint, and then become instantly lost in the El Paso traffic before disappearing altogether. During 1988 and 1989, the Sylmar conspirators had succeeded in smuggling more than two hundred tons of cocaine through this conduit.

Following the September 1989 seizure at the Sylmar warehouse, federal agents moved with the haste of the monumentally chastened. Through seized smuggling ledgers and plea-bargain arrangements with some of the conspirators, they learned that members of the Medellin cartel were working with a Juárez trafficker named Rafael Muñoz Talavera. The Colombians transported their cocaine to a ranch airstrip in Villa Ahumada; from there Muñoz drivers moved the product seventy miles up the road into Juárez and across the international border in the trunks of old model LTDs and Oldsmobile Cutlass Sierras. Every Monday through Friday for two years, four or five of Muñoz's smuggling vehicles crossed into El Paso nightly, each carrying 150 to 170 kilograms of cocaine in the trunk; not a single one was searched at the bridge. The drugs were repackaged and warehoused in El Paso until Saturday afternoons, when the cocaine was reloaded into hidden compartments of Peterbilt tractor-trailers and the trailers filled with hundreds of breakable Mexican artifacts. The drivers set out for Ruidoso, New Mexico, bearing bills of lading for a dummy corporation called Ruidoso Arts and Crafts and receiving information along the way from conspirators about Border Patrol activity along U.S. 70. From Ruidoso, new bills of lading were inked indicating that the truck was ferrying contents from that city rather than El Paso. Then, assisted by road surveillance teams, the trucks drove on the back roads of New Mexico into Arizona, where they rejoined Interstate 10 and headed for the Colombian distributors who would meet them at the Sylmar warehouse.

The scheme was at the same time extravagant and maddeningly simple, but after the seizure at Sylmar, the conspiracy was dismantled. Between 1990 and 1993 almost all of the Mexican organizers, including the Juárez *patrón* Talavera, were brought to justice. But the corridor still beckoned. The conditions that made El Paso-Juárez so appealing to the Colombians in 1983 have only intensified. In 1994 more than 16 million vehicles crossed the three bridges linking Juárez to the United States. Less than 10 percent of those vehicles are submitted to a detailed inspection by U.S. Customs and Immigration agents at the border checkpoint. George McNenney, the special agent in charge of the U.S. Customs Service Office, in El Paso, observes, "It's not so much a matter of resources as a matter of other realities. Yes, we're a law enforcement agency. But we're also an agency that facilitates trade. If we checked every vehicle, there would be lines all the way to Mexico City."

That more than 90 percent of the vehicles enter the U.S. from Juárez unsearched instantly guarantees, as one senior federal agent puts it, "odds that are far greater than Las Vegas odds." To increase the odds in his favor, the agent adds, a trafficker "would send several cars across the bridge and assume that one of them will be seized, just to help discern the pattern of detection." (The drivers often times are ignorant Juárez peasants paid a nominal sum to drive the vehicles across the border to an El Paso safe house, no questions asked.) The traffickers improve the odds further by creating hidden compartments such as detachable dashboards that harbor the drugs within the vehicle. Then there are the spotters -- individuals paid by traffickers to loiter around the checkpoint and monitor the border inspectors. One afternoon while standing by the Bridge of the Americas station, I asked a Customs inspector if there were any spotters in the vicinity. Hesitating only for the moment that it took for him to snicker darkly, the inspector pointed out four likely suspects: two leaning against the pay telephones twenty yards away, another hunched in the shade near the employee parking lot, and a fourth positioned near the center of the bridge, some fifty yards distant. The latter was an elderly man in rumpled clothes and a straw hat. I could just make out the cellular phone in his hand. The vehicles idling in the traffic pattern between Mexico and the U.S. would receive a coded message on their digital pagers from the spotters -- 333, for example, meaning that the driver should make haste for lane three, or 000, indicating that the Customs agents with drugsniffing dogs were checking the driver's lane and that a hasty return to Juárez would be in order.

Yet the crude ingenuity of spotters and custom-designed drug vehicles could be dispensed with. At the El Paso-Juárez corridor the deck is hopelessly stacked in the smugglers favor. At issue is not the viability of the conduit, but rather which trafficker will become its master -- and thus the primary link between Colombian drugs and their American consumer. After the Sylmar bust in 1989, the link was severed, but not for long. Someone would step forward. Someone would take charge of the Juárez *plaza*.

TO TELL YOU THE TRUTH, we're just not getting much intelligence about him because no one is talking," a veteran federal agent said to me on the subject of Amado Carrillo Fuentes. "His circle is small, and he doesn't come out of it. And everyone else is afraid to tell us anything."

American anti-drug agencies know embarrassingly little about their biggest nemesis. Intelligence reports list three different dates of birth for Carrillo, placing him between 40 and 45 years of age. He is either a third-grade dropout or a law school graduate. He has two children, a wife of unknown name and origin, and he is said to have a girlfriend in Ojinaga and another in Sonora, each with a child that is his. The three existing photographs of Carrillo are dated but suggest a tall, unremarkable-looking man with hazel eyes, soft cheeks, sullen lips and a youthful head of dark hair. Though rumor has it that he alters his appearance with colored contact lenses and hair dye, most federal agents are doubtful. He is his own disguise, conveniently nondescript.

Even his exact birthplace is a matter of dispute, though everyone agrees that Carrillo was born in one of the agricultural villages outside of Culiacan, the capital of the Pacific coastal state of Sinaloa. Like Sicily in Italy and Medellin in Colombia, Sinaloa is a hothouse of mobsters, a violent and provincial region surrounded by marijuana plantations and opium fields. In the midsixties, when Pedro Aviles Pérez -- the acknowledged godfather of the Mexican drug trafficking federation -- rose out of Sinaloa to claim smuggling supremacy, "you could hear gunfire in Culiacan every night," recalls a senior U.S. official.

Carrillo didn't have to seek out strangers to learn about the drug trade. His uncle Ernesto Fonseca Carrillo was one of the country's biggest traffickers. Fonseca had the dim, addled visage of a born thug – "To look at him," says one agent, "you wouldn't hire him to sweep your sidewalks." Yet Fonseca was also Aviles' bookkeeper, and he maintained ties to Colombian suppliers following Aviles' assassination by Mexican federal judicial police in 1978.

Carrillo started at the bottom, loading and driving marijuana to safe houses. Eventually, and most likely through his uncle, he made his acquaintance with the Herrera family, Mexico's notorious heroin-smuggling family from Sinaloa's neighboring state, Durango. The Herreras were the last of a breed in Mexico, an exclusively family-run operation that controlled every single aspect of their trade, from planting marijuana and poppy seeds in the foothills of Las Herreras to distributing the product in Chicago. The godfather, Jaime Herrera Nevares, was a functionally illiterate ex-cop with a nonetheless dignified Old World bearing. He despised the rude and arrogant Colombian drug lords and refused to sell their cocaine. Carrillo helped tend the Herrera opium fields, and it is likely that he fell into the company of Jaime Junior, the godfather's son, who was about Carrillo's age and who epitomized a new style of trafficker: the Concorde-flying, thousand-dollar-boot-wearing, gold-and-diamond-ornamented internationalist.

"During Jaime Juniors era, we began to see something we hadn't seen before," says Travis Kuykendall, a former head of DEA operations in El Paso and now an administrator of the West Texas High Intensity Drug Trafficking Area, an organization that disperses federal funds to antidrug agencies. "Traffickers began to show their money on the American side. They bought big mansions, invested in racehorses and feedlots, and partied in Las Vegas. They believed they were invulnerable." Prominent among this ilk was Rafael Caro Quintero, a brutal Sinaloan who owned a magnificent estate in San Diego, California, as well as a pet lion. In the early eighties Caro Quintero recruited thousands of Sinaloans to tend to his marijuana plantations near the Chihuahuan town of Ciudad Jiménez and the nearby village of Colonia Búfalo. Amado Carrillo Fuentes showed up in Chihuahua about this time. In this northern border state, Carrillo received a crucial apprenticeship under the most flamboyant trafficker in modem times: Pablo Acosta Villarreal, the *patrón* of the Presidio-Ojinaga *plaza*.

Acosta was the bridge that connected the old drug lords with the new. His grandfather was a bootlegger who switched over to smuggling marijuana after Prohibition. Acosta started out smuggling pot in mule carts and melon trucks, by the mid-eighties, he was using twin-engine planes to ferry grass, heroin, and cocaine across the border. "He set the standard for moving multi-ton quantities and for flaunting it," says one federal agent.

Carrillo moved to a house, on a hill north of downtown Ojinaga and became Acosta's lieutenant. They rode together on drugrunning expeditions and freebased cocaine together. Carrillo curried favor with his boss by buying him gold wristwatches and necklaces. In turn, he learned the intricacies of staging and moving major loads into Texas: how to set up a transportation network, how to time a delivery, whom to bribe, and whom to trust. Just as valuably, he learned from Pablo Acosta's excesses. For all of his generosity toward the Ojinaga peasants, Acosta recklessly trigger-happy, given to ambushing rivals and being ambushed himself. That he freebased incessantly made his conduct that much more erratic. By 1987, Acosta had so undermined his authority that Mexican law enforcement officials felt sufficiently emboldened to take him down. In April they surround his ranch in Santa Elena, just across the Rio Grande from Big Bend National Park. After a ninety-minute shoot-out, Pablo Acosta lay dead.

By that time, Carrillo was long gone. He had fled to Torreón in Durango, where he resumed his partnership with the Herreras. In 1988 he relocated westward to Hermosillo in Sonora, the state just north of Sinaloa and bordering Arizona, where his brother Cipriano had set up shop. It was an unsettling time for Mexican traffickers. Following the torture and murder of DEA agent Kiki Camarena in 1985, Mexican authorities had arrested two men allegedly responsible, Rafael Caro Quintero and Ernesto Fonseca Carrillo, Amado's uncle. A mass arrest of more than a hundred American-based Herrera affiliates had decimated that organization. The warring federations most able peacemaker, Juan Esparragoza Moreno, had been jailed, and by 1989 the most powerful Mexican kingpin, Miguel Félix Gallardo, had been arrested in Guadalajara and charged with conspiring to murder Camarena. That year as well, Mexican authorities announced that they had discovered the body of Cipriano. The official ruling was suicide -- but a senior U.S. official told me, "Yeah. He put an AK-47 in his mouth and shot himself fifteen times."

When the smoke lifted, the Mexican drug federation was in tatters. A gaping power vacuum spanned practically all of western Mexico. Cipriano wasn't there to control Sonora. Acosta had fallen in Ojinaga. And in the burgeoning Juárez *plaza*, two drug lords -- Gilberto "El Greñas" ("the Mophead") Ontivero Luccro and former Mexican Federal Security Police regional director Rafael Aguilar Guajardo -- had been hauled into custody in 1986. Following the dismantling of Rafael Muñoz Talavera's Sylmar operation in 1989, the *plaza* was there for the taking.

HE ARRIVED IN JUÁREZ WITH IMPECCABLE credentials: nephew of Aviles' bookkeeper, brother of Sonora's drug lord, Acosta's right-hand man a smooth veteran of the trade who had worked his way up from the fields of Durango and Chihuahua and acquired his share of Colombian contacts along the way. He was handy with an automatic, but he preferred alliance building to Acosta-style gunslinging. The dirty work he left to the underlings of his brother Vicente, who accompanied Carrillo to Juárez but kept an even lower profile.

In the vein of his predecessors Aviles, Gallardo, and Esparragoza, Carrillo united the drug lords of Mexico and convinced them that if they let him broker the major deals with the Calí cartel in Colombia, everyone would benefit. He established ties with the traffickers who served as gatekeepers of the twelve Mexican ports of entry, from Tijuana and Mexicali, along the California coast, to the three Arizona corridors and Matamoros, on the western lip of the Gulf. His cross-country smuggling operations served dual purposes: to maintain his alliances and to avoid detection by the U. S. intelligence agents stationed in Mexico. Along the way, he bankrolled industrialists and bought off Mexican law enforcement officials -- almost always in private, except in Juárez, where periodic public appearances were necessary to preserve his status in the *plaza*.

The nature of his deals with the Colombians varied according to the vagaries of the market and the conditions in the corridors. Having received several barrels of Peruvian coca paste and processed it into white powder in their labs, the Calí traffickers would establish where demand in the U.S. was highest. Then the cartel honcho, Miguel Rodriguez Orejuela, would call his close friend Carrillo. Taking into account the size of the load, Carrillo would consult with the Mexican drug federation's division heads to determine the optimal means of delivery into Mexico. Sometimes the cocaine would be ferried through the Pacific and transferred onto fishing boats and pleasure crafts controlled by Carrillo. More often than not, however, the drugs would arrive by air. The planes would fly with their lights off and land on an obscure airstrip somewhere in the rural interior. A fuel truck would be waiting, along with half a dozen or so other trucks. The truck drivers would load the cocaine into their vehicles, the Plane would be refueled, and then the airstrip would be deserted. The cargo trucks would be driven to warehouses along the border -- usually in Juárez -- where the drugs would be repackaged and stored.

When the time was right, the gatekeeper -- in Juárez's case, Vicente Carrillo Fuentes -- would select the best method for getting the product across the border, as well as the *pasadores* (border crossers) to do the honors. Some shipments might be flown across, though American radar balloons and Air Force pursuit planes have proven an effective deterrent to this approach. Or the goods might reach the tunnels -- like the one federals covered this past summer in Nogales, which originated in the floor of an abandoned downtown church hooked up to the city's sewer system, and passed directly underneath the checkpoint into Arizona. (Though tunneling into Juárez would require the difficult measure of digging underneath the Rio Grande, one federal analyst cautions, "Amado's imagination is the key. If you try to pin him down with the overland method, he'll kill you with a tunnel.") But the *pasadores* would in all likelihood cross in vehicles -- though the type (cargo trucks, vans, Ford Tauruses) and the timing of the crossing would be matters of deliberation. Once in America, the drugs might be stashed in safe houses throughout El Paso, repackaged once more, and moved by different vehicles out of Texas; or the *pasadores* might simply take the border access ramp to the freeway and slip into the flurry of interstate traffic.

Compromising law enforcement officials on either side of the checkpoint would surely enter into the equation, though to what extent is difficult to gauge. Carrillo's pesos-or-bullets offer would be tendered throughout Juárez; where, as one veteran federal agent in El Paso puts it, "All the officers, both federal and local, are either afraid of Carrillo or compromised." On the American side U.S. Customs officials frequently order random and spontaneous searches of border traffic with drug-sniffing dogs to keep both traffickers and corrupt inspectors off-balance. Still, as one senior American law enforcement official in the area observes, "The sheer numbers of vehicles coming across the border explain the success of drug dealers more than corruption world. Yes, corruption may be there. But how much is even needed?"

Throughout Mexico, and even in Juárez, other enterprising traffickers continued to ply their trade. But what distinguished Carrillo's organization from the rest was size. The Colombians wanted huge volumes moved and moved in a hurry. Carrillo was fortunate to be firmly in control of the Mexican drug federation and thus a major beneficiary when the Calí cartel began purchasing massive Boeing 727's and French Caravelles to replace their twin-engine planes. Bigger planes meant bigger deals -- assuming, of course, that the *patrón* could provide larger airstrips, more smuggling vehicles, and greater numbers of *pasadores*. Carrillo could provide. Unlike the Herrera family-run organization, he contracted the services of numerous outsiders. This meant that he could handle shipments both vast and small, keeping costs down by not maintaining a bloated payroll and, at the same time, keeping various factions happy -- and, not coincidentally, making his operation's activities less traceable. Though he had a strong relationship with cartel principle Miguel Orejucia. Carrillo's business did not seem to suffer in the least when Orejuela was arrested by five hundred Colombian policemen and soldiers in Calí this past August. The 727's continued to land on his airstrips. His value to the Colombians meant that the Lord of the Skies enjoyed sweetheart deals. Frequently they would pay him 50 percent in cash and 50 percent in product -- a huge boost in profit because Carrillo's people could cut the pure cocaine and, in doing so, double or triple the dividend.

The Colombians regarded Carrillo as one of their own. He went about his business with cool, impersonal precision. He wasn't an egotistical hothead like Juan Garcia Abrego, the Matamoros *patrón* who seemed to enjoy the notoriety of being the only international trafficker ever to wind up on the FBI's Ten Most Wanted Fugitives list. Carrillo didn't go ordering the deaths of government officials as Abrego was suspected of doing, or spraying bullets at his rivals as the Joaquin "El Rapido" Guzman and Arrellano Felix factions had been doing to each other for years. As a result of their brashness, Abrego and the Arrellano Felix brothers were on the lam (the latter for allegedly murdering a Roman Catholic cardinal by mistake while trying to assassinate Guzman in 1993), and Guzman was behind bars. Unlike the other *patrones,* Carrillo never partied in America, where drug-trafficking indictments awaited him and justice was not so easily compromised. The Lord of the Skies remained standing because he didn't shoot himself in the foot.

Yet Carrillo was not untouchable in the Colombians' eyes. Like anyone else, he would be held accountable for the efforts of his organization. In August 1993 more than nine tons of cocaine -- believed to have been sent from Calí chief Orejuela to Carrillo's organization -- were seized off the coast of Mazatlán by the Mexican navy. The seizure, likely made possible by an informant among Carrillo's ranks, amounted to a $20 million loss for the Colombians. Not long after that, Carrillo, his wife, their two children, and a few friends were dining at Bali Hai, a restaurant in a suburb south of Mexico City. when several hitmen walked in and opened fire with their automatic weapons. In the shower of bullets, two of Carrillo's dining companions were killed.

If, as was speculated, the assassination attempt was ordered by the Calí cartel as payback for their loss at Mazatlán, the Lord of the Skies and the Colombians apparently managed to patch things up in a hurry. Perhaps it was the cartel's basic admiration for Carrillo that made appeasement possible. After all, the hitmen apparently hadn't seen enough photographs of the camera-shy Carrillo to know whom to take aim at. As a result, they went after the two dining companions who had tried to flee; in the meantime, Carrillo simply ducked under the table. His stealth, once again, had carried the day.

IN JANUARY OF THIS YEAR DEA AND customs officials took aim at one ring of Carrillo's Juárez *pasadores:* the port runners. Throughout 1994 this particular smuggling ring had employed a crude but surprisingly effective means of transporting cocaine across the border. They simply drove their cars up to the checkpoint and, if motioned over to a secondary search lane by an inspector, stomped on the accelerator and barreled across into El Paso. More than 250 port runners had successfully sped their way into the U.S. in 1994, ferrying an estimated ten tons of cocaine. Acting in conjunction with the El Paso Police Department, the Department of Public Safety, the Immigration and Naturalization Service, and the Internal Revenue Service, DEA and Customs agents infiltrated the port-running operation and on January 30 arrested eighteen members of the organization, seizing 7,034 pounds of cocaine and 2,559 pounds of marijuana.

One of the men in charge of the interagency roundup, Travis Kuykendall (then with the DEA). Was both pleased and worried. "We took down too much coke for there not to be repercussions in Juárez," he now says.

Four months later, Choy Márquez, a port runner who had managed to avoid arrest, was sitting with his girlfriend in his car outside the Juárez fairgrounds when the two were met by a hail of bullets. At least Marquez's body would be accounted for. "Everyone above him in the operation has just disappeared," says Kuykendall. "We have pretty good information that they were all assassinated."

It has become a matter of grim predictability in Juárez: Whenever a major seizure of Carrillo's drugs takes place on the American side, there is hell to pay. "He immediately orders the assassination of everyone who *could have* turned the shipment in," says Kuykendall, "and bodies fall left and right."

More often than not, they fall in familiar fashion: hands cuffed or tied behind the back and a single bullet to the back of the head. A few of the bodies have been found in the city garbage dump. Others have been strewn about in Lote Bravo, just south of Juárez. A few hits have taken place farther afield, as in the case of Rafael Aguilar Guajardo, a rival Juárez drug lord who was believed to have cooperated with U.S. agents on the Sylmar case. For his sins, Aguilar was shot to death while vacationing at the Hyatt Cancún Caríbe in April 1993. Back home in Juárez, seven of Aguila's associates were also executed.

Some of the bodies found in the past year were informants on the DEA or FBI payroll, but most of the rest were individuals killed without any evidence that they had given law enforcement authorities any information of any kind. In the court of Amado Carrillo Fuentes, to be suspected -- or to be close to someone suspected – is to become immediately eligible for the death penalty, according to U.S. intelligence officials. In November 1994, in the trunk of a Honda Accord abandoned on the Bridge of the Americas, El Paso police officials found the bodies of retired Mexican police official José Muñoz Rubalcava and his two sons. The word on the streets of Juárez was that the ex-cop was a DEA informant, and as if to punctuate this suspicion, his mouth was bound with a yellow cord and bow-gift wrapped, as it were.

The Juárez authorities argued that the bodies were found on the American side of the bridge, and that the matter was therefore outside of their jurisdiction. Not that the location of the corpses makes much difference: In the two hundred to four hundred drug-related homicides in Juárez over the past three years, no one can point to a single arrest that has been made. The Juárez government's failure to prosecute Carrillo in connection with the killings corresponds with its failure to curtail his trafficking in any recognizable way. Those failures, in turn, reflect a failure that is national in scope. Despite Mexico president Ernesto Zedillos declaration at the White House on October 10 that "we are determined to use every resource at our disposal to fight tirelessly against the evil of illegal drugs" the only warrant possibly outstanding for the Lord of the Skies in Mexico is a weapons charge -- "the equivalent of jaywalking," as one federal analyst dryly notes.

They're not looking for Carrillo, they're not investigating Carrillo," says Kuykendall. "We are, but they're not. It's a shame that the citizens of Juárez are under siege by his group and nothing is being done." Indeed, the shared silence among the Mexican media, law enforcement authorities, and government officials hasn't fooled the Juárez public. They know all too well that since Amado Carrillo Fuente, took charge of the *plaza*, their city has become a far more dangerous place. And though their outrage has compelled them recently to elect a new mayor who pledges to fight drug trafficking, they have heard the rumors that high-ranking federal police officials break bread with a billionaire smugglers and they are under no illusions as to who runs their *plaza*.

There is a peculiar irony in all of this for the city that stands a stone's throw away from the carnage. Despite the tons of cocaine, marijuana, methamphetamine, and heroin that surge through Juárez and across the Rio Grande, El Paso seems at ease. Its homicide rate is low, its legal system appears far less tainted by corruption than the drug corridors along the Rio Grande Valley, and its streets seem no more or less blighted by drug abuse than any other city with more than half a million residents. Instead, drugs have lent El Paso a kind of false prosperity. The city enjoys a monthly cash surplus ranging from $50 million to $70 million -- meaning that upwards of half a billion dollars annually circulates through El Paso without actually being generated by its economy. Though local officials protest that the surplus comes from tourist dollars, federal officials point to the tens of millions in currency actually seized in El Paso from drug transactions as a more likely indicator. In any event, the correlation between the El Paso-Juárez corridor's premier trafficking status and the ranking of El Paso's cash surplus as fifth highest in the nation is difficult to dispute. The hot money has helped buoy the local real estate market and has boosted car and liquor sales; it is providing El Paso with an economic stimulus that the city has neither earned nor can count upon.

"One day we're going to wake up and realize that much of the economy of El Paso is reliant on drug money," says Tom Kennedy, an assistant special agent in charge of the DEA's El Paso office. "If we're ever successful at putting away Carrillo and shutting down the drug traffic here, numerous businesses in this city will crash and burn. El Paso is not a big city like Miami; it won't be able to absorb the impact. It'll be like a cancer -- something we can't feel and can't diagnose until we experience it. And then it will be too late."

Perhaps we owe a debt of gratitude to Amado Carrillo Fuentes for the clarity he has lent to the never-ending debate over American drug use. For while the Lord of the Skies reigns unfettered, one need not even attempt to calculate what his drugs are doing to our street", or our children. We can instead stick to the inarguable: In Juárez, the killing is done with bullets: across the bridge, the killing is done with pesos. We can look at the era of high-volume drug trafficking as an era of high-volume killing, first and foremost. And we can await the day that a killer meets a killer's justice.

MCDUFF WAS FREE TO KILL
by Gary Cartwright

TWENTY-ONE YEARS AFTER HE SHOULD HAVE DIED in the electric chair for the savage murder of three teenagers, Kenneth McDuff was back on the streets, as cocky and mean and dangerous as ever. In the small Central Texas community of Rosebud, where McDuff grew up, people pumped shells into shotguns and shoved heavy pieces of furniture in front of double and triple-locked doors. "This is a walking town," said John Killgore, the editor of the *Rosebud News,* "but these days you see very few people on the streets. McDuff's return has scared the hell out of this town." At Festival Days in the Falls County seat of Marlin word spread like wildfire that McDuff had sworn to show up and kill one person for every day he spent in prison. Tommy Sammon, who had humiliated McDuff in a playground fight in the eighth grade, worried about his teenage children. A man who had once prevented McDuff from crushing the throat of a young woman with a broomstick-a dress rehearsal for what McDuff would do to a teenage girl in southern Tarrant County some months later-pushed the button on his telephone answering machine and was greeted with the sound of three gunshots. No question about it: Kenneth McDuff was back in town.

It was October 11, 1989, Falls County Sheriff Larry Pamplin telephoned his longtime friend deputy U.S. marshal Parnell McNamara in Waco and told him, "You're not going to believe what happened, Parnell. They've paroled Kenneth McDuff." There was a brittle silence as McNamara processed this totally illogical piece of information, then McNamara laconically inquired, "Have they gone crazy?" There didn't seem to be any other explanation. McDuff wasn't just another killer who had fallen through a crack in the system; he was the most violent, sadistic, remorseless criminal either of these veteran lawmen had ever come across. Their association with McDuff went back more than a quarter of a century, because their fathers, the late deputy U.S. marshal T. P. McNamara and the late Falls County sheriff Brady Pamplin, had seen McDuff's savagery up close. Brady Pamplin was the lawman who had arrested McDuff in 1966 for the three murders -- literally shooting McDuff's car to pieces as he tried to escape. People had always wondered why Brady Pamplin didn't kill McDuff when he had the chance; no telling how many lives that would have saved. Larry Pamplin and Parnell McNamara and his brother, Mike-who is also a deputy marshal in Waco-were teenagers at the time, about the same age as McDuff, and the incident had made a permanent impression on them. Parnell McNamara remembered how Pamplin's voice broke as he described killings to Parnell's father. "Then he put a broomstick across the throat that poor little girl up in Tarrant County and broke her neck just like a possum." Brady Pamplin was as tough and as able as any lawman who ever lived, a legendary figure who had been a Texas Ranger before World War II and had served as sheriff of Falls County for nearly thirty years, a man who had stood toe to toe with the worst that society could spit up, but his voice quivered and his hands shook when he talked about Kenneth McDuff.

What really burned in the guts of the lawmen was how the system had failed so utterly, how at every juncture McDuff had thumbed his nose at authority and sent it reeling. Brady Pamplin and other Central Texas lawmen had been handling McDuff since he was a teenager, had seen flashes of his sadistic nature and his complete contempt for the rules of society. They finally put him away on a series of burglary charges in 1965, or so they thought. McDuff was assessed penalties totaling 52 years, but because he was only eighteen, the sentences were assessed concurrently instead of consecutively. McDuff made trusty in three months and was back on the street in less than ten, the smirk on his face suggesting that the time had been well spent. Eight months after he was paroled, McDuff went on one of his periodic rampages and killed the three teenagers. A jury gave him death, but after a 1972 Supreme Court decision effectively overturned all the death sentences in the United States, McDuff's sentence was commuted to life. In 1976, ten years after the murders, McDuff had served enough time to be eligible for parole, though the parole board was certainly under no obligation to grant it-and hardly anyone supposed that it ever would.

But McDuff had time on his side. He applied for parole, and when the board turned him down, he kept on applying until he succeeded-and now law enforcement officers say that as many as nine women may be dead as a result. This spring the entire nation learned what the Texas Board of Pardons and Paroles couldn't figure out. Kenneth McDuff is an unrepentant habitual killer. He was featured on America's Most Wanted and became the object of a national manhunt. In Texas the story of his twisted career was front page news, especially along the Interstate 35 corridor, where he had stalked his victims. By the time he was reapprehended Kenneth McDuff had come to personalize the violent crime wave that swept Texas in the past year — a crime wave abetted by a cynical parole policy whose aim has been to empty the prisons rather than safeguard the streets.

To gain parole from the Texas Department of Criminal Justice-as the superboard that controls paroles, pardons, and the prison system is now called -- an inmate needs two votes from a three-person parole board team. In 1979 and again in 1980, McDuff got one of the two votes he needed, falling short by what must have seemed to him just a matter of bad luck. When he came up for parole the following year, McDuff tried to jigger the odds by offering a $10,000 bribe to a member of the parole board. He was subsequently tried and convicted for the bribery attempt. Despite the brutal nature of the murders, the fact that he was a three-time loser, and his bribery conviction, the parole board continued to view him as a good risk for release. In 1984 and 1985, McDuff again came within a single vote of gaining freedom. Finally, he got a second vote in 1988 and was approved for parole but the approval was rescinded when new information was received. The parole board refuses to reveal the nature of that new information but normally it would be letters of protest from the judge and the prosecutor at his trial. A year after that, to the shock of those same trial officials — and to law enforcement officers as well — the parole board saw fit to return McDuff to society. No, McDuff hadn't fallen through the cracks in the system; he had slithered through, cleverly, insidiously, like a rodent in the shadows.

On the day that McDuff was let out of prison and told to report to a parole officer in Temple, where his parents had moved, Sheriff Larry Pamplin made a prediction. "I don't know if it'll be next week or next month or next year," he told Parnell and Mike McNamara, "but one of these days, dead girls are gonna start turning up, and when that happens, the man you need to look for is Kenneth McDuff." Three days later, the naked body of 29-year-old Sarafia Parker was discovered in a field of weeds in southeast Temple, beaten and strangled.

ACHING TO PROWL

The McDuff's weren't the friendliest family in Rosebud when Kenneth was growing up — in fact, they were downright weird — but they weren't white trash either. They worked hard saved their money, and regularly attended the Assembly of God church. Kenneth s father, J.A. McDuff was a cement finisher who made a lot of money in the business during the building boom in Temple in the late seventies and early, eighties. Addie McDuff was a large, domineering woman who ruled over her four daughters and two sons, maintained the family's purse and operated a washateria across the street from the family home, just off Main Street. Newspaper editor John Killgore recalls, "The McDuff's were very dedicated to their children. Attentive, protective making sure they grew up knowing how to work and work hard."

Some people thought they were a little too protective. Addie McDuff and her three eldest daughters lavished attention on Kenneth and treated him as though he were a young god, somehow above the rules that restrained other children. Though Kenneth had a younger sister, he was regarded as the baby of the family. Classmates remember that Kenneth always had money in his pocket and usually wore nice clothes. When he was older his mother bought him a motorcycle that was probably the loudest machine in Rosebud. Kenneth's father was a tight-lipped man who went about his business and left family matters to his wife, although apparently he did not share her unwavering devotion to Kenneth. When Kenneth was charged with the three murders in Tarrant County, J. A. McDuff told a lawman: "If I believed he did what you say, the state wouldn't have to kill him. I'd do it myself."

In the late fifties the real troublemaker in the family was Kenneth's elder brother, Lonnie, who once pulled a knife on the popular (and tough) Rosebud school principal, D. L. Mayo, and got thrown down the stairs for his insolence. Lonnie, who was tongue-tied, liked to refer to himself as Rough Tough Lonnie McDuff, — "Wuff Tuff Wonnie McDuff," it sounded like. While Kenneth was in prison for murder, Lonnie was shot to death by the ex-husband of a woman he was seeing.

An entry in Kenneth McDuff's prison file notes that as a youth he was never required to assume responsibilities or observe standards of conduct adding, "If any problem arose [at school]... the school was to blame and Kenneth was completely innocent." Any attempt to discipline Kenneth was certain to bring Addie McDuff hurrying to the school in full fury, sometimes carrying a pistol or at least claiming to. Teachers referred to her as Pistol-Packing Mama McDuff. "Every teacher in school was afraid of her," says Ellen Roberts, a special education teacher. Many people in Rosebud had heard the story about Addie McDuff flagging down a school bus with her pistol, then giving the driver, who had thrown her son off the bus the previous day for fighting, a tongue-lashing. The story may or may not be true, but it illustrates the cloud of intimidation the McDuff's cast over the small town.

Kenneth took pleasure in bullying classmates and intimidating teachers. A classmate remembered how he would goad other kids into flipping quarters — Kenneth loved to gamble — until he had relieved them of their lunch money. Ellen Roberts recounts a strange experience when Kenneth's sixth-grade teacher sent him to her office for consultation. "He never said a word, no response whatsoever," she says. "He just sat there in stony silence and refused to make eye contact. That was most unusual in a young boy."

With an IQ of 92, Kenneth was not the brightest guy in class. He liked to call attention to his negative impulses. "When he scored zero on a test," a classmate remembers, "Kenneth would make sure everyone in class knew about it, make some kind of joke just to let everyone know he did it on purpose and he didn't give a damn." What this classmate remembers most is McDuff's maniacal laughter, usually at something in his class that no one else thought was funny and how, in an instant — "like turning a light on and off" — the laugh would dissolve into a glare so hard and cold it stopped conversation.

People who grew up in rosebud with Kenneth McDuff recall with enormous satisfaction that day in the eighth grade when McDuff challenged Tommy Sammon to meet him after school. Tommy was one of the most popular boys in school, a good athlete, modest, unassuming, not easily provoked. McDuff had been trying to goad him into a fight. He finally succeeded one day between classes, bumping against Sammon in the hallway and calling him a chickenshit in front of his friends. Ellen Roberts says, "Kenneth was so hated that when word got around that he was going to fight Tommy Sammon after school down by the drainage ditch, my whole class talked of nothing else." The fight, such as it was, lasted only a few minutes. Though McDuff was larger than Sammon — or almost anyone else in school — Sammon easily overpowered him. McDuff was big, but he wasn't strong. Sammon got him in a headlock, and McDuff bit him. The incident went down in Rosebud history as the day Tommy Sammon liberated the town (or at least the eighth grade) from the bully McDuff. Kenneth never bothered Sammon or anyone else in his class after that. A few months later, he quit school for good and went to work for his father.

The only close friend Kenneth had, either before or after he dropped out of school, was his brother, who listened to the stories of how society had mistreated Kenneth and counseled him on the proper response — screw 'em, was Lonnie's advice. Sometime in the fall of 1964, when Kenneth was about seventeen and spending his evenings breaking into buildings and prowling for sex, he confided to Lonnie that he had raped a woman, cut her throat, and left her for dead in a ditch. Lonnie told him to go to bed and forget it. Not long after that, McDuff was sent to prison for burglary. The rape and attempted murder were never reported; otherwise the parole board might not have looked so casually on McDuff when it decided to release him in December 1965.

Kenneth McDuff underwent a subtle but deadly change following that first parole. The belief that he had committed murder and gotten away with it — coupled with the short, easy prison term he served for pulling more than a dozen burglaries — hardened him, gave him an exaggerated sense of invulnerability. He wasn't a boy any longer; he was a man, having grown to six feet three inches and two-hundred-plus pounds, his broad shoulders and large hands causing him to look even larger. The evil of his countenance was accented by a crooked smile and bulblike Popeye nose. Though prison had not taught McDuff how to make friends, it had taught him how to attract smaller, weaker sidekicks who could be controlled through intimidation and counted on to take part in whatever twisted schemes appealed to McDuff's appetites. Kenneth seemed to enjoy having a witness to his debauchery.

One such unfortunate companion was Roy Dale Green, who lived with his mother in Marlin and worked for Kenneth's dad. Green was two years younger than Kenneth and was mesmerized by McDuff's tales — and sometimes exhibitions — of sadistic sex. One of McDuff's more brutal amusements, which he demonstrated once in a bedroom of Green's mother's home, was pinning a girl to the floor and squirting a tube of Deep Heat into her vagina. Kenneth bragged that he had raped and strangled several women in his time. "Killing a woman's like killing a chicken," he told Green. "They both squawk." Green wasn't certain that he believed McDuff — until the evening of August 6, 1966.

It was Saturday and McDuff was aching to prowl. He and Green had worked that morning pouring concrete at a construction site in Temple, and after work they cleaned up and headed for Fort Worth in the new Dodge Charger that McDuff's mother had given him when he got out of prison. Green, who was eighteen at the time, had never been to Fort Worth, but McDuff had worked there a few years earlier and said he knew some girls. They cruised the small town of Everman, just south of Fort Worth, drinking beer and visiting with friends, including a girl that Kenneth knew from church. Later that evening, after they had taken the girl home, Kenneth found what he was looking for — a pretty teenage girl in a red-and-white striped blouse and cutoff jeans—a total stranger, standing near a baseball field talking to two boys in a 1955 Ford. Purely by chance, McDuff selected his three victims — sixteen-year-old Edna Sullivan, her boyfriend, seventeen-year-old Robert Brand, and Robert's cousin, fifteen-year-old Mark Dunnam, who was visiting from California. Roy Dale Green watched with fascination as McDuff took a .38 pistol from under his car seat and walked over to the three young people. First, McDuff demanded that the boys hand over their billfolds, then he forced all three into the trunk of the car and locked them in. "They got a good look at my face," he told Green. "I'll have to kill them."

McDuff drove the Ford, with the teenagers in the trunk, down dark and narrow country roads, and Green followed in McDuff's Dodge, still not convinced that McDuff intended to harm his hostages. Presently, McDuff turned into a field and stopped. He opened the trunk and said, "I want the young lady out," pulling her by the arm. He instructed Green to lock her in the trunk of the Dodge, which Green did. Still in the trunk of the Ford, the two boys were on their knees, begging for their lives, when McDuff brought the gun up to chest level and shot them both in the face. He shot Brand twice and Dunnam three times, then lifted Dunnam by the hair and shot him again. Green saw the fire from the gun and covered his ears, looking away from the horror but not before seeing the look on McDuff's face, an expression of inner peace that seemed to say, How do you like it so far, Roy Dale? For some reason the trunk wouldn't shut, so McDuff backed the Ford, with the trunk open, against a fence, then McDuff and Green drove away in the Dodge, the terrified Edna Sullivan still a prisoner in the Dodge's trunk.

With McDuff driving, they headed south, crossing the Johnson County line, eventually stopping along a dirt road about eleven miles from where they had left the Ford with the boys' bodies. McDuff took Edna Sullivan from the trunk, made her undress, then threw her in the back seat and began raping her. He raped her two times, made Green rape her, then he raped her again. In all this time, Green heard the girl say just one thing, "I think you ripped something," she cried out as McDuff brutalized her for the third time. His sexual appetite momentarily in check, McDuff drove them to another location, down a gravel road. Stopping, he took the girl to the front of the car and told her to sit down on the road. Green wasn't sure what McDuff had in mind. Then he saw McDuff force the girl's head to the ground and begin choking her with a section of broomstick. "He mashed down hard," Green told lawmen. "She started waving her arms and kicking her legs, and he told me, "Grab her legs."' While Green held Edna Sullivan's legs, Kenneth McDuff crushed the life out of her. Then they threw her body over the fence and headed home, stopping along the way to bury the boys' billfolds and discard their own bloody underwear.

Roy Dale Green never fully recovered from the horror of that night. The next afternoon, while he was taking a Sunday ride with friends, news of the killings came over the radio and suddenly Green was blurting out the whole story. "My God, I've got to tell somebody!" he cried. He became the prosecution's star witness in the case against Kenneth McDuff, served five years for his part in the crimes, and returned to Marlin, where he lives to this day. "He stays out at the old family home and spends most of the day in his sister's beer joint, the Town Door," says Sheriff Larry Pamplin, who has known Green all his life. "To say he's messed up is a real understatement."

Vowing Kenneth's innocence, Addie McDuff hired a lawyer from Waco and sat in the courtroom with her daughters throughout the trial. McDuff denied any knowledge of the killings, of course, suggesting that Roy Dale Green was probably responsible and, in an aside to the jury, whining that Falls County sheriff Brady Pamplin had had it in for poor Kenneth McDuff for years. During one recess, Mama McDuff told reporters that Kenneth had been with a girl from his church at the time the three teenagers were murdered, that her son was willing to risk death in the electric chair to spare the girl's reputation. "He's too good for his own good," she said.

JUSTICE FOR MCDUFF, INC.

Two times in 1969 and again in April 1970, Kenneth McDuff came within a few days of his execution date, and each time he was granted stays. McDuff probably wasn't sweating it. Only a handful of executions had taken place in the United States in the two years before he was convicted and none in the time he had been on death row. And the case of *Furman v. Georgia* was working its way through the system. In 1972 the Supreme Court handed down its landmark decision, ruling that the unlimited discretion given to juries in capital trials-the ability, for example, to sentence someone to death without first focusing on the particular nature of the crime and the particular characteristics of the accused-amounted to cruel and unusual punishment and thus was unconstitutional. In effect, all the capital convictions in the country were overturned. Within a few months, the death sentences of all 88 inmates on death tow in Texas were commuted to life.

McDuff was transferred to the Ramsey Unit and assigned to work in the fields, which was where prison officials put inmates who needed the tightest supervision. "We considered McDuff to be extremely dangerous and a high escape risk," says David Christian, who was an assistant warden at the unit in the seventies.

In 1977, Addie McDuff hired a new lawyer, and the Kenneth McDuff story took on the trappings of a Hollywood melodrama. A Dallas attorney named Gary Jackson began a long and costly effort to prove that McDuff had been framed and that the true killer was his evil running mate, Roy Dale Green. Over the next decade, Kenneth McDuff became more than merely a client for Gary Jackson; he became an industry, incorporated in 1989 under the name of Justice for McDuff, Inc. There was, until recently, talk of book and movie deals. Jackson, who refused to be interviewed for this article and no longer represents McDuff, seemed a curious candidate to lead the McDuff crusade — he and his wife were both active in the Republican party of Texas, and Jackson had a career in the U.S. Army Reserve, where he holds the rank of colonel. He didn't usually practice criminal law. Nevertheless, Gary Jackson became a zealous advocate for the convicted killer. Poring through old trial records and newspaper accounts and crossing the country to interview witnesses, Jackson devised a new scenario for the events of August 6, 1966.

In a 26-page, single-spaced letter written to the chairman of the Board of Pardons and Paroles in 1979, Jackson presented what he considered dramatic new evidence. At the trial thirteen years before, McDuff had testified that on the night of the killings he handed over the keys to his new Dodge Charger to Green so that Green could go on a date. In the revised version, Gary Jackson charged that Green needed the car to pull a robbery — the implication being that McDuff wanted no part of the robbery but had no objection to loaning his car to Green. In both versions McDuff had waited for Green in a burned-out shopping center in Everman, napping while Green satisfied his lust for murder. The problem, of course, was how Green could have driven both the Dodge and the Ford.

To get around this apparent impossibility, the lawyer developed a theory in which Green rendezvoused with the teenagers, whom he had met earlier that evening, to do some "underage drinking" in the field where the boys' bodies were later discovered. Running out of beer, Green and his new friends left the Dodge in the field and took the Ford to buy more, which they consumed at the second location-the spot in Johnson County where Edna Sullivan's body was found. There, Green made his move. Forcing the boys into the trunk at gunpoint, he proceeded to rape Edna Sullivan. While Green was occupied, the boys forced open the trunk. Realizing the impending danger, Gary Jackson wrote, Green "jumps out of the car and, without thinking, shoots the boys . . . using all six shells in his pistol." The six shots were a nice romantic touch, -- it always is in the movies -- because it meant that Green was out of bullets and had no choice except to strangle Edna Sullivan with a broomstick. He leaves her body there and returns the Ford, with the two dead boys in the trunk, to the first location, where he picks up the Dodge and heads for the shopping center where McDuff has been waiting. This scenario had the added advantage of placing all three murders in Johnson County, out of the jurisdiction of the judge and jury that found McDuff guilty in the first place.

Gary Jackson's letter impressed at least one member of the parole board enough to vote for McDuff, but it did not result in a parole for his client. In 1980 the Dallas attorney came up with additional evidence, alleging in a writ of habeas corpus several incidents of jury misconduct and tampering. Rumors of improper conduct had first surfaced back in 1966 in a newspaper report that one of the jurors had carried a flask of "needful intoxicant" into the room where the jury was quartered and in a story in the old *Fort Worth Press*, alleging that the sheriff of Tarrant County had come to the dorm and told jurors about another crime that he believed McDuff had committed. This one involved a rape and disfigurement, and the sheriff supposedly told jurors that because of "stupid" laws, they hadn't been permitted to hear about it. The story had been leaked to the media by a bailiff named Rose Marie Anderson, who had vanished after the trial, claiming that she had been threatened by the sheriff for speaking up. Gary Jackson tracked the ex-bailiff to Arizona, where she repeated her allegations in an affidavit. Jackson was able to get McDuff an evidentiary hearing in Fort Worth in 1982, but the court found the allegations not worthy of belief. During that same time period, McDuff wrote several letters of his own, one of them to the Court of Criminal Appeals in Austin, reporting a rumor that his trial judge in Fort Worth had taken $750,000 from the Mafia.

"MY FAMILY'S GOT THE MONEY"

In his six years on death row and his seventeen years among the general prison population, Kenneth McDuff wasn't necessarily a model prisoner, but he knew how to keep his shirt clean. Hard cases like McDuff are given maximum leeway; As long as they are not putting a knife into someone or openly smuggling drugs, they can do almost what they please. After transferring to the Retrieve Unit, near Angleton, McDuff became boss of his tier of cells. In that position, a man of McDuff's talents would have enjoyed not only the blessing of the wardens but substantial clout among inmates, meaning, among other things, that McDuff was able to influence which inmate was assigned as his cell mate. While McDuff was at Retrieve, his cell mate-or punk, to use the vernacular-provided whatever McDuff required in the way of sex and drugs which he squirreled away in a red balloon inserted up his rectum-keistering drugs, they call it. Not your garden variety punk, this particular one was large and cold-eyed, with an excess of body hair and tattoos, but his menacing appearance was handicapped by the fact that he had offended the Aryan Brotherhood and faced the daily threat of assassination. It was a measure of McDuff's prestige that he was able to protect his punk without tarnishing his own good record.

Mastering the angles came naturally to Kenneth McDuff. The parole board looked favorably on inmates who tried to better themselves -- so this eighth-grade dropout enrolled in correspondence courses. If there was a shift in policy, or a subtle trend among parole board members, McDuff was one of the first to sniff it out. The procedure for considering which inmates deserved parole was-and is-for one of the three members of the parole team to interview a batch of inmates (usually fifteen to twenty in a single day) as they become eligible, then vote yes or no on each one and pass the files to the second member. Most of the time the members don't even bother to discuss the cases with each other. In the early eighties, during Bill Clements' administration, the governor had to approve paroles, which is no longer the case. Scuttlebutt among prisoners held that if a Clements appointee voted yes on an applicant that he had personally interviewed, at least one of the other members was likely to go along and so was the governor.

When McDuff's name came before the parole board in 1980, he received the vote of one member, Helen Copitka, who had been a parole commissioner since 1975 (before 1989 both commissioners and board members voted on parole). Copitka was swayed by the material that attorney Gary Jackson had sent to the parole board. Copitka was still on the board in 1981, but McDuff asked to be interviewed by Glenn Heckmann, who had been appointed by Governor Clements in January 1980. As soon as he was alone with Heckmann in the chaplain's office, McDuff said, "If you can get me out of this pen, I guarantee that $10,000 will be left in the glove compartment of your car. I know you're the governor's man. Word is, I get your vote, I'm out of here. My family's got the money." Heckmann mumbled that he would take McDuff's offer under advisement and went straight to the office of the Brazoria County district attorney, who held a charge of bribery against McDuff.

The charge resulted in McDuff's third conviction, which meant the jury had an opportunity to give him life under the state's old habitual felon act; another life sentence would have pushed McDuff's eligible parole date into 1992. Instead, McDuff (with help from Gary Jackson) once again displayed his uncanny talent for slithering through the system. Over the objection of prosecutor Ken Dies, the judge granted McDuff considerable latitude to tell the jury about his criminal past-not the details of his murder spree in 1966, but his own fantasy of how the system had conspired against him time after time, injustice heaped upon injustice, the good name of "McDuff" besmirched by charlatans. It was a soliloquy of soap opera proportions, and McDuff carried it off with a straight face.

Under the provisions of the habitual felon act, the jury first voted on McDuff's guilt or innocence in the charge of bribery; that part was easy. The law then called for a separate deliberation, one that was strictly technical in which the jury was required to find that the Kenneth A. McDuff they had just found guilty was the same Kenneth A. McDuff that two previous juries had found guilty. But the jury misunderstood the instructions. "They got confused by McDuff's testimony, which was partly my fault," Ken Dies admits. "They thought that they were supposed to rule on McDuff's guilt or innocence in the two previous cases." Of course, they couldn't be sure, since it didn't hear the evidence in those cases. So instead of giving McDuff life, the jury opted for two years — a meaningless punishment, since McDuff had accumulated more than two years of good time merely waiting for his trial. In effect, McDuff offered a bribe to a parole officer and got away with it.

So why did a 1989 parole board — fully aware of McDuff's criminal history and cognizant that the jury that found him guilty of murder also found that he was likely to kill again — decide to put him back among us? The quick answer is that by 1989 Kenneth McDuff was no longer a name or even a case history; he was just a number. Two years before, Bill Clements, the parole board, and the prison system had decided that to prevent Texas prisons from becoming over crowded in violation of court-imposed ceilings, 750 inmates a week had to be paroled. That meant the fifteen members of the parole board (the number was elevated to eighteen in 1989) had to interview and study the files of at least 1,000 inmates every five working days. Old timers like McDuff, convicts whose names came up year after year, weren't even interviewed anymore but were lumped with similar inmates in special review groups. Their files — if board members bothered to study them at all — contained only the most basic and banal information, hardly anything to suggest the true nature of an inmate. By the time McDuff was paroled, eight of every ten parole applications were being approved, and the system was still falling behind. All the good risks for parole had been exhausted; the parole board was getting down to the bottom of the barrel. And then the bottom was lowered. Time was awarded so liberally that an inmate could get credit for serving one full year in just 22 days. In a prison system with a capacity of 60,000 inmates, more than 36,000 received paroles in 1989, the year Kenneth McDuff went free. The goals of the state became not to keep the streets safe but to keep the tap flowing and the federal courts at bay.

Chris Mealy, the parole board member who cast the deciding vote that freed McDuff, recalls that when McDuff came up for special review in September 1989, he was impressed by two things. First, McDuff had begun to improve himself by taking college-credit courses, and second, the file showed that in six of the fifteen years since he had become eligible for parole, McDuff had received one affirmative vote. In hindsight, Mealy admits that maybe he made an error. "If any of what we know is true, then obviously a mistake was made. It's a human system. Errors will be made. Some of them will be very costly. I wish that I could take it back."

But in the case of Kenneth McDuff the parole board blew it not once but twice. In July 1990, nine months after he was released, McDuff was charged with a new crime, making a terroristic threat — a misdemeanor, but also an offense sufficient to put him back behind bars for the remainder of his life, because it was committed while he was on parole. The charge grew out of a racial incident in downtown Rosebud. McDuff directed some slurs at a group of black teenagers who were minding their own business, then chased one of them down an alley with a knife and threatened to kill him. At his preliminary parole revocation hearing, McDuff spewed forth his loathing for blacks with such intensity that Gary Jackson had to shout at his client to prevent him from doing additional damage to his claim of innocence. McDuff was returned to TDCJ

Crime and Criminals

in September, but once again the system faltered. After conferring with Sheriff Larry Pamplin, Falls County district attorney Tom Sehon made the fateful decision to drop the misdemeanor charge — most of his witnesses were too frightened to testify, anyway — and allow the parole board to deal with McDuff. To make sure the board understood that the people who knew McDuff best considered him a continuing menace, Sehon wrote a letter in which he called McDuff "the most extraordinarily violent criminal ever to set foot in Falls County," and advised the board against ever reinstating McDuff's parole.

Nevertheless, Gary Jackson filed a motion to have McDuff's parole reinstated. He made the point that the charge that had caused it to be revoked had been dismissed. What happened next was bureaucracy at its worst. The board had long considered the revocation and rein statement process a waste of time and, for years, had delegated to its staff (known as hearings officers) the power to revoke and reinstate paroles, even though some lawyers believe that the practice is illegal. There was no hearing, no testimony, no advocacy of any kind. The board made no formal decision to reinstate McDuff's parole. Some anonymous hearing officer simply decided that there was no reason to keep Kenneth McDuff locked up. On December 6, 1990, Kenneth McDuff went free again.

"PLEASE, NOT ME"

Sheriff Larry Pamplin and his friends in the U.S. marshal's office in Waco, the McNamaras, sensed that McDuff was back on the prowl long before they could prove it. "The most frustrating part," says Pamplin, "is that we knew he was going to kill someone. We just didn't know when or where." In any case, he wasn't clear what they could do about it. Unless McDuff committed a crime in Falls County, Pamplin wouldn't have jurisdiction, and the only way the McNamaras would be able to investigate would be if McDuff became a federal fugitive. Still, the three lawmen did what they could to keep track of McDuff. In the beginning, at least, McDuff was cool enough to keep on the good side of his parole officer, and no other law enforcement agency seemed at all interested in his activities.

McDuff moved frequently — Temple, Rockdale, Cameroon, Bellmead, Tyler, Dallas — usually staying close to his mother or one of his sisters, most of the time with no apparent means of support, driving new cars, spending freely, robbing crack dealers on the street. The randomness of his movements made connecting him with specific murders almost impossible for Pamplin and the McNamaras. They didn't even learn about several of the killings McDuff is now suspected of committing until weeks after the fact.

In the spring of 1991, McDuff enrolled in Texas State Technical College in Waco and moved into a dormitory on campus. Starting then, and in the months that followed, several Waco-area prostitutes were reported missing, a fact that didn't appear to alarm Waco police or prompt them to ask hard questions of McDuff. A woman named Regina Moore was seen kicking and screaming in the cab of McDuff's red pickup truck as it ran through a police checkpoint, and though the police did look up McDuff several days later and questioned him, nothing came of the incident. He seemed to be living a charmed life; he beat up and nearly blinded a fellow student at TSTC and threatened several others, and still nobody reported him to the police. It was a cool life, student by day, drug-crazed prowler by night, nobody asking questions.

Then, a week before he was scheduled to take his final exams, McDuff abandoned all pretense of cool. Sometime late in the evening of March 1, 1992, he parked his tan Thunderbird at the New Road Inn just south of Waco and vanished into the shadows. That same night, less than a block away, 22-year-old Melissa Northup was kidnapped from a convenience store where she worked. Her body was found weeks later, bound and floating in a gravel pit in Dallas County, near the spot where the killer had left her car. A few weeks after Northup's disappearance, police discovered the naked and badly decomposed body of Valencia Kay Joshua in a shallow grave in a wooded area behind TSTC. Joshua was one of the missing prostitutes. She was last seen alive on the night of February 24, on the TSTC campus, looking for McDuff's dormitory room. McDuff's sudden disappearance caught the parole board and everyone else by surprise. Addie McDuff was so worried that she filed a missing persons report.

Knowing McDuff's history, the McNamaras realized they had to act quickly, and for once, the system cooperated. McDuff had made a mistake that played into the hands of the law. He had sold drugs to an informant. Using information provided by two informants, assistant U.S. attorney Bill Johnson of Waco charged McDuff with possession of firearms and distribution of drugs. McDuff had unwittingly become a federal fugitive, which was all the McNamaras needed to get on his trail. The U.S. Marshals Service had already assigned 250 investigators to Operation Gunsmoke, a nationwide effort to target violent offenders and get them off the streets. McDuff fit the mandate of Operation Gunsmoke right down to his evil smirk.

By early March, a formidable Kenneth McDuff task force had been assembled in Waco. It consisted of lawmen from several county and local police departments, agents from the Bureau of Alcohol, Tobacco, and Firearms and the Drug Enforcement Agency, Texas Rangers, an investigator from the Texas Department of Criminal Justice, and about two dozen federal marshals from Operation Gunsmoke, including two of the agency's international supersleuths, Mike Carnevale of San Antonio and Dan Stoltz of Houston. Capturing McDuff was becoming a national priority. "Until I actually got on the scene down in Texas," says Mike Earp, a supervisory inspector of the Marshals Service's enforcement division in Washington, D.C., "I didn't realize what an impact McDuff had had on those small communities, that people were absolutely terrified of the man." Earp, a distant relative of the most famous marshal of all, Wyatt Earp, dispatched one of the service's mobile command centers, a double tractor trailer rig called Red October. Parked on the lot behind the federal building in Waco for the duration of the search, Red October put the task force in communication with every law enforcement agency in the country. It seemed somehow appropriate that the job of tracking down one of the worst killers in modern times should fall on the Marshals Service, the oldest law enforcement agency in the country, founded in 1789 by George Washington. It seemed appropriate, too, that Parnell and Mike McNamara (assisted by another Waco-based deputy, Alonda Guilbeau) should take the point in this deadly race against time.

Many of McDuff's ex-convict running mates lived in Temple and nearby towns, so that's where the task force focused its search. Layer by layer, McDuff's sordid past was overturned. In the community of Holland, they questioned some people whose family album consisted almost entirely of photographs taken at TDCJ. One marshal said matter-of-factly that one of the boys told them that after his daddy killed his mama, "the old man had only stabbed him once and beat him twice with a tire tool." A major shock was the discovery that Kenneth McDuff had a daughter. The woman that he raped and left for dead in 1964 not only survived but also had his baby. The daughter, Theresa, was 21 when she learned that her real father was a convicted killer named Kenneth McDuff. Theresa told the marshals that she had visited McDuff in prison and became fascinated by him. He tried to persuade her to smuggle drugs. After his parole, McDuff offered to take her to Las Vegas and be her pimp. She also told the marshals that McDuff's family had paid $25,000 to a former member of the parole board to secure his release from prison in 1989, an accusation that has led to an ongoing investigation of several former parole board members. Disenchanted with the man she once found so fascinating, Theresa has moved out of state, as far from Kenneth McDuff as possible.

At first McDuff's associates were too loyal — or maybe they were simply too frightened — to give up much information. The McNamaras developed a technique for softening them up. They would launch into a bloody description of McDuff's murder spree in 1966, watching the reaction as the story spilled out. Sure, his friends knew from being in prison that McDuff had killed some people, but nobody inside went into details. They didn't realize that there were three of them, that they were kids, for Christ's sake, that the boys had begged on bended knees as McDuff blew off their faces, that Edna Sullivan's eyes had filled with terror as McDuff leaned his full weight onto the broomstick pressed across her throat. The story always got a reaction, even from the sorriest of criminals.

The search was as arduous as it was intense, requiring the lawmen from the various agencies to pull eighteen-hour shifts, usually without a day off. Sometimes they didn't bother going back to their motel room to sleep, curling up instead on the floor of the marshal's office in Waco for a few hours. But piece by piece, they began putting things together. The first big break came when they cornered McDuff's onetime punk in the parking lot outside of Por Boy's Lounge in Temple. After some persuasion, he told them about a woman drug dealer in Harker Heights, who in turn directed them to a thug in Dallas, who told about spending Christmas Day with McDuff in Austin. This was an especially interesting revelation because it established that McDuff had been in the Capital City five days before 28-year-old Colleen Reed was abducted from a car wash west of downtown. Witnesses had reported that two men in a tan car with rounded tail lights — a good description of McDuff's Thunderbird -- had grabbed Reed and sped off going the wrong way on West Fifth Street. Driving the wrong way on one way streets was a McDuff trademark, one of the many ways he demonstrated his contempt for the rules of society. The Austin police were under enormous public pressure to solve the Reed case but they had dismissed McDuff as a suspect because, according to their sources, McDuff had not been in Austin since October.

But the McNamaras were sure that McDuff was their man. They began running through a list of McDuff's buddies looking for someone who fit the description of the second occupant of the tan car-a Hispanic or dark-complected white male. They stopped at the name of Alva Hank Worley. A 34-year-old concrete worker who hung out with McDuff, Worley fit the description fairly well, but more than that he was a textbook example of the kind of weak-willed sidekick McDuff liked to have around. They saw Hank Worley as a nineties version of Roy Dale Green, a man haunted by what he had done, a man ready to talk. . .

Worley lived with his fourteen-year-old daughter at Bloom's Motel, south of Temple, and late one night the McNamaras, along with a deputy from the Bell County Sheriff's Department, knocked on his door. The late hour was calculated for maximum psychological effect. They didn't expect much out of Worley on the first visit and that's what they got. He claimed that he barely knew Kenneth McDuff. When Mike McNamara went into his bloody account of McDuff's murder spree, Hank Worley didn't blink. "That was not a normal reaction," Mike told his brother as they drove away. "He knows something."

Over the next two weeks, the marshals and the deputy dropped by Bloom's Motel at odd hours, always taking Worley by surprise -- what lawmen call "driving a suspect up." One thing Mike McNamara had learned in his 21 years on the job: Criminals are basically lazy, you drive them up by outhustling them, by working while they're sleeping (or trying to), by imprinting on their brains the relentlessness of your pursuit and the hopelessness of their attempts to outrun or outlast it. On the fifth visit, several marshals found Worley barbecuing and drinking beer with some friends. Over Worley's shoulder Mike McNamara could see Worley's young daughter, and he kept his eyes on her as he began his litany. "Hank, you're hiding a kid killer, you know that? You're protecting a man who raped and brutalized and strangled a girl not much older than your daughter over there. Pinned her on the ground, a broomstick across her throat, crying out to you for help, begging you to speak out, to do what's right, to save the life of some other young girl, to . . " About that time Hank Worley began to scream.

When Worley had calmed down, this is the story he told. Four days after Christmas, he rode with McDuff to Austin to look for drugs. They cruised the university area and scouted the bars on Sixth Street, then they crossed Lamar and turned south on a side street to double back in the direction they had come. That's when McDuff spotted Colleen Reed, washing her black Mazda in one of the bays at the car wash on Fifth.

She was a random choice, just as Edna Sullivan had been in 1966. McDuff parked his Thunderbird in the adjacent bay and disappeared for a moment. When he returned, he had Colleen Reed by the throat, holding her up so that just her toes touched the cement floor. "Please, not me," she cried. "Not me." McDuff threw her in the back seat and put Worley back there to control her.

A few miles out of Austin, McDuff pulled over and changed places with Worley. While Worley drove along I-35, McDuff stripped Colleen Reed naked, stubbed out a cigarette between her legs, and began raping her. When Worley stopped again to change places, he noticed that her hands were tied behind her back. While McDuff drove, Worley took off his own clothes and forced her to perform oral sex. Then he raped her. North of Belton, McDuff turned off the interstate onto Texas Highway 317, close to the house where his parents lived. He stopped on a narrow dirt road and raped Colleen Reed again.

When she was able to stumble to her feet, the young woman put her head on Worley's shoulder and said in a quivering voice, "Please don't let him hurt me anymore." McDuff grabbed her by the back of the neck, shoved her into the trunk of the Thunderbird, and slammed it shut. When McDuff dropped Worley off that night, Worley asked what he intended to do with the woman. "I'm gonna use her up," McDuff grinned. That was one of McDuff's pet phrases. It meant that he intended to kill her. Police believe that McDuff buried Colleen Reed in a field a few hundred yards from the frame house where J. A. and Addie McDuff live, but her body hasn't been found.

Worley's statement was released to the media, giving the McDuff task force what it needed most-national attention. On May 1, America's Most Wanted featured the search for Kenneth McDuff, generating fifty tips. Three days later, Kansas City, Missouri, police received a call from a viewer who had suddenly realized that a womanizing garbage truck worker known as Fowler was in fact a killer from Texas named McDuff. A few hours later, at the city dump, McDuff surrendered without a struggle.

While the investigation continues, authorities believe that McDuff may have killed as many as nine women going back to Sarafia Parker, whose body was found near Temple three days after he was paroled. He has been charged with capital murder in Waco in the deaths of Valencia Kay Joshua and Melissa Northup, and almost certainly will be charged with the kidnapping and murder of Colleen Reed. Federal and state prosecutors are discussing the appropriate way to deal with McDuff, but they are in general agreement that the prosecutor who can make the best capital case should get the first chance at him. This time, God willing, the system will do the right thing. If there has ever been a good argument for the death penalty, it's Kenneth McDuff.

THE PUBLIC HELL OF BOB CARREIRO

*The Houston trucker turned grief for his
murdered daughter into a publicity campaign that
led to her killer's conviction. Now, as a
victims' rights advocate, he's a star in a world he
never wanted to be a part of.*

by Mimi Swartz

THERE WAS STANDING ROOM ONLY IN A SMALL HARRIS COUNTY COURTROOM this past September on the day Robert Carreiro stood before the man sentenced to death for killing his only daughter. The occasion was Carreiro's reading of his victim's impact statement, a relatively new and quixotic end-of-trial proceeding meant to provide "closure" for those who have experienced or lost someone to violent crime. But for Carreiro it reflected the moment he let go of one life and embraced another. Behind him was his life as a private individual; before him was a future as a public victim, an inhabitant of that niche in American society where one man's pain is another man's diversion. If you lived in Houston in the summer of 1992, his story was familiar to you: He was the father of Kynara Carreiro, who until July 20 had been a particularly pretty seven-year-old with shimmering blond hair and knowing blue eyes. The photograph most often featured by the media at the time of her death was the one in which she posed with her arm around her best friend, Kristin Wiley, a ten-year-old with a tumble of curls and the sweet but tentative smile of an older girl before the camera. Both children were found stabbed to death on a blood-soaked bed in the Wiley home. They had been sexually assaulted and then murdered in the middle of the day, in the middle of a suburb northwest of Houston previously believed to be safe, while Kristin's brother played across the street, while Kynara's mother was engaged with chores a few doors down.

For almost nineteen months no arrest was made, though the investigation eventually focused on a neighbor who had lied to Harris County Sheriff's Department Homicide Investigators about having seen two men, an African American and a Hispanic, jump the fence into his yard around the time of the killings. That man, Rex Mays, pale and bespectacled, who sometimes performed as Uh-Oh the Clown at childrens parties in and around Houston, confessed to investigators in the winter of 1994. He had killed the girls after having "a bad day" – he'd been fired from his job, and Kristin and Kynara had enraged him by refusing to turn down the Christian music they were listening to as they played. Mays had stabbed Kristin 18 times and Kynara 23, and yet before the younger girl died she had had the courage to tell Mays: "You are going to be sorry you did this," which, when Carreiro learned of it, inspired in him a mission at first devoted to Mays's conviction and then to something much larger and much more necessary to his survival.

"Keep it short " the judge had advised, and Carreiro planned to do just that. He had seen his share of emotional and incomprehensible outbursts by victims -- in fact, they had become a staple of tabloid TV shows -- and that was not what he wanted. Carreiro stood up and in a gentle, almost abject cadence, did not speak to Mays at all, but to those around him. He thanked the judge and the jurors, the district attorney's office and the sheriff's department. He suggested that childhood trauma, an explanation employed briefly by the defense, was no excuse for the horrific violence visited upon his daughter. Inflated childhood or 'my mother didn't love me as much as my sister' are no longer acceptable," he said.

It was not so much the substance of Carreiro's talk that drew people to him as his style. For his speech he had changed out of the suit he had worn for the seven-day trial into the clothes in which he was most comfortable: a suede vest over a button down shirt and jeans and his boots. At 46 he wore his long silver hair braided down his back and his eyes were the kind of bottomless blue that, under the circumstances, could only be described as haunted. He looked as if he had been no stranger to violence before Kynara's murder, which happened to be the truth. "I ask everyone to keep informed and keep involved so we can rid society of predators such as Rex Mays," Carreiro said and then, feeling the onset of tears, sat down. He had spoken for no more than three minutes.

After the court was adjourned, cameras blocked the courtroom exit, their lights turning the dingy corridor as bright as midday. Carreiro emerged and was swamped by reporters, while family members, pushed to the periphery, fell into one another's arms. The crowd reflected the world that had enveloped him since Kynara's murder: Along with the media, there was Andy Kahan who ran the mayor's crime victims' office, and Randy Ertman, the huge, barrel-chested man with whom Carreiro had fashioned a friendship out of mutual grief. Representatives of Justice for All – the state's most influential victims' rights group, which Carreiro had helped establish – and Parents of Murdered Children were there too. After the Wileys emerged from the courtroom, the contingent moved outside for a final press conference. Had justice been served? The reporters wanted to know. Would Carreiro attend Mays's execution, as a new state policy allows? Where would he go from here?

Carreiro answered their questions as best he could – witnessing the execution, he said, "was not retaliation but justice" – and then, little by little everyone drifted away. After more than three years in the spotlight, Bob Carreiro was left alone with the life his daughter's death had created for him.

IN MID-OCTOBER 1995 THE PINK CONSTRUCTION-PAPER ribbon bearing Kristin's and Kynara's names still hung on the front door of Bob Carreiro's modest northwest Houston home. Inside he most often settled in the small living room that remained a shrine to his daughter: Portraits of Kynara lined the wall, videos of her surrounded the TV, and her belongings lay entombed in a cedar chest. Laid off from his job as a truck driver sixteen months before, and long divorced from Kynara's mother, Carreiro had lately given into drift. Other parents of murdered children had warned him that the period following the trial, when the cameras went away, could be the worst.

He let the phone direct his day. Carreiro had an answering machine and a pager so they could find him: the parent who had lost a child and could get no help from the police; the victims' rights advocated who wanted him to attend a conference; the grieving family member who needed a friendly face in court. With Kynara gone, he had little use for a private live. The Harleys upon which he used to lavish so much attention now languished in his garage; his girlfriend, Lesli – the young, beautiful one friends hoped would help him get past his grief – had joined the victims' rights crusade herself, selling gimme caps or getting signatures on petitions at Justice for All meetings. It was perhaps the bitterest irony of Carreiro's life that Kynara's death had transported him into a world much broader than the one he had previously inhabited, and he would give anything that this were not so. At night, when Lesli slept, he went into the spare bedroom and talked to other crime victims on the Internet.

Bob Carreiro had stepped into an ever-expanding role on the American stage. The victims' rights advocate has become the official griever for a nation in decline. As the judicial system has disintegrated and fear of crime has grown, the advocacy groups of old – those that represented the rights of the accused – have been replaced by those of the harmed. Across the country, the children of socialite Sunny von Bulow, who started the National Victim Center after their stepfather was acquitted of attempting to murder their mother, and Vanity Fair's Dominick Dunne, who watched the man who killed his daughter receive a seven year sentence, have become symbols of the movement to make the criminal justice system more responsive to victims; Fred Goldman and Denise Brown, casualties of the O. J. Simpson trial, will no doubt join their ranks.

But nowhere are crime victims more active than in Houston, where fifty such groups make their home. Justice for All boasts almost four thousand members there, and the mayor's crime victims' office, headed by Kahan, is the only one of its kind in the nation. ("I want victims' rights to be to the nineties what civil rights was to the sixties," Kahan likes to say.) These organizations have been instrumental not just in defeating judges perceived as soft on crime but also in pressing for much harsher criminal legislation around the state: an automatic capital murder charge for the killing of a child under six, community notification of a sex offender's imminent release from prison, limitation of the number of appeals granted death row inmates, the opportunity for crime victims to testify against their assailants in front of parole boards, and most recently, the right to witness executions.

Not every surviving crime victim becomes a victims' rights advocate, of course. Those who do usually share certain experiences -- a particularly heinous crime and the accompanying media attention it engenders, for instance. Many advocates also possess a powerful personal need for community that sometimes preceded the crime itself. Those who join this world will find that it is not the redemptive one of Sunday newspaper-supplement stories as much as it is a mirror of modern life, where social movements become religions, religions become recovery movements, and grief becomes another form of entertainment. The day that Kynara Carreiro was killed was the day her father's education in this world began.

SIX WEEKS AFTER THE TRIAL CARREIRO sat in the jury box of a Humble courthouse, fingers to his cheek, studying the crowd. Along with other members of local victims' rights organizations, he had come to address a group of teenage probationers. Everyday violence was a foregone conclusion here. Carreiro waited his turn while a representative of the Harris County Probation Department presented a "weapons workshop" -- a primer on which weapons would land her audience back in trouble with the authorities. "Swords are not to be carried around on an illegal basis," the compact, no-nonsense woman droned. "A tomahawk is in the category of a club and is illegal to carry."

Carreiro let his gaze play across the crowd -- the worn faces of the parents, the insolent bravado of their children, mostly boys, wore as proudly as their fade haircuts, oversized jeans, and Rage Against the Machine T-shirts. Carreiro was searching for the ones he might be able to save, and it looked to him like a friendlier group than the kids he sometimes talked to in juvenile detention, the ones who laughed outright when he told his story. He got tired of telling his story over and over again, but since Kynara's death, testifying this way seemed, simply, the right thing to do. "I used to wonder why this happened," he said. "Now I think God has got this other plan for me, and I don't want to mess it up."

"This is reality folks, this is not a movie," Andy Kahan said, pacing in front of the group. The mayor's crime victims' director was a tall, balding man with the belligerent air of the parole officer he had been. His was a sensible admonition, given the attention span of those present. Most of the kids had been charged with lesser crimes like car theft and burglary, and it was hoped, perhaps vainly, that a dose of Kahan's medicine would keep them from graduating to something worse.

It was up to each speaker to make his or her story as dramatic as possible; a generation raised on television required as much. On this night Carreiro followed two women he had appeared with often, Gilda Muskwinsky, the former president of Parents of Murdered Children, and Kathy McCrory, a victims' rights advocate from Fort Bend County. Muskwinsky's daughter had been murdered in 1984 by drug dealers in search of her boyfriend; McCrory had been kidnapped, beaten, and raped while on a business trip several years ago. The presentation was something like a television talk show crossed with an Alcoholics Anonymous meeting, particularly with respect to the confessional style the speakers used and the way the audience wept at painful moments and applauded at moments of personal triumph. But it was Carreiro who used this style to its most powerful effect; he had a flair for the theatrical that drew people to him.

"I was born and raised in a dysfunctional family," he began, forming quotation marks in the air around the word "dysfunctional." "My father was a violent alcoholic -- the most time I spent with him was in a beer joint. I grew up hating my father for what he did, but I grew up just like him. That," he said, letting his eyes pass slowly over the crowd, "was my idea of what it was to be a man."

He was the son of a Portuguese construction contractor and a German homemaker and grew up in Connecticut watching his father drink himself into oblivion when he wasn't pummeling Carreiro's mother. Carreiro grew up to be angry and self-pitying -- "it was always me against them" -- someone who found himself living in a run-down shack and having to choose between a loaf of bread and a sixpack of beer when he went to the store for food. Carreiro left one bitter marriage and one child behind when he drifted to Texas in 1977 with Diane Kelly, whom he battered and married and who later became Kynara's mother. Carreiro stopped drinking with the help of Alcoholics Anonymous in 1979, after he blackened both of Diane's eyes in a fight.

"I feel my daughter was born to teach me how to love," he said of Kynara. Though he and Diane divorced, they shared custody of Kynara and made peace in the process. With the passion of a changed man, Carreiro took his daughter everywhere, to AA meetings, on motorcycle and fishing trips. He built her a playhouse, took her shopping, and found he wanted for nothing. He began to work with drunks at AA and discovered he was good at it; he reconciled with his father. And then one phone call proved that a reformed man's peace is as fragile as anyone else's.

"That's the way I'm gonna have to remember her," Carreiro said to the kids. He had unfurled a poster, a blowup of the familiar snapshot of Kristin and Kynara arm in arm. "No graduations, no first kiss, no grandchildren." As he recounted the crime, his voice coarsened with anger. "These precious little girls' lives were lost forever. *Forever,*" he repeated furiously. When he was done, the crowd rewarded him with thunderous applause.

"Lemme just tell ya," Kahan said, thanking the audience and opening up the meeting to questions, "this is the best group I've seen," The kids pressed for more dramatic details. One young man asked how Kynara had died. "Did he beat her or shoot her?" To Kathy McCrory: "How did that guy *get* you? To Gilda Muskwinsky: "Was this a random killing or did they plan it?"

After the meeting, a small group surrounded Carreiro to thank him for coming. "This is my little girl," one woman said, stroking the head of her shy, smiling child, who looked to be about seven. Carreiro bent down toward her and looked urgently into her eyes. "Be careful," he said. "Be real careful, okay?"

THE SCRAPBOOK IN WHICH KYNARA Carreiro's father chose to put newspaper clippings about her murder was covered with a Norman Rockwell print of a pretty blonde teenager showing off her corsage to a soda jerk while her date looks on proudly -- a mournful symbolism that could be lost on no one. The extensive video library of Kynara consisted of home videos -- Kynara on an Easter egg hunt, Kynara on Christmas Day, Kynara hovering near the water at a friend's beach house -- as well as tapes of her father clearing a bayou near the Wiley home, seeking clues to her death. "KC birthday/Cemetery 11/1/93" one tape is labeled; another "Oprah," another "Jerry Springer." Because Kynara's murder went unsolved for so long it happened that Bob Carreiro's grieving was both public and protracted, which, in turn, led to his rise as a public figure.

Like many high-profile murder cases, this one was played out almost entirely in front of the cameras. The earliest news reports showed Carreiro seated upon bags of mulch in his ex-wife's front yard with his head in his hands. He had come upon the scene to find the street blocked by police officers and reporters, and his former wife, now remarried, pacing in front of the Wiley house, carrying her screaming newborn son. "No one would talk to us," Carreiro said. At first he thought Kynara had been wounded in an accidental shooting; he did not learn that she was dead, and how she had died, for more than four hours. "It looked like a zoo," he said, and his suspicions about the competence of the sheriff's department were born at that moment. He was not reassured when a deputy he had known for some time gave him this warning about his colleagues: "Get on 'em and stay on 'em."

In the first few weeks after Kynara's murder, he was incapable of doing so. When public interest faded. Carreiro retreated into himself. In those earliest days, his emotional makeup, which tended toward the mystical and the sentimental, saw him through. Searching Kynara's room, he divined portents in the way she had numbered every day of her July calendar except the one on which she died and in the tombstonelike crosses she had taken to drawing on the inside covers of her coloring books. He formulated a theory in which his daughter was an angel whose time on earth had been brief but purposeful, and then, when he heard his daughter's voice telling him it was time to rejoin the living, he went back to work at the trucking firm. Passing a tattoo parlor near a sandwich shop he and Kynara had frequented, he had her face, surrounded by roses and a unicorn tattooed on his upper arm. "What better way to honor my daughter?" Carreiro asked. "She's in my head, my heart, she's on my skin too." He took to caressing his shoulder, as if warding off a chill.

It also happened that the investigation into the murder of Kristin and Kynara stalled in August, just one month after the crime was committed. What is clear in retrospect was not clear at the time: Rex Mays was one suspect of many, and the sheriff's department set up a task force to investigate everyone from suspicious drifters to Kristin Wiley's fourteen-year-old brother. The notion that his daughter was dead and her killer was free ate at Carreiro, and he directed his anger at the authorities. The county sheriffs homicide division, understaffed and ill equipped compared with its Houston police counterpart, had no use for a father who was hysterical and hostile. "If you don't find him I will, and I will take him down," Carreiro told the investigators in one early encounter. "Just get a confession before you do," they told him.

I was between a rock and a hard place," Carreiro explained. "I started doing my own investigation." He worked with three private detectives, gave up on sleep, ignored his girlfriend, began carrying a gun, and plunged himself into a world of paranoia and panic. The calls were constant: One woman said her boyfriend had washed out his truck on the day of the murder and had bite marks on his chest; another woman said she had found a little girl's sock with blood on it. Carreiro received word that a psychic in Tomball, near where the girls were buried, wanted to see him. The man, a self-described Indian named White Bear, told Carreiro that Kynara was sending him messages in his sweat lodge. A neighborhood security guard seemed overly brusque, members of the Wiley's church overly solicitous. When Carreiro sat down with sheriffs department homicide investigators, he felt no more secure: "There were five different officers in charge of five different suspects, and each one could convince you his guy had done it," Carreiro said.

He turned more and more to the press, which gladly obliged. Television had found a perfect subject in Bob Carreiro. "I was not gonna let this die down," Carreiro explained. "Every time it was gonna die down, I'd find something to keep it in the news." He called the media when the reward for finding Kristin and Kynara's killer was created. He let a reporter watch him tearfully pack up Kynara's room. Another filmed him grieving at the sweat lodge. He learned to negotiate: "I'd call up and say I wanted to do a news conference about raising the reward money, and they'd say okay, but we want an exclusive," he said.

Two months after the girls' deaths, in September 1992, when media interest had flagged and the investigation remained at a standstill, Carreiro had his grandest idea to date. It hit him when he was driving home from work with the helpless feeling that his daughter's killer would never be apprehended. "My baby's gonna be on billboards all over town," he told himself.

WHO KILLED THESE GIRLS? the enormous letters of the billboard cried. Alongside the question was the picture of Kynara and Kristin arm in arm and an offer of a $40,000 reward donated by family members and businesses. Representatives of the sheriff's department attended the unveiling of the two hundred billboards only because the Houston newspapers had sported damaging information about the investigation -- involving contamination of the crime scene, delays in polygraphing Rex Mays, among other things. Privately, the sheriffs department saw Carreiro as a bum out for attention.

If the publicity did not serve to flush out a killer, it did have the usual effect: it created more publicity. "Tell us what happened," Oprah would ask, as would Jerry Springer and many others. Carreiro became a regular on segments devoted to unsolved crimes. "When we come back we'll meet a sixty-six-year-old woman who survived a hired hit -- someone wants her dead," Jerry Springer chirped after Carreiro had, once again, related that his daughter had drowned in her own blood. Carreiro's tears made for powerful television, but they also inducted him into the new American pastime of vicarious misery. He didn't care. He thought only of reaching his daughter's killer. "I wanted that sumbitch to hate it every time he turned on the TV and saw me there."

The year ended, and the authorities had nothing to show for their efforts. The sheriff's department had contacted the FBI for help, and the bureau had produced a profile of a killer who was white and between 25 and 35, the proverbial loner who might have taken an unusual interest in the case. The description fit Rex Mays, the neighbor who had lied to investigators immediately after the murder. Unfortunately, Mays's ruse had bought him enough time to destroy most of the physical evidence that could have been used against him. The only way to apprehend him was the most difficult of all: Someone would have to get him to confess. That job fell to a two-time cop of the year by the name of Bill Valerio, a heavyset, taciturn man with four daughters of his own. For the next fourteen months, he took Mays drinking and to strip joints, and got nowhere.

Once he learned that Mays had been targeted, Carreiro took to threatening the former neighbor, an activity that ran counter to the FBI's advice that the killer would confess only if treated kindly. ("There were times when I probably hindered the investigation," Carreiro would later admit.) He had his biker buddies gun their cycles outside Mays's home. He had friends send May, birthday cards -- "Roses are red, violets are blue, the girls are dead, wish you were, too." He followed Mays to bars, waiting outside while he drank, and when Mays applied for jobs -- particularly those involving children -- Carreiro saw to it that he wasn't hired. When Carreiro heard that Mays was bragging about being the prime suspect in the murder investigation, he thought he would go mad. He imagined hanging him up and peeling his skin off, or simply snapping his neck. Said Carreiro: "I was getting real close to killing him."

OUTSIDE A HIGH-RISE OFFICE BUILDING on the West Loop South, Bob Carreiro, finishing a cigarette, served as the unofficial greeter for the October meeting of Justice for All. It was a pretty night, the kind that promised the end of another interminable summer, but the people entering were somber. They approached with their heads bowed, not unlike the way people enter church. This was not coincidental: Justice for All served many of the functions most people once found, in a less complicated world, in organized religion. They joined for communion, and they joined to mourn.

In an era in which practically everyone purports to be a victim of one thing or another, these people had a legitimate claim on the word. Dressed in T-shirts and jeans or wrinkled workday clothes, they could he mistaken for guests at a company retreat or a PTA meeting; they were, instead, living memorials to some of Houston's grisliest crimes. Carreiro accepted an embrace from Jeanne Bayley, a sunny woman whose teenage stepson Robbie was murdered in the woods west of town; his schoolmates had played soccer with his head and taken pails of his body home as souvenirs. Patsy Teer updated Carreiro on the status of the man who had been on death row for twenty years for murdering her son, a state trooper. "This guy is running several businesses from prison," she told him. Randy Ertman graced his friend with a gruff hello, his wife, Sandra, trailing behind. Jennifer Ertman, along with her best friend, Elizabeth Peña, had been brutally raped and murdered by six gang members just a year or so after Kristin and Kynara had been killed. Greeted with both affection and deference, Carreiro was, in turn, both giving and contained. People were drawn to what they perceived as a calmness within him, though Carreiro defined it differently. "The worst thing that was gonna happen to me has happened," he said simply.

The topics of tonight's meeting reflected the group's need for both solace and social change. Inside the small auditorium containing about a hundred people, Pam Lychner, a movie-star-pretty blonde, opened the meeting by making a plea for financial assistance for a Honduran immigrant who lost both legs after a shotgun attack by her husband. Then she turned the podium over to Andy Kahan, who introduced the widow and teenage daughter of a police officer named Bruno Soboleski, murdered in the line of duty in 1991. "They've received the dreaded parole notice," Kahan said of the family, meaning that they must now perform a new social ritual -- that of acquiring signatures on petitions to keep a criminal from being released. "It would mean a lot to us to keep this man where he is," Sue Soboleski implored, as her daughter studied the floor, as if embarrassed.

The content of the meeting, which would be almost unendurable for people who were not victims of violent crime, was comforting to those who were. There was a mother trying to find her son's killer and another woman trying to pressure the district attorney into asking for the death penalty for her son's murderer; while one woman caressed the contents of her dead son's wallet another railed against medical examiners who removed corneas without the family's permission. "They're making a profit off our loved ones," Carreiro snarled under his breath. In each case, members offered to help or offered a hug, anything so that the person would not feel alone or abandoned. After one woman mentioned that the district attorney had suggested she avoid the arraignment of the boys accused of killing her son, Carreiro was adamant. "You be there," he said. *"You be there."* Later, he made arrangements to meet her at the courthouse.

Shorty after Kynara was murdered, Carreiro attended a Parents of Murdered Children meeting in the basement of a downtown church. He had gone with Diane and her husband, Patrick Taylor. Diane found that she could not return -- the sadness in the room overwhelmed her -- but Carreiro was drawn back. Unlike his former wife, who had a new baby to attend to, and unlike the Wileys, who could take solace in their church, Carreiro had no one but the people at the meetings. "It was an avenue, and I didn't know any way else to go." Carreiro said.

This association also gave him a framework with which to manage another change in his life. Within a few months of the murder, the media exposure had made Carreiro the man to call whenever a child was missing. His phone rang constantly. One parent wanted to meet White Bear. Another wanted help in dealing with a coroner's report she suspected was bungled. Another wanted to know how to look up criminal records at the courthouse. Andy Kahan had gone to the unveiling of Kynara's billboards and at the time had known that Carreiro was too involved with his own case to become an effective advocate; still, he sensed Carreiro's potential, "Within six months he began making himself available and known, as he began talking about the system and not just his daughter's case," Kahan recalled. Carreiro became a regular at rallies in support of victims. By the summer of 1993, he felt the need to supplement the cloistered emotional atmosphere of Parents of Murdered Children with something broader and more, political. Following Pam Lynchner's lead, Carreiro and several friends formed Justice for All, which has a tax status that allows the group to lobby. He began working as a public speaker, telling Kynara's story to everyone from funeral directors to Parole officers.

A little more than a year after Kynara's death he was at one such event when a large man with long hair and a beard approached him: His daughter had been missing for three days, and the police were ignoring his pleas, assuming she, was a runaway. Carreiro gave him the number of a network for missing, children. "I hope I never have to see you again " the man told Carreiro. "I hope I never see you either." Carreiro replied. The man was Randy Ertman, the next day, his daughters body was found, along with her best friend's, near some railroad tracks in northwest Houston. Right away he called Carreiro for help. He arrived to see kids, in a car passing by slowly, like sightseers. Ertman, enraged took off after them, cursing and kicking at the car. Watching him, Carreiro was overcome with envy. He longed to lose control.

Instead, he began to believe that Kynara's death held some meaning for him that he had yet to grasp. He took it as a sign when his company closed and he could spend more time working with crime victims. On a trip to Washington, DC, he met with senators Phil Gramm and Kay Bailey Hutchison and spoke at a reform legislative dinner on crime. "Maybe, we could talk to him about getting a haircut," Beaumont congressman Jack Brooks muttered, following Carreiro to the podium. Carreiro, impervious, did not change his look; he knew it made him easier to remember.

What be really wanted people to remember was Kynara. When the first of Jennifer Ertman's murderers came to trial in 1994 Carreiro was there, every day, performing the ritual known among victims' advocates as court sitting. By then he was on the brink of despair. On the day of sentencing, detectives had picked up Mays for questioning one last time. "Valerio had told me this was the last shot at it. If they didn't get anything this time, they would have to drop it." Carreiro said. He sat Through the proceedings with his body quaking. As Jennifer's killer received the death penalty, Carreiro wondered if God would forgive him for killing Rex Mays. And then, just outside of court, Valerio got word to him: Mays had confessed.

The news interrupted regularly scheduled programming in Houston. Two daughterless fathers embraced while the TV cameras rolled, recording what passed for a happy ending. Back in Kynara's old neighborhood, residents rejoiced. "Was it Rex? *I knew it was Rex!*" one exulted, as if she had just guessed the end of a made-for-TV movie.

THE HARRIS COUNTY CRIMINAL COURTHOUSE is an ugly building, a slab of muddy pink granite and glass, oafish in comparison with its graceful, cupolaed civil counterpart across the street. But what the building lacks in architecture it makes up for in personality; from the dispossessed on the sidewalk to the cynical lawyers in the basement cafeteria and the teenage mothers weeping on hallway benches, it is perversely vibrant, offering a drama in real life, every single day. This was Bob Carreiro's community now. That he had made the transition from guest star to series regular might be seen as tragic, proof of his addiction to grief, but for this: He seemed happy there. Over the years, some people had come to view Carreiro's high profile with suspicion, branding him a publicity hound. But the courthouse was more forgiving. People there seemed to understand that he stayed close because the place provided the last link to his daughter.

On one day nearing the end of October, he had in mind to sit in on the preliminary stages of the murder trial of Eric Charles Nenno, who was being tried for a 1995 murder eerily evocative of Kynara's. Seven-year-old Nicole Benton was playing in a neighbor's front yard when Nenno, another neighbors lured the child into his home, where he raped her, killed her, and hid her body. He too confessed to the crime, though in a matter of days, rather than the months it took to extract the truth from Mays. The family had called Carreiro for help soon after Nicole had disappeared.

He had found that such court sitting -- a ministry of sorts -- had helped him prepare, for Mays's trial, as had his AA experience. "The twelve-step program taught me to wait," he said. "Every day, I'd get up and think, 'I'll kill him tomorrow.'" Then Carreiro would head for the courthouse to take a seat behind Mays at the trial. The psyche of Rex Mays remained beyond Carreiro's comprehension. Detectives had no idea what prompted him to confess they had merely asked him to come in, saying they had a new lie-detector test that could clear him once and for all, and he had agreed. (He was diffident to the end: "I can't eat this," he told them, as he chewed the burger they had bought him for dinner. Detectives believed he had stopped because he was overcome with remorse, or sickened by his actions. Then he explained: "I can't eat this with mustard on it.")

Carreiro, who by then had become knowledgeable about the admissibility of certain pieces of evidence and wise to the ways of defense lawyers, anticipated that Mays's attorney would try to get the confession thrown out, but he could not stop the fear that gnawed at him as he listened to the debate. Likewise, he was in agony when he heard Mays's attorney establish running objections to certain portions of testimony, building the record for an appeal. When it came time, for the coroner's report, the crime-scene video, and the reading of Mays' confession, Carreiro fought the impulse to flee and instead sat stoically through Mays's description of the way he had gouged out the girls' eyes and used his Marine Corps training to slit the backs of the girls, necks. Carreiro calmed himself by pretending he was attending someone else's trial. He knew, then, that his pain would end only with Mays's execution and tried to reconcile himself to the wait.

And so he had made a home of sorts for himself here at the courthouse. He felt good: He had a warehouse job starting in a week or so, with a schedule flexible enough to allow him time to continue his work with crime victims; and he imagined that one day he might have a job with the governor's office, maybe something like Andy Kahan's.

He went up top the windowless courtroom where the, Benton family sat alone behind the prosecution's table. Pretrial hearings were scheduled for today. So the courtroom' was almost empty. Nenno, the defendant, sat against a wall in handcuffs. Aside from the Orange hair that matched his jumpsuit, his resemblance to Mays was at most uncanny -- another pale, bespectacled man wearing, a thousand-yard stare. Carreiro regarded him briefly as he entered then nodded to Nicole's great grandfather and gently touched the shoulder of the small, birdlike woman who had been her stepmother.

An FBI agent was called to the stand, the same man who had investigated Kynara's murder. The questions began: *Did you find the body? Yes. How did you find the body? The defendant told me where to look.*

When Kynara was small, she had been like so many children, afraid the dark. To soothe her, Carreiro would prop her door open with a shoe so a tiny crack of light shone through. Later, it became a kind of joke between them. "Put a shoe in the door, Daddy," she would say when she felt a little bit scared, and that had always given him the simplest satisfaction, that she knew he would always be there to protect her.

Did you find the body right away? No, the defendant's first directions were insufficient. I had to return to the attic after he told me to look behind a stack of boxes where he had hidden her.

Carreiro directed his gaze to the man speaking in the witness stand, but his eyes were vacant and his hands we pressed tightly together in front of his lips, as if he were praying, as alone as one person could possibly be.

FAMILY VIOLENCE INTERVENTION: ATTITUDES OF TEXAS OFFICERS

by Sylvia D. Stalnaker,

Patricia M. Shields and Daniel Bell

ALTHOUGH A DOMESTIC DISTURBANCE FAILS to fit the police image of criminal activity, when an officer responds to a call, he places life and limb in jeopardy. Family disturbance calls typically comprise a significant portion of all calls for service. For example, a comprehensive survey of Texas police officers and administrators revealed that 13 percent of all calls were for family disturbances, and accounted for 26 percent of all injuries. In addition, Texas police officers unanimously agreed that the danger of responding to domestic disturbance calls is second only to an armed-robbery-in-progress call. A further complication is that family violence cases involve non-traditional compliancy because they include judicial involvement (obtaining protective orders), and they connect offender, victim and officer to a broader social service network.[1]

Given the threatening nature of family violence and the pivotal role of police, we will examine police attitudes toward the criminal justice system response to family violence. Such attitudes have been a neglected area of study, since domestic disturbance calls fail to fit the traditional criminal categories studied in either police training or criminal justice scholarship. Family violence has long been considered a family problem, not criminal activity. Although family violence has received considerable attention in the human service field, the attitudes of police are seldom considered. Hence, neither the criminal justice field nor the human service field have given police attitude on this topic sufficient consideration.

THE TEXAS FAMILY CODE

Protective orders, the legal documents that mandate police intervention, are designed to provide the victim immediate protection from further abuse. The protective order process begins with the filing of an application for a protective order with the clerk of the court in the county where the applicant resides or where an individual alleged to have committed family violence resides.

Several elements of the Texas family code that deal with the protective orders are relevant to the day-to-day activities of an officer. Chapter 71 deals with protective orders for the family or household members where a divorce petition has not been filed. Here "family" is defined liberally, including former spouses, biological parents (without respect to marriage or illegitimacy), foster children and foster parents. The "household" is a unit composed of persons living together in the same dwelling regardless of their relationship. "Family violence" is defined as the intentional use or threat of physical force by a member of a family or household against another member of that family or household. Chapter 3 specifies the special circumstances associated with the dissolution of a marriage. Chapter 11 provides for temporary orders governing possession, access to and support of children.

Given the pivotal role of the protective order, it would be interesting to learn police officers' attitudes toward the effectiveness of the instrument and the enforcement process.[2]

ISSUES OF EFFECTIVENESS

Much of the literature on family violence law and process points to its inaccessibility to victims. Many battered women want to go to the courts because they believe the legal system exists to protect them. However, critics of the courts maintain that the laws were made by and for white, middle-class men. Most people working in the legal system have conservative/traditional views regarding family roles and conduct. Because the court has a vested interest in keeping families together and preserving the status quo, it will often downplay or ignore outright dangerous living arrangements and discourage an abused woman from taking legal action.[3]

JUDICIAL SYSTEM: TIME ISSUES

Delay is considered a common problem associated with the implementation of current family violence law. There are many sources of delay within the system. In district courts, many judges and clerks consider abuse cases family matters that do not belong in their courts. It is not unusual, for instance, for a married woman to be told that she must go to probate court and file for divorce, or for a single woman to be told either that she must go to district court or that she is not entitled to a protective order because she is single.

In fact, the law gives both married and single women the right to file and to request protective orders in the district, probate or superior court. The choice belongs to the individual woman, not the court. In some cases, the clerk or judge may accuse the woman of exaggerating or even lying about the violence. Some judges are more concerned with protecting a man's due process rights than preserving a woman's physical safety.

A woman may have come all the way fighting fear, embarrassment, lack of knowledge about the law and, perhaps, a difficult clerk, only to be denied orders by the judge. If she gets her orders, she must then try to get the police to enforce them. The abuser may ignore the orders and continue to harass the woman in the absence of police enforcement. The police have the power to arrest a man who has violated protective orders as long as they have reasonable cause to believe that he violated them. When the police refuse to enforce the protective orders, the woman may decide to press criminal charges against the abuser for violation of orders.

In most cases, the woman will have to press charges against the abuser on her own in the district court or the place in which the violation occurred. Women trying to press criminal charges for violation of orders are often shuffled back and forth between probate and district court, each telling her that she must go to the other, or between the district court that issued her orders and the district court for the area in which the violation occurred.[4]

This type of system affects the day-today life of a police officer because the delay increases the number of calls per household, as well as the likelihood of violent encounters. As inefficient and frustrating as this is to action-oriented police officers, one would anticipate police dissatisfaction with judicial system procedures and lack of specific time frames.

CHANGES IN JUDICIAL SYSTEM: REFERRAL SYSTEM

Even though the primary function of the criminal justice system is the prosecution and punishment of offenders, there is an increasing awareness that the system may also be used to encourage offenders to enter treatment. This use, however, is hotly debated. Those who oppose the use of the justice system to force offenders into treatment argue that one cannot "treat" a crime and that forcing perpetrators into treatment denies their due process. Those favoring the use of the justice system to force offenders into treatment stress that many offenders have no insight into their behaviors and tend to rationalize their acts of violence.[5]

Most health and human services target the abuse victim rather than her assailant; however, violent men are often willing to seek help or will respond positively to court programs. Counseling abusive males helps them accept responsibility for their acts, recognize the consequences of these acts, understand that their reactions are unacceptable and develop alternative ways to manage stress and interpersonal conflict.

Clearly, counseling is an alternative to incarceration. Police, however, have not been asked about their attitudes toward counseling. On the one hand, police may question counseling as treatment because they have insights into additional problems. On the other hand, officers may be supportive of the process. Abusive men may be more likely to trust the judgment of a police officer than that of a social worker. Hence, police attitudes are critical to effective implementation of the counseling alternative.

PREVENTION: EDUCATION

The enforcement of family violence laws involves the courts, police and the community. The literature suggests that the nature of family violence, its seriousness, consequences and prevention are poorly understood. Many advocate increased education as a way to cope with the problem. Given the police officers' unique perspective, what is their point of view on the need for further education?

EDUCATION FOR POLICE / JUDICIAL SYSTEM

The judicial view of family violence still needs much improvement, as many a defense attorney can attest. Despite encouraging decisions at the upper levels, many local judges still react to trials involving family violence in a knee-jerk, traditionalist fashion. Many female victims fail to call in the police because the police have failed to respond in the past and the abuser was not arrested. Overworked prosecutors, who live by the professional standards of winning cases, sometimes fail to prosecute domestic assault cases because of the gray, rather than black and white, nature of family violence. Judges face overcrowded court dockets and may be poorly informed about family violence —in some cases still regarding it as a civil or domestic, rather than criminal, matter. The family violence problem, in other words, is perceived as a no-win situation at each step of the criminal justice system.[6]

EDUCATION IN SCHOOLS

School systems can be involved in the prevention of family violence by integrating information on the problem of family violence and types of intervention into their curricula. Most junior and senior high schools offer courses in home economics or health, as well as some progressive courses that try to expose teenagers to the realities of adult living. But it would be a rare course indeed that discussed child abuse and woman battering or included anger management techniques among its topics. Students may need to have an opportunity to discuss family conflicts and analyze alternative methods for resolving them, as well as to express their feelings of anger, hostility and helplessness.[7]

EDUCATION FOR THE COMMUNITY

Community intervention programs attempt to assist the social institution of the family and other social institutions (educational, legal and medical) that support the family. These programs include public education efforts directed to parents and teachers, and innovative changes in legal and medical procedures for assisting the family in need.[8]

Table 1
Effectiveness on Current Laws (Percent Distribution)

	Yes	No	No Experience	Total %	Sample Size
Referred client to use a protective order	91.6	7.2	1.2	100	470
Protective orders deter family violence	77.0	19.5	3.5	100	470
Local judges cooperative in granting protective orders	71.2	8.3	20.5	100	470
Courts have method to deliver copies of protective orders to local police	78.5	11.9	9.6	100	470
Effective process to enforce protective orders	78.1	12.2	9.6	100	470

METHODOLOGY

A survey that solicited police officers' views about the Texas family violence law enforcement system was used to test hypotheses. All police chiefs and sheriffs in departments in Texas were sent questionnaires and asked to forward them to appropriate personnel. Chiefs in larger departments, such as Dallas and Houston, were asked to photocopy the questionnaires for wider distribution because they have a larger volume of family violence cases. One thousand questionnaires were sent out; 470 were returned. The results of the survey are presented below.

EFFECTIVENESS OF THE PROTECTIVE ORDER

Police attitudes toward the effectiveness of the protective order process are highlighted in Table 1. The most striking thing about these results is the strong support for the protective order process found among law enforcement officers —over 90 percent of whom have referred a victim to use a protective order. Almost 80 percent of the officers maintained that protective orders deter violence and that they represent an effective process of enforcement. Further, they are generally pleased with the role of judges and the courts. For example, over 70 percent found judges cooperative in granting protective orders. It should be noted, however, that for this question, over 20 percent of the group indicated having had no experience. When those with no experience were removed from the sample, approximately 90 percent of the remaining officers believed that judges are cooperative.

JUDICIAL SYSTEM ISSUES

Although police officers believe that the protective order is an effective method to deal with family violence, they strongly advocate the need for procedural improvement in the judicial system (see Table 2). The officers considered timeliness an overriding issue. They indicated that the legal system should simplify and expedite procedures (75.1 percent), time frames should be written into the code (87.1 percent) and the legal system should monitor family violence cases to ensure rapid resolution. Further, a striking 95 percent maintained that the judicial system should evaluate its family violence decisions and enforcement record.

The officers seemed to support the notion that counseling was an alternative to incarceration. Over 73 percent believed a referral mechanism to family counseling would be helpful. Coincident with their otherwise reported ambivalence about the criminal nature of family violence, only 28.7 percent believed that the abuser should be referred to the county attorney for criminal charges. It is interesting to note that for this question, over half of the officers indicated no opinion.

Table 2
Judicial System Issues (Percent Distribution)

	Yes	No	No Opinion	Total %	Sample Size
Time Issues					
Legal and judicial system should expedite and simplify procedures	75.1	18.9	6.0	100	470
Time frames need to be written into code for protective orders	87.1	7.6	5.4	100	470
Legal system should monitor family violence cases to ensure rapid resolution	70.4	18.0	11.6	100	470
Simultaneous Referral Mechanism					
Mandatory family counseling	73.1	17.6	9.4	100	470
Refer to county attorney for possible criminal charges	28.7	20.0	51.3	100	470
Evaluation					
Judicial system or state bar conduct evaluation of judiciary's family violence decisions and their enforcement	94.8	4.3	0.9	100	470

THE ROLE OF EDUCATION

Table 3 summarizes officers' perceptions of the importance of education and training in the application of family violence laws. In fact, the respondents strongly support the use of education and training. For example, over 90 percent believe there should be public service announcements on local media. In addition, they maintain that family violence laws should be part of the curriculum in elementary (87.8 percent) and junior high or high schools (78.8 percent). They also believe that professionals who deal with the public, such as local teachers (59 percent), law enforcement personnel (70.3 percent) and judicial system personnel (77.7 percent), should receive training in family violence law.

CONCLUSIONS

The results of the empirical analysis indicate that Texas police officers have strong opinions about family violence law enforcement. Paradoxically, they believe that the protective order is effective (see Table 1) yet maintain that there is room for vast improvement in implementation (see Table 2). They are particularly concerned with the system's ability to reach a suitable resolution in a timely manner. Nearly 95 percent of those surveyed believe that a formal evaluation of the judicial system's family violence decisions and enforcement is merited. Lastly, they indicate that there is a need for more training both among the general public and professionals such as teachers, police officers and judicial system personnel (Table 3).

Table 3
Education or Training (Percent Distribution)

	Yes	No	No Opinion	Total %	Sample Size
General Public Public service announcement in local media about family violence laws	90.2	6.2	3.6	100	470
Students Family violence laws part of elementary curriculum	87.8	8.3	3.8	100	470
Family violence laws part of junior high and high school curricula	78.8	12.8	8.3	100	470
Professionals Faculty and staff of local schools receive training in family violence laws	59.0	21.2	19.8	100	470
Law enforcement personnel should receive training in family violence law	70.3	20.3	9.4	100	470
Judicial system personnel should receive training to increase knowledge and understanding of the judicial responses to family violence	77.7	17.6	5.1	100	470

[1] Texas Department of Human Services and Southwest Texas State University, "Survey Results: Family Violence and Law Enforcement" (Austin, TX: TDHR & SWTSU 1983), p. ix; and Texas Department of Human Resources, "Evaluation Report in Family Violence Centers in Texas 1979-1980" (Austin, TX: TDHR, 1979-1980), p.13.

[2] Senate Committee on Human Resources, *Safe at Home: Breaking the Cycle of Violence in Texas Families* (Austin, TX.: TDHR, 1982), p. 29; and E.J. Patterson, "How the Legal System Responds to Battered Women," in D.M. Moore (ed.) *Battered Women* (Beverly Hills, CA: Sage, 1979), p. 83.

[3] Massachusetts Coalition of Battered Women Service Groups, *For Shelters and Beyond: An Educational Manual for Working Women Who are Battered* (Boston, MA: Massachusetts Coalition of Battered Women Service Groups, 1981), p. 44.

[4] *Ibid.*

[5] H. Levy, S. Shelton and J. Conte, "Special Programs for Children Victims of Violence," in Lystad (ed.) *Violence in the Home* (New York: Brunner/Mazel, Inc., 1986), pp. 172-173.

[6] A Shupe, W. Stacey and L. Hazelwood, *Violent Men, Violent Couples* (Boston, MA: Livingston Books, 1987) pp. 8, 127.

[7] U.S. Department of Health and Human Services, *Family Violence: Intervention Strategies* (Washington, DC: DHHS, 1980), Pub. N (OHDS) 80-30258, p. 80.

[8] Lystad, p. xxv.

MERCHANT OF DEATH
*Overpaid price gouger or legitimate entrepreneur?
Either way, Houston's Robert Waltrip has turned the
Funeral business into quite a profitable undertaking.*

by Robert Bryce

WHEN ROBERT L. WALTRIP'S TIME COMES, he will likely get the same treatment accorded any of his customers at Houston's Service Corporation International (SCI). Two men will pick him up, place him in a black plastic bag, lift him onto a stretcher, load him into a dark-colored vehicle, and drive him to a low-slung metal building at Thirty-Fourth Street and Ella Road -- what SCI insiders call the prep center. No matter that Waltrip built SCI into a multinational funeral home conglomerate with $1.7 billion in annual sales. One of the company's nearly 29,000 workers will treat his body just like the others they handle each day: It will be sprayed with disinfectant, and his throat and anus will be packed with gauze to prevent fluids from leaking. His mouth will be closed with glue or sewn shut by a thread run through his septum and lower gum. His eyes will be closed with plastic eyecaps or glue. Then an incision will be made in his throat, upper arm, or pelvis, and embalming fluid -- a solution of methyl alcohol or formaldehyde will be pumped into his body, forcing all the blood out. Waltrip, a large man of perhaps 250 pounds, will require about five gallons of embalming fluid. Upon completion, another worker will dab a bit of makeup on his face and hands and ship him back to the SCI location handling the arrangements, where he'll be dressed in one of his many dark suits.

There's nothing romantic or sentimental about preparing a corpse for the grave, but that's the point: Waltrip, who is 65, has made himself a very rich man by taking sentimentality out of the funeral trade and replacing it with a tough -- some might say ruthless -- business mentality. Over the past four decades, he has parlayed a single funeral home on Heights Boulevard into the world's largest provider of "death care" by exploiting advantages that other CEOs would die for: His industry is recession resistant; the logistics and cost of entering the market keep competitors at bay; customers rarely if ever shop for prices; and everyone needs the service eventually. Best of all, many people pay in advance -- SCI currently has more than $2.4 billion in prearranged funerals on the books.

"People who don't buy our stock just don't like money," Waltrip once said. He's right: profit margin in 1995 was 11 percent, nearly twice the average of all American companies, and it's revenues were more than twice what they were only three years earlier. Over more than decades, SCI has buried more than two million people, everyone from regular Joes and Janes to such luminaries as John Lennon, Howard Hughes, Jacqueline Kennedy Onassis, and J. Howard Marshall II; in fact, an SCI home held two funerals for Marshall last year – one given by his wife, Anna Nicole Smith, the other by his son E. Pierce Marshall. This year the company will handle one out of ten services in the U.S., about 230,000 in total. And Waltrip is just getting started. During the past three years, his company has nearly quadrupled its holdings; at the end of the first quarter of 1996 SCI operated 2,795 funeral homes, 324 cemeteries, and 138 crematoriums, making it ten times larger than its closest U.S. competitor, Stewart Enterprises of New Orleans. He's already the largest funeral services provider in the United Kingdom, having acquired two chains there in 1993, and last July he snatched up France's largest funeral home operator, Lyonnaise des Eaux, for $423 million. Now he's looking at other purchases in western Europe and the Pacific Rim. "Germany is a very attractive place to be," he says. "We will be there one of these days."

Pale and dour, Waltrip speaks in measured sentences with a distinct Texas twang. He is always clean and wears the standard uniform of the funeral director; starched blue shirt, conservative tie, dark blue suit, polished black tassel loafers. "I always wanted to be a funeral director," he says, resting his hands in his lap. "I liked it, I was good at it, and I never wanted to do anything else." In particular, he adds, he has always understood the power of emotion when dealing with the customers. "The relationship a funeral director has with the people he serves is very rewarding," he says. "If you don't have empathy and a desire to serve, you won't be very good. You'll come across as cold."

Waltrip's office, on the twelfth floor of a nondescript tower on Allen Parkway, is just a few miles from his boyhood home. Growing up, he knew he would someday be an undertaker, just like his father, Robert E., who co-owned the Heights Funeral Home with his grandmother, Mrs. S.P. Waltrip. But in 1951, while he was a student at Rice University, his father died suddenly, and Waltrip had to leave school so he could help manage the business. Young Robert ran the funeral home while completing his degree at the University of Houston. By 1957 he had come to see the profit potential of buying more funeral homes, and the family acquired two more in Houston. Five years later he founded SCI, and by 1974 he owned three hundred funeral homes and the company's stock was trading on the New York Stock Exchange.

Just as Ray Kroc, the founder of McDonald's, brought efficiencies of scale to fast food, Robert Waltrip did the same for funeral homes. The analogy isn't perfect -- while patrons of McDonald's may spend $5 per visit, SCI's customers often spend a thousand times that much -- but as Waltrip explains, "Things about each business are the same." Like McDonald's, SCI has fixed costs. Buying in quantity such commodities as coffins and embalming fluid allows the company to increase its profits. Once the fixed costs are met at an SCI home, between 60 and 80 percent of the remaining revenues go straight to the bottom line. And like McDonald's, SCI cuts costs and ups income by employing mass-production techniques. For instance, rather than have an embalmer at each home, SCI sends most Houston-area corpses to its prep center. A centralized livery system dispatches hearses and limousines to the company's funeral homes; thus one hearse, which costs $60,000 to $80,000, can work two or more funerals in a single day. SCI slashes its overhead, staffing, and transportation costs -- and offers customer one-stop shopping -- by building funeral homes at its cemeteries.

No wonder Wall Street loves Waltrip's company. From 1989 to 1994, SCI's stock, which traded for nearly $53 on May 1 of this year, nearly doubled the performance of the Standard and Poor's 500 Index. "The entire time I have been covering the company, we have always been recommending it," says Susan R. Little, a stock analyst with Raymond James and Associates of St. Petersburg, Florida, who thinks SCI is as close to a slam dunk as there is in the market. Is it a sure thing? "There are only two sure things in life -- death and taxes," she says, acknowledging that the surety of death, combined with the aging of America, means SCI should have no problem maintaining double-digit growth rates. "Conservatively, you are looking at net income growth of twenty to twenty-two percent over the next few years," she says. "That means the stock price could go to sixty by early 1997."

But if Wall Street loves Waltrip, federal regulators are less impressed. Last Year, after SCI purchased a funeral company in Medford, Oregon, the Federal Trade Commission ordered the company to sell two funeral homes, a cemetery, and a crematorium in town for fear that there would not be enough local competition. Since 1992, the agency has required SCI to perform similar divestitures in the southeastern U.S. and California. In Britain, the Monopolies and Mergers Commission recently asked SCI to identify its funeral homes as corporate-owned and to provide customers with lists of competing cremation rates. In Australia, where SCI controls 20 percent of the funeral business, it is said to be under investigation for possible violations of that country's antitrust laws.

And if the FTC is unimpressed, funeral industry watchdogs are downright mad. "SCI figures it has the mortuary business and consumers by the tail and it can twist them around any way it wants, says the Reverend Henry Wasielewski, a Catholic priest in Phoenix who is a member of the Interfaith Funeral Information Committee, an organization that publishes the wholesale costs of caskets on the Internet. According to the committee's Web page, SCI's markup on caskets averages about five times the wholesale price. Wasielewski notes that based on the volume of its business, the company could charge half to a third of what it currently charges and still make a profit. Karen Leonard, a consumer representative for the Sonoma, California-based Funeral and Memorial Society, is equally puzzled that while SCI gets deep volume discounts -- paying for caskets about half of what the independents pay -- its funeral prices are among the highest in the nation. The National Funeral Directors Association estimates that an average funeral costs $4,470, but Leonard alleges that the average SCI funeral in Houston costs between $8,000 and $14,000.

And it's not just big-budget funerals. Brian Sergeant, who owns Sergeant Memorial Funeral Home in admittedly less expensive La Grange, says he pays $25 wholesale for a cremation container, which he sells to his customers for $100 -- yet SCI's Memorial Oaks Funeral Home in Houston charges $392 for its least expensive cremation container. When Sergeant needs low-budget caskets, he buys plain twenty-gauge steel non-sealing caskets for $235 from a wholesaler in Houston. Memorial Oaks sells a similar casket for $2,395 ten times the wholesale price. "It's a free market, and everybody is entitled to a fair profit." Sergeant says. "But what's fair?" In response, SCI spokesman William R. Barrett says, "Everybody wants to pick a single piece of merchandise and say, 'You are charging a thousand percent too much.' What you need to do is look at the whole package. There's a lot more that goes into a funeral besides the casket."

One possible reason for SCI's high prices: They pay their executives very well. While Barrett insists that SCI's executive compensation "is in line with other major corporations in America." last year corporate compensation expert Graef Crystal included SCI in a group of ten companies that grossly overpay their top bosses. Using a formula he calls competitive pay, which factors in elements like company size, stock performance, and comparable pay at companies of a similar size, Crystal figured that SCI's board members are paid nearly twice as much as their counterparts. Crystal told me that while SCI's directors earned $102,000 in 1994, they should have earned $52,300, putting them 95 percent over the market. Among the members of SCI's board are Tony Coelho, the former U.S. representative and House majority whip who left Congress under an ethical cloud, and auto racer A.J. Foyt, a lifelong friend of Waltrip's.

Crystal also assails Waltrip's pay saying he is the twelfth most overpaid executive in the U.S. In the February issue of his newsletter, *The Crystal Report,* Crystal examined 896 large and midsize companies from 1992 to 1994. Crystal estimates that Waltrip earned an average of $9,334 million a year over that three-year period. "An average CEO salary at a company of that size and performance would be $2.259 million per year," Crystal told me. "He is three hundred and thirteen percent over the market." And Crystal isn't the first to cast a critical eye on Waltrip's pay. In 1991 *Forbes* reported that Waltrip made $3.2 million in 1990. When added to the money paid to his son Blair, SCI's executive vice president, his mother, Wanda McGee, and his son-in-law, T. Craig Benson, a vice president, the magazine said, "The Waltrip family owns about 3 percent of SCI stock, but took in 8.5 million all told, a lush 8 percent of the company's 1990 profits."

Although he claims not to know or care what he is worth, Waltrip is indeed a wealthy man. His 500,000 shares of SCI stock are worth more than $26.4 million, and he also sits on the board of and owns stakes in Cash America International, a pawnshop chain, and Tanknology Environmental, a wastewater processor. He works behind a leather-topped antique desk in an ornate office decorated with numerous pieces of Western art, airplane models, and several massive bronze statues. He makes his home at what he calls a "little place" in Waller County that is registered at the courthouse in his mother's name. The 133-acre spread which is covered with live oak trees and ringed by, a freshly painted white wood fence, is valued by the local appraisal district at just over $8.1 million. Waltrip also owns a 3.021-acre ranch near Taos. New Mexico, and 17.748 acres near Steamboat Springs, Colorado. When he travels for work he takes the company jet, a Gulfstream IV. And he owns a stable full of superb cutting horses. His most famous, Colonel Flip, was born of a $13,000 investment. In 1983 Waltrip turned down an offer of 81 million for the stallion, which he still breeds.

But Waltrip seldom rides. Why not sit in the saddle awhile? "I don't have time," he says with a dismissive wave of his hand. Instead of enjoying the fruits of his labor, he concentrates on making SCI bigger and even more profitable. "I was up at ten to four this morning and at my desk by six-thirty." Why work so hard? "There aren't many people still alive who have built a company to this size," he says. "Now I can see it being huge worldwide. What are there -- fifty, sixty, seventy million deaths worldwide? That's big. There's a need in every community in every country for what we do.

"We have to weigh the economies and the stability of the governments," he cautions. "We, are very concerned about currency risk." Yet his only apparent currency problem is what to do with all the money rolling in. "We want to place our bets on aces, straights, and cinches," he says.

By betting on death, Robert Waltrip has found a cinch. And he is making sure that lots of people pay him before they pay, the piper,

Robert Bryce writes for the Austin Chronicle and the Christian Science Monitor.

CRITICAL THOUGHT AND ANALYSIS WORKSHEET

Crime and Criminals

I. Describe the type of crime that was committed:

    a) When and where did it happen?

    b) What factors contributed to this crime or type of crime?

    c) What appears to be the relationship between the victim and the suspect?

2) Ethical Issues:

    a) List at least two ethical issues involved in this investigation:

    b) What makes these two issues "ethical" in nature?

    c) What could have been done to eliminate the possibility of these two ethical issues developing?

Criminal Investigation

SEE NO EVIL

by Skip Hollandsworth

CHARLES ALBRIGHT PATIENTLY WAITED BEHIND AN UNBREAKABLE GLASS WALL, watching as the prison guard escorted me through three sets of steel-barred doors. "I apologize for not being able to shake your hand and say hello," he said, formally rising as I approached his window in the visiting room. "They do not allow me to have face-to-face visits "

The steel doors clanged shut. Then the man whom the Dallas police had called the coldest, most depraved killer of women in the city's history gave me a long gentle stare, his dark deep-set eyes never wavering, an encouraging half-smile on his lips. At 59, he had a finely sculpted face and carefully groomed gray hair. Even in his prison uniform, he looked positively distinguished. "Ask me anything you want," he said. "I'm not going to tell you anything that's not true."

Throughout his life, Albright had been described by many who knew him as the portrait of happiness, untroubled and troubling no one. He was, they said, a kind of Renaissance man—fluent in French and Spanish, a masterful painter, able to woo women by playing Chopin preludes on the piano or reciting poetry by Keats. It was simply impossible to believe that he could have viciously murdered three Dallas prostitutes in late 1990 and early 1991. The person who should have been arrested, Albright's friends and lawyers insisted, was Axton Schindler, a paranoid, fast-talking truck driver who lived in one of Albright's rental homes. The evidence pointed to him, they claimed, not to their beloved Charles Albright. Perhaps Albright was a touch eccentric, but he was certainly harmless; he was even squeamish when it came to violence.

"You won't find any woman who'll say anything other than that I was always a perfect gentleman in their presence," he said softly. Behind the glass wall, he wore an almost childlike expression— weak and perplexed and, yes, oddly appealing. "I was always trying to do things for women. I would take their pictures. I would paint their portraits. I would give them little presents. I was always open for a lasting relationship."

In most cases, serial killers are brutal, woefully uneducated young men, lifelong sadists who kill for their own twisted reasons. How, then, could someone so charming, so exceedingly polite, suddenly decide in the later years of his life to become a blood-thirsty sex monster? "Look, I've known Charlie for thirty years," sighed one Albright friend, a retired Baptist minister. "In all that time I think I would have seen his dark side slip out at least once. Believe me, if he really was a psychotic killer, he couldn't have kept it a secret all this time—could he?"

DECEMBER 1944: LIFE WITH MOTHER

HE WAS KNOWN AS THE MOST good-natured, eager-to-please of children, a precocious boy who could do just about anything: name all the constellations in the sky, catch snakes without getting bitten, even perform a tap dance routine on stage at the famous Texas Theater. "Charlie was like a Pied Piper to the rest of us kids," a childhood friend recalled. "We always wanted to see what he would do next. He was just so much damn fun."

In 1933, when he was three weeks old, Charles was adopted by a young dark-haired woman, Delle Albright, and her husband, Fred, a Dallas grocer. The Albrights lived in the all-white middle-class neighborhood of Oak Cliff, then a beautiful residential area across the river from downtown. According to the story Delle would later tell Charles, his birth mother was an exceptional law student, just sixteen years old, who had secretly married another student and had become pregnant. When the girl's father found out, he demanded that she annul her marriage and give up the baby for adoption; otherwise, he would cut her off from the family.

Delle Albright made sure that Charles knew she would never abandon him. She pampered her boy: She kept goats in the back yard so he could drink goat's milk, which she said was better for him than cow's milk. Yet sometimes her mothering went to extremes. When Charles was a small child, she occasionally put him in a little girl's dress and gave him a doll to hold. Two or three times a day she would change his clothes to keep the dirt off him. Afraid that he might touch dog feces and get polio, she took him to Parkland Hospital to see the polio patients locked in huge iron lungs. "You can spend the rest of your life here," Delle would solemnly tell her son. When he was less than a year old, Delle put him in a dark room as punishment for chewing on her tape measure. When he wouldn't take a nap, she would tie him to his bed. When he wouldn't drink his milk, she would spank him.

Indeed, people around the neighborhood talked about Delle Albright's odd, grim nature. No one could ever remember her buying herself a dress. She kept a scarf over her head and wore clothes from Goodwill. Although she and Fred were far from poor, she usually scrimped at mealtimes; even picking up the old bones the local butcher threw in a box for his dogs. She could use them, she would say, for soup.

Not that Charles ever openly complained. He always appreciated that his mother taught him manners. Delle told him to speak politely about other people or "say nothing at all." She told him to respect women, especially when it came to sex. She lectured him about the way his father acted "greedy" with sex: Whenever Fred saw her in the bedroom in her bra and panties, he tried to grab her. She was going to have none of that, and she was going to make sure Charlie never tried anything like that with his girlfriends either. As he grew older, she insisted on chauffeuring him every time he was on a date. She would even call the girl's parents to let them know that her son would not do anything untoward.

If Delle seemed overprotective, friends said, surely it was because she had never raised a child before. Charles himself recognized how fiercely she wanted him to succeed. Each morning, before the school bus arrived, she had him practice the piano for at least thirty minutes. She taught him so much reading, writing, and arithmetic that he was moved up two grades in elementary school.

Delle also introduced Charles to the world of taxidermy. When he was eleven years old, she enrolled him in a mail-order course—the Northwestern School of Taxidermy, taught by Professor J. W. Elwood. "You are beginning to learn an art that is second only to painting and sculpturing," Professor Elwood wrote in the first book of lessons Charles received. "A true taxidermist must be an artist." As Charles set to work on the dead birds he found, Delle was right beside him. She showed him how to use all the tools: the knife used to cut the skull, the little spoon used to scoop out the brains, the scalpel required to cut away the eyes from their sockets, the forceps that pulled out the eyes. She even skinned the first bird for him, teaching him not to cut too deep.

Dutifully, Charles spent hours on his taxidermy courses, stuffing and mounting his birds, making them look as lifelike as possible. Then he would be ready for the crowning touch—the eyes. He used to go to a taxidermy shop and stare at the boxes and boxes full of gloriously fake eyes: owl eyes, eagle eyes, deer eyes. He loved their iridescent gleam. He wished he could collect them the way other boys collected marbles.

Yet Delle wouldn't let him. Taxidermists' eyes were too expensive, his frugal mother would say; there was a better, cheaper way. She would open her sewing kit, look for exactly what she needed, and get to work. Then she and her son would place the birds in the oak china cabinet in the front of the house.

They were, indeed, Charles Albright's first works of art, just as the mail-order booklet had promised. Everyone who came to the house would peer into the cabinet to see what he had done. And there, peering back, would be his birds, beautiful, lifelike . . . and blind.

The birds had no eyes. Instead, sewn tightly against their delicate feathered faces, were two dark buttons, each shimmering dully in the living room light.

"You never knew a prostitute in Dallas?" I asked. He shook his head, baffled by the question. "Never! I knew absolutely none of them. At the time I was arrested, I couldn't tell you the names of the motels they stayed in, any of the motels' locations, or anything else. It is a crime that the police never put me on the lie detector to find out what I did know and what I didn't."

"Could the prostitutes possibly have seen you somewhere?"

"None of these girls had ever seen me. They never saw me drive slowly by like I wanted to pick somebody up. Believe me, if I had anything to do with any prostitutes in Dallas, I would tell you."

DECEMBER 1990: MARY PRATT

THE FIRST VICTIM TURNED UP IN an undeveloped, almost forgotten lower-class area of far south Dallas. She was a large woman, 156 pounds, naked except for a T-shirt and a bra, which had been pushed up over her breasts. Her eyes were shut; her face and chest were badly bruised. Apparently, the killer had thought it best to beat her before firing a .44-caliber bullet into her brain. A resident of the neighborhood was so horrified by what he saw that he rushed inside his home and brought out a flowered bed sheet to cover the body.

A police officer on the scene immediately recognized the woman as Mary Pratt, age 33, a veteran prostitute who worked the Star Motel in Oak Cliff.

While it was not unusual for the "whores of Oak Cliff," as the police called them, to get their share of beatings—almost nightly, a girl would complain about a trick "jumping bad" on her, punching her, kicking her, even trying to run her over with a car—for a whore to be murdered was unusual, especially when it happened to someone as well liked as Mary Pratt. Mary wasn't one of the brazen hookers who stood in the street and flagged down tricks. Because she rarely had any extra spending money—the money she got usually went for drugs—she never bought sexy clothes. Standing quietly on her corner, she wore blue jeans, tennis shoes, and small T-shirts that showed off her breasts. Occasionally, at the end of a night, she asked one of her regulars to drive her to her parents' home in the south Dallas suburb of Lancaster. Mary's parents—older retired people— never knew about her other life. They would call out good night as she climbed into her childhood bed.

Pratt's file was handed to John Westphalen, a short, ruddy-faced homicide detective at the Dallas Police Department. With his thick East Texas accent and a wad of Red Man chewing tobacco permanently packed in his cheek, Westphalen looked more like a rustic county sheriff than a street-smart urban cop. In homicide circles he was something of a character: Defense attorneys loved to complain about his blustery, intimidating interrogation tactics. But Westphalen was also one of the department's most tenacious investigators. He took one look at the Pratt file and realized the case would depend more on good luck than on good detective work. Pratt's killing was a "dumped body" case—one of the hardest types of murders to solve. She had obviously been killed in one location and dumped somewhere else. There were no witnesses to either the killing or the dumping, no murder weapon, little forensic evidence, no fingerprints, and no apparent motive. Considering the kind of felonious characters who nightly swing by the Star Motel, Mary Pratt could have been shot by just about anyone.

Accompanied by his partner, homicide detective Stan McNear, Westphalen drove to the Dallas County medical examiner's office to watch the autopsy of Mary Pratt. It was a routine trip; both men knew the autopsy would show a gunshot wound as the cause of death. As Dr. Elizabeth Peacock, one of the staff's younger pathologists, put down her coffee cup to begin the examination, Westphalen and McNear stood a short distance from the blue plastic cart where Pratt's body lay. Peacock noted the needle tracks on Pratt's arms, the Playboy bunny tattoo on her chest, the bullet hole in her head. She opened Pratt's right eyelid. Then she opened the left.

"My God!" she exclaimed. "They're gone!"

There were no eyeballs, no tissue—nothing. Mary Pratt's eyes had been cut out and removed so carefully that her upper and lower eyelids were left undisturbed. Peacock was dumbfounded. This was not an operation taught in medical school. The killer had to know how to slip a knife around the eyes, making sure not to injure the adjoining skin, and then cut the six major muscles holding each eye in the socket, as well as the rope tough optical nerve. With the eyelids shut, it was impossible to tell the eyes were missing. Surely, whoever did this had to have had a lot of practice on someone, or something, else.

Quickly Westphalen contacted the FBI's Violent Crimes Apprehension Program unit. Through its computers, the FBI keeps data on the nation's most unusual, depraved mutilations—bodies chopped up, organs removed, even eyes punctured with a knife as a result of a frenzied attack. But an FBI agent told Westphalen that he found no listing anywhere of such a surgically precise cutting.

Longtime Dallas cops take pride in acting utterly unaffected by anything that comes their way. But this time, Westphalen couldn't help it.

"What kind of person," he asked McNear, "would want a girl's eyeballs?"

SEPTEMBER 1952: CLASS CLOWN

WHEN CHARLIE ALBRIGHT TRANSFERRED to Arkansas State Teacher's College in Conway, Arkansas, it didn't take him long to become one of the school's most popular students. He was remarkably well rounded: president of the French club, business manager of the yearbook, member of the school choir, halfback on the football team. When he signed up for a drawing course, the art professor was so impressed with Charlie's good looks that he made him the class model.

Yet Charlie wasn't known as just a goody two-shoes. He was the all-American fraternity boy, a great college prankster. One time he sneaked into the home economics building, got a load of food out of the refrigerator, and cooked a steak dinner for his buddies. Another time, on a dare, he broke into a physics professor's office in the middle of the day, picked the lock on his cabinet, stole what was known around school as "the unstealable physics test, raced downtown to make a copy of it, and had the test back in its place within an hour. The professor, who was teaching a class next door, never suspected a thing.

Frankly, Charlie Albright had to feel some relief in being away from home. He was considered a very bright boy in Dallas—he graduated from Adamson High School at fifteen—and he was something of a celebrity. When Charlie was fourteen, Delle and Fred purchased a piece of property in their neighborhood and gave it to Charlie. Charlie sold it to buy more lots, and the *Dallas Times Herald* published a story about him under the headline WORLD'S YOUNGEST REAL ESTATE MAN AMASSING NEST EGG FOR COLLEGE. Yet Charlie's love for mischief had tainted his reputation. He had received bad deportment grades in school for shooting rubber bands and crawling out of study hall. He had "accidentally" set fire to his chemistry teacher's dress. And he had flunked a few courses because he was "too bored" to study. (Of course, if his mother had found out, he would never have heard the end of it. So he sneaked into the school office, filched some report cards from a desk, filled them in with all A's, and proudly showed them to his parents—his teachers' and principal's signatures perfectly forged.)

It was minor stuff, really. It wasn't like he went to jail. As Charlie himself would later explain, "I just didn't know what I was doing. If anybody tells the truth, they will say I never did a mean thing in all my life. But I did a lot of mischievous things just to show off for the older kids."

Well, there was the time he was caught breaking into a neighborhood church. Then there was the time he was caught breaking into a little store and stealing a watch. And there were the visits he and his mother received from Alfred Jones, a twenty-year-old psychology student working part-time as a Dallas County juvenile probation officer. But what did Jones know back then? And what right did Jones have to say, forty years later, when he was a well-known psychologist in Dallas, that of the dozens of juveniles he saw back in the forties, the one he remembered most clearly was Charlie Albright? "He could divorce reality sufficiently from his value system," Jones said, "so that he could tell you something false and at the time actually believe he was telling you the truth."

Maybe, one of Charlie's relatives said, he pilfered things from stores because his mother was so stingy. Or maybe he just wanted to rebel against her. Granted, Delle Albright did whatever she could to keep a close watch on her son. She took him to the Methodist church each Sunday. She made him go to bed, even when he was in his teens, at eight each night. Whenever she chauffeured him on a date, she watched him so closely that he would joke about the way she drove "with her eyes on the rear-view mirror." Charlie loved his mother—that much was clear. But there were little things that sometimes bothered him. He was never certain, for example, that his biological mother had been the brilliant law student that Delle claimed she was. He so hated Delle's cooking that he would stuff his food on a ledge under the table or give it to his dog. Delle fussed over him so regularly, he said, that he began to get headaches. (Delle decided the headaches were from bad eyesight and promptly made Charles wear glasses, even though he had twenty-twenty vision.)

Yet Delle couldn't protect Charlie the first time he left home. Right after high school, he enrolled in North Texas State College in Denton—but by the end of his freshman year, he was arrested for being a member of a student burglary ring that broke into three stores and stole several hundred dollars' worth of merchandise. Charlie swore he stole nothing. The other boys, he said, had asked him to keep some things in his dorm room for them. How was he to know the things were stolen?

Delle Albright went to the store owners and tried to reimburse them for what was taken. She tried to persuade the judge to let her act as Charlie's lawyer. She even asked that she take his place in prison. Yet the boy went to prison for a year, spending his eighteenth birthday there. Delle, meanwhile, worked to keep the matter hushed up, so that no one in the neighborhood knew that Charlie Albright had become a convicted felon.

Arkansas State Teacher's College was Charlie's chance for a new start. As he told a probation officer, he was going to mend his ways. He began to date a lovely young English major, Bettye Hester, and made plans to marry her. He did truly brilliant work in science; although he hardly studied, he made an A in his human anatomy course. It was said around school that Charlie Albright was going to go far. He even talked about going to medical school and becoming a surgeon.

But Charlie never stopped playing the role of class clown. Of all his great pranks, no one would forget the one he played on his friend Andrew (not his real name). In a fit of anger, Andrew had broken up with the most beautiful girl on campus, a woman with almond-shaped eyes. After the separation, he tore up several photographs of her and threw them in a trash can in his dorm room. Weeks later, Andrew got a new girlfriend and asked her for a photo. One night, while Andrew was staring at his new girlfriend's picture, he realized that something was wrong. He looked closer. It seemed that her eyeballs had been cut out and replaced with—Good, Lord!—the eyeballs of his old girlfriend. In disbelief, Andrew looked up at the ceiling. There, staring down at him, was another pair of his old girlfriend's eyeballs. More eyeballs were above the urinal in the men's bathroom down the hall. No matter where Andrew turned, he was confronted by the sight of his old girlfriend's almond-shaped eyes.

The story soon raced through school. That jokester Charlie Albright had pulled the old photographs out of the trash and saved her eyeballs for just the right moment. Did any of his fellow students, in retrospect, find the stunt a bit strange? Of course not, they said. It was pure Charlie. Who else could have been so inventive?

"Why do you think the eyeballs were missing?" I asked.

"I don't understand either." He sighed. "Why the eyeballs?"

"Well, what kind of person would be able to cut out the eyeballs of some hooker?"

"Someone who is sadistic? Just one mean son of a gun? I don't know the purpose behind it, unless that person thought the women wouldn't be able to see without their eyes in the next world—which is sort of ignorant."

DECEMBER 1990: A CLUE

BECAUSE THE POLICE HAD NOT RELEASED any information about Mary Pratt's missing eyeballs, her death had only warranted a two-paragraph story in the back sections of the local newspapers. In fact, when patrol officers John Matthews and Regina Smith began their daytime shift on December 13, just a few hours after Pratt's body was found, they had not even heard about the crime.

Only two and a half months before, the two officers had been assigned to a newly created beat on Jefferson Boulevard that included Pratt's streetwalking territory. Once the most popular shopping district in Oak Cliff, Jefferson had deteriorated over the previous 25 years, a victim of urban blight. Some storefronts were shuttered; others were barely profitable. The Texas Theater, infamous for being the site where Lee Harvey Oswald hid out after the Kennedy assassination, was padlocked. Matthews and Smith's assignment was to provide a police presence for the area—to become acquainted with the merchants, shake a lot of hands, and crack down on small-time crime such as burglary, car theft, shoplifting, and prostitution. In police circles, it was far from a glamorous beat. Other officers, used to the action of the streets, considered it more of a public relations position.

Each morning, Matthews and Smith began their day by cruising down Jefferson, herding the prostitutes back toward the Star Motel. On a busy day, about forty women—mostly black, some white, and a few Hispanic—worked the area, charging anywhere from $15 to $50 for a "flatback" (straight sex). The Star was not a high-class call girl operation; Matthews snidely called the forty-room motel "the prostitute condominium." The women there, most of them drug addicts, would have sex in a customer's car in a nearby alley or use a room shared with other prostitutes. Then, money in hand, they would walk down a well-worn dirt path to one of the nearby dope houses and purchase heroin or crack. After a quick hit, they would be out on the street again. Some hookers would work nonstop for two or three days—never changing their clothes, never even taking the time to eat—until they finally crashed back at the motel or in the house of their "sugar daddy" (a regular customer who cared for the woman enough to provide her with food, clothes, and a place to sleep).

Such a dreary scene did not faze Matthews, a stocky, no-nonsense 28-year-old; little on the streets did. The son of a patrol officer in New York State, he had grown up with cops-and-robbers stories. He had been with the Dallas Police Department since he was 21, when he went to work patrolling Harry Hines Boulevard, one of the city's high crime and prostitution areas. On the other hand, when 31-year-old Regina Smith decided to become a police officer, she had never fired a gun, seen a dead person, or even been in a fight. She was a former supermarket cashier, a graduate of a two-year fashion merchandising college, and the single mother of a 6-year-old child. Nonetheless, inspired by a newspaper story about the need for more black female police officers, she entered the Dallas Police Academy in 1988. Her instructors berated her for wearing too much jewelry, mocked the way she shot a gun, and laughed when she couldn't finish her push-ups, but she refused to quit. After graduation she was assigned to one of the rougher night shifts—and still she wouldn't quit.

On the Jefferson beat, Smith discovered she had a knack for talking to prostitutes. She wanted to talk to them; she felt it was her duty as a police officer to try to improve people's lives. "Tell me, girl," she would say to a new prostitute, "what are you doing whoring out here? You know you can make more money working at Burger King than you do here." She even started a "hook book," a kind of photo album that contained the mug shots of the whores on the street. She would wistfully leaf through her hook book the way some people pore over their high school annuals.

On this particular morning, Smith was not surprised to see Veronica Rodriguez, a brazen charcoal-eyed prostitute who would try to flag down tricks even when she knew the cops were watching. Usually, when she spotted Matthews, she would lean forward so he could see her cleavage and say, "How ya doing, Officer?" Rodriguez, barely 26 years old, had lived a miserable life. She had been arrested for prostitution numerous times, once when she was nine months pregnant. Although that baby was stillborn, she was the mother of at least one child— a baby born on a raggedy bed in a whore motel down the road from the Star.

As Matthews pulled the squad car alongside Rodriguez, Smith rolled down her window. She noticed a nasty gash across Rodriguez's forehead and what looked like a thin knife cut across the front of her neck. "Girl, what happened to you?" she asked. "Don't arrest me," Rodriguez gasped. "I almost got killed!"

Rodriguez told the officers that the previous night, she had been picked up by a trick, driven a long way south to a field, and raped. The man—a white man, she said—then tried to kill her, but she escaped and ran toward a house. The man at the house just happened to be someone she knew. He also just happened to know the man who was trying to kill her.

Matthews and Smith gave each other a look. Rodriguez was a notorious liar. No doubt she had been in some kind of fight, but in the middle of nowhere she ran right into the house of someone she knew? This was probably another of Rodriguez's "pity stories," which she often told the cops so they would feel sorry for her and leave her alone.

Yet two days later, on an afternoon drive past the Star, Matthews and Smith saw Rodriguez again. She was sitting with a balding middle-aged white man in the cab of an eighteen-wheeler. While Matthews went to one side of the truck to get Rodriguez and escort her to the squad car, Smith went to the other side to speak to the man. She asked him for his driver's license, which he produced: His name was Axton Schindler, of 1035 Eldorado. When Smith ran Schindler's name through the computer, he came up clean, except for some unpaid traffic tickets. Suddenly, Rodriguez started shouting, "Oh, don't arrest him! That's the man who saved me from the killer! That's him!"

The officers looked at the address again: 1035 Eldorado. It was not out in south Dallas, where Rodriguez's attack allegedly took place. It was in an Oak Cliff neighborhood, just a five-minute drive from the Star. The man—a sort of nervous guy who spoke incredibly fast—said he had no idea what Rodriguez was talking about. He said he had known her for years and was just giving her a ride to the motel. He didn't protect her from any killer. He didn't even have sex with her. He was just a long-distance truck driver doing her a favor. Rodriguez, the officers decided, was lying once again. They carted her to jail for prostitution and hauled Schindler in for his unpaid tickets.

Although Matthews and Smith would not know it for months, a clue to the murderer's identity had fallen right in their laps.

SEPTEMBER 1969: CON MAN

CHARLES ALBRIGHT WAS 36 WHEN he began teaching high school science in Crandall, a small town east of Dallas. The principal at Crandall, who had been looking for—a teacher the entire summer, was ecstatic when the astute young man called him up right before the school year was to begin. According to his college records, Charles Albright had a master's degree in biology from East Texas State University and was working on another master's in counseling and guidance. He was also about to enter ETSU's Ph.D. program in biology.

Albright's students found him fascinating. On field trips, he could recite, in flawless Latin, the scientific name for every plant he came across; he could split open a rotted log and talk about each insect he found inside. He drove a green Corvette to school and wore lizard-skin shoes. (A few girls, smitten by his charm and masculine looks, wrote him love letters.) He even helped coach the football team. After a heroic play by one Crandall player won a game for the school, Albright lifted him up and carried him off the field.

How, the principal would later ask, was anyone supposed to know that the promising young teacher had forged all of his transcripts? He was simply flabbergasted when an ETSU official told him that Albright had never even earned a bachelor's degree. Everything—his degrees, his teacher's certificate—had been faked. Apparently, he had slipped into three different offices at East Texas State, grabbed all the necessary forms, copied them, added his name, forged signatures, and then sneaked them back into the files. He had even stolen the registrar's typewriter so the typeface on his records would look the same. Had an ETSU administrator not realized that he had never met the Charles Albright whose name kept popping up on the school's list of graduate students, Albright would have gotten away with the scam.

When Albright was confronted, he grinned ruefully and admitted to the crime. He needed to bend the rules a little, he explained, in order to get a teaching job. After he quit Arkansas State Teacher's College—well, okay, he was kicked out for being caught down at the train station with suitcases full of stolen school property, including his own football coach's golf clubs—he didn't think he was going to get a second chance to prove how smart he was. By then, he had married his college sweetheart, Bettye, and she had given birth to their daughter. Frankly, he didn't have time to begin all over at a university. It was a crying shame, he said. If only he could have finished his degree, there was a professor at Tulane University in New Orleans who would have hired him to do biology research.

Because the forgery was a victimless crime—and because Albright himself, according to one ETSU administrator, was such a nice, repentant fellow—the university decided to keep the transcript scandal out of the newspapers. It was embarrassing, after all, that a school could get bamboozled. Albright pleaded guilty to a fraud charge and received a year's probation.

As the seventies began, Albright was back in his old Dallas neighborhood with his wife and daughter, living in a house not far from his parents' home. Once again, no one had any idea of what he had done. The Charlie Albright the neighbors knew was a happy-go-lucky figure who could master anything but simply didn't care about settling down in a nine-to-five job. He had some money from his parents, and his wife had a job as a high school English teacher. He was free to latch on to one new project after another; he rarely had a job that lasted longer than three months. He worked as a designer for a company that built airplanes. He worked as an illustrator for a patent company. He was a well-regarded carpenter. He collected wine bottles from the famous Il Sorrento restaurant in Dallas, hoping to start his own winery. He bought a lathe and made baseball bats. He collected old movie posters. He regularly went to the Venetian Room at the Fairmont Hotel to get autographs from the stars performing there. On a lark, he went to a Mexican border town and became a bullfighter—"Señor Albright from Dallas," the posters read.

Albright still had a Pied Piper-like ability to captivate people. After visiting a friend who worked at the beauty salon in a Sanger Harris department store, Albright promptly went off to beauty school, got his beautician's license, and then persuaded the salon to hire him, with no experience at all, as a stylist. Albright took to calling himself Mr. Charles. He would spend at least an hour with each woman to get her hair exactly right.

When Albright told his stylist friend that he was also an accomplished artist, the friend paid him $250 to paint a picture of his wife. Albright was indeed a good painter; self-taught, he had won a prize at the Texas State Fair for his portrait of a dark-haired woman in a long green gown. His goal, he said, was to be like Dmitri Vail, the famous portrait artist of Dallas.

Albright worked for weeks on the woman's painting without finishing. He insisted that he needed to keep working on one special feature, the most difficult part of the painting. Tired of waiting, the friend decided to go to Albright's house to look at the work in progress. There, in the living room, was the six-by-three foot portrait. It was richly colored and remarkably realistic. The woman's hair, her mouth, her nose, her ears, her neck—everything was finished. Well, not everything. The stylist stared curiously at his wife's painting. In the center of his wife's face were two round white holes.

After all this time, Albright hadn't even begun working on the eyes. It was as if something held him back, as if he preferred the portrait to remain as it was on his living room easel. "Charles," asked the friend, "when are you going to paint the eyes?"

"When I am ready to," Albright replied.

Months later, Albright finally painted the eyes. He then painted them again, to get them just right. He painted the proper shadows under the eyelashes; he gave the eyelids just the right droop in the corners; he shaded the eyeballs to make them look perfectly round. When Albright was finished, his friend could not believe how well the painting had turned out. It was, he realized, a mesmerizing portrait—especially the eyes. His wife's eyes were so perfectly recreated that they seemed to follow a person across the room.

"There's no question you love eyes," I said.

"Well, I do want to paint fine eyes. That's every other artist's weakness—they can't paint eyes."

"Would you ever love eyes enough to—"

"No, no, I've never taken the eyes out of anything. I've never had the desire to. To me, what matters is what the eyeball looks like in the woman's face, or the guy's face—not what the eyeball itself would look like."

"Could you figure why someone might want to keep the eyeballs? Would they want them as sort of a souvenir?"

"I don't think anybody would want to keep eyeballs. That would be the last thing I would want to keep out of a body. It would be a hand or a whole head, maybe, if you were a sick artist and you thought the woman was fabulous. You might not want to see that beauty go to waste."

FEBRUARY 1991: SUSAN PETERSON

THE SECOND VICTIM WAS FOUND on a Sunday morning, on the same south Dallas road where Mary Pratt was dumped. Like Pratt she was mostly naked. Like Pratt, she was a prostitute. Her name was Susan Peterson, age 27. She had been shot in the head, chest, and stomach. Her eyelids were closed.

Because her body was discovered on the other end of the road, just outside the city limits, the jurisdiction for the case fell to the Dallas County Sheriff's Department. A detective named Larry Oliver, who had not heard about the Pratt killing, was called to the scene. Eerily, the same scenario unfolded. Oliver accompanied the body to the autopsy room, where a pathologist began the standard external examination. The pathologist opened one eyelid, then the other. He motioned for Oliver to come closer to the table. Oliver couldn't believe what he was seeing: The dead woman's eyes had been expertly cut out.

When the pathologist mentioned that the Dallas Police Department had had a similar case just two months earlier, Oliver did some checking. Within 24 hours he traveled to the police department's homicide offices to see John Westphalen. Soon there were meetings with sergeants and lieutenants and with the chief in charge of homicide. While police officials deliberately avoided the phrase "serial killings" to describe what was happening—Westphalen kept referring to the killer as "a repeater"—everyone in the room knew what they were hunting for: a twisted, brilliant murderer, someone who dropped bodies on quiet residential streets, where they were certain to be found the next morning.

At that point, a contingent of detectives favored keeping a lid on the story. If the press discovered that the killings were linked and turned the spotlight on the Star Motel, the killer might get nervous and start picking up women from other areas. But homicide supervisors decided that the police department had a greater obligation to warn the community that it might be in danger—even if it meant warning low-dollar hookers. Besides, publicizing the case might bring in some leads. Lord knows, there was little else to go on.

As flyers were posted around the Star asking prostitutes to stay off the streets, detectives met with the press to discuss the two killings. Although no information was officially divulged about the missing eyes, word quickly leaked to reporters that the women's faces had been strangely mutilated. "The guy was almost surgical in the way he did it," one detective told a reporter. To the police department's dismay, a media frenzy ensued. The prostitute murders sent the city's imagination into overdrive; calls came in from reporters all over the country.

As John Matthews and Regina Smith sat in their squad car reading the front page newspaper stories about the prostitutes' deaths, they too were shaken. These were women from their beat, women they were supposed to protect. They knew Susan Peterson: She used to be the most beautiful white prostitute in Oak Cliff. Although her five years on the street had taken their toll—her once-alluring smile had turned winter-hard and her body had grown plump—she was still able to put on her brown go-go boots and denim miniskirt and pick up ten to twelve tricks a night. And she was a fearless hooker. She threatened other prostitutes who tried to work too close to her corner. She even cursed Matthews and Smith when they tried to move her off Jefferson Boulevard. Like a good pickpocket, she was an expert at clipping a trick—stealing money from his billfold while he was having sex with her. If the killer could get Peterson, Matthews and Smith said, then he could get any of the women. They surmised that the killer knew every corner of the whore district, all the alleys and all the streets. He was able to pick up Peterson and vanish within seconds. He also must have been one of her regular customers. Otherwise, she never would have let her guard down. Certainly she wouldn't have allowed him to shoot her three times. She would have pulled out a razor and fought back.

This time when Matthews and Smith pulled up to the Star, the prostitutes didn't keep their distance. They poured out of their rooms, surrounded the squad car, and began to pass on their own personal lists of suspects. The women talked about their kinkiest tricks, the men who wanted to tie them up or whip them. Smith made her usual impassioned speech, asking the girls to get off the street, but the black prostitutes, at least, were not buying it. "He's after the white girls, honey, not us," they said. Oddly enough, the black prostitutes saw the killings as an opportunity for them to get more business.

And then there was Veronica Rodriguez. Rodriguez had been telling a lot of people—reporters, other prostitutes, and Matthews and Smith, as well as other officers—any number of stories since the killings began. At first, she said she had witnessed Mary Pratt being shot. Then she said she had met a man who had only bragged about having killed Pratt. Then she said she knew nothing at all about Pratt's death. About her own rape in the south Dallas field, she no longer said the killer was white; now he was Hispanic. Then she said he might have been black. Almost everyone who spoke with her thought she was "brain-fried" from drugs.

What bothered Matthews, however, was that Rodriguez had never changed her basic story about being attacked. Usually, she would forget whatever pity story she had told the day before. Did someone really try to kill her in that field? Could the man who supposedly saved her, Axton Schindler of 1035 Eldorado, know the killer too? Or could Schindler have something to do with the killing himself? Could it be that the real reason Rodriguez was changing her story was simply because she was afraid?

Matthews and Smith didn't know what to do next. They had already told the homicide division that Rodriguez claimed to have information about Mary Pratt. They had mentioned the attack and the possible Axton Schindler connection. With that, they figured they had done their job; it would have been way out of line for the two young officers to cross into homicide's territory and conduct a murder investigation on their own. Later, Westphalen would say that he never got the officers' tips. Among all the phone calls, all the messages, all the reports flooding in, the name "Axton Schindler" never crossed his desk, he said.

Whatever the case, a potential break was slipping away—and the killer was preparing to strike again.

MARCH 1985: DARK SECRETS

THE INCIDENT WAS KEPT VERY, very quiet. There would be no trial, no headlines. The district attorney had arranged for him to serve a probated sentence of ten years, which meant no jail time. Probation was fine with him—just as it was in 1971, when he was arrested for forging some cashier's checks, and in 1979, when he was caught shoplifting two bottles of perfume. In 1980, when he was sent to prison for stealing a saw from a Handy Dan, he had to serve six months. But then, at least, his mother could tell everyone that he was leaving Dallas temporarily to take an important job at a nuclear power plant in Florida.

This case, however, was different. If the news got out, it could humiliate him. Not that he was guilty, he kept saying over and over. He had never touched that little girl. The girl's family was just looking for a scapegoat—and they had picked him, Charlie Albright, one of the most dedicated members of St. Bernard's Catholic Church in East Dallas. He had first met the family in 1979, when he began singing in the church choir. People admired his voice, even if it was untrained. In one hushed service, he performed the tenor solo, "Comfort Ye My People," from Handel's *Messiah*. Soon he was acting as a eucharistic minister, standing before the altar in a robe, reading Bible passages, helping with Communion—almost like an assistant priest, for goodness sake. He loved to help people; everyone knew that. The monsignor at St. Bernard's called him Good Old Charlie. Albright was known to slip a $100 bill to someone who was down on his luck. After he met the little girl's family, he brought them a big box of steaks. He dressed up as Santa Claus and gave the girl and her siblings presents. Did anyone seriously believe he would sneak into her bedroom and molest her?

The girl's parents tried to keep the matter quiet—especially at the church— because they did not want to stigmatize their daughter. But they also wanted Good Old Charlie to pay. Albright worried that if he fought them, the story would leak. So on March 25, 1985, in a nearly empty Dallas courtroom, he stood before a judge and confessed to "knowingly and intentionally engaging in deviate sexual intercourse" with a girl under the age of 14. He was 51.

For the first time, Charles Albright's mask seemingly had slipped. Was there, on the other side of his gentlemanly Jekyll-like personality, a kind of sexually perverted Hyde? Women who heard the story couldn't believe it. After Albright dissolved what he called his loveless marriage to Bettye in 1975, he developed a reputation as an old-fashioned ladies' man. He was still getting by with odd jobs and family money, but women saw him as a grand romantic figure, someone who showered them with flowers and music boxes and candy. To one woman, he recited from memory all 42 verses of "The Eve of St. Agnes," by John Keats. To another, he gave a slew of presents, along with a fully decorated Christmas tree. Women found him virile and sexy; one said he could do six hundred pushups without stopping. Yet Albright never made a sexual advance toward a woman until she asked him to first—at least that's what he proudly told his friends.

In late 1985, Albright fell in love with Dixie Austin, a pretty, shy widow whom he had met on a trip to Arkansas. It was one of the most romantic times of his life. At dinner, he charmed Dixie with stories about nature and art. He showed her the autographs he had collected from Ronald Reagan, Marlene Dietrich, and Bob Hope. He took her hunting in the country for salamanders. His dream, he told her, was to find a new species of salamander that could be named after him. Sex with Albright, Dixie later said, was gentle and satisfying. He never talked dirty to her, and he never wanted her to do anything that might be considered unconventional. He certainly did not sneak off and have affairs.

By the time he met Dixie, however, Charles Albright had already created another life for himself. Although he masterfully hid his secret from everyone who knew him, he was a veteran of red-light districts all over Dallas. To some prostitutes, he was a whoremonger—a regular trick. To others, like Susan Peterson, he was even a sugar daddy. At Ranger Bail Bonds, the company she used to bail her out of jail, Peterson listed Charles Albright as her cosigner on bond applications. On one form, she listed him as her best friend in the event that she skipped town and the bondsmen had to hunt her down.

There is also evidence that Albright was a friend of Mary Pratt's long before she became a prostitute. In the early eighties, Mary lived in a south Dallas neighborhood where Albright's parents had long ago invested in cheap rental property. At the time, Albright was temporarily living in one of the rental homes. According to several sources, Albright had a brief fling with one of Pratt's female friends and brought that woman and Pratt over to his house for parties.

Other prostitutes say that when Pratt started turning tricks at the Star, Albright became one of her customers. Pratt told them that "Old Man Albright" was a good trick, willing to pay a little more than the going rate. Soon Albright was making the rounds. With some of the girls, he had a platonic relationship. He would pick them up, talk to them, take them to get a hamburger, and drop them back off, never even attempting sex. With others, he had standing sexual appointments—always in the afternoons, when Dixie was at work as a sales clerk at a gift shop in Redbird Mall.

Every Friday afternoon, for instance, he had sex with a married woman who hit the streets after her husband had gone to work and her children were at school. Albright, whom she called Pappy, felt sorry for her, she said: "He was a sweet gentleman. If I ever needed extra money, I would call him and he would drop it off." But the married woman said that by late 1987 she had to put an end to her dates with Albright because he began to get more and more aggressive. She said he asked her to beat him—"to spank him like a child." Another prostitute, Edna Russell, remembered meeting Albright when her friend Susan Peterson asked her to do a "double." She said she and Peterson went with Albright into a motel room. There, he handcuffed them to the bed and began hitting them with a belt and an extension cord, all the while shouting, "Scream, bitch! You know you like it!"

Perhaps it was no coincidence that Albright's life began to spin out of control after the death of his parents, Delle and Fred. Without them around to look out for him, a repressed part of Albright may have finally unleashed itself. He and Delle, who died of cancer in 1981, were not close in her last years. Delle was disappointed in the way her son had turned out, while Albright found her to be a pest—especially when she would bang on his door early on Saturday mornings to get him to help her with one of her little fixup projects.

But as his final gesture of devotion to his mother, Albright went out and bought a dress for the undertaker to put on her body—the first new dress he had ever seen her wear. Surprisingly, he wept at her funeral, wracked with grief or maybe guilt over the way he had let her down.

He also cried at Fred's funeral a few years later. Frankly, it had not been until after Delle's death that Albright and his father became close. Albright remembered how Delle constantly nagged at her quiet husband, bickering with him about problems around the house. With her gone, Fred seemed more relaxed. Several nights a week, Albright would take him to dinner at a nearby cafeteria.

After Fred's fatal heart attack in 1986, Albright inherited at least $96,000, along with all of his parents' homes and property in south Dallas. For what friends said were sentimental reasons, he kept the property in his father's name. To bring in some extra money, he rented out one of the tiny ramshackle frame homes, on a street called Cotton Valley, to a truck driver named Axton Schindler. Known as Speedee because he talked so fast, Schindler was a singularly weird individual. He stacked the rooms of his house with trash up to three feet high. He put an automobile engine in the living room. He lived without electricity and running water: He used a Coleman lantern for light and bottled water to wash himself. Albright's friends said he should get another renter, that Speedee was too unusual. But the always agreeable Albright, who had met Schindler through a female friend, said he wasn't that bad of a fellow, so he let him stay.

At this point, Albright had made the decision to move back into the old family home in Oak Cliff, which, like the rental homes, was still listed in the property rolls under Fred's name. Although the neighborhood had grown somewhat shabby over the years and the house was definitely in need of a new paint job, Albright said the place would do nicely. He brought his new love, Dixie Austin, down from Arkansas, and together they settled in for a quiet, romantic life.

The address of their home was 1035 Eldorado.

"You know Irv Stone, the head of the Dallas County forensic science department, which studies physical evidence found at crime scenes."

"Yes," he said. "We played on a softball team together. He was sort of a standoffish person. Everyone would call him 'Dr. Stone.' So finally I said something to him about my supraorbital foremen bothering me. He'd say, 'Huh?' I'd say, 'You know, where the ophthalmic division of the trigeminal nerve comes through and feeds my eyebrow up here. It's really been bothering me.' And Irv, sort of cocky, said, 'I hate to inform you that I am not a medical doctor.' I'm surprised he didn't know his anatomy.'

"What were you describing, the area above your eye?" I asked.

"Yes, the little ridge there, right where the nerve comes through."

MARCH 19, 1991: SHIRLEY WILLAMS

JOHN WESTPHALEN HAD FILLED UP four black spiral notebooks with notes on the prostitute murder case. He had gone back and reexamined the crime scenes. Special undercover units had been sent to stake out the prostitution areas and run computer checks on the license plates of vehicles that cruised by, just to see if the owners might have any unusual criminal records. Everything added up to zip. This was a killer in total control, a man who refused to panic. "We've got to answer three questions," Westphalen said again and again at meetings about the case. "Number one, Why is he after prostitutes? Number two, Why were both bodies dumped on that same street? And number three, Why are those eyes cut out?"

Sitting around Westphalen's battleship-gray metal desk in the heart of the fluorescent-lit homicide office, detectives started throwing out theories. Maybe the killer had gotten AIDS from a prostitute and was out for revenge. Maybe he believed the old superstition that a murderer's image always remains on the eyeballs of the person he kills. Maybe he believed a dead person's eyes would follow him forever. Or maybe the killer took the eyeballs to fuel some sexual fantasy. Maybe he wanted to eat them—or cook them. The only thing Westphalen knew for sure was that the killer came out late at night, was strong enough to drag those girls in and out of a car, and had surgical skills. He also probably needed a well-lit room to do his surgery. Hell, somebody said, maybe this guy is a whacked-out doctor.

Suddenly, in the early morning hours of March 19, the killer changed tactics. On Fort Worth Boulevard, another whore hangout a few miles from the Star, a black prostitute named Shirley Williams emerged from the Avalon Motel, where she worked as a maid during the day and turned tricks at night. According to another prostitute who saw her, Shirley was wearing jeans and a yellow raincoat and appeared to be in a stuporous drug high as she tottered alone on the sidewalk.

She was found at six-twenty the next morning, dumped on a residential street half a block from an elementary school in the heart of Oak Cliff. As children walked to school, they could see the naked woman crumpled against the curb. An unopened condom was beside her body. "Go look at her eyes and tell me if they're there," Westphalen said to the medical examiner's field agent at the scene. The field agent flipped open the eyelids. "Gone," he said.

Westphalen turned to his partner, Stan McNear. "We've got number three," he said.

The autopsy on Shirley Williams' body would show that the surgery had been hurried. The broken tip of an X-Acto blade was found embedded in the skin near her right eye. But there were still no witnesses, no murder weapon, no fingerprints. Worse, the killer had now murdered a black woman, and he had moved locations. Just as the detectives had feared, the publicity about the case had sent the killer away from the Star and his south Dallas dumping ground. There was no telling where he would hit again.

OCTOBER 1990: A SON'S VENGEANCE

IN THE AUTUMN BEFORE THE KILLINGS began, Charles Albright was the model of domestic propriety. During the day, he put his carpenter's skills to use around the house, installing new cabinets for the kitchen, adding a skylight in the bathroom. If he was preparing to become a modern-day Jack the Ripper, none of his friends or family had any idea.

But on October 1, Albright did something that, even for him, seemed a little peculiar: He took a job delivering newspapers in the middle of the night for the *Dallas Times Herald*. Albright told Dixie, who by now was his common-law wife, that he needed more spending money. He had never been good with his finances; in four years he had gone through his inheritance, and he had yet to get a full-time job. Because Dixie got a monthly annuity check and worked daily in the gift shop, she paid most of their bills. Dixie wasn't exactly pleased with Charlie's decision—she said she couldn't get a good night's sleep with him gone. But Albright said it would work out fine. He would wake up around three in the morning, deliver papers on an Oak Cliff route between four and six, and then be back in bed by six-fifteen.

He and Dixie agreed that most of the money he made would go for the trips he took with his softball team. The well-built Albright was one of the better players in the city's senior slow-pitch softball league. He played for both a day team and a night team, and he was chosen as an outfielder for a local all-star team that went to the Senior World Series in Arizona. Albright, of course, was the league's most colorful personality: He wore red shoes while everyone else wore black, and he twisted a coat hanger inside his cap so the cap would sit perfectly upon his head. He brought a cooler of soft drinks to every game for the other players to share. At the end of the game, there was nobody who could regale an audience with a funny story the way he could.

"No one ever saw Charlie upset—I literally mean that," said a man who managed one of Charlie's teams in the fall of 1990. "He went out of his way to try to be liked," said a longtime friend who also played ball with him. "Every now and then there would be some jawboning during a game, maybe a scuffle between two players from opposing teams. But if somebody came after Charlie, he would back down, as if he was scared. He literally could not stand the idea of fighting. He would rather give you a present. Every time he saw one of my daughters, he gave her a gift or a ten-dollar bill."

Because Albright's former teammates were so fond of him, it is difficult even today for them to talk about a certain incident that took place a few months before the murders. Many of them still deny knowing anything about it; others say they have only heard about it secondhand. But at least two men have confirmed that Charlie Albright let his mask slip again.

At the end of one game, some players for the Richardson Greyhounds, Charlie's day team, were sitting around the ballpark, shooting the breeze and eating some candy that Charlie had brought, when two women in a car drove slowly by. After the men joked that the women must be prostitutes, the team's manager shouted, "Hey, Charlie, you're single. Why don't you take after them whores?"

Albright said, "Hell, I'd kill them if I could."

Stunned, the men turned toward their mild-mannered friend. On his face was a dark scowling look. "What do you mean?" the manager said, trying to keep the conversation light. "We've got to have whores. It keeps men from chasing married women."

"The hell it does!" Albright snapped. Then he marched off to his car and left.

It was the first time anyone had ever seen Albright show any kind of anger. When the team assembled again for practice a few days later, the manager tried to apologize. "We were just shooting the bull," he said.

"Well, that's a touchy subject with me," Albright replied. "My mother was a prostitute."

He was not talking about Delle, he said, he was talking about his birth mother. The other men were speechless.

Was this just one of Albright's tall tales? In the months to come, a number of people tried to verify the story, including an FBI agent and a private investigator working for Albright's defense attorney. They learned that while his biological father could not be traced, his biological mother was a nurse who had lived and died in Wichita Falls. Perhaps she never was the brilliant law student whom Delle Albright had described to her son. But there was no way they could determine if she had ever been a prostitute. Albright's relatives, in fact, insisted that after a lengthy search through court records, Albright had been thrilled to find his biological mother. As an adult, he had visited her several times in Wichita Falls and had brought her gifts. He had even introduced her to Fred Albright and to his own daughter.

Yet somewhere in Albright's mind, the connection between prostitution and motherhood had been made. It is possible that Charles Albright was wrestling with a very twisted version of the madonna-whore complex, unconsciously seeking revenge on the mother figures who disappointed him by associating with prostitutes—the worst possible women he could find. On one hand, he seemingly cares for prostitutes like Susan Peterson and Mary Pratt. He helped them financially, bought them dinner, and gave them presents. On the other hand, he wanted to punish them. Perhaps he hated what they had become. Perhaps he hated what he had become in their presence.

Whatever the reason, if Albright had truly decided the time had come to kill, he had put himself in a perfect position to do it. His paper route gave him an excuse to be out at night. He had prostitutes who trusted him enough to let him take them on a little trip. He had his parents' old property just a ten-minute drive south of the Star, where, unseen, he could carry out the murders and mutilations. And because the property was in his father's name, nothing could be traced back to him.

There was only one flaw in the plan— one Albright didn't even know about. Charlie's truck-driving tenant, Axton Schindler, had decided a few years back not to list his south Dallas address on his driver's license. As he liked to say, he preferred to keep his privacy; he wanted the government to stay out of his business. Instead, he put down 1035 Eldorado, the address for Charles Albright.

"The police told me you had a number of true-crime books in your house," I said.

"Oh, hell, there were other books—books of poetry, several Bibles, cookbooks, all kinds of books on art, watercolors, oils, and some books on science. It was as well-rounded a library as you wanted to find."

"But in any of those murder books you read, did you learn why a serial killer acts the way he does?"

"Well, just for the sheer pleasure of killing a girl, I would imagine."

"A serial killer," I said, "would not have —

"Would not have dumped them on the street where they would be easily found," he quickly said. "Look, if I made up my mind I wanted to be one, I wouldn't have been caught on the third killing. If I had decided to be a serial killer, I sure would have been a good one. You can ask anybody about anything I have ever done. I tried to be the best at what I did."

MARCH 22, 1991: CAUGHT

ONCE WORD OF SHIRLEY WILLIAMS' killing spread, the Star Motel turned into a ghost town. Some prostitutes, black and white, told officers John Matthews and Regina Smith that they were leaving Dallas. Others said they were getting out of the business. A few women, so desperate for drug money that they couldn't leave, moved together to a street corner next to the home of a man who promised to serve as their lookout and bodyguard.

Cruising the area, Matthews and Smith spied a black prostitute, Brenda White, a seventeen-year veteran of the neighborhood. White tended to work alone on a street corner in front of a church, away from the other prostitutes. The officers decided to stop and make sure she knew about the murders. "Girl," Smith said, "don't you know there's a killer loose? He's now killing the black girls too." "Well, I'm going to get my black ass out of here," White replied. "I just had to mace a man who jumped bad on me the other night."

White told the officers that a few days before, a trick in a dark station wagon had pulled up alongside her and that she had gotten inside the car. He was a husky-looking white man with salt and pepper hair, cowboy boots, and blue jeans. "Let's go to a motel," she told him. "No," he said. "I've got a spot we can use." As a way to protect herself, White never allowed a new trick to take her anywhere but a whore motel, so she told him to drop her off immediately. Suddenly, "a change came over his face," she recalled. "It was like anger, rage. He said, 'I hate whores! I'm going to kill all of you motherf—ing whores!'" Before he had a chance to grab her, White shot a stream of Mace into his face, threw open the door, and jumped out, breaking the heel of one of her favorite red leather pumps.

For the rest of the day, Matthews and Smith could not shake White's story from their minds. They flipped through their notebooks. They thought about everything the whores had told them since the killings began. Always, they returned to Veronica Rodriguez's rambling talk about being raped.

The next morning, as they were checking in for work at their police substation, Smith said, "We need to run a computer check on that Axton Schindler." Because county government computers contain more information about citizens than city computers, she and Matthews drove to the Dallas County constable's office near Jefferson Boulevard. There, a deputy constable on duty, Walter Cook, agreed to help them. Seated around the terminal, the officers asked Cook to type in Schindler's address: 1035 Eldorado. The name Fred Albright popped up as the owner of the property.

Fred Albright? Where was Axton Schindler?

Cook punched in another code. It turned out that this Fred Albright also owned property on a street called Cotton Valley. Wasn't Cotton Valley in the very neighborhood in south Dallas where the first two prostitutes were found? Cook kept typing. Fred Albright, the computer reported, was dead.

Matthews and Smith stared at the screen: The only clue in the case led them to a dead man. Then, after a pause, Cook said softly, "Maybe this has something to do with a man named Charles Albright."

Several weeks before, Cook explained, he had come to the office early one morning and had answered a call from a woman who would not identify herself. The woman had been friends with Mary Pratt, she said, and through Pratt had met a man whom she briefly dated. He was a very nice man, she said, but he had an odd love for eyes. She also happened to mention that he kept X-Acto blades in his attic. Cook asked for the man's name. "Charles Albright," she said.

If any other constable's deputy had been helping Matthews and Smith that day, the link to Albright might never have been made. But good fortune prevailed. Cook typed in another code, and personal information for Charles Albright popped up on the screen: "Born—August 10, 1933. Address—1035 Eldorado."

Somehow, they said, Schindler and Albright were connected. Perhaps Albright was Schindler's "friend," the one who had tried to kill Veronica Rodriguez. Their hearts racing, Matthews and Smith rushed to the county's identification division and asked to see Albright's criminal record. The officers discovered a string of thefts, burglaries, and forgeries and the charge of sexual intercourse with a child. The clerk then pulled out a mug shot of Albright, a photo of a rather handsome well-built man with grayish hair, angular features, and deep-set dark eyes—just like the man Brenda White had described. In the picture, Albright was frowning, his face perplexed, as if he was surprised he had been caught.

The clerk wondered why Smith was so excited. "Honey," Smith said, "I think we've got the killer."

On their way to the homicide department, Matthews and Smith rehearsed everything they wanted to say. They could not seem unprepared, Matthews insisted; it was nervy enough for two raw patrol officers to visit the legendary Westphalen and tell him they believed they had found the killer—although they had no solid evidence to prove it.

Westphalen greeted them politely. Matthews started, then Smith interrupted, and soon they were both talking at once. Westphalen sighed. "Calm down," he said. "Let's take it slow." A few minutes later, after they had finished their presentation, Westphalen decided they were on to something. He put together a photo lineup of six mug shots and told Matthews and Smith to show it to Brenda White.

Immediately, Smith and Matthews tracked White down on her usual street corner and asked her if she recognized any of the men in the mug shots. White unhesitatingly pointed to Albright's picture and said he was the man who had attacked her. A little while later, they showed the same lineup to Veronica Rodriguez. According to Matthews, when Rodriguez got to the third picture—Albright's—she started trembling. Suddenly fearful, she refused to identify anyone. Matthews called Westphalen with the bad news. Rodriguez is so afraid of the killer, he said, that she won't pick out his picture. "Bring her down here to see me," Westphalen growled.

Westphalen knew if he could not get Rodriguez to break, he wouldn't have the evidence to go after Charles Albright. Brenda White's story offered only the prospect of a misdemeanor assault charge. But if Rodriguez identified Albright, the Dallas police could file charges for attempted murder, get a search warrant, and look through his house for evidence that might connect him to the three murders.

Smith and Matthews dragged Rodriguez downtown. In a small interrogation room, Westphalen stared with his icy blue eyes at the crack-addicted Rodriguez. Rodriguez began to shake again. Tears poured out of her eyes. She wouldn't look at the pictures laid out before her. Trying to control his anger, Westphalen took a different tack. He told Rodriguez about the three girls, how they were brutally killed, how the police couldn't get the killer off the street without her help. "This is so easy," he said. "Pick out the picture of the guy who assaulted you, and we will get him and put him in jail, where he can't hurt you." Slowly, Rodriguez looked over the mug shots. While Westphalen and another officer watched, she reached for Albright's photo, turned it over, and signed her name.

At two-thirty in the morning on March 22, as a gentle rain fell on Oak Cliff, a team of tactical officers burst through the front door of 1035 Eldorado. Despite the home's shabby exterior, the treasures of Charlie Albright's eclectic life decorated room after room. One cabinet was filled with exotic champagne glasses; another held delicate expensive Lladro figurines of pretty young women. On one wall were *Life* magazine covers and valuable Marilyn Monroe movie posters.

As Charles Albright was handcuffed and led away, he never said a word. Stumbling out of bed in her nightgown, Dixie Austin looked incredulously at Albright and then back at the police. Unable to imagine what the man she loved could have done, she began to scream.

DECEMBER 1991: CONVICTED

FOR A LONG TIME AFTER CHARLES Albright's arrest, most everyone involved in his case wondered whether the police had enough evidence to convict him of murder. Despite a withering all-night interrogation by Westphalen, Albright refused to confess to anything. He acted as if he had never heard the names of the murdered prostitutes. Police searched through every square inch of the south Dallas properties. They searched his Oak Cliff house six times. The FBI even brought in a high-tech machine that could see through walls. Although the searches produced an array of interesting items—carpenters' woodworking blades, X-Acto blades, a copy of *Gray's Anatomy,* at least a dozen true-crime books—they never came up with the eyeballs. Behind Charlie's hand-built fireplace mantel, police discovered a hidden compartment filled with pistols and rifles. None, however, turned out to be the murder weapon.

Nor could police find anyone who would admit to seeing Charlie with the three prostitutes on the nights they were killed. Dixie claimed that on the nights in question, Charlie did not leave the house early for his paper route and that he always came home on time. As the trial date arrived, Veronica Rodriguez decided to testify as a witness for the defense. She claimed that she and Albright had never been together and that Westphalen had coerced her into picking Albright's photograph from the lineup. Axton Schindler continued to deny that he had saved Rodriguez from Albright. He said a Hispanic man named Joe had brought her to his door.

But Toby Shook, a low-key 33-year-old prosecutor working for the Dallas County district attorney's office, had a trump card. For the first time in its history, the DA's office was going for a murder conviction based solely on controversial hair evidence. Days after Albright's arrest, the city's forensic lab reported that hairs found on the bodies of the dead prostitutes were similar to hair samples taken from Albright's head and pubic area. As evidence goes, hairs are not as conclusive as fingerprints—it's impossible to tell how many other gray-haired men's hairs might look similar to Albright's hairs under a microscope— yet in this case, the lab kept running tests. Lab technicians said that hairs found on the blankets in the back of Albright's pickup truck were similar to hair samples from the first two prostitutes killed, Mary Pratt and Susan Peterson. Hairs found in Albright's vacuum cleaner matched the hair from the third prostitute killed, Shirley Williams. An additional piece of the puzzle came from John Matthews and Regina Smith. The officers found a prostitute, Tina Connolly, who claimed that Albright was one of her regular afternoon customers on Fort Worth Boulevard.

She never saw him cruise after dark, she said, except for one time—the night Shirley Williams disappeared. Connolly took Matthews and Smith to a secluded field near Fort Worth Boulevard where Albright used to take her for sex. There, they spotted a yellow raincoat, just like the one Williams was last seen wearing, and a blanket. Hairs on the coat and blanket matched Albright's hair.

Albright's defense attorney, Brad Lollar, tried to convince the jury that the case against Albright depended on the flimsiest circumstantial evidence. The killer, he said, was probably Axton Schindler, who just happened to skip town the week of the trial. Admittedly, the police had many unanswered questions about Schindler. Westphalen had spent hours interrogating him, trying to determine if he assisted Albright in the killings or was at least aware that Albright was murdering women on the rental property. But there was nothing to tie him to the case except for an empty .44-caliber bullet box found behind the house, which Albright might have dropped there himself. When Schindler's and Albright's photos were shown to dozens of prostitutes, none recognized Schindler, but many recognized Albright. Nor were there any hairs found on the dead prostitutes that could be linked to Schindler. Most important, no one who had ever met Axton Schindler could imagine he would have the slightest skill required to perfectly remove a set of human eyes.

Albright never testified. Throughout the trial, he sat quietly in his chair, his shoulders slumped, like a weak, humbled figure. Shook, in his closing argument, derisively called Albright "this former biology teacher, bullfighter, college ace, smart man who just can't seem to have a job." But Shook warned the jury not to underestimate Albright—that he had grown much smarter during this trial, that if he ever got out of jail, he wouldn't make the same mistakes again.

On December 19, when the jury returned with a guilty verdict and a life sentence, Dixie collapsed in the courtroom. Albright's friends avoided the reporters in the courthouse hallway; it was as if they did not want to be blamed for having lived with a vicious killer without recognizing him for what he was. But a stunned Brad Lollar, who genuinely thought he was going to get his client acquitted, strode tight-lipped out of the courtroom. "It's always a miscarriage of justice," he told the press, "when an innocent man is convicted."

He was confident, he told me, that he would win his case on appeal. Another judge, he said, would see through the lies told at the first trial. He leaned forward in his chair and grinned optimistically. He couldn't complain about prison life, he said. He was reading two books a week on the Civil War; he was taking notes for a book he wanted to write on the wives of Civil War generals. He was busy working as a carpenter in the prison woodworking shop, coaching the prison softball team, and writing letters to Dixie. He had just sent a request to Omni magazine for a back copy of its first issue because there was a painting on the cover that he liked. He grinned again and told terrifically funny stories about how crazy the other inmates acted. For a moment, it was hard for me to remember exactly what Charles Albright had been accused of doing.

But then I'd lock on the image of an eyeless young woman lying faceup on a neighborhood street. Why would such a kindly, lighthearted man want to cut out a prostitute's eyes? Why was he so plagued by eyes, that potent and universal symbol, the windows to the soul? In the ancient myth, Oedipus tore out his own eyes after committing the transgression of sleeping with his mother. Did Charles Albright, a perverted Oedipus, tear out the eyes of women for committing the transgression of sleeping with men? Perhaps he removed their eyes out of some sudden need to show the world he could have been a great surgeon. Maybe he dumped that third body in front of the school to show his frustration over never having become a biology teacher. Or maybe a private demon had been lurking since his childhood, when the eyes were left off his little stuffed birds. Just as he long ago wanted to have a bagful of taxidermist's eyes, maybe he decided to collect human eyes for himself.

"Oh, really, I have never touched an eyeball," Albright declared again, for the first time becoming indignant with me. "I truly think— and this may sound farfetched—that the boys in the forensics lab cut out those eyes. I think the police said, 'We want some sort of mutilation.'" Almost cheered by his reasoning he returned to his psychologically impenetrable self. Whatever secrets he had would remain with him forever.

Weeks after that conversation, I remembered Albright's comment about wanting the first issue of Omni magazine. Intrigued, I went to look for it at the library. I opened a bound volume to the cover of the first issue, which was published in October 1978. There, staring out from the center of a dark page; was a solitary human eye, unmoored, as if floating in space. The eyelid slid down just to the top of the eyeball; the eyeball was lightly shaded; the eyelashes were curved like half-moons.

It was, I thought, exactly the kind of eye Charles Albright would wish he had painted.

THE SWEET SONG OF JUSTICE

It took the jury less than three hours to find Yolanda Saldivar guilty of murdering Selena. But for two weeks in October, all of Texas followed the most sensational trial in years. A behind - the - scenes look at what happened in the courtroom.

By Joe Nick Patoski

"YOU MIGHT NOT WANT TO SIT DOWN HERE," Douglas Tinker said wearily, holding a glass of white wine. "Man I haven't won a case in so long." The rotund balding man with the expansive white beard who recalled both Santa Claus and Ernest Hemingway was slouched in a booth at Buster's Drinkery, an anonymous dive frequented by the lawyers who work nearby at the Harris County Courthouse. It was a Monday afternoon in late October. While the boys at the next ran table were engrossed in their usual game of gin rummy, a loud party was going on in the street outside, with honking horns, blaring music, and cheering crowds filling the sidewalks. Most of the several hundred revelers were Hispanic – Mexican American Texans to be precise -- and they had plenty to celebrate. Yolanda Saldivar had just been found guilty of murdering their heroine, Selena. Tinker and his court-appointed co-counsel, Arnold Garcia, a hard-boiled former prosecutor from Jim Wells County, had just finished the thankless task of defending Selena's killer, and they were already second-guessing their defense strategy. Believing they had discredited key prosecution witnesses, they had decided not to ask that the jury consider a lesser charge of voluntary manslaughter, which might have meant a shorter sentence. They had rested their case without calling Abraham Quintanilla, Jr., Selena's Father, whom they had portrayed as a controlling stage dad and manager and the catalyst behind the murder. They had decided against putting their client on the stand.

The honking of the horns grew more persistent. Tinker had had clients accused of unsavory crimes in his thirty years as Corpus Christi defense attorney, including George B. Parr (the Duke of Duval County) and a Branch Davidian, but no client had generated the pure hatred that Saldivar did. There had been death threats, and more than once he had spoken of going out in a blaze of bullets, like Marlon Brando in *Viva Zapata!* "They saw us walk in. They know we're here," Tinker said in a low voice. "Let's have another round." When the evening news came on the television in Buster's it touted coverage of the "Selena trial." Tinker talked back to the tube: "The Selena trial? What about the Yolanda Saldivar trial?" As the celebration outside continued. Tinker smiled at Garcia and raised his glass. "Well," he said, "at least this reduces our chances of getting shot."

The same could not be said for Yolanda Saldivar. Ever since that drizzly day in March when she shot Selena, she had been a marked woman. With millions of fans still distraught over Selena's murder, it is debatable whether the 35-year-old Saldivar is safer in prison or out.

In life, the 23-year-old Selena Quintanilla Perez was the undisputed queen of tejano music and an international superstar. In death, she has become bigger than ever. Since the shooting, the legend of the talented, beautiful, smart, clean-living vocalist who proved you can assimilate and have your culture too has spread from her hometown of Corpus Christi throughout the world. Street murals in barrios around the state have elevated her to a saint-like status almost equal to that of the Virgin of Guadalupe. More than six hundred babies born in Texas between April and September have been named Selena. Her posthumous album, *Dreaming of You*, debuted at number one on *Billboard* magazine's album chart in July, making it the second fastest-selling release by a female singer in the history of popular music, after Janet Jackson. Selena's appeal has always been strongest in South Texas, where she lived and worked, and for this reason, state district judge Mike Westergren moved the trial from Corpus Christi to Houston, where finding a fair jury would be easier.

Throughout the trial of *State of Texas vs Yolanda Saldivar*, Nueces County district attorney Carlos Valdez kept saying, "This is a simple murder case." The evidence seemed to support him. Immediately following the shooting at the Days Inn Hotel in Corpus Christi on March 31, 1995, Saldivar, the former president of Selena's fan club and close business associate, sat in a pickup in the motel's parking lot for nine and a half hours with the murder weapon pointed at her head, negotiating her surrender to the police. After she gave up, she signed a confession admitting her guilt. This was an open and shut case, one that Valdez, a native of Molina, the sane humble neighborhood on the southwestern edge of Corpus Christi where Selena had grown up and resided, was determined to win.

In his opening statement Douglas Tinker presented a much darker picture of the events surrounding the murder. Saldivar was Selena's best friend, and she was trusted by the entire Quintanilla family; with, among other evidence, the audiotapes of her negotiations with the police, the defense would prove the shooting was an accident. Also, it would show that the confession she had signed didn't include her claim that the shooting was an accident. Paul Rivera, one of the Corpus police officers who had interrogated her, had left that part out. Texas Ranger Robert Garza would reluctantly testify that he had witnessed Saldivar protesting to Rivera that the written confession he had prepared said nothing about the shooting being an accident. Furthermore, the defense would prove that Saldivar was forced into this confrontation and its unfortunate conclusion by Selena's father, who lived his life through his daughter and was involved in a power struggle with Saldivar, even telling Selena that Saldivar was a lesbian. The defense believed that Abraham did not approve of Selena's expanding her fashion business, with which Saldivar was intimately involved, into Mexico. (Selena had had a salon-boutique in San Antonio and another in Corpus Christi.) Her father, the defense said, thought she was doing so at the expense of the family band.

But once the trial got under way, Valdez preempted the defense's blame-the-father strategy by calling Abraham as the first witness. Quintanilla obliged by speaking affectionately about the family and the band he managed and promoted. He forcefully denied ever threatening Saldivar, calling her a lesbian, or raping her, as she claimed on the hostage audiotapes. (His initial response to prosecutors when informed of the rape accusation had been "Have you ever seen the woman?") The surprise of the trial was Tinkers decision not to cross-examine Quintanilla or recall him later. It meant the defense was not going to pursue the sordid details it had alleged. "He suffered through this," Tinker said after the verdict was announced, explaining what seemed to be an about-face. "He and his family are hurt by what happened, and I decided not to put him through it." Cross-examining Abraham, the defense had concluded, was too risky: It might backfire and stir up sympathy for him. Therefore, the defense stuck to the evidence concerning the accidental-shooting claim and the incomplete confession.

The jury didn't buy any of it. But before and after the verdict and the life-in-prison sentence were handed down, there was much drama at the Harris County courthouse, involving aggressive lawyers, the grieving families, the eyewitnesses and the Selena faithful. Over the course of the fourteen-day trial, which was the most closely watched murder trial in Texas in years, one thing was certain: Selena's ghost hung over the courtroom and the hundreds of fans keeping vigil outside.

THE TESTIMONY

EYEWITNESS TESTIMONY BY FAMILY MEMBERS, boutique employees, gun shop employees, and hospital nurses filled in some blanks about the events leading up to March 31. One revelation was Saldivar's ambivalence about the murder weapon. She bought the Taurus 85 .38-caliber double-action revolver on March 11 at *A Place to Shoot* in San Antonio, telling the clerk she was an in-home nurse who was getting death threats from family members of a terminally ill patient she cared for. Two days later, on March 13, the same day she had her lawyer, Richard Garza draw up a resignation letter to Selena, Saldivar picked up the gun. She returned it on March 15, saying her father had given her a .22 and she no longer needed the Taurus. On March 26 she returned to repurchase the gun.

Part of Saldivar's indecisiveness about the gun seemed to be a result of her uncertain employment status throughout March. According to the testimony of Chris Perez, Selena's husband, Selena told Saldivar over the telephone that she was fired on March 10, the day after Abraham, Selena, and her Sister, Suzette, had confronted Saldivar claiming to have discovered evidence that she had stolen up to $30,000 from the fan club. But both Suzette and Celia Soliz, one of Selena's boutique employees, testified that Selena had not made a final decision until March 30, the day before the shooting. Perez also testified that Saldivar was to continue working with Selena only to help set up the fashion ventures in Mexico and that Saldivar had bank records Selena wanted back.

There was also some gripping testimony about Selena and Saldivar's visit to Doctors Regional Medical Center the morning of shooting. Saldivar had said that she was raped earlier that week in Mexico, a medical examination proved inconclusive, Selena realized Saldivar was lying, according to two nurses at the hospital. The murder took place less than half an hour after the two left the hospital. Perhaps a fatal mistake was made in dragging out Saldivar's firing. Having most of the month of March to contemplate that her relationship was over with the person she described as "the only friend I ever had" was too much for Saldivar to take. As she told hostage negotiator Larry Young "I had a problem with her and I just got to end it."

THE DEFENSE: If Douglas Tinker wasn't exactly a one-man dream team, the 61 year-old attorney had a long record of impressive acquittals. The criminal justice section of the State Bar of Texas had recognized him as the state's outstanding criminal defense lawyer for 1995. After Judge Westergren appointed Tinker to defend Yolanda Saldivar, Richard "Racehorse" Haynes said that she had lucked into $50 million worth of representation. At Tinkers request, Westergren appointed Arnold Garcia to assist him because Garcia spoke Spanish, as did Saldivar, and was a tireless investigator. Before the trial many Houston lawyers had offered to assist Tinker in the high-profile case. Tinker took on Fred Hagans, a personal-injury attorney and a former partner of superlitigator John O'Quinn. This was Hagans' first criminal case, and he invested considerable sums of money for the experience. He offered the services of his co-counsel Patricia Saum, hired jury consultant Robert Gordon, and staged a mock trial at an expense of more than $20,000. It was during the mock trial, with cameras filming the reactions of every "juror," that Tinker first sensed his case might not be as strong as he had thought. Though one third of the "jury" voted to acquit, not one of the test jurors seemed bothered by the actions of Paul Rivera, the officer who took Saldivar's confession but didn't include her claim that the shooting was accidental. If the real jury didn't buy the bad-cop theory, would they buy the accident?

THE PROSECUTION: Carlos Valdez had never tried a felony case, before he was elected district attorney for the 105th Judicial District two years ago. His presentations and examinations in court left room for improvement, but the boyish 41-year-old DA had the evidence and he knew how to delegate. Valdez's chief prosecutor, Mark Skurka, a garrulous 36-year-old, tried the bulk of the case and ably demonstrated why he has prosecuted more murder cases in Nueces County than anyone else. During closing arguments in both the verdict and the sentencing phases, Skurka posted a picture of Selena in the jury box and repeatedly spoke to it, especially when he was referring to the defense's claim that the shooting was accidental, which he labeled "hogwash." He called the defense strategy the "squid defense," attacking Saldivar's defenders for putting out a black cloud of inky doubt to get away from the essence of the case. Elissa Sterling became part of the team when the case was assigned to Westergren's 214th District Court, where Sterling prosecutes cases. Between the three of them, the prosecution got the desired verdict by sticking to the indisputable evidence, by calling both friendly and hostile witnesses before the defense could, and by keeping the jurors focused on the victim: Selenas screams and her last steps and words immediately following the shooting were recounted by five motel employees, one of whom, Norma Martinez, said she had heard Saldivar shout. "Bitch" at Selena. Their testimony, more than anything else, convicted Saldivar.

THE JURY: It took two days to select the twelve-person jury. Judge Westergren had decided that to keep things moving, he wouldn't seat alternates or sequester the jurors. Throughout the trial, the jury paid close attention, took notes, and showed little emotion, except for one blond Anglo female, who cried at the sight of the autopsy photographs and during the teary testimony of Frank Saldivar, the father of the accused. Up until the verdict, Tinker kept saying how much he liked this jury, in particular the three Anglo men sitting on the back row, one of whom was an ex-Marine. Tinker liked them so much he thought he could make his case without getting into the seamier aspects of the alleged split between Selena and her father. He liked them so much he called only three witnesses for the defense and recalled only two prosecution witnesses before resting, without asking the judge to consider a lesser charge. The guilty verdict was returned in less than three hours. The sentence of life in prison took nine hours. Charles Arnold, who was one of the jurors Tinker liked so much, had held out for a forty-year-sentence before giving in.

THE JUDGE: The bow-tied Mike Westergren was the anti-Ito, the kind of judge who would have kept O. J. Simpson's dream team on a short leash. If nothing else, the unsuccessful candidate for the state Supreme Court was going to make the trial run on time and not let it get out of hand. Despite pretrial petitions from the Univision and Court TV networks, the 48-year-old judge ruled that cameras would not be allowed in his courtroom.

He showed a less serious side after the jury began deliberating punishment, when he visited with spectators in the gallery. As everyone began to relax, the din grew so loud that a bailiff had to shout, "Quiet in the courtroom!" Westergren, talking and laughing with two young lawyers had sheepishly raised his hand and said, "I'm afraid it was me."

YOLANDA: Seeing the accused up close, it was hard to imagine that the tiny four-foot-nine woman could hurt a flea, much less pull the trigger of a murder weapon. Whenever a witness was asked to identify her, she stood up and tossed her head back with an air of pride. But when the five hours of hostage-negotiation tapes were played in the court -- a grueling listening experience, the eerie sound of her sobs and hysterical moans filling the room -- Saldivar quietly began crying along with the tapes. It was a sad sight, but it humanized the cold-blooded murder that the prosecution had portrayed. She broke down sobbing after the verdict was read, quietly saying she wanted to kill herself, while defense investigator Tina Valenzuela comforted her.

WHERE'S LARRY? The most potentially explosive evidence was the recordings of conversations between Saldivar, sitting in the motel parking lot with a gun to her head, and the Corpus Christi Police Department's hostage negotiation team. Lead investigator Paul Rivera testified that he had been aware of the tapes in April. But they didn't surface until late August, after Tinker called police Chief Henry Garrett and asked for them. Played in their entirety, they depicted Saldivar as distraught and panicky. Between her wails, Saldivar said over and over, "I didn't mean to do it," suggesting the shooting was an accident. She also blamed Abraham, saying, "He made me do it. He was out to get me . . . This man was so evil to me. My father even warned me about him. My father said I should get out before I get trapped."

The special two-way phone line used by the hostage negotiation team was a flawed piece of technology. A portable phone would have allowed Saldivar a conference call with her mother in San Antonio, which she had asked for from the start. The two-way phone picked up the broadcast signal from the KSIX-AM transmitter located one hundred yards from the motel parking lot, which is why the voice of Milo Hamilton calling a Rangers--Astros exhibition baseball game and the melody of "The Theme From M*A*S*H* (Suicide Is Painless)" could be heard when the tapes were played in court. It was through this interference that Yolanda heard a news report that Selena was dead, at which point she became even more hysterical. The tapes also reveal that hostage negotiators promised Saldivar that her mother and her lawyer, Richard Garza would be waiting for her when she gave up. She wasn't and he wasn't. One thirty-minute tape consisted of little else but Yolanda repeating the mantra "Where's Larry?" -- an appeal to bring negotiator Larry Young back on the line. The mantra was accompanied by a mysterious and extremely irritating electronic buzz. The bizarre audio conflagration inspired "Where's Larry?" T-shirts, which were hawked on the street the next day.

THE FAMILIES: Both the Quintanilla and the Saldivar families came from humble Mexican-American roots and had survived and flourished by sticking close to their kin. The Quintanillas lived in three adjacent homes on Bloomington Street in the Molina neighborhood of Corpus Christi, the Saldivar's in four houses and a trailer on five acres just beyond the southern limits of San Antonio. While the Quintanilla's showed signs of wealth – they wore expensive clothes and brought along their own family spokesman and publicist – the Saldivar's were a true blue-collar family.

The 56-year-old Abraham Quintanilla, a forceful presence, was a dominant figure at the trial not only because the defense portrayed him as the one who drove Yolanda to buy the murder weapon but also because he was Selena's father and her business manager. On many occasions since the shooting he had shown himself to be a tough business manager, cutting deals and maximizing profit from all things Selena. He held countless press conferences to announce, among other things, the creation of the Selena Foundation; to introduce his new discovery, twelve-year-old Jennifer Peña, who resembles a young Selena; and to reveal his role as executive producer of the movie being made about Selena's life, which filmmaker Gregory Nava was writing from the fathers perspective.

He became increasingly hostile to the media, though, after the value of Selena's estate was published in the *San Antonio Express-News* in September. Probate court documents revealed that her net worth was only $164,000 and that Chris Perez had given up his right to administrate the estate to Abraham.

At the trial, Perez appeared thoroughly devastated by the loss of his wife, though the handsome, ponytailed 26-year-old is a delicate figure by nature. Before the trial, he said that he wanted to continue playing guitar, focusing on rock music. He also answered critics who questioned the handling of the estate, saying, "I didn't have a lawyer just like Selena didn't have a lawyer. We didn't need a lawyer because this is family. And why should I worry about losing something? I have already lost what I always wanted. I would trade everything I had if I could have her back."

Marcella Quintanilla, Selena's attractive mother, had said little publicly following the shooting in March. She was having just as much trouble as Perez coping with her daughter's death. When motel maintenance worker Trinidad Espinoza began recounting Selena's last moments, Marcella was overcome and had to leave. The next day, she was admitted to the coronary unit of St. Joseph's Hospital for overnight observation.

Yolanda's mother, Juanita, was the only Saldivar to attend the entire trial, usually accompanied by one of her six other children and various nieces and nephews. Gray-haired and wrapped in a sweater, she was the living embodiment of the *pobrecita abuelita*, the "poor little grandmother." On several occasions, she too had to be escorted out of the courtroom, overwhelmed with emotion. Yolanda's father, the diminutive Frank Saldivar, had recently retired after forty years of balancing enchilada plates and glasses of iced tea as the headwaiter at Jacala Restaurant in San Antonio. He spent his sixty-ninth birthday on the stand, fighting back tears and imploring jurors to have mercy on "our baby girl." After sentencing, Juanita and Frank crossed the rail and hugged and kissed Yolanda good-bye.

THE STREET: Everyday, Selena fans gathered outside the courthouse and made their feelings known by holding signs, wearing shirts, or shouting chants such as "ju-sti-ci-a!" or "Cien años!" As the trial neared conclusion, their numbers swelled and the mood took on a vindictive streak, evidenced by a "Hang the Witch" placard, posters that depicted Saldivar in cuffs standing in the middle of a target with the words "*la marrana*" ("the sow") written underneath, and a "Kill Yolanda" message painted in white shoe polish on the windshield of a Toyota. But imagination was at work too. One sign paraphrased a line from the new crossover country hit of Selena's old labelmate and duet partner Emilio Navaira: "There Can Never Be Enough Justice for Selena, But It's a Damn Good Start."

The celebrations around the courthouse following the guilty verdict and the sentence were marked by the strange sight of tears on the faces of many fans, especially older women. For them, Selena had already evolved from a pop star into an icon of grief.

THE MEDIA: There were more than two hundred media credentials issued for the trial, with almost as many Spanish-language media as English-language media. The most thorough TV coverage came from the two Spanish-language networks, Univision and Telemundo, both of which aired at least ninety minutes' worth of coverage daily. Univision's Marie Celeste Arraras -- the doe-eyed, henna-haired anchor of "Primer Impacto," a news program seen throughout the United States and in fifteen foreign countries -- was the trial's undisputed media star, judging from the fans' wolf whistles and the way they crowded her on the street. Her program had the most knowledgeable courtroom analyst, former Corpus state district judge Jorge Rangel, who knew Texas law and the players in the trial.

THE O. J. EFFECT: As murder trials go, the one in Houston had little to do with the O. J. Simpson trial in Los Angeles other than it involved homicide and a celebrity. Nevertheless, comparisons were frequently made. Before the trial, Abraham Quintanilla observed that after the O.J. verdict anything was possible. Once the trial began, the fear spread through barrios in Texas that Saldivar might get off as a result of police officer Paul Rivera's questionable handling of the confession. Selena's own Mark Fuhrman was going to mess everything up.

The verdict shored up trust in a legal system that has come under increasingly close and critical scrutiny. It proved to Texas' largest minority group that the criminal justice system, flawed as it may be, really does work. Following the trial, the of United Latin American Citizens announced a campaign to urge Hispanics to seek jury duty.

WAITING FOR THE JURY: While the jury deliberated the sentence, the mood in the courtroom turned informal and almost jovial. Sheriff's deputies ceased patting down media when they reentered the courtroom. A bailiff approached Yolanda Saldivar and whipped out a court pass, asking her to sign it. Pretty soon, members of the press were slipping their passes to Arnold Garcia for Saldivar to sign. Westergren and Valdez were signing autographs too. The Saldivar family sought out the autographs of several reporters. Tinker posed for sketch artists and quipped, "If the jury never comes back, it would be fine with me." Two spectators dozed off. So, briefly, did Abraham Quintanilla, sitting alone in the family-seating section. This was hardly the stuff of a trial of the century.

When the sentence of life in prison was returned, Carlos Valdez saluted the jury. Douglas Tinker announced that he would appeal. Following the final press conference, the same man who was fretting about being followed by angry Selena fans was still being hounded. But the fans didn't want Tinker's head. They wanted his autograph.

THE FUTURE: In addition to the Selena movie, her bands farewell tour next spring, and other Selena memorial projects, Abraham Quintanilla has been building a roster of young talent for his custom label distributed by Capitol EMI. A 900 number has been set up for fans to telephone condolences to the family for $3.00 per call. Selena's sister, Suzette, handles the boutiques and Selena merchandising. Selena's brother, A. B. Quintanilla III has been busy producing acts in the recording studio and writing. His composition "Estúpido Romántico," co-written with former Selena backup singer and popular solo act Pete Astudillo, was a big hit for the tejano supergroup Mazz, and he recently composed a theme song for a Mexican soap opera. He has just moved his wife, Vangie, and their two children to a palatial new home west of Corpus. Chris Perez is looking for a new place too. The three Quintanilla homes on Bloomington Street will soon be an empty nest.

FAMILY MATTERS: Back inside the friendly dimly lit confines of Buster's Drinkery two hours after the jury had returned its verdict -- the conversation shifted from law to family. Tinker had spent the previous weekend camping out in the woods of Alabama. "My son attends boarding school there and it was parents' weekend. I hadn't seen him in several months," he said. Garcia spoke lovingly of his son, Javier, a metal sculptor. They agreed that no matter how hard you try, you can never tell how your kids will turn out. Abraham and Marcella Quintanilla loved their daughter and had tried to protect her; Frank and Juanita Saldivar loved their daughter too. And they all wound up in a court of law in Houston, where twelve strangers passed judgment on why everything turned out so badly.

THE LAST RIDE OF THE POLO SHIRT BANDIT

William Guess was his name - and it was prophetic.
When he shot himself while surrounded by the police,
he left unanswered the question that had stumped his pursuers:
Why did an ordinary middle-class Texan turn into the most
prolific bank robber in the state's history?

By Helen Thorpe

ON NOVEMBER 27,1996 William Guess sat in a rented maroon Nissan Maxima surrounded by Harris County sheriff's deputies, holding a blue steel semiautomatic to his head. Guess was 46 years old, and he was a big man -- more than six feet tall, around 240 pounds. He had graying blond hair and a square face. At that moment he was wearing a windbreaker, blue jeans, low-heeled boots, and glasses, bearing little resemblance to the person who had just robbed Guaranty Federal, a small bank north of Houston. About fifteen minutes earlier, however, Guess had been wearing a fake beard and mustache, sunglasses, a baseball hat, and the shirt that had come to be the signature of his alter ego, a serial bank robber known as the Polo Shirt Bandit. Once he had driven away, he had hurriedly pulled off the disguise, and a heady surge of relief probably had flooded through him -- he thought he was going to escape once more, back to the part of his life that was ordinary and respectable. On the floor of the car on the passenger side was $12,460. The money had been in Guess's briefcase when he had walked out of the bank. He could have dumped it out shortly after getting into the car to see how much was there, or it could have tumbled out during the fast turns he had taken in his unsuccessful attempt to shake the deputies who had cornered him. Either way, all those crisp-as-if-starched bills were now spilled out over the carpet: all that easy money, obtained at such immense risk.

Guess had just wrecked the Nissan on FM 1960, a busy four-lane stretch bordered by strip malls, Chinese restaurants, and auto body shops that intersects Interstate 45 and U.S. 290, the Northwest Freeway. The banks that stand along the road's length are quintessentially modern; they are small outfits, staffed by three or four, that sit next to day care centers and Hunan Palaces and Big and Tall clothing stores. The branches are as homey and cheerful as a Hallmark greeting card, and you wouldn't think a robber would ever happen inside one of them. But to Guess, they must have once looked like a row of cherries, his personal jackpot. This was where he had started robbing banks. Over the span of his career, he is suspected of pulling off at least 38 robberies making him the most prolific bank robber in the history of the state stealing in the vicinity of $600,000. He robbed more banks than Jesse James, John Dillinger, Willie Sutton, or Bonnie and Clyde, although he never hurt anyone. Guess committed one robbery in a town called Salado, two in Austin, and nine within the limits of Houston, but he always came back to FM 1960 or Texas Highway 6 (as the road is known south of 290). Of the 26 additional bank robberies that he is believed to have committed in parts of Harris or Fort Bend counties, 21 occurred somewhere along the road where he now sat. There were never many witnesses around, never that many bank employees to control, and afterward he would slip into the speeding stream of traffic on U.S. 290 or I-45 and vanish.

Not this time. The front of Guess's Nissan was stuck under the bed of a red pickup truck, and the back of it had been rear-ended by a Harris County Sheriffs Department patrol car. Two other squad cars had swerved to stop beside the Nissan. What kind of desperation filled Guess, knowing that he was trapped? It would not have been the kind that a crime victim feels -- the sudden shock of an entirely unexpected threat. It would have been the sort of dread that steals over a person when he finally confronts a scenario that he has been courting yet running away from for a long time. Four uniformed deputies hurried out of the patrol cars with their guns drawn and took aim at the Polo Shirt Bandit. But Guess had already taken aim at himself.

AS DETECTIVES LEARNED AFTER THEY DISCOVERED HIS IDENTITY from his driver's license, William Guess lived in Oenaville, an unincorporated town six miles northeast of Temple, in a redbrick ranch house. He shared it with his wife, Geneva, and the youngest of their three sons. Oenaville is far removed from the urban sprawl of roads like FM 1960; the town consists of a main crossroads, one convenience store, half a dozen ranches, and some houses surrounded by a vast expanse of rolling prairie. The revelation of the Polo Shirt Bandit's identity was greeted by the residents of Oenaville with total disbelief. "This is a farming community," said a neighbor who lives two houses down from the Guess family. "This is the least likely place in the world for something like this to happen."

William Guess grew up in Temple, where his father worked as the director of the city's utilities. His family life was unremarkable. He was known to be friendly but reserved -- he rarely initiated conversations, although he was happy to stop and talk if you did. "He was quiet, confident, calm, self-assured, intelligent, and a natural athlete," remembered one friend. As a student at Temple High School, he had achieved nearly perfect grades without having to study hard, and he was an all-around athlete who served as the captain of both the basketball and the golf teams in his senior year (class of 1969). He dated one of the school's homecoming princesses, Geneva Sanderson. "When I saw hi for the first time, it was, like, wow, love at first sight," Geneva told me over the phone. "We got engaged right after high school."

Guess' single quirk was his apparent lack of drive. Classmates had assumed that because things came to him easily, he would go on to become something of importance, but he didn't. While friends like Brad Dusek won a football scholarship, left for Texas A&M, and went on to play professionally for the Washington Redskins, Guess attended local colleges but never obtained a degree. As his athletic and academic successes faded, his relationship with Geneva must have taken on an even greater significance. They were married on August 7, 1971. In the mid-seventies, after floundering for a while, Guess found work in Houston as a deliveryman, driving all over the city and its outlying suburbs. On the weekends he would return to Temple, three hours away. Within a few years he gave that up to work as a cleaning-supplies salesman in Temple and then he started a used-car business with a friend; they called it Two Guys Car Lot. "Many of us felt he was badly underutilized," said one friend. "He just never seemed to have much ambition."

After he started Two Guys Car Lot, Guess began spending a lot of time with Cliff Lambert, who worked as a mechanic in an auto shop at a local salvage yard. At the same time, he maintained ties to many Temple residents who were in the conventional sense, far more successful, such as Brad Dusek and Joel Garrison, who had become homebuilders. He played golf regularly at the Wildflower or Mill Creek country clubs with some of the most prominent people in town, including one of the city's former mayors, John Sammons. If the disparity between the public images of these people and his own bothered him, he didn't let on. But he had a big ego, and he liked to prove himself; he played golf to win, and he liked to bet on the outcome. He started off betting $40 or $50 on a round, but in recent years he sometimes wagered ten times that amount.

After friends learned about his secret life, as a bank robber, they came to see Guess as an enigma, as if his name proved to be prophetic. They found it impossible to reconcile the character of the man they knew with the activities of the bank robber who wrecked his Nissan on FM 1960. "He was a good friend and a good guy," said Joel Garrison. "I guess he was just a different person than we all knew." But in truth Guess's public life and his hidden one were linked, and the frustrations Guess felt with his daily routine fed the growth of his alternate persona. Those frustrations piled up over time, particularly after he sold his interest in his car business and his marriage began to founder. There were days, and I mean days, when I wouldn't hear from him," said Geneva. "I would stand at the window wondering if he was dead or alive. Then he would show up again thinking everything was hunky-dory." In 1989 William made an attempt at a permanent break, leaving a note that said, "I can't go on like this," but he returned in several days, and the couple decided to stay together for the sake of their children. He was drinking too much; he was twice charged with driving while intoxicated and once checked into an alcohol-abuse treatment clinic. And he started to gamble more.

While people who live in Temple like to think of their city as the last place that would spawn a bank robber, it is a place where a person can easily develop a serious gambling problem, if he has the inclination. The city has always catered to Fort Hood soldiers looking for action, and several used-car businesses in the area (though not Guess's) have been investigated by the police for serving as fronts for local bookmaking operations. Temple is also home to two weekly high-stakes poker games; the first is strictly private and includes a number of prominent businessmen, while the second is run by local bookies and hard-core gamblers and is more open. Guess played in both. On a routine night, he might win or lose anywhere from $500 to $5,000. If he had been looking for a warning of how far afield the cards might lead him he had only to look across the poker table: Another regular at one of the games was a man from Temple who had once served time in federal prison. As a young man, he had forced his way into the home of a wealthy widow and held her hostage until she wrote a check for $11,500, which he supposedly needed because of gambling debts.

But if Temple provided the temptation, Guess was willing to be tempted. Besides betting on golf and poker, he started wagering as much as $15,000 on professional football games with two bookies in the Temple area known to their clients (and later to police investigators as well) as Shorty and Champ. Guess started trips to the horse track at Manor Downs, east of Austin, where he would drop as much as $1,500 on a horse, and then he started going to the Isle of Capri casino in Bossier City, Louisiana. He even played the lottery heavily. Nobody seems to have been aware of the extent of his gambling habit. "When I cleaned out his office, I found all these tickets," said Geneva. "I said, 'What are these?'" They were from the racetrack. But people who saw Guess bet could see that he liked to take risks. "William lived on the edge," said one person who used to bet with him. "He would play blackjack for any amount you wanted. He kept wanting to play for more and more." So much did Guess come to define himself in terms of his risk taking than when his children were asked what he did for a living, they sometimes replied that he was a professional gambler.

NOBODY KNOWS PRECISELY WHAT went through Guess's mind as he decided to slide into criminal behavior, but the broad outlines of the situation are plain: He was gambling too much, he probably needed money to pay off a debt, perhaps he felt intrigued by images of himself usurping control of something as solid and as reputable as a bank. Did the idea of robbing banks hold some gritty, Western romance for him? Was it his way of getting even with all the people who had grown up to lead ordinary, dull, successful lives? Or maybe he studied the idea with a cold pragmatism, concluding that sticking up banks was a sure way to make easy money.

Several years before he started robbing banks on a regular basis, he apparently committed one isolated robbery in Harris County. That stickup wasn't linked to others committed by the Polo Shirt Bandit until recently (when a woman who had worked at the bank called the Houston Police Department after seeing Guess on TV and said, "That's the asshole that robbed me back in 1985"). Four years later, however, Guess started robbing on a systematic basis. On September 29, 1989, he was in Houston -- probably to attend an automobile auction -- and had checked into a Holiday Inn on 290 where he often stayed. It's likely that he went somewhere else to change clothes. The branch of San Jacinto Savings that he had decided to raid was in a strip mall on Texas Highway 6, next to a Montessori Children's Cottage, a

Kids Kuts barbershop, and Copperfield Family Dental Care. It was a small bank, only women worked there, and Guess knew he could keep an eye on all of the employees at once. When he walked into the place at around noon, Guess looked like any nine-to-five businessman. He was wearing a dress shirt, a light blue vest, a tie, dress slacks, a driving cap, and dark sunglasses. He had painstakingly applied a realistic looking false beard and mustache (a crepe beard, as the disguise is known, involves brushing spirit gum on the face, then attaching fake facial hair clump by clump), and he was carrying a large zippered daily-planner case, but the only thing inside was a small blue revolver, probably a .38. Guess took out the gun and told the tellers to dump the cash from their tills into the daily planner. From behind his pitch-dark sunglass lenses, he might not have been able to make out the tellers' features, but he must have sensed the fear and vulnerability that he aroused. One minute the employees had been in charge of the bank, and the next minute he was. After warning the tellers that he had an accomplice outside who was also armed, which wasn't true, Guess drove away in a brown Mercedes that he had probably bought at the auction.

Guess lifted a total of $1,000 from San Jacinto -- not that much money. None of his early robberies was particularly lucrative; he knew tellers usually trigger a silent alarm, and he had only minutes before the police would arrive. Typically he got away with between $4,000 and $15,000. Only much later did he get larger hauls. But he must have found that first job rewarding enough, because it wasn't long before he struck again. One month after robbing San Jacinto Savings, he held up tellers at an NCNB (as NationsBank used to be known) on Highway 6, in Fort Bend County. Two weeks later, he returned to Harris County to rob First Federal Savings and Loan on FM 1960. Witnesses saw him flee in another Mercedes, this time dark blue, license plate number 437 HFT. In December he hit the same NCNB again, and in January 1990 he returned to rob the branch for the third time. Then there was a lull.

SOMEBODY HAD JUST PULLED OFF FIVE bank robberies in less than four months, which was galling to the detectives assigned to solve the cases. Among the law enforcement agents who converged on San Jacinto Savings after the first robbery in 1989 were Lieutenant Grace Hefner, who was in charge of the Harris County Sheriffs Department robbery division, and Detective Tom Keen, who reported to her. Hefner is a reserved, soft-spoken, tenacious woman who is known for her ability to crack tough cases by carefully cataloguing large amounts of data. Keen, by contrast, is a gung ho, right-off-the-streets detective. Keen and Hefner would spend the next seven years trying to solve the San Jacinto robbery, but at the time it looked like a run-of-the-mill crime, and there was no reason to suspect that the investigation would prove inordinately long. Later they came to realize that the robbery was unusual in one respect: "That was the first time we saw such an elaborate disguise," said Hefner recently. "Usually they just wear a hat and sunglasses. We don't usually see fake beards." But back then, nobody knew that the bank robber's beard was false. They did notice the luxury automobile that he had driven off in, which was how Guess acquired his first nickname -- originally the police referred to him as the Mercedes Bandit.

Most bank robberies are solved within a matter of weeks, but the robberies attributed to the Mercedes Bandit continued to mount, while Keen and Hefner made no progress. At least in his secret life, Guess must have felt charmed. Once he was almost caught when a police officer arrived in the middle of a robbery, but the officer mistakenly accosted another bearded man as Guess drove away from the scene. Another time Guess robbed a bank while an armed security guard was in the back of the institution fixing a cup of coffee. "This man was just fortunate." said Keen. "He had lots of breaks."

Guess was also smart; when Keen checked his computer system, the license plate number that the teller at First Federal had written down popped up as belonging on a Hyundai. The owner of that car had reported its plates stolen from the parking lot of a medical office building on FM 1960. Guess was taking off the stolen plates and removing his false beard as soon as possible after each robbery (he had abandoned the crepe beard in favor of a prefabricated one that he could rip off all at once) to confuse any law enforcement officers he encountered. He also coated his fingertips so that they left no prints. About the only clue Keen and Hefner had to the bank robber's identity was his peculiar ability to get his hands on different cars, none of which were being reported stolen; this seemed to indicate the used-car business. The detectives also believed the bank robber had to be from Houston, because he knew his way around. In the spring of 1990 the theory that the Mercedes Bandit was a local car dealer led the sheriff's office to charge an innocent man with some of the robberies that Guess is now suspected of having committed. Frustrated by the lack of progress, the sheriff's office distributed a surveillance photograph of the Mercedes Bandit to television stations and newspapers in the Houston area. Somebody called in and said the person looked a lot like Aubry Lee Kelley, who was in the vehicle-repossession business. Several witnesses picked him out of a lineup. Although Kelley immediately protested that he was innocent, he spent the next two months in jail – until Guess returned to San Jacinto Savings, the first bank he had held up and one of the two that Kelley was accused of robbing. This time he fled in a black Mazda, but the tellers were certain he was the same man who had robbed them before. The charges against the Kelley were dropped. "Nobody listens to you in that jail," Kelley told the *Houston Chronicle* shortly after his release. "They don't care if you're guilty or innocent. They're just pushing people through court." If he sounded bitter, he had good cause; while Kelley was in jail, he lost his repo business, was kicked out of his apartment in the Woodlands, and his wife suffered a miscarriage.

SOON AFTER GUESS RESURFACED, INADVERTENTLY springing Kelley from jail, he decided to move into new territory and alter his disguise, as if he felt he had to vary his routine to keep ahead of the police. On May 21, he ventured into Houston and hit Mason Road Bank (now called Comerica), a small adobe-style building much like the institutions he had been robbing up and down FM 1960. On July 3, he robbed the same, bank again. Despite its name, the bank lies on Blalock Road, which runs directly into I-10 and after both robberies Guess simply disappeared into traffic. By now he had abandoned his Mercedes for cars that were less noticeable. In the second robbery of Mason Road Bank he also abandoned the Mercedes Bandit's business attire for a more casual look: He was still using a fake beard and mustache and sunglasses, but now he wore a white polo shirt with blue stripes, blue jeans, low-heeled boots and a baseball hat. From that point on, he wore a polo shirt in every robbery he committed.

Why Guess reconfigured himself as the Polo Shirt Bandit remains an unanswered question; maybe he adopted the look to make the police think they were dealing with a different bank robber. Whatever the reason, the new disguise was an improvement: While the Mercedes Bandit had posed as a typical businessman, the Polo Shirt Bandit was even more, ordinary, and therefore more invisible. The new apparel seemed to transform Guess into a generic Bubba, a Texan Everyman, just another big guy in a gimme cap.

The two Houston robberies brought Guess's heists to eight and the number of law enforcement agencies hunting for him to five, as the Houston Police Department joined the Harris County Sheriffs Department, the Fort Bend Sheriffs Department, the Sugar Land Police Department, and the FBI. Guess must have spent some time conjecturing about his pursuers, but he must have felt secure enough once he made it back to Oenaville; the town was surely too tiny, too rustic, and too remote to be the scene of his unmasking. And if his occasional trips to Houston began to acquire an element of serious risk, well, Guess had long had an appetite for risk. Before, he had chanced his livelihood now he was gambling with his freedom.

During his next jobs, Guess displayed an unusual ability to think fast under pressure. On September 18, 1990, he visited a branch of Guaranty Federal Savings that sits in a shopping center on Jones Road, near FM 1960. He was wearing his disguise, and he issued the same set of instructions, but before he left the bank, a dye pack that he had scooped into his briefcase along with the money exploded, shooting a fine red powder that looked like smoke into the air, staining his skin and clothing, and spraying a chemical agent that made his eyes burn and water. If he had taken the time to look for clean money, Guess might have been caught, but he immediately threw the briefcase down and ran off, leaving the cash behind. Apparently he had a pressing debt to pay, however, because only three weeks after the dye pack went off, Guess returned to rob a bank called Commerce Savings. The following year, he robbed Guaranty Federal for the second time. "Okay, girls," he said to the tellers with characteristic aplomb. "Let's do it right this time: No dye packs."

Several months later, the same audacity helped Guess brazen his way through the most harrowing moment of his criminal career. In the summer of 1991, perhaps because he was concerned about hitting too many banks near Houston or the target was too tempting, Guess decided to rob a branch of Taylor Bane in Austin. The one-story, redbrick building stands on the crest of a hill at the intersection of Braker Lane and I-35. It is clearly visible from the highway, and Guess probably spotted it on a trip to Manor Downs. As soon as he saw the building, he must have imagined how easily he could rob it: The bank was just the right size, and a getaway looked simple -- although as it turned out, it wasn't.

At eleven-fifteen in the morning on July 18, Guess drove up to Taylor Bane in a two-tone Chevy pickup. He walked into the lobby wearing a fake beard and a polo shirt and carrying a Titan chrome .32-caliber semiautomatic in his briefcase. The robbery went off without a hitch, but the Austin police responded within minutes, and when Guess tried to disappear into the northbound traffic on I-35, he kept running into patrol cars. A police helicopter soon appeared overhead. Spooked, Guess finally drove down a dead-end street and got rid of every piece of evidence that could tie him to the crime. He shucked off his shirt, jeans, belt, boots, hat, and beard -- everything he had worn into the bank -- shoved them into a plastic trash bag and heaved it out the window of the truck. He also dumped the money, the stolen plates on the truck, and the Titan semiautomatic. "He got naked," said one detective. Then he pulled on different clothing and drove away. The police didn't have a vehicle description, and they were looking for a bearded man in a baseball cap and a polo shirt; if any officers encountered Guess, they didn't recognize him as their suspect. Shortly after Guess left, a patrol car turned onto the street. A woman who had seen Guess change his clothes pointed out the pile of belongings in the trash bag, but by then Guess was gone.

On that occasion the debts that Guess had amassed must have been particularly onerous. One day after leaving Austin empty-handed he showed up in Harris County and robbed a Bank of America, and the day after that, as if he still hadn't gotten the amount he required, he robbed a branch of San Jacinto Savings. Before the end of 1991, he robbed four more banks, all in Harris County, boosting the number he had hit to nineteen.

KEEN, HEFNER, AND THE OTHER detectives looking for the Polo Shirt bandit obtained the first and only items of physical evidence they ever got during their investigation from the pile of stuff Guess left in Austin, From the fake beard, they learned that their suspect had been using a disguise. The investigators had already decided that the bank robber probably had a steady source of income, since his robberies took place in an irregular sequence; considering his actions after the botched Austin robbery, Keen and Hefner felt certain that their suspect had a gambling problem. "Who else would be going through that kind of money other than somebody with a drug problem?" asked Keen. "And he didn't look like somebody who was into drugs. He stayed the same weight."

But the evidence and the suppositions led nowhere. Keen and Hefner contacted casino officials around the country, but their quest turned up no useful tips; partial fingerprints recovered from the license plate Guess left behind in Austin didn't match any on file. The Harris County Sheriff's Department turned to the media for new leads. On December 17, 1991, the *Houston Chronicle* published a surveillance photograph obtained the week before, and after the picture ran, the sheriffs office got a tip that the bandit resembled another man who owned a car-repossession business. The suspect's partner also looked like the Polo Shirt Bandit, however, and detectives decided the two had been taking turns at wearing the same disguise. Early in 1992 the sheriff's office arrested both men and charged them with some of the Polo Shirt Bandit's robberies. "In each case they would wear sunglasses, a baseball hat, and a beard," someone from the sheriffs department told reporters at the time. "If you look at the surveillance photos, it's hard to tell the difference."

Both men were released, but they soon would have been cleared anyway: On February 19, 1992, the Polo Shirt Bandit returned to Harris County to rob a branch of Cypress National Bank on Jones Road that he had robbed once before. "This is the last time I'm going to rob a bank," Guess told the tellers at Cypress National. "I need this money for my son." And then the robberies stopped, as abruptly as they had begun.

WILLIAM GUESS DID NOT HAVE A SICK SON. Detectives now believe he was just trying to justify his actions to the people he was holding up. However, it is possible that the strain of leading a double life had begun to affect him; Geneva recalls that William had constant stomach problems and was always eating Tums. (Three years later Guess would suffer a heart attack.) If he was ever to interrupt the cycle of compulsive gambling and criminal activity he had fallen into, this would have been the occasion. However, whatever qualms he may have felt were no match for the pull of his addictions: On February 23, 1993, a year after saying he was through with crime, Guess packed up his gun, his fake beard, one of his polo shirts, and resumed his bank-robbing spree. He stole the license plates off a car that belonged to an employee of a fast-food restaurant on U.S. 290 and put them onto the white Ford Thunderbird he was driving. Like many of the cars he used from then on, it looked new; apparently Guess started using rental cars instead of used ones. Guess then headed for the Bank of America on FM 1960 and held it up for the second time.

Three months later Guess committed a robbery that was the one most likely to have led to his capture -- it was like a beacon announcing his approximate home base, although none of the detectives searching for him understood this at the time. On May 20, 1993, Guess held up Peoples National Bank in the scenic town of Salado. It was the only robbery that he ever committed in Bell County, where Oenaville is located -- Salado is only about twenty miles from Guess's home. While his success in evading capture thus far was largely because he had avoided robbing banks in places where he might be recognized, Guess must have found Peoples National irresistible: The old stone building sits so close to I-35 that the highway entrance ramp is visible from the bank's parking lot, and Salado has no police department of its own. Law enforcement agents had to come from Belton, ten minutes away. Breaking from the routine he had used in the past, Guess stayed inside the bank long enough to force the employees to open its vault, and while the police have never disclosed how much money he got, it was far more than his usual plunder. One week later the *Temple Daily Telegram* linked the Salado robbery to "a professional bandit" who was described as being from around Houston. The article outlined the Polo Shirt Bandit's methods and appearance, and it included a photograph of Guess in disguise. "Authorities do not believe the robber remained in the Central Texas area," reported the paper. "However, anyone able to confirm the true identity of the man pictured in the photograph is urged to call the sheriffs department." Half of Temple must have read the story -- Guess probably saw it himself. In the meantime, FBI agents showed photographs of the Polo Shirt Bandit at work in other banks to Jerry Kopriva, who was in charge of security for Peoples National in the area at that time. Kopriva had known Guess in high school, and they had become reacquainted when their children started attending the same schools. Kopriva studied the photographs and never realized he was looking at William Guess. "I had no earthly idea," he said recently.

In retrospect it seems weird that a beard, a gimme cap, and a pair of sunglasses were enough to render Guess unrecognizable, but apparently people who knew him were incapable of seeing through his disguise because the idea that he might be a bank robber was unthinkable. And Guess never revealed any sign of his illicit career to his friends or neighbors; he never changed his lifestyle in any obvious fashion, and he was never suddenly and inexplicably rich. "He never flashed a hundred dollar bill," said a neighbor in Oenaville. "He's lived here for ten years, and he's always driven around in an old vehicle." Geneva and William had separate bank accounts, and his family was never aware of any change in William's finances. "He was a penny-pincher," said Geneva. "It was a big joke with the kids: 'Daddy's cheap, cheap, cheap.' When we went on vacations, he would want to stay in some dumpy old motel. He was happy buying clothes at WalMart." He never boasted of his illegal exploits, not even when he was drunk.

Perhaps he never slipped because nobody knew him that well anymore. After selling the car business, Guess had drifted into buying old cars at auctions, fixing them up, and selling them to other car dealers, and he was spending almost all his time at the garage owned by Cliff Lambert. The property sits on a bluff, and it is strewn with every model of vehicle imaginable, including two-doors, four-doors, old pickups, a few Winnebagos, and even an old powerboat. When friends asked if he was going to get back into the used-car business on a more formal basis, Guess replied no, not unless he had to. "Gradually he built a shell around himself," said an old friend. "In the last five, or six years, it was like he had a chip on his shoulder. He was more aloof."

As if Guess was alarmed by the publicity the Salado bank robbery attracted, he committed no more robberies that year. He started up again in 1994, however, and from that point on he became more and more effective as a criminal. Guess had been learning on the job, and in the last phase of his career, he figured out how to avoid security measures like dye packs and how to coerce employees into letting him into the vaults. While the life went out of William Guess, who was sitting in a junkyard for hours at a time, the Polo Shirt Bandit grew more potent; it was as if one waxed and the other waned.

EARLY IN 1994 ROBERT DAVENPORT, A detective newly assigned to the Houston Police Department's robbery division, was handed material on the serial bank robber. The police department's interest in the Polo Shirt Bandit had been reignited on January 4, when the bank robber hit his third institution within the city limits. A subsequent Houston robbery -- at Pinemont Bank, on Memorial, on May 19, 1994 -- provided Davenport with what he thought was a big break. "We got an excellent video," he said. "it showed his every movement. It showed him pointing, holding his weapon, walking. There was a strong front-on facial shot, a good profile, even a shot of the back of his head. It was perfect." The videotape of the Polo Shirt Bandit robbing Pinemont first ran on the TV show *City Under Siege,* then appeared on local news, and eventually aired again on America's Most Wanted. Davenport researched every name that turned up and found many people who bore, a striking resemblance to the Polo Shirt Bandit, but nobody who had committed his crimes. "One woman was so upset she went into convulsions because, she thought it was her ex-husband," he remembered. Investigators began to feel certain that the bank robber didn't live in the Houston area since the publicity would have unearthed him if he did. Davenport distributed wanted posters at police roll calls around the city and held seminars for bank employees to teach them about the bandit's habits. He worked until he had the sense that he knew the Polo Shirt Bandit, even though he didn't know his name, and still the bank robber wasn't caught. He robbed eight more banks in the next year and a half. Then he started using a semiautomatic that carried more firepower than any he had used before. On April 11, 1996, Guess showed up at a Compass Bank on Bissonnet in Houston. The wedge-shaped bank building looked small from the outside, but once Guess was inside, he discovered that it was much bigger, Guess was forced to spend far longer in the bank than he wanted to, he had to round up employees from various offices before he could get his money, and he grew visibly jittery n the process. During his next robberies, his manner became increasingly ominous. Guess started getting more aggressive, more nervous, and more demanding; he began pointing the gun directly at bank employees, whereas before he had only displayed a weapon to show them that he was armed. How had the years of assuming the role of the Polo Shirt Bandit changed William Guess? What actions was he now capable of? On July 24 Guess got into the vault of a Savings of America on Post Oak and walked off with $31,823 -- a vast difference from the $1,000 he had taken from San Jacinto Savings almost seven years before,.

As Guess's behavior became more threatening, law enforcement officers began to put more and more effort, into his capture. The Harris County Sheriff Department formed a task force to catch the man that everyone in the robbery division had come to think of as their nemesis and put Grace Hefner in charge. In the middle of 1995 a bank association had offered a $10,000 reward for information leading to the capture of the Polo Shirt Bandit. By last summer, when Guess showed up with a bigger gun, the reward being offered was up to $26,000. Davenport said, "We didn't know whether he was making a statement: 'I've got more bullets. I'm ready for a shoot-out.'"

And then Hefner noticed a pattern. Beginning in February 1996, as if he had been lulled into complacency or was getting sloppy, Guess had started robbing a bank every 50 to 56 days. He had robbed on February 15, April 11, May 31, and July 24. By September 11, the Harris County Sheriffs Department, the FBI, the Houston Police Department (HPD) and the Texas Rangers convened to figure out how to respond. One week later Guess cleaned out the vault at a branch of Coastal Banc, scoring more than $60,000, and that caused law enforcement agencies to disagree about what he was going to do next: The FBI and the HPD argued that the robber had just gotten so much money that he wouldn't rob again for some time, while Hefner thought his gambling had become so compulsive that he would strike again within the 56-day time frame. The sheriff's department and the Texas Rangers decided to set up a surveillance operation over a three-week period in November, when they thought the Polo Shirt Bandit was going to hit, but the FBI and the HPD decided not to participate.

After juggling schedules and rearranging long-planned vacations, a team of eighty uniformed and non-uniformed officers was assembled. Hefner briefed them about the bandit's habits. She also told them to anticipate that the bank robber would try to kill himself or shoot his way out of a corner if he faced with the prospect of arrest -- the Polo Shirt Bandit was relatively young and had committed dozens of serious crimes, meaning that he was facing an extremely long prison term. Beginning on November 5, the officers sat in parked cars outside of banks that looked like the kind of places that the Polo Shirt Bandit liked to stick up, and waited. He never showed. By November 25 the three weeks were up, and the sheriffs department was about to call off the surveillance. Then bank executives requested that the extra protection remain in place through the Thanksgiving holidays. The sheriff's office decided that it couldn't afford to keep all 80 officers on the lookout for a bank rubber who might not show up, but it did keep about 25 officers on the alert.

ON SUNDAY, NOVEMBER 24, WILLIAM Guess got a phone call from a friend in the car salvage business in Houston. The friend told Guess that there was going to be a big automobile auction on the following day. On Monday, Guess drove to Houston, checked into the Holiday Inn he often stayed in, and went to the car auction. On Wednesday morning, he put on his bank-robbing attire and drove a rented Nissan over to Guaranty Federal, at 3902 FM 1960. Apparently he sat in the car for some time police officers later found a cooler and a lot of empty beer cans in the car). At ten-thirteen Guess went into the bank, where he displayed his gun and ordered the tellers to fill his briefcase with cash. But then, as if a fickle wind turned the weather vane of his fortune around, everything started to go wrong.

A woman who worked at another branch of Guaranty Federal had stopped by the location on FM 1900 that morning, and as she was leaving, she noticed Guess enter the bank. As it happened. the woman had attended one of Davenport's briefings, and she recognized Guess as the Polo Shirt Bandit. Recalling what Davenport had said to do during such a situation -- "If you ever see this man, call 911" -- she dialed the emergency number on her cellular phone. The dispatcher kept her on the phone until Guess emerged, and the woman was able to report that he left the bank in a maroon Nissan Maxima, license plate STS 05X, heading west on FM 1960.

Ron Fleming and Mitch Hatcher, who were normally assigned to a narcotics unit, were among the only Harris County deputies still out looking for the Polo Shirt Bandit that morning. After patrolling up and down Jones Road for a while. Fleming, who was driving, had said. "There's nothing going on here, lets cruise over to 1960." Right after they turned onto FM 1960, the dispatcher announced that the Polo Shirt Bandit had struck again and gave them a vehicle description and location. "He was heading right to us," Fleming recalled afterward. As the dispatcher was repeating the bank robber's vehicle and license plate number, Hatcher and Fleming spotted the maroon Nissan in oncoming traffic. Thirty seconds later, and they would have missed him. Fleming made a U-turn "We got him! This is him!" he started yelling to his partner.

When the patrol car pulled up behind him, Guess waved as if to show that he would pull over momentarily. His mind must have raced to consider whether he had committed a traffic violation or whether this was the confrontation that some part of himself must always have been anticipating. The patrol car moved up behind him, close enough for him to study the faces of the two deputies in his rearview mirror. Apparently something told him that they knew exactly who he was. As soon as he saw a break in traffic, Guess took off, running a red light. The patrol car turned on its siren and followed. Guess led Hatcher and Fleming on a chase through a Builders Square parking lot, several other red lights, and up and down streets that intersected with FM 1960. Two other Harris County Sheriff's Department patrol cars joined the caravan along the way. Guess kept leaving the main thoroughfare in a vain attempt to shake the cars on his tail, but he always came back to his primary getaway route.

About ten minutes after the chase began, Guess and the three patrol cars came tearing down FM 1960 toward the intersection at Perry Road. Sitting in a red pickup in the far-left lane was Steve Sharum, a Deer Park plumber. Sharum had been just a few cars ahead of Guess when Hatcher and Fleming had first spotted the Nissan, and he had watched as the patrol car turned around, and the maroon car had zipped out to run the red light. Sharum's younger brother had been killed in a car accident, and the reckless driving of the man in the Nissan had ticked him off. "That guy's driving ignorant," Sharum had thought. "He must have stolen that car." Now when Sharum looked up and saw the same Nissan Maxima in his rearview mirror, hearing down fast, he thought, "Well, if I stop, he'll either have to stop too or go around me." Sharum closed his eyes, held on to his steering wheel, and punched the brakes. He felt two jolts -- Guess smashing into his pickup, and the third patrol car slamming into Guess. Then Sharum heard someone yell, "He's got a gun!" so he lay down on the front seat of his truck and didn't move.

Once he rear-ended Sharum's pickup, Guess knew his long charade was finished. He had planned what he would do in such a moment. Perhaps he knew the moment was inevitable, because he robbed banks like he gambled -- he didn't stop until he was completely out of luck. Guess put the blue steel semiautomatic to his temple. When the deputies jumped out of their cars and surrounded him, he fluttered his other hand at them, as if he could shoo them away. "It's over," he said. "I haven't hurt anybody. I don't want to hurt you. It's over." Guess let the gun slip down a little bit, then lifted it back up and fired. His head slumped forward on his chest.

Tom Keen was the first detective to arrive at the crime scene. He took one look and knew that he wasn't going to learn much about the hidden life of the man in the car. All the essential facts were bleeding out of him. "Fellah, I've been looking for you for a long time," Keen said to the slumped-over man. "Now I finally get to see you, and look how it's ending." Robert Davenport had learned that a chase was in progress from an HPD dispatcher; once it ended, he started to head over there, but he changed destinations once he learned that Guess was being flown to Hermann Hospital. Davenport was waiting at the emergency entrance when Guess arrived. "I was hoping that I could look at him and just know, but a self-inflicted gunshot wound to the head is a pretty ugly thing," said Davenport. While doctors hurried to stabilize Guess's condition, Davenport snapped photographs of his immobile figure. The hospital staff also allowed the police to take fingerprints of the still-unconscious man. Davenport immediately contacted the police department's lab and had them compare Guess's prints with those left by the Polo Shirt Bandit in Austin. "Lo and behold," said Davenport. "Bing. They were his."

Geneva was at home preparing for Thanksgiving when she learned from a reporter that her husband was the Polo Shirt Bandit. She never went to Houston to visit him. "I didn't want to," she said. "I was just so angry that he could do such a thing. What really upset me was the statement he made to the police about how he had never hurt anyone. I thought, 'Well, who are we?'" William Guess died without regaining consciousness on January 4. Since his secret life was unmasked, Geneva has discovered bills for credit cards that she didn't even know he had. William had been taking out large cash advances on the cards and Geneva had been left with the bills. "I just cannot figure out what happened to the money," she said. "There is no money. His savings account, everything, it's all wiped out. I think he left me with $184."

To his surprise, Davenport felt none of the elation he had expected to feel, no sense of satisfaction, at the conclusion of his investigation. Even though Guess had been found, it was as though he had eluded capture after all. "I was just so disappointed," the detective said. "I was mad, I guess, mad at him, more than anything. I was crushed to see him and know that he would never answer the biggest questions I had. I knew the what, where, when, and how. But why? What made this man turn to a life of crime?"

GANG RAPE

By Bill Minutaglio

"Maybe," they hear a fat man saying, "we could get stoned with that stuff."

The dozens of other men laugh as Angela, 16, fiddles with a red-and-white striped can of Aquanet she has fished out of her purse. It's early Saturday -- just after midnight. Next to the normally chatty Angela is Dolores, another black-haired 16-year-old from Dallas. Next to her is Sandy, a thin 12-year-old from Plano who likes to watch cartoons.

They are sitting in a dimly lit front room on Columbia Avenue in East Dallas. A messy kitchen is just beyond the front room; to the left is a short hallway. A bedroom is off the hall, across from a 5-by-9-foot tiled bathroom.

Empty beer cans litter the soiled carpet of Apartment 205. A magazine centerfold of a nude woman hangs on a wall. The refrigerator is covered with graffiti. A small mirror catches the image from a color TV. A black VCR is on top of the TV.

Dolores, who celebrated her birthday two weeks earlier, has already decided she wants to leave. Nothing, she thinks, is good about this. Dolores hates Angela for getting them into this apartment — with dozens of strange men — in the first place.

Almost as if she didn't hear what the fat man said, Angela idly sprays her hair. More men walk in through the front doorway. In a corner, a few of them huddle and snort coke.

One man adjusts the VCR. A videotape box marked Purple Rain is nearby. The girls assume it is the movie made by pop star Prince. Instead, grainy images appear on the screen; couples snake their way through lurid sex games.

The girls stare straight ahead and try not to look. The movie rolls for 10 minutes. Although there are about 30 men in the room, there is an unsettling and heavy sense of quiet.

"Come on, girls," says Angela. "Let's go." Dolores is already ahead of her, walking toward the door. Angela steps right behind. Sandy stands up to follow.

For several weeks before this evening, Dolores has been having the same dream. In it, she is in trouble and is reaching for a doorknob but is never able to open the door. Sometimes she dreams things — and they happen.

Now, she is reaching again. As her hand wraps around the knob, all the lights in the apartment go out. It is inky black and she is suffocating with dread. A thought pounds through her mind: "Is this real or my dream?"

Before she can turn the knob, several hands are clutching at her arms and pulling her backwards. Someone locks the door. She kicks her legs and knocks over a chair. The VCR crashes to the floor. Twelve men surround her.

She screams: "We have money if you just let us go."

From somewhere, she hears: "You rich bitch, we don't want your money."

As she is dragged she can see other men forming a circle around Angela. Choked with fear, she watches as Sandy, a sixth-grader at a middle school in Plano, bolts away from one man and is grabbed by another.

The fat man, holding what looked like a .22, shoves Sandy into the small, dirty bathroom. She can see moonlight coming through the window. She is forced to the grimy floor. Hands tear at her black pants. Words are whispered and the handgun is jabbed at her head. She grows quiet.

With her head near the toilet, she listens as the bathroom door repeatedly opens and closes. She is relentlessly raped, sodomized and forced to perform oral sex. A pool of blood forms. After the third stranger has pressed down on her, she loses track of how many different men come and go.

Several men beat Angela and rape her in the living room. More men wait their turn to sodomize Dolores in the bedroom. A sweating, huge man covered with tattoos is replaced by a reed-thin teenager.

Dolores tries to move. She is choked. With every struggle, knees and arms slam down harder. Filled with rage, she can't speak. As time stands still, as she is savagely molested, she doesn't care if she is living or dead.

"Shoot me," she manages to say. "Blow my head off."

It is after 1 a.m. Outside the apartment, 15 yards away, a Dallas policeman named Ken Witt is routinely making the rounds and talking to night people who have straggled back from the It'll Do nightclub.

He is in the parking lot of The Bogota. He has no idea what is happening in Room 205. As he talks to people in the parking lot, the three girls are hauled into the bedroom. They are shoved to their knees. At gunpoint they are made to perform oral sex on the men.

Angela and Dolores are bleeding, but not as much as Sandy. "Please," begs Dolores, "she is going to die."

The night is far from over. The three young women are enduring the worst case of gang rape the police say has ever been reported in Dallas.

Though it occurred Aug. 25, 1989, the case is still open. It appeared as a blip on Dallas' consciousness -- and then quickly disappeared.

By 2:30 a.m. the apartment is empty of all but Dolores, Angela, Sandy and a handful of men. Three men still form a tight circle around Dolores and Sandy. Suddenly three others appear in the apartment. "Get out of here, man," Dolores hears the new arrivals say.

The girls struggle into their torn clothes. Someone tightly wraps bandannas around their faces. Like prisoners in a Central American torture camp, they're hustled down the concrete stairs.

Pushed from behind, they are forced to walk across a patch of grass and in between a row of houses. They go for a block and a half down Elm Alley.

"Don't take off the blindfolds," someone orders.

After a minute, there is silence except for the sound of an occasional car. They reach behind their heads and untie the bandannas. Dolores, unable to produce any tears, simply screams and shakes.

Huddled together, they finally see a police car driving by and flag it down. "We've been raped," they tell Officer Gail Kansier. As they talk to the police officer, the three see another car go by.

Staring back at them are several of the men from Apartment 205. Dolores is sure the men will shoot her. Instead of pointing them out to the police, the girls look away and say nothing.

At 3 a.m., the phone rings at Detective Robert E. Rommel's home. Rommel, as everyone calls him, is a burly, mustachioed man with graying sideburns and thin ribbons of hair combed sideways over his scalp. Driven to wearing cowboy boots and tucking his horn-rimmed glasses into his suit pocket, he is a 12-year veteran of the Dallas Police Department.

His partner with the Dallas Police Department's sex crimes unit is on the phone.

Rommel bolts wide-awake when he hears his partner say: "There are 18 to 20 suspects. Probably more." He dresses and drives straight to 4531 Columbia, the Bogota.

The foot soldiers in the police department have always enjoyed the irony inherent in the Bogota's name and location. For years, the area it is in had been considered by police researchers to be the most dangerous in Dallas.

When Rommel arrives, he sees the three girls sitting in the back of a police car. Two other squad cars are on the scene. Members of the physical evidence unit arrive. It is a typical August early morning, temperature around 75 degrees and no wind.

And no one in the neighborhood knows anything. The apartment manager has no lease records. She scribbles the name "Carlos" on a piece of paper, hands it to Rommel and shrugs. Rommel wonders if the manager is renting the place out without telling the owner and pocketing the rent.

Another woman emerges from the dark. She stares into the police car and is relieved that it's not her daughter in the back. "The cops need to do something about all these gangs," she mutters. The mention of gangs registers on Rommel. But the woman, like everyone else, has no information.

Back outside after viewing the apartment, Rommel is in a strangely forgiving mood about the way everyone is so reticent.

"You can't blame these people," he says to himself. It is as if an invisible army has occupied the area. He can sense the fear.

Rommel knows that no one will talk to him. He holds the useless piece of paper that the apartment manager gave him and watches the girls being taken to Parkland Hospital. It is 5 a.m.

"This case," he says to himself, "will never be solved."

Dolores knew Sandy was lying.

Even though Sandy said she was 15, she didn't act like it -- certainly not like any of the 15-year-olds Dolores knew.

In fact, Sandy was 12. Her parents were divorced and she lived with her mother and baby brother in Plano. Her grandparents lived in Pleasant Grove, but they came as often as they could and, in a way, she considered them as important in her life as her mother.

People who knew her thought she was a bit of a dreamer, someone who liked to take chances. She enjoyed theater classes best of all in school, and had thought about being an actress when she grew up. She liked roaming around her Plano neighborhood -- and she hated baby-sitting her 1-year-old brother while her mother worked.

That summer, the baby-sitting was almost more than she could bear. Each night she would dread the next morning and the thought of having to stay cooped up inside.

In the middle of the last week of August she left the house. Dressed in her white vest and button-down white shirt, she slipped out a window and into the night. She headed to a friend's home in an apartment complex. But no one would come to the door. In the parking lot, a slightly older Mexican-American girl walked by. They struck up a conversation.

"I've been a runaway, too," she told Sandy. Sandy had never met anyone like the voluble, streetwise Angela, who said she was visiting friends in Plano. When Angela suggested going to where she lived in Oak Cliff, Sandy jumped at the chance.

Later, in Oak Cliff, the girls met another friend of Angela's. Dolores had a bit in common with Sandy: Dolores' father left home when she was a year old. She had lost interest in school back in Fannin Elementary. Her mother worked at a series of minimum-wage jobs to keep Dolores and her two older sisters afloat. Now, her mother was a cashier at an Eckerd store.

On a Friday evening, the girls went to an Oak Cliff club called The Prerogative on Jefferson Boulevard. Denied admission because they didn't have the proper ID, they crossed the street and were instantly stopped by a policeman in a patrol car.

He checked their IDs, told them not to jaywalk again and ordered them home. The police car disappeared. The girls began walking west on Jefferson. Two blocks later, a black Monte Carlo pulled alongside.

Three young men in the car called them over. The boys were funny and energetic. They flirted, offered pizza — covered with jalapenos — from two boxes. They said they would give the girls a ride.

It was late; it would be a long walk back to Angela's place. As usual, Angela took charge and led the way into the front seat of the car. After a short drive, the Monte Carlo pulled into a 7-Eleven. One of the men left to make a phone call.

"We're going to take you to Mexico," one of the young men said.

"OK," said Angela, going along with the joke.

When the young man came back from the phone, the driver headed for East Dallas and The Bogota. Dolores, Angela and Sandy thought they were going to a party.

At the Bogota, the men in the car sped away after the girls got out. It was approaching midnight. They had no idea how to get back to Oak Cliff. Confused, scared, the three headed down Elm Alley. They wanted to find a phone, a cab, something.

They walked the short distance to the It'll Do Club, a place that years ago used to be known as a hothouse favored by afternoon lovers. Turned away from the nightclub, Angela, Dolores and Sandy found themselves surrounded by 40 men.

Some insisted the girls go with them back down the alley. "You can get a drink of water," Dolores heard one of them say.

With some of the men leading the way, and others following, the girls walked to Apartment 205. Fifteen minutes later, the lights went out and the door was locked.

"I need your help," said Rommel.

"Man, I don't know that I have much for you," he remembered the other detective replying. They made an arrangement for Rommel to bring over his files the next day.

Some of the kids on the streets of East Dallas called Detective R.L. Dorsey an old hippie. He never blinked. "I used to be a hippie," the round-faced father of two young girls would reply, "until I lost my hair."

Detective Dorsey grew up in Dallas and spent 15 years working different details for the police department, including a stint with intelligence. He had endured a decade trying to get close to the secretive Asian-American underground. At one point the department loaned him out to work with the FBI. Now, he was one of two original members in the new gang unit. In October of 1989, he got his first big gang unit assignment when Rommel appeared with his files.

Rommel had already been in touch with regular patrol officers, the people who cruise the area. But he needed someone to get inside the gang underworld. He knew that this case was in danger of just sliding from that hot August night into oblivion.

He also knew that he was dealing with a world that he barely understood. A world where young men wear shirts with pictures of the Virgin Mary on the back -- but where women are sometimes considered property to be traded, raped and disposed of at will.

He was hoping that Detective Dorsey, who had spent the last five years trying to figure out life in East Dallas, would have a key. The detective had seen and heard plenty over the years.

There was the time Snoopy was in the driver's seat and his confederate in the passenger seat was firing bullets out the driver-side window, right in front of Snoopy's face. The shooter misjudged, and one of his bullets thudded into Snoopy's head.

And there was the yuppie urban pioneer who got so fed up with the gunfire that he literally had his whole house picked up off of Fitzhugh and hauled to another location.

Rommel knew Detective Dorsey had knowledge about East Dallas. But for the two men there was one glaring hurdle. Both Dolores and Angela had disappeared.

There were only three possibilities: They were hiding. They had left town. They were dead.

At Parkland Hospital, Angela gave the admitting nurse a fake name. It was the same false name that she had given Rommel. She was still scared -- of how her family would react and of the men who had raped her. She was sure they would come for her.

Dolores was also scared. When the nurse came to give her a blood test, she lost control. Sandy's grandparents were at the hospital, but no one was there for Dolores. Ashamed and certain that everyone was staring at her, she ran out of the hospital.

Meanwhile, in an examining room, Sandy was told to lie down on a table. It was after 7 a.m. For two hours, technicians with plastic gloves probed and scraped, collecting fluid and tissue samples from every part of the sixth-grader's body. The technicians told her they would keep her underwear.

Close to 9 a.m., her grandparents took her home. And, over the next few months — as Dolores and Angela hid with relatives and friends — only Sandy remained accessible to the police.

Detective Dorsey began the tedious task of literally stopping young men on the streets near the Bogota — showing he wasn't frightened by them, sometimes befriending them. He began to assess the magnitude of the crime. It especially hit home when he visited Sandy at the counseling center.

She would stare, a blank look on her face, as he walked toward her down the hall. When he got near, she would burst into tears.

"Why are you crying?" Detective Dorsey asked.

"I don't know," Sandy replied, her whole body convulsing.

The counselors told him that she never expressed any anger. All she did was cry. She was never able to explain why.

"I've seen a lot of things, but I have never seen anything quite like this before," he said. "This is the worst crime I have ever seen. This is a nightmare."

Early in 1990, Rommel received a note from Detective Ron Hale, assigned to the intelligence division. He had a source, a snitch, who had been dead accurate for years. The snitch was offering up details about what happened at the Bogota.

The information was so specific it could only come from someone who had been there. The snitch said he had gotten all the details from an East Dallas man named Mario Ortiz Garcia.

It was the first big lead in the case. And the name jogged something in Rommel's memory. He pulled all the pictures of the crime scene from his files and pored over them. In one shot he saw the initials "MGO" written with a marker on a mirror.

The informant had said that Mario Garcia liked to "tag" his name and initials on things. Rommel called Detective Dorsey. The gang division detective knew all about Mario Garcia.

Despite publicity given to other Dallas gang members—false gods who courted the media —Mario Garcia was considered by the police to be the real deal.

Within the ever-changing gang world — the East Side Homeboys, the Little Locos, the East Side Juniors, El Barrio, El Casper, Los Vatos of The Grove, Porkchop, the Cash Mob, Rat Face, Charlie Brown, the Wayne Street Bad Boys, White Larry, the Solo Posse, the Devastating Home Boys, the Sunset Posse, Crazy Albert — he allegedly had a special claim to fame:

Some said he was the co-founder of the largest East Dallas gang of all, a loosely organized unit of dope-heads and criminals, many of whom were known to each other only by their nicknames -- many of whom rarely surfaced elsewhere in the city.

The different gangs with their roots in the crumbling bungalows and apartment complexes usually confined their drive-by shootings, armed robberies and car thefts to nearby zones. But, on occasion, they did spill over their boundaries and alerted Dallas to their presence:

There was the murder in tranquil Kidd Springs Park. The trashing of the card shop and mom-and-pop grocery store in the quiet Elmwood area of Oak Cliff. The break-in at the Garland hunting store, where they only had time to steal bows and arrows and black powder rifles.

The East Dallas gangs have never been steeped in traditional organized crime, but there were patterns, certain codes, to their chaos. It was understood that no one talked to the police; that you backed up your homeboys; that there was territory worth defending.

Now, it was also understood that the Bogota had been declared a temporary headquarters for one of those gangs, the one that MGO had allegedly helped start.

Detective Dorsey began to learn other things about MGO: He grew up poor and attended Zaragoza Elementary. He had been living with a woman named Laticia Morales and had worked at laying carpet and tile.

And now, even though MGO was normally a fixture on the blocks around the Bogota, no one could tell Detective Dorsey where to find him. No one had seen him for weeks. In the end, not many even claimed to know him that well.

As the detective continued his hunt, the police adamantly refused to release any substantial information about their investigation. Gangs compete for attention, and a decision had been made at high department levels to avoid giving them any publicity — or to endanger the still-missing Dolores and Angela.

In essence, the police had very little to work with. All the detectives had was a suspect's name — and an informant who was scared to go public.

Finally, three months after the rape, the police agreed to release some details. And when they did, even the detectives in charge of the investigation were stunned that the city largely ignored the news accounts. Quietly, among themselves, they talked about how jaded Dallas had become.

Months had passed since the assaults.

Dolores had shocked the police by contacting them and agreeing to come downtown, maybe to look through 500 photographs Detective Dorsey had been assembling.

The police waited, but Dolores never showed up. In a small Oak Cliff apartment with her mother, she shifted between extreme fear and anger — and never left the building. Angela was still missing. Sandy, an emotional cripple, was still in counseling and being watched by her grandparents.

Finally, in mid-1990, Rommel received another call. Someone matching MGO's description was being held, on suspicion of an unrelated offense, in the county jail.

Rommel instantly made arrangements for an interrogation.

Sitting before him was a thin, black-haired man who looked younger than his 19 years. He was polite, well groomed and almost fresh-faced. It was MGO.

"I don't know a thing about it. I don't know anybody else involved. I don't know the girls involved. I don't know," Rommel remembers him saying.

Rommel thought the barely audible MGO was surely schizophrenic. In person, he didn't match the ferocious reputation he had on the streets. Rommel sat across from him and kept questioning.

"Even if I ever did go to court, I'd be put on probation," he remembers MGO saying.

The comment made Rommel certain that MGO was one of the men in Apartment 205. After a decade of interrogations, he had developed a theory. If they begin to hedge just a bit, then they just might be guilty.

Rommel stood up. "It may take me a while," he said. "But I am going to get you. I will get you." He paused between each word of his last sentence to MGO.

When he left the jailhouse, Rommel had big doubts about what he had just said.

MGO was eventually released. But Rommel had decided that since he had evidence, including his initials at the scene of the crime, there was probable cause to have him arrested again. MGO promptly bonded out.

Before he did, though, he found himself assigned to the same cell as the man who would break the case. That man — Thomas White III — would turn into a disgusting miracle for the police.

A 42-year-old with several convictions, he had gone by a variety of aliases in Florida and Texas: Tom Smith, Thomas Jason Smith and Joseph Jimmy Williams. His rap sheet was filled with offenses including robbery, delivery of cocaine, delivery of speed, possession of cocaine and burglary of a motor vehicle. There was one other item — aggravated sexual assault of his daughter.

After a series of 1990 convictions, Thomas White wrote a letter to a sergeant in the burglary unit of the Northeast Division. He had information about a rape in East Dallas.

The letter was transferred to Rommel. He arranged a meeting with the prisoner, who quickly agreed to a written affidavit with some pinpoint details. Thomas White III said his county jail cellmate, Mario Ortiz Garcia, had told him everything about the rape.

Rommel knew this was his best bit of evidence so far. "He was ready to deal," admitted Rommel. "I don't care if he is a child rapist or a murderer, he was credible."

Through 1990, Rommel's best hope continued to write letters to the police:

"Help me get the aggravated (sexual assault) dropped on my charge since I am helping and willing to go into open court to testify. Mr. Rommel, help me, sir. I don't think I am asking much ... Mr. Rommel, if a person wants something bad enough they can get it. What I am saying is will you and your supervisor really, honestly and truly go to bat for me to get the aggravated dropped? Please give me this last chance, I am begging. Respectfully, Thomas White."

He was facing a 12-year sentence.

Meanwhile, Detective Dorsey had finally succeeded in finding Dolores. Her level of anger had surpassed her level of fear -- Dolores seemed to sputter and boil with rage. And this time she kept her appointment downtown. The police showed her line-ups and pictures.

She identified Oscar Martinez, a 21-year-old native of El Salvador. Detective Dorsey had early tips that Monkey, as he was called on the street, might be involved. He had been telling people that he had found religion, that he wanted to become a priest -- or a police officer.

Oscar Martinez became the first person in Apartment 205 to go to jail for what happened at the Bogota. In January 1991, he pleaded guilty to sexual assault and was sentenced to five years in prison. The police understood that he was to be deported upon his release.

By last summer, there was finally enough information to take Mario Ortiz Garcia to court for raping Sandy.

Investigators with the Dallas County District Attorney's office had at last succeeded in finding Angela. She seemed as combative as Dolores. And now, all three girls were ready for the June trial.

Sandy took the stand first, answering Assistant D.A. Larry Jarrett's questions in a flat voice devoid of emotion.

Q. While you were in the bathroom, Sandy, what were you doing while these people were having sex with you?

A. Laying there.

Q. Say it again.

A. Just laying there.

Q. Were you kicking, screaming, yelling, fighting or anything like that?

A. Yes.

Q. At what point did you stop kicking, screaming or yelling?

A. When they put the gun to my head.

An angry Dolores took the stand, followed by a firm-voiced Angela.

They pointed prosecutors to the young, neatly groomed man in the green shirt -- Mario Ortiz Garcia.

Rommel took the stand next and said, in a dry voice, that he "developed a man by the name of Mario Garcia as a suspect." Thomas White III was next. He also pointed to the man in the green shirt. He said that Mario Garcia told him he was a member of a gang called the East Side Locos.

Two days later, Judge Gary Stephens heard arguments for the punishment phase of MGO's trial. Prosecutors wanted a life sentence; the defense wanted probation. Detective Dorsey matter-of-factly testified that MGO "is not law-abiding in the community."

MGO's attorney called one character witness. Laticia Morales, MGO's 21-year-old girlfriend, said she had been living with him for two years. No, he was never head of the East Side Locos. Never a founder. Never a member. Never convicted of anything before.

He had no time to do any of that because he spent all his time with her. She and MGO had a month-old baby, she said.

The jury recommended a sentence of 20 years. After he dismissed the jurors, Judge Stephens turned to MGO's attorney: "Counsel, is there any reason in law why I should not sentence Mr. Garcia at this time?" The lawyer said no.

MGO was given the full 20 years for aggravated sexual assault. His attorneys immediately began planning an appeal. On the way out of the courthouse, Dolores and Angela exchanged heated words with MGO's friends and family. Sandy's grandparents quickly shepherded Sandy away.

In 1991, two other gang members were convicted of sexual assault. Two other cases are pending. The police say at least four additional rapists are in prison for other crimes.

Three more men alleged to be in Apartment 205 have since died violently -- including one who apparently was held by his arms in front of a speeding Monte Carlo.

Detective Dorsey still works the neighborhood for information that he can give to Rommel. He still sees people on the street who he is convinced were at the Bogota that August night.

And in Elm Alley there is a small neat piece of graffiti shoehorned in amid the endless scrolls and splotches of paint sprayed by the gangs. It reads: Sentenced To Life In East Dallas.

"I guess," says Detective Dorsey as he guides his unmarked car down the dirty, rutted alley, "that's an example of East Dallas activism."

At the final arguments in MGO's trial, Detective Dorsey had brought along his two daughters. His wife was working, and he was essentially baby-sitting, showing the kids what he did for a living.

That afternoon, after court was recessed, he received a call from a patrol officer who specialized in picking up tips in East Dallas: "Did you go to court today?"

Detective Dorsey: "Yeah, why?"

The patrol officer: "Did you go to a rape trial?"

The detective answered yes again.

"Did you take your daughters?" asked the patrolman. This time, the detective insisted that the patrolman tell him why he wanted to know.

"Because they tried to follow you home. Because they know what kind of car you drive. Because, without your knowing it, you lost them. Because they said they were going to get your daughters just like they got the other girls."

Today, Dolores still says the same thing three times, maybe to convince herself more than anyone who might be listening. It sounds like a chant, like liturgy.

"It's not as if I'm going crazy. I'm not going crazy. I'm not crazy," she says. She is angular-faced with dark eyes. Now 18, she looks like a 14-year-old wearing a bit of baby fat.

She absent-mindedly twists a golden bracelet on her right wrist. Though it's sunny outside, the room she's in is dark except for the TV whining off to one side. The sink is filled with dishes, and...

THE TEXAS RANGERS REVISITED: OLD THEMES AND NEW VIEWPOINTS

.. there is glamour in the names
Of the men who made the Rangers, as the record still proclaims:
The lifter left the cattle and the outlaw hid his gat
When they thought about the rider in the tall-white-hat.[1]

By Harold J. Weiss, Jr.*

SUCH VERSE CONJURES UP TIMELESS IMAGES OF RANGERS battling desperadoes in furious gun battles. The Rangers as heroic figures can be seen as Cossacks on horseback, Mounties without uniforms, six-shooter Sir Galahads who knew no fear and persevered as guardians of law and order. In their relentless pursuit of lawbreakers, these fearless Rangers "rode the border and the outlaw rode for life."[2]

Continuity in historical analysis has two important elements: enduring traits in a time continuum, and the imprint of such long-standing characteristics on the public. From events in their early history the Texas Rangers gained a reputation as a mounted body of officers capable of pursuing their foes in Indian country or along the Mexican border; were identified with a particular weapon—the six-shooter—that contributed to their image as fighters who neither gave nor asked for quarter; and were an irregular force with no uniforms, some privately supplied equipment and provisions, and a noticeable lack of military discipline. This rough-and-ready image, which first appeared in the fight for Texan independence and the Mexican War, left its imprint on the imagination of those writers who have recorded the exploits of outlaws and lawmen.

Although tradition played an important part in Ranger affairs, different eras in Texas history produced different types of Rangers. Through the decades of settlement, revolution, and statehood; the period of the Civil War and Reconstruction; the growth of agriculture and industry; the rise of urban Texas; and American involvement in two world wars, the operations of the Texas Rangers can be divided into three distinct periods:

1. 1823-1874: the heyday of the Rangers as citizen soldiers. Within this time frame ranging companies and other volunteer units engaged in a military struggle with Indian tribes and Mexicans for control of the land.

2. 1874-1935: the age of the Rangers as old-time professional lawmen. In 1874, to protect the frontier and suppress lawless segments of the population, the legislature created a Special Force of Rangers under Capt. L. H. McNelly and the Frontier Battalion, commanded by Maj. John B. Jones. By the beginning of the twentieth century, the Frontier Battalion had evolved into a complex organizational structure with a chain of command and career-minded officers who carried out administrative duties and investigative work, from tracking criminals to collecting and analyzing evidence. Such processes were the hallmarks of the old-style professional peace officers throughout the American West.

---

[1] William B. Ruggles, Trails of Texas (San Antonio: The Naylor Co., 1972), 17.

[2] Ibid.

3. 1935-present: the period of the Rangers as new-style modern police. In 1935 the Rangers became part of the modern state police movement in the United States when they were transferred along with the Highway Patrol to the newly created Department of Public Safety. The move reinforced professionalism, as political patronage decreased and bureaus were created for communications, education, intelligence, and identification and records.[3]

Each generation must use its experiences to reinterpret—some might say reinvent—the actions of the Texas Rangers in the field. The historiographical map of the Ranger companies is covered with accounts that chronicle dates and events, narrate the adventures of intrepid Rangers, or criticize the same body of men for using force beyond the line of duty. The highlights of this historical literature are twofold. First, there is the professional stature of Walter Prescott Webb. Although it did not stress a central thesis as did his other works, Webb's monumental study of the Rangers brought together a vast array of factual information and attracted public attention to the exploits of nineteenth century Ranger captains. J. Frank Dobie called this classic work the "beginning, middle, and end of the subject".[4] Yet before his untimely death Webb realized that his Ranger book needed to address more fully events in the twentieth century, as did his articles for the Michigan *State Trooper,* and that a fresh approach to the conflict between Anglos and Hispanics would contribute to a more balanced view of law enforcement in modern Texas.[5]

This interplay between the Rangers and Mexican Americans, another major theme in the historical literature on Ranger operations, has resulted in endless controversy. Too often the story of the border conflicts has been framed in dichotomous relationships. For some the Rangers have become heroic figures who saved Texans from foreign invasion and rampant crime. As one Ranger captain said graphically, "Hell, . . . whenever there's a mean ass, they call on us."[6] For others, though, the image of the Rangers is just the opposite: from iron-fisted range riders with the "sensitivity of a rattlesnake" to the derogatory verse *"'Rinche, pinche, Cara de chinche"* (Mean ranger, face of a bug)."[7] Such opposing viewpoints, with each side emotionally defending its position, do not create an atmosphere that

---

[3] For a comprehensive survey of the Rangers in the nineteenth century, see Walter Prescott Webb, *The Texas Rangers: A Century of Frontier Defense* (Boston: Houghton Mifflin Co., 1935). For an historical sketch of the twentieth-century Rangers and their heroic deeds, see two works by Ben Procter: *Just One Riot: Episodes of Texas Rangers in the 20th Century* (Austin: Eakin Press, 1991), and "The Texas Rangers: An Overview," in *The Texas Heritage*, ed. Ben Procter and Archie P. McDonald (St. Louis: Forum Press, 1980), 1991-131. For a look at the Rangers and other peace officers in the West, see Frank R. Prassel, *The Western Peace Officer: A Legacy of Law and Order* (Norman: University of Oklahoma Press, 1972) and Harold J. Weiss, Jr., "Western Lawmen: Image and Reality," *Journal of the West*, XXIV (Jan. 1985), 23-32.

[4] J. Frank Dobie, *Guide to Life and Literature of the Southwest* (1943; rev. ed., Dallas: Southern Methodist University Press, 1981), 60.

[5] Llerena B. Friend, "W.P. Webb's Texas Rangers," *Southwestern Historical Quarterly,* LXXIV (Jan., 1971), 293-323 (cited hereafter as *SHQ*). See also Stephen Stagner, "Epics, Science, and the Lost Frontier: Texas Historical Writing, 1836-1936," *Western Historical Quarterly*, XII (Apr. 1981), 165-181. Webb enjoyed writing a second book on the Rangers—*The Story of the Texas Rangers* (2nd ed.; Austin: Encino Press, 1971)—without the deadening facts and scholarly notes of his other work. For Webb's professional career, see Necah Stewart Furman, *Walter Prescott Webb: His Life and Impact* (Albuquerque: University of New Mexico Press, 1976).

[6] Procter, *Just One Riot,* 16.

[7] The rattlesnake quotation is from W. Eugene Hollon, *Frontier Violence: Another Look* (New York: Oxford University Press, 1974), 42. For the Texas-Mexican taunt, see Archie P. McDonald (comp.), *The Texas Experience* (College Station: Texas A&M University Press for the Texas Committee for the Humanities, 1986), 80.

encourages asking new questions and seeking new answers in order to understand the complex world of modern law enforcement.[8] Viewing the Rangers in white hat-black hat terms will freeze their historiography in time, with more ties to local interests than regional and national concerns.

Citizen soldiers were an age-old instrument of British military policy that became embedded in American culture. Non-Texan rangers engaged the enemy on the battlefields of eighteenth-century America. While the Native Americans in Texas were encountering the northward expansion of New Spain, ranger units fought in the woodlands and valleys east of the Mississippi River in the French and Indian War and the American Revolution. At that time rangers, like those under Robert Rogers in both wars, gained fame as a "flying army" of sharpshooters who could either fight alongside other soldiers or carry out guerrilla operations. In addition, the use of rangers in the late 1700s coincided with the use of light infantry to protect the flanks of an army and the recognition by the military of the battlefield abilities of buckskin-garbed frontiersmen who held rifled long guns and knew how to fight Indian-style. Thus, before Anglo-Americans settled in Texas, ranger-frontiersmen had a distinctive role as soldiers in irregular warfare: unmilitary dress with the firepower of a special weapon."[9]

To play this role before and after their formal organizations in 1835, the Texas Rangers needed an implacable foe. They found not one, but several: the unyielding Mexicans and the indomitable Apaches, Tonkawas, Comanches, and other Indian tribes. In this multifaceted struggle through the movement for independence and early statehood, Texans were repeatedly mustered in and out of ranging companies. A recent critic of the Rangers maintained that they were "born out of vigilantism" because they "developed out of private ranger companies."[10] More to the point is the fact that in the days of Stephen F. Austin the Rangers began as citizens acting as occasional soldiers. In the 1820s Mexican law called for the training and use of the militia and allowed Austin to handle local governmental matters. Austin, who first placed the Rangers under a militia officer, and other militia representatives realized that mounted Rangers could patrol the Indian frontier until other military units could take the field.[11] Although the existence of the angers in pre-Civil War Texas was sporadic and no career-minded captains arose from the ranks, a few officers left their marks on Ranger traditions of martial skills. These included John S. "Rip" Ford, Richard A. Gillespie, Benjamin "Ben" McCulloch, and Samuel H. Walker.

---

[8] An analysis of dichotomous relationships is in David Hackett Fischer, *Historians' Fallacies: Toward a Logic of Historical Thought* (New York: Harper and Row, Publishers, 1970), 9-12.

[9] Don Higginbotham, *Daniel Morgan: Revolutionary Rifleman* (Chapel Hill: University of North Carolina Press, 1961), 121 (quotation). For an introduction to the varied use of the rangers in the revolutionary war, see Mark Mayo Boatner III, *Encyclopedia of the American Revolution* (New York: David McKay Co., 1966), 149, 153, 586, 664, 909, 934-936, 945-946, 1009-1010.

[10] Alfredo Mirandé, *Gringo Justice* (Notre Dame, Ind.: University of Notre Dame Press, 1987), 67 (2nd quotation), 68 (1st quotation).

[11] The Austin Papers, ed. Eugene C. Barker, *Annual Report of the American Historical Association for the Year 1919* (2 vols.; Washington D.C.: Government Printing Office, 1924), II [I], Pt. 1, 678-679; and two works by Eugene C. Barker, *The Life of Stephen F. Austin: Founder of Texas, 1793-1836* (1925; reprint, New York: Da Capo Press, 1968), 98-108, 162-167, and *Mexico and Texas, 1821-1835* (1928; reprint, New York: Russell and Russell, 1965), 21-23. Also see Mark E. Nackman, "The Making of the Texas Citizen Soldier, 1835-1860," SHQ LXXVII (Jan. 1975), 231-253, and Allen R. Purcell, "The History of Texas Militia, 1835-1903" (Ph.D. diss., University of Texas at Austin, 1981), 62-106. For a succinct account of the field operations of the first Rangers, see D.E. Kilgore, *A Ranger Legacy: 150 Years of Service to Texas* (Austin: Madrona Press, 1973).

The concepts of rangers and citizen soldiers have become umbrella terms for a variety of roles and occupations on both sides of the Atlantic. Rangers can be defined simply as wanderers, or as officials involved in the care of parks and forests; military raiding parties; or armed groups who range over a region for its protection. From Scotland and the royal parks of England to the colony of Georgia to frontier Texas, and with a mixture of Celtic culture, English traditions, and modern attitudes, rangers took part in search-and-destroy missions and won public acclaim. A recent historian described the first Rangers in Texas as men who "fought under no flag, wore no uniform, and in practice observed no prescribed length of service. One would even have to stretch the definition of the term to call them militia, for militia mustered at regular intervals for drill."[12] Yet by the time of the settlement of Anglo Texas, volunteer rangers in western states with an Indian frontier did align themselves with organized militia units, which could be called into federal service.[13] Although the exact relationship between Ranger companies and militia units in antebellum Texas remains unclear, one Texan made an important point: "every settler was a minuteman . . . ready to start at a moment's warning."[14] To stand and fight for family and community was the essence of the citizen soldier. "The Texas Ranger," according to one expert, "was none other than the *ordinary citizen soldier.*"[15]

The steadfast attitudes in favor of citizen soldiers in American society in the eighteenth and early nineteenth centuries made the rise of the Rangers in Anglo Texas inevitable. Two points about the first Rangers are clear: in the 1820s small groups of from ten to thirty Rangers were periodically formed to protect property and settlements from Amerindians, and in November 1835, during the Texas Revolution, three companies of fifty-six men were organized, with John J. Tumlinson as one of the company captains and Maj. Robert M. "Three-Legged Willie" Williamson directing their operations. Ranger activities reached their zenith in antebellum Texas in the 1840s. Armed with rifles and revolvers, mustered in more organized bodies in small numbers or by the hundreds, used as scouts and spies, ordered to fight in defensive lines or attack in hit-and-run style or make frontal assaults on enemy positions, Rangers under the command of "Devil Jack" Hays gained a reputation for initiative and bravery as mounted gunmen in their battles with Comanches and as state volunteers under the American flag in the Mexican War. In retrospect, the exploits of Hays's volunteer soldiers played an important role in reinforcing the traditional American dislike of large standing armies and their professional codes.[16]

The intermittent use of the Texas Rangers as either a state force or as troops taken into federal service continued for the next two decades. Ranger leaders like "Old Rip" Ford and James H. Callahan stood out in violent encounters with Comanches and Mexicans in the 1850s. Two significant developments, which have been underplayed in Texan chronicles, were the actions of Henry McCulloch,

---

[12] Stephen Hardin, *The Texas Rangers* (London: Osprey Publishing, Ltd., 1991), 4.

[13] Jim Dan Hill, *The Minute Man in Peace and War: A History of the National Guard* (Harrisburg, Pa.; The Stackpole Co., 1964), 11, 14-15.

[14] Nackman, "The Making of the Texan Citizen Soldier, 1835-1860," 231. For the relationships between the militia, Rangers, and regular troops in antebellum Texas, see Purcell, "The History of the Texas Militia, 1835-1903," 75-100.

[15] Nackman, "The Making of the Texan Citizen Soldier, 1835-1860," 246 (quotation). For stimulating accounts of American military attitudes, Celtic culture, and the southern heritage to the Texas Rangers, see Marcus Cunlifffe, *Soldiers and Civilians: The Martial Spirit in America, 1775-1865* (Boston: Little, Brown and Co., 1968); Hardin, *The Texas Rangers,* 3-4; and Grady McWhiney, *Cracker Culture: Celtic Ways in the Old South* (Tuscaloosa: University of Alabama Press, 1988).

[16] Hardin, *The Texas Rangers,* 3-20.

veteran Ranger and Confederate officer, in handling the Indian frontier and the activities of draft dodgers, deserters, and bushwhackers in Texas during the Civil War;[17] and Gov. Edmund J. Davis's creation not only of the state police to enforce Reconstruction, but also of organized companies of Rangers—the "governor's police"—to pursue Indians and outlaws and recover stolen cattle and horses in the 1870s.[18] Thus, the Texas Rangers continued their sporadic existence, remained distinct from professional soldiers, and began to adapt to changes in the period between 1823 and 1874.

Scores of minor skirmishes and major battles since the era of New Spain took place between European settlers and the Indian tribes in Texas. One can argue that battle-hardened Anglos, Hispanics, and Amerindians fought each other on equal terms. What, then, allowed the Native Americans to win battles but lose the war? For one thing, the feared Comanches came up against superior firepower in Hays's Rangers, with their five-shot Paterson Colts. After battles at Walker's Creek and other places, more Comanches than Rangers lay dead on the field.[19] Another important factor was the inability of the Indian tribes to unite in order to plan strategy and build villages that could withstand a prolonged siege. Flacco, the Apache leader, fought with distinction alongside Hays, and in 1858 a combination of Rangers under Ford and reservation Indians under Shapley P. Ross took the offensive and won a significant victory by destroying Iron Jacket's Comanche village in a six-hour running fight on the north bank of the Canadian River.[20] Primitive Indian arms could not stand up against state and federal troops allied with other Indians.

Most historians agree that the pivotal event in the making of the early Ranger mystique was the Mexican War. For decades the search for a decisive victory in a bloody battle dominated the relations between Mexico and Texas. Then in 1846 came the North American Invasion, as it is called south of the border. The role of the Rangers in this conflict can be viewed in three different ways. First, the Texans under Hays became effective soldiers whose mobile tactics allowed them to carry out varied assignments, from scouting missions to leading a charge against an enemy stronghold to protecting supply lines by engaging Mexican guerrillas. Second, a Ranger image recognized throughout the United States developed from these assignments. Into Mexico rode Hays's Rangers. Out of Mexico came a mounted irregular body of Rangers armed with revolvers and knives and celebrated in song and story for their rough and-ready appearance and their fearlessness. Finally, the most controversial aspects of the role of the Rangers in this war resulted from their contacts with Mexican civilians away from the battlefields. That the Rangers took

---

[17] David Paul Smith, *Frontier Defense in the Civil War: Texas' Rangers and Rebels* (College Station: Texas A&M University Press, 1992).

[18] John L. Davis, *The Texas Rangers: Images and Incidents* (1975; rev. ed., San Antonio: University of Texas Institute of Texan Cultures, 1991), 46 (quotation); Bern Keating, *An Illustrated History of the Texas Rangers* (New York: Promontory Press, 1980), 93-97. For a study of the state police and Reconstruction, see Ann Patton Baenziger, "The Texas State Police during Reconstruction: A Reexamination," *SHQ* LXXII (Apr., 1969), 470-491. For a recent scholarly work that shows the mix of Rangers, volunteers, militia, and other troops in early Anglo Texas, see John H. Jenkins and Kenneth Kesselus, *Edward Burleson: Texas Frontier Leader* (Austin: Jenkins Publishing Co., 1990).

[19] James K. Greer, *Colonel Jack Hays: Texas Frontier Leader and California Builder* (New York: E.P. Dutton and Co., 1952), 22-125; Dorman H. Winfrey, "John Coffee Hays," in *Rangers of Texas,* ed. Roger N. Conger et al (Waco: Texan Press, 1969), 5-25.

[20] Thomas W. Dunlay, *Wolves for the Blue Soldiers: Indian Scouts and Auxiliaries with the United States Army,* 1860-90 (Lincoln: University of Nebraska Press, 1982), 20-23; W.J. Hughes, *Rebellious Ranger: Rip Ford and the Old Southwest* (Norman: University of Oklahoma Press, 1964), 129-159; Harold B. Simpson, "John Salmon (Rip) Ford," in *Rangers of Texas,* 95-99.

clothing, chickens, pigs, and whiskey can be seen either as plundering a helpless people or as foraging in the accepted military tradition. That they killed civilians for taking horses, throwing stones, stealing handkerchiefs, or knifing a Ranger in the streets can be viewed either as unnecessarily harsh retaliation or as following the rules of an uncivilized war. In a guerrilla war both sides can be accused of using terrorism, of believing in war for war's sake. At the end of the fighting, however, the Rangers stood tall. Santa Anna was leaving the country with an American military escort Although the Rangers talked about shooting their old nemesis, they lined the road instead and watched his carriage disappear. For the Rangers the bloodshed had come to an end.[21]

Since the mid-1800s Texas and the United States had undergone vast changes. For America the Industrial Revolution and involvement in two world wars had brought the country into the modern age. For Texas a wave of new settlers pushed settlements into the Panhandle and West Texas and diminished the importance of the Mexican American population. Railroads crisscrossed the state and the search for oil and gas became part of the new industrialism. In urban America the war against crime and disorder led to changes in big-city police departments, the creation of new agencies like the FBI, and the spread of the state police movement from Texas and Massachusetts.[22]

With the creation of McNelly's Rangers and the Frontier Battalion in 1874 under Gov. Richard Coke, the Rangers continued to engage Indian tribes in combat and guard the border against forays by Mexican nationals, but increasingly their duties turned to arresting those Texans suspected of breaking the law. The rate at which the Rangers changed from citizen soldiers to professional lawmen accelerated as each Ranger officer (an important term in future legal disputes) was given "all the powers of a peace officer" and had the "duty to execute all criminal process directed to him, and make arrests under capias [writ] properly issued, of any and all parties charged with offense against the laws of this State."[23] Armed with this authority, Rangers would arrest those who committed arson, embezzlement, and murder; those who stole horses and cattle; and those who tried to get away with such crimes by fleeing to another state.[24]

---

[21] For the secondary literature on the Rangers in the Mexican War, see Henry W. Barton, "The United States Cavalry and the Texas Rangers," *SHQ* LXIII (Apr., 1960), 495-510; Greer, *Colonel Jack Hays,* 126-216; Hughes, *Rebellious Ranger,* 22-56; Stephen B. Oates, "Los Diablos Tejanos!" *American West,* II (Summer, 1965), 41-50; Webb, *The Texas Rangers,* 91-124; Harold J. Weiss, Jr., "The Bloody Texans in the Mexican War: The Reasons Why," *Westerners Brand Book* (New York Posse), XVI, No. 1 (1969), 1-5, 21-22; and Frederick Wilkins, *The Highly Irregular Irregulars: Texas Rangers in the Mexican War* (Austin: Eakin Press, 1990).

[22] The most recent histories of Texas with up-to-date information on the Texas Rangers include the following: Robert A. Calvert and Arnoldo De León, *The History of Texas* (Arlington Heights, Ill.: Harlan Davidson, 1990), and David G. McComb, *Texas: A Modern History* (Austin: University of Texas Press, 1989). For an older study, see T.R. Fehrenbach, *Lone Star: A History of Texas and the Texans* (New York: American Legacy Press, 1983).

[23] H. P. N. Gammel (comp.), *The Laws of Texas, 1822-1897* . . . (10 vols.; Austin: Gammel Book Co., 1898), VIII, 91.

[24] An informative study of criminal violence in Texas in the nineteenth century has yet to be written. For a recent look at Texan violence with emphasis on gunfighters and the struggle between settlers and the Amerindians, see Bill O'Neal, "Violence in Texas History," in *Texas: A Sesquicentennial Celebration,* ed. Donald W. Whisenhunt (Austin: Eakin Press, 1984), 353-369. For two older views of violence in Texas and the Southwest see W.C. Holden, "Law and Lawlessness on the Texas Frontier, 1875-1890," *SHQ* XLIV (Oct., 1940), 188-203, and C.C. Rister, "Outlaws and Vigilantes of the Southern Plains, 1865-1885," *Mississippi Valley Historical Review,* XIX (Mar., 1933), 537-554. Interpretative frameworks to study Texas crime and violence will be found in Richard Maxwell Brown, "Western Violence: Structure, Values, Myth," *Western Historical Quarterly,* XXIV (Feb., 1993), 5-20, and Gary L. Roberts, "Violence and the Frontier Tradition," in *Kansas and the West: Bicentennial Essays in Honor of Nyle H. Miller,* ed. Forrest R. Blackburn et al. (Topeka: Kansas State Historical Society, 1976), 96-111.

After the 1870s, the Texas Rangers had to mesh two interrelated but somewhat discordant factors: organizational structure and charismatic leaders. The former provided the operational network for the Rangers to act as police; the latter produced heroic images that kept the Rangers in the public limelight. In their role as organized police, the Rangers had to answer for themselves a question common to law enforcement work throughout the American West: in fighting crime, were they justified in bending the rules limiting the use of intimidation and violence? Whenever they answered in the affirmative, the lines between the Rangers and the outlaws they pursued became blurred. But those Rangers who tried to carry out their duties with a minimum of gunplay deserve the highest praise. A peace officer in this frame of mind was "truly the one who tamed the west."[25]

Although the number and size of Ranger companies varied from decade to decade between 1874 and 1935, stability remained a hallmark of the organization and operations of the Frontier Battalion. Initially this force consisted of six companies with seventy-five men each (reduced to forty within a few months to handle budgetary problems). By the 1890s four companies remained, with sometimes less than a dozen Rangers left with each captain to patrol the countryside, investigate crimes, and arrest felons from the Panhandle to South Texas. Dressed in broad-brimmed hats, "round-a-bout" vest-like jackets, and possibly wearing a shield-type badge or one with the more popular wagon-wheel, fivepointed star design, the privates in the companies of the Frontier Battalion reported to their sergeants and captains, and the officers, in turn, kept open lines of communication with headquarters in Austin.[26]

In 1901 and 1919, Texan state authorities made important modifications to this organizational structure. By 1901 a legal dispute arose over whether commissioned officers, and not the rank and file of the companies in the field, were peace officers who could make arrests. Some Rangers faced charges of false arrest. To solve this problem the governor's office and the legislature changed the name of the Frontier Battalion to the Ranger Force and stipulated that all Rangers be given all the powers necessary to make arrests and execute criminal processes. The number of companies and their manpower, however, remained basically the same. The demise of the Frontier Battalion, in name at least, did not result from a fiery gun battle, but from words spoken from a judge's bench.[27]

By the beginning of the twentieth century the Frontier Battalion or the Ranger Force had evolved into a complex organization. The most important characteristic of the old-time Ranger captain was the ability to recognize the centralizing forces connecting field offices to the main headquarters and at the same time handle the decentralized aspects of the organizational structure. In the chain of command power flowed from the governor to the adjutant general and his staff, including the battalion quartermaster, to the officer in command of a company in the field to the Ranger in charge of a subcompany stationed at various locations. At the top of this pyramid one adjutant general, John A. Hulen, kept track of Rangers and their companies by using numbered and colored pins on a Texas map, and Battalion Quartermaster W. H. Owen criticized one captain for making the central office wait for his reports "all the time."[28] At the bottom of the pyramid Capt. William J. "Bill" McDonald acknowledged

---

[25] Dennis Brennan, "Who Really Tamed America's Wild West?" *The Lion*, LIV (May, 1972), 8.

[26] Webb, *The Texas Rangers*, 307-342; Webb, *The Story of the Texas Rangers*, 116 (quotation).

[27] Harold J. Weiss, Jr., "'Yours to Command': Captain William J. 'Bill' McDonald and the Panhandle Rangers of Texas" (Ph.D. diss., Indiana University at Bloomington, 1980), 147-156.

[28] For Hulen's method, see Austin *Stateman*, July 14, 1906. For Owen's quotation, see Owen to Captain William J. "Bill" McDonald, Aug. 7, 1896, *Letter Press Book*, Ranger Records, Records of the Adjutant General of the State of Texas (Archives Division, Texas State Library, Austin; cited hereafter as AGR).

his instructions by ending some of his letters with the phrase "Yours to command."[29] Initially, Major Jones gave personal leadership and discipline to this organization in the 1870s. But the high-water mark of operational effectiveness came with the career-minded "Four Great Captains" by the early 1900s: McDonald, John A. Brooks, John R. Hughes, and John H. Rogers. The old-time Rangers became organizational Rangers.[30]

For a police agency to perform in a professional manner, it must achieve administrative efficiency. Captains and other commissioned and noncommissioned officers in the Frontier Battalion or the Ranger force carried out administrative duties that ranged from the selection of recruits and the dismissal of Rangers to maintaining company stations and obtaining supplies and equipment, assigning personnel to details to scout and investigate crimes, and handling citizen complaints and making reports to superiors. At one pint George W. Arrington, the "iron-handed" captain of the Panhandle, even submitted to central headquarters monthly weather reports, with twice-daily citations such as "Clear & Cold Wind S."[31] A more important responsibility, however, was the hiring and firing of personnel. A century ago, men who joined the Rangers could ride, shoot, scout, track criminals, act like detectives, speak Spanish, and control mobs. In 1901 Adj. Gen. Thomas Scurry instructed company commanders to "enlist only such men as are courageous, discreet, honest, of temperate habits and respectable families."[32] Yet Rangers were discharged for desertion, drunkenness, insubordination, lack of judgment in the use of firearms, being in league with outlaws, and what one captain called "low down ungentlemanly things."[33] After some new enlistments this same captain was able to "boast of having a sober company and one that is not gambling and drinking all the time."[34]

Besides a command structure and centralized administrative work, three other factors characterized the old-time professional Rangers between 1874 and 1935: their use of deadly force; their ability to track criminals and collect and analyze evidence; and their need to adapt to technological change and relate to other lawmen, local, state, and national. Recently a Texas historian tried to find a new approach to the study of the history of the Rangers. He stressed the use of force and made the point that the "Rangers did not always get their man." This writer went on to show that outlaw Tom Ross escaped from a shoot-out with Rangers and other peace officers and that Ross even got the drop on Captain Rogers in another episode.[35] Although such events were humiliating to the Rangers, the

---

[29] See the complimentary closing in the letter from McDonald to Adj. Gen. William H. Mabry, Feb. 19, 1891, Gen. Corr., AGR.

[30] For sketches of the careers of the "Four Great Captains" see William W. Sterling, *Trails and Trials of a Texas Ranger* (Norman: University of Oklahoma Press, 1963), 305-362, 363 (quotation), 364-396. For a revisionist account of the career of Captain McDonald, see Weiss, "'Yours to Command.'" For the modernization of American society in this era, see Robert H. Wiebe, *The Search for Order, 1877-1920* (New York: Hill and Wang, 1967).

[31] Webb, *The Texas Rangers*, 422 (description of Arrington); "Weather Report, Month Ending Feb. 29, 1880, Co. C," Ranger Records, AGR.

[32] General Order No. 62, July 3, 1901, typed transcript of message, Ranger Correspondence, Walter Prescott Webb Papers (Center for American History, University of Texas, Austin; cited hereafter as CAH).

[33] McDonald to Captain E. M. Phelps, Oct. 6, 1900, Gen. Corr., AGR.

[34] McDonald to Mabry, Sept. 30, 1891, ibid.

[35] James I. Fenton, "Tom Ross: Ranger Nemesis," *Quarterly* of the National Association and Center for Outlaw and Lawman History, XIV (Summer, 1990), 4 (quotation), 19-21.

important point is that the use of coercion is not the distinguishing feature of a police officer; it is only a tool to consider in pursuit of a legitimate goal.

The reality of the Rangers in the late nineteenth and early twentieth centuries lay between the images of the good guys in white hats and *"Los Diablos Tejanos"* (the Texas devils) in black hats. On the plus side, a few Rangers scattered over vast distance carried out hundreds of scouting expeditions, arrested thousands of lawbreakers, and guarded jails and courts on numerous occasions. More dramatic were the cases that brought fame and renown to the Ranger organization. In 1876, during the bloody Sutton-Taylor feud, Lt. Lee Hall and his Rangers surrounded a house during a wedding celebration, arrested seven of the Sutton faction without bloodshed, and then stood guard in the courtroom with their Winchesters ready.[36] The next year, during the Horrell-Higgins feud, Sgt. N.O. Reynolds and his men got the drop on the Horrell brothers and talked them into surrendering without firing a shot.[37] Then came encounters with well-known bandits and gunmen: the arrest more than once of John King Fisher (who knew, as did Mexican prisoners, that any attempt at rescue or escape would bring instant death); the manhunt for and shooting of Sam Bass; Lt. John B. Armstrong's role, with other lawmen, in the capture of John Wesley Hardin (he knocked Hardin unconscious with his six-shooter); and the part played by ex-Ranger Frank Hamer in the slayings of Clyde Barrow and Bonnie Parker in 1934.[38] Such intrepid Rangers had one thing in common; they did their duty to the best of their ability in difficult times.

Yet some of these same Rangers had blots on their records. A few were removed from their posts; others learned from their experiences and became better Rangers. From the time that William G. Tobin carried out his orders in an incompetent manner in pre-civil War Texas to a pickpocket's theft of cash and a diamond pin from McDonald in 1910, Rangers failed to solve cases and make arrests and some allowed their prisoners to escape.[39] Even famed Sgt. Ira Aten suffered a "loss of face" when a fugitive he was watching escaped while Aten was drinking a cup of coffee.[40] Furthermore, Major Jones had to remove about fifteen Rangers from the service when they sided with an ex-Ranger in the Mason County War.[41]

---

[36] Hughes, *Rebellious Ranger*, 38 (*"Los Diablos Tejanos"*); Dora Neill Raymond, *Captain Lee Hall of Texas* (Norman: University of Oklahoma Press, 1940), 69-78. For a history of the Sutton-Taylor feud, see C.L. Sonnichsen, *I'll Die Before I'll Run: The Story of the Great Feuds of Texas* (New York: Harper and Bros., 1951) 19-87.

[37] James B. Gillett, *Six Years with the Texas Rangers,* 1875 to 1881, ed. M.M. Quaife (New Haven: Yale University Press, 1925), 69-80. A sketch of the Horrell-Higgins feud is in Sonnichsen, *I'll Die Before I'll Run*, 97-118.

[38] For the events in the lives of these bandits and gunmen, see O.C. Fisher, with J.C. Dykes, *King Fisher: His Life and Times* (Norman: University of Oklahoma Press, 1966); H. Gordon Frost and John H. Jenkins, *"I'm Frank Hamer": The Life of a Texas Peace Officer* (Austin: Pemberton Press, 1968); Wayne Gard, *Sam Bass* (Lincoln: University of Nebraska Press, 1969); Chuck Parsons, *The Capture of John Wesley Hardin* (College Station: Creative Publishing Co., 1978); and Webb, *The Texas Rangers*, 297-304 (Armstrong), 519-546 (Hamer).

[39] The analysis of Tobin's action is in Hughes, *Rebellious Ranger*, 167-170. For the episode with McDonald, see the summation of a newspaper story from Wichita [Falls] *Daily Times*, n.d., Card File Index 144, newspaper collection of Wichita Falls *Times*, WPA Historical Survey Project (CAH). According to an account in another newspaper, McDonald apprehended but then lost the pickpocket after the thief had passed his valuables to a confederate. Austin *Statesman*, Oct. 15, 18, 1910. For an example of a Ranger losing a prisoner, see Gillett, *Six Years with the Texas Rangers*, 192-193.

[40] Harold Preece, *Lone Star Man: Ira Aten, Last of the Old Texas Rangers* (New York: Hastings House, 1960), 117-121, 122 (quotation), 123-125.

[41] Gillett, *Six Years with the Texas Rangers*, 46-52.

Most humiliating to the old-time Rangers, however, was the surrender of Lt. John B. Tays and his entire command to armed Hispanics from both sides of the border in the El Paso Salt War in 1877.[42]

By the late 1800s the most controversial aspect of the law enforcement work of the Frontier Battalion was its use of weapons—revolvers, rifles, and shotguns—in investigating crimes and maintaining order. The Rangers as peace officers could legally make arrests with or without warrants, and could use "all reasonable means" to do so. Justifiable homicides could also be committed by peace officers in Texas in preventing arson, burglary, castration, disfiguring, maiming, murder, rape, robbery, or theft at night. In addition, in Texas and other states in the nineteenth century, judges changed the English common-law tradition, which required one to retreat before defending oneself, to the American legal doctrine of self-defense, by which one could-stand one's ground and fight. Thus, Texans and their police forces had ample legal authority to use violent means.[43]

Yet the Texas Rangers were not extraordinary gunfighters in the Old West. Only one prominent old-time Ranger-Captain Hughes—had the honor of being named to the roster of the most deadly gunfighters of all time.[44] One of the more bizarre gun battles took place between two feuding one-time Rangers, G. A. "Bud" Frazer and James B. "Deacon' Miller. In two shoot-outs between them, the steel breastplate that Miller wore for protection saved his life. Then in 1896 Miller found Frazer in a saloon and killed him with a blast from a shotgun.[45] In retrospect, the reputation of the horseback Rangers as gunmen rested not only on their involvement in gunfights, but also upon their proven marksmanship, their use of their weapons to intimidate opponents, and the fanciful stories woven around their exploits.

Particularly troublesome for the Rangers as lawmen after 1874 were their role of guarding the Rio Grande border and their use of force against Mexican Americans in southern Texas. Cultural, ethnic, and religious differences between Anglos and Hispanics persisted in the decades after the Mexican War. From Sam Houston's "Grand Plan" to conquer Mexico in 1860 with thousands of Rangers, Indians, and Mexicans to the 1915 Plan of San Diego for an uprising of people of Spanish descent on both sides of the border to retake the Southwest, American expansionism and Mexican territorial beliefs came into conflict with each other and kept some individuals dreaming of conquest.[46] In this charged atmosphere, people

---

[42] Webb, *The Texas Rangers*, 345-367.

[43] Richard Maxwell Brown, *No Duty to Retreat: Violence and Values in American History and Society* (New York; Oxford University Press, 1991); William M. Ravkind, "Comments: Justifiable Homicide in Texas," *Southwestern Law Journal*, XIII (1959), 508-524; Geroge W. Stumberg, "Defense of Person and Property under Texas Criminal Law," *Texas Law Review*, XXI (1942-43), 17-35; John P. White, *The Code of Criminal Procedure of the State of Texas, Adopted at the Regular Session of the Twenty-fourth Legislature, 1895...*([Austin]: Gammell Book Co., 1900), 159 (quotation).

[44] Bill O'Neal, *Encyclopedia of Western Gunfighters* (Norman: University of Oklahoma Press, 1979), 4-6, 160-163.

[45] Ibid., 113-114, 230-233. See also Glenn Shirley, *Shotgun for Hire: The Story of "Deacon" Jim Miller, Killer of Pat Garrett* (Norman: University of Oklahoma Press, 1970), and C.L. Sonnichsen, *Ten Texas Feuds* (Albuquerque: University of New Mexico Press, 1971), 200-209.

[46] James A. Sandos, *Rebellion in the Borderlands: Anarchism and the Plan of San Diego, 1904-1923* (Norman: University of Oklahoma Press, 1992); William M. Hager, "The Plan of San Diego: Unrest on the Texas Border in 1915," *Arizona and the West*, V (Winter, 1963), 327-336; Webb, *The Texas Rangers*, 197-216 (Houston's "Grand Plan"). For an introduction to the course of empire and the cultural conflict between Americans and Mexicans, see Arnoldo De León, *They Called Them Greasers: Anglo Attitudes toward Mexicans in Texas, 1821-1900* (Austin: University of Texas Press, 1983), and Reginald Horsman, *Race and Manifest Destiny: The Origins of American Racial Anglo-Saxonism* (Cambridge: Havard University Press, 1981). Of the numerous accounts about life along the Mexican-American border, see Linda B. Hall and Don M. Coerver, *Revolution on the Border: The United States and Mexico, 1910-1920* (Albuquerque: University of New Mexico Press, 1990), and

found reasons to cross the border for nefarious purposes whenever necessary. As late as 1917 Mexican raiders crossed the Rio Grande, attacked the L. C. Brite ranch near Marfa, looted stores, and killed several individuals. In addition, Rangers (like Captain McNelly) and federal troops found it necessary to invade Mexico in warlike manner.[47] In the tug-of-war along the border, which involved cattle rustling, gunplay, liquor smuggling, and violations of American neutrality laws, some participants, such as Juan "Cheno" Cortina and Gregorio Cortez, have been seen by Anglos as bandits and murderers and by Texas Mexicans as revolutionaries and Robin Hood heroes.[48] The Rangers in South Texas gained notoriety for executing their Hispanic prisoners. The companies under the "Four Great Captains" at the turn of the twentieth century did not follow such a policy. On the other hand, Capts. H. L. Ransom and J. M. Fox shot a number of Mexican prisoners on the spot during World War I.[49] Such treatment of those of Spanish descent tarnished the Rangers' heroic reputation.

Important in the Rangers' transition from soldiering to policing was the rise of the professional police movement in this country, with its stress on careerism, the science of detection, and the use of technology derived from industrial America. The Rangers as mounted state police or, as one Ranger wrote, "mounted constables," were using modern techniques of police work by the early 1900s.[50] Long before the advent of computerized information systems, a list of fugitives, sometimes called "Bible II" and published by the state from reports received from county sheriffs, with colorful descriptions of thousands of criminals, allowed the Ranger organization to apprehend wanted men in a more efficient manner and integrate their activities more fully with those of local peace officers.[51] Equally important to the professionalization of the Rangers was their participation in the movement to prevent crime and improve the techniques of criminal investigation. From the 1877 sweep through Kimble County by several companies to arrest lawbreakers to the 1889-1890 use of undercover agents and dental information by Aten and Hughes and the 1905 use of handprints by McDonald, Rangers acted aggressively to deter crime.[52] In addition, the adoption of new technologies, such as repeating handguns

---

Oscar J. Martinez, *Troublesome Border* (Tucson: University of Arizona Press, 1988). See also Matt S. Meier and Feliciano Rivera, *Dictionary of Mexican American History* (Westport, Conn.: Greenwood Press, 1981).

[47] James R. Ward, "The Texas Rangers, 1919-1935: A Study in Law Enforcement" (Ph.D. diss., Texas Christian University, 1972) 1-3; Webb, *Texas Rangers*, 255-280; Michael G. Webster, "Intrigue on the Rio Grande: The *Rio Bravo* Affair, 1875, SHQ LXXIV (Oct., 1970), 149-164.

[48] Mirandé, *Gringo Justice*, 50-99. See also John B. McClung, "Texas Rangers along the Rio Grande, 1910-1919" (Ph.D. diss., Texas Christian University, 1981); Américo Paredes, *With His Pistol in His Hand": A Border Ballad and Its Hero* (Austin: University of Texas Press, 1958); and Ward, "The Texas Rangers, 1919-1935," 98-103.

[49] For information about Captains Fox and Ransom, see Ward, "The Texas Rangers, 1919-1935," 9-11, 15.

[50] The quote is taken from Gillett, *Six Years with the Texas Rangers*, 19.

[51] Erik Rigler, "Frontier Justice in the Days Before NCIC," *FBI Law Enforcement Bulletin*, LIV (July, 1985), 16-18, 19 (quotation), 20-22.

[52] Helen F. Bonner, "Major John B. Jones: The Defender of the Texas Frontier" (M.A. thesis, University of Texas at Austin, 1950), 51-55 (Kimble County); Jack Martin, *Border Boss: Captain John R. Hughes—Texas Ranger* (1942; reprint, Austin: State House Press, 1990), 66-75, 85-100; Webb, *The Texas Rangers*, 328-333 (Kimble County); Weiss, "'Yours to Command,'" 169-176.

and rifles, trains and cars, telegraph and telephone lines, and typewriters, improved investigative methods in a changing society.⁵³ The Rangers had become more professional since the Jones-McNelly era.

Through the early decades of the 1900s two problems brought grief to individual Rangers and forced organizational changes: the interrelationship between Rangers and politics, and the troubles along the border between 1910 and 1920. The tactic of direct action and the practice of *la ley de fuga* used by McNelly's force in the 1870s along the Rio Grande were resurrected in grand style in the second decade of the twentieth century. On the one hand, a few Rangers made a gallant effort to cope with outlaw bands, Mexican revolutionaries seeking arms and public support, wartime spies and draft-dodgers, liquor smugglers, and a *gringo*-hating generation along the border. On the other hand, as one historian wrote, "instead of meeting these challenges, of acquitting themselves heroically in such critical times, the Rangers fashioned a dismal record of murder and injustice."⁵⁴ In 1919 Rep. J.T. Canales initiated a legislative inquiry that heard testimony about intimidations, pistol whippings, and cold-blooded killings during Ranger operations. A reorganization of the Rangers resulted from the investigation. Four companies remained, each with seventeen Rangers including the captains. The legislation also created a headquarters company with six men under a senior captain. Although it helped to restore public confidence, the new law failed to address the issue of political influence and patronage in Ranger affairs. The next generation of political leaders could follow the policies of those, like Gov. James E. Ferguson and James B. Wells of Cameron County, who had hampered Ranger attempts to administer even-handed justice.⁵⁵

The new-style Texas Rangers developed for several reasons. Most important was the fact that the governors between 1911 and 1935 did not follow a consistent policy for the selection, upkeep, and deployment of the Rangers. The appointment of hundreds of Special Rangers cheapened the badge, and the corrupt "Ferguson Rangers," like Capt. James Robbins who took bribes and embezzled funds, further tarnished the reputation of the organization.⁵⁶ Other Rangers, however, especially in the era of Governors Dan Moody and Ross S. Sterling, carried out their duties with distinction, from the closing of vice dens in the oil boom towns by veteran Capt. William L. "Will" Wright to the capture of the Cisco bank robbers in 1927 by a posse led by Capt. Tom Hickman.⁵⁷ Yet Wright called for less politics in Ranger affairs and Hickman talked about combining the force with other Texas lawmen and using experts in fingerprints and ballistics.⁵⁸ Such reform movements to reduce political patronage and modernize police operations have been common in police work in this country since the time of Theodore Roosevelt.

---

⁵³ The use of science and technology in police work affected law enforcement agencies throughout the western United States. Weiss, "Western Lawmen," 25. For information about Ranger weapons, see two articles by Charles Askins: "The Texas Ranger and His Guns," *American Rifleman*, CXXX (Nov., 1982) 44-45, 78-79, and "The Texas Ranger and His Guns, Par II," ibid. (Dec. 1982), 28-29, 75. See also Charles Askins, *Texans, Guns & History* (New York: Winchester Press, 1970).

⁵⁴ Procter, *Just One Riot*, 4.

⁵⁵ Ibid., 3-7; Evan Anders, *Boss Rule in South Texas: The Progressive Era* (Austin: University of Texas Press, 1982), 9-10, 37-38, 227-228, 252-254.

⁵⁶ Procter, "The Texas Rangers," 123; Ward, "The Texas Rangers, 1919-1935," 223 (quotation).

⁵⁷ Ward, "The Texas Rangers, 1919-1935," 145-209.

⁵⁸ Ibid., 229-230; Stephen W. Schuster IV, "The Modernization of the Texas Rangers, 1930-1936" (M.A. thesis, Texas Christian University, 1964), 38-39.

The year 1935 was crucial in the history of the Texas Rangers. A time of questioning had come to an end. Using the Griffenhagen study of Texas law enforcement and the work of Dallas attorney Albert S. Johnson, Gov. James V. Allred and the state legislature created a Department of Public Safety, which included the Rangers, the Highway Patrol, and a Headquarters Division, to act as a modern center for the science of detection. Special Rangers had their numbers reduced and their powers limited. And the appointment of former Ranger Manuel T. 'Lone Wolf' Gonzaullas to head the Bureau of Intelligence eased the transition of the rest of the Rangers into the DPS and the field of criminalistics. Texas had joined the list of states that had developed and modernized their police forces and organized central crime labs.[59]

The new-style Rangers resembled their pre-1935 counterparts in two ways: they maintained law and order in disputes between labor and management, and they investigated criminal cases that required working with other lawmen in Texas and across the nation. Like state police elsewhere, Rangers have been sent to keep the peace in violent confrontations between labor and management. In these difficult situations the actions of the Rangers have received mixed reviews. In some strikes, like the dispute between cowboys and ranch owners in the Panhandle in the late 1800s, the arrival of the Rangers aided the cause of management. In other violent encounters, such as the railroad strikes of 1922, the entire Ranger force was insufficient to handle the affair and the military had to be called in. In the strike by Texas-Mexican workers in Starr County in the late 1960s, Capt. A. Y. Allee and his Rangers kept order, but their use of force in making arrests and their methods of handling the mass media and the union movement among Mexican Americans resurrected the image of the brutal, Hispanic-hating Rangers.[60] One can argue that the use of the Rangers in such labor-management confrontations has had adverse effects on their ability to collect information and solve criminal cases.

For more than a century both the old- and new-style Texas Rangers have had to work with numerous officials on the local, state, and national levels of government: army officers, county sheriffs, district attorneys, federal marshals, judges, mayors, and town police forces. Their formal and informal collaborative arrangements have ranged from the exchange of information about the modus operandi of Texan criminals to conducting joint manhunts to working out arrangements for the detention of prisoners and the presentation of evidence in the courtroom. From the time that a Ranger subcompany set up tents in San Saba County to assist local officials in solving murder cases in the late 1800s to the involvement of the DPS in disaster relief after Hurricane Carla in 1961, Rangers and other public authorities in the state stood shoulder to shoulder in maintaining law and order. Relations between the Rangers and law enforcement officers of the national government and of the states have taken two basic forms: the exchange of information and collaboration in the pursuit of outlaws, particularly with federal marshals in Oklahoma and U.S. Army units in South Texas, and the extradition of fugitives between the states and

---

[59] Duayne J. Dillon, "A History of Criminalistics in the United States, 1850-1950" (Ph.D. diss., University of California at Berkeley, 1977), 156-162; Brownson Malsch, *Captain M T. Lone Wolf Gonzaullas: The Only Texas Ranger Captain of Spanish Descent* (Austin: Shoal Creek Publishers, 1980), 119-150; Schuster, "The Modernization of the Texas Rangers, 1930-1936," 34-66.

[60] David Montejano, *Anglos and Mexicans in the Making of Texas, 1836-1986* (Austin: University of Texas Press, 1987), 87-88 (cowboy strike); Ward, "The Texas Rangers, 1919-1935," 76-81 (railroad strikes). For the troubles in the Rio Grande valley in the 1960s, see Ben H. Procter, "The Modern Texas Rangers: A Law-Enforcement Dilemma in the Rio Grande Valley," In *Reflections of Western Historians,* ed. John A. Carroll with James R. Kluger (Tucson: University of Arizona Press, 1969), 215-231, and Julian Samora et al, *Gunpowder Justice: A Reassessment of the Texas Rangers* (Notre Dame, Ind.: University of Notre Dame Press, 1979), 89-156.

with foreign countries. Such interaction has highlighted the cooperation and conflict in American intergovernmental relations.[61]

In recent decades the Texas Ranger Service continued to investigate felonious crimes, apprehend fugitives, and suppress riots and insurrections. Under DPS directors such as Homer Garrison Jr. and Wilson E. "Pat" Speir, appropriations increased; computerized equipment modernized information systems; and regional centers appeared in the organizational charts. Rangers were older, more experienced, and better trained and educated than their predecessors.[62] This was especially important in an era of procedural justice in which strict rules governed the admissibility of evidence in American courtrooms.

In the chronicles of the American Southwest the Texas Rangers ride into history in a dual role: as Texans and as Rangers. As Texans, some married and had children; others used their literary talents to write poetry and newspaper stories; and still others carried their Bibles with their guns. As Rangers, different labels can be attached to their actions in the field: intrepid heroes, brutal lawmen, organized peace officers, and professional state police. To look into the complex world of the Texas Rangers one must go beyond the good-evil syndrome embedded in Ranger historiography. The dichotomous views of some writers of Ranger roles—heroes or devils for the military deployment as citizen soldiers against Amerindians and Mexican nationals, white hats or black hats for their actions as peace officers against desperadoes and Robin Hood bandits-cannot withstand the scrutiny of historical research. Yet the image of the Rangers will not really change until old stories are told in new terms. An army officer once wrote about Captain McDonald, "It is said here [in Brownsville] he is so brave he would not hesitate to "charge hell with one bucket of water."[63] Maybe Jack Hays would have done that as a citizen-soldier Ranger, but McDonald was a police officer. And as a cop, he would have followed procedures: investigate and call for more Rangers and more buckets.[64]

---

[61] For a work with some emphasis on the theory and practice of American intergovernmental relations and the Rangers, see Weiss, "'Yours to Command.'"

[62] Procter, "The Texas Rangers," 124-130; Erick T. Rigler, "A Descriptive Study of the Texas Ranger: Historical Overtones on Minority Attitudes" (M.A. thesis, Sam Houston State University, 1971), 20-24, 30-34.

[63] *Message from the President of the United States, Transmitting a Report from the Secretary of War, Together with Several Documents, Including a Letter of General Nettleton, and Memoranda as to Precedents for the Summary Discharge or Mustering Out of Regiments or Companies*, 59th Cong., 2nd Sess., S. Doc. 155, Pt. 1 (Ser. 5078), 65.

[64] Numerous topics for original research in Ranger history remain to be addressed. These include traditional subjects, such as Ranger captains and heroic deeds, and the fields of class, gender, and race of the new western historians. A list of unexplored topics for research in Ranger history would include the following: American intergovernmental relations and the operations of the Rangers; beliefs and actions of the Christian Rangers, as, for example, Captain Rogers and Thalis T. Cook; a comparative study of the Texas Rangers and other notable police forces (the Arizona Rangers, Canadian Mounties, and Mexican Rurales); the image of the Rangers in novels and other media; the impact of criminalistics on the new-style Rangers since the 1930s; labor-management strife and the Rangers since 1874; law enforcement, the Rangers, and black Texans; the life-styles and thought patterns of the wives of the Rangers; literate Rangers who excelled in the use of the written word; the origins of the organizational Rangers, from Captain Jones to Battalion Quartermaster L. P. Sieker; recreational pursuits of the Rangers in camp; and the work of the Rangers in World Wars I and II. For examples of publications that are useful to such research, see Chuck Parsons, *"Pidge," A Texas Ranger from Virginia: The Life and Letters of Lieutenant T.C. Robinson, Washington County Volunteer Militia Company "A"* (Wolfe City, Tex.: Henington Publishing Co., 1985), and Mrs. D.W. Roberts, *A Woman's Reminiscences of Six Years in Camp with the Texas Rangers* (1914; reprint, Austin: State House Press, 1987).

*Harold J. Weiss Jr. is professor emeritus of history, government, and criminal justice at Jamestown Community College, Jamestown, New York. He received his doctorate in history from Indiana University at Bloomington in 1980. His primary field of interest is law enforcement in the west, and he is currently working on a study of the transition of the Texas Rangers from soldiering to policing. He presented a version of this paper at the thirty-first annual meeting of the Western History Association in Austin in October 1991.

THE TWILIGHT OF THE TEXAS RANGERS
by Robert Draper

IN THE SUMMER OF 1993, JOAQUIN JACKSON, the senior member of the Texas Rangers, drove from his outpost in Alpine to the Austin headquarters, where he informed his superiors that he was hanging up his spurs. Assistant commander Bruce Casteel was visibly upset by the news. "Joaquin, you're not ready to quit," he protested. "You need to stay."

Jackson shook his head. "I just can't do it," he said.

Everyone present knew what Jackson meant. Though he had been a Ranger for the past 27 years, the strapping six-foot-five lawman was only 57 and had several good years left. The murderers and drug smugglers, he could handle just as capably as always. What Joaquin Jackson could not handle were the changes taking place within his beloved Texas Rangers. "Well," said one of the secretaries after a long silence, "I guess this is the end of one era and the start of another."

In fact, the new era had already begun, and it had made Jackson sick to his stomach. Forty Department of Public Safety employees had recently been made finalists for nine new Ranger positions. Five of the forty applicants were women. Friends within the DPS had told Jackson that two of the nine jobs were going" to be filled by women, no matter what. Since no woman had ever been named a Ranger before, this information came as a shock to Jackson. As veteran lawmen went, Jackson had a reputation for open-mindedness. He had vocally encouraged the 1973 hiring of the Rangers' first Hispanic officer in more than fifty years. He believed that any good law enforcement agency had to adapt with the times and was hopeful that by the year 2000, Rangers would be computer experts who primarily tangled with white-collar criminals. Now, women Rangers-that was something else again. Jackson knew a few excellent female FBI agents and always thought that a woman's intuitive powers were useful investigative tools. But a Ranger had to be more than an investigator. A Ranger had to live off the land, had to withstand days of sleepless pursuit, had to fight back mobs and overpower psychopathic murderers. That was what a Ranger did. That was what Joaquin Jackson had done for the past 27 years. Could a woman do all that? Jackson was skeptical, but he waited to see who the DPS would come up with.

When Jackson found out, he was infuriated. Cheryl Steadman was promoted from a clerical job that involved processing warrants. The other newly appointed female Ranger, Marrie Garcia, had spent the past several years in San Antonio's driver's license service. Like Steadman, Garcia had never worked a criminal case in her life. Neither Jackson nor any of the other Rangers he talked to could remember a Ranger being plucked from the ranks of the driver's license service.

This was hardly a trivial matter. After all, the elite force of 87 Texas officers has a hand in the state's biggest criminal cases, from the crime-scene investigation of the Branch Davidian compound to the pursuit of mass murderers, serial rapists, and drug lords. Arguably, Steadman and Garcia were two of the least qualified recruits in the Rangers' 170-year history. And, Jackson thought bitterly, that was obviously beside the point. DPS director Jim Wilson and Ranger chief Maurice Cook had turned their backs on tradition and responded to the political lash. So a new era was dawning, all right, and the men of Jackson's era wanted no part of it. "When they hired those two women that clinched it for me," Jackson says today. Another Ranger, with 18 years on the force, turned in his badge as well, citing the women as his reason. A third veteran, after putting an end to his 23 years of service, was heard to say, "Well, I'm the last rat getting off this sinking ship."

Even so, the veterans left quietly, their disenchantment with the brotherhood surmounted only by their aversion to airing dirty Ranger laundry. The hiring of the women Rangers was seen as a quirky sign of progress by the media, which did not bother to investigate whether these particular women possessed even the most rudimentary qualifications for the job. When reporters asked Marrie Garcia's father if she was up to the challenge, he declared, "Watch her shoot," as if Rangers were ever known for their marksmanship. For her part, Cheryl Steadman told the media how she placated the DPS interviewers by saying, "A good female Ranger will wear whatever she's told," as if Rangers were ever known for conformity. But then again, this was the new era.

To Joaquin Jackson and his peers, the quota-hiring of women Rangers suggests a kind of political emasculation, one that makes a mockery of the legendary law enforcement corps. To critics of the Rangers, the event was twenty years behind schedule, further proof that the state's most sanctimonious good old boys could not be trusted to march in step with the modern world.

Certainly it is true that the recent history of the Texas Rangers is the history of an organization at odds with the changing times. In a sense, however, the Rangers have always been in sync with Texas — or rather, with the part of Texas that, for better and for worse, distinguishes Texans from the rest of the world. No other state boasts an equivalent to the Rangers, and in no other state would the Rangers survive its many controversies. The question, Are the Rangers necessary? involves matters so deeply embedded in the Texas psyche that it is almost never addressed. For that matter, America as a whole is entranced by this indigenous lawman; hence the recently released movie *A Perfect World* (starring Clint Eastwood as a Ranger), the television series *Walker, Texas Ranger,* and the innumerable movies and books preceding them. As such, the movement to overhaul the Texas Rangers, and the Rangers' cynical and defensive reaction to that movement, are knotted together in our state's tangled web of romance and realpolitik, honor and progress, myth and mortality. The knot is what binds us, and what forms the noose we cannot slip.

A retired ranger stared dreamily at the plaque he kept on his wall, bearing the name of his most famous predecessors. "Leander McNelly," he murmured at last, and his voice almost caved in with emotion as he quoted one of McNelly's men, "Lord, how I would have charged hell with a hand bucket behind the leadership of that man!" Rangers are faithful keepers of Ranger mythology, and it all begins with McNelly, the youthful captain under whose command a pint size brigade slaughtered countless criminals and Mexicans from 1874 until 1877. To the Rangers and their admiring historians, McNelly is an appealing composite of warlord and Christ figure: courageous and gentlemanly, utterly devoted to his men and his mission, a remorseless killer, and dead himself by the holy age of 33. From McNelly flows the rich blood of Ranger lore.

And that is oddly fitting, since in fact Leander McNelly was never a Texas Ranger. Muster rolls, vouchers, and state correspondences indicate that from 1874 until 1876, McNelly was the captain of the Washington County Volunteer Militia, and from 1876 until his departure in January 1877, captain of a brigade worded in state legislation as "special state troops." His troops were structurally and budgetarily set apart from the six companies making up the separately legislated Frontier Battalion of Texas Rangers. McNelly did not report to the head of the Rangers, Major John B. Jones, but rather to Adjutant General William Steele. Occasionally reporters and McNelly referred to his men as Rangers, presumably as a descriptive term — and indeed, McNelly's brigade performed just as bravely as Major Jones's Rangers did. But to say that McNelly was a Texas Ranger simply because he killed Mexican bandits on behalf of the state would be like saying that Oliver North was a CIA agent simply because he went on a few spying missions.

Yet historians, including the Rangers' eminent biographer-booster Walter Prescott Webb, have woven Leander McNelly into Ranger history with little regard for the facts. Numerous biographers have written that McNelly's troops were known as the Special Force of Rangers, though the historical record plainly indicates that his battalion was never given that official designation. True, McNelly was a remarkable leader, when he was well, but it is also true that he spent much of 1876 laid up with ailments and was finally determined by the adjutant general to be "an incompetent man" and discharged. True, McNelly often seared death in the face, but it is also true that as a state policeman in 1870, McNelly stared a gang of Harrisburg outlaws in the face promptly surrendered to them. (Perhaps that was a prudent act on McNelly's part, but in any event this rare display of "Ranger" capitulation does not appear in any known historical text, though a copy of the newspaper article citing the surrender can be found among Webb's papers at the University of Texas.) McNelly's lionized exploits include the killing of unarmed men and the raiding of innocent homesteads-enough wanton bloodlust to have reportedly scared off Robert Redford from a Leander McNelly movie project.

But Webb is perhaps right to conclude that McNelly and the Rangers were reared in desperate times, when, as he puts it, "neither the rules nor the weapons were of the Ranger's choosing." The first Rangers were hired in 1823, when Stephen F. Austin employed ten men to protect settlers from Indians. Some fifty years later, after subduing the Indians, the Rangers turned their attention to the precarious conditions along the Mexican border. After the banditos came the bootleggers, bank robbers, and lynching mobs; later still, the oilfield thieves and striking steelworkers.

In that rough rural terrain, no officer excelled like the Texas Ranger. He knew his prey and his territory, but tenacity was his greatest asset. Indeed, a Ranger's charge was to range the frontier: to cross city and county lines, to spend a week or a month or a year in pursuit of his quarry, to suppress lawlessness with any weapon at his disposal. It fell to other Texas officers to mingle with the public and wear starched uniforms. A Ranger was a Ranger because he was bred for the prairies and the backwoods. He personified the frontier and lived by its rough-hewn ethic. In the city he always seemed out of place. When Joaquin Jackson visited New York a few years back and toured the Harlem projects with the city vice squad, he believed he had stepped into Ranger hell. "I could never do what y'all do," Jackson told the city cops. A Ranger belonged in the wilderness. He was the earthiest of Texas lawmen, and yet there was always a little bit of the dreamer in every Ranger, for he lived the dream of the virtuous wanderer, slaying serpents in God's garden; every man who coveted Rangerhood sought his mythic place among the wanderers.

In their domain the Rangers were champions. Big Foot Wallace, John Coffee Hays, Rip Ford, Ben McCullough, J. B. Gillett, Lone Wolf Gonzaullas—the names themselves are expressions of frontier heroism. The Rangers made it possible to settle Texas. By protecting South Texas from cattle rustlers and East Texas from oil-field plunderers; they guarded the soft flanks of the state's burgeoning economy. They were the Klan's greatest foe and the most-dogged trackers of murderers, from Clyde Barrow to Animal McFadden. In the line of fire the Ranger force produced dozens of bona fide legends, a handful of scoundrels, and hundreds who simply performed as the times demanded. For the vast majority of Rangers, it might be enough to say that they were merely actors in the unholy theater of the frontier, beyond good and evil.

Yet Ranger scribes cannot resist the holy detail: that McNelly "would not enlist a man who did not come from a good family," that feared "border boss" Captain John R. Hughes "is a devout church minister" who "will not keep a man in his Ranger company who swears or drinks," that famed Bonnie and Clyde tracker Frank Hamer, killer of more than fifty men in his lifetime, loved to whistle for birds and "talk to his feathered friends." Far less is said about Ranger sergeant Bass Outlaw, murderer and drunk, or about Geronimo captor Tom Horn, who was hanged for murder in 1903. For that matter, former Ranger commander and historian William Sterling wrote much about his own exploits on the frontier but nothing about his being tried in 1915 for murdering a South Texas rancher with a bullet to the back. (The jury bought Sterling's self-defense plea, though no weapon was found on the deceased.) And while the credo "One Riot, One Ranger" originated around the turn of the century, its validity was called into question only a few decades later, following the lynching of an accused black rapist at the hands of a mob in Sherman in 1930. Writing of the incident, the *Wichita Falls Times* lamented, "We are afraid that story (one riot, one Ranger) is passé from now on. Not just one Ranger, but several, constituted the force at Sherman, and proved all but helpless against the mob."

Today's Ranger does not pretend to be able to stifle a riot single-handedly. But another turn-of-the-century Ranger motto remains in force, this one coined by Captain W. I. McDonald: "No man in the wrong can stand up against a fellow that's in the right and keeps on a 'coming." It is the romance of this statement that has kept the Rangers alive in the hearts of Texans, and it is the sanctimony of the motto that has gotten them into so much trouble. By 1919, the notion of a lone officer's being given the authority to determine what is "right" was called into question. That year — for the first time, but by no means the last — the Rangers were investigated by the Legislature for torturing and killing civilians who had been deemed "in the wrong." The Ranger force endured the investigation and also survived the 1933-through-1934 reign of Governor Ma Ferguson, who filled the force with cronies as punishment for the Rangers' diligent efforts in the 1932 campaign to keep Governor Ross Sterling in power.

When the Department of Public Safety was created, in 1935, Walter Prescott Webb glumly predicted the demise of his heroes. But Webb had underestimated the tug of the Ranger mythology he himself had promulgated. The Rangers were simply incorporated under the DPS and kept on a 'coming.

Progress, however, was a 'coming even faster.

"The men I worked with used to chase criminals on horseback," says Lewis Rigler, who joined the Rangers in 1947. "The captains all got cars around 1921, and the number one private was the one who got to drive and wash the captain's car. There were only fifty-one of us by the time I came along and they put a tremendous responsibility on all of us. No bothering the captains with picky-picky things-just go where you need to go and work as long as it takes to get the job done. And anytime you needed something, you picked up the phone and called the Colonel direct."

The Colonel was Homer Garrison, Jr., the head of the DPS and the Rangers from 1938 until 1968. Garrison had come up through law enforcement ranks; he knew his men, and their trust in him was unwavering. When the Colonel's door was closed, he was most likely telling the governor what his men needed. When it was open, anyone was free to tell the colonel what was on his mind. In 1965 Sid Merchant was a 32-year-old DPS patrolman when he took advantage of Garrison's policy, walked in, and said, "Colonel Garrison, I'd like to be a Texas Ranger." The DPS chief said, "I could tell that the moment you walked in," and eventually hired him. Garrison relied on his hunches but was not an intractable man. Twenty days after Lewis Rigler was promoted to a command post at the Austin headquarters in 1957, he told Garrison, "Colonel, I appreciate your confidence in me. But I'm used to dealing with robbers, rapists, and cattle thieves. Here I'm just staring at the walls. Please just make me a private again." Garrison nodded and said, "You head on back to Gainesville, Lewis." Rigler did, and happily remained a Ranger private for the next twenty years.

Garrison kept the politicians at bay and let his Rangers police themselves. Each of the six Ranger companies was led by a captain stationed at each of the six officers (In Houston, Dallas, Lubbock, Corpus Christi, Midland, and Waco), with Ranger privates scattered throughout the hinterlands. Each Ranger assembled his own work load from the cases originating in his jurisdiction. If a Ranger needed to leave his region, or even the state, no advance permission was required. When Garrison needed to hire a new Ranger, he usually took the advice of his subordinates. "A lot of Rangers put in a good word for me," says Glenn

Elliott, who joined the force in 1961 and left in 1987. "But I had been in the trenches with them. During the Lone Star Steel strike in 1957, I was a patrolman working side by side with Lewis Rigler, Bob Crowder, Jim Ray, and Red Arnold. The first night of the strike, we fought a mob of twenty five hundred mad people blocking the gates. That night, those Rangers learned how I would react in the dark against a mob. If anyone should know whether I'd be a good Ranger, it was them."

"The Colonel stressed individuality," says Rigler, though only up to a point: Garrison's Rangers were white males. Equal opportunity was not yet an issue, but Garrison had his hands full with other matters. Criminals were smarter in postwar Texas, their methods far more sophisticated than in the days of bank robbers and bootleggers. So that his frontier battalion would not be consigned to obsolescence, Garrison's Rangers were made to learn state-of-the-art investigative and forensic techniques. His last Ranger hiree, Joaquin Jackson, says, "The Rangers would never have survived the modern era if not for him." But no amount of laboratory schooling could prepare the veteran Rangers for the avalanche of laws and court rulings that descended upon them in the sixties. The Civil Rights Act. Miranda. Laws of arraignment. Habeas corpus writs. No longer could Rangers hide suspects from their attorneys by means of the "East Texas merry-go-round," ferrying them from one town to the next in the dead of night. No longer could a suspect be tossed in jail without being charged with a crime and given access to a telephone. And the age-old Ranger specialty—coaxing confessions out of suspects by any means necessary—was suddenly in serious jeopardy.

"All the way up to the early sixties, a Ranger was apt to kill you as look at you," says one Ranger who served among the old-timers. "He was the law, and on occasion he was above the law." The methods employed by tough cusses like Walter Russell, Jerome Preiss, Clint Peoples, Jim Nance, and Levi Duncan weren't pretty, but they produced results. When a man got his face held down in a river, it tended to refresh his memory. Putting a milk bucket over a fellow's head and beating on it with a nightstick often yielded some useful information. "After Miranda," says Sid Merchant, "we needed to use more finesse in getting confessions. Some of those old boys said to hell with it and left."

Those who stayed found that the new rules, however aggravating, were going to be enforced. "They issued us each a little card that had the suspect's rights printed on it, and we were supposed to read it aloud," recalls a retired Ranger. "Some of us didn't bother doing it at first-and we had some cases overturned as a result."

The changes were especially apparent in South Texas, where a century's worth of animosity had accumulated. To Mexican Americans, the Rangers were not romantic stalwarts but rather "Los Rinches," oppressors of the poor and flunkies of wealthy Anglo ranchers. Captain A. Y. Allee, the head of Ranger Company D since 1947, was the focus of their fear and contempt. Allee had been sued and investigated countless times for his conduct in South Texas. He readily owned up to assaulting attorneys, smacking a Mexican labor organizer over the head with a rifle butt, and pistol-whipping George Parr, the Duke of Duval County. During a 1968 U.S. Commission on Civil Rights hearing, Allee said of his Rangers, "We are not instructed in any way about the use of force. We use what force we deem necessary to make any kind of arrest."

When the United Farm Workers organized a strike in Starr County in 1967, Allee and his company waded in with characteristic vigor. The Rangers arrested a minister and his wife who were not carrying pickets, delivered a concussion to an organizer, and informed demonstrators that the Rangers would do whatever it took to break the strike. For both the Rangers and the South Texas residents, nothing about the scenario was unfamiliar except for the response it generated. Allee's behavior was vilified in the statehouse, in the national media, and by the federal government. Eventually the U.S. Supreme Court ruled that Allee's Rangers had violated the farm workers' right to peaceful assembly; Allee remained unrepentant, but the damage to the Rangers' reputation was considerable. In 1975 Allee's son, Ranger Alfred Allee, Jr., volunteered to assist in a Presidio case involving a strike organized by César Chavez. The younger Allee's superiors adamantly refused. "We saw what mess your dad got us into before," he was told.

Captain Allee departed in 1970, done in by mandatory retirement. Homer Garrison's retirement from the DPS in 1968 ended a thirty-year reign, which would be followed by a succession of Ranger commanders. In 1972 Sissy Farenthold ran for governor and made the abolition of the Rangers one of her major campaign issues. The stance was intensely unpopular, and Ranger veterans guffawed when Farenthold lost. But Farenthold was of a newer time, and the Rangers were not impervious to it. No longer could a Texas lawman earn his Ranger badge simply by virtue of a veteran's blessings; now he had to pass a written test that many old-timers doubtless would have failed. A regulation instituted by DPS director James Adams in the early eighties stipulated that new Rangers would have to be plucked from the Department of Public Safety, rather than from a police or sheriff's office, as had been the case with so many Rangers in the past. As civil procedures tightened, paperwork demands increased. With Captain Allee's antics known throughout Texas and Garrison no longer around to take the flak, Ranger captains reined in their men and demanded an account of their comings and goings. "Rangers were notoriously unsupervised," recalls Sid Merchant. "I'd go a month at a time without seeing my captain. And things worked, because the old captains would back you. My captain, Tim Riddles, had balls as big as two brass bathtubs. Cap Allee was as mean as a snake, but damn it, he stood up for his men. Those fellows left, and the ones who came in after them were all caught up in covering their asses."

New federal labor regulations that severely restricted overtime took effect in the mid-eighties. While unions across America rejoiced, the Texas Rangers were aghast. A Ranger didn't punch a clock. How could he, when criminals didn't? "I remember they forced me to take off twenty straight days because I had worked too many hours," says Max Womack, an East Texas Ranger from 1969 until 1988. "It was ridiculous, and it brought a hardship on the rural counties that depended on me to work their cases." Many Rangers went about their business and simply fudged on their time sheets. "You'd have to lie," says Glenn Elliott, "and then if a case you were working on went to trial, they'd get you on the witness stand and shove your time sheet in front of your face and make a fool out of you in front of the jury."

The Ranger force had always been full of ancient lawmen who had lied about their age to keep the their post, but now the rules conspired with their advancing frailness to goad them into retirement. Charlie Miller in Mason, Jim Nance in Sierra Blanca, Homer Metton in Benjamin, Frank Kemp in Paris, Hollis Sillavan in Columbus, Bill Baten in Pampa, Lewis Rigler in Gainesville-these men had served their country outposts for as long as anyone could remember, and the silence of their passing was like a lonely death on the prairie. They would have successors, but they would not be replaced. "Coming up, I knew that old bunch," says Alfred Allee, Jr., now retired from the Rangers. "They were just different. Had a sense of honor. Knew how to get the job done. That old bunch—they were Rangers *all the time.*

"Now, the new bunch, they're something else again. You might run into them on the street and see them in Bermuda shorts and tennis shoes."

"I served on the oral interview boards when Tom Almond and Lloyd Johnson were made Rangers," recalls Lewis Rigler. "Before we did the actual interviewing, a captain would tell me, `Now, Lewis, I know this Johnson and he's good.' And another captain would tell me, `Almond, he's a hell of a guy.' So that's who we'd select. Sure, the fix was in. And I was part of the fix."

To the Rangers, that was a perfectly legitimate hiring practice. To those outside, looking in, it smacked of old-boy inbreeding. In the wake of the 1967 farm worker strikes, critics began to ask DPS officials why there hadn't been a Hispanic Ranger in many years. The question seemed to take Rangers aback, and their stock response—that there weren't any qualified Hispanic officers available—no longer seemed to wash. "I don't see any Japanese here," A. Y. Allee snapped at a reporter. "I don't see any Chinamen. We can't hire every doggone breed there is in the United States." But the pressure did not relent, and in 1969 a 31-year-old highway patrolman named Arturo Rodriguez was given a Ranger badge. Rodriguez was a rough investigator, highly thought of by Allee and Joaquin Jackson. Yet those connections, along with Rodriguez's mere five and a half years of law enforcement experience, only reinforced criticisms about the Rangers' good-old-boy network. In 1971 a Ranger captain approached DPS narcotics investigator Ray Martinez and said, "Ray, we really need another Mexican American Ranger." Martinez, who as an Austin police officer in 1966 helped gun down sniper Charles Whitman in the University of Texas Tower, thought the proposition sounded like tokenism and declined. He later changed his mind, and though Martinez served contentedly as a Ranger from 1973 until the end of 1991, he acknowledges that his efforts to be promoted in the Ranger ranks were unsuccessful. "Did I feel like I had an equal opportunity to compete for promotion?" he muses. With a wry smile, Martinez then says, "Let's just say I would hope I that I did."

In 1986 the Ranger oral interview board turned away a veteran DPS trooper named Michael Scott, despite the eight commendations in his personnel file and the high score he had achieved on the written test. Scott had grown up in Waco a mile from the Texas Ranger Hall of Fame. His childhood dream was to be a Ranger. He was an intelligent, well-built, clean-cut family man. The oral interview seemed to have gone well, and yet he was given a score sufficiently low to deny him a promotion to the Ranger force. In 1987 Scott again scored high on the written test. Again he went before the oral board. Again he received a low score and was denied a Ranger position.

Michael Scott could not help but notice that the Rangers had no blacks on the force and wonder if the fact that he was black had something to do with his treatment. Other black troopers began to wonder the same thing, and in 1987 they approached the NAACP, which led a federal Equal Employment Opportunity Commission complaint on behalf of the troopers in 1988. DPS officials agreed to enter into negotiations, and later that year, two black Rangers were hired. Neither of them was Michael Scott, who had committed the unpardonable sin of airing his frustrations to the media. Nor were the hirees among the group of black troopers who had contacted the NAACP. "Scott was as good or better than any Ranger who got in," recalls a state official who was part of the negotiations between the DPS and the NAACP. "But that's the pattern that emerged alter 1988. Individuals who refused to go along with the company line have continued to be denied justifiable promotions. "

Never before had the Rangers been the least bit concerned about appearances, but the EEOC complaint changed all that. The traditional Ranger oral interview board, consisting of veteran Rangers who happened to be white, was now seen as an invitation to a job-discrimination lawsuit. By 1992, the new interviewers tended to include one of the two black Rangers as well as a 32-year-old Hispanic woman from the DPS narcotics division and a black woman from the DPS safety division — "People who don't know 'come here' from 'sic 'em' abut the Rangers, to tell you the damn truth," says Joaquin Jackson.

But the cosmetic reforms were not enough to suit the state legislature. By 1993, the growing power of the Hispanic and Black caucuses had seeped into the Texas House Appropriations Committee. During the 1993 session, new committee members like Mario Gallegos, Pete Gallego, and Karyne Conley took it upon themselves to review the minority-hiring situation at the DPS and the Rangers. DPS colonel James Wilson and Ranger chief Maurice Cook were called to a conference session, where, according to Gallegos, "We raked them over the coals. The low numbers of minorities just stuck out like a sore thumb. Their promotional test hadn't been validated since the early seventies. To us, that justified what was happening over at DPS."

The committee members made it clear: If the DPS and the Rangers wanted to survive the 1993 session unscathed, they would have to make a demonstrative commitment to minority hiring. "You hate to write policy through appropriations, but that's the only way you get people's attention," says Conley. "The Rangers are the last bastion of the good-old-boy system. We sent them a message that their ranks would have to be reflective of the state as a whole."

It was a message that the Rangers had been hearing from Governor Ann Richards as well, with an additional twist: The Ranger force should include women. The lawmen had been wary of Richards from the start. At a Ranger reunion in Waco in the spring of 1992, Richards addressed the current and retired lawmen over dinner. Among the old-timers was former senior Ranger captain Clint Peoples, who had told a reporter in 1990 that he would vote against Richards because "I don't care to see any petticoats in the governor's office." Now Richards' blue eyes fell on the 81-year old retired Ranger. "I'm glad to see y'all eating some good steak," she cracked, "but in my opinion, ol' Clint ought to be eating some crow. "

Women had been employed by the Rangers in the past for security detail, and in 1935 a "petticoat brigade" of four female Rangers was used in undercover nightclub work. But these were only brief assignments. Word spread among Ranger ranks that Governor Richards had something far more lasting in mind. On an instinctive level, the notion was anathema. What would McNelly and Big Foot Wallace and Frank Hamer and Cap Allee have thought? Former Ranger chiefs had vowed that as long as they were in charge, no woman would ever wear a Ranger's badge. When Maurice Cook became chief in 1992, he reaffirmed the sentiment. But on August 1, 1993, DPS officials announced the hiring of nine new Rangers: two white males, three Hispanic males, one black male, one Asian American male . . . and two women.

The appointments fulfilled Representative Karyne Conley's demand that the Rangers "be reflective of the state as a whole." Beyond that, they fulfilled little else. One of the Hispanic males hired, Duane Henderson, happened to be the nephew of House Hispanic Caucus chairperson Irma Rangel, who had previously been critical of Ranger hiring practices. As a nine-year veteran of the highway patrol, Henderson had no formal investigative experience but had been hired over 62 applicants who did. The new black Ranger was once again not Michael Scott but rather a highway patrolman named Marcus Hilton. Hilton was hired despite having logged fewer years in law enforcement than 246 of the 261 DPS employees who applied for a Ranger position. Of the 19 female applicants, only 2 of them were criminal investigators —and those were not the 2 who were hired. The Ranger interview board had chosen from a woeful limited field of minorities and women to begin with and compounded the problem by selecting individuals who were clearly less qualified than other minority and women applicants. Word circulated throughout the Ranger force that the only thing these new Rangers had in common, besides their inexperience, was their willingness not to rock the boat. And while Rangers saw nothing wrong with the hiring of Richard Shing -- who had been a DPS veteran for seventeen years and looked, notes Glenn Elliott with approval, "just like George Strait" -- they thought it unseemly that the DPS was openly advertising Shing as the Rangers' first Asian American officer. The Texas Rangers had now become politically correct and were the worse for it.

When Sid Merchant heard the news about the hirings, he vowed never to attend another Ranger reunion. "The damn women," he mutters today. "Some things ought to remain sacred, and the Rangers are one of them."

Three weeks after the hirings were announced, Chief Maurice Cook addressed a conference room filled with criminal investigators from around the state. The attendees worked for cities and counties that had relied on the Texas Rangers for law enforcement leadership for more than a century. But today Cook was not here to offer advice. Instead, the Ranger chief told the attendees that his newest Rangers lacked experience and would benefit greatly from any guidance those present could give the rookies.

It was a startling admission by the Ranger chief. To some, however, Cook was merely stating what had been obvious for some time. "A sheriff told me not long ago, 'When we call the Rangers, it's because we need help,'" says Alfred Allee, Jr. "He said, 'These new Rangers, they're nice folks, but they're just inexperienced troopers, and we can't get any help from them.'"

Today's Rangers find themselves hemmed in by bureaucratic absurdities and civil rights edicts. But they must share the blame for their own decline. Once media darlings, the modern Rangers are thin-skinned when it comes to their public image and generally-as Chief Cook did for this refuse to explain themselves to the press. Cook, the Ranger chief since July 1992, is a 26-year veteran of the DPS, a lifer like Homer Garrison, but his ascension through the ranks has not garnered him the admiration of his men as Garrison's rise did. Then again, Chief Cook inherited a force that is now paying dearly for the insularity of the Garrison era. In their stubborn arrogance, the Rangers did not think to prepare for the inevitable equal-opportunity demands and had a shallow talent pool at the DPS from which to draw qualified women. For every Michael Scott who has patiently reapplied for the Rangers every year, there are several other talented black law enforcement agents who have given up waiting on the force and sought employment elsewhere. The cynical recent hirings, combined with prior hirings based purely on the old-boy spoils system, have produced a roster that would not fit anyone's description of an elite force.

Many outstanding Rangers remain, of course, and the best of them are greatly admired and relied upon by sheriffs and district attorneys throughout the state. Even a run-of-the-mill Ranger can move with more freedom than the average deputy, can devote more time to a case than the average investigator, can make use of the DPS's sophisticated crime labs, and can cut through the department's red tape at will. For these reasons, the Rangers remain useful. Nonetheless, the performance of the force over the past decade suggests an organization still struggling to square the utter rightness of its holy frontier ethic with the imperatives of the modern world.

The infamous Brandley case epitomized the wrong-headedness of the Ranger Way. On August 28, 1980, Texas Ranger Wesley Styles was called in to investigate the sexual assault and strangulation of a Conroe High School cheerleader. The following day, before interviewing a single witness, Styles arrested high school custodian Clarence Brandley and charged him with capital murder. A Montgomery County jury sentenced Brandley to death. Today a number of Rangers contend that Styles had collared the right culprit. After all, Brandley had recently been arrested for an attempted rape and abduction, was on felony probation for a weapons charge, was spotted near the scene of the crime, had no solid alibi, and had failed a polygraph in connection with the offense.

The Rangers believed they had gotten their man. But he ultimately slipped through their fingers, due entirely to the Rangers' outmoded methods. In 1989 the court of Criminal Appeals determined that Styles had conducted his investigation with a "blind focus" on Brandley, ignoring crucial evidence that incriminated other potential suspects. Styles had led other janitors on a "walk-through" of the crime scene that "contributed a due process violation by creating false testimony." He had roughed up and threatened to kill the state's star witness. He had suppressed crucial tape recordings of witness interviews. Finally, presiding judge Perry Pickett determined that Ranger Styles had lied on the witness stand. The court was thereby left with no choice but to reverse the conviction in 1989 and set Brandley free after seven years on death row.

The Brandley episode indicated that the classic Ranger style could not survive modern legal scrutiny. But as an embarrassment to the force, it paled in comparison to the Henry Lee Lucas fiasco. Lucas, a drifter who had served time for killing his mother, stunned a Montague County courtroom audience in June 1983 when he pleaded guilty to two murders and then added that he had committed at least a hundred more across the nation. Later Lucas revised the body count to more than six hundred. The Rangers dove into the fray, spearheading the Henry Lee Lucas Task Force, which would oversee the clearing of unsolved murder cases to which Lucas was now confessing. The Ranger in charge of the task force, Bob Prince, would later insist that its role was purely to facilitate interviews with Lucas by outside law enforcement parties, that it played no role in the confessions. But that was not the case at all. As Ranger memos confirm, the Rangers helped "refresh Lucas' memory" by providing him with details of specific cases that Lucas had more or less claimed were his offenses-crimes that, as evidence would later show, he could not possibly have committed.

The task force's role looked fishy to some from the outset. An Arkansas district attorney learned that Lucas had confessed to a Little Rock murder that had already been solved and that Lucas provided details of the case only after the Arkansas State police, in the presence of the Rangers, obligingly showed him a videotape of the crime scene. West Virginia officials learned that Lucas, at the urging of the Rangers, was now confessing to the murder of a West Virginia policeman despite an official ruling that the death had been a suicide. The attorneys for a Delaware murder defendant sent the task force their client's case file, and once again Lucas confessed. But a tape of the confession later indicated that the Rangers had been, according to a Delaware prosecutor, "incredibly leading" in discussing the case with Lucas, and ultimately the defendant admitted that he, not Lucas, was the killer.

Through these dubious methods, the Rangers extracted literally hundreds of confessions from Henry Lee Lucas. But in 1985, a *Dallas Times Herald* article documented that Lucas had been out of the state and at times in jail when many of the murders were committed. McLennan County district attorney Vic Feazell, spurred by these revelations and two questionable confessions in his home county, brought Lucas before a grand jury, where the drifter admitted that he had taken the Rangers for a ride. Rather than own up to their mistakes, the Rangers continued to insist that Lucas was a mass murderer, even as they sought to distance themselves from some of his confessions. Feazell has testified that Ranger Prince assured him outside the grand jury room, "I'm going to make you regret this if it's the last thing I do." Indeed, DPS officials undertook a full-scale investigation of the district attorney's activities culminating in a trial in which Feazell was found not guilty of various infractions.

The Lucas hoax drew international attention and brought shame to the Rangers of a magnitude not seen since the A. Y. Allee years. Today a number of retired Rangers, including Joaquin Jackson and Glenn Elliott, say they had interviewed Henry Lee Lucas about certain cases in their jurisdictions and could see for themselves that the task force was dealing with a habitual liar. "I remember him trying to cop to one he didn't do" says Elliott, "but there was another murder case where I'll kiss your butt if he didn't lead us right to the deer stand where the murder took place. Ain't no way he could've guessed that, and I damn sure didn't tell him. I think he did that one." Yet the hoax aura of Lucas' many confessions has left the resolution of this case in doubt.

The eroding credibility of the Rangers meant that defense attorneys no longer shuddered when a Ranger took the stand on behalf of the state. In 1986 an East Texas school principal named Hurley Fontenot stood trial for the murder of a football coach who had been dating a woman Fontenot had been in love with. Much of the evidence incriminated Fontenot, and as one of the jurors later said, "A lot of us felt that he was guilty, but the evidence just wasn't trustworthy." Specifically, Fontenot's attorney, Dick DeGuerin, based his defense largely on the dubious investigation and testimony of Ranger Tommy Walker. As Wesley Seyles had done in the Clarence Brandley case, Ranger Walker focused exclusively on Fontenot as a suspect, ignoring numerous leads along the way and emphasizing physical evidence that withered under DeGuerin's cross-examination. "All of us thought Walker's investigation was very slipshod and his credibility on the witness stand was blown from beginning to end, the juror remembered. "Right after we looked at some of his conflicting testimony, we took the vote and decided to acquit Fontenot. It was not at all what I would have expected of a Ranger."

Nor did the citizens of Brownsville expect the kind of investigation the Rangers conducted of their city officials in 1987. Following a grand jury's determination that there were irregularities in Brownsville City Hall's purchasing procedures, Ranger Rudy Rodriguez undertook a highly visible, leak-plagued, seven-month investigation that led all of Brownsville to believe that a massive scandal was about to be unearthed. Those suspicions hardly abated when Rodriguez's investigation led to 23 indictments of city officials, including Mayor Emilio Hernandez. Yet as one of the attorneys involved in the cases noted, "It was a results-oriented investigation from the start. The Ranger knew what he wanted and wouldn't let the facts get in the way. Indeed, 21 of the indictments were thrown out and another resulted in a not-guilty verdict. The lone conviction, that of Mayor Hernandez, was later reversed after the Ranger's main witness would not confirm in court information he had given Rodriguez. Far from cleaning up a corrupt city hall, the Rangers left Brownsville in a state of confusion and bitterness, with nothing to show for their efforts except a number of damaged reputations, including their own.

So tarnished was the Ranger image that by the beginning of the nineties, it was just as easy to suspect the Rangers of covering up evidence as it was to assume that they were doing their jobs honorably. When David Joost, the Texas Racing Commission's chief financial officer, his wife, and their two children were found shot to death in March 1990, the Rangers promptly took charge of the case-and for the next four years seemingly did nothing. Though the Hays County sheriff's department's ruling had been that Joost had shot his family and then himself, numerous clues pointed to a multiple murder. Joost's brother begged the state to let him know what the evidence in its possession suggested, but the Rangers refused to disclose anything, saying that the investigation was ongoing. Their silence, along with their refusal to pursue a number of angles to the case, led the media (including the news show *20/20*) to speculate that the Rangers might be covering up a contract killing at the behest of powerful racing interests. Individuals involved in the Joost investigation say that this is not the case-that in fact the Rangers have been gathering evidence and are in the final stages of producing a documented finding. But the Rangers' arrogant refusal to respond to earnest questions surrounding a high-profile case virtually guarantees that their conclusion about the Joost murders, whatever it happens to be, will not be accepted on faith.

This past year has seen the Texas Rangers consistently in the news yet somehow incidental to the day's events. The Rangers were called upon to investigate the crime scene of the Branch Davidian compound near Waco; they comported themselves professionally but seemed all too willing to accept the FBI's word on critical matters of dispute, such as whether or not helicopters from the Bureau of Alcohol, Tobacco, and Firearms had opened fire on the Davidians. When a black man named Craig Thomas died last June at the hands of white Corsicana police officers, the Rangers were called in. Yet the "investigation" promised by the Rangers was in fact a slender report that took only a day to produce and exonerated the Corsicana officers. City leaders promptly connected the U.S. Justice Department in hopes of a more penetrating inquiry, swatting aside the Rangers' work like a feeble first draft. Later in the year, the Rangers hired Marrie Garcia and Cheryl Steadman and put the latter to work processing extradition warrants. By the fall of 1993, Ranger Steadman had been assigned her first criminal case, but the media had already lost interest in the women Rangers—maybe in all Rangers. When it was announced this past December that the Rangers would be investigating the matter of an Odessa Permian High School football player's stolen transcripts, no one seemed to be wondering whether the Rangers didn't have something more important to do. Perhaps it was one of those questions that hit too close to home and was better left unasked.

"It used to be we'd have a controversy every two or three years by someone who wanted to do away with us," says Lewis Rigler. "Now there's no noise, and that means we're not doing something right."

The Rangers have seen through their own myths and are confronting their worst fear: that they may become uncontroversial and in fact irrelevant. It is the only threat that could drive a proud lawman like Joaquin Jackson out of his life's work. "The sheriff's department county budgets have gotten bigger than when I first got here," he acknowledges over chicken-fried steak in an Alpine restaurant. "They're not as dependent on us as they used to be. And the city police- hell, they don't need us. Normally I work about two homicides a year, where a Houston Police Department homicide detective works four or five a week."

But Jackson lives upon the changeless West Texas prairie, and on its vistas he sees, through eyes both cold and unabashedly romantic, that a changeless struggle persists: good versus evil. In what remains of the frontier, the Rangers must still roam-if they can. "I see the brotherhood slipping," he says quietly as he chews. "The government won't let us pick our own people. The ones we're recruiting are there strictly to meet federal standards. Politics and law enforcement don't mix. They never did. A lot of us got tired of it. It just got to be too much.

And so Jackson left the Rangers, the better to keep them in his heart. He looks down at a piece of paper that lists the Rangers who retired in 1993. Jackson's name is there. His eyes go down the list. Robert Steele, the Yankee from the New York Police Department who had been worked over by the mob in a failed sting operation and left to die on the Long Island Expressway. Steele survived, relocated his family to San Antonio, then flew back to New York and testified against the mobsters at their trial. A hell of a Ranger for thirteen years . . . George Frasier, a fine investigator, now gone on to be a preacher . . . Bobby Prince and Clayton Smith, the men who had headed the Henry Lee Lucas Task Force. Maybe they got in over their heads a little on that one, but generally speaking, they did excellent work . . . Jack Dean, the captain of Company D for damn near forever. Now about to be a U.S. marshal . . . Joe Bailey Davis, been in Kerrville thirteen years. Hard to imagine anyone else in Kerrville. Or in Alpine, for that matter . . .

"Good men," says the Ranger. "These are all good men."

THE DEATH BEAT

by Christine Wicker

OF ALL THE DIRTY TASKS THAT GO WITH THE DIRTY WORK of chasing a killer, notifying the next of kin is the job that homicide detectives hate most. It's worse than getting up at 3 a.m. on a February night to slog through a field of freezing mud toward a body that needed burying two days ago. Worse than staring into the flat, cold eyes of a teen-ager who bragged about dragging a man through the streets to his death. Worse than visiting every sleazy dive in town until you finally find the one person who can put the murderer away and having that person say as cool as a debutante with a full dance card, "I don't think I want to get involved."

You might think that years of breaking the bad news—sometimes two and three times a month—would toughen a detective until he'd be able to slough off a thing as common as a mother's grief. But it doesn't work that way.

"You never get used to it," says homicide Detective Howard Johnson. "It never gets any easier."

The Dallas officer still remembers one woman who watched them as they walked toward her door. The car was unmarked. They were not in uniform. But she knew. "Just don't tell me," she called out from the door, fear shrilling through her voice like an electric current. "Don't tell me."

So they didn't. But it made no difference.

"I introduced myself," Detective Johnson remembers. "I said, 'You're right.'" Her son was dead.

Homicide detectives offer little in the way of divine comfort. Their manner toward the bereaved can seem rough. "The only way we know is to just straight out and do it," says homicide Detective D.A. Watts.

But as they bring death, cold, clumsy and rough, to the door, they also bring the only earthly solace that remains: a promise of justice. The fact that justice is slippery, chancy and often overturned can't matter. It is all the world has to offer, and, in most cases, homicide detectives are the only ones who can secure it.

Only the promise of justice gives them heart to go on.

The 36 homicide detectives in the Dallas Police Department work on an end of downtown that has become increasingly scuzzy. They pay for their own parking, and they office in an old building so grim that even the potted plants look dispirited. Their base pay is less than that of a patrol officer's.

But dedication to the job is intense. Turnover is low. For one three-year stretch in the late '80s, not one member of the department took a sick day. They solve a lot of cases. Dallas' lock-step parade of killing provides plenty of work.

A preacher is pumping gas. An elderly man is picking up pecans in his back yard. A young woman is driving home from a bookstore. A child is on the playground. And somebody kills them. Somebody who doesn't know them, doesn't know anything about them, has no reason to kill them.

That kind of death takes a toll on everyone in the city. Homicide detectives deal with it every day.

"We never close a murder case," homicide Lt. Ron Waldrop says.

"How could we? How could we tell a relative that we've worked on their case for five months or five years and now we're giving up?"

To be a big-city bloodhound, you need a bit of terrier in you. Being tough isn't as important as being tenacious. You get a little rag of a notion between your teeth, the idea that a certain somebody knows something that will break the case, and you hang on.

It's nothing like TV. There's a lot of paperwork, a lot of legwork, a lot of knocking on doors and talking to people who have nothing to say. Mundane factors such as interdepartmental cooperation can mean the difference between clearing a case or losing a suspect's trail.

"I wish I lived the life a TV star has," says Detective Watts. "I wouldn't want all the shootouts, but other than that I."

Dallas homicide detectives are generally closemouthed. Suspicious by nature and trade, they like asking questions better than answering them.

Ask too many and they begin to shift in their chairs. They balk when asked about certain subjects, wary of revealing secrets that might make getting away with murder easier. But once the detectives begin telling stories, they can talk for hours.

The murder of the people they call innocents sticks with them most: elderly couples killed at home, convenience store clerks executed, children playing in the line of fire. One detective remembers a murder victim who looked a lot like his daughter. Another remembers a 12-year-old girl murdered and left in a gravel pit 17 years ago. "I would like someday for that case to be cleared," she says, sorrow shadowing her face.

Things that bother other people don't bother them. The scene of a killing, for instance, doesn't generally depress detectives. "You have to get away from that pretty fast, or you can't do this job," says Detective Linda Erwin, 17 years in the department and the only female homicide detective until five years ago.

Threats don't bother them either. "You get threatened a lot. They say, 'I'm going to go out and I'm going to find you and kill your family, and this and this and this.' You just say, 'Come on,'" says Detective Virgil Sparks, beckoning an imaginary person forward. "You don't worry about that because if you did, you couldn't do your job."

There is a lot not to like in this job. For one thing, murder has no schedule. The summons to join those standing around a body in the street may come just as grace is being said over a family supper. Or it may come while the house is asleep, in the gray lull before sunrise when the city's earliest workers, yawning and stretching their way into the day, stumble onto the night's bloody remnants.

And it often involves getting close to things that most people don't even want to think about. "There's a lot of personal satisfaction in knowing that you did something not everybody can do, not every police officer can do," says Detective Sparks. Some people can't get down amid the body and the flesh and the gore and the maggots and everything else you have to do to do the job."

What detectives do or don't do at the crime scene can never be undone. Nobody knows that better than Detective Sparks, and nobody works a crime scene harder.

Detective Sparks' grayish-brown hair, parted slightly off-center, gives him a mild look, one that would type him as a middle-level civil servant if he were cast in a British movie. It's a deceiving image.

He wears cowboy boots with his suit and carries Marlboros in his shirt pocket. He has a degree in mechanical engineering and wanted to be a pilot, but law enforcement got him first.

Nicknamed Sparky, he doesn't trust anything that talks.

At any crime scene, most especially a homicide, most everybody you talk to is going to lie to you, even when they don't have a reason to lie to you," he says, "or they will omit telling you something that is vital."

Only the scene does not lie. "It is inanimate," Detective Sparks says. "It has no motives."

He and partner Linda Erwin always split their duties at the scene. She interviews the people; he supervises the gathering of evidence. He has a reputation for being meticulous and skeptical.

The site is measured, photographed, sketched. Scrapings are taken, fibers collected, surfaces dusted for fingerprints. The victim's hands are covered with paper bags before being taken from the scene to preserve whatever might be on them or under the nails.

In the best circumstances, the evidence speaks so loudly that even the murderer feels shouted down - just like in the movies. Several years ago, Sgt. Jerry King had such a case while investigating the rape and murder of an elderly woman.

There was reason to suspect her grandson, but Sgt. King had only one good piece of evidence: the print of an athletic shoe left in the mud near her backyard fence. The teen-ager repeatedly denied knowing anything about his grandmother's murder. But detectives searching his house had turned up a pair of athletic shoes.

Sgt. King pulled out the cast of the footprint and held it next to the tennis shoe so the grandson could see them both. A perfect match. All right," the boy said. "I did it."

One homicide textbook calls the crime scene the only unimpeachable witness." It's all there for anyone who has the wit to see it," says Detective Sparks.

He remembers one case that fell together like a dream. It began when an East Texas man came to Dallas for a night on the town and made some new friends in a topless bar. Before the sun was up, he was dead.

"The victim was found in a muddy parking lot of a city park. Real cold that night, lot of mud. You get out to the crime scene, and you see these (car) tracks going into this muddy parking lot and then you see the body.

There's no mud on the bottom of the tennis shoes of the victim, so you know he wasn't marched out there. He didn't walk out there. You know he was shot at another location and then the car was driven out there and the body thrown out.

We didn't know who this individual was because he'd been robbed. No identification, nothing on him in the file, no fingerprints."

But later, when the victim's parents called from out of town to report him missing, police ran a check. The man's car had been impounded the night before. There was blood in the back seat. You knew this guy was shot in the car. You knew which side of the car he was shot on.

Right after they killed this individual, they took off in the car and wrecked it out. When they wrecked out, the driver hit his head on the windshield," Detective Sparks continues. "We had some evidence on it, hairs, blood."

They climbed out of the car after it went in a ditch. And about a mile, a mile and half away, some patrol officers stopped these two people walking. One didn't have a shoe on. They were dirty, muddy, wet..

The patrol officers didn't know about the murder, but while talking to the men, they noticed that one had a head wound. Shortly afterward, the officers heard about the murder and reported that they'd stopped two men.

Detective Sparks remembers: "We went to talk to them, and they said, 'Oh yeah, we got robbed.' Their story was 'We went to such and such a place. A guy picked us up and hit us on the head with a gun.'"

But the physical evidence spoke differently. "We rapped them out on fingerprints. They'd been in that victim's car. The hair matched." Both were convicted. "The funny thing about it is when it came to trial, I was accused and the D.A., both of us, were accused of putting electronic eavesdropping stuff in these individuals' cells because we had gotten so close on how the sequence of events happened and how the victim was shot."

The first stop after leaving the crime scene is to visit the next of kin. In Dallas, two homicide detectives announce every murder, unexplained death or suicide to relatives. "We always try to do it partners because you don't know what you're going to be into," says Detective Watts, who has worked homicide 12 years.

Telephone calls are never substituted. "It might be 3 or 4 o'clock in the morning," says Detective Johnson. "I come wherever they are. I find them."

The first order of business is to make sure they have the right person. "Do you know so-and-so? Are you the mother of so-and-so?" Some relatives are too stunned to speak. Others turn immediately toward the phone to tell someone else. Some curse and call the officers liars.

"It's anywhere from simply fainting in front of you to wanting to fight you," says Detective Watts. They're mad and hurt, and you're the nearest thing. We've had people actually run out of their homes. You don't want to chase them because that wouldn't look good. So you just sit there in their home until they come back.

"A few, there's nothing you can say to them. Hysterical. We went into one house, and I had to talk to a woman whose son was killed, and she said, 'Something's happened. Who is it?' She got to screaming, and about this time, here comes her husband, and she's screaming and crying. He sees these two guys standing there in his house, and the first thing he says is, 'What did you do to my wife?' I put my hands up."

An added complication is the unsavory possibility that the next of kin could be the perpetrator. Even as they offer comforting words, detectives are watching for a reaction. Time is short. Common wisdom says that a case not solved within the first 48 hours becomes much harder to crack. As soon as possible, they begin asking the family questions. Detective Sparks even prefers to ask a few questions before he breaks the news.

Everyone involved is more likely to tell the truth in those first hours, says Detective Bobby Hammer.

"They'll tell you, 'My son's a drug dealer,' right then. But a month later, the family thinks, 'He's already gone. We can't do anything about it.' They begin to be concerned with preserving whatever reputation their loved one had left."

Detective Hammer says friends follow a similar pattern. "When it's still a tragedy, that's when they're going to tell you. Later, then they've had time to get over it, then they decide that they don't want to get involved because it really doesn't matter anymore. He's dead."

When someone is killed in an average American city of more than a million people, the chances are a little better than 50-50 that a suspect will be charged. But in Dallas, more than three-quarters of homicide cases were cleared in 1993.

Dallas' homicide rate has fallen for three straight years, but it doesn't feel that way - 321 people died violently at the hands of others in 1993. Murder is messier than it used to be. One shot from a Saturday night special was once thought sufficient; now killers use semiautomatics and big guns with bullets that tear gaping holes.

Not so long ago, the victim nearly always knew the killer. It wasn't too hard to track a murderer, and it wasn't too hard to understand why the killing took place. Mom and Pop got into a fight, two guys in a bar got drunk, a drug deal went bad.

Marry the right person, make the right friends, stay out of the wrong places, and you would be safe. The old rules no longer apply.

The level of violence leaves even seasoned detectives mystified. "I think, 'Who would do something like this? What's going through their minds?'" says Detective Johnson. "I couldn't beat someone to death, stab someone to death. Ain't no way I could get so mad that I'd shoot somebody to death. Sometimes people give up their property, give them what they want, and they still shoot them. Break in on old women, all they have to do is just walk in. They don't have to kill them, probably can't even identify them or anything. It seems like the younger people, they have no regard for human life."

In 1984, two teens under the age of 17 were charged with homicide; by 1992, that number had grown to 64. "It's scary," says Detective Watts." The thing that just sends chills up you is that you're talking to some kid who's only 16 years old, he's killed someone. It's like they're talking about the weather. There's no emotion, no remorse. I can't tell you the last suspect that actually cried in front of me. I mean they look at you-no expression, no nothing."

Detective Johnson, a big, quiet, churchgoing man who believes in treating everybody with respect, was in a neighborhood one day talking to some 13- and 14-year-old kids. "They knew I was a police officer investigating a murder, and they cussed me out. They showed me no respect at all. One particular one cussed me out. He wasn't 5 feet tall."

"I'm afraid to say something to a kid. They might just pull out a gun and shoot you. And a lot of people in the neighborhood feel like that. I've seen people locked up in their houses, afraid to go out because these young people are roaming the streets."

These days bargaining for information during the investigation can be tricky. Witnesses often are criminals themselves. "Sometimes they have worse records than the suspect," says Detective Sparks.

That means detectives find themselves cozying up to people they wouldn't ordinarily care much for. "Some people call them informants," says Detective Hammer. "I call them friends. Informants sounds cold to me. These are people who help us, and I think of them as friends."

Other people who know about a murder will refuse to talk because they don't want to get involved. "It's a small percentage of fear and a large percentage of apathy," says Detective Sparks, who sometimes finds such attitudes harder to understand than the murder itself. "I've had citizens tell me, 'I know what happened, but I'm not going to tell you because it didn't happen to me. It didn't happen to somebody I know or love.'"

These conversations, along with every other detail of an investigation, are enough to keep homicide detectives awake at night. They try to leave the job at the office, but that's difficult. In a society as gaga over murder stories as this one is, there's always a movie or a television episode to bring work matters crashing back. Or acquaintances who want to hear all about a killing they've seen on the news.

The stress never lets up. "I don't know what stress is, I've been under it so long," says Detective Hammer, whose high blood pressure disappeared during a long vacation and came back immediately when he resumed work.

"A lot of times you just stay tired," says Detective Watts. "I don't think too many people want to admit there's an emotional factor involved and there's a stress factor. There's time in the middle of the night I've woke up thinking about a case. Something I hadn't done and it was just there. As soon as you get to work, you're hitting the streets with that thought in mind."

"Working murder tends to put life in perspective. A lot of things that bother people, normal citizens, your family, whatever, don't bother you. Somebody's mad at somebody or the car's not working right. Things of this nature."

Detective Watts, married and the father of four, says, "As far as friends, I don't make outside friends that much. Maybe it's the trust factor. Maybe it's that I don't want to be involved with a bunch of 'Have you shot anybody? Have you ever killed?' That sort of thing. I go off a lot of times just to be by myself. I've got a small place near a lake, and I go down there for the weekend by myself, and I just sit there. I don't talk to anybody. Sometimes I just read."

He doesn't read detective novels.

The detectives are reminded every day that murder can happen to anyone, anywhere. It causes Bobby Hammer to warn his two children repeatedly about the dangers of confrontation. He hopes they will hear his words in these moments and walk away rather than risk their lives.

Howard Johnson's children are 22 and 17. "Certain functions I would never let them go to, like dances after a football game. It's too dangerous. You've got kids doing drive-by shootings. They're not aiming at anyone in particular."

"My wife, she would say that I was a mother hen, but I see death all the time. Nobody is immune to this. You could stop and get a newspaper, a cup of coffee, walk out to get in your car. I'm very cautious when I go out. When I go to the grocery store, I'm very cautious. I look at everybody around me."

They sit knee to knee with the suspect in a cubicle the size of a big closet. A small table sits to the side so that it doesn't come between the questioner and the suspect. Interview rooms, they call them, not interrogation rooms. That kind of tough terminology went out of favor along with bright lights shining in a suspect's face. No tape recorders. Just the two of you talking.

The walls are covered with a carpetlike fabric that muffles sound. Until a few months ago, gang graffiti decorated the walls. But a recent remodeling covered it up. Lt. Waldrop says that witnesses would sit in the rooms, reading the graffiti, and by the time the detectives came in, they would be too scared to say anything.

Homicide detectives guard the secrets of their questioning techniques. They don't want suspects to know what's coming. But they will debunk a few myths.

Good cop-bad cop is a rarely used technique. "The bad cop's going to get them mad," says Detective Watts. "Well, why get them mad to begin with?"

D.A. Watts is one of the department's best interviewers, so good he teaches techniques to new detectives. Like other seasoned investigators, he knows how to hold a silence. He listens with his face perfectly still, no expression, no feedback. It's a habit that tempts a nervous person to babble a bit.

When the detective does begin to talk, he's often accommodating. One of the common jokes around here is, if you're talking to an ex-con, you don't talk to him about what he did. You ask, 'What did they say you did?'"

Most killers grew up on the streets, and they're used to being bullied, so Detective Watts believes in treating people with respect. "You get a lot more results than being forceful or looking down on anybody."

The urge to tell some version of the truth is so strong that a large percentage of people give statements about their involvement in the crime.

"These people have done something that's traumatic in their life, too," says Detective Hammer. "They do something out of rage, or anger, and they usually want to tell somebody about it because they feel like they're going to be caught, but they want to tell it in a light that might make them look a little better."

"Some just see the writing on the wall," says Detective Watts. "The evidence is there. You've got to let them know you've got the evidence. Others, they don't feel good about what they've done. Some, in a few cases, were boastful about it.

"One of the cases I had was a gang deal in Oak Cliff. They beat a guy up and drug him, tied his neck to a pole. One of the biggest problems I had was that all the young kids in the neighborhood were bragging about how they did it. It caused me to waste a lot of my time on a lot of false leads."

A confession is helpful, but detectives rarely take it for the truth. "They're going to omit things they don't want you to hear, maybe because something is real gruesome, or maybe they don't want you to know that they did this particular thing to this person before they killed them or after they killed them," says Detective Sparks. "You don't get a hundred percent truthful confession from anybody, even on a self-defense-type situation because there's something in their mind that they think might get them in worse trouble."

Homicide detectives reconcile themselves to all the vagaries of justice: plea-bargains, light sentences, early parole, convictions overturned on technicalities. And they learn to accept that no matter what they do, some murderers get away with it.

Especially galling are cases in which detectives think they know who the murderer is but don't have enough evidence to file charges. "I have one guy that I see occasionally," says Detective Watts. I'll always ask him how he's doing.

"Luckily, he's not doing well."

Sometimes a case is lost because witnesses don't stand up under questioning or don't show up for the trial. Detectives may hit the streets alongside prosecutors to help round up witnesses before trials. A lot of their time is spent sitting outside courtrooms waiting to testify.

And what looks like a sure bet occasionally turns out to be a matter of the wrong people being charged. "We've had it happen," says Detective Erwin. "But (if you know it) you set it right. No doubt about it."

A well-publicized case tested her convictions 10 years ago. Dallas had 13 unsolved murders that fit the kind of crimes Henry Lee Lucas was confessing to all over Texas. Detective Erwin was sent to talk to Mr. Lucas.

Even in this stony-faced department, Detective Erwin has a reputation for never giving anything away. She likes to describe her manner as businesslike, but she knows others call it brusque. On this occasion, she was even more steely.

"Henry Lee Lucas wasn't going to pull any stuff with me," she says. She kept her files closed, showed him no crime scene photos and watched his every move. "He'd pick up on little things, on a little look. I saw him. A couple of agents were in the room with us, and he'd look from one to the other and try to pick up on little moves and little glances."

She came back convinced that Mr. Lucas was lying. Her bosses wanted to be sure, so Dallas put together a bogus case.

"I carelessly laid it down to see what would happen, and he told me a pretty good story about how he crept into this woman's house. He described what she had on, the color of nightclothes, gown and robe, and how he killed her, and what articles he took from the house. And there wasn't any murder."

She brought a tape of the interview back to her captain; Dallas didn't file any cases on Mr. Lucas. A year or so later, his stories began falling apart in other cities.

Last year, Detective Sparks had his own chance to let a case go forward or halt the proceedings. Two or three days after arresting two men, he realized his source was lying. The men charged were "drug dealers and they steal and they rob, but I couldn't live with myself if I tried to let that slide to a conviction," he says.

He asked the grand jury to drop the charges; the case has not been solved. Part of his motive was fairness to the accused. Another part was personal pride. "You don't want to know that you've been taken for a ride by somebody," he says.

Detective Watts gives yet another reason: The real murderer would get away, and one murder might not be enough. "Murder is just like anything else you do. Once you've done it, you can do it again more easily," he says.

If a case isn't solved quickly, it usually fades from media attention. Public interest shifts. Only the family and friends of the victim still care. Only the murderer will remember. And the detective. There is no statute of limitations on murder.

Detective Johnson once worked for a year on the killing of an elderly couple before he solved the case. "I just kept going out in the community," he says. One day, someone mentioned a woman's name that he'd never heard before. "I think they got tired of me coming around. I went down there, and she told me who did it and what was taken out of the house."

In the last year, the department has concentrated especially hard on old cases. "Things change over the years," says Sgt. King, who is directing the effort. "People get older and feel differently about things. People who were friends aren't friends anymore, and they'll tell things they wouldn't have."

One case from the 1950s and another from the '70s went to trial last year. Both suspects were convicted. Detective Watts is working on the 1991 murder of Keow Gove, who was stabbed to death during her regular early morning walk. Her husband, Ken, is still offering a $10,000 reward for information, and he continues to distribute fliers asking for help.

Many relatives never give up hope. They often phone detectives on the anniversary of the murder. At Thanksgiving and Christmas, detectives take lots of calls from people asking if anything has turned up on unsolved cases.

"We've had them call from 20 years ago," says Detective Watts. Some are regular callers, including one who began referring to him as `my detective.' "I had one old woman, bless her heart. I wasn't able to solve her husband's murder, and she would call me, it started out once a week, then once a month. And, I mean, I'm talking for years."

Unsolved cases never leave the detectives' memories. "I have some I think about daily," says Detective Johnson. Detective Watts often refers to victims as complainants, as though their voices can still be heard demanding justice.

Names of the dead and the stories of how they died stay in the detectives' minds for years. Ami Sanders, abducted in her apartment's parking lot in 1992. Barbara Hoppe, raped and stabbed to death in 1980 by two men who burst into the apartment where she was watching a football game with two male friends. Christopher Lee Bates, shot in the head by the same men. Terrina `Jade' Chivers, stabbed to death inside her home in 1989.

"They're yours," Detective Watts says of all the cases he has worked and all the murderers he still hopes to catch, "and they'll always be on your mind and your memory. You just never get away from them."

Christine Wicker is a staff writer for Dallas Life Magazine.

Unsolved Murders

In 1992, 32 percent of the time, the murder suspect knew the murder victim, and 68 percent of the time the suspect was a stranger (as best police could determine).

Police say homicides of women are sometimes more difficult to solve than other crimes because there may be a sexual motivation, and killers are less likely to tell anyone what they've done. The following are six homicides police need help in solving.

On Nov. 7, 1991, Myra Barrett was found murdered in her antique shop on Miller Avenue, near Henderson Avenue. Ms. Barrett, 44, had been beaten, stabbed and set on fire. Police have no leads in the case. Ms. Barrett's family is offering a large reward for detailed information leading to the arrest of a suspect.

On Dec. 28, 1992, Natalie Fontenot was found strangled in the trunk of her 1982 Ford Mustang, which had been abandoned in a grocery store parking lot on Skillman. On Nov. 20, the Paul Quinn College freshman checked into Room 227 of the Deluxe Inn in Garland with an unidentified person. At 5 a.m. the next day, she made a call from a pay phone at the motel, according to phone records. That is the last detail known about her life. Police would like to question the person who was with her at the hotel.

On Dec. 31, 1993, shortly after noon, Bessie M. Jackson was found stabbed to death in a garage behind a vacant house on 10th Street in Oak Cliff. She had left her home about 9:30 the night before to go to her job at Presbyterian Nursing Home on Ann Arbor. The 62-year-old woman is believed to have gotten off a bus at Jefferson and Ewing Avenue and begun walking toward a bus stop on Marsalis Avenue. Robbery appears to have been a motive.

Twenty-year-old Christina Marie Gill was last seen leaving On the Rocks, a Deep Ellum club, at about 2 a.m. on May 4, 1990. Her 1989 black Ford Mustang was found later that day, abandoned at an apartment complex in the 8600 block of Park Lane. Seven months later, her remains were found in the Trinity River bottoms.

A neighbor called police on Aug. 13, 1993, at 11:57 p.m. after noticing that Anne Hammons' outside water had been running for several hours. Police found Ms. Hammons, 87, slumped onto the bed, strangled. Apparently, a burglar entered by a side door of the house on Miles Street in the Love Field area and killed Ms. Hammons. Schepps Dairy has posted a $5,000 reward.

On the morning of July 25, 1991, Keow Gove was killed as she took her regular morning walk around Spruce High School in Pleasant Grove. The 54-year-old woman was stabbed five times in the chest and suffered a 4-inch cut to her face. Mrs. Gove's husband, Ken, is offering a $10,000 reward for information leading to the indictment of a suspect or suspects.

1. The workday of Dallas police detectives is nothing like that of TV cops - it includes lots of tedious clue sifting and plenty of paperwork. Detectives R.D. Carney (left) and Julia Tafalla and Sgt. B.R. Little study photographs of a crime scene, while Detective Maria Espinoza (seated) translates a document written in Spanish.

2. Detective Virgil Sparks, nicknamed "Sparky," spends two to six hours on the phone each day while working a case. Securing information sometimes can be tricky, he says, especially because witnesses may "have worse records than the suspects."

3. In one of the last killings of 1993, a 62-year-old woman was found dead in an Oak Cliff garage. Detectives say that the pathlike area inside the building suggested that her body had been dragged away from the door to hide it from view.

4. Detective Sparks examines a knife that was found near the Oak Cliff garage where 62-year-old Bessie Jackson's body was found. Two brothers who lived nearby discovered the knife and called police after reading that she had been stabbed. Police later determined that the knife had not been used in the crime.

5. Murder doesn't take a holiday. From left, Detectives Bobby Hammer, Maria Espinoza and Carlton Marshall, uniform Sgt. Edwin Dresser, and homicide Sgt. Roger Martin work a murder scene on Christmas Eve.

6. Sgt. John Boyle of the physical evidence section dusts a victim's car for fingerprints. Details of every crime scene are meticulously recorded through measurements, photographs and sketches.

7. Detective D.A. Watts revisits the spot where Keow Gove of Pleasant Grove was stabbed to death 4 years ago during her regular morning walk. Her husband still brings flowers to the site. Unsolved cases, Detective Watts says, "are always on your mind and your memory. You just never get away from them."

8. (Cover) Homicide detectives have to live with death. There's how they do it. (1-8. DMN: Paula Nelson)

9. Myra Barrett

10. Natalie Fontenot

11. Bessie M. Jackson

12. Christina Marie Gill

13. Anne Hammons

14. Keow Gove

Copyright: Copyright 1994 The Dallas Morning News Company Accession Number: DAL1392106

CRITICAL THOUGHT AND ANALYSIS WORKSHEET

Criminal Investigation

1) Briefly describe the crime and the type of investigation that was conducted.

    a) When and where did it happen?

    b) How was it investigated?

    c) What was good and bad about the investigation?

    d) What would you do to improve the investigation?

2) List at least two ethical issues involved in this investigation.

Prosecution and Judgment

RUSH TO JUSTICE

An East Texas cop, a drug addict, a convict, a novelist and now a policy wonk?
Absolutely, says Kim Wozencraft, whose rallying cry is prison reform.

by Keith Kachtick

ON A COLD FEBRUARY AFTERNOON in 1979, several years before, the success of her autobiographical novel Rush would take her far from her life in Texas as an undercover narcotics cop and eventual drug addict, Kim Wozencraft made a choice that forever changed her life: While making a drug buy from one of the nearly one hundred Tyler-area dealers whom she was trying to send to prison, she decided that she would rather shoot up than risk blowing her cover.

At the time, Wozencraft was in her early twenties. She had recently graduated from Lake Highlands High School in Dallas, where she ran track, played church league softball, and -- at her wildest -- sipped strawberry wine on Saturday nights with her girlfriends. Soon after joining the Tyler Police Department, she started working undercover in local honky-tonks, befriending anyone who might be willing to sell drugs. Often without her partner, and never with any official police backup, she would meet the dealers in cheap motels or dingy apartments and buy anything from a few ounces of pot to several hundred dollars worth of speed or heroin. Unbeknownst to the dealers, the drugs went straight into an evidence locker. But unbeknownst to the police, not all the drugs Wozencraft and her partner bought were turned over. While still a rookie cop, she became addicted to drugs.

In the early pages of *Rush*, Wozencraft describes through her characters the harrowing nature of buying, and for the first time using, hard drugs:

> *I sat next to [my partner] Jim, on a beaten green couch in a dumpy one-bedroom apartment.... Across from us sat Willy Red, dealer in stolen merchandise and drugs.... He was huge and coffee-skinned, with pale red hair shaved close along his scalp. As he spoke, he pulled a nickel-plated .38 from a stack of newspapers on the floor next to his Stratolounger ...*
>
> *"Now you be showing me you ain't the man, " he said, flopping his hand back and forth, shaking the gun first at Jim then at me."*
>
> *Jim reached slowly toward his ankle. Willy Red tightened his grip on the pistol..*
>
> *"Easy, dude, just my works, " Jim said, and pulled a syringe from his sock... He took out his pocketknife and scooped a small amount of powder from the packet on the table, delicately tapping it into the spoon Willy had provided. . . . While he was cooking the dope, I removed my belt and draped it over his thigh.... Jim put the needle in smoothly, expertly, and left the syringe resting on his arm while he loosened the belt from his biceps....*
>
> *"Oh, yeah, " Willy Red said. "Sweet I heaven, here we come.... What about you, Sister, you wanna taste? Huh?"*
>
> *"No man, " Jim mumbled, head nodding gently, eyes half closed. "She don't fix. The lady don' t fix.*
>
> *"Oh, man," Willy Red moaned. "I think she fix or she don't walk out of here.... I be . . . talking bullets in about a half a minute if I she don't wanna get down. Like I said, I don't be knowing you. . . . "*

> *I picked up the syringe ... and copied what I'd, seen Jim do to prepare the shot. I was shaking, trying to control my hands and not let Willy Red see just how scared I really was ... I didn't know how I was going to get that needle through my skin and into my vein, and I didn't know whether or not it would kill me....*
>
> *I sat motionless, waiting, trying to feel it inside me, flowing, and then my body was melting and my eyes where closing....*
>
> *"Yeah," Willy Red falsetto-drawled "Yeah. The bitch caught a rush. Dreamland."*

"Looking back now, I feel a tremendous guilt about having ever been involved with any drug cases," Wozencraft explains over lunch at a Tex-Mex restaurant in Rhinebeck, New York, near the two-hundred-year-old house where she lives and is currently working on her third novel, *Home Sweet Home*. Now 41, Wozencraft has a tomboyish beauty about her, with an easy smile, an athletic figure kept trim by running the hills on her property, and hazel eyes flecked with the various colors of her Welsh, French, Mexican, and Canadian Indian heritage. "I no longer think setting people up is the right thing to do," she says in a warm and pleasant voice. "I think it not only does amazing damage to the individual, who has probably got a drug problem in the first place, but it has completely corrupted law enforcement and the whole criminal justice system."

Today Wozencraft and her husband, writer Richard Stratton (whom she met several years ago at a prison-writing awards ceremony), take care of their two small sons, Maxwell and Dashiell, while struggling to put out the controversial *Prison Life*, a two-year-old glossy bimonthly magazine for what she calls "the captive audience." Many of the articles are penned by prisoners and ex-cons and contain everything from legal and medical advice to work-out routines and in-cell recipes. In recent issues, Wozencraft and Stratton -- the magazine's editor-at-large and editor in chief, respectively -- have published features on celebrated Philadelphia death row inmate Mumia Abu-Jamal. Texas prison gangs, and the flurry of three-strikes-you're-out crime bills, as well as poignant examples of short fiction, poetry, and artwork produced behind bars.

And now, for the first time, they're getting to expand the franchise. On January 8, HBO will air *HBO and 'Prison Life Present: Prisoners of the War on Drugs*, an hour-long documentary produced and directed by Emmy nominee Marc Levin. Wozencraft was an adviser for the project and believes that its look at the dark reality of life in American prisons is unprecedented: "There's footage I can't believe they let him out the front gate with." The film has sobering images of inmates using and selling readily available drugs, including cocaine and heroin (one prison dealer claims to make $3,500 a week providing smuggled drugs to his fellow inmates), and interviews with first-time, nonviolent female drug offenders serving what could be life sentences.

Wozencraft knows firsthand the complicated connection between drugs and jail. Eventually in 1979 there came a "bustout" -- a night when the Tyler police swooped in and arrested the drug dealers Wozencraft and her partner had accumulated evidence against. "It was frightening knowing that I would now have to confront many of them in court," she recalls. "To know that that many people who, on sonic level, had come to trust me now hated me and wanted to destroy me."

In fact, Wozencraft learned from the Texas Department of Public Safety that someone -- presumably one of the several dozen defendants facing long prison sentences -- had hired a hit man to kill her. "That just about sent me over the edge," she says. "I was just waiting to die. Everyday I was thinking. "When are they going to get me?"' Holed up in a trailer on the outskirts of town during the trials, Wozencraft and her partner finally had their worst fears come true: One night, under the cover of darkness, the barrel of a shotgun poked through an open window and tapped her on the forehead while she lay asleep on a couch. She grabbed the gun barrel as the unseen assailant blasted her partner's leg and arm, almost killing him.

Soon after the shooting, Wozencraft quit the police department, got free and clear of her drug addiction, and moved to San Antonio, where she joined the Air Force. "I was going to study Russian at the Defense Language Institute and learn how to translate Russian broadcasts," She smiles and sighs. "But the day I got out of basic training, there was a little news blip on the radio about the FBI looking into our undercover investigations back in Tyler, and I knew right then that this was it, that I wasn't going anywhere.

Word had spread that Wozencraft and her partner had been pressured by their superiors to plant evidence on certain defendants and that while undercover they had used illegal drugs. "I had gotten on the stand in several trials and of course the defense attorney always asked if I smoked marijuana with his client or did cocaine with his client, and I would say no. Initially I stayed with the story when the FBI agents came to talk to me. I kept up the blue wall of silence -- that we never used drugs, that we never set anyone up. But eventually I decided to tell the truth, to deal with it, and then maybe start over. I certainly had hopes of probation, but I understood that most likely I would go to jail. I knew that if I went to trial, I could have lied and the jury would probably have believed me, because they chose to -- no one wanted to believe that the local police in a town of eighty thousand are corrupted by drugs. But I'm glad that I made the decision to come clean. I would do it again."

In 1981, after her admission to prosecutors. Wozencraft was convicted of perjury and civil rights violations and sentenced to eighteen months at the federal prison in Lexington, Kentucky. (Her partner was sentenced to three years. The Tyler chief of police went to trial, testified that he knew nothing about the illegal activities, and was promptly acquitted. "I was terrified," Wozencraft says. "The prison had a capacity of eight hundred and there were thirteen hundred of us. They had started to double-bunk. The noise level at this place was just astonishing. Initially I told the other inmates that I was in for cocaine -- here I was pretending I hadn't been a cop, working undercover again. But eventually I was honest about what I had been on the outside, and to my surprise, everyone was great about it. They were interested in it. They said, 'My brother-in-law was a cop, my cousin was a cop, I used to date a cop.' It's a cliché, but it became clear that the line between criminals and cops is thin. They function in the same world."

Wozencraft describes the three-hundred-acre prison as a small town where the inmates did all the labor. Wearing her fatigue pants, T-shirt, and steel-toed boots, she spent her days riding around the warden's vegetable garden on a 1940 Ford tractor; she spent her nights in her cell reading, writing in her journal, and sharing stories with the other inmates. Oddly enough, she says her time in prison was good for her. "It was one of the best things ever to happen to me. I had grown up thinking, naively, that this is America, the land of the free, being in prison was the first time in my life that I truly understood the value of intellectual freedom."

After her release in 1983, Wozencraft spent time in a halfway house in Dallas and then moved to New York, where she fleshed out her prison journals in hopes of becoming a writer. She enrolled at Columbia University, earned a bachelor's degree in literature and writing in 1986, and was accepted into the school's master of fine arts program. "I wrote a six-hundred-page thesis, a novel," she says. "Robert Towers, the director of the program at the time, suggested that I get rid of the first three hundred pages, which I did. I rewrote the second half, which became *Rush*, submitted it to an agent, and within a few weeks got a $30,000 advance, which was an astonishing figure for me. I thought, 'You mean I can now stay home and write?'" *Rush* quickly became a best-seller and earned Wozencraft critical praise from around the country. The *New York Daily News* called it "a great book [that] ... can be read as both an immorality tale and a classic of street lit." The *Houston Chronicle* said the novel was "intensely written, [with] ... the wallop of a shotgun blast."

In 1991 a movie version of *Rush* hit theaters, with a screenplay by Pete Dexter, a soundtrack by Eric Clapton, and terrific performances by Jennifer Jason Leigh, Jason Patric, and Gregg Allman as a drug-dealing nightclub operator. "I was pregnant when I saw the movie in a theater for the first time," Wozencraft says. "I was scared that I would go into labor just from the visual impact of the stuff, but I loved the flavor of it. The film captured the total sense of menace of the East Texas drug world." Two years later she published her second novel, *Notes From the Country Club*, a gritty look at life in the psychiatric ward of the Fort Worth Federal Corrections Institute. At its heart, the book is about domestic violence and the difficulty many women -- even someone like the protagonist, who is a well-educated public relations executive -- have in leaving abusive mates.

In 1994 the founder of *Prison Life* invited Wozencraft and her husband to contribute their editorial skills and much of their personal savings to help keep the foundering magazine in print. "When I got out of prison, my first impulse was to get as far away from that world as possible," Wozencraft concedes. "But I've gradually come back to it. *Prison Life* is not about letting all the criminals free -- it's about making justice more just. People who do horrible crimes need to be locked up, but there's a myth that prisons are filled with violent people. Even in the state joints, the level of violent offenders hovers around fifteen or twenty percent. Much of crime is not violent in nature. These people could do community service, clean up the parks, make restitution to their victims, do something other than be stuck in a cage.

"If it was up to me," she continues, "I would change the way we regulate drugs -- legalize marijuana like alcohol and tobacco, and keep hard drugs under the supervision of a doctor, as is done in England -- which would cut the prison population by half and would help people instead of hurting them. I'm also really opposed to the privatization of prisons. It's slavery. We've locked up more than a million people in this country, and we're doing it so corporations can make money, so politicians can get votes -- it has nothing to do with justice and helping people straighten out their lives."

Wozencraft glances down at the copies of her two novels and the most recent issue of *Prison Life* next to my plate -- accomplishments born directly of her experiences with the criminal justice system. "I mean, I messed up, and I went to prison, and I've tried to come back out and contribute to society. Many prisoners don't get that chance. I believe in justice. But I believe in *restorative* justice."

Freelance writer Keith Kachtick lives in New York.

THE HIGH TIMES OF GERRY GOLDSTEIN

The San Antonio Lawyer Started Out Defending Friends Who Had Been Busted For Smoking Pot. Twenty-Five Years Later, His Clients Are Big-Time Dope Dealers and International Cocaine Kingpins -- And He Believes He's Saving The World

THE ARREST AND EXTRADITION IN JANUARY OF REPUTED MEXICAN drug lord Juan García Abrego created something of a stampede among criminal lawyers. The McAllen office of Abrego's longtime counselor, Roberto "Bobby Joe" Yzaguirre, was overwhelmed by sales pitches from attorneys all over the country forceful or flattering letters and faxes explaining why they and they alone should be hired as part of the defense team. Farther north, in Houston, speculation about who would get the job was rampant. Florida dope lawyers, pumped their Texas colleagues "Is it you?" they wanted to know. One lawyer sparked a blaze of gossip after spying the name "Frank Rubino" on the visitors log at the Harris County jail, where Abrego was incarcerated. ("Wasn't me," the Miami attorney for dictator-drug smuggler Manuel Noriega said.)

Though Abrego could be quite charming and humorous – "You'd feel very comfortable if he was selling you a car," said one acquaintance -- he would not hold much allure for the average person. After all, the 51-year-old car thief turned kingpin was alleged to have presided over the flow of Colombian cocaine through northern Mexico into the U.S., an operation that reaped $20 billion a year, according to estimates by the Drug Enforcement Agency. He was believed to be armed and dangerous -- Abrego's indictment charged him with authorizing "the murders of numerous individuals," which were thought to include everyone from business rivals to nosy journalists. There were additional charges of money laundering, drug smuggling, and attempted bribery. There were dark hints of political assassinations, of corruption within the now tainted administration of former president Carlos Salinas de Gortari. There was the dubious distinction, in 1995, of a spot on the FBI's Ten Most Wanted list. Innocent until proven guilty, okay, but either way, Juan García Abrego looked at best like a pretty bad guy.

Unless, of course, you were a criminal lawyer: then you knew that everyone was entitled to the best defense possible, that if society cannot treat the worst of us with fairness, then what of the rest of us? Maybe the extradition wasn't legit. Maybe the investigation was fishy -- the DEA and the FBI were rumored to have cut deals with more than seventy felons to get their man. There were lots of maybes, except, of course, for one: The Abrego case was the legal equivalent of a gusher. Along with a fee that could hit seven figures, it offered lots of media coverage that doubled as free advertising -- in other words, big money up front and down the road in the form of future clients. Juan García Abrego might get life without parole, but the lawyer who represented him couldn't lose.

Roberto Yzaguirre knew this as well as anyone, of course, but as the only lawyer actually hired by Abrego, he had other concerns. Having represented clients facing drug-related charges in the Valley for more than twenty years, he knew that alone he lacked the resources to go against the federal government in a case of this magnitude. And as a man whose courtliness belied his shrewdness, he had known whom he wanted as partners from the beginning. Tony Canales, a criminal lawyer from Corpus, was an obvious choice: The former U.S. attorney was an old friend who spoke Spanish and knew the ways of the federal government, particularly the federal government in South Texas, better than just about anyone. But Yzaguirre, needed someone else to complete his team, someone who was not just a great trial lawyer and a great drug lawyer but a great book lawyer, someone with the intellect to, at a moment's notice, tip the vagaries of the Constitution in his client's favor. Someone who, if need be, could work out the negotiations should Abrego decide to cooperate with the government, testifying against an even bigger fish like, say. Salinas himself. Someone who had no problem representing the worst of us and, in fact, saw that as a matter of conscience. When you came right down to it, there really was just one man for the job.

"Goldstein!"
"GOLDstein!!"
"GOLDSTEIN!!!"

THE ATTORNEY'S GATHERED IN MIAMI'S Fountainebleau hotel for the 1996 midwinter meeting of the National Association of Criminal Defense Lawyers make way for Gerald Goldstein like supplicants in a temple. He has flown in from his San Antonio home this morning and will fly out shortly after his speech. Whipping a cart of visual aids through the hotel's gilded warrens, he has the air of a man unable or unwilling to downshift. Even without his haste, Goldstein would stand out amid these cheerful conventioneers in their sport shirts and jeans. His salt-and-pepper hair is slicked back, taming curls that twenty years ago approximated an Afro long past the age of love beads and bellbottoms, when he first made a name for himself defending conscientious objectors, Goldstein now wears scholarly tortoiseshell glasses, which complement his impeccably crafted sport coat, which is enhanced by a contrasting orange-and-green tie and the crispest white shirt. At 52 he is trimmer than he was at 42, his hawk-like nose and deepening crow's-feet telegraphing wisdom, not age. The enfant terrible has become an éminence grise, simultaneously elite and egalitarian. "Hey brother! Hey, brother! Hey, brother!" he says by way of greeting, having his cake and eating it too.

So it has always been with Gerald Goldstein, a man who has made his reputation championing civil rights and his fortune defending dopers, two activities that frequently and fortuitously overlap. He has never shied away from a controversial case -- in 1974 Goldstein, no fan of government censorship, defended a San Antonio theater manager's right to show *Deep Throat* and, in 1990, rap group *2 Live Crew's* need to be as nasty as they wanted to be, infuriated by overzealous prosecutors, in 1980 he represented one of Texas House Speaker Billy Clayton's cronies in the kickback scandal known as Brilab. Even so, it is safe to say that drugs have been Goldstein's life. It was his 1978 appeal that reversed the convictions in what has come to be known as the Piedras Negras Jailbreak Case, in which two Texans stormed the border city's jail and, Rambo style, freed fourteen American inmates charged with drug offenses. Goldstein was an early and influential supporter of the National Organization for the Reform of Marijuana Laws. He is a counselor and loyal friend to superhead Dr. Hunter S. Thompson, wrote an amicus brief on behalf of Noriega, and has defended on drug charges the sons of such prominent men as BeBe Rebozo and assorted San Antonio swells. The majority of newspaper clippings framed on his office walls have to do with his victorious work in the field of drug-related defense work: a 1979 *High Times* article that named him one of the top ten dope defenders in America; a 1983 *San Antonio Express* story headlined POT CONVICTIONS THROWN OUT, POLICE SURVEILLANCE WAS TOO ORWELLIAN; a 1985 *Texas Lawyer* story titled "U.S. Must Return $10 Million to Drug Smuggler"; a 1989 *San Antonio Express-News* story headlined FEDERAL CASE DEAD IN RECORD DRUG DEAL. Let the general public scowl -- "Rich libertarian is druggie mouthpiece" the late, irascible *Express-News* columnist Paul Thompson declared in another clipping on the wall -- Gerald Goldstein loves his work.

And why shouldn't he? It has earned him the profound respect of his colleagues, who elected him president of the Texas Criminal Defense Lawyers Association in 1992 and president of the National Association of Criminal Defense Lawyers in 1994 and 1995. He is a sought-after commentator on CNN, a frequent contributor to op-ed pages, the kind of guy whose number is in the Rolodexes of reporters around the nation. If Americans are ambivalent about drugs – outraged by their destructiveness but bitterly divided over what to do about them -- then Gerry Goldstein is the embodiment of that ambivalence, and has profited mightily from it.

Nowhere is this ambivalence more apparent than here, in Miami, a place revitalized in part by a TV show about two drug-busting cops in silk suits, a place that now pays the price for its drug culture in the form of murdered tourists. The lawyers gathered here seem immune to this irony, absorbed in the investigative databases on display or in swapping war stories ("I got a reversal in my drug case that means my client will only have to serve ten years back to back," says one. Says another: "I just won a two-billion-dollar forfeiture!") They gossip "I hear Abrego's cooperating, so it'll be an easy case for y'all," one lawyer says, baiting Goldstein -- or they make plans for drinks at the Delano, the hot new hotel owned by Ian Schrager, the man who helped make cocaine a glamour drug in the eighties with his club in Manhattan, Studio 54. The drug culture isn't just a culture nowadays but an economy, one that is so pervasive that many Americans regard it as unavoidable.

So, predictably, when it comes time for Goidstein's speech, drugs aren't the problem, the government is. The subject of the seminar is "Motions That Win Cases," and Goldstein's topic is "Bail and Detention Hearings: Making the Best of a Bad Situation," but it's really the Gospel According to Gerry. He flips through case after case on the overhead projector, using an illuminated pointer for emphasis. His voice picks up velocity as he speaks; five minutes into his subject, he is furious. "No, no, said the Queen," he intones, paraphrasing his favorite quote, from *Alice's Adventures in Wonderland*. "First the punishment, then the verdict." To Goldstein, we are seeing a serious threat to liberty as we know it. The evidence: minimum mandatory sentences in drug cases; the Comprehensive Crime Act of 1984, which revamped the federal criminal code to make way for more police officers, more prisons, and more prosecutors while eliminating parole ("The Incomprehensible Crime Act," he calls it, paid informants as witnesses for the prosecution ("What do you think they'd do to you or me if we paid five hundred thousand dollars to a witness?"), Senate Bill 3, which proposes to make it felonious for an attorney to incorrectly cite the law in a criminal case ("They would indict us like a ham f--ing sandwich if they *think* we misspoke"); cops who beat prisoners ("I call this the South Texas Miranda warning ... you have the right to remain silent as long as you can stand the pain"); the national disgrace that is the warehousing of young African American males, one out of three in California either awaiting trial, in prison, or on parole ("They could be sending these f--rs to Harvard for thirty thousand dollars a year!").

In Goldstein's world, every person is always just one lawyer away -- one clever motion, one shrewd objection -- from jackboots kicking in doors at the direction of elected officials. "There really is just *us*," he warns, pronouncing the words as one.

Two hours later Goldstein is still in overdrive. He's back at the airport, heading for home -- San Antonio tonight and then, for the next few days, a frenzied itinerary that includes Houston the next morning, another swing back to Miami, and as soon as possible, a return to Aspen, where Goldstein has a second home and where he indulges his passion for skiing. If he lives in flight, so be it. Life is good, you can have it all. You can have a house in Aspen and your business in San Antonio. You can be a civil liberties hero and a kingpin-defending pariah. You can live on the edge and you can be part of the establishment. You can be a man of ideas and a man of action. You can, you can, you can. Even an airport yogurt dispenser, offering two distinct and traditionally opposing flavors, gets the Goldstein treatment. Faced with the choice of vanilla or chocolate, he opts for a swirl. "I hate giving anything up," he mutters, an admission that speaks to far more than his preference in snacks.

"YOUR MAMA WAS FINE," GOLDSTEIN says, consulting a client on a phone he has answered, with a cuff-shooting flourish, at the reception desk in the lobby of Goldstein, Goldstein, and Hilley. "Your family looked good. I explained to them what I thought was going to happen." It's a jail call, a client trying to decide between copping a plea or risking a trial. "Often," he continues, "we have to choose between difficult and unsatisfactory results. We have to choose between what's bad and what's worse. There was a large quantity of drugs found on those premises. You were charged with possession. It's almost a slam dunk." Goldstein listens for another moment and then takes off his glasses. Today he wears a blue blazer, gray flannel slacks, and a yellow tie, somewhere between canary and lemon. His cowboy boots are buffed to an inky black. "She's your mama," he says patiently. "She's gonna hear what she wants to hear. She's a wonderful mama and she's right there. And it's downhill from here. The court has ruled in our favor and has agreed not to add the gun charge . . ."

So begins a real-world morning for Gerald Goldstein. The office on the top floor of San Antonio's Tower Life Building looks like it could have belonged to a criminal lawyer practicing in the sixties: thirty-year-old paneling, dingy floors, fluorescent lighting hanging from oppressively low ceilings, worn leather chairs, and fraying rugs. Maintaining the decor is to some extent a tribute to Goldstein's 87-year-old father, Eli, who founded the firm, a business-law practice, as a young man. But it also speaks to an essential truth about Gerald Goldstein: He has always been more a creature of time than place, and that time was the civil rights era.

He is a descendant of rabbis and scholars; his great-grandfather played chess with Venustiano Carranza, the great Mexican revolutionary who was elected president in 1914. Goldstein was an only child, pampered, indulged, and inculcated with the liberal politics that were an article of faith in many Jewish homes of the fifties and sixties. "About forty-one years ago his parents were living around the King William area," Maury Maverick, Jr., explains, in a rumbling, grumbling godlike voice that befits his role as the long-standing liberal conscience of San Antonio. "I was at this Hanukkah party. All of a sudden there's this little boy who is about ten years old and is being this absolute pain in the ass. 'Who is that little boy?' I asked Aileen Goldstein. 'I don't know,' she said. 'He must be some kid from the neighborhood.'" It's lunch-time and Goldstein has driven his ancient bronze-colored Mercedes to the Liberty Bar, a social nexus of San Antonio's arts and politics set. Goldstein and Maverick, 75, try to meet for lunch at least once a week -- maintenance on the father-son relationship they've forged over four decades. They make an odd pair: the rumpled, contentious, barely solvent son of a much-beloved congressman and mayor, and his rich, polished protege, but the affection between them is palpable. "Maury represented an attitude that I thought was righteous and wanted to emulate. He radicalized my concept of the practice of law," Goldstein says.

"He's made so goddam much money it's unbelievable," Maverick counters when asked for comment on Goldstein's career. "And he's spent twice as much." Goldstein grins gamely but squirms a little under the ribbing.

"I expect to see Tigar tomorrow," he offers, a reference to an appointment in Denver. He'll be meeting with members of a law firm there who, along with Michael Tigar, a University of Texas law professor, and former federal prosecutor Ronald Woods, are currently representing Terry Nichols, who is accused of murder and conspiracy in the Oklahoma City bombing case. (Such is life now for high-profile guardians of civil liberties. With the country's swing to the right, they have found themselves representing not draft resisters, civil rights marchers, and marijuana puffers, with whom they were politically simpatico, but drug lords and religious or property-rights fanatics like the Branch Davidians or Randy Weaver, whose wife and child were killed in an FBI raid.) Goldstein speaks rhapsodically about the firm Tigar is dealing with in Colorado. "It's all public defenders," he says, "top to bottom."

"Gerry takes every now and then some death-penalty cases and poor-boy cases," Maverick says, ignoring Goldstein as he thoughtfully slathers goat cheese on a piece of bread. "He's better about that than most lawyers. He's got a lot of old-time Jewish radicalism in him."

In the spirit of compromise, the two into storytelling. In the late sixties Goldstein had a bachelor's degree in art from Tulane University and a law degree from the University of Texas, but he lacked ... direction. "His problem was he was bored to death with his father's law practice," Maverick says. "He came to see me and said, 'My father is having me send collection letters to people who can't pay their bills.'" Rather than continue, Goldstein had decided to light out for Europe with his soon-to-be wife, Christine Sayre, a stunning blonde with a British pedigree. (The Goldsteins' 1969 wedding reception -- which could have doubled for a *Hair* movie set -- was a high point hippie era in San Antonio.) Maverick a better idea: The Vietnam War was raging, and he needed help defending conscientious objectors. Goldstein, who had a medical deferment, took to the work instantly, traveling around the country in a Volkswagen bus equipped with a Persian rug and a slobbering St. Bernard. He had found his calling.

Goldstein was a true believer. So fired up that he seemed, at times, in danger of self-immolation, he found that practicing Maverick's kind of law was the perfect outlet for his passions. It satisfied his desire to make a difference ("Law is the primary vehicle for social change," he likes to say) and his craving for the dramatic and the unpredictable ("It's first-rate street theater," he also likes to say). Being anti-war and antigovernment was not just morally justifiable but glamorous then, a seductive combination for an angry but ambitious young man. Over the next decade, Goldstein, often with Maverick's help, took a host of heroic stands against the status quo. He represented black clients against racist forces in East Texas, sued for reforms at the Bexar County jail, and served as the call of last resort in death-penalty cases. If veteran liberals like Maverick were fueled by fail -- his losses were victories, proof of the struggle -- Goldstein, craving accolades, played to win. He was thorough, relentless, creative, and intellectual, which was unusual in a trial attorney; early on he distinguished himself as a good book lawyer, swiftly able to turn the tiniest drop in the vast sea of case law to his advantage. "Once he signed on, he would do whatever he had to do to get the perfect defense, even if he had to pay for it out of his own pocket," says Ed Mallett, a Houston lawyer with whom Goldstein tried many cases. Of course, Goldstein wasn't as strapped for cash as many of his contemporaries because he had the backing of his father's firm. "What a lucky little sucker I was to do all this and not starve to death," Goldstein says.

But after being in practice for just a few short years, Goldstein had found another method of keeping the wolf from the door. The conscientious-objector business was often accompanied by the drug business in those days, smoking marijuana was part of the left-wing political package. It was then a counterculture credo that marijuana was harmless; nevertheless, the government was leveling harsher and harsher penalties for its use. Pot smokers barely out of their teens could find themselves sentenced to life in prison for having an ounce of the drug. To Goldstein and many others defending drug users was the moral thing to do. "In those days we only defended nonviolent criminals -- our friends in law school, for instance," says Tom Pearl, an Austin attorney who tried cases with Goldstein.

But taking drug cases had other advantages. San Antonio was then a small city with few lawyers interested in such work; fewer still who were interested in the intricacies of constitutional law. It didn't take long for word to circulate among local Mr. Bigs that there was a sharp Jewish kid who knew his lawbooks. Goldstein had no problem representing them -- their Fourth Amendment right to be protected from illegal searches deserved to be guarded as much as anyone else's. "How we treat the least of us is how we can ultimately expect to be treated ourselves," he says. "Bottom line, the Bill of Rights was not designed to protect the majority -- it was designed to protect the most offensive and despicable among us." If his skills got the baddest guys off, well, sometimes an ethical, adversarial system worked that way. Lawyers weren't paid to make judgment calls.

In 1970, just two years after his admission to the bar, Goldstein had caught the attention of the National Organization for the Reform of Marijuana Laws (NORML) -- he represented the founder, Keith Stroup, after a drug bust. From NORML came a string of referrals, which further enhanced Goldstein's reputation. At age 34, he made an even bigger name for himself with his work in the Piedras Negras Jailbreak Case. Though the defendants, Sterling Davis, Sr., and William McCoy Hill, became heroes in

Texas for freeing fourteen Americans incarcerated on drug charges under harrowing conditions in a Mexican Jail, the Mexican government was outraged and demanded punishment. Bowing to international pressure, the U.S. government indicted the two men on the grounds that a sawed-off shotgun they had used violated gun-running laws, for which they went to prison. In his appeal, Goldstein argued that the two had unwittingly, as opposed to intentionally, violated U.S. law because neither had known the length at which a sawed-off shotgun was illegal. He won. "You don't often find a case where ignorance of the law can be cited as a defense, but this particular statute requires an individual to have specific intent to violate known legal duty," Goldstein told Playboy. In another big case, he represented Carlos Gerdes, who was believed to be the moneyman for the so-called Cowboy Mafia, in a marijuana-smuggling conspiracy case that involved fifteen other defendants.

He was a star. It had not taken long for Gerry and Christine to abandon their hippie digs, which were near the site of what is now Fiesta San Antonio (old friends recall with fondness the lack of portable water, the barber's chair in the living room, and the frequent explosions from the limestone quarry nearby), and move into a house in the King William Historic District. (Helping them with the restoration was a client, the founder of the local chapter of the Student Non-Violent Coordinating Committee, who faced charges of assaulting a police officer and for smashing a pawnshop window during the Fiesta parade and throwing guns into the crowd. "He thought the revolution had begun," Goldstein cracks). Goldstein could be seen tooling about town in an old Bentley he had taken in lieu of a fee from a drug client in Austin. He liked the finer things in life, 'Sure, but he had stayed true to his beliefs. Why should you suffer for success?'

"Think about this, Maury," Goldstein posits, back in the present, stabbing his tomato and basil salad with a knife and fork. "Think about the federal sentencing system. Minimum mandatories. The only way you can get around 'em is to satisfy a prosecutor ... You get off only if the truth helps the prosecution! Can you imagine?" Something catches Goldstein's eye, a small distraction. He picks up his napkin and tenderly dabs at a spot on Mavericks beleaguered tie. "I don't see how you can call a system fair that metes out justice that way," he says, continuing his dialtribe without missing a beat.

ON A BLUSTERY NIGHT IN ASPEN, Hunter Thompson is late for dinner, but no one seems to mind. "Hunter helps Gerry keep his edge," Christine Goldstein offers, as if this was a critical role, but not one she aspires to. In that way Chris resembles the wives of venerated rock stars. A striking, reed-thin woman with a tumble of blond hair, she is cool and glamorous and has constructed a life that does not require her husband's presence. Hence, Aspen: This sprawling, airy log cabin with its impeccable interiors began as a home away from home, but as Goldstein's passion for skiing grew and his passion for privacy along with it, the vacation home became, essentially, the real one. Aspen might seem a curious choice for a civil rights attorney; it is by Goldstein's own admission "full of healthy white people," so fatuously devoted to the rich that it makes New York's Upper East Side or Beverly Hills look positively proletarian. But the Goldsteins' sense of the place was shaped by an earlier time, when Thompson ran for sheriff and the town was divided between hip, dope-smoking kids and doughy middle-aged, middle-class types.

Goldstein has had the kind of day that would exhaust a normal man, even a normal attorney. Up at six in the morning, he has flown from San Antonio to Denver for various appointments around town and then, in the afternoon, represented a client in a hearing in federal court. The woman, a pretty blonde in her forties, was facing a ten-year mandatory sentence for the delivery of one pound of cocaine; he had represented her before, a decade or so ago, in Texas. Anyone who spends time with Goldstein cannot help but notice how much the drug culture has become his culture. He has rescued friends time and again from jams, some who are now nothing more than walking casualties of a different sort of war, a fact he seems oblivious to.

Thompson could fall into this category. The erstwhile gonzo journalist, whose drug experiences were extensively chronicled in the brilliant *Fear and Loathing in Las Vegas* and *Fear and Loathing on the Campaign Trail*, now has, at 56, the air of a wounded veteran. He's a tall, anxious, bald man with a penetrating but perpetually shifting gaze, someone whose sentences dip, soar, and then trail into the unknown, like an aircraft on a reckless but unavoidable mission. How much of this is the result of decades of substance abuse is impossible to tell, and of no consequence to the Goldsteins, who dote on him like an errant child. "Do I have a claim on this, Gerry?" Thompson asks, displaying a newspaper ad for a new cable TV cartoon character called Duckman, which quotes from Thompson's work.

"Sure you do," Goldstein says.

Because Thompson is not only a friend but also a client, dinner -- Chris's stunning creation of leeks and salmon in a fish-shaped puff pastry, salad, and pasta *puttanesca* -- must wait just a bit longer while Goldstein attends to business. Thompson was arrested for impaired driving last November and, with Goldstein and four other lawyers, is looking forward to his trial. Goldstein has alleged that the police had no probable cause to stop the car, and he shows Thompson how the transcripts of police radio conversations can be read to support his claim. "Okay, okay, Hunter," Goldstein says, excitedly scrolling the text on his computer screen to highlight places where the police seem to be speaking in code to protect themselves. "Now we're getting some fun here."

Only the most privileged could ever dream of converting their DWIs into a Fourth Amendment showdown, but that is one of the pluses of being in Goldstein's orbit. In return, he gets access to the kind of secret social frequency that most people could never get on their dials. He knows which national celebrity has a girlfriend who needs help on her dope charge, which prominent executive had a son who narrowly escaped a grand jury indictment in Florida. Gossip, like fine food or fine wine, should be of the best quality. Someone brings up CBS newsman Ed Bradley, in town for a bit. "He's fighting for his job," Thompson cracks. "You know CBS is a Nazi group, don't you?"

The conversation veers rightward to militia members and the fallout from Oklahoma City. Thompson, something of a gun nut, is not entirely unsympathetic, but Goldstein grows glum. He doesn't see them as the same kind of freedom fighters as his generation of sixties radicals. "I fear it is that politically we were unable to effect change because we expressed a hedonistic Spock-baby philosophy," he says.

As anyone over forty knows, the pacific hedonism of the seventies gave way to the materialistic hedonism of the eighties, and the drug of choice changed to cocaine in all its variants, a drug for the very rich or the very poor, perfect for a society losing its middle. Drug dealing was no longer a casual enterprise; the dealers weren't just college kids with VW buses anymore, but foreigners with guns or ghetto kids with nothing to lose. And as the federal government became more successful at stopping drug smuggling in Florida, the game shifted to Texas. For Goldstein -- who believes the cocaine explosion was a result of the government's destruction of the marijuana industry -- business was never better.

Throughout the eighties, he represented bigger and bigger fish. In 1985 Goldstein forced the federal government to return $10 million in assets to a Sherman drug smuggler, the largest forfeiture in the country at the time. He freed the men arrested in the biggest marijuana seizure in San Antonio history -- $5.7 million worth. He represented Miami businessman Danny Vilarchao (a "mobster," according to columnist Paul Thompson), who was charged with selling DEA agents 4 kilos of cocaine with the promise of 160 more. Florida congressman Richard Kelly hired Goldstein to represent him in the political kickback scandal known as Abscam because of his success in the Cowboy Mafia trial. In every case, Goldstein was as scrupulous about his professional ethics as he had been in the early days, when he felt protective of his father's practice: When a client called and contest to jumping bail, for instance, Goldstein wasted no time in ordering the man to turn himself in. "He would use words that he would be proud to hear replayed in a courtroom, because they might be," says colleague Ed Mallett.

Goldstein became known for the kind of legal legerdemain that astonished his colleagues and, as the drug crisis deepened, infuriated the general public. He overturned the conviction of three marijuana growers by proving that the police telescope used by the investigators was too strong (powerful enough to see through partially closed blinds, it violated the defendants' "legitimate expectation of privacy"). In what has come to be known as the Mr. Jake Case, Goldstein won probation for a client arrested while unloading 100,000 pounds of marijuana by proposing that evidence used in a previous drug trial, which produced a hung jury, should be subject to the double-jeopardy standard -- and therefore was inadmissible in a second case. He went after the federal government's drug-courier profile (used to justify searches) by proving that, counter to the objective criteria required by law, officers were using their intuition to stop suspects. "He looked like a dirtbag, but he was traveling first class" is the way Goldstein describes the officers' modus operandi. In all cases, constitutional rights were indisputably protected and, most likely, the guilty went free. "In spite of my lifestyle and having succumbed to greed," Goldstein told a reporter in 1989, "I'm still a child of the sixties. It's fun to go up against that system."

But as the eighties progressed, Goldstein looked less like a counter-cultural icon -- an advocate for the down trodden -- and more like a prosperous member of the establishment. He began to take time off. He took up sailing, buying a forty-foot boat from Racehorse Haynes called the *Esprit Libre,* and raced national competitions. Tired of sailing, he took up skiing and traveled as far as Argentina in search of perfection on the slopes. He spent money faster than even he could make it -- whether he was chartering planes or finding just the right white shirt. "Anything he does, he does with a vengeance," says one friend, "whether it's skiing, defending somebody, or anything else." "Anything else," according to friends and associates, was Goldstein's passion for drugs. Those who know him well say that he used drugs on more than a casual basis, which became a topic of local gossip. Talk of his own drug use, however, is one of the few subjects that causes the loquacious Goldstein to turn reticent. "I'm a child of the sixties," he says. "Let's just say I probably couldn't pass the security check for a Supreme Court nomination."

THE HEARING AT THE FEDERAL COURTHOUSE in downtown Houston on this February day has not attracted much media attention. In the matter of *United States of America v. Juan Garcia Abrego,* there is only a bit of scheduling to attend to. Present for the government in the windowless, fluorescently lit, high-cellinged room is special prosecution chief Bernie Hobson and the lead prosecutor in this case, Melissa Annis, a thirty-something straight-arrow known for her prosecutorial zeal -- she has devoted almost a decade to bringing Abrego to justice. Across the room sits Roberto Yzaguirre with his team, Tony Canales and Gerald Goldstein. The defense wears good suits and appears confident and amenable; they are middle-aged men, old friends at the peak of their careers, for whom a case like this appears to hold little mystery. Today the parties swiftly agree on a trial date of September 16, adjourn, meet briefly with reporters, and then head for the office or, in the case of the defense, the airport. If you happened by, the proceedings might have resembled any big corporate case, which, of course, it is.

The gossip among Texas criminal defense lawyers has been that Abrego isn't such a big fish -- he's past his prime, they say, nothing more than a sop offered by Mexican president Ernesto Zedillo to Bill Clinton. The real guys remain in the shadows, international investors protected by their money, their anonymity, and most likely their lawyers. The drug business is now worth billions -- $60 billion is grossed annually on the black market; $100 billion is spent fighting it by the government. It is a global enterprise in which so many competing interests are involved that shutting it down seems impossible. For that reason the drug business and the epidemic of crime it has spawned looks, to most people, far, far more dangerous and all-powerful than Goldstein's lifetime adversary, the federal government, which, however misguided, is trying to stop the flow of drugs into homes and communities. To those citizens, the enemy is the people who are perpetuating enterprise that is killing American children, generations of them. Not so, to Goldstein of course. "It's poverty, not drugs, that causes crime," he insists.

Even so, most defenders of constitutional rights know they've come a long way from those suburban kids protesting the war with a toke or two. History has fashioned a test for the prominent attorneys who declare that they represent high-profile but despicable defendants for our sake. Sometime after the Oklahoma City bombing, for instance, the judge in the case, David Russell, heard Gerry Goldstein and the late Abbie Hoffman's attorney, Gerald Lefcourt, on Charlie Rose's show, talking about the duty of all lawyers to represent unpopular clients. An intermediary for the judge telephoned Goldstein the following morning, looking for representation for Terry Nichols, who, his defenders believe, is a victim of an overzealous criminal investigation by the government. "We had lunch the next day and [Goldstein] was freaked," recalls Lefcourt. "Fortunately, two very good lawyers stepped up to the plate." Representing a white male who allegedly murdered 168 innocent men, women, and children to prove his hatred for the federal government did not stoke the flames of Goldstein's sense of righteousness. At least the drug lords' victims, though they may be numerous, are, anonymous; Oklahoma City was not his kind of war.

Goldstein is slowing down, anyway. His firm continues to do pro bono work, and he still devotes time to causes. Citing civil rights violations, he is currently fighting the Internal Revenue Service's attempt to force lawyers to report the names of clients who paid fees of more than $10,000 in cash. But he longs for the slopes of Aspen in the way he once longed for the courtroom; he loves the feel of his body smashing through the racing flags at breakneck speed, of winning in that way.

Leaving the Houston hearing, Goldstein is undecided about his plans. Should he go to Cumberland Island, a speck of sand off the coast of Georgia, where his wife and son are visiting her family? Or should he just head home to Aspen, where he could get in a few more days of skiing? Faced with such a dilemma, he telephones his San Antonio office to consult his secretary, Diane Doege, a wise and witty woman who has worked for him for more than twenty years. "It's not as if you've never been skiing before," she tells him, and Goldstein nods, agreeing to go to Cumberland Island. "It's the right thing to do, isn't it?" he asks her. "Isn't it?"

DOES DaROYCE MOSLEY DESERVE TO DIE?

Raised in Kilgore's poorest black neighborhood, he was an honors graduate with a bright future -- until he was convicted of killing four whites. But the case is still hotly disputed, and the question remains...
by Skip Hollandsworth

IN THE EAST TEXAS TOWN OF KILGORE, KATIE'S was just another beer joint perched next to Texas Highway 135. Inside, there were a few tables the size of hubcaps, a small pool table, a jukebox, and some Dallas Cowboys posters tacked to the plywood walls. The customers were white, working-class people. Most of the men who stopped in for the $1 bottled beer were oil-field workers still trying to make a living from the dregs of what was once the largest oil field in the world. They arrived in unwashed pickup trucks. They wore shirts that had their first names sewn above their pockets. Their wives or girlfriends often came along sitting at separate tables, smoking cigarettes and calling each other "honey." The owner, a rusty-voiced woman named Katie Moore who had been operating East Texas honky-tonks for more than thirty years, liked to call Katie's a "quiet little family place." But on the night of July 21, 1994, Sandra Cash, the 32-year-old barmaid who was paid $30 a night to serve the beer crawled to the phone and made a 911 call. "Please help me," she rasped. "I am choking."

A young Kilgore police officer, one of the first to arrive at Katie's, was so horrified by what he saw that for months afterward he needed counseling. Behind the bar, Cash was barely alive, her spinal cord severed by as many as six shots that had been fired into her. The four customers who had been at Katie's that night were crumpled on the floor, each one shot in the head. Patricia Colter, a 54-year-old Wal-Mart employee, and her 44-year-old husband, Duane, who worked at a Kilgore company that built ceramic toilet fixtures, were closest to the front door, face down, blood from their heads seeping into the carpet. Alvin "Buddy" Waller, a 54-year-old oil-well worker, was lying a few feet away with a pool cue in his hand. He had been shot once in the leg, once in the back the head, and once through the left eye. Because of the gunpowder on his face, investigators knew that the killer had stuck the gun right up to Waller's eye and pulled the trigger. Luva Congleton, a 68-year-old retiree, had crawled under the pool table to hide. The killer had walked to the pool table, leaned down, and shot her. The only item missing from Katie's was a gray fishing tackle box that Cash used to keep the bar receipts. It held $308.

Throughout the night and into the next morning, officers and agents arrived from the Federal Bureau of Investigation, the Bureau of Alcohol, Tobacco, and Firearms (ATF); the Texas Rangers, the Department of Public Safety's mobile crime laboratory, two sheriffs departments and the Kilgore Police Department. The Mayor came. The local press showed up too. Describing Patricia Colter in her younger years, a reporter for the *Kilgore News* Herald wrote, "[She] looked like she could have gone to Hollywood and become a movie star." Katie's regulars stood behind the yellow police tape and told anyone who would listen that the killer or killers had to have come from Goat Hill, a poor black neighborhood just down the highway. "Crack city," one called it. "Nigger heaven," said another.

Two days later, the police announced they had found the killer: nineteen-year-old Goat Hill resident DaRoyce Mosley, a former honors student at Kilgore High School, member of the student council, and starter on the basketball team who had gone on to Kilgore College. Tall and smooth-skinned, with a dazzling, broad smile, DaRoyce was one of the few black teenagers whom any Kilgore resident knew by name. "He was just about the first kid to cross the racial lines in Kilgore, which is saying a lot for a town that's still got some Old South in it," said his friend William Linn, a former high school classmate who is white. "I mean, it's no secret that whites and blacks here keep their distance from one another. But DaRoyce made a point of making white friends. He kept saying that he wanted to be successful and that he didn't want to be stuck in his part of town."

DaRoyce's arrest – and the district attorney's decision to seek the death penalty -- was unfathomable to many Kilgore residents. This was a kid, people said over and over, who talked about becoming a doctor or a lawyer. "I'd have called him studious," said former Kilgore mayor Bob Barbee. "'Respectful' is the word I would always use to describe him," added Kathy McMillan, a schoolteacher whose son was one of DaRoyce's closest friends. "He'd come over to spend the night here and he'd always carry on an intelligent conversation with us in this very gentle voice."

But after an all-night interrogation, DaRoyce had signed a confession in which he admitted that he had agreed to accompany his 31-year-old uncle, Ray Don Mosley, on a robbery along with Marcus Smith, a 16-year-old Goat Hill teenager with a juvenile record. DaRoyce said that although he had tried several times that night to back out of the robbery, his uncle Ray Don, one of the most feared criminals in the Goat Hill neighborhood, persuaded him to come inside the bar. "I had never done anything bad before, and I felt like doing something bad," DaRoyce said in the confession. After they walked in, he said, Ray Don shot Sandra Cash. "The people looked at me and it scared me and I shot a lady at a table," DaRoyce said. He then said Ray Don pointed a gun at him and ordered him to kill everyone else or be shot himself.

For the police, the case was open and shut. But plenty of Kilgore's citizens were convinced that the confession was not the truth. DaRoyce's friends insisted that he hated guns: When he had gone along with them on camping trips, he wouldn't hold a gun, let alone shoot one. A psychiatrist and a psychologist who arrived separately to interview DaRoyce said that nothing about his personality fit the profile of a mass murderer. It was also peculiar, they said, that DaRoyce had given a series of different stories during his all-night interrogation before finally saying that he did the killings. "I believe that during the night he confessed, he was under intense pressure, emotionally broken down, his mind almost dissociated from reality," said Louis-Victor Jeanty, an Austin psychiatrist who spoke to DaRoyce for several hours. "He was trying to please a group of angry police officers because that is his nature."

After his arrest, DaRoyce told his attorneys that he had been so scared during his interrogation that he had lied to the police. The real story, he said, was that in a moment of weakness, trying to prove to a belligerent Ray Don that he was not a "punk," he went along on the robbery but ran out the door once Ray Don started shooting. To those who knew the strapping, insolent Ray Don – once described by a lawyer as a walking piece of dynamite" -- it was absurd that the police were apparently believing his confession in which he said that he shot Sandra Cash but then threw down his gun once DaRoyce began shooting everyone else. Did the police really think that Ray Don Mosley, the man who organized the Katie's robbery, deliberately dropped his gun? At least five Goat Hill residents later gave sworn statements that they personally heard Ray Don claim he had murdered everyone at Katie's. (Ray Don would not be interviewed for this article.) Charline Jackson, Ray Don's sister and DaRoyce's mother, said Ray Don came by her house, told her he had committed the killings and then added that he enjoyed looking at the blood coming out of the backs of the white people's heads.

For a death penalty case, in which the truth is supposed to be obvious, there seemed to be as many questions as answers. Indeed the case sent the town into turmoil, forcing its citizens to confront the fine line between guilt and innocence -- and between justice and compassion. As one longtime teacher at the high school would later say, "After DaRoyce arrest, none of us here were ever the same again."

"THIS DOESN'T FEEL RIGHT, DOES IT?" DAROYCE asked me when I first met him in a holding cell at the courthouse just before his trial this past October. He gave me a sympathetic smile, his liquid brown eyes blinking behind his wire-rimmed glasses. "No matter what the district Attorney says, people here know I'm not some monster," he said. "They know this isn't right."

About 155 miles east of Dallas, Kilgore's population of 11,000, is still very much a part of the South, not the Southwest. A Confederate flag flies over the local police department, and Gregg County (where Kilgore is located) is named after a Confederate hero. Because of the town's past -- in the thirties it was a kind of Texas Eden, its land brimming with oil -- some remarkably wealthy, sophisticated residents live there. But the oil patch is also home to a large number of blue-collar workers whose talk would chill even the bravest black man. Sitting one night in Katie's, I listened to some roughnecks discussing a black employee at an oil-drilling operation. One man said to his buddy across the table, "I told that nigger boy, 'Get your ass in the truck or I'll put my pipe wrench around your scrawny nigger neck.'" Goat Hill residents say that when they walk past Katie's, patrons occasionally stand in the doorway and shout, "Get on out of here, niggers!" According to Sandra Cash, Katie makes it clear to her barmaids that black people are not welcome.

Although other black neighborhoods are scattered around Kilgore, which is about 15 percent black, none is as dilapidated as Goat Hill, which is on the northwest edge of town. Many of the frame homes look like their roofs are about to buckle. Concrete blocks prop up the front porches. Few homes have air conditioning units; one has carpet stapled to the outside wall, to provide insulation in the winter. A ditch runs through Goat Hill where water and oil dripping from a leaky pipeline settle for weeks at a time. It is a barren world of unwed pregnant teenage girls, aimless young men who don't finish high school, mothers and grandmothers who, if they work, usually find jobs as domestics for the richer whites, and a few grown men who have not abandoned their families. About the only white people who set foot in Goat Hill are members of a new drug-prevention program called Tom Around Kilgore. On Saturdays the mostly prosperous white citizens march in front of the homes of suspected drug dealers and chant, "Hi-de-hi-dc-hi-de-ho, drug dealers got to go."

Charline Mosley Jackson was only fourteen and unmarried when she gave birth to DaRoyce. She told me that she had been a teenage drug abuser. Charline had four more children. But she spent much of her time on the streets, moving from man to man, often leaving home for a couple of days. DaRoyce is not sure who his father is. When he was eight, he got a job bagging groceries in return for meat and bread to feed his younger brother and sisters. On nights when the electricity in the house was turned off because Charline hadn't paid the bill, DaRoyce built a fire in the bathtub to keep him and the other children warm.

One evening the children heard Charline screaming in the front part of the house. Her brother, Ray Don Mosley, had come by, started an argument, then pulled out a knife and slashed Charline across her breasts. To those who knew Ray Don, the attack was no surprise. "When we were growing up, we all ran the other way if we saw him," said Tracey Arch, a student at Kilgore Junior College and a former Goat Hill resident. "He'd rather hit you than talk to you." Ray Don's parents, Raymond and Francis Mosley, couldn't control him when he was younger. "Ray Don's mind was just different, that's the only way I can explain it," said Francis, who works as a cook at a local nursing home. "He always talked about how he hated white people and wanted to get them." As a teenager, Ray Don turned to small-time crime. By the late eighties his adult rap sheet included aggravated assault, sexual assault, drug possession, attempted burglary, and fraud. In a statement to a private investigator, a Kilgore woman said that after she had accepted Ray Don's offer of a ride home from a party, he drove down a dirt road and held a gun to her head while another man raped her. Another woman, an ex-girlfriend, said in a separate affidavit that Ray Don had gotten angry and held a shotgun to her head. "Oh my, you should have seen him," Francis told me, "jumping on his women and dragging them up and down the yard."

Francis Mosley had made it a point to warn her grandson about Ray Don. She took DaRoyce to see him at the county jail. "This is my own son I'm talking about now." Francis would tell young DaRoyce, "but you be careful of him. He gets so mad his eyes turn blood red."

Through most of his childhood DaRoyce hardly saw Ray Don. When DaRoyce was in elementary school, his mother dumped her children at the home of her uncle and aunt, Joe Rogers and Johnnie Mae Johnson, who lived just outside Kilgore in the community of Fredonia. Charline didn't return to see them for at least a year. While the other children were split up among various relatives, DaRoyce stayed with Joe Rogers and Johnnie Mae. The Johnsons didn't have much money for their own children -- Joe Rogers was a self-employed auto repairman and welder -- but they treated DaRoyce like a son. Most important, they kept him away from Goat Hill. "Before he came to us, he lived in a shack that half the time didn't have water or gas," said Johnnie Mae. "I remember when his mother came back around and told him he could move back in with her in Goat Hill, he said he'd rather stay with us."

It was astonishing, people said, how DaRoyce pushed himself to succeed at school. He made A's and B's, earning the name "bookworm" from his family, most of whom hadn't made it through high school. "I was the only black kid in the honors advanced classes at school," DaRoyce said. "So who else was I supposed to talk to, other than the white guys?" He started to go to white kids' parties. He even went along with one of his white friends to Kilgore's August First Presbyterian Church. DaRoyce was remarkably outgoing: He loved teasing people and being a class clown in high school. But he told me he didn't always like hanging around other black kids or going to their parties because there was usually a fight. "DaRoyce would get upset at the way the tougher black kids would act," said Kathy McMillan, the mother of DaRoyce's friend Aaron, who is white. "One night Aaron and DaRoyce were driving around and stopped to talk to some girls. Then another car of black kids came by to talk. Well, the girls went back to their own car a few minutes later and their purses were gone. Everyone knew who took them -- the black kids. DaRoyce was so upset. He kept saying this was the kind of thing that gave all blacks a bad name."

It had to have been a difficult balancing act for DaRoyce. "The black guys in the neighborhood would say, 'Look at DaRoyce. He's trying to be, better than us. Look at that honky lover, that Uncle Tom,'" DaRoyce told me. "I didn't want to be white. I just wanted to make something of myself." But many white students refused to accept him. Some taunted other whites who were close to DaRoyce. In his senior year in high school, he lost his starting position on the basketball team after he broke his hand in a fight with a white classmate, who had called his buddy Aaron a "nigger lover." "I went over to that guy's house," DaRoyce said, "and I told him I don't disrespect people and I hadn't given him any reason to disrespect me. And I said I didn't appreciate that 'nigger' shit. One thing led to another and we ended up fighting." At another party he attended with Aaron, a fight broke out and DaRoyce got in the middle of it. He suddenly found several white guys surrounding him, including some members of the Kilgore College football team. "Everybody started shouting, 'Let's lynch the nigger,'" said William Linn, who was also there. "DaRoyce got the crap beat out of him. Then, after he left, the cops arrived and one of the white guys hosting the party told them, 'Man, everything was fine until that nigger DaRoyce came around.'" When I asked DaRoyce about his exposure to racism in Kilgore, he shrugged as if it was of little importance to him. "You have your prejudiced people, you *expect* that," he said. His white friends said DaRoyce never seemed especially angry about race relations or felt a need to settle any scores. The polar opposite of his uncle Ray Don, DaRoyce never had a single brush with the law. As the superintendent of schools would later say, "DaRoyce was a happy-go-lucky student -- part of the better class of students who obeyed authority and followed directions."

But after graduation in May 1993, when some of his white friends headed to Austin or San Marcos for college, DaRoyce made a fateful decision. He decided to spend a year at Kilgore College to get some basic courses out of the way and save money to attend the University of Texas at Austin. Because he didn't own a car, he moved back to Goat Hill to live with his grandparents, Francis and Raymond Mosley. "DaRoyce kept saying, 'I'll be joining you, I'll be joining you,'" said Aaron McMillan, a handsome UT pre-med major who dresses in starched shirts, pressed khakis, and Roper boots. "Now all I think about is how different things would be if he had just gotten out of town."

No one can say for certain what happened that year at the Mosleys' rickety three-bedroom house, where a painting of the Lord's Supper hangs on the living room wall and a lucky horseshoe is nailed to the front porch. Ray Don was not around: He was on his way to prison for violating the conditions of a probated sentence he had received for stealing a Pontiac Firebird. DaRoyce spent much of his spare time in Goat Hill hanging out with a teenager named Chris "Caboo" Smith, his teammate on the Kilgore High basketball team until he had been shot by a neighborhood teenager after an argument, leaving him paralyzed. In the afternoon Caboo would wheel himself out to the street and talk to whoever came by. Among the young men who whiled away their time in front of Caboo's house, it was crucial not to be considered soft -- not to cave in when challenged at basketball games in the park or act too sweet for a girl. Some of the homies liked to talk about "jack moves" and "gang moves" -- Goat Hill slang for robberies. "But DaRoyce acted very polite," said Tracey Arch. "My mother was always surprised by the way he addressed her as Mrs. If we were hanging out by Caboo's, and someone's mother drove by, DaRoyce would hide the beer he was drinking to show respect."

One thing, however, did change in DaRoyce's life: His academic work started to suffer. By the end of the 1994 spring semester, his grade point average had plummeted to 1.5 and he was placed on scholastic probation. "I was goofing off," DaRoyce told me, obviously embarrassed. He spent chunks of his days at the student union, playing pool and table tennis and talking to "the honeys." He found himself hanging around Caboo's in the evenings until midnight. By the end of his freshman year he had lost his $2,250 annual grant for student aid, though administrators said he could get it back if he took classes in summer school to improve his GPA. But DaRoyce said he would pay for school himself the next fall and prove what he could accomplish. He never got that chance. In June 1994 Ray Don Mosley returned from state prison to Kilgore and moved into the same cramped house where DaRoyce was living with his brother, sisters, and grandparents.

HE SMOKED CRACK, HE REFUSED TO GET A JOB. He peppered DaRoyce with insults to see if he would fight or cry. He called him "Mr. Kilgore," "punk," and "pussy." He liked to say DaRoyce was "too much," meaning he, acted too white. "He said DaRoyce had too many big ideas," said Francis. "For whatever reason, Ray Don was determined," said DaRoyce's great-aunt Johnnie Mae Johnson, "to bring DaRoyce down to his level. I'll never forget Ray Don saying. 'If I have to go to the Big House again, then I'm going to take someone with me. And whatever I do, it's going to be something big.'"

DaRoyce told me that Ray Don and Marcus Smith, a sixteen-year-old who lived down the street, would often regale one another with stories of burglaries and other crimes they had committed. Inevitably, Ray Don would turn to DaRoyce and say, "Man, you need to do something. You're acting too nice."

"No, man," DaRoyce would reply, "I'm not down for that. It's not my style."

"One time, you punk, it ain't going to hurt you," Ray Don would say.

What outsiders don't understand is that in that poor neighborhood, being called a sissy, a punk, is a terrible blow," said Louis-Victor Jeanty, the psychiatrist who interviewed DaRoyce. "And the man saying this to DaRoyce was Ray Don, this evil legend in the community who had nearly killed DaRoyce's own mother. I'm certain DaRoyce was so scared of Ray Don that there was no question of following him, because if he didn't, something bad would happen to him."

I asked DaRoyce directly why he couldn't walk away from Ray Don. "I guess. You know," he said hesitatingly, "Ray Don was my uncle and I never had done anything with him and I guess I'd do that to get him off my back. If we robbed somebody or stole something, then I could say, 'Yeah, I did it, now get off my back. You can't say I haven't done it before.' So I just thought I'd get it out of the way, get him off my back, so he would leave me alone and quit throwing it up in my face." What doomed DaRoyce, however, was his decision to go along on a robbery of Katie's, a place that made Ray Don seethe. In sworn statements to the police, many Goat Hill residents said they heard Ray Don say that he wanted to either burn Katie's down or shoot the people in there. DaRoyce told me that Ray Don would say, "I want to rob all them prejudiced m—f--s up there at Katie's. Somebody needs to rob them."

DaRoyce insisted to me that neither Ray Don nor Marcus said anything to him about shooting anyone when they planned the robbery. He said he made it clear that he was not going to participate actively in the robbery. "I told them, 'If ya'll grab the money, that's just you doing it. I'll just be there.'"

On the night of July 21, 1994, Ray Don showed up at Caboo's with a .38 semi-automatic pistol he had bought from a fifteen-year-old crack dealer. He showed it to Marcus and DaRoyce. Marcus later told investigators that DaRoyce said to Ray Don, "We're going to chill." But when Ray Don and Marcus began to head off to get a second gun, also a .38 semi-automatic, from a young man who lived behind Caboo's house, DaRoyce suddenly said, "No, I'll get it." Why would DaRoyce, who hated guns, make sure to get one for himself? DaRoyce told me he did it to keep Marcus from getting the gun. "I knew that if both Ray Don and Marcus had guns, they probably would kill somebody, because they would both try to be bad; so I got the gun, because I knew I wouldn't shoot anybody."

Exactly what happened the remainder of that night is hotly disputed. But according to witness statements obtained by the police, this much is known: The trio went back to the Mosley house to put on gloves, bandannas, and ski masks. As they walked to Katie's, a neighborhood acquaintance named Napoleon Wheat drove by in his pickup truck and shouted to Marcus, "What's up, Cuz? Is you trying to rape somebody?" Ray Don then went to the nearby home of Napoleon's brother, Darrell, to see if he could borrow a gun. Ironically, Darrell, who had been drinking throughout the night, had gone into Katie's just a couple of hours earlier and ordered a beer. The barmaid, Sandra Cash, called the police, who came and took Darrell outside and asked him what he was doing there. A few minutes later, Darrell left.

Back at his house, Darrell told Ray Don that he didn't have a gun. Ray Don, DaRoyce, and Marcus then headed toward Katie's. According to one of DaRoyce's statements, he kept "begging off" because he was scared. He said too many people in the neighborhood knew what they were going to do. "And they [Ray Don and Marcus] started cussing me, calling me a damn punk and stuff like that. I said, 'I ain't no punk, I'm just scared.' They were like, 'Naw, naw, we said we was going to do this. We was all in this together.'"

When they got to Katie's, Ray Don, who was in front, told Marcus to bring up the rear so DaRoyce wouldn't run off. A few minutes later, the three of them returned to Darrell Wheat's house. One of the Wheat brothers gave the trio a ride back to Caboo's house, where they divided the $308 taken from the bar. DaRoyce then went home, and Ray Don went off to buy some crack with his money. But like a psychopath who needed to return to the scene of his crime, Ray Don showed up at Katie's at one-thirty in the morning to watch the police coming in and out of the bar. He also came back the next morning to watch the bodies being carried out. Two young Goat Hill women later said that when they gave Ray Don a ride the day after the murders, he proudly told them he had done the shootings because a man at Katie's had once called him a nigger. Three other residents later signed affidavits saying Ray Don told them he had committed the murders.

Meanwhile, DaRoyce spent the day after the slayings buying a used car. His down payment was money he had received in an insurance settlement over a minor car accident. He then picked up some friends -- including Caboo and Marcus -- and drove to the Longview where he bought some new shoes, and a sweat suit. Either out of utter remorselessness or because he was in some state of denial, DaRoyce, was going right along with his life. "I was shocked, so shocked," DaRoyce told me. "I felt bad about what had happened. But what am I supposed to do? Break down and cry? Do you want everybody to know?"

Right off, the police went looking for Darrell Wheat. He told them about DaRoyce, Ray Don, and Marcus. That Friday evening, less than 24 hours after the shootings, the three of them were picked up by the police and interviewed at the Kilgore Police Department. Initially, DaRoyce told FBI agent

James Hersley, who was asked by Kilgore officials to assist on the case, that he spent the evening at Caboo's house and had never gone to Katie's. In another room, Marcus was saying that he had turned and fled before the shooting started. But in a third room, Ray Don was talking. He said DaRoyce had gone into Katie's and told everyone to lie on the floor. Ray Don said that after shooting Sandra Cash twice, "I threw [my] gun down and DaRoyce was shooting the people sitting at the table in the back of the head.... The people at the table were just falling on the floor. I saw a man near the pool table raise up a pool stick that he had. DaRoyce shot the man with the pool stick several time's. DaRoyce also told me later that he had shot a lady up under the pool table."

Around three in the morning, FBI agent Hersley confronted DaRoyce with the new information and told him that he was being arrested for murder. According to Hersley, DaRoyce cried out, "Oh, what have I done. I've ruined my life. I'm going to spend the rest of my life in jail." DaRoyce then said he had shot two people and Marcus had shot two. After more, time passed, Hersley and a Texas Ranger asked DaRoyce if they could tape-record his statement. During that session, DaRoyce changed his story again, saying that he had panicked and that Marcus had pulled the gun from his hand and shot everyone. When Hersley asked DaRoyce why he had earlier said that he and Marcus had each shot two peoples DaRoyce replied that Ray Don and Marcus "had told me that if anybody went down, they were going to say that I shot two people, even though I didn't shoot anybody ... They were going to say that we all had something to do with it."

After sunrise, about seven in the morning, ATF agent Larry Smith asked DaRoyce to show him where he threw the ski mask that he had worn in the robbery. When they got to the scene, Smith saw a glove, which DaRoyce, admitted was his. Smith recalled that he said to DaRoyce, "You know, we can run gunpowder tests of your glove to find out if you were the shooter at Katie's." At that point, said Smith, DaRoyce said he was ready to change his statement and admit that he had shot all four people at Katie's. (DaRoyce heatedly told me that he never made a confession to Smith at the scene.) Instead of taking the new statement from DaRoyce immediately, Smith suggested that everyone get some sleep. Six hours later, DaRoyce said he killed the Katie's customers because Ray Don had pointed a gun to his head. According to witnesses in the room, after the eight-page, single-spaced confession was printed out, DaRoyce read it carefully for at least thirty minutes before signing it. It was 3:50 on a Saturday afternoon, more than sixteen hours after the police had started questioning him.

ALTHOUGH THE CASE LOOKED AIR tight, there were significant problems. The glove and clothes that DaRoyce wore that night showed no trace of blood from the four victims and no trace elements of gunpowder residue. Ballistics and autopsy tests showed that the gun DaRoyce got from the man who lived behind Caboo had been the one used to murder the four customers at Katie's. But a blood spot inside the small box where the gun was kept when the police recovered it matched Ray Don's. Blood matching that of Buddy Waller, one of the victims, was also found all over the side of one of Ray Don's tennis shoes. "Blood spatter" tests showed that Waller's blood had hit Ray Don's shoe, at a high velocity, undoubtedly as a result of the force of a bullet entering Waller's flesh. In other words, Ray Don had to be standing very close to Waller when he was shot. To further complicate matters, Marcus Smith said that when he saw Ray Don and DaRoyce after the shootings, Ray Don was covered with blood, but DaRoyce had no blood on him at all.

Ronald Dodson and Richard Stengel, two longtime firearms and toolmark examiners for the Bexar County Forensic Science Center in San Antonio, were asked by the defense, attorneys to study the Crime scene. They studied the shell casings that had been ejected from the two pistols. By noting the location of each casing on the floor, it was possible to determine where, the, killer or killers were standing when the shots were fired. Dodson and Stengel found that a shell casing lodged under the pool table next to Luva Congleton's body had come not from the gun DaRoyce supposedly used but from Ray Don's gun. If Ray Don had shot his gun only when he first came into the bar, as he said he did, his gun's casings would have flown toward the right corner. Although police investigators suggested that the casing had been kicked by officers and ambulance attendants when they got to the bar, Dodson said it was impossible for someone to have kicked that casing on a carpeted floor all the way across the room and around the other side of Luva Congleton's body.

Trying to understand how Ray Don's blood got inside the gun box, Dodson and Stengel wondered whether Ray Don had used both guns that night. Dodson had been a homicide detective in St. Louis for ten years; before coming to San Antonio. He was a hard-boiled cop who had investigated more than five hundred homicides and written a major paper in college on the importance of the death penalty. He almost never testified for defense attorneys. "But the more I kept looking at the evidence from the crime scene," he told "the more I was convinced that DaRoyce froze at the door and didn't shoot anybody, and Ray Don took the gun from DaRoyce." I asked Dodson about the police department's theory that Ray Don didn't shoot Buddy Waller because the blood spatter was only on the side of Ray Don's shoe, meaning that Ray Don had to be standing on the side of or away from Waller when he was shot. "Oh, that's easy," said Dodson. "I think after Buddy Waller had been shot in the leg and the head, Ray Don stood right over him, his foot at a sideways angle to his face, and he shot him through the eye. You have to ask yourself if DaRoyce Mosley could be capable of doing something that vicious."

When I asked DaRoyce to tell me what really took place that night, he did admit that he had followed Ray Don into the bar. "Ray Don told me to shoot the lady in front of me. I said, 'I'm not going to shoot anybody.' He said, 'Shoot her, goddammit.' I said, 'I'm not going to shoot anybody.' He snatched the gun out of my hand and I turned to run."

"But why didn't you ever go back to the police and tell them that Ray Don had killed those people?"

DaRoyce's body seemed to sag, and it appeared for a moment that he was about to break into tears. "I don't know. I honestly don't know," he said. "I didn't know I could just go back [to the police]. I felt [that since] I had already given several different statements, they would think that this one was also a lie."

AFTER DAROYCE'S ARREST, SOME supportive Kilgore citizens anonymously placed an ad in the Kilgore newspaper announcing the DaRoyce Mosley Benefit Fund. "Friends of DaRoyce Mosley plead for your help to SAVE HIS LIFE," read the ad, which also showed a picture of DaRoyce from his high school yearbook. There were, however, plenty of townspeople convinced that DaRoyce was a cold-blooded killer. Relatives of the Katie's victims began showing up at pretrial hearings wearing black armbands with the word "justice" emblazoned on them in gold letters.

The tension escalated when DaRoyce's great-uncle Joe Rogers Johnson used his entire life savings, $15,000, to hire Austin attorney Gary Bledsoe, the head of the Texas chapter of the National Association for the Advancement of Colored People, to defend DaRoyce. The 43-year-old Bledsoe -- a tall, surprisingly gentle-voiced man who prefers cowboy hats, boots, and bolo ties -- asked Cynthia Orr, a San Antonio defense attorney who specializes in capital punishment cases, to be his partner. (She worked pro bono.) They immediately caused an uproar when they alleged that the police were desperate to convict DaRoyce because they needed to prove they could successfully solve a case. The Kilgore Police Department had been embarrassed by the infamous 1983 Kentucky Fried Chicken murder case, in which five Kilgore citizens had been abducted and were later found dead in an adjoining county. Although the police quickly identified four suspects, they were never brought to trial because of a lack of evidence. "There have been a feeling in the community that maybe its police department isn't up to snuff," Bledsoe told me.

The two attorneys further inflamed the community when they said that the police and prosecutors didn't care about the facts in the case because DaRoyce is black. In one motion to the court asking for a change of venue, Bledsoe and Orr wrote, "The local criminal justice system is still infected with racism, and many members of the community still hold racist beliefs that have not changed since the Civil War." Bledsoe said that during one of his visits to the county jail to see DaRoyce, a jailer unleashed a large German shepherd just to scare him. It was no different, Bledsoe said, than police using German shepherds to attack civil-rights demonstrators in the sixties. Gregg County sheriff Bobby Weaver said the dog was never unleashed. "I am not calling him a liar," Weaver snapped about Bledsoe, "but he is coming close."

In their most damaging attack, Bledsoe and Orr charged that Ray Don had worked out a deal with prosecutors to keep himself off death row. At a pretrial hearing, Ray Don was brought to the witness stand. Although Ray Don invoked the Fifth Amendment to keep from answering most questions, the judge did order him to answer one question Bledsoe posed about his making an agreement with the district attorney to testify against his nephew in exchange for DaRoyce's being tried first. Ray Don said yes. Bledsoe then asked if "high-ranking public officials" had assured him that he would not get the death penalty if he took the stand against DaRoyce. Again, Ray Don invoked the Fifth Amendment, and this time the judge ruled that Ray Don didn't have to answer to avoid self-incrimination. "Something stinks," Ronald Dodson told me. "I've been around too long not to smell a deal."

As the capital murder trial began this past October, the case could be seen either as a small-town version of the O.J. Simpson trial, with defense attorneys blatantly playing the race card, or as a reenactment of *To Kill a Mockingbird*, with callous white officials unfairly prosecuting a black man. Rumors had swept through Kilgore that the Ku Klux Klan was planning to bomb DaRoyce's grandmother's house if DaRoyce was acquitted. There were also rumors that a group of black men had vowed to burn down Katie's if DaRoyce was convicted. Because of the publicity, it had been difficult to find jurors. When 500 county residents were summoned to the courthouse for jury selection, only 207 showed up.

After the jury of eleven whites and one black was finally seated, Gregg County district attorney David Brabham -- a wiry man with a thick East Texas drawl and a forceful speaking style -- told jurors that DaRoyce's confession superseded any of what he called the "technical arguments" of defense attorneys. "DaRoyce went into Katie's Lounge for the thrill of it, for the thrill of doing something devious," Brabham said. DaRoyce, who had turned 21 the day before testimony began, sat quietly at the defense table in a gray jacket, dark pants, and a purplish tie. There were days when he softly waved to some nicely dressed white spectators who sat toward the back: parents and former high school classmates from the wealthier side of town. His grandmother Francis, and his mother, Charline, who had gotten off drugs and started singing in the church choir, whispered "We love you" as he was escorted in and out of the courtroom each day. It was hard for the people in the courtroom not to like him. During a recess, state district judge Alvin Khoury, who was presiding over the trial, gave DaRoyce a chocolate-chip cookie.

One of the trial's most dramatic moments came when Chris "Caboo" Smith was wheeled to the witness stand. In a mumbling voice, he told the jury that on the night of the shootings, DaRoyce came back to his house and said, "We did it." He said DaRoyce told him that he had shot the woman under the pool table. When Caboo was asked if DaRoyce had ever said that Ray Don had threatened or intimidated him, Caboo said no. DaRoyce appeared flabbergasted. Bledsoe tried to show that Caboo was biased because he is Marcus Smith's first cousin. (Marcus earlier had been given only a two-year sentence at a juvenile facility because the juvenile judge concluded that he had left Katie's before the crime was committed.) But Caboo said in court that he was DaRoyce's "best friend." Desperate, Bledsoe tried to paint Caboo as a drug dealer who couldn't be trusted, based upon the fact that Caboo sat out in front of his house while people drove by. Caboo just shook his head and said he didn't deal drugs.

Later, when DaRoyce's final confession was read aloud, jurors could be seen giving angry looks his way. In response, Louis-Victor Jeanty and Gary Mears, a Tyler psychologist who also had seen DaRoyce, testified that they thought the confession was unreliable. They gave various explanations of why DaRoyce might have said those things: He was already guilt-ridden about going along with Ray Don's burglary scheme, he was slightly delusional because he had been kept up throughout the night, or he thought the police would stop badgering him if he just said what he thought they wanted him to say.

The explanations might have been more persuasive if the jurors had heard from DaRoyce himself. But the defense lawyers didn't call him to the stand. (Bledsoe told me he was worried that DaRoyce would be "too susceptible" to Brabham's suggestions.) What's more, when the defense tried to present testimony showing Ray Don to be a murderer, Judge Khoury ruled it inadmissible, proclaiming, "Ray Don Mosley is not the one on trial here."

The law in a death penalty case required prosecutors to prove beyond a reasonable doubt that there was a "probability" DaRoyce would commit future acts of criminal violence which they never did. The lone witness they could find to testify about DaRoyce's allegedly violent personality was a longtime Kilgore High School history teacher named Marita Ann Ater, who had a reputation, one former student later said, as "a busybody meddling type." Ater testified that when she taught DaRoyce in 1992, he was so disruptive that she sent a small stack of disciplinary notes about him to the office. More than just being the class clown, she said, "he craved attention." She said when she once told him that he could do great things some day if he just harnessed his energy, he replied, "I will be famous some day, but it won't be by following your dumb rules."

It seemed preposterous that prosecutors believed DaRoyce should be put to death based on a teacher's assertions that he had acted up in her classroom. The defense presented other teachers who said DaRoyce was not a discipline problem, and the school's vice principal testified that he never received any notes from Ater about DaRoyce. But in their final arguments, prosecutors asked the jurors to imagine DaRoyce standing behind them when they are at a convenience store. "Wouldn't your heart skip a beat?" assistant prosecutor Rebecca Simpson asked. The jurors listened closely and after an afternoon's deliberation, they returned to the courtroom to announce their decision. They had determined that DaRoyce would constitute a constant and violent threat to society and that there were no mitigating circumstances to justify a life sentence in prison. Judge Khoury asked DaRoyce to stand before the bench. "DaRoyce, he said in even tones, "by law, I have no choice but to assess your punishment as death."

For a moment DaRoyce didn't move. Then he looked at Bledsoe, the man who had become his father figure, and mouthed. "What?" Charline rose, then collapsed on the floor, her body convulsing spasmodically. The victims' relatives hugged and wept outside in the hallway, a distraught black woman told a television reporter, "You people know that if it had been a white person who had killed all those people, he wouldn't have gotten the death penalty." But Brabham was unmoved. "DaRoyce was exposed to opportunities," he said "He had the intelligence and the ability to do something with his life, and he chose to go the other way." When I later asked Brabham whether he would also seek the death penalty in Ray Don's case, he paused, then finally said, "The case is still pending, and that's all I can say on the matter."

WEEKS LATER, KILGORE CITIZENS were still talking about the trial. Some were able to explain away the discrepancies in DaRoyce's case by saying that as long as he was involved in something in which innocent people were killed, he should pay. If DaRoyce hadn't gone along, maybe Ray Don would have backed out," one Kilgore resident who sat through the trial told me. But when I talked to Ron Dodson, he shook his head and said, "Goddam, I hate to sound liberal, I really do. But there are too many questions about this case for it to end with the death penalty. This kid participated in a robbery in which four people were killed -- and that should definitely involve a jail term. But putting this kid to death? Oh, man, no."

At the all-black, 122-year-old Kilgore Baptist Church, where Charline sang in the choir, the Reverend Gary Walker preached about Jesus' followers in the New Testament who had been thrown in jail. "The Lord opened the prison doors for them, and he can do it for us." Walker said. Meanwhile, at Katie's, where the dark bloodstains from the killings were still visible on the carpet, I heard a man cheerfully tell a new barmaid. "Don't you worry, honey. As long as I'm sitting here, no niggers going to come through that door alive."

In mid-December I parked outside the red-brick walls of the Texas Department of Criminal Justice's Ellis I Unit, near Huntsville. A prison guard in a watchtower buzzed me through the barbed-wire gates. In the small front yard of the unit ... as a nativity scene; a banner reading "Merry Christmas" had been placed above the front door. In the room where visitors are allowed to talk to death row inmates, DaRoyce came out in handcuffs, followed by a Prison guard. A thick wire screen separated us, but then I leaned forward, I was able to see DaRoyce giving me that same sympathetic smile. "It's unreal," he said. "It's unreal."

He told me that just before his transfer to the Ellis I Unit, he had seen Ray Don in the county jail. He said Ray Don promised to tell the police the truth about the shootings. "But saying and doing are two different things," DaRoyce said. "I have no way of knowing what he'll do, I don't know how to get him to tell the truth."

Eventually, I got to the question I had been wanting to ask, him since the trial. Why did he confess to all the killings after the ATF agent told him there might be gunpowder residue on his glove? DaRoyce shrugged and told me that on the way to Katie's that night, when the three of them were in some woods, he had pulled out the gun and shot it into the air just to see what it felt like. "You got to realize," he said, "that I had the glove on when I shot the gun. And Ray Don had told me that was the gun he had used to kill the people. So I felt like it [the murder rap] was going to come back on me." I stared at him. In their earlier statements, no one -- not Ray Don, not Marcus, not DaRoyce himself -- had said anything about DaRoyce's shooting a gun in the woods. He could tell I was skeptical about this latest story. "But what did you possibly think was the advantage of confessing?" I asked.

"I thought it would be a lot easier on me if I said I was forced to do it, that Ray Don made me do it against my will."

DaRoyce might have been telling the truth. Ballistics experts testified that any gunpowder residue on his glove could have been washed off by the heavy rain that fell in Kilgore shortly after the shootings. And the police had never been able to locate all the bullets in Katie's that supposedly came from his gun that night. Still, it was a difficult story for me to swallow. I doubted that I was ever going to know for sure what DaRoyce had done on that one crazed, panic-stricken night in which he gave in to the diseased culture of Goat Hill and the relentless prodding of his uncle.

A prison official walked by to notify me that my time was up. The official had other work to do: The execution of a young black man who had shot a Dallas police officer was scheduled for that night. The man had been kept in a cell just three cell blocks away from DaRoyce's. "You know I shouldn't be here. You know I shouldn't be here," DaRoyce said to me as I rose. "I'm different than these other guys. They're like Ray Don -- his type of people, people always in trouble."

A guard put the handcuffs on DaRoyce and began to lead him away. But DaRoyce turned and asked, "You aren't going to give up on me, are you?" I didn't know what to say. There was a metallic sound as the prison door closed behind him.

CRIME AND PUNISHMENT IN DALLAS

by Richard L. Fricker

THE SPRING THUNDERSTORMS HAVE PASSED, the Trinity River flood waters have abated, and Dallas has settled in for the 100-degree days of summer. But unlike the torrents of spring, the cloud over the Dallas district attorney's office refuses to dissipate. The storms created by cases involving defendants with names such as Adams, Geter, Gardner and Brown still linger.

For 36 years, until he departed the scene in 1986, the man at the top of the Dallas DA's office was Henry Wade (the "Wade" of *Roe v. Wade*). He was a mighty figure who brooked no dissent and made no apologies. He judged his prosecutors, it is said, on their won-lost records: They were given raises and promotions according to their success in obtaining criminal convictions. According to those who worked under Wade, the DA never questioned their methods in obtaining guilty verdicts.

One of those convicted during Wade's tenure was Randall Dale Adams, the man who in 1977 was found guilty and sentenced to death for the murder of Dallas police officer Robert Wood. Adams became the subject of a 1988 movie, "The Thin Blue Line." In Errol Norris' film, it not only becomes obvious that Adams did not commit the murder, it suggests that prosecutors knew he didn't.

But they went after him anyway, presumably on the ground that it would be easier to get a death sentence against him than against one David Ray Harris. The man who virtually confesses to the murder in the movie, Harris was only 16 at the time, and therefore ineligible for the death penalty.

The Adams case is sensational by any standard, and has gotten national press play even beyond the bounds of the movie. But the case is only one piece of the disturbing mosaic that is the district attorney's office of Dallas County, Texas a place where "law and order" means law and order and where prosecutors don't lose.

Wade's "win at any cost" philosophy survives in the DA's office, and his successor, John Vance, appears to lack the stature and public-relations dexterity to dampen the flames of discontent.

Judges are openly critical of weak cases filed by Van's office. Defense attorneys claim he has squelched his prosecutors' ability to negotiate plea agreements by requiring unreasonably high minimum sentences. Judges and attorneys claim Vance's office is overcharging cases, and overworking the "habitual criminal" provisions of state statutes.

And, at the core of the criticism is the claim by judges, defense attorneys, and former prosecutors alike that the current DA has not abandoned his predecessor's bankrupt philosophy of winning by any available means.

On March 1, 1989, the Texas Court of Criminal Appeals unanimously set aside Adams' conviction and had some sharp words for Vance's office, which made noises about retrying Adams even though some of the prosecution's key witnesses had been caught lying.

Emily Miller, for instance, had testified at Adam's trial that she and her husband were driving past as Wood approached the car from which the fatal shots were fired. She identified Adams in a police lineup as the driver of the stopped car. But, said the Court of Criminal Appeals, Miller pointed to Adams only after a police officer told her that she had picked the wrong man and gave her Adams' number in the lineup.

The court found that the prosecutor, Douglas Mulder, knew this. It also said Mulder failed to turn over to the defense until after Miller's testimony her statement to police that the suspect was either a Mexican or a very light-skinned black man. It concluded that Mulder lied to the trial court about Miller's whereabouts, claiming she was unavailable for cross-examination when he knew she was staying in a Dallas motel.

"Mulder advised the trial court that Miller had already left Dallas for Belleville, Illinois, and that he had gone to her apartment that morning and discovered she had moved," said the Court of Criminal Appeals. "Responding to such assurances, the defense then sought to have [Miller's conflicting description] admitted into evidence as impeachment. Mulder objected to this as being unfair because Miller would not have a chance to explain the differences between the two statements....

"While this was occurring Miller was still in Dallas at the Alamo Plaza Motel. After she completed her testimony she told Mulder that she would be at the Alamo Plaza Motel if he needed her any further. And, significantly, [the trial court concluded] 'Mr. Mulder's statement to the court that Mrs. Miller was en route to Belleville, Illinois, was incorrect.' Further the presence of Miller's motel telephone bill in the State's file, along with Mulder's notations in it, was corroborative of the State's knowledge of Miller's whereabouts."

Armed with the appeals-court reversal, Adams' attorneys, Randy Schaffer and George Preston, went before Criminal District Judge Larry Baraka. Baraka, who all but proclaimed Adams innocent, recommended that the Texas Department of Corrections grant parole as quickly as possible. The TDC declined. Adams went back to court with a bond request. Assistant District Attorney Winfield Scott fought the request vigorously, calling Judge Rusty Duncan, who authored the opinion for the state's highest criminal appeals court, "as liberal as they come."

When Baraka ruled that Adams could go free on his own recognizance, Scott said, "We'd be a fool to try this case before Judge Baraka without a jury'" and went on a forum-shopping spree that ended in Judge Ron Chapman's court. Chapman overruled Baraka and set a cash bond.

Outside Chapman's courtroom, Scott, unhappy that Adams would be allowed to make bond at all, threw another tirade in front of reporters, television cameras, and anyone who would listen.

Scott never seemed to understand that no one believed Adams was guilty. It was never clear if he actually believed Adams was guilty or was just trying to keep faith with the long-held Dallas axiom that if a police officer is killed, someone must be killed in exchange.

Vance who tried to remain neutral, at least publicly, about a trial and conviction that occurred under the Wade administration, finally announced on March 24 all charges against Adams were being dropped on the ground that no reliable witnesses could be found for a new trial.

But Vance's damage control efforts were too little, too late.

Scott, who had been with the office for 17 years, was fired on April 5. Vance cited a lack of harmony and Scott's unwillingness to adapt to new policies as reasons for the departure.

The state's appellate attorneys in the Adams case, Leslie McFarlane and John C. Creuzot, quit the same day. McFarlane had been ordered to file a writ for a new trial on Adams. When the press discovered that Vance actually might want a new trial, Vance ordered her to withdraw the writ and disavowed any knowledge of the writ. McFarlane said she was leaving simply to move on to other things, but she confided to friends that she had lost faith in Vance and his office.

Adams' lawyer Schaffer also blasts Vance. "I sent Vance a letter detailing the circumstances and asking far a pardon," he says. "My pitch to Vance was that this happened in a former administration, you can come out looking like a good guy, there's no need to defend Mulder. He had his chance to take a leadership role; he never gave me the courtesy of a phone call.

"Misconduct permeated the case," Schaffer adds. "There was never an attempt at justice." The Dallas DA's office, he says, "is morally bankrupt, it's an attitude that reached its apex in Dallas. It's the attitude from the top."

More than giving the office a black eye, the Adams affair opened it up to criticism, something unheard of in the Wade administration. Wade maintained strict control over public opinion and subordinates. During his tenure Wade is said to have been able to hand-pick judges and dethrone those who failed to comply with his standards. Those usually receiving his blessing for public office were attorneys who had served in his office. If defense attorneys questioned his methods too closely, their court appointments dried up.

Vance took office in 1987 and initially received good reviews. Three months into his term the president of the Dallas Criminal Bar Association, Bradley Lollar, told the *Dallas Times Herald* that his bar was pleased with the Vance approach.

Almost a year to the day later, however, Lollar was at Vance's heels, saying the office was trying to chill "legitimate criticism" of newly enacted policies.

The criticism stemmed from a Vance-ordered policy that an accused person with two prior prison terms would be declared a habitual criminal and, if convicted, given a minimum of 25 years in prison, regardless of the offense or the time span between offenses.

When defense attorney Balon Bradley publicly called the rule "stupid," Vance and First Assistant Norman Kinne instructed prosecutors to bring all of Bradley's cases to them for review. Lollar and the defense bar sprang to Bradley's aid, but the rule remains in effect.

Bradley refuses to back down, despite the DA's pressure. "I don't believe he [Vance] ever actually reviewed any of my cases," he says. "My chief criticism is, why waste time and energy and space to prosecute nickel-and-dime people? Why fill up the pen with petty thieves when there are people committing aggravated robbery and dealing dope?"

Judge Baraka agrees, citing a recent case in which the prosecutor attempted to "habitualize" a man for steeling two cartons of cigarettes. "We [the bench] are not going to participate in the stupidity," he says. "Each case is different and the policy is making a hard job even harder." The criticism from Baraka and Lollar is especially stinging as both men worked as prosecutors under Wade.

The director of the Public Defender's office, Carl Hays, cites a case in which a "street person" attempted to take a pair of sunglasses from a car. The district attorney sought a life sentence for the man.

Other attorneys have similar stories, but the overriding complaint is that the policy has jammed the system. The inflexibility in plea agreements and Texas' overcrowded prisons combine to leave defendants with little choice but to opt for trial.

Currently the Texas prison system grants one-year reductions in sentence for every month served awaiting trial. As a result, defendants are willing to wait for trial because even if they are convicted, each month spent awaiting trial translates to credit for a year in prison. Jailed defendants today wait about five months before going to trial. Lollar expects the gap to widen to as much as seven months in the near future if the current trend continues.

Vance concedes there may be flaws in the "habitual offender" rule, but he defends the policy itself. "The criminal element does not fear the criminal justice system," he says "I don't feel you can rehabilitate one in 100 adults."

A greater source of public opprobrium has been the "win at any cost" philosophy that Wade bequeathed to the office.

The Adams case swept through the media just as the ripples from the Lenell Geter case were beginning to settle. Geter, a black electronics engineer at E-Systems, a defense contractor in Greenville, about 60 miles northeast of Dallas, was convicted of an armed robbery in the Dallas suburb of Balch Springs in

1982. The prosecution relied on testimony from a Greenville police officer and a photo identification by a victim, and ignored testimony from Geter's coworkers at E-Systems that he was at work the entire time the robbery was taking place.

Geter was convicted primarily on the photo identification and statements from the Greenville police officer that Geter and other black engineers hired by E-Systems were known as "bad characters" in Orangeburg, S.C., where Geter attended South Carolina State. The officer claimed to have talked with a police officer in Orangeburg, but the South Carolina officer denied having such a conversation and said that Geter and his co-workers were unknown to his department.

Outraged at Geter's conviction, his fellow workers launched a public campaign to win his release. Geter came to national attention following a CBS-TV "60 Minutes" segment that established the guilt of another man and the likelihood that prosecutors knew Geter was innocent. Geter was released in 1984. Then-District Attorney Wade was asked if the state owed Geter an apology. Wade said he saw no reason to apologize for any actions taken by his office.

These bungled prosecutions have given rise to the perception that the Dallas district attorney's office will —as the Court of Criminal Appeals observed in Adams' case—use any means to obtain a conviction.

"In the old days it was at any cost, that was always policy and the individual prosecutor dealt with it in his own way," says Lollar. "The word on the street was that you didn't want to be the prosecutor that followed Henry Wade. Anyone who followed would have to un-teach that policy of 36 years."

Baraka is harsher. "Getting a conviction suffers no consequences, no matter how it's done," he says. "Conviction is the main line rather than truth and justice." The investigation of cases, he says, "is done toward conviction, not in seeking truth."

The state's problems in this area may not be over.

Keith Jasmin is appellate attorney for Billy Conn Gardner, sentenced to death in 1983 for the slaying of a school cafeteria worker during an armed robbery. Gardner's appeals in state court have been exhausted and are now in federal court.

Jagmin suggests that the state has gone overboard in its efforts to prevent Gardner from obtaining a new trial. He points to inconsistencies in statements by prosecutor Gerald Banks.

At the time of Gardner's trial, Banks told the court the state was not in possession of a confession. During a pretrial hearing, prosecutor Banks, in response to a question from the court, said, "There's no written confession of the defendant. There's no oral confession of the defendant, whether recorded or not."

But at a hearing on a motion for a new trial on Dec. 12, 1988, Banks testified there was a confession he had planned to use if Gardner had testified.

Joyce Ann Brown was convicted of murder in the 1980 death of a fur store operator in a robbery. Her attorney, former prosecutor Kerry FitzGerald, and private investigator Jun McCloskey contend she is innocent and that the DA's office and the police used faulty evidence to convict her. McCloskey claims that the state's key witness testified in exchange for favors from the prosecution. The person who actually committed the crime, McCloskey says, is in a Colorado prison. And he claims to have evidence that the district attorney's office ignored because it would have aided in Brown's acquittal.

McCloskey notes that the victim's wife identified Brown from a photo shown her just five minutes after being told her husband had died. The state's prime witness, Martha Jean Bruce, previously had served a jail sentence for filing a false police report. Following her testimony against Brown, Bruce was released from prison on a felony charge which prosecutor Norman Kinne said the state had discovered she did not commit—

even though she had entered a guilty plea. The witness later recanted her testimony against Brown to investigators, and then recanted her recantation. Prosecutor Kinne has denied knowledge of Bruce's prior conviction for perjury five months before she testified against Brown.

Brown was convicted of being one of two women who committed the robbery. Her co-defendant, Rene Taylor, pleaded guilty to shooting the store owner and has passed a polygraph test during which she denied knowing Joyce Ann Brown. A second woman, Loran Germany, is a known associate of Taylor's and is serving a sentence in Colorado for another armed robbery.

As with Geter, Brown's co-workers testified that she was at work at the time of the robbery.

Since 1974 the DA's office has not lost a death-penalty case including those of Adams and Gardner. Vance, office expects to seek the death penalty 10 to 14 times this year, double the cases from 1988. As to the possibility of convicting innocent people Vance says, "We're pretty careful.

While capital crimes capture the public's attention, the day-to-day operation of the DA's office is of great concern to defense attorneys and judges. Much of the discretion previously enjoyed by prosecutors in plea agreements has been removed and replaced by absolute minimums. The DA's office also is said to have boosted theft charges to robbery and to have sought indictments in weak cases that previously would have been no-billed by grand juries.

"Wade had a policy in the grand jury to no-bill bad or weak cases so the cases that wound up in court were good cases," says Lollar. "Vance has a problem in that he asks for a true bill with every case that has prima facie [evidence] regardless of problems. Now we're getting a bunch of weak cases—it raises my acquittal rate and lowers their convictions.

But Dallas juries are considered extremely conservative and, according to Lollar, "will convict on weak cases." The Adams case is important, he says, because "it brings home the point that some of these people really are innocent.'"

Adams' attorney, Schaffer, says that "juries came to trust Henry Wade," referring to what he sees as the prevailing attitude among prosecutors in Dallas: "The juries trust us and give us our way."

Others claim Wade, Vance and the Dallas Police Department have preyed on public fear, promoting the belief that even if defendants did not commit the crimes they were charged with, they had committed some other crime or were likely to commit a crime.

Baraka sees a need for "radical reform" in the district attorney's office. "The office needs a new spirit of dedication and to view itself in the light of the '90s," he says.

"The DA's office is going to have to move out into the community because we are filling prisons with people that need to be in some other program. Most of the people who come before this court are guilty, but which ones? That is the key to justice."

CRITICAL THOUGHT AND ANALYSIS WORKSHEET

Prosecution and Judgment

1) Describe the type of trial and the type of defense or prosecution that was used:

    a) When and where did it happen?

    b) Did the defense and prosecution do an adequate job of using available information?

    c) What was good and bad about the trial?

    d) What would you do to improve the fairness of this situation?

2) List at least two ethical issues involved in this investigation and prosecution. How might these ethical issues have been avoided?

Corrections and Punishment

WHO DETERMINES WHO WILL DIE?
EXECUTION LAWS SHOW A WIDE VARIANCE

by Tamar Lewin

AMONG THE 37 STATES WITH THE DEATH PENALTY, Texas has been the undisputed leader in executions, putting 92 people to death since the U. S. Supreme Court allowed capital punishment to resume in 1976.

But within Texas, the odds of a convicted killer's being put to death depend largely on where the crime took place: of those executed so far, 37 are from the Houston area, where District Attorney Johnny B. Holmes Jr. is an aggressive and vocal proponent of the death penalty.

In Dallas, with a population two-thirds the size of Houston's and a district attorney's office that is more cautious in its approach, only five people have been executed.

The disparity between the state's two largest cities illustrates one of the enduring truths of the nation's return to the death penalty: despite two decades of court decisions attempting to define when capital punishment is constitutional, vast differences persist in how the death penalty operates from state to state -- and even county to county.

And as New York prepares to restore the death penalty, just how it will work remains an open question -- both because significant elements are still undefined and because, in practice, the use of the death penalty depends as much on prosecutors and juries as on the letter of the law.

Prosecutors' enormous discretionary power is nowhere more apparent than in two sensational murder cases now under way: in South Carolina, Susan Smith, who has been charged with drowning her two sons, faces the death penalty, while O. J. Simpson, who is on trial in Los Angeles for stabbing his former wife and a friend of hers to death, does not.

In every state with the death penalty -- and experts say New York will be no exception -- prosecutors seek capital punishment in only a tiny fraction of the cases in which it is allowed.

While there are some predictable patterns in how the death penalty is used, such a low proportion of the nation's murderers are executed that there are no clear-cut predictors of who will be put to death.

"There are 22,000 homicides a year, 18,000 arrests and maybe 300 death sentences, leading to maybe 50 or 60 executions," said Victor Streib, a law professor at Cleveland State University, who is assisting in Ms. Smith's defense. "How do you figure out why lightning strikes one defendant and not another? It's been studied for 20 years, and all I can say is, it's not a rational process."

Still, he and others say, there are certain factors that make it more likely that a particular murderer will get the death penalty.

"A key factor is what kind of attorney you can afford, so the death penalty is most commonly imposed on poor people," Streib said. "That often correlates with people who are poorly educated, or people of color, but the issue is really less about race or class than whether they have the resources to pay lawyer fees."

And many studies have found that a killing in which the victim is white is more likely to be punished by death than one in which the victim is black.

Another important predictor is whether the crime took place in a state, and county, where the culture -- and the district attorney -- support capital punishment.

"In Connecticut, the death penalty is basically symbolic," said Eric Freedman, who teaches constitutional law and legal history at Hofstra University. "No one has been executed, and no one is near execution. But in the Deep South, the death penalty is a commonly used part of the criminal justice system."

Indeed, nine Southern states -- Arkansas, Alabama, Florida, Georgia, Louisiana, Missouri, North Carolina, Texas and Virginia -- account for 226 of the 266 people executed since the Supreme Court allowed the resumption of capital punishment in 1976. And more than a dozen states with the death penalty on the books have not executed a single criminal in that time.

LOCAL ISSUES: WITHIN STATES, "DEATH BELTS" ARISE

There are many cultural factors that come into play in determining how widely the death penalty will be used. For example, some experts suggest that in New Mexico, no one has been executed partly because the Catholic Church has sermonized against capital punishment, and many Hispanic jurors will not vote for the death penalty.

Just across the border, Texas has become the nation's leading user of the death penalty.

Stephen Bright, an Atlanta lawyer and Yale University law professor, said the attitude there reflects "a Western macho thing, the justice of the Marlboro man."

But even there, the use of the death penalty is sporadic. Of 254 counties in Texas, only 42 have put inmates on death row -- and half of those counties have only a single criminal there.

But Harris County, which includes Houston, is more then well represented, accounting for 113 of the 397 inmates on the state's death row. Although Holmes, the district attorney, would not be interviewed for this article, he has previously pronounced himself a proud supporter of the death penalty.

In Dallas, the district attorney also supports the death penalty. But Norman Kinne, the Dallas County first assistant district attorney responsible for deciding when to seek the death penalty, said his office seeks the death penalty only in cases where "we're 99 percent certain that's what we're going to get."

Harris County, he said, seeks death in all cases that meet the legal requirements.

"Lots of states have death belts," said James Liebman, a Columbia University law professor who is an expert on the death penalty. "In southern Georgia, there are lots of death sentences; in northern Georgia, there aren't. In Tennessee, there are tons of death sentences in Memphis and East Knoxville, but not in Nashville."

While it is difficult to predict how New York's law would be applied -- especially since the precise contours of the law have yet to be defined -- experts on capital punishment are already puzzling over where in the state the death penalty is likely to be used most, and least.

In New York City, Manhattan District Attorney Robert M. Morgenthau has made no secret of his opposition to capital punishment. In an article on the front page of The New York Times earlier this month, he wrote that it "actually hinders the fight against crime."

But many lawyers say the death penalty is likely to be sought relatively frequently in suburban counties, like Westchester and Nassau, where voters, and prosecutors, tend to be more conservative. They predict that upstate cities, too, will make steady use of the capital punishment law.

In Syracuse, District Attorney William Fitzpatrick, a Republican who favors the death penalty, said that he would probably seek the death penalty in about a third of the murder cases his office handles.

"I don't want to be the leading death DA or anything," he said. "I'd say that of the 25 murders we get each year, about two-thirds would meet the criteria for capital punishment, and off the cuff, I'd estimate that we'd seek the death penalty in half of those."

Local politics, too, often play a role, experts say. "It may depend less on the crime than on whether the prosecutor sees the case as a viable vehicle to ride into a higher elective office," said Streib of Cleveland State University.

"We had a notorious cult killing case, east of Cleveland, that helped sweep an obscure prosecutor right into Congress," he said, referring to Steven C. LaTourette, a Republican.

PRACTICAL ISSUES: JURIES LOOK TO THE VICTIMS

As a practical matter, prosecutors say, the decision to bring capital charges depends in part on their sense of what local juries will accept.

In the district attorney's office in Los Angeles, Fred Sunstedt heads the Special Circumstances Committee, which meets weekly to decide whether to seek the death penalty. His panel reviews about 180 cases a year, and goes forward with about two dozen.

"If you have a victim who is a totally innocent child or a totally helpless older person," he said, "the jury is more likely to vote for the death penalty. But the major source of cases that come before the committee are hard-core gang shootings, drive-by shootings or drug transactions, and jurors tend to look at victims in those crimes a little differently."

And when it comes time to decide on a sentence, Sunstedt said, many jurors are not as willing to choose the death penalty as they initially say they will be during jury selection.

Criminal justice experts agree that the identity of the victim plays an important role in determining who will get the death penalty. When the victim is a woman or a child, capital charges are far more likely.

And those who kill strangers are more apt to get the death penalty than those who kill family members, lovers or friends.

"People identify more with the victim when it's a total stranger, because that random killing is what people have the most horror of," said David Baldus, a criminal law professor at the University of Iowa who is an expert on the use of the death penalty.

Women are far less likely to get the death penalty than men, perhaps because the victims of women who kill are almost always lovers or family members. Since 1976, only one woman -- a North Carolina nurse convicted of poisoning several family members -- has been executed.

While mass murderers and those who torture their victims are more likely than other killers to be sentenced to death, experts say they make up only a small percentage of those on death row.

"If New York gets the death penalty, I guarantee that of the 20 people who will commit the most spectacular crimes, maybe five will get death sentences, four will be reversed, and the one poor schnook who gets executed will hardly be the worst of the lot," said Freedman of Hofstra.

While opponents of the death penalty argue that it is inherently arbitrary, supporters stress the many safeguards the Supreme Court has established since 1972 to insure that it will not be capricious.

"You now have what I call 'super due process' built into the system that makes it much harder to get a death penalty," said Paul D. Kamenar, executive legal director of the Washington Legal Foundation, a conservative law and policy group.

"All the laws have safeguards built in, and in some cases, I think, go overboard in making it tough for prosecutors to get capital punishment. People like Charles Manson, in cases that almost everyone would agree were particularly heinous, may not be eligible for death because they don't fit the strict categories in the state law."

Since 1972, when it ruled in Furman vs. Georgia that the death penalty worked in such an arbitrary and random manner as to make it unconstitutional, the U. S. Supreme Court has issued opinion after opinion clarifying what is constitutionally acceptable.

It has established guidelines requiring, for example, that juries must be allowed to consider evidence of mental retardation, that defendants under 16 cannot be executed, that the death penalty cannot be mandatory, and that juries must be told if there is an option of life imprisonment without parole.

The high court also requires consideration of aggravating and mitigating factors, such as the defendant's criminal record, motivation, mental or emotional disturbance, and the means of the killing.

But here, too, state laws vary. Some states do not define which factors to consider. And even states that list specific factors, as is likely in New York, emphasize different issues: in Idaho, killing without feeling is an aggravating factor, but in Arizona, it is an aggravating factor to kill with a feeling of pleasure.

STATEWIDE ISSUES: VARYING CRIMES AND PUNISHMENTS

On almost every level, the death penalty differs from state to state. Even the method of execution varies, with most states favoring lethal injection, but some prescribing electrocution, hanging, the gas chamber or the firing squad.

In some states, capital punishment can be imposed for a few crimes. In New Hampshire, for example, the only crimes punishable by death are contract murder, murder of a law enforcement officer or kidnapping victim, or killing after being sentenced to life imprisonment without parole.

But in many states, the death penalty can be imposed for any first-degree murder -- or, in Georgia, any murder.

Experts on capital punishment say the majority of those on death row have been convicted of felony murder; that is, a killing that occurs in the course of another serious crime like robbery or kidnapping. The New York law is likely to include as capital crimes some felony murders, but not enough to make it one of the broadest in the nation.

While some states, including Texas and Georgia, give the jury the final word on whether the defendant should be sentenced to death, others, including Florida, Arizona, and Alabama, leave the final decision to the judge.

A few states guarantee two lawyers to defend every death penalty case, or require that lawyers handling such cases have special qualifications or training.

New Jersey -- a state whose legislation New York is likely to emulate -- has created a statewide office to train, assign and oversee lawyers who handle capital cases for indigent clients.

But Texas requires no special training or qualifications, and provides no counsel beyond the first appeal. And in Louisiana, lawyers may be paid nothing at all -- and may even be appointed to a case they have no interest in handling.

"They keep two lists of lawyers to appoint, a voluntary list and an involuntary one," said Bright of the Yale law school. "In some parts of Georgia, lawyers have to handle court appointments for the first five years after they're admitted to the bar, so you can get someone starting a tax practice, with no criminal experience at all, appointed to a capital case."

While federally financed resource centers in several states struggle to provide legal representation to indigents facing execution, they cannot handle all the cases.

So much of the burden of handling such cases has been carried by volunteer lawyers from outside the state. But the pool of volunteers is shrinking even as the number of death penalty cases grows.

"When I started in Georgia 15 years ago, we got a lot of help from Chicago, but as capital punishment became an issue in Illinois, fewer came South," Bright said. "As Virginia's death penalty cases grew, more D. C. lawyers did their work there. When New York gets the death penalty, there's no question that a great deal of our help will disappear."

DEATH ROW GRANNY

By Glenna Whitley

THE WORK IS PAINSTAKING, BUT BETTIE BEETS says she likes it. Certainly it beats doing nothing.

Every morning at 7, she and three other women settle down in a big room cozily decorated with craft projects they have completed -- doilies, afghans, lap quilts.

For years, Bettie made toddler-sized dolls, with painted faces and black, white, or brown skin. Buyers put their names on a yearlong waiting list to get one, for $25. Now she spends six hours a day making quilts.

Bettie and her co-workers earn nothing from their labors; that goes to the Texas Department of Corrections.

At 57, Bettie is the oldest of the four women in the group. She has eight grandchildren and three great-grandchildren. Once bottle blond, her hair is now a soft gray, permed in the prison beauty shop. She wears hearing aids. But her eyes, fitted with blue contact lenses, still can see well enough to sew. She wears a white shirt, white pants, a gold ring, and a tiny gold cross on a chain. Well-groomed, pleasantly plump, and matronly, Bettie Beets looks every bit the East Texas grandma — the kind you might see shopping at Wal-Mart.

NOT AT ALL THE SORT OF WOMAN TO MURDER A COUPLE OF HUSBANDS.

Inside the big room, the four women chat while they work. They've been together nine years now, and conflicts occasionally surface. Bettie says they talk through those, praying to find answers.

But they never, ever talk about why they are there.

When Bettie first arrived at the Mountain View Unit of Gatesville State Prison in October 1985, she says she was convinced she was not in a penitentiary, but in a mental institution — a shadow of her family's past. Her cell was near a treatment center and at night there were screams and moans, floods and flames. Female inmates brought in for psychiatric care would stop up toilets or sinks and turn the water on to flood the room. One terrible night, a woman set herself on fire.

About six months after her arrival, Bettie and two other inmates were moved to a remodeled area. Each has a private cell; they share a day room. Later, after being joined by a fourth woman, they decided to give their home a new name. It was too depressing to say they lived on Death Row. Now, when their laundry is done, it arrives in a bag marked "Life Row."

"We call it that 'cause Jesus lives here," says Bettie. Every Wednesday there's Bible study. Bettie spends much of her time reading 'anything scriptural,' and books about battered women.

Whatever the name, the truth is that Bettie lives in a place where death draws nearer everyday.

There are more than 400 inmates on Death Row in Texas. Only four are women. All four of the members of Bettie's sewing circle are convicted killers.

Pamela Perillo, 39, robbed and strangled a Louisiana man. Karla Faye Tucker, 35, was convicted of the pickax murder of a man in Harris County. Francis Elaine Newton, 29, was sentenced to death for the murder of her husband and two children.

Bettie Beets has not been on Death Row the longest. But her conviction nine years ago in the capital murder of Dallas Fire Department captain Jimmy Don Beets, her fifth husband, has been upheld by the Texas Court of Criminal Appeals and is furthest along in its path through the federal court system.

The system follows no hard-and-fast timetable, stretching out Death Row appeals to an average of eight to 10 years. But since Texas reinstated the death penalty in 1982, executions have come more frequently. In 1994, Texas executed 14 prisoners more than any other state in the nation. In the last 12 years, 85 inmates have been strapped to a gurney and given a lethal injection. So far Bettie Beets has survived two dates with the executioner.

In interviews with the Dallas Observer, Bettie insists she was wrongly convicted, that she killed no one. She says her defense attorney was motivated by greed to botch her defense so that he could cash in from the sale of media rights to her story.

Appellate attorneys have filed documents contending that her lawyer failed to introduce evidence that Bettie suffered from battered wife syndrome, post-traumatic stress disorder, and organic brain damage — that she is herself a victim of a life filled with poverty, violence, and sexual abuse.

And they contend that her attorney negligently failed to challenge the most bitter fact about her case: the testimony of her own children, who described how their mother methodically planned and carried out two murders. Bettie says her son and daughter lied, putting their mother on Death Row in exchange for a prosecutor's promise to let them go free.

Bettie's lawyer now is trying to convince the U.S. Fifth Circuit Court of Appeals that she deserves a new trial. If that fails, Bettie Lou Beets could become the first woman the state of Texas has ever executed.

FISHERMEN FOUND THE BOAT ADRIFT ON CEDAR CREEK LAKE, about 60 miles southeast of Dallas, on the evening of August 6, 1983. The propeller of the green-and-white Glastron was missing, and nitroglycerin pills were spilled across the bottom of the boat.

The fishermen towed the boat to the Redwood Marina near Seven Points. On board they found a fishing license in the name of Jimmy Don Beets, a 45-year-old Dallas fire department captain who lived at the lake on the days he wasn't commanding the No. 9 station in southeast Dallas.

Beets had lived for years on Cedar Creek Lake, site of expensive lake homes as well as more middle class subdivisions, making it a popular getaway for Dallasites. It's where his parents had bought a mobile home when his father retired.

Jimmy Don spent his off-hours puttering around the house, helping his neighbors and hunting and fishing. Jimmy Don was aiming for retirement in 1987. That meant a comfortable pension, and the day when he could do anything he wanted with his time.

The owner of the marina, Lil Smith, called Beets' home several times. Finally, about 9 p.m., she reached a woman who identified herself as Bettie, Captain Beets' wife.

Bettie said she had been shopping in Dallas all day. When she got home, she had started working in her yard planting flowers, so she hadn't heard the phone.

Friends drove Bettie to the marina about 10 p.m. She was wearing clean jeans, and her face was carefully made up. She told Smith that her husband had gone out fishing the night before and hadn't returned home. She had notified the Henderson County Sheriff's Department at 8 that morning, she said, and filed a missing-person report.

Bettie seemed upset that her husband of one year was missing. But to Smith, whose own husband had drowned a few years before, it seemed she was holding up unusually well. There were no tears.

By then, the sun had dropped and the wind began to whip across the lake. No search for the missing Beets could be mounted until morning.

Daylight brought hundreds of volunteers, many from the fire stations of Dallas, to look for Beets' body. A fire department deputy chief set up a command post and drew a grid map of the lake. Under the coordination of the Coast Guard, people piled into boats to search the area where Jimmy Don's boat was found. The media from North Texas descended with camera crews and satellite trucks.

Jamie Beets woke up that dawn at his home in Balch Springs to find his aunt, Bettie Henderson, leaning over him. "Get up and get dressed," she said. "They think your dad has drowned."

Jamie thought it was a joke. His father — strong, fit, an outdoorsman — drown? Impossible.

Jimmy Don Beets was a brawny man. At 5-foot-11, he weighed about 235 pounds. Beets had thick black hair and arms as big as his grown son's thighs.

The fire captain was well-known and liked in the Cedar Creek area. But it had been months since Jamie, 25, had seen his dad. In fact they hadn't spoken to each other in almost six months.

Jamie raced to Cedar Creek, arriving at the public boat ramp on Chamber Isle about 8 a.m. There were more than 100 boats on the lake. A few helicopters and small planes had joined in. A bass fishing tournament was going on; the participants had been enlisted to help. Though only a few hours into the search, the Red Cross had set up a recreational vehicle to feed the hundreds of volunteers.

The game warden and a deputy sheriff took Jamie to his father's boat and asked him to look it over. Did anything seem strange or out of place?

In shock, Jamie studied the Glastron, his father's pride and joy. Jimmy Don had traded for the 19-foot inboard-outboard. Though used, it was in perfect condition. During the good times, Jamie often had gone fishing with his father; he knew his fastidious habits. Jamie took in the scattered pills, the missing propeller, and knew something was very wrong.

His father was extremely safety-conscious. He'd taught Jamie that the first item to put in the boat before taking it out was the CB radio. But it wasn't there.

After the CB, his dad drilled him to put his billfold in the boat, so he'd have identification if necessary. There was no billfold. The wrong pair of glasses. No checkbook.

And the propeller — how could it be gone? His father needed a tool to take the propeller off, and it was still in the bottom of the tool box. Could he have had a heart attack while taking off the propeller, put the tool back, then fallen overboard?

The final straw was the nitroglycerin pills scattered on the bottom of the boat. Jimmy Don had indeed had a heart attack about five years before while pouring a concrete sidewalk for a blind neighbor. But after a year's leave of absence from the fire department, he'd been cleared to return to active duty, and hadn't taken the medication in at least two years.

Jamie was convinced that his father had not been in the boat. "Bettie knows something about this," he insisted to several firemen assisting in the search.

Calm down, they told him. "Don't let your imagination run away with you."

Someone drove Jamie to his grandparents' house a few miles away to give him time to compose himself. He returned to the dock about 5 p.m. It was muggy and hot — at least 100 degrees. Jamie watched as boats crisscrossed the area. He turned and saw his father's red and white Silverado pickup truck bouncing across the bridge. He felt a flood of relief.

But it was short-lived. The pickup stopped, and Bettie stepped out.

"Have you found anything?" Bettie asked several officials. To Jamie, she seemed nonchalant.

A friend in the Coast Guard saw Jamie's anger and hustled him into a boat to help the searchers find his dad's favorite fishing holes.

On August 8 — just two days after Jimmy Don's disappearance — Jamie heard that Bettie had gone to the fire department to pick up his paycheck. Jamie visited Bill Manning, an attorney in Gun Barrel City. Manning had used his personal airplane to help search for Jimmy Don.

Jamie was adamant that his father couldn't have drowned — that Bettie had something to do with his disappearance. He asked Manning to tie up his father's assets to keep Bettie from getting them at least until they knew what had happened.

"I thought it was a fantasy of a grieving son," the lawyer recalls. "He seemed motivated by his dislike of Bettie." Manning knew something of Jamie's troubled past — his problems with drinking, drugs, and his disputes with his father. "Don't you think your emotions are running away with you?" Manning asked.

Bill Bandy, the Henderson County district attorney, was also skeptical. He had no probable cause for a search warrant, no evidence of foul play. That seemed to agitate Jamie even more. No one — his aunt, his wife, his friends, the police, even his own attorney — took his suspicions seriously.

Bettie seemed resigned to the fact that her husband had drowned. Though his body had not been found, two days after he disappeared, Bettie went to a Scagoville funeral home, where she picked out a casket and burial plot.

"I NEED TO TOUCH YOU," THE PSYCHIC TOLD JAMIE.

They were riding in a Coast Guard boat as it slowly cruised the shoreline of Cedar Creek lake. Reluctantly, Jamie extended his hand.

The short matronly woman with coal black hair closed her eyes and began gently rocking back and forth.

Jamie was edgy and skeptical, but willing to try anything. Back at the Red Cross mobile home, the grandmotherly psychic from Georgia, after stroking a framed picture of his father, had experienced a vision. Your daddy is buried somewhere near a castle," she said softly. "He has sand on his face."

The massive search for Beet's body had been going on for more than a week, making front-page news across the state. Dallas psychic John Catchings had been brought in after the boats, planes, and helicopters failed to turn up anything. Catchings told authorities he "saw" Beets clutching his shoulder and falling into the water after a heart attack. But his powers failed to lead searchers to a body.

The Henderson County Sheriff's Department then brought in the second psychic. After she had her vision, a Coast Guard officer asked Jamie and the psychic to get in a boat to look for any structure along the shoreline resembling a castle. Evening was coming on; the hot August day was cooling off. As the boat cruised slowly, the psychic turned to Jamie.

"I need to touch you to get a better vision of your daddy" she said. "Just let me hold your hand."

Reluctantly, he complied. The psychic closed her eyes and began talking about Jamie being thrown from a horse when he was small, growing up torn between two parents, about his volatile relationship with his father.

It was all true.

Jamie felt panicked. Take him back to the shore, he demanded — "or I'm jumping out." They found no "castle" that day. The official search was called off after 13 days. But Jamie remained convinced that something terrible had happened to his father — something that meant he would never have a chance to make his peace with Jimmy Don.

To Charlene Pullen, Jimmy Don Beets' first wife, it seemed like the fire station was his real home and the other fire fighters real family. "He was more true to them," she says, "than he was to us."

After joining the Dallas Fire Department in 1957, Beets toiled his way from first driver to captain. One of the only times Jimmy Don ever missed his shift was on Christmas Eve in 1957, when Charlene went into labor, and he took her to the hospital. Jamie was born an hour after they arrived. In the years after Jamie's birth, another son was born but lived only five hours; a few years after that, a daughter was stillborn, leaving Charlene deeply depressed.

Jimmy Don began drinking heavily after work. Over the years, the arguments over his drinking escalated, and one day, he simply didn't come home. The couple divorced in 1968, when Jamie was nine. "Jamie took the divorce hard" says Charlene. "He felt it was his fault."

Jamie lived with his mother until he was 12, then moved in with his dad, who in 1967 had married a robust cheerful woman named Suzy. But as Jamie grew into a young adult, father and son frequently fought. Jimmy Don didn't like his son's hair, his recreational drug use, or Jamie's refusal to keep a job and be responsible for his own wife and two small children.

When Jamie was arrested for possession of THC while a teenager, his dad bailed him out — though only after making him sit in jail for five days. Later, Jimmy Don made sure his son's family didn't go hungry when Jamie couldn't get a job as a carpenter. But no matter how hard they tried, the two just couldn't seem to get along.

In the early '80s, it appeared to Jamie that his father was frightened, scared of growing old alone. Jimmy Don and his second wife Suzy had divorced, then remarried, then divorced again in 1981. Jimmy Don next married a woman he'd known only a few weeks; that marriage lasted less than a year.

Then, in the summer of 1982 at The Cedar Club in the lake town of Seven Points, Jimmy Don met the woman who would become his fourth wife: Bettie Lou Barker.

Bettie, a slim, attractive woman in her mid-40s, tended bar. They quickly became inseparable.

In the rough-and-tumble world of the private clubs and bars around the lake, Bettie seemed out of place. Friendly, soft-spoken, always conservatively dressed, she was not the prototypical barmaid. A hard worker, she dreamed of buying her own club one day.

The suddenness of the relationship surprised Jimmy Don's ex-wife Suzy. The two had begun dating each other again when Jimmy Don abruptly turned up with Bettie. Still, when Suzy saw them around town, always together, it seemed that Jimmy Don and Bettie were very much in love. Says Suzy: "I think she really cared for him, and he did for her."

On a weekend during the summer of 1982, Jimmy Don brought Bettie to meet his son.

He told Jamie the big news: they were planning to get married. Though Jamie didn't know it at the time, Jimmy Don would be Bettie's seventh marriage — and fifth husband.

Jamie instantly disliked Bettie. There was something about her that seemed manipulative and hard. When they were alone, with characteristic bluntness, Jamie, then 24, told his father just what he thought.

Jimmy Don was furious. "I love her," he declared.

Not long after that exchange, on August 19, 1982, they were married at the courthouse in Kaufman County. Bettie Lou Barker became Bettie Beets.

Jimmy Don owned a three-bedroom lake house in a subdivision called Glen Oaks. By doubling up on the payments, he owned the house free and clear. It was his own little piece of heaven — the place where he planned to retire.

But even before the wedding, Jimmy Don already had moved into Bettie's place, a two bedroom mobile home tucked away in a grove of cedar trees about 50 feet from the water in Cherokee Shores. Bettie had added a redwood deck and surrounded the place with flowers. Jimmy Don docked his boat in the rear of the lot, on an inlet to the lake.

Not long after their marriage, Jimmy Don asked Jamie to come over. His new wife thought that, to make Jamie grow up, he had to cut off the generous support he had given him over the years. Jamie and his family could live in Jimmy Don's lake house, but "the only thing I want to do with you is to see my grandchildren," he told his son.

For the rest of the year, Jamie saw little of his father. For Christmas, he took his wife and their two small children to her mother's home in Celina. Four days later, a neighbor child called them there to report that his dad's lake house, filled with all their possessions, had burned down. Jimmy Don had been on duty in Dallas when it happened.

With everything destroyed, Jamie and his wife moved in with her mother. In early 1983 Jamie met at Bettie's house with his father who gave him $850 of the insurance settlement to replace the possessions they had lost in the fire. He was rebuilding the house with the rest. "I'd give you more, but Bettie says I need to take out everything you owe me from the past," his father told Jamie. Jamie owed him $3,000; Jimmy Don considered that debt paid.

Jamie tried to hug his father. "I love you," he told Jimmy Don. But his father pushed him away. "All I care about," he told his son, "is seeing my grandchildren."

By August 1983, Jamie and his wife had gotten back on their feet. Jamie was working in the air conditioning and heating business during the day and as a bartender at night; he'd bought a new mobile home and a new car.

He dreamed that his show of responsibility would help him to mend fences with his dad.

But he never got the chance.

THROUGH THE GLASS PARTITION IN THE VISITORS' ROOM of the state prison in Gatesville, Bettie Lou Beets offers an easy, slightly nervous smile.

Her voice is low and pleasant, as she earnestly presents the saga of Bettie Lou Dunevant, the "good little girl" from Newport News, Virginia.

For years, many of her childhood memories were blocked, she says, brought back only a few years ago when a lawyer assigned to her appeal came to visit. As the attorney began to ask Bettie questions, memories came trickling back. "I didn't know until a few years ago who Bettie was and what Bettie had missed and what Bettie's life could have been like if I'd had some help," she says bitterly.

Bettie was born in March 1937, in a pine cabin in North Carolina where her parents, Louise and James Dunevant, were sharecroppers on a tobacco farm. There was no electricity, no running water, no indoor plumbing, no glass in the windows. There was little to eat but salt pork and corn.

When Bettie was five, her parents moved to Newport News to work in the cotton mills. That year, Bettie contracted measles; the resulting high fever and ear infections produced profound hearing loss.

Bettie's mother was a quiet woman who kept an immaculate home, decorated with beautiful drapes and hand-made doilies. But when Bettie was about 13, her mother suffered a psychotic breakdown. Severe depression and hallucinations put her in and out of the state hospital for years, according to court records.

While her mother was hospitalized, Bettie says, she cooked, cleaned house and cared for her two younger siblings. She says her father drank heavily and hit her. "I grew up doing everything I was told to do. I learned that if you didn't, you got hurt." She says other children taunted her, telling her that her mother was crazy — and that she would end up that way too.

Louise Dunevant returned to her family when Bettie was 14. A year later, in the late spring of 1952, desperate to get away from home, Bettie dropped out of the ninth grade to marry Robert Branson, a local boy with olive skin and black wavy hair. He was 18 and worked at a zipper factory. She was 15.

Branson went to work in the shipyard. In 1956, the first of their six children, Faye, was born. But their marriage was stormy. He asked for a divorce. During a six-month separation, Bettie says, she twice attempted suicide.

The two reconciled and had a second child, Connie. By then, they'd moved to Mesquite, and Robert found a job as a welder. Shirley, Phyllis, Robert (Robby), and Bobby followed. There were happy times: family vacations, outings to the zoo, Easter egg hunts, Thanksgiving dinners.

But her husband, Bettie claims in court records and interviews, was mentally and physically abusive. She says he was so jealous and possessive that he didn't want her to work or leave the house, driving her to attempt suicide a third time. The marriage finally ended in December 1969, after 17 years, when Bettie filed for divorce accusing Branson of cruel treatment. (Branson did not return phone calls.)

Affidavits filed by her children describe the divorce as a turning point in Bettie's life. Still just 32, she had few skills and only a ninth-grade education; that, combined with her hearing problem, made it difficult to find a good job. Branson fell behind on child-support payments for the six kids. "I remember after the divorce she would cry a lot and say how she loved daddy," said Connie. "She was never really happy with anybody after that."

The family began to disintegrate. Bettie started drinking heavily, going out to clubs at night and ignoring her children. At 15, Faye married and moved out. Bettie sent Robby and Phyllis to live with their father and his new wife. Connie went to live with sister Faye. The youngest child, Bobby, stayed with his mother; Shirley moved in and out.

In 1970, Bettie married Bill Lane, a house painter. Family members portray Lane as physically abusive, beating Bettie and threatening her with guns. The two divorced only months after their marriage. But they couldn't stay apart.

On January 17, 1972, Dallas County sheriff's deputies were called to Bettie's apartment in Hutchins at 1:45 a.m. They found Lane lying face down in the yard behind the building. He was taken to Parkland Hospital in critical condition with two gunshot wounds in the back.

Bettie told investigators Lane had "run her out" of the Roundup Club on Industrial Boulevard earlier that night and threatened to come by her house and hurt her. After she went home to bed, she said, Lane began banging at the back door of her apartment, then broke the door down. That's when, Bettie said, she fetched her .22-caliber pistol from a china cabinet and shot "until she didn't see him anymore."

Lane told deputies a different story — that it was Bettie who summoned him to the apartment, asking to talk, and that when he arrived, the back door was dark. "I asked her to turn a light on, and she said that she had decided not to talk to me and to get out of here," Lane told investigators. "I started backing out the door and she stuck a gun against my back and fired one time.

"This didn't seem to faze me, but then she fired again, and it paralyzed me and I fell off the porch to the ground. I then remember her saying not to move, that if I did she would shoot again."

Bettie was charged with "assault with intention to commit murder with malice." But the charges were dropped to a misdemeanor aggravated assault a few months later when Lane signed an affidavit saying he was at fault. He paid Bettie's $100 fine and $50 court costs. The judge gave her back her pistol.

Not long after the incident, the two remarried — then divorced again, in September 1973. She packed up Shirley and Bobby and moved several times, eventually landing in Little Rock, Arkansas, where she went to work at a convenience store.

Bettie was at a country-western club in Little Rock when she met a salesman named Ronnie Threlkeld. He saw a shapely, attractive blond nursing a drink at a table, refusing all the men who asked her to dance. "She was a little blond fox," recalled Threlkeld, in a recent interview.

Threlkeld persuaded her to dance, assuring her he wasn't like all the others. That night, he went home with Bettie and stayed. She was 39; Threlkeld was 36. "She wanted you to like her," Threlkeld says.

In fact, Bettie often raged that people didn't love her enough that her children and men were always taking advantage of her. After one argument, Bettie slashed all four tires on Threlkeld's car. Another night, she came after him in a bar with a tire iron. Recalls Threlkeld: "She was a hellcat. Nobody messed with her."

Today, Bettie accuses Threlkeld of beating and choking her; an affidavit from her son Bobby backs up her claims. Threlkeld says he did nothing more than slap her once during an argument. Yet the two lived together off and on for two years. When Bettie moved back to Dallas to be closer to her children, he followed. They were married in February 1978.

Bettie's stormy relationship with her four daughters — Faye, Connie, Phyllis and Shirley — made the marriage difficult. "The most anger I ever heard from her was about those girls," says Threlkeld. She complained that they were always getting into trouble and asking for money. But the biggest problem, says Threlkeld, was that "she seemed to think they were a threat."

Their relationship ended one night in Dallas after she accused her husband of sleeping with one of her daughters, who was living with them at the time. Threlkeld says he was having a drink when the teenage daughter appeared in the kitchen and dropped her robe — and that Bettie then walked in the room. Though he swore there was nothing going on between them, Bettie refused to believe it.

The next day, Threlkeld says, he was loading his belongings in his car when Bettie tried to run him over; he managed to dodge between two cars as his wife roared past. (Bettie insists Threlkeld tried to ram her car.) Threlkeld returned to Little Rock.

Beginning in the late '70s, it seemed to Bobby, Bettie's youngest child, that his mother was developing two different personalities. Bettie drank and gobbled diet pills, but the transformation didn't take place when she was drunk. And it was more than being in a bad mood — more like Dr. Jekyll and Mrs. Hyde. "One minute we got along real well, and the next thing you know she was different," Bobby later recalled in an affidavit. "It was like she got hateful all of a sudden."

After Threlkeld left Bettie and returned to Little Rock, she called to advise him that she had filed for divorce and was going to marry a man who was good to her — a construction worker named Doyle Wayne Barker. They tied the knot in October 1978 and moved to Cedar Creek Lake, where Bettie had bought a lot, purchased a nice mobile home, and found work as a bartender and waitress.

"Bettie would always call me when she got married," recalled her mother, Louise Dunevant, in an affidavit. "Every one of them was just what she had been looking for."

Repeating the pattern, Bettie divorced Barker in July 1980, then remarried him in July 1981; once again, she claimed her husband beat her. "I never understood how someone could remarry the very person who beat you up so bad, just months before," Mrs. Dunevant said. "It was really sad."

Faye's husband, Leon, remembered seeing his mother-in-law on several occasions with black eyes, bruises up and down her arms and split lips. "I'd ask her what the hell happened and she'd tell me Wayne did it," Leon said in an affidavit.

Bettie threatened to leave, but never did. It was as though she were addicted to the abuse. She would deal with the problem in her own way.

One day in 1981, Leon saw Bettie after an especially bad beating. Both her eyes were black, there were choke marks on her neck, and her arms were covered with bruises. Leon and Faye took pictures. Bettie talked about pressing charges.

But it wasn't necessary. Barker dropped out of sight.

Bettie explained that after yet another beating, he had walked out, saying he was going to get some cigarettes — and never returned. He even left his new pickup truck in the driveway.

Bettie's husband had simply vanished.

AT NIGHT, DREAMS ABOUT HIS FATHER TOPPLING INTO WATER jarred Jamie Beets awake.

Jamie Beets was obsessed. In the weeks after his father's disappearance, he couldn't work, couldn't sleep, couldn't talk about anything else. He had to find out what had happened.

Jamie was certain his stepmother, Bettie, knew something. But the sheriff's department dismissed the notion of foul play. They thought Jamie was losing touch with reality, haunted by his failure to reconcile with his dad.

A month after the empty boat was found, Jamie moved some of his belongings to his dad's lake house, which had been rebuilt after the fire. Though the house was legally Bettie's — certainly for as long as Jimmy Don was officially missing, rather than declared dead; possibly for as long as she lived — he was intent on keeping her from claiming it.

Jamie began driving back and forth from his Dallas home, trying to make it appear that he was living in the Cedar Creek house. In late October, he returned home to Dallas to find a note. His wife had left him.

Jamie and Bettie then began a guerrilla war over Jimmy Don's house. One night, he returned to Cedar Creek to find that Bettie had thrown his belongings into the yard and moved some of her things in. Jamie returned the favor and had the locks changed. She tried to sell it for $42,000; he called the title company and blocked the sale.

In January 1984, Jamie took a job at The Western Club, a giant country-and-western club near Cedar Creek Lake where big stars often played, tending bar and helping with the sound system. It was a place for lakeside gossip; Jamie hoped he could pick up some tips that might unravel the mystery of his father's disappearance.

Several times a week, he went to his attorney's office with rumors he had picked up tending bar. One day, he came in with the news that Bettie's fourth husband, Doyle Wayne Barker, had also disappeared.

Not long after that, the manager of the Western Club hired a new waitress: Bettie Beets. Jamie confronted her, telling her he knew she had something to do with his father's disappearance, that he was going to find out what really happened.

That night, Jamie was at the lakehouse when he heard someone outside. He found a four-foot stick wrapped with a gas-soaked rag in the front window of his truck, ready for someone to light it. Gun in hand, Jamie chased two men away from the truck into the woods; he lost them in a neighboring subdivision.

The next day, the manager of the Western Club, a friend of Bettie's told him he was fired.

By then, Bettie was living with a new boyfriend — Ray Bone, a handsome, muscular man with blond hair and blue eyes. Bone was on parole for manslaughter.

One day during the early summer, Jamie went to Dallas for the day. He came back to discover that his father's house had, once again, been set on fire.

The blaze had begun on the bed in the master bedroom, stoked with a pile of his father's files that had been soaked in coal oil before being lit.

State fire investigator Gil Harper, called in to investigate both blazes, summoned Jamie in July to meet with him at a local restaurant. Harper had startling news: several witnesses said they had seen Bettie Beets enter and leave the house before each of the fires began. But DA Bandy still didn't believe there was enough evidence to file charges.

Anguished and frustrated, Jamie hit bottom. He started using drugs again — "everything I could find except heroin." He couldn't hold a job for long. He began dreaming of revenge against Bettie, fantasizing about elaborate, sadistic schemes to make her suffer.

In January 1985, Jamie — completely sober, for a change — was driving home when a 78-year-old man in a Ford Pinto slammed into his car head-on. The old man was killed; Jamie suffered nothing more serious than a broken kneecap. The accident put Jamie's leg in a cast from thigh to ankle for five months. He moved in with his mother in Longview, his monomaniacal pursuit of Bettie abruptly suspended until he healed.

A year after Jimmy Don's disappearance, Bettie sold his boat for $3,250, using a forged power of attorney. Then, in March 1985, her attorney, E. Ray Andrews, persuaded a Henderson County judge to sign an order declaring Jimmy Don Beets dead and naming Bettie as administrator of his estate.

Andrews was trying to collect fire insurance benefits on Beets' house for Bettie too, but the insurance company was balking because of the arson investigation. Finally he retained a Dallas law firm to petition the Dallas Fire and Police Pension Board to pay Bettie a widow's pension, about $790 a month, plus Beets' back pay and life insurance benefits — worth a total of about $180,000.

The board was scheduled to meet on June 13, 1985, to approve the claim.

It seemed that Jimmy Don Beets' disappearance would remain a mystery forever.

WHEN THEY HEARD WHAT THE DIRTBALL THEY'D PICKED UP HAD TO SAY, the two Henderson County investigators, Rick Rose and Mike O'Brien, raced to the department's file on the disappearance of Jimmy Don Beets.

Rose, then a patrol deputy, had participated in the search of the lake when the Dallas fire captain had disappeared. That was almost two years earlier — but there was little in the file except the missing-person reports and a note from someone who swore he'd seen Jimmy Don at an Ennis truck stop.

Now it was late April 1985, and Rose had arrested a local small-time troublemaker, who had asked for leniency in exchange for information on another crime. Rose had dealt with the man before as a confidential informant. His tips had always been reliable.

But after hearing *this* story, he and O'Brien insisted the man take a polygraph. Hooked up to a lie detector, the informant repeated his account.

He'd gone to a motel with a woman named Bettie Beets. Both of them were drunk, and after they had sex, she made a comment that stunned him. "We're laying up here fucking and having fun," Bettie said. "You wouldn't think it was so funny if you knew that the last son-of-a-bitch I laid up with I buried in the front yard."

The polygraph indicated he was telling the truth.

The investigators realized no one had ever investigated the case — or even really questioned Bettie. Still they needed more to get a search warrant. They located one of Bettie's daughters, Phyllis Coleman, in Dallas, and asked a Dallas homicide investigator to talk to her.

Confronted by the detective, Phyllis squawked: she had heard from her younger brother Robby that her mother had killed Jimmy Don — and buried him in the yard.

But that wasn't all. While Phyllis and Shirley were drinking one night, Shirley blurted out that their mother had killed and buried her fourth husband, Doyle Wayne Barker, as well. What's more, Phyllis told the detective, Bettie hadn't done it alone: Robby and Shirley had helped with the murders.

The Henderson County investigators spent six weeks questioning friends, neighbors, and Bettie's lover, Ray Bone. But Robby and Shirley refused to talk.

On June 8, Henderson County sheriffs had Bettie Lou Beets arrested in Mansfield with Ray Bone. Bettie was charged with two counts of murder. Her bond was set at $1 million.

After the arrest, O'Brien obtained a search warrant, then asked a deputy to fetch Bettie from her cell.

"I'm going to look for Jimmy Don's body in your yard," O'Brien told her.

"Jimmy Don drowned," Bettie told him in a sad voice.

"After that, I'm going to look for Doyle Wayne Barker's body," O'Brien said. "Do you want to go with me? You can keep me from digging up the whole yard."

Bettie's sweet, doleful manner changed. "She gave me the meanest, coldest look I've ever seen," O'Brien recalls.

"I want my lawyer," was all Bettie Beets said.

Leading a squadron of cops to Cherokee Shores, O'Brien cordoned off the street around Bettie's lot, then directed a backhoe onto the tidy yard. He ordered the backhoe operator to knock over the ornamental wishing well in front of the porch. Jimmy Don had built the brick-and-wood planter — a cube about four feet square and four feet tall — just days before his disappearance, and Bettie had filled it with peat moss and flowers.

Was this the "castle" the psychic had seen?

Even though it was almost 6 p.m., the heat was sweltering. As the backhoe retreated, the scene grew tense. O'Brien began digging through a foot of soil, peat moss, and plants.

He quickly found a blue sleeping bag and opened it. The smell staggered him; he could see part of a skull. If his information was accurate, it was Jimmy Don Beets. His decaying body had lain only 30 feet from Bettie's front door for almost two years. He had built his own grave.

After summoning the Dallas Medical Examiner's office, O'Brien directed the backhoe to the rear of the lot. The backhoe knocked over a shed that Jimmy Don had built. An indented area was immediately visible. Three feet down, O'Brien found bits of blue canvas and green plastic.

Another sleeping bag. And another body.

"What the hell is going on?" Jamie Beets asked, after passing the crowd of police cars, TV news vans, and helicopters surrounding Bettie's property.

A friend who owned a motorcycle had come to take Jamie to his grandparents' home near Cedar Creek Lake. The cast had just come off his leg a few weeks earlier, and Jamie had been lying low, contemplating fresh ways to ensnare his stepmother.

Two days earlier, there had been a fire at Bettie's mobile home. Fire investigators had determined that it was arson; diesel fuel had been dripped throughout the trailer. And Bettie was blaming it all on Jamie.

But now, as they pulled up to his grandparents' home, he found his entire family waiting to explain the scene he had noticed on the way over.

"Jamie, they found two bodies at Bettie Beets' house'" his mother told him. "They think one of them is your daddy."

FOR TWO MONTHS, 48-YEAR-OLD BETTIE LOU BEETS and her 26-year old daughter, Shirley Stegner, shared adjoining cells in the Henderson County jail in Athens.

Shirley had been arrested at her home in Balch Springs the day after the bodies were found, only hours after returning from a second honeymoon. She was charged with two counts of murder. Her bail was also set at $1 million.

The media attention started a procession of the curious to Bettie's lot. "Every time we would walk by their place, my dog would run straight to that wishing well and stand there and bark," one neighbor told a reporter. "I guess he knew something we didn't."

Concerned that Bettie's third husband might also have met an untoward end, sheriff's deputies tracked down Ronald Threlkeld in Little Rock. Threlkeld was shocked, but thought back to the day his "little blond fox" had aimed her car at him. "I felt lucky to be alive," he says.

O'Brien soon discovered that Bettie had attempted to take out a $10,000 insurance policy on Jimmy Don's life in May 1983, just three months before his death. Bettie had given her daughter Faye's mailing address for the premium notices. But a relative of Jimmy Don who worked at the insurance agency, curious about the unfamiliar address and signature, had taken the policy back to the fire captain, who ordered it canceled.

Though Bettie contended that she had thought the policy form was for a credit card, the DA now felt he had a motive for the murder: Beets' insurance and pension benefits. He upgraded one charge against Bettie to capital murder.

Mother and daughter both told the grand jury they knew nothing about the deaths of the two men buried in Bettie's yard.

After years of battling a drug problem, Shirley was struggling to get her life together. She was working as a management trainee at a Mesquite Taco Bell.

One morning, her father, Robert Branson, came with his wife to speak privately to Shirley. When she returned to her cell, she began changing clothes.

"Where are you going?" Bettie asked.

"I'm going home," Shirley told her mother.

THE EAST TEXAS TOWN OF ATHENS (pop. 10,000) is known for its annual Black-Eyed Pea Jamboree and as the place where the hamburger was invented in the 1880s.

But the October 1985 capital-murder trial of Bettie Lou Beets was the biggest event in its history.

Reporters from across the nation descended, setting up satellite trucks and interviewing everyone in sight. Neighbors told stories of a hot-tempered woman who threw hatchets and knives at a target tacked to a tree in her yard — and shot dead a neighborhood dog who had molested her poodle. Then there was her 1980 arrest for lewd conduct. O'Brien found a police report that revealed Bettie had been auditioning at a Dallas topless bar called Charlie's Angels when one of her pasties fell off. Bettie was arrested after she invited an undercover vice officer to put it back on. She pled guilty to a misdemeanor and received one year's probation

With residents jockeying for seats in the courtroom, the trial finally got under way. E. Ray Andrews, Athens' best-known criminal attorney, was representing Bettie. Known locally as a genial rogue, Andrews was a witty, gregarious country lawyer. His corn pone approach hid an effective legal talent — at least when he wasn't drinking.

Forensics experts had identified Jimmy Don's badly decomposed body with dental records. An autopsy indicated he'd been shot twice — once in the torso and once in the back of the head — probably while in bed. Two bullets had been found in the sleeping bag. The murder weapon was a .38-caliber handgun much like the .38 Colt Special found in Bettie's mobile home.

Jimmy Don's skull was brought into the courtroom in a box to show the wound in the back of his head. Barker had been shot in the head with a similar weapon.

But the most shocking testimony was that of Bettie's children.

After she agreed to testify against her mother, Shirley's bond had been lowered from $1 million to $5,000. She and Robby painted a picture of young adults who simultaneously loved and feared their mother.

Robby had come to live with his mother and Jimmy Don right after he turned 17, following years of separation and his arrest on a burglary charge in Corsicana. Robby and his stepfather got along well until the summer of 1983, when Bettie and Jimmy Don returned from a Virginia vacation to find that Robby had messed up the house and Jimmy Don's boat.

Nervously chewing gum, Robby told the packed courtroom how his mother had brought him into her plan. At about 9 p.m. on the night of August 5, 1983, Bettie calmly informed her son in the kitchen that she was going to murder Jimmy Don that night.

Bettie sent Robby out of the house; she didn't want him to be around when she did the deed. Robby climbed on his motorcycle and drove around the lake aimlessly, returning to his mother's place about midnight.

In the living room, he found Bettie, who quietly told him she had taken care of Jimmy Don. Robby walked to the back of the trailer, and there, near the back door, was a large shape encased in a blue sleeping bag.

Bettie asked him to help drag the body to the empty wishing-well planter. Robby and Jimmy Don had recently built it together, at Bettie's request.

They dumped the body in the planter. Bettie spent much of the rest of the evening cleaning house and doing laundry.

The next day, after a shopping trip to Dallas with Robby and Bobby, Bettie began putting flowers in the planter, which she had filled with peat moss. Then she put her cover story into place. Bettie told Robby to take Jimmy Don's boat out into the lake and set it adrift, after making it look as if Beets had drowned.

Robby drove the boat out, removed the propeller, and scattered the heart pills Bettie had given him. Then he swam back to Big Chief landing, where his mother picked him up on the bridge and drove him home.

Robby testified that he had liked Jimmy Don, but didn't go to the authorities because he cared about his mother and had to protect her.

On cross-examination, Andrews charged that Robby, not Bettie, had killed Jimmy Don, in an argument over his use of the boat — and that Bettie covered it up out of love for her son, who was on six years' probation.

"She always been good to you?" Andrews asked.

"Up until now," Robby said.

"What has she done to you now?"

"She's lying now, saying that I killed him when *she* killed him."

Shirley took the witness stand next. She testified that Bettie had called her to talk one evening about midnight in August 1983. Sounding upset, Bettie told Shirley she planned to kill her husband. Shirley says she was shocked. "I cared very much for Jimmy Don Beets," she testified. "He was the best stepfather that I'd ever had."

Shirley and her husband arrived at Bettie's house that night at 2 a.m. Her mother said she had "everything taken care of," that Shirley could go home.

Several weeks later, Shirley went down to the lake to see her mother. Flowers were growing in the new wishing well. Bettie explained that she and Robby had buried Jimmy Don in the planter.

Why hadn't she called the police — or warned Jimmy Don? Andrews demanded.

"I was afraid of my mother," Shirley said.

Though Andrews fought to bar any mention of Barker's death, for which Bettie was not on trial, the jury heard that she had offered her daughter a similar revelation two years before Jimmy Don's murder. In October 1981, Shirley, then 22, was sitting at a campfire outside her mother's home when Bettie explained that she was fed up with Barker. But there was a problem with them splitting up: the mobile home was in his name; if they divorced, she would have no place to live.

"She told me that she was going to kill him [Barker] because he had beat her so many times, and she couldn't stand it anymore and that she didn't want him around," Shirley testified. As mother and daughter drank White Russians around the campfire, Bettie confided that she was going to shoot Barker after he fell asleep.

A few days later, Bettie brought Bobby to Shirley's house to spend the night. The next morning, Shirley testified, "she told me that it was all over with, that she'd done what she intended to do ... that after he had gone to sleep, that she took the gun and covered it with a pillow and put it to his head and fired the gun and the pillow interfered with the trigger on the gun ... She thought the noise would awaken Wayne, so she hesitated for a minute and then recocked the gun and fired again."

Bettie took her daughter to the back bedroom of her mobile home. There, lying on the floor of the closet, was a large shape wrapped in plastic and covered with a blue sleeping bag.

Afraid of what would happen to her mother, Shirley volunteered to help her dispose of the body. After dark, the two women dragged Barker's body to the back yard. "I helped her bury him in the back of the trailer where the shed is," Shirley testified.

Earlier that week, Bettie had asked an acquaintance in the development to dig a hole for a barbecue pit in the rear of the lot. The two women filled the hole with dirt, and the next day, they bought some red cinder blocks and built a patio over the top of the grave. Jimmy Don Beets later moved the cinder blocks and built a storage shed on the site.

Bettie Beets took the stand in her own defense on the tenth day of the trial.

Dressed in a feminine blouse and skirt, Bettie softly explained that she had heard Jimmy Don one night, after drinking all day, argue loudly with Robby over his decision to quit a job. "They were fighting in the bedroom ... yelling at each other," Bettie testified. "I had started to the bedroom and I heard a shot." She said she found Jimmy Don lying on the floor, with blood on his head and oozing out of his mouth.

"I was sitting beside Jimmy Don and Robby told me, he said, 'Mom,' he said, 'I'm sorry. I didn't mean to.'"

Bettie said she knew she had to help Robby — she had been separated from him for years when Robby lived with his father and couldn't abandon him again.

Bettie told the jury she reached up and got a bedspread and began wrapping her dead husband's body in it. "I held Jimmy's body for a few minutes and tried to tell him what I was doing and why." She and Robby put his body in the planter, Bettie testified, and the next morning she got up early to buy some peat moss.

On cross-examination, Bandy pointed out to the jury that Bettie had shed no tears on the stand. He asked her about her feelings for her husband. "I loved Jimmy Don, Bettie testified. "Nobody's ever been as good to me as he was."

Jurors deliberated for six hours into the evening of October 12 before returning at about 9 p.m. The verdict was guilty.

In the courtroom, Bettie's children began crying when they heard the verdict. Bettie collapsed and was hospitalized overnight.

The next Monday, the jury reconvened to determine her punishment. The judgment again was swift: death by lethal injection.

Since her 1985 trial, the U.S. Supreme Court has twice refused to hear Bettie Beets' appeals. Twice, she's received last-minute stays of execution. At one point, her conviction was briefly overturned.

One jurist, Texas Court of Criminal Appeals Justice Marvin Teague, accorded her mythic status in a 1989 opinion. "Ms. Beets is evidently a greedy and insensitive killer, the kind of succubus who has managed to capture the romantic imagination of Americans in such modern cinematic classics as Body Heat and Black Widow," the judge wrote.

After exhausting her appeals in the state courts, Bettie's attorneys have been making their pleas in the federal system. Contending that Andrews was ineffective, her attorneys filed an affidavit from his co-counsel, Gil Hargrave, who said Andrews did very little investigation on Bettie's case and spent every afternoon during the trial at the VFW Hall drinking five or six Wild Turkey doubles.

But they also contended that Andrews had a conflict of interest, after persuading Bettie, on the second day of her trial, to assign him all media and literary rights to her story. (In fact, there's no indication those rights ever brought the lawyer a penny.) The appeals lawyers also claimed, Andrews had a conflict because Bettie, before ever being charged, had once told her lawyer she was unsure whether she was entitled to Jimmy Don's pension and life-insurance benefits.

If she knew nothing about being eligible for money, that would scuttle the state's accusation that she had murdered Jimmy Don for profit — the basis for her death sentence. That prospect, her appeals lawyers contend, means Andrews should have declined to represent Bettie -- and instead testified as a witness on her behalf.

The state rebutted the argument by noting that others had told Bettie how she might become eligible for death benefits after Jimmy Don's demise; and that Bettie had sold her husband's boat and tried to sell his house.

In 1991, the Fifth Circuit Court of Appeals in New Orleans ruled there was no conflict of interest. But various appeals points remain to be heard. It is now likely that resolving Bettie's case — either by setting aside her sentence or clearing the way for her execution — will take at least three more years.

Beets' trial attorney, Andrews, is now himself facing a prison term. After winning the post of Henderson County district attorney, he was charged last year with soliciting $300,000 to drop murder charges against a Corsicana businessman accused of killing his wife. After his indictment, Andrews checked himself into a hospital for treatment of substance abuse and gambling addiction. After negotiating a plea bargain, he awaits sentencing to a federal prison.

FOLLOWING HIS STEPMOTHER'S TRIAL, JAMIE BEETS was declared his father's sole heir and received about $150,000 in benefits and property. Jamie felt vindicated after laboring for months to try to direct investigators toward Bettie.

Jamie suffered psychiatric problems for years, including nightmares about being shot in his sleep by a faceless woman lying next to him. But last year, he began to pull himself together. He is engaged to be married and has his own heating and air conditioning business; he's off drugs and alcohol and has started going to church.

Jamie was relieved when his father's skull was finally buried with the rest of his body in November 1989, four years after the trial. He lives with the dread that Bettie's appeals will result in a new trial. And he's determined to be there when — and if — Bettie is executed.

The trial was especially painful for Bettie's children — especially Robby and Shirley. "Those kids loved their mother," notes DA's investigator O'Brien. "They were very torn, very mixed up. What does a child do when his mother asks him to bury his stepfather?"

The courts have yet to deal with Bettie's contention that her behavior results from battered-wife syndrome, brain damage from abuse and a 1980 car accident, a learning disability, her hearing impairment, and, according to experts retained by her attorneys, "an abnormally low IQ."

One psychologist posits that Bettie attempted to escape the torment of her life during the 1980s by drinking alcohol and popping large quantities of diet pills, a combination that could have induced paranoia and psychosis, making her more likely to overreact to perceived threats. Is that what created the "different" Bettie that her son Bobby saw?

That might explain Barker's murder. According to her son-in-law, Leon, the day before he "disappeared," Barker had beaten Bettie unmercifully.

But Bettie was convicted of killing Beets, and there was no evidence that he ever physically abused her.

None of those who came into contact with Bettie felt she was brain-damaged or possessed far below average intelligence. In fact, she has received a GED while in prison.

In opening arguments at her trial, Bandy dismissed such defenses, calling Bettie's behavior part of a carefully calculated pecuniary scheme and branding her "cold as a well-chain."

"What kind of wife would shoot her husband as he lay sleeping in her bed?" the prosecutor demanded. "What kind of a mother would seek to pin a murder on her own child? The female of the species protects the young, above all — above her own life."

Investigator O'Brien, who is now in law school, dismisses suggestions that Bettie was some sort of feeble-minded victim. "She was not a shrinking violet," he says. "Those men were lying in bed asleep when she shot them. I think Bettie was just meaner than hell."

In the nine years since her trial, Bettie Beets' children have rarely come to see her on Death Row. The last time Bettie saw Shirley — whose testimony helped put her on Death Row — was Mother's Day 1993. Bettie says they didn't talk about her case.

Shirley has remarried and is living in Pleasant Grove; she refused to talk about her mother. Neither Robby nor Bettie's other daughters could be reached for comment. Bobby died after being struck by a car a year ago.

Today, Bettie still contends that Robby killed Jimmy Don Beets and Shirley made up the story about her murdering Barker. "Shirley blamed me for her being in jail," Bettie says. "It was all my problem. She hadn't been married long. She just wanted to go home."

How did Barker end up buried in her yard? Bettie blames her second husband, Bill Lane, who died of a heart attack in 1982. Lane killed Barker in an attempt to get her back, Bettie suggests. "A lot of things went on in my house that I didn't know about," she says.

Her children lied; everybody lied. But most of all, her attorney, Andrews, lied. "I just did what he told me to do and hung myself," she says bitterly.

Bettie still clings to hope. "I believe with all my heart that somebody's going to believe me," she says.

But if, for some reason, those appeals fail, Bettie Beets says, she's not afraid to die. "God has forgiven me for everything in my life," she says, breaking into tears. "He forgives and forgets."

PRISON GUARDS AND SNITCHES

by James W. Marquart
and Julian B. Roebuck

IN PRISON VERNACULAR "RATS," "SNITCHES," "STOOL PIGEONS," "stoolies," or "finks" refer to inmates who "cooperate" with or discretely furnish information to staff members. By and large, the popular imagery and folk-beliefs surrounding these inmates are particularly negative. Typically, prison movies present "rats" as the weakest, most despicable and pitiful creatures in the prisoner society. "Rats" are usually depicted as outcasts or isolates that undermine the solidarity of the cons by breaking the inmate "code" of silence (see Sykes, 1958). Whenever a "rat" appears in a movie scene, groups of inmates stop talking, disband, or mumble obscenities. Some prison researchers, like McCleery (1960), contend that uncovering snitches is an obsession for the majority of inmates. This may be true in many correctional institutions because "rats" are often the victims of "accidents" or savage reprisals from other prisoners, as evidenced by the New Mexico prison riot in 1980. The inmates in many other prisons have developed an inmate society, enabling them to define, label, and punish "rats" as deviants.

The sociology of confinement, especially prison role research, has for decades noted the negative perception of "rats" by the other inmates (see Bowker, 1977.) Yet, despite the fascination with and knowledge of "rats," prison researchers (unlike police researchers) have offered little systematic research on snitches. Johnson (1961) and Wilmer (1965) are the only prison investigators who have examined informing, but their work focuses on the types and personal attributes of "rats" rather than informing as a mechanism of social control. Perhaps the best descriptions of the exchange relationships between staff members and stood pigeons come from former inmates (see Bettelheim,1943; Solzhenitsyn, 1975; and Charriere, 1970). Nevertheless, little is known about how officials use inmate-intelligence as a management strategy.

This paper examines a southwestern state penitentiary control system wherein a network of "paid" inmate informants functioned as surrogate guards. Although known "rats" may be typically loathed and disparaged by the staff and captives in most institutions, the "rats" in the prison under study were hated, but also envied, feared, and respected. No stigma was attached to their deviant role. We focus on the snitch recruitment process, the types of intelligence gathered, the informers' payoff and the use of this intelligence to maintain social order -- in short the dynamics of this guard-surrogate guard society.

SETTING THE METHOD OF STUDY

The data were collected at the Johnson Unit, a maximum security recidivist prison within the Texas Department of Corrections (TDC), that housed nearly 3200 inmates over the age of twenty-five (47% black, 36% white, and 17% hispanic). Many of these hard-core offenders had been convicted of violent crimes. Johnson had a system-wide reputation for tight disciplinary control, and inmate trouble-makers from other TDC prisons were sent there for punishment. Structurally, the prison had eighteen inside cell blocks (or tanks) and twelve dormitories branching out from a single central hall-a telephone pole design. The Hall, the main thoroughfare of the prison, was a corridor almost one quarter of a mile long, measuring sixteen feet wide by twelve feet high.

The data for this paper are derived from field research conducted from June 1981 through January 1983. The first author entered Johnson as a guard, a role which enabled him to observe and to analyze first-hand the social control system. A number of established field techniques were used: participant observation, key informants, formal and informal interviews, and the examination of prison and inmate documents and records. The investigator directly observed and participated in the daily routine of prison events (work, school, meals, sick call, cell and body searches, counts, etc.) as well as various unexpected events (fights, stabbings, suicide attempts, drug trafficking). He also observed and examined officer/officer and officer/inmate (snitch) interaction patterns, inmate/officer transactions, leadership behavior, rule violations, disciplinary hearings, and the administration of punishment. With time, he established rapport with guards and inmates, gaining the reputation of a "good officer." (He was even promoted to sergeant in November 1982).

During the fieldwork, the observer developed, as did most ranking guards, a cadre of "rats" and channeled their information to supervisors (sergeants, lieutenants, captains, majors). These inmates routinely brought him information about prisoners (e.g., weapons, gambling, stealing) and even other officers (e.g., sleeping on the job, drug smuggling, having sex with inmates). The vast majority of snitches were shared, but the "rats" dealt primarily with officers who had the reputation of using good judgment (not overreacting, keeping cool) when handling sensitive information. Enmeshed in the intelligence network, the researcher frequently discussed these matters with the officers and "rats."

THE SNITCH SYSTEM

Johnson employed 240 officers and housed nearly 3,200 inmates. One guard was generally assigned to supervise four cellblocks totaling 400 prisoners. Obviously this situation obviated individual inmate supervision. Therefore, to facilitate control and order, staff members enlisted the "official" aid of the inmate elites as informers and surrogate guards. These snitches, called building tenders (BTs) and turnkeys, in turn cultivated their own inmate snitches. Johnson was managed via a complex information network facilitating a proactive as well as a reactive form of prisoner management. These surrogate guards acted with considerable authority.

STRUCTURE AND WORK ROLE

The BT system involved four levels of inmates. The top of the hierarchy consisted of the "head" building tenders. In 1981, each of the eighteen cell blocks had one building tender designated by the staff as the "head" BT. These BTs were responsible for all inmates and staff members alike who referred informally but meaningfully, for example, to "Watson's tank" or "Robinson's tank." Head BTs were the block's representatives to the staff and were held accountable for any problems that occurred therein. Besides procuring information (described in the next section), head BTs mediated problems (e.g., lover's quarrels, petty stealing, gambling, fighting, dirty or loud cell partners) within the living areas. The listened to and weighed each inmate's version of an argument or altercation. In most cases, the head BT warned the quarrelers to "get along with each other" or "quit all the grab-assing around." In some cases, they even let two antagonists settle their differences in a "supervised" fistfight. However, those inmates who could not or would not get along with the others were usually beaten and then moved to another block. BTs unofficially and routinely settled the mundane problems of prison life in the blocks without the staff's knowledge but with their tacit approval (see Marquart and Crouch, 1983).

The second level of the system consisted of the rank and file building tenders. In every block (or dormitory), there were generally between three and five inmates assigned as BTs, totaling nearly 150 in the prison. BTs "worked the tank" and maintained control in the living areas by tabulating the daily counts, delivering messages to other inmates for the staff, getting the other inmates up for work, procuring information, and protecting the officers from attacks by the ordinary inmates. BTs also socialized new inmates into the system; that is, they educated them to "keep the noise down, go to work when you are called, mind your own business, stop 'grab-assing around,' and tell us [BTs] when you have a problem. BTs broke up fights, issued orders to the other inmates, protected weak inmates from exploitation, protected the officers, and passed on information to the head BT and staff members.

Finally, the BTs unofficially disciplined erring inmates. For example, if an inmate was found stealing another's property, he was apt to receive a slap across the face, a punch in the stomach, or both. If the erring inmate continued to steal, he was summarily beaten and, with the staff's approval, moved to another cell block. The BTs were "on call" twenty-four hours a day and the head BT assigned the others to shifts (morning, evening, and night). It was an unwritten rule that cell block guards were not to order the BTs to sweep the floors, wash windows, or perform other menial tasks. Those officers who violated this "rule" were informed on and frequently disciplined (e.g., reassigned to gun towers, never assigned to that particular block again). This further underscores the building tenders' proprietorship of the tanks as well as their ability and power to curtail the lower ranking guards' authority and behavior.

The third level consisted of inmate runners or strikers. Runners were selected and assigned to work in the blocks by BTs on the basis of their loyalty, work ability, and willingness to act as informants. They also worked at regular jobs throughout the prison (e.g., laundry, shops kitchen). Runners performed the janitorial work of the block such as sweeping, cleaning windows, and dispensing supplies to the cells. More importantly, runners, who were also called hitmen, served as the physical back-up for the BTs by assisting in breaking up fights and quelling minor disturbances. As a reward for their services, runners enjoyed more mobility and privileges within the block than the other inmates (but less than the BTs). Many runners were also friends or acquaintances of the BTs in the free world, and some were their consensual homosexual partners. Some blocks had three or four runners, while others had seven, eight, or even nine. Altogether, there were approximately 175 to 200 runners.

The fourth level of the BT system consisted of turnkeys, numbering 17 in 1981. The Hall contained seven large metal barred doors, riot barricades that were manned by turnkeys in six-hour shifts. Turnkeys shut and locked these doors during fights or disturbances to localize and prevent disturbances from escalating or moving throughout the Hall. These inmates actually carried the keys (on long leather straps) which locked and unlocked the barricades. Every morning, turnkeys came to the central picket (a room containing all the keys for the prison and riot gear) and picked up keys for "their" barricades. Turnkeys routinely broke up fights, provided assistance to the BTs, and physically protected the officers from the ordinary inmates. These doorkeepers passed along information to the BTs about anything they heard while "working a gate." When off duty they lived in the blocks where they assisted the BTs in the everyday management of inmates. Turnkeys occupied a status level equal to that of the BTs.

SELECTION OF BTS AND TURNKEYS

As "managers" of the living areas and Hall, these inmate-agents obviously performed a dangerous task for the staff. Vastly outnumbered, BTs and turnkeys ruled with little opposition from the ordinary inmates. In fact, most of the ordinary inmates feared their "overseers" because of their status and physical dominance. They were formally selected by the staff to perform an official job within the living areas. Unwritten but "official" departmental policy existed on the appointment of inmates to BT and turnkey positions. The staff at Johnson (and other Texas prisons) recommended certain inmates as BTs/turnkeys to the Classification Committee (a panel of four TDC officials all with prison security backgrounds). This committee then reviewed the inmate records and made the final selections. Recommendations to the Classification Committee from the staff were not always honored and less than half of those recommended were selected for BT/turnkey jobs. One supervisor, an active participant in the recruitment process at Johnson, expressed a typical preference:

> I've got a personal bias. I happen to like murderers and armed robbers. They have a great deal of esteem in the inmate social system, so it's not likely that they'll have as much problem as some other inmate because of their esteem, and they tend to be more aggressive and a more dynamic kind of individual. A lot of inmates

steer clear of them and avoid problems just because of the reputation they have and their aggressiveness. They tend to be aggressive, you know, not passive.

The BTs and turnkeys were physically and mentally superior inmates, "natural leaders" among their peers. All were articulate and had physical presence, poise, and self-confidence. Generally, they were more violent, prisonized, and criminally sophisticated than the ordinary inmates. Of the eighteen head BTs, eight were in prison for armed robbery, five for murder (one was an enforcer and contract style killer), one for attempted murder, one for rape, one for drug trafficking, and two for burglary. Their average age was thirty-nine and they were serving an average prison sentence of thirty-two years. Of the seventeen turnkeys, three were murderers, three were armed robbers, six were burglars, two were drug traffickers, one was a rapist and one was doing time for aggravated assault. Their average age was thirty-one and they were serving an average sentence of twenty-two years. All were physically strong, rugged, prison-wise, and physically imposing. BTs and turnkeys were older than most prisoners and often they were violent recidivists similar to the inmate leaders noted by Clemmer (1940) and Schrag (1954). In contrast, the average TDC inmate in 1981 had been given a twenty-one year sentence and was between twenty-two and twenty-seven years old. Almost half (48%) were property offenders or petty thieves.

INFORMATION ACQUISITION

The most important means of controlling inmates' behavior in the cell blocks was the presence of BTs. These inmate-agents, while carrying out their other duties, spent most of their time sitting around the entrance to the block talking with other inmates, especially the runners. Conversations with and observations of other prisoners enabled the BTs to gather a variety of intelligence about inmates' moods, problems, daily behaviors, friends, enemies, homosexual encounters, misbehaviors, plans, plots and overall demeanor.

The runners, who worked throughout the prison, had more contact with the ordinary inmates than did the BTs. This contact facilitated eavesdropping and the extracting of information. For example, while mopping the runs (walkways on each tier), runners talked to and observed the inmates already in their cells. At work, these inmates listened to, watched, talked to, and interacted with the others. Runners secured and relayed to the BTs information on work strikes, loan sharking, stealing of state property, distilling liquor, tattooing, homosexual acts, and escape and revenge plans.

INFORMATION SOURCES IN THE CELL BLOCKS

Though informing was expected from runners, they were not formally instructed to inform. A head BT explains this situation:

> You don't pick these people and tell them now you've got to go in there and tell me what's going on inside the dayroom [a TV and recreation area in each living area]. By becoming a runner it is expected that you will tell what's going on; it's an unspoken rule that you will inform on the rest of the people in here. If you hear something you are going to come to me with it.

With the runners' information, the BTs penetrated the tank social system. Ordinary prisoners knew they were under constant surveillance and thus were amenable to the prisoner social control system -- a system based on inmate intelligence reports, regimentation, strict rules, and certain punishments. For example, when the BTs found out that two or more inmates were "cliquing up" for any purpose, they immediately told the staff, who disbanded the group through cell changes.

Atomized and lacking solidarity, the ordinary inmates "ratted" on each other, especially when they felt the need for protection. Ordinary inmates rarely if ever, sought out the staff to solve a block problem because this brought punishment from the BTs. Instead they sought the counsel and help of the BTs, the power block they were forced to deal with. From the ordinary inmates, the BTs learned about a variety of things such as gambling pools, illicit sex, petty thievery, tattooing paraphernalia, liquor making, weapons, and numerous other forms of contraband, misbehavior, and planned misbehavior (e.g., plots of revenge, possible attacks on an overbearing guard). This knowledge enabled the guards to take a proactive stance, thereby preventing rule violations. Not all block residents were informers. Those who snitched did so for several reasons.

Like anyone else, prisoners react negatively to certain repugnant behaviors and situations. Most were followers and refrained from taking action themselves. Citizens often call the police, for example, about a neighbor's barking dog or loud stereo rather than complain directly to the neighbor. Inmates took similar action. They told the BTs about various illegalities (especially those that threatened them in any way) because they knew the problem would be resolved in the block without involving themselves or attracting official intervention. The BTs usually took swift action when resolving problems. For example, one inmate told the BTs in his block that his cellmate was making sexual advances to him. After investigating the claims, the BTs solved this problem by beating the sexually aggressive inmate and, with staff approval, moving him to another block. In another cell block, an inmate told the head BT that his cell partner was scaring him by turning off the cell's light bulb. The BT struck the pranking inmate on the head with a pipe and threatened to have him moved to another block. The prankster "got his message."

Inmates were not always straightforward and sometimes informed for revenge. For example, some inmates informed on those they desired to see the BTs punish and/or move to another cell block. Some inmates "planted" contraband in their enemies' cell and then "tipped off" the BTs. Some inmates gave the BTs false information about other inmates, a variety of snitching called "dropping salt" or "crossing out." However, revenge-informing was restricted because the BTs were especially aware of this maneuver and severely punished the disclosed instigator. Those who gave spurious information of any kind (or who deceived the BTs in any way) played a dangerous game. If discovered, they were beaten. The BTs (like the guards) weighed and checked the informer's information, considered his motive, and noted the relationship between him and the one informed upon before taking action.

Some ordinary inmates reported illegalities to the BTs in return for favors and to get on their good sides. For example, when an inmate told the BTs about someone who was fashioning a weapon, he expected something in return. Favors assumed many forms such as selection as a runner or maybe even a job recommendation. BTs often recommended "helpful" inmates to the staff for jobs in the garment factory, shops, laundry, or showrooms-and these allies served as additional snitches.

A number of ordinary inmates "ratted" on other inmates as a sort of game playing device. They planned a scenario, informed, and then sat back and enjoyed the action and reaction. Several inmates told me that this kind of game playing relieved their boredom at others' expense. The BTs received most of their information from regular legitimate snitches. However, in some cases when the regular channels did not suffice, they resorted to threats and the terrorization of ordinary inmates to gather information.

BTs, like guards, could not be everywhere at once and therefore relied on stool pigeons. For example, BTs could not observe homosexuality in the cells, but their snitches could. Bob, a head BT, sums up the situation: "The tanks are run through an information system. Whether this information comes from runners or even other inmates, this is how trouble is kept down." The BTs' snitching system was officially recognized as part of the prisoner control system whereas their snitches' behavior was informal, though expected.

INFORMATION GATHERED OUTSIDE THE BLOCK

Runners and ordinary inmates worked throughout the prison and routinely informed the BTs about activities in the work areas, school, hospital, laundry, dining rooms, and shower rooms. Gary, a head BT, described this activity:

> We [BTs] all have our people, but we don't fuck with each other's people. If you walk down the Hall and hear somebody say "he's one of mine" that means that that particular inmate owes some type of allegiance to a particular BT. The reason he owes that allegiance or loyalty is perhaps he [a BT] got him a job someplace, got him out of the field and into the Garment Factory. These people are loyal to me. I put them there not for me but for the Man [the warden] and they tell me what's going on in that particular place. If you don't help me then I'll bust you. I got Bruce the job in the Issue Room [clothing and supply room]. I own Bruce because I got him that job. He tells me if clothing is being stolen or if inmates are trying to get more than they deserve.

Misbehavior, plots, and plans were not confined solely to the living areas and the BTs had extended "ears" in all areas where inmates interacted. Consequently, they kept abreast of developments everywhere and relatively little happened without their knowledge.

Turnkeys were not isolated from this spy network because they too had snitches. The turnkeys worked in the prison corridor and therefore gathered much information about illegal behavior outside the cell blocks. They acquired information about weapons, drugs, or other contraband being passed in the Hall, a vital area in the prison because large numbers of inmates were in constant movement there from one point to another. The turnkeys had to keep a constant vigil in the Hall to keep out unauthorized inmates and to maintain order in a very fluid and potentially explosive situation. The Hall was divided into the north and south ends and inmates who lived on the north end were forbidden to walk to the south end and vice versa. No inmates were permitted in the Hall who were not enroute to an official destination. Turnkeys generally knew in which end of the building inmates lived and vigorously watched for "trespassers." Holding down the illegal inmate Hall traffic suppressed contraband peddling as well as general disorder.

EFFICIENCY OF THE SYSTEM

At first glance, this snitching system appears cumbersome and inadequate because (apparently) BTs, and turnkeys' snitches could end up snitching on one another and the guards, creating an amorphous situation without accuracy, consistency, or legitimacy. However, the system worked effectively because the BTs and turnkeys, for the most part, knew "whose snitch was whose." Loyalty to key individuals and reciprocity were the key conditions underpinning the snitch system. BTs and turnkeys interacted amongst themselves and generally knew whose "people" were working where, and their grapevine facilitated the necessary communication. Some snitches were "shared" or owed allegiance to several BTs (or turnkeys). The snitches did not owe their allegiance to the guards or to the BTs as a group, but rather to a particular BT or the BTs who ran their cell block or who were in close supervisory contact with them. When a BT's snitch was "busted," he was expected to intervene with the staff to help his snitch get off or obtain light punishment. The snitches were not completely immune from the rules, but they had an edge over other inmates in circumventing certain rules and in receiving lighter punishments when caught in rule breaking.

TYPES OF INFORMATION

The major organizational role of the BTs and turnkeys was to gather information on ordinary inmates' behavior, but they did not report every rule violation and violator. They screened all information and passed to the staff only intelligence about actual or potentially serious rule infractions. As Jerry, a head BT, says:

> Look, we don't tell the Man (Warden] about everything that goes on in the tanks. That makes it look bad if I'm running down to the Major's office and telling somebody, old so and so, he's playing his radio too loud, or so and so, he's got an antenna that goes from his cell up to the window. That shows the Man up there that I don't have control of that tank and I can't let that happen. That makes me look bad.

The BTs handled "misdemeanors" or petty rule violations themselves in the blocks. The BTs and turnkeys regularly informed the staff about five types of serious rule violations, commonly called "Major's Office Business."

"MAJOR'S OFFICE BUSINESS"

First and foremost, the BTs and turnkeys were constantly on guard to detect escape plans because TDC considered escape the most serious of all violations. For example, one night when the first author was on duty, a cell block officer found several saw marks on the bars of a cell's air vent which provided access to the cell house plumbing area and ceiling fans. Should an inmate stop the fan, he could conceivably climb to the roof and perhaps escape. When a shift supervisor arrived to examine the marks, the block's BTs were assembled and asked about the situation. They knew of no hacksaw blades in the block and doubted that the two suspected inmates were the types to be preparing for an escape. They suggested that the cell's previous occupants were the most likely culprits. In any event, the BTs assisted several officers (including the researcher) in searching the inmates' belongings for escape tools. Nothing was found and everyone was allowed to go back to bed.

Second, BTs informed the staff about ordinary inmates' homosexual behavior. The staff considered this behavior serious because it frequently led to envy, fights, lover's quarrels, retaliation, stabbings, as well as to the buying and selling of "punks." Homosexuality also went against the legal and moral rules of the prison system. The guards, a moralistic conservative group, despised homosexuality and punished it severely, officially or otherwise. BTs were very adept at discovering this form of illicit behavior. For example, one night while I was on the third shift (9:45 to 5:45 A.M.), the head BT on 13-block informed a captain that one well-known homosexual (or "bitch") had entered the wrong cell on the second tier. I accompanied the shift supervisor and head BT as they slowly crept along the walkway and caught the inmates "in the act." Both were charged and punished. The BTs made sure the inmates entered their own cells and not someone else's, thus also keeping stealing to a minimum.

Third, the inmate-agents told the staff about inmates who strong-armed weaker inmates into paying protection, engaging in homosexual acts, or surrendering their property. Extortion or strong-arming was considered serious because of the potential for violence and the prison's legal obligation to protect inmates from exploitation and physical harm. In most cases, these problems were handled informally within the blocks (i.e., a warning). If the behavior persisted, the offending inmate was generally beaten up ("tuned up") and reported to the staff. Staff members usually gave the erring inmate a few slaps across the face or kicks in the buttocks and transferred him to another cell block.

Fourth, BTs and turnkeys informed the staff about drug trafficking. The introduction of drugs into the population was extremely difficult but occasionally small quantities were smuggled inside. Again, the inmate-agents kept this activity to a minimum and assisted the staff in making "drug busts." For example, one head BT and a turnkey briefed the staff about an inmate who worked outside the prison compound (farm operation) and who was supplying marijuana cigarettes to a certain block. Plans were devised to catch the inmate with his supplies. As he came in from work the next day, another guard and the investigator detained and searched him. Although no marijuana was found, it was later reported to us that the "dealer" quit trafficking because he knew he was being watched.

The BTs and turnkeys also told ranking staff members about guards who brought in drugs. In fact, one head BT was notorious for convincing (or entrapping) officers, especially new recruits, to smuggle narcotics into the institution. If the officer agreed, and some did, the staff was informed, and plans were made to catch the unsuspecting officer. Officers caught bringing in drugs (or any other contraband such as pornography) to the inmates were immediately dismissed. The BTs in one block even assisted the staff in apprehending an officer who was homosexually involved with an inmate. This officer was promptly terminated.

Last, the BTs and turnkeys informed staff members about inmates who manufactured, possessed, or sold weapons, especially knives. Inmates with weapons obviously placed the officers and their inmate-agents in physical jeopardy. One day, John, the head BT on 18-block, came to the Major's Office and told the captain about a knife in the eighth cell on the first row of "his" block. Two officers, two BTs, and the researcher searched the cell and found a knife wedged in between the first bunk and the cell wall. The owner of the weapon received a disciplinary hearing, spent fifteen days in solitary confinement, and was then moved to another cell block. It was common for the BTs to help the guards search suspected inmates' cells because they knew the tricks and places that inmates used to conceal weapons. Many officers learned how to search cells from the BTs. On another occasion a turnkey told the first author that an inmate, who had just exited a dining hall, was carrying a knife in his ankle cast. The cast was searched and a small homemade knife was found. The turnkey later revealed to the investigator that one of his snitches spotted the inmate putting the "shank" in his cast just prior to leaving the block for the dining hall.

ROUTING OF INFORMATION

The actual passage of information did not always follow a formal chain of command. Though runners and ordinary inmates "reported" directly to the BTs and turnkeys, these latter inmates relayed information only to those ranking officers (sergeants, lieutenants, captains, majors, wardens) with whom they had developed a personal relationship. Some guards were trusted by few if any inmate-snitches and were essentially left out of the informer process. Others who had displayed sufficient consistency and common sense in handling sensitive information were trusted, respected, and admired by the inmate elites. Inmate-agents actively sought alliances with these officers. Indeed, only a "man" could be trusted with confidential information. Such officers were briefed each day about events on and off their work shifts. Some of these inmate-agents were so loyal to a particular staff member that they refused to "deal" with other officers in that particular staff member's absence.

Staff members who had a cadre of inmate-agents "working" for them were in a better position to anticipate and control problems in the prison. Somewhat ironically, therefore, inmates were in a position to confer status on officers and even to affect indirectly their promotions. Some officers often gave their favorite BT or turnkey special jobs generally performed only by staff members. These jobs included stakeouts, shadowing, or entrapping a suspected inmate or officer to gather evidence about rule violations or plans of wrongdoing. These special assignments brought the staff member and inmate together in an even tighter, symbiotic relationship, leading sometimes to mutual trust and friendship. Some of these snitches were so fanatical in their loyalty that they openly stated they would kill another inmate if so ordered by "their" officer.

AN OPEN SYSTEM OF INFORMING

Unlike "rats" in prison movies, BTs and turnkeys did not hide the fact that they were snitches. It was not uncommon to see some of these inmate-agents point out the misdeeds of another inmate to a guard in the presence of other inmates. It was quite common to see BTs and turnkeys "escort" their officer "friends" as companions and bodyguards while these guards were making their rounds. While accompanying "his" officer, the inmate-agent openly informed the staff member about what was "going on" in a particular cell block or work area. The "betrayer-betrayed" relationship was not hidden and when the guards searched an inmate's cell or body, the suspected inmate knew full well in most cases who had "tipped off" the staff. One could argue that the BTs and turnkeys were not "rats" because they officially, voluntarily, and openly worked for the staff. Following this reasoning, the only "real" snitches were the BTs' and turnkeys' informers who were ordinary inmates. These inmates were mildly stigmatized by other inmates, but rarely punished because all inmates feared the BTs' presence and wrath.

Although informing occurred throughout the prison, the Major's Office was the official focal point of such activity. This office, located directly off the main corridor, was the place BTs-turnkeys conducted their "business;" that is, turned in intelligence reports and discussed plans of action. This site was divided into two rooms; the front part (off the Hall) housed the inmate bookkeepers and the back room contained two desks for the major and captains. Disciplinary court was convened in the back room where such punishments as slapping, punching, kicking, stomping, and blackjacking were administered.

The staff and their "inmate-guards" socialized here as well as conducted the daily "convict business." Throughout the day, BTs and turnkeys came in to visit their bookkeeper friends and mingle with the ranking guards. Together, in this office area, the guards and their inmate-agents drank coffee, smoked, discussed the point spreads for sporting events, joked, chatted, engineered practical jokes, roughhoused, and ate food from the prison canteen. Whenever a captain, major, or warden entered, these inmates (sometimes there were eight or nine) would, if sitting, stand and say "hello sir." However, all was not fun and games. These inmates also kept the staff abreast of what was "going on," especially in terms of Major's Office business. All day, a steady stream of these inmate-agents filed in and out. BTs and turnkeys entered this office at will. However, the Major's Office was off-limits to the ordinary inmates except for official reasons. It was a status symbol for the "rats" to hang around this office and interact with the guards.

THE INFORMER'S PAYOFF

Skolnick (1966: 124), in his account of police informants, maintains that "the informer-informed relationship is a matter of exchange in which each party seeks to gain something from the other in return for certain desired commodities." Similarly, BTs and turnkeys expected to receive rewards for the information they procured beyond a sense of accomplishment for a job well done.

In addition to status and influence, BTs and turnkeys also enjoyed a number of privileges which flowed from and defined their position. Some of these privileges appear relatively minor, yet they loomed large in a prison setting. The privileges included such scarce resources as specially pressed clothes and green quilted jackets. Ordinary inmates, meanwhile, wore white, ill-fitting coats. Some BTs possessed aquariums and such pets as cats, owls, rabbits, and turtles. BT cell block doors were rarely closed, permitting BTs to move freely about the block and to receive "visits" in their cells from friends and homosexuals. The latter were not threatened or forced to engage in sexual behavior; they voluntarily moved in to share the benefits. Head BTs roamed the halls and spent considerable time in and around the Major's Office.

Furthermore, BTs were able to eat whenever they desired and often ate two or three times in one meal period. Part of this special freedom stemmed from the fact that BTs and turnkeys were on call 24 hours a day. Nonetheless it was viewed by them and others as a special privilege. These inmate-agents were permitted to carry weapons with which to protect themselves and the guard force. These weapons, usually kept concealed, included wooden clubs, knives, pipes, blackjacks, "fistloads," and hammers. A special privilege was relative immunity from discipline. For example, if a fight occurred between a BT (or turnkey) and another inmate, the non-BT might receive several nights in solitary or ten days in cell restriction; the BT might receive a reprimand or, more likely, no punishment at all. This differential treatment reflected the understanding that the BT was probably "taking care of business." The BTs also used their influence to persuade the staff to "go lightly" on their runners who faced disciplinary cases for "helping the Man." In short, the BTs and turnkeys did "soft" time. Because of their position and privileges, the BTs-turnkeys were hated, but also feared, envied and respected by the other prisoners.

On an interpersonal level, many of the BT-turnkey-officer relationships transcended a simple *quid pro quo* of exchange of favors for instrumental purposes. That is, upper level staff members called their favorite BTs and turnkeys by their first names. Sometimes, they even took the word of a head BT over that of a cell block officer. In this way, the status differential between the staff members and their inmate agents was decreased. As one supervisor put it:

> Look, these guys [BTs-turnkeys] are going to be here a while and they get to know the cons better than us. I can't depend on some of these officers, you know how they are, they're late, they're lazy, they want extra days off, or just don't show up. Hell, you've got to rely on them [BTs and turnkeys).

This preferential treatment of a subset of inmates caused frustration and low morale among many low ranking officers, contributing to a high turnover rate among the guard staff, especially weak guards.

INMATES, INFORMATION, AND SOCIAL CONTROL

The prison staff's primary duty is to maintain social order and prevent escapes. Although Johnson's barb-wire fences, lights, alarm system, perimeter patrol car, and rural isolation reduced the possibility of escapes and mass disorder, routine control and order were achieved proactively by penetrating and dividing the inmate population. Walls, fences, and alarms were the last line of defense as well as symbolic forms of social control. Moreover, the staff's guns, tear gas, and riot gear were also an end of the line means of control and were infrequently utilized. The prison guards, like police officers, rarely employed weapons to achieve order.

The day-to-day maintenance of order at Johnson depended on the cooperation of inmate elites, a snitching system, and the terrorization of the ordinary inmates. The constant surveillance and terrorization of ordinary inmates prevented them from acquiring the solidarity necessary for self-protection and the cohesion needed for organized resistance. Although the ordinary inmates were atomized, they lived in a regimented and predictable environment. The staff's power, authority, and presence permeated the institution.

The role and identity of the inmate-agents was not hidden and they did not suffer from role strain or spoiled identities. Even though the ordinary inmates surreptitiously called the BTs-turnkeys "dogs" among themselves, they avoided physical confrontations with the "dogs" at all costs. They lacked the influence, prestige, power and organization necessary to stigmatize the BTs'-turnkeys' status or define their roles as deviant (see Lofland, 1969). To compound deviancy, one must be caught committing an inappropriate act, and snitching by the BTs and turnkeys was not considered inappropriate (see Matza, 1969: 148-9). At Johnson, informing was a means to enhance one's status and well-being. The inmate-agents were pro-staff and openly sided with and protected the guards. As one building tender stated: "I'm proud to work for the Man [Warden] because I know who butters my bread." They rationalized away their snitching behavior by denigrating and dehumanizing the ordinary inmates, referring to them as "scum" and "born losers." Ordinary inmate-snitches were looked down upon but rarely punished.

The guard staff used this snitch system to penetrate the inmate population and thereby act proactively to reduce the likelihood of such breaches of prison security as escapes, murders, rapes, narcotic rings, mob violence, loansharking, protection rackets, excessive stealing, and racial disruption. The officers, protected by the elites, were rarely derogated or attacked and never taken hostage or murdered. The staff was rarely caught off guard. This totalitarian system virtually destroyed any chances among the ordinary inmates (as individuals or groups) to unite or engage in collective dissent, protests, or violence. Those ordinary inmates who were docile and went along with the system were generally protected and left alone. This proactive system was so successful that only two inmate murders and one riot occurred from 1972 through 1982.

The aggressive use of co-opted snitches was not, however, without problems. Ordinary inmates under this system were non-persons who lived in continuous fear, loneliness, isolation, and tension. They never knew when they might be searched or, for that matter, disciplined on the basis of another inmate's accusation. BTs and turnkeys were not above occasionally falsely accusing "insubordinate" inmates of wrongdoing. The staff routinely backed up their allies. Some "unruly" inmates were "set up" by the BTs (e.g., having a knife thrown in their cell while they were at work) and then reported to the staff. Every ordinary inmate was suspect and even lower ranking guards were sometimes terminated solely on the word of a head BT. Furthermore, a federal judge, as part of the class action civil suit Ruiz v. Estelle (1980), stated that this form of prisoner control at TDS was corrupt and deviant in terms of progressive penology. The snitch system at Johnson is now defunct and the staff no longer uses BTs and turnkeys (see Marquart, 1984).

CONCLUSION

This paper examined the structure and workings of an informer-privilege system within a penitentiary for older recidivists. At Johnson, the official informers, called BTs and turnkeys, worked for and openly cooperated with the staff. These snitches, the most aggressive, older, and criminally sophisticated prisoners, were not deviants or outcasts. In turn, they cultivated additional snitches and, with the staff's help, placed these allies in jobs or positions throughout the institution. Ordinary inmate behavior as well as that of lower ranking guards was under constant scrutiny. Therefore, the staff knew almost everything that occurred within the institution, permitting proactive control and thereby preventing in many instances, violent acts, group disturbances, and escapes.

The ordinary inmates considered the inmate-guards "rats." However, they lacked the influence, prestige, and power to define and label them as such-to impute deviancy to the BT turnkey role. Selection as a BT or turnkey was not assignment to a deviant category, but rather to an elite corp of pro-staff inmates. Within this system, the only deviants were the unruly ordinary inmates and weak lower ranking guards. Both of these groups were stigmatized and labeled deviant by the staff and their inmate-agents within the prison. From the standpoint of progressive penologists and reform-minded citizens, this entire system would be considered deviant, inhumane, and morally corrupt. Although the system described in this paper may be unusual, it remains to be seen if and how other prison staffs co-opt elite inmates to help maintain social order. Past prison research has demonstrated some informal alliances between prison staffs and inmate elites. However, the form of this alliance may vary widely from prison to prison.

NOTES

1. Perhaps the epitome of the hatred of "rats" was in the movie "Stalag 17" (1952) wherein William Holden was falsely accused of being a "plant" in a German POW camp during World War II.

2. The use of informants in police work, especially in vice and narcotic operations, has been well documented (see Greene, 1960; Skolnick, 1966; Westley, 1970).

3. Johnson is a pseudonym.

4. For a more thorough analysis of the BT/turnkey system see Marquart (1983).

5. The exact format or guidelines used by the Classification Committee is not known. However, this committee was composed primarily of security personnel and these members probably exerted the greatest voice in the selection process.

6. The Major's Office is simply an office area where the ranking guards (sergeants, lieutenants, captains, majors and wardens) conducted disciplinary hearings and other forms of prison "business."

7. Weak guards were easily bullied by the inmates, could not or would not enforce order, failed to break up fights, failed to fight inmates, and were basically ignored and laughed at by the other guards and inmates.

REFERENCES

Bettelheim, B.
    1943 "Individual and mass behavior in extreme situations." Journal of Abnormal and Social Psychology.

Charriere, H.
    1970 Papillon. New York: Basic Books.

Clemmer, D.C.
    1940 The Prison Community. New York: Holt, Rinehart and Winston.

Greene, E.
    1960 War on the Underworld. London: John Long.

Johnson, E.H.
    1961 "Sociology of Confinement: Assimilation and the prison 'rat.'" The Journal of Criminal Law, Criminology, and Police Science. 51: 528-533.

Lofland, J.
    1969 Deviance and Identity. Englewood Cliffs, NT: Prentice Hall.

Marquart, J. W.
    1984 The Impact of Court-Ordered Reform in a Texas Penitentiary: The Unanticipated Consequences of Legal Intervention. Paper presented at the Southern Sociological Society Annual meetings in Knoxville (April).

Marquart, J. W. and B. M. Crouch
    1983 Co-opting the Kept: Using Inmates for Social Control in a Southern Prison. Paper presented before the American Society of Criminologists Annual meetings in Toronto.

Matza, D.
    1969 Becoming Deviant. Englewood Cliffs, NJ: Prentice Hall.

McCleery, R.
    1960 "Communication patterns as bases of systems of authority" in Theoretical Studies in Social Organizations of the Prison. New York: Social Science Research Council.
Ruiz v. Estelle, 503 F. Supp. 1265 (S.D. Texas) 1980.
Schrag, C.
    1984 "Leadership among prison inmates," American Sociological Review. 19: 37-42.
Skolnick, J. H.
    1966 Justice Without Trial: Law Enforcement in Democratic Society.
Solzhenitsyn, A. I.
    1975 The Gulag Archipelago II. New York: Harper and Row. Sykes, G. 1958 The Society of Captives. Princeton, N.J.: Princeton University Press.
Westley, W.
    1970 Violence and the Police. Cambridge, MA: MIT Press.
Wilmer, H. A.
    1965 "The role of a 'rat' in prison." Federal Probation 29 (March): 44-49.

STUDY QUESTIONS

1. What are "BTs" and "turnkeys"? How are the BTs organized at Johnson Unit?

2. From an administrative perspective, what moral value seems to dominate the snitch system? Explain. What moral values are sacrificed? Explain.

3. From an inmate perspective, what moral values are most protected under the snitch system? What values are least significant? Explain.

4. Given your understanding of mainstream contemporary correctional theory, what was wrong with the Johnson system? Does the success of the system reveal a theoretical inadequacy, in your view? Why? Defend your position.

5. Describe your ethical reaction to the snitch system. Assess the system from a utilitarian perspective and then from a deontological perspective. Do you agree with the Court's decision to terminate the system? Why? Defend your position.

A GUARD IN GANGLAND

by Robert Draper

"HEY, BOSS, YOU GOT A LIGHT?" Every newly hired prison guard, or "new boot," hears the question. It is seemingly a simple, humble favor asked of men in gray by men in white. The impulse is to accommodate the inmate, since prisons — spiritual wastelands of concrete and metal — cry out for random acts of human kindness.

By the time 21-year-old Luis Sandoval, a new boot at Huntsville's Ellis I Unit in the summer of 1985, was approached by an inmate with an unlit cigarette, his ears were still ringing from a more desperate request he had heard during his first week on the job. That first week, as he chatted with one of the old boots, the cry came from somewhere behind him: "Help me, Boss!" Turning around, Sandoval saw a Hispanic inmate standing behind a hallway crash-gate, clinging to the bars with both hands. His neck had been slashed; his head was all but severed. A long, metal object — a homemade knife, or shank — protruded from his jugular. The assailant was nowhere in sight.

Sandoval took a step toward the crashgate but was held back by the more experienced guard. "Don't go in there," said the veteran, who then correctly hollered, "Fight!" Presently other guards arrived, along with a lieutenant, who ordered, "Open the gate."

The gate opened. The inmate staggered forward, blood gushing from his head and neck. "Bring a gurney!" called the lieutenant. A gurney was produced, but the inmate ignored it. He continued to walk, step after tortured step, a full fifty yards, before collapsing, dead, in the doorway of the infirmary. Sandoval marveled at the river of red the inmate had left behind.

The brutality of the murder, coupled with Sandoval's complete inability to prevent it, made quite an impression on the young guard. Nothing during three weeks of by-the-book lectures at the Texas Department of Criminal Justice Training academy had prepared him for the helplessness he felt as a lone correctional officer constantly surrounded by violent criminals. It was their house, not his or the state's. At a given time, Sandoval would stand guard over hundreds of inmates. Anytime they chose — anytime — they could kill him. The thought worked away at his nerves. He took up smoking, two packs every eight-hour shift. The new boot's new habit, like everything else, was duly noted by the inmates.

"Hey, Boss, you got a light?"

Lighting an inmate's cigarette is considered an act of friendship or favoritism, and favoritism is forbidden by TDCJ rules. Sandoval knew this. And perhaps he was vaguely aware that the request, if honored, would be only the first of many — that later he would be asked for cigarettes, chewing gum, packs of sunflower seeds and more. His refusal would prompt the reply, "Then I'll tell your supervisor about when you lit my cigarette."

At first the young guard spurned the inmates who pestered him, and threatened to write them up for disciplinary action. But as the weeks rolled on, as the do's and don'ts of the training manual began to look more and more like some bureaucrat's idea of a joke, his resolve cratered. "It's a society," Luis Sandoval told me of the world he inhabited five days a week, eight hours a day. "They have their money. They have their prostitution, their gambling, their extortion. Just like in the free world. It's a society all its own. And we're there in it. And as you work there, you tend to become a product of your environment. In a sense, you become a convict also."

When Sandoval told me that, he was sitting in the interrogation room of the Walker County jail in Huntsville, wearing prison whites. The short, apple-cheeked Hispanic man with the neatly combed hair and the Howdy Doody grin looked too soft to be an inmate or even a guard. Apparently the inmates at Ellis I had noticed this as well, for their sweet talk had gotten to him. Over time, Sandoval got sucked into the under-tow of prison life. He lit cigarettes, which led to other small favors, which led to bigger ones. In his first year on the job, Luis Sandoval found himself delivering drugs to a self-described drug runner on behalf of the state's deadliest prison gang, the Texas Syndicate. Two years after lighting his first cigarette, Sandoval was arrested and charged with murder for allegedly aiding a gang plot to kill an inmate.

Now it was May 1991, and Sandoval was behind bars, his fate in the hands of a Huntsville jury. The first Texas prison guard ever to be tried for the murder of an inmate seemed eager to describe, to me and to the jurors, the pressures and temptations a correctional officer faces. "I was a damn good officer," he told both me and them. But he also acknowledged that he had made mistakes; and to me, though not to the jury, he confessed that one of those mistakes was bringing drugs into Ellis I. (After the trial, Sandoval became less talkative on the subject of drugs. Several weeks after the jury's verdict, he told me over the phone that he wished to recant everything he had said to me on tape about his involvement with drugs.)

The Sandoval trial was a rare public washing of the Texas penal system's bloodstained linen. It revealed a world where drugs and weapons are freely available to inmates, where murderous prison gangs control inmate behavior far more than prison guards do, and where the guardians of law and order have just as much trouble distinguishing right from wrong as do the inmates they are watching. The prosecutors of Luis Sandoval not only conceded this but went out of their way to make it part of their case. "If you work at any time for the TDCJ," said assistant prosecutor Burt Neal "Tuck" Tucker during the first day of testimony, "you know how powerful the Texas Syndicate can be."

With the impersonal manner of assassins who have long since become intimate with the odor of death, the witnesses — guards, inmates, and prison officials — readily supplied evidence that gangs are calling the shots in our prisons. A host of documents relating to the trial, as well as interviews with numerous sources involved in the case, have provided chilling details of how Texas prisons really work today. To the public, the saga of Luis Sandoval will be a shocking revelation of how Texas prisons have spawned an organized crime wave that afflicts the entire state. But to prison officials, the story is as familiar as the smell of marijuana in a cellblock and the sight of an innate with a hand-tooled shank.

A FLY IN THE SALT SHAKER

"Who's on trial here, Louie?" demanded the intense and steely-eyed chief prosecutor, Travis McDonald, during his two-hour grilling of Luis Sandoval on May 24, 1991. "Are you on trial or is TDCJ on trial?"

"I'm on trial, sir," conceded the polite young man in the pin-striped suit who sat in the witness stand. But the defendant's earnest tone suggested that this was itself an injustice-that the prison system had asked the impossible of prison guards and was now punishing Sandoval for the state's shortcomings. The only witnesses who said that Sandoval had anything to do with the murder of inmate Joe Arredondo were two convicted felons: Carlos Rosas, a Texas Syndicate member who confessed to actually stabbing Arredondo but was offered a favorable deal in exchange for his testimony; and Ruben Ortiz, a convicted murderer and Texas Syndicate sex slave who was paroled after he agreed to testify.

Ten Ellis I guards who worked with Sandoval testified that they had no knowledge that Sandoval was involved in drug transactions with prison gangs. Nearly all of them, however, confessed that they knew TDCJ had its share of dirty guards. Sandoval is one of more than sixty TDCJ guards who have been indicted by McDonald's Special Prison Prosecution Unit over the past six years for felony offenses. That statistic does not come close to reflecting the actual number of TDCJ employees suspected of involvement in corrupt activities. The real picture presents gloomy evidence of who really is in charge at TDCJ -- not the state, not the guards, but the convicts themselves.

Unlike most state crises, there is absolutely no mystery to the takeover of our prisons by violent gangs. Virtually everyone saw it coming. The ink from U.S. district judge William Wayne Justice's signature on his 1980 *Ruiz. v. Estelle* decree had not yet dried before critics were predicting that the prison reforms specified in the judge's order would leave a dangerous power vacuum.

Until judge Justice's decree, TDCJ's inmate population was essentially governed by brutal trusties known as building tenders, whose methods -- which included beating and sodomizing inmates into terrified submission -- went largely unchecked by prison officials. Everyone agreed that the building tender system was a cheap and crudely effective method of maintaining order. But the evidence gathered by justice clearly added up to a violation of the Eighth Amendment's protection from cruel and unusual punishment. Justice therefore ordered that the two thousand building tenders be replaced by more prison guards, who would police the inmates with a firm but civilized hand.

The guards were hired. But they weren't enough: A guard like Luis Sandoval would be assigned to a hallway filled with hundreds of inmates. "They're coming in from work, they're coming out of the tanks to go eat or recreate or go to school or go to the chapel," said Sandoval. "And all you see is white shirts. It's like a fly in a salt shaker."

Today the numbers still favor the inmates: There are 47,751 of them and only 3,500 security personnel -- none of whom carries a gun -- per eight-hour shift. At the close of the eighth hour, the shift changes, but the inmates remain. "In your house you can walk around in the dark and not bang your shins because you know every square inch," said a former Ellis I officer. "Well, so does the inmate. After you sit there for twenty-four hours a day with nothing else to do, you discover all sorts of good hiding places." Added a current officer, "The only time that we can find drugs is if an inmate snitches and tells us."

Inmates know their surroundings, and they know that the surroundings are theirs. And as in any society, some lead while others are led. We in the free world classify inmates according to motivation: those who do not wish to live a life of crime and those who know no other life; those who wish only to do their time and get out and those who function best in a kill-or-be-killed environment. As the free world would have it, there are good inmates and bad inmates. But such sentiments are meaningless down on the farm. There are only weak inmates and strong inmates.

Prisoners join gangs, thereby becoming strong, and prey upon the weak. The first major TDCJ gang, a Hispanic group known as the Texans, consisted of former residents who were doing time in California penal institutions in the mid-seventies. To defend themselves against harassment and assault by California prison gangs, they formed their own protection group. Push inevitably came to shove: In two separate gang confrontations, the Texans murdered one California inmate and seriously wounded another. Word spread that the Texans were a force to contend with. Upon their release from prison, gang members returned to Texas, renamed themselves the Texas Syndicate (TS), committed crimes, and wound up in TDCJ, where they developed an extensive network of drug trafficking, extortion, prostitution, and contract murder behind Texas prison walls.

Other inmates reacted to the TS as the TS members had first responded to California gang harassment. Hispanics who were not TS members formed their own gang, the Mexican Mafia, which today outnumbers the TS two to one but is not considered as well organized by prison officials. (Officials also say the Texas Syndicate is far more selective and does not, for example, recruit homosexuals.) Meanwhile, white inmates, tired of being robbed and sexually assaulted by the larger population of black inmates, began the Aryan Brotherhood of Texas. The blacks, in turn, formed the Mandingo Warriors. Other gangs also sprang up: the Hermanos de Pistoleros, the Self-Defense Family, the Texas Mafia, the Nuestra Carnales. Each gang had its own hierarchy and its own rules; each member was not permitted to leave his gang, even outside of prison, except by his own death. And each gang, after accomplishing the first objective of protection from other gangs, preyed on inmates who would buy drugs or sex or who could be intimidated into giving sex or buying protection.

Throughout the Sandoval trial, guards on the witness stand were asked if they had ever stopped a gang member from murdering an inmate. The answer was always no. Said former Ellis I officer Nolan McCool, "If the opportunity exists, they're gonna make the hit. If you tell him, 'Put that knife down,' he'll look up at you and say, 'I ain't through yet.' These people are serious. If they don't make this hit, they'll become the person to get hit. So it may be a week or a month or a year.... but that hit is on."

Today supervisors advise guards: "We cannot stop a hit. So don't try." Guards have been instructed to monitor gang activity but have shown an embarrassing inability to do so. At the Ferguson Unit, for example, guards wore special caps sporting a patch designed by an inmate. It took months before someone looked closely at the gas mask featured on the patch and realized that every correctional officer at the unit had been wearing the letters TS across his forehead.

Gangs didn't worry about guards; they worried about each other. The field for their activities, though fertile, was finite, thus making turf wars inevitable. During August and September of 1985, a long-standing rivalry between the Mexican Mafia and the TS exploded into a free-for-all throughout the prison system, leaving eleven inmates dead. For about three months thereafter, while state officials sought a long-term solution, every prison unit experienced a total lockdown. Every inmate was confined to his cell, stripped of recreation and visitation privileges, and fed sandwiches that guards tossed through the bars of the cell. By the spring of 1986, prison officials had examined every inmate for telltale tattoos, weeded out identifiable gang members, and ordered that they spend the rest of their sentences in administrative segregation, away from the general population.

After the lockdown, the murder rate plunged. Peaceable inmates who had lost faith in TDCJ's ability to protect them now felt less inclined to carry shanks everywhere they went. A certain order prevailed, which stilled the critics and deflected the interest of the media. Prison officials could boast that their residents stood less chance of being killed than did the average Texas city dweller. By the end of the eighties, the public fretting over prison gangs had dissipated.

But the sudden absence of gang wars did not mean that the gangs had gone away. On the fourth day of the Sandoval trial, as if to punctuate the implicit warning in the testimony that gangs still thrived within the system, a member of the Mexican Mafia stabbed a Hermano de Pistolero to death at the Eastham Unit. Around the same time, prison officials expressed concern about the fifty or sixty members of the two Los Angeles based black street gangs, the Bloods and the Crips, that had recently entered the system. The youth gangs haven't caused trouble yet, but the realities of prison life suggest that this will surely change.

The Bloods and the Crips will likely adapt to their new environment just as other inmates do. To make identification difficult for prison officials, most gang members no longer wear tattoos. Uneasy truces between gangs have developed. The 1,577 gang members currently housed in administrative segregation represent only a fraction of those inmates who actually do the gangs' bidding. Many of the gang leaders who had been doing time are now in the free world, spreading the gang network across the state, beyond prison walls. TDCJ intelligence files indicate that by the close of the eighties, the TS, the Mexican Mafia, and other prison gangs had developed active memberships in every major Texas city, as well as in several small towns. Our prisons, far from turning out reformed citizens, have instead become incubators of a statewide crime wave.

The gang murders that once took place inside prisons now take place on the streets. Prison officials believe that the rivalry between the TS and the Mexican Mafia has produced homicides in Austin, Dallas, Houston, El Paso, and especially San Antonio, where nearly one hundred suspected prison-gang-related murders were committed last year. This past May, the bullet-riddled body of Mexican Mafia member Andres Sampyro was found in a San Antonio barrio.

What sustains the gangs is money, which inmates use to bribe prison employees. The money chiefly comes from drugs. Drugs come from the free world. Prisons, crammed with thrill-seekers and outright junkies, provide the ultimate captive consumers. Each society sustains the other, but the economic cycle depends on a vital link, for the supply will not meet the demand unless the product reaches the consumer. To get drugs out of the free world and into prison cells, there must be a courier. And the courier must possess a particular power: He must be able to walk through walls.

A CALL FROM EL CARPINTERO

"Hey, Boss, you got a light?" Luis Sandoval pulled out his lighter and, as he had before, lit the cigarette held by Armando Garcia. (This inmate's name has been changed as a condition of his interview.) Garcia, a four-time loser serving a life sentence for repeated theft and heroin offenses, was one of the friendlier inmates: 33 years old but actually grandfatherly in demeanor — a gentleman, you could almost say — quiet and unthreatening. And Sandoval welcomed his company.

Sandoval felt more at home with fellow Hispanics than with the black inmates, who terrified him. The five-foot-six, soft-voiced young man had spent most of his life in the South Texas town of Alice, where blacks were scarcely seen. His mother and stepfather lived in a middle-class neighborhood, but most of Sandoval's friends lived in the barrios or in the projects in Kingsville, where Sandoval attended college for three years. In the tenements across the street from the Texas A&M University stadium lived a fifteen-year-old girl named Veronica, whom he married on June 22, 1985, after learning that TDCJ had accepted his application for employment as a correctional officer, or CO.

The next day, a Sunday, the newlyweds threw their possessions into a suitcase and a grocery bag, and drove Sandoval's Datsun to Conroe. On Monday, at eight in the morning, Sandoval reported for duty at the Ellis I training academy in Huntsville.

"I've seen about five new boots take one step out of the control riot-gate and into the main hallway and turn around and say, 'See you later,' " said Sandoval. "If you last six months in there, you'll make it. But the first six months is hell." Sandoval was determined to tough it out. The new boot suffered the usual abuse from veterans and inmates. But he stayed out of trouble, in large part because of two hall porters, Bubba Ray Smith and Johnny Abrams. The two inmates snitched for Sandoval and herded him away from troublemakers, admonishing him, "Boss, stay away from those guys."

Somehow an inmate by the name of Vicente had gotten past the new boot's boys. Perhaps it was because Vicente was so quiet and servile or perhaps he had such a talent for lingering that the porters simply paid him no mind. It seemed that everywhere Sandoval went, there was Vicente, pushing his broom across the floor, sometimes waving or offering a greeting to the new boot, but never badgering him. Eventually the guard found himself engaging in polite conversation with the inmate. Sandoval came to enjoy these moments. It was a pleasure to deal with an inmate man to man, for once. When Vicente and his friend Armando Garcia -- also a pleasant, nonconfrontational fellow — began to ask Sandoval if he had a light, the guard refused at first, and finally decided, after repeated requests, what the hell. Some rules were just too silly to heed.

Eventually, however, Vicente and Garcia began to ask for more than a light. The inmates handed Sandoval a letter, wondering if the guard could mail it for them. "I don't have any money to get any stamps," Garcia explained.

Sandoval weighed his choices. If he refused to do the favor, they could always snitch on him for lighting an inmate's cigarette -- though Sandoval didn't think either was that type of inmate. On the other hand, if his superiors caught him delivering inmate mail, they could fire him on the spot. But that was if they caught him. Or if they cared to enforce the rule. Neither possibility seemed likely, given what Sandoval had learned about TDCJ in his first few months on the job.

At Ellis I, Sandoval had never seen so many rules enforced so haphazardly. Homosexuality was prohibited, yet punks strutted about in their cells, wearing women's panties and makeup. Alcohol was forbidden, yet "chock," or homemade wine, was made in a variety of ways in cells, the crudest method being by letting food wrapped in a plastic bag fester in a toilet tank. One Ellis I officer reported that in 1986, between one hundred and two hundred gallons of chock was discovered on a weekly basis within the unit.

Compared with Luis Sandoval's quite life in Alice, Ellis I must have seemed like an opium den. The 1985 lockdown put a damper on the atmosphere but not on the flow of drugs. Guards could still smell burning marijuana and still see inmates giggling to themselves.

Inmates fashioned shanks out of road signs, door hinges, food trays, typewriter platen rods, and field equipment. After the big lockdown, metal detectors were installed in every prison unit to discourage the carrying of shanks. Thereafter, inmates made their blades out of hard plastic or made do with whatever crude instrument was within reach, like the cast-iron weight an inmate found in the recreation yard and used, with one vicious swing, to lop off the ear of another inmate. Other weapons were by-products of inmate ingenuity, as in the case of Cosmo, the death row inmate who fashioned a bomb out of matchstick tips and an asthma inhaler and blew a hole in his cell wall.

Though inmates weren't allowed needles for tattooing, resident artists took to using the metal pieces of windup toys. Convicts made primitive ovens out of foil-lined cardboard boxes equipped with a light bulb, and cooked deer or rabbit killed by inmates working in the fields. Sandoval caught one inmate with a homemade oven and a laundry basket filled with about fifty prime-cut steaks.

The steaks would have come from the kitchen; the laundry basket that held them would have been wheeled past a guard. Either the guard didn't know what was going on, or he did. Sandoval figured the odds were about even. In prison, he had come to learn, if you gave, you got. Rumor had it that inmate Jesse Turner had stood between an inmate and a prison official and had taken the blade himself. Now Turner could be seen pushing trash cans down the hall, twirling his knife in the air; nobody took his knife away. According to Sandoval, Howard Digby, a runty burglar with a pug nose and heavily tattooed arms, was known as a captain's boy, a snitch who filled his boss's cup with coffee and his ear with prison gossip. In return, the snitch had an oversized cell to himself, plus a hall pass that gave him the run of the unit.

Sandoval did not know any warden, ranking officer, or CO at Ellis I who did not have at least one snitch. Everyone wanted information on the inmates, on their superiors, on their peers. Seemingly everyone in Ellis I would snitch or be snitched on. If you didn't treat your snitch right, he would scurry off to a more grateful listener and begin his new relationship by snitching on you. It was not the most hospitable climate for trust, which was something Sandoval felt inclined to consider when Armando Garcia and Vicente held out a letter and asked Sandoval to mail it for them.

Today, Sandoval says he mailed the letter and others like it "with a kind heart but with bad judgment." And in an institution where judgment allowed some inmates to flaunt dangerous weapons while officials looked the other way, mailing the letter seemed like a minor transgression. He did so and, he told me, was then given $50 by the inmates. Later, Vicente asked the guard if a free world individual could mail Sandoval two money orders, which Sandoval would cash and then bring the $250 to the inmates. Sandoval did as he was asked. For his trouble, the inmates offered the guard $75. Sandoval told me that he took the money, though he denied it in court. Later, when Vicente asked the guard to phone a number in Brady and ask the person who answered when Vicente's family would make their next visit, Sandoval had no objections. On another occasion, Vicente asked Sandoval to deliver the phone message that Vicente needed money to buy arts and crafts supplies. The guard made the call, apparently unaware that such messages, and the letters, might contain coded instructions from a prison drug-runner to a high-ranking member of the Texas Syndicate.

Garcia himself was not a TS member. Murder wasn't his thing. He was a drug dealer, with connections dating back to his days peddling heroin in El Paso. Like any good businessman, Garcia kept a close eye on the marketplace. When cocaine was cheap, he sold coke; when pure coke became scarce and heroin became abundant, Garcia seized the opportunity. "I just want to take care of my business," he would tell gang members who tried to recruit him. A deal was struck between the gang and Garcia: Garcia would acquire the drugs, give half to the Texas Syndicate, and sell the other half himself. All Garcia and his friend Vicente lacked was a reliable "drug mule" who could be counted on to transport drugs into the prison.

Eventually, Sandoval agreed to bring drugs into Ellis I. The drug trade was lucrative, and Sandoval always seemed to be hurting for money. But other factors have caused guards to agree to be drug mules. One of them is fear. The moment Garcia asked Sandoval to bring marijuana into TDCJ, it did not take superhuman deductive powers for the guard to figure out the Hispanic inmate's clientele. Recalling the letter deliveries and phone messages, Sandoval might have wondered just what he had gotten himself into and how deeply. Garcia, of course, could snitch to the Ellis I authorities. But now that seemed the least of Luis Sandoval's worries.

The other factor that has led guards to traffic in drugs is the peculiar morality of Ellis I, where rules are never universally applied and the use of drugs is so widespread that officials have to know — and accept — that prison guards are involved in the supply chain. On Sandoval's shift alone, at least four or five guards had been busted for bringing drugs into prison, but there were others who hadn't been busted and probably never would be. One was an officer who muled marijuana and cocaine for a black inmate known as Apple Jack, whose activities were no secret at the unit. "He would stand at the searcher's desk like he was running the building," Sandoval said. "Everybody knew about this scum." Yet Apple Jack went unpunished: He tithed a share of his profits to the Texas Syndicate and gave the supervisors something to crow about by setting up a guard now and then. Apple Jack protected his mule, however, and though many knew of the officer's extracurriculars, the hammer never fell on him.

One day Garcia told Sandoval to expect a call at home that evening. The caller, known as El Carpintero, was a convicted child molester from El Paso who nonetheless had managed to obtain a job, under an assumed name, as an x-ray technician at Ellis I. El Carpintero instructed Sandoval to drive to a location in Huntsville where a sack containing marijuana awaited. Sandoval picked up the marijuana and smuggled it into Ellis I — frightened every step of the way, he told me, that someone might notice the smell of marijuana and search him. But no one suspected a thing.

After that first transaction, Sandoval went back for more -- a total of "three, four, or five times," he told me, though he vividly described six transactions to an investigator hired by his family. (For that matter, Garcia testified during the trial, outside the presence of the jury, that Sandoval muled drugs "countless times." Sandoval was never searched, he told me, and came to learn that "the only way they bust you is if they're told by a snitch, 'This guy's coming in today.'"

While Sandoval said there were other guards — and even supervisors — involved in drug activity, the Texas Syndicate preferred that Garcia deal directly with Sandoval, a fellow Hispanic. Sandoval's apparent relationship with the gang did not escape the attention of the Ellis I population. "I'd say about eighty percent of the inmates knew he was dealing," claimed one inmate who was close to the action. "They'd say, 'Don't mess with him.' "

The new boot thereby became a feared boss among bosses. To the newer guards, Sandoval's stature among the inmates was something to behold. "Sandoval was one of the officers I wanted to be like," said one correctional officer whom Sandoval helped train. "I could watch him deal with inmates and think, 'This guy knows something I don't know.'"

One evening, while gazing out from his apartment balcony, Sandoval saw a car drive slowly by. Paranoia overcame him. He grabbed the stash of marijuana he had recently picked up, ran to the bathroom, and flushed it down his toilet. "Look, man, I think I'm being watched," Sandoval told Garcia the next day. "Armando, I can't jeopardize my life, man."

Garcia took the story to the Texas Syndicate. They didn't believe Sandoval. The mule, they believed, had done the drugs himself. Either way, Sandoval was out. The next day, Sandoval recalled, "I walked into work feeling good. I had the burden lifted from my shoulders."

THE HIT

"You have these inmates," said an Ellis I correctional officer, "where you write 'em up [for rule infractions] and nothing happens. Rank is taking care of them."

Joe Arredondo was one of those inmates, an arrogant squirt barely over five feet tall who frequently provoked guards but never got in trouble for it. In fact, his disciplinary record was almost spotless, and he enjoyed the privileged position of commissary clerk.

By the fall of 1986, several months after the gang lockdown policy had been instituted, Joe Arredondo's cockiness began to catch up with him. Arredondo was a Texas Syndicate member. He had been ordered to carry out a hit on another inmate and had failed to do so. Arredondo did take part in a different contract killing, but when all the conspirators except Arredondo were placed in administrative segregation, TS members concluded that Arredondo had snitched on the rest to save himself. The decision was reached: Arredondo would be taken down. The question was when. He had a one-week prison furlough coming up; the gang didn't want to spook him, fearing that he might not return to Ellis I. To keep him at ease, the Texas Syndicate requested that the inmate return from his furlough with two hundred dollars' worth of heroin and marijuana. Arredondo took the two hundred dollars, went home, and blew the money.

Ellis I officials caught wind of the deal through a snitch. Upon Arredondo's return, they ushered the inmate to an infirmary cell, where a guard stood nearby, waiting for Arredondo's bowels to evacuate a container of drugs. But Arredondo had brought back nothing. Word spread through the unit the way it always had, at bewildering speed: Joe Arredondo was a dead man.

The roles in the Arredondo hit were decided in either the chow hall or the chapel, where numbers were drawn from a cup. According to testimony, the man who drew the magic card, number one, was TS sergeant Carlos Rosas, a 31-year-old Dallas resident who was serving thirty years for aggravated robbery. Rosas would do the killing, while another TS member held Arredondo and two others stood by as lookouts. The murder would take place in a corridor abutting the B-wing: the maximum-security area where Luis Sandoval often worked.

The B-wing, a loud an grossly overcrowded area, "was considered the hellhole," in the words of Cade Crippin, the CO who worked the B-wing with Sandoval the afternoon of the murder. Some of the state's most violent criminals were housed there. At certain times, more than five hundred of them might flood the B-wing hallway en route to the gym, the chapel, the woodshop, or the chow hall. When asked on the witness stand if the hallway was ever undermanned, the reply of Nolan McCool — another officer working the B-wing that afternoon — was emphatic: "Constantly."

Conditions were no different on December 17, 1986, which was why Sandoval was given the assignment of B-wing hall boss that afternoon. He had long since survived the new boots' six months of hell. By now he was a CO III, an old boot, and he had trained many of the guards who now worked with him. His assignment was one of the toughest jobs in Ellis I. The west end of the B-wing hallway was left unguarded after three-thirty every afternoon, when the guard normally stationed there was transferred to the chow hall. This practice violated the *Ruiz* stipulation that an officer must be present at all times at any entrance or exit of the main building. It was also a dangerous practice in light of the fact that a narrow corridor intersected the west end of the B-wing and only an officer standing at that end could see what was going on in the corridor.

But Ellis I officials, like so many other wardens in the post-*Ruiz* era, were playing a numbers game. Chow time meant that vast numbers of inmates would be crowded together in one room. Extra guards to supervise the gathering had to come from some other post. Officials knew this meant that every day from three-thirty until after chow time, activities in the narrow corridor went unmonitored. It was a blind spot, and unit officials hoped the inmates wouldn't notice. But according to one Ellis I officer, "Inmates watch everything we do. That's all they do-look for our weaknesses."

At about five-thirty that afternoon, Sandoval approached CO II Cade Crippin, who was inside a cellblock, observing the inmates. "Take over the hallway for me," Sandoval said to his subordinate while handing him his keys. Then he headed for the bathroom, a route that took him through a confined area guarded by CO II Nolan McCool. McCool opened the picket gate to allow Sandoval into the rest room. Just as he entered, Sandoval heard someone yell, "He's on the floor! He's bleeding!" He whirled and burst into the B-wing hallway. Looking toward the chapel, he could see Crippin ahead of him, heading for the hidden narrow corridor at the west end of the B-wing.

When they got there they found Joe Arredondo lying on his back. Blood was gushing out of a hole in his neck; he was unconscious but gasping wildly. An eight inch metal shank lay nearby. Sandoval put his hand against the wound, looked up, and saw Crippin and McCool standing there, gaping. "Yell 'fight,' " he said, but the two officers seemed paralyzed. Sandoval got up, ran into the hallway, and yelled "fight" twice. Then he returned to Arredondo. "Give me your shirt," he ordered an inmate and with it applied pressure to the wound. Crippin knelt and lifted the inmate's legs. "Leave them on the floor!" said Sandoval. "You'll drain all the blood to his head." Three other officers arrived on the scene. "Get these inmates in the chapel," he told them. "And call for a gurney."

Joe Arredondo was taken to a hospital in Huntsville. He was pronounced dead at seven that evening, a victim of twenty stab wounds. By that time, things were quiet again at Ellis I. There was no further violence, a signal to those who understood gang behavior that Arredondo had been snuffed out by one of his own rather than by a rival gang. The following day, Chaplain Alexander Taylor, who witnessed Sandoval's efforts, wrote the CO III a letter of commendation. That afternoon, Ellis I warden Jerry Peterson called Sandoval into his office to congratulate him on a fine job. The warden would later testify that Sandoval's actions were "somewhat heroic." But, Peterson added, the hero had seemed awfully calm in the midst of all the bloodshed-perhaps too calm.

ON A WESTBOUND BUS

Ten months after the murder, on October 23, 1987, Sandoval was again summoned to the warden's office. This time, however, four Internal Affairs officers greeted him inside by reading him his rights and charging him with murder. He was accused of leaving a door unsecured and unguarded as part of a murder plot. Sandoval was then ordered to take official uniform and replace it with inmate furlough clothes. The officials fitted Sandoval with handcuffs, leg irons, and a belly chain. He was whisked off to the Walker County jail.

That afternoon in the interrogation room, Special Prison Prosecution Unit investigator Royce Smithey bore down on Sandoval. You were in the hallway, Smithey said. A man was stabbed twenty times. Whoever killed him had to have come through the B-wing hallway and had to have been dripping with blood. You're telling us you saw nothing? You're telling us it's a coincidence that you weren't down at that end of the hallway? Come on, Sandoval. We know who you're tied to. We know who you take orders from.

Sandoval insisted that he didn't know anything about the Arredondo murder other than what he filed in his report. The guard said he wasn't tied to anyone. But things got more interesting when Internal Affairs investigator Dale Schaper walked into the room and handed Sandoval copies of his phone records, showing that 25 phone calls he had made on Vicente's behalf were to a high-ranking TS official named Felix Benavidez.

Sandoval buckled. Yes, he had made the phone calls. Yes, he had mailed Vicente's letters, had cashed two money orders for the inmate, and on three different occasions, had delivered packages from a parking lot to a telephone booth. The packages, he admitted, most likely contained drugs. Dale Schaper dutifully typed up his report and sent it through the proper channels. (Today, Sandoval says that statement was coerced.) Six weeks later, in December 1987, Luis Sandoval was terminated from the Texas Department of Criminal Justice.

It took more than three years for the Arredondo murder case to come to trial, during which time a number of things happened to Sandoval. His wife divorced him. His father died. He was arrested for driving while intoxicated, following a one-car accident that left his limbs temporarily paralyzed. To pay for his legal expenses, his mother sold the family home. Sandoval, in the meantime, worked at J. C. Penney in Plano.

One day Sandoval received a phone call at work. The caller advised Sandoval not to show up for his March 18, 1991, trial, and then hung up without identifying himself. On the witness stand, Sandoval suggested that the caller was someone from TDCJ Internal Affairs; more likely, he was a Texas Syndicate member delivering the message that the TS would not be amused if Sandoval blew the whistle on their activities. Even before the call, Luis Sandoval had been sweating bullets. Armando Garcia had seen this coming. Garcia would later say that he told Sandoval shortly after the Arredondo murder, "Man, you're in deep shit. They're gonna be looking at you, and all that stuff in the past is gonna come up. They're gonna say you were in on it. You better get the hell out of here, Sandoval."

Sandoval took the advice three years after Garcia gave it. On March 19, the name of Luis Sandoval was called three times in the Walker County courthouse, but the defendant did not respond. He was on a westbound bus, fleeing the state. Sandoval got off in Los Angeles and found his way to Van Nuys, where a cousin put him up in his apartment. For several days, Sandoval read the Bible and considered his options. He called his mother, who begged him to turn himself in. He told her that he feared the Texas prison authorities, who by now had surely discovered that the murder of Joe Arredondo was, if anything, a result of prison mismanagement. It was their fault, not his, but someone would have to take the fall. Sandoval did not tell his mother why he was such a vulnerable candidate.

He did not turn himself in. Instead, he wrote an impassioned, handwritten 24-page letter that his mother sent to a few members of the media. The letter was not what one might expect from a former prison guard. It criticized TDCJ's good ol' boy system, which Sandoval claimed "has ruled with an iron fist since the penal system was first established." Hispanic guards, he said, were "either coerced into quitting or found doing something wrong." Supervisors treated inmates "like animals." He further wrote, "I am not the only one who worked there that knows that TDCJ is linked to the gangs and their illegal activities. Inside the walls of each prison is drugs, prostitution, gambling, extortion, and grand theft, but no investigation into any of these things has ever been made." The letter did not say what such an investigation would say about Luis Sandoval.

When he sent the letter off to his mother, he knew it wouldn't be long before law enforcement officials discovered his whereabouts. With what was left of his final J. C. Penney paycheck, Sandoval and his cousin drove to Las Vegas, a place Sandoval had always yearned to visit. They blew the paycheck on the slot machines; they had a wonderful time. On the way home Sandoval asked his cousin to drive the scenic route. "I want to see the mountains," he said.

A few days later, on April 12, 1991, FBI agents showed up at the apartment where Sandoval had been hiding and took him to the Los Angeles County jail. Twelve days later, Texas chief prison prosecutor Travis McDonald flew to L.A., took custody of Sandoval, and flew him back to Huntsville, where he was held without bond at the Walker County jail.

NOT GUILTY

For all of Sandoval's claims that the system was making a sacrificial lamb out of him, the system came to his rescue in the end.

The two inmate snitches who testified against Sandoval understated their criminal history, contradicted each other, and came off looking like dirtbags who would say anything for the right price. In contrast, sixteen current or former Ellis I employees testified. Not one of them pinned the murder of Joe Arredondo on Sandoval. Not one of them said that Sandoval was a bad officer; many, in fact, went out of their way to laud his abilities. Several of them testified vigorously that Ellis I was understaffed and overcrowded, and that the unit was riddled with blind spots.

None of them knew anything about Sandoval and drugs. Asked point-blank by his attorney, Did you ever bring drugs inside TDCJ? Sandoval lied: "No, sir." Contradicting this claim, Internal Affairs investigator Dale Schaper took the stand and read his report of the night Sandoval was arrested. But the report was not a signed confession. When asked about it, Sandoval testified that the report merely contained Schaper's accusations, which Sandoval denied then and would deny now, under oath. Had Schaper's investigation been thorough, this denial might have seemed implausible to the jury. But the report made no mention of Armando Garcia and El Carpintero; nor did it officer any evidence that Sandoval had actually smuggled drugs into Ellis I.

It took the jury 33 minutes to decide that Sandoval was not guilty. After their verdict was announced on Wednesday, May 29, the jurors milled around outside the courtroom and vented their disgust with the state's case to the media. One juror phoned Sandoval's brother that afternoon and told him that in her view the case against Sandoval was racially motivated. A week later another juror wrote Sandoval a four-page letter, expressing her chagrin that he had been put through all the agony.

Not everyone was so sympathetic, however. After the trial, Sandoval's attorney, Steve Fischer, contacted TDCJ officials and asked them to let bygones be bygones. "Louie would love nothing more than to be a guard again," Fischer told them. The attorney was advised that his client would never again wear gray in a state penal Institution.

Were he to pay his old workplace a visit, Luis Sandoval would notice several changes at Ellis I. Video cameras monitor the hallways. The corridor where Joe Arredondo was murdered is now permanently guarded. Beneath the cosmetic alterations, however, things at Ellis I are just as Sandoval left them. On August 26, 1990, a death row inmate proved his loyalty to the Aryan Brotherhood during his daily recreation hour by strangling a black inmate in a recreation yard with a jump rope while the latter was performing oral sex on the former. And in March 1991, McDonald's prosecution force indicted yet another Ellis I guard. "He was muling," said McDonald.

Sandoval described Ellis I warden Jerry Peterson as "a good man but a figurehead. His assistant wardens run the building." Indeed, Peterson said to me that his unit's drug problem "isn't rampant," but he also acknowledged that much has escaped his attention over the years. Even after Arredondo's murder, when the Special Prison Prosecution Unit began to gather incriminating evidence against Sandoval, Peterson showed little interest in the details. "The investigators didn't tell me much, nor was I particularly inquisitive," he said.

Gangs still terrorize the prisons. "There's no way to shut them down," Sandoval said. Yet a former prison drug-runner confirmed the obvious — that without the help of TDCJ employees, the flow of drugs into state prisons would dry up. Without drugs, gangs would have little income; without income, they would have little power over the system. But the system will not change. Employees come and go unfrisked, unobserved. The system snitches on one mule while protecting another. "And there's always somebody," the ex-drug runner told me "who'll do, something for you."

"I didn't do it," Sandoval announced to me in a recent phone conversation. Reminded that our earlier on-the-record on-tape conversation contradicted this, he said, "I have my life to think about.... I made my mistakes. But I was a good officer." Thus, the former good officer now wished to disavow everything he had told me earlier. As to everything he had told his investigator — none of that was true either, he said. He had lied to his own investigator, just as inmates and Internal Affairs had lied to the jurors. No one, he seemed to be suggesting, was capable of telling the truth about Luis Sandoval — not even Sandoval himself.

A GOOD KID

The inmate, a former gang operative now in protective custody, pulled a hand-rolled cigarette out of his white shirt and lit it. He squinted through the smoke and the bars and the memories. "I can't honestly tell you why he did it," said the inmate of Sandoval. "There were many times when he said, 'I ain't gonna do this shit anymore.' And we'd think well, maybe we're putting too much pressure on him. So we'd just lay back, let him cool down. Then he'd say, 'Damn, I wish I had twenty dollars to go buy a couple of beers.' And I'd say, 'Just wait here, I'll be back.' And I'd collect fifty dollars for him. Then he'd have to do something for us.

"When Arredondo got killed, Sandoval was just in the wrong place at the wrong time. If the Texas Syndicate had told him there was a murder happening, he wouldn't have gone for it. I remember when he yelled fight. I was in the dayroom. I looked up, and as he was running by, he looked at me . . . like he wanted to cry, you know? I knew he didn't have nothing to do with it.

"Sandoval, he was a good kid," said the inmate of the guard who had once done him favors. "He just got involved with the wrong people."

JUDICIAL REFORM AND PRISON CONTROL: THE IMPACT OF *RUIZ V. ESTELLE* ON A TEXAS PENITENTIARY

During the past two decades, federal courts have become increasingly involved in upholding the rights of prisoners in state correctional facilities. Judicial decisions ordering administrators to implement procedures and standards that meet constitutional requirements have often had widespread and unintended consequences.

By James W. Marquart
Ben M. Crouch

IN THE 1960S A "DUE PROCESS REVOLUTION" OCCURRED in which the judiciary addressed and attempted to remedy aspects of many of this society's institutional ills. Almost since the start of this revolution jails and prisons have been an important focus of judicial attention. In general, the courts have expanded the constitutional rights of prisoners at the expense of the so-called "hands-off" doctrine (Calhoun 1978; Jacobs 1980). That is, the courts have rejected the traditional view that prisoners were socially "dead" and managed at the discretion of the prison staff. Courts for the past fifteen years have responded sympathetically to prisoners' grievances and have issued as well as administered many rulings forcing prison organizations to modify or cease numerous institutional policies and procedures. To illustrate, as of December 1983 thirty state prison systems were operating under court order or consent decrees designed to alleviate prison overcrowding (U.S. Department of Justice 1984). This change in court posture has made possible the fuller integration of the penitentiary within the central institutional and value systems of the society (Shils 1975: 93; Jacobs 1977).

Despite the proliferation of "prisoner rights" cases, there exists relatively little empirical research on the impact of judicially mandated reforms on prison structures and operations. The sociology of confinement literature typically describes court-ordered reforms as part of or ancillary to changes wrought by shifts in prison administration (Carroll 1974; Jacobs 1977; Colvin 1982), goals (Carroll 1974; Stastny and Tyrauner 1982), or inmate populations (Irwin 1980; Crouch 1980). When researchers have directly examined court-ordered reforms (for example, Kimball and Newman 1968; UCLA Law Review 1973; Champagne and Haas 1976; Turner 1979), their analyses have been narrowly focused and do not assess the long-term effects of intervention on the prison community. Because systematic empirical research is lacking, we have only some general ideas about what happens in prisons when courts intervene and alter an established order. Jacobs (1980) summarizes those general ideas and notes that court-ordered reforms often lead to a demoralized staff, a new generation of prison administrators, a bureaucratic prison organization, a redistribution of power within the prison, and a politicized and often factionalized inmate society.

The most general observation made about the consequences of judicial intervention has been that prisons have become increasingly bureaucratized (Jacobs 1977; Turner 1979). Authority in prisons is no longer unrestricted but based instead on formal procedures and policies. The days of the autonomous "big house" warden are history. Bureaucratization has also affected prisoner control. The harsh disciplinary measures of the past have been replaced with a legalistic due process model, similar, in some respects, to hearing procedures in nonprison settings. We do not know, however, how the bureaucratization of prisons and prisoner control that judicial intervention has engendered has affected day-to-day life within the prison community. We need to know what transpires within prisons after court-ordered reforms have been implemented by the administrators. In particular, we need to know more about the consequences of court-ordered reforms for prison control systems and for relationships among the parties-inmates, guards, and administrators-on whom control ultimately depends.

This paper is a case study and institutional analysis that examines the impact of legal intervention on a Texas penitentiary -- the Eastham Unit. This study, unlike many legal impact studies, is not primarily concerned with the "gap" question -- whether or not compliance has been achieved. Rather, it analyzes the institutional implications of a judicial remedy that has been implemented in good faith. The case in question is *Ruiz v. Estelle* (1980), a massive class action suit against the Texas Department of Corrections (TDC) in which a federal district judge ordered TDC to make wholesale organizational changes (for example, in health care, overcrowding, inmate housing). Our focus is on a central feature of *Ruiz* which ordered TDC and Eastham to abandon certain official and unofficial methods of prisoner control. Our objective is to analyze the prisoner control structure at Eastham prior to this case, the specific changes that were ordered, and how these changes affected the prison community. In the last section, we contrast several organizational elements of the old order with the emerging bureaucratic-legal order and discuss the implications of this shift in structure and philosophy for daily control. In effect, this analysis examines a penitentiary before, during, and after the implementation of a legal reform.

THE SETTING AND METHOD OF STUDY

The research site was the Eastham Unit of the Texas penal system. Eastham is a large maximum security institution located on 14,000 acres of farmland, which housed in 1981, nearly 3,000 inmates (47 percent black, 36 percent white, 17% Hispanic). Inmates assigned to this prison were classified by the Texas Department of Corrections as recidivists over the age of twenty-five, all of whom had been in prison (excluding juvenile institutions) three or more times. Eastham has a reputation for tight disciplinary control and so receives a large number of inmate troublemakers from other TDC prisons. Structurally, the prison has eighteen inside cellblocks (or tanks) and twelve dormitories which branch out from a single central hall-a telephone pole design. The Hall is the main thoroughfare of the prison and is almost one-quarter of a mile long, measuring 16 feet wide by 12 feet high.

The data for this paper were collected in two phases through participant observation, interviews with guards and inmates, searching documents and inmate records, and informal conversations resulting from the participant observation. In phase one, the first author entered the penitentiary as a guard and collected dissertation data on social control and order for nineteen months (June 1981 through January 1983). He worked throughout the institution (for example, in cell blocks, shops, dormitories) and observed firsthand how the guards cultivated "rats" and meted out official and unofficial punishments. In addition, he cultivated twenty key informants among the guards and inmate elites, with whom he discussed control and order as a daily phenomenon. The first authors close relationship with these informants and their "expert" knowledge about prison life and prisoner control were essential to the research (see Jacobs 1974b: Marquart 1984). Most important, his presence allowed observation and documentation of the control structure before, during, and for a short period after the reform measures were implemented.

In the second phase of research, the authors returned to Eastham and collected data from late September 1984 until January 3, 1985. Data collection procedures involved intensive observation and open-ended structured interviews (tape-recorded) with a cross section of thirty officers and sixty inmates. The inmate interviews addressed such issues as race relations, gang behavior, violence, relations with guards and prison rackets. The officer interviews focused on such topics as morale, violence, gang behavior, unionism, and relations with inmates. While formal and taped interviews were conducted, the researchers also obtained valuable insights from daily observations of and informal conversations with guards on and off duty throughout the prison as well as from inmates at work, recreation, meals, and in their cells. Furthermore, we closely interacted with seventeen key informants -- ten inmates and seven officers -- who provided a constant source of support and information. Available official documents (for example, memos, inmate records, solitary confinement logbooks) were used to substantiate and corroborate the interview and observational data.

THE CHANGE AGENT: *RUIZ V. ESTELLE*

In December 1980 Judge William W. Justice (Eastern District of Texas) delivered a sweeping decree against the Texas Department of Corrections in *Ruiz v. Estelle*. That decree, a year in the writing following a trial of many months, was the culmination of a suit originally filed with the court in 1972. The order recited numerous constitutional violations, focusing on several issues. First, TDC was deemed overcrowded. Prison officials were ordered to cease quadruple and triple celling. (1) To deal with the overcrowding problems, TDC erected tents, expanded furloughs, and in May 1982 even ceased accepting new prisoners for approximately ten days. Moreover, a "safety valve" population control plan passed by the legislature in 1983 and a liberalized "good time" policy have been used to expand parole releases. Nevertheless, overcrowding continues. A second issue was TDC's security practices. The judge ordered the prison administrators to sharply reduce and restrict the use of force by prison personnel. He also demanded the removal and reassignment of special inmates known as "building tenders" since the evidence clearly indicated that these inmates were controlling other inmates. To further increase security, the decree called for TDC to hire more guards and to develop a much more extensive inmate classification plan. Third, the judge found health care practices, procedures, and personnel in need of drastic upgrading. A fourth shortcoming involved inmate disciplinary practices. Problems included vague rules (for example, "agitation," "laziness"), the arbitrary use of administrative segregation, and a failure to maintain proper disciplinary hearing records. Fifth, the court found many problems with fire and safety standards in TDC. Finally, TDC was found to have unconstitutionally denied inmates access to courts, counsel, and public officials.

To implement this sweeping decree, Judge Justice appointed Vincent Nathan to serve as special master. Because TDC encompassed twenty-three units in 1981 (it now has twenty-seven), a group of monitors was hired to visit the prisons regularly and gauge compliance. The nature and extent of noncompliance with each aspect of the decree are contained in a series of lengthy monitors' reports and have served as the basis for ongoing negotiation and policy changes by the prison system.

Since our concern in this paper is with the official and unofficial means of prisoner control that were ruled unconstitutional by the court, we limit our analysis to those parts of the court order (for example, removal of building tenders and changes in security practices and personnel) relevant to that concern. To appreciate the effect of the order, we must first understand how Eastham was organized and how it operated prior to the courts intervention.

PRISONER CONTROL UNDER THE OLD ORDER

The control of older, hard-core criminals presents special problems in any prison. At Eastham, the staff maintained tight discipline and control through a complex system of official rewards and punishments administered by an elite group of prison officers. Basically, this control system rewarded those inmates who had good prison records with such privileges as good time, furloughs, dormitory living instead of a cell, and jobs other than fieldwork. On the other hand, the staff severely punished those inmates who challenged the staff's definition of the situation. The most unusual and important element in controlling the prisoners in the old order centered on the staff's open and formal reliance upon a select group of elite inmates to extend their authority and maintain discipline. It was this latter system of prisoner control, called the "building tender (BT) system," (2) that the court ordered TDC to abolish.

THE BUILDING TENDER/TURNKEY SYSTEM

The staff employed a strategy of co-opting the dominant or elite inmates with special privileges (for example, separate bathing and recreational periods, better housing, uniforms, open cells, clubs or knives, "friends" for cell partners, craft cards) in return for aid in controlling the ordinary inmates in the living areas, especially the cell blocks. The use of select inmates to control other inmates is ubiquitous and has been documented in such various prison settings as the Soviet Union (Solzhenitsyn 1974; 1975), India (Adam, n.d.), Australia (Shaw 1966), and French Guiana (Charriere 1970), as well as in Nazi concentration camps (Bettelheim 1943; Kogon 1958) and the management of slaves (Blassingame 1979). The most notable as well as notorious use of pro-staff-oriented inmates (convict guards) has occurred in the Mississippi, Arkansas, and Louisiana prison systems (see McWhorter 1981; Murton and Hyams 1969; Mouledous 1962). In these prisons, selected inmates were issued pistols and carbines to guard the other inmates. However, these elite inmates, unlike the inmate agents at Eastham, were housed in separate living quarters.

Structure and Work Role

The BT system at Eastham involved three levels of inmates. At the top of the hierarchy were the "head" building tenders. In 1981, each of the eighteen blocks had one building tender who was assigned by the staff as the "head" BT and was responsible for all inmate behavior in "his" particular block. Indeed, "ownership" of a block by a head BT was well recognized: inmates and officers alike referred informally but meaningfully to, for example, "Jackson's tank" or "Brown's tank." Essentially, the head BT was the block's representative to the ranking officers. For example, if a knife or any other form of contraband was detected in "his" living area, it was the head BT's official job to inform the staff of the weapons whereabouts and who had made it, as well as to tell the staff about the knife makers character. In addition, these BT's would help the staff search the suspected inmate's cell to ferret out the weapon. Because of their position, prestige, and role, head BTs were the most powerful inmates in the prisoner society. They acted as overseers and frequently mediated and settled disputes and altercations among the ordinary inmates. This role frequently called for the threat of or use of force. They stood outside ordinary prisoner interaction but by virtue of their position and presence kept all other inmates under constant surveillance.

At the second level of the system were the rank and file building tenders. In every cellblock or dormitory, there were generally between three and five inmates assigned as building tenders, for a total of nearly 150 BTs within the institution. These inmates "worked the tank," and their official role was to maintain control in the living areas by tabulating the daily counts, delivering messages to other inmates for the staff, getting the other inmates up for work, cleaning, and reporting any serious misbehavior by inmates to the head BT who, in turn, told the staff. Another important duty of the BTs was the socialization of new inmates into the system. When new inmates arrived at a living area, BTs informed them of the "rules," which meant "keep the noise down, go to work when you are supposed to, mind your own business, and tell us [the BTs] when you have a problem." In addition to these tasks, the BTs broke up fights, gave orders to other inmates, and protected the officers in charge of the cellblocks from attacks by the inmates.

The BTs also unofficially meted out discipline to erring inmates. For example, if an inmate had to be told several times to be quiet in the dayroom (the living area's television and recreation room), stole another inmates property, or threatened another inmate, he was apt to receive some form of physical punishment. If this initial encounter did not correct the problem the BTs, with tacit staff approval, would severely beat the inmate (sometimes with homemade clubs) and have him moved to another cellblock. This process, called "whipping him off the tank" or "counseling," was not uncommon, and some inmates were moved frequently throughout the prison. Although the BTs were "on call" twenty-four hours a day, the head BT assigned the other BTs to shifts (morning, evening, and night) to provide the manpower needed to manage the block. The living areas were their turf, and the staff basically left the management of these areas in their hands.

The third level of the building tender system consisted of inmates referred to as runners, strikers, or hitmen. Runners were not assigned to work in the blocks by the staff rather, these inmates were selected by the BTs for their loyalty and willingness to act as informants. They also worked at regular jobs throughout the prison. Runners performed the janitorial work of the block, sweeping and dispensing supplies to the cells. They also served as conduits of information for the BTs since they had more contact with the ordinary inmates than BTs and picked up important information. More important, runners served as the physical backups for the BTs. If a fight or brawl broke out, the runners assisted the BTs in quelling the disturbance. As a reward for their services, runners enjoyed more mobility and privileges within the block than the other inmates (but less than the BTs). The BT crew in each tank recruited their runners, and selection was based primarily on the inmate's ability to work and willingness to inform. Moreover, many runners were friends of or known by the BTs in the free world; some runners were also the homosexual partners of their BT bosses. Some tanks had three or four runners, while others had seven, eight, or even nine. The numbers of runners totaled somewhere in the vicinity of 175 to 200 inmates. The final aspect of the building tender system consisted of inmates referred to as turnkeys, who numbered seventeen in 1981. As mentioned earlier, the prison contained a large corridor known as the Hall. Within the Hall were seven large metal barred doors, or riot barricades. Turnkeys worked in six-hour shifts, carrying on long leather straps the keys that locked and unlocked the barricades. They shut and locked these doors during fights or disturbances to prevent them from escalating or moving throughout the Hall. In addition to operating the barricades, turnkeys routinely broke up fights, assisted the BTs, and protected the prison guards from the ordinary inmates. These doorkeepers also passed along information to the BTs about anything they heard while "working a gate." More important, turnkeys assisted the cell block guards by locking and unlocking the cell block doors, relaying messages, counting, and keeping the Hall free of inmate traffic. In fact, the block guards and turnkeys worked elbow to elbow and assisted one another so much that only their respective uniforms separated them. When off duty, the turnkeys, who lived in the block, assisted the BTs in the everyday management of the block. In terms of power and privileges, turnkeys were on the same level as the regular BTs.

The building tender system functioned officially as an information network. Structurally, the staff was at the perimeter of the inmate society but the building tender system helped the staff penetrate, divide, and control the ordinary inmates. BTs and turnkeys in turn had snitches working for them, not only in the living area, but throughout the entire institution. Thus, the staff secured information that allowed them to exert enormous power over the inmate's daily activities. As mentioned earlier, the BTs and turnkeys were handsomely rewarded for their behavior and maintained power and status far exceeding that of ordinary inmates and lower ranking guards. Unofficially, these inmates maintained order in the blocks through fear, and they physically punished inmates who broke the rules.

Selection of BTs and Turnkeys

These inmate "managers" of the living areas performed a dangerous job for the staff. Vastly outnumbered, BTs and turnkeys ruled with little opposition from the ordinary inmates. In reality, most of the ordinary inmates justifiably feared their "overseers" because of their status and physical prowess. The BTs and turnkeys were selected through an official appointment procedure to perform a "formal" job within the living areas. The selection procedure began with the staff at Eastham (and the other TDC prisons), who recommended certain inmates as BTs/turnkeys to the Classification Committee (a panel of four TDC officials, all with prison security backgrounds). This committee then reviewed each inmate's record and made the final selections. Recommendations to the Classification Committee from the staff were not always honored, and fewer than half of those recommended were selected for BT/turnkey jobs. One supervisor who was an active participant in the recruitment process at Eastham expressed his preference, which was typical:

> I've got a personal bias. I happen to like murderers and armed robbers. They have a great deal of esteem in the inmate social system, so its not likely that they'll have as much problem as some other inmate because of their esteem, and they tend to be a more aggressive and a more dynamic kind of individual. A lot of inmates steer clear of them and avoid problems just because of the reputation they have and their aggressiveness. They tend to be aggressive, you know, not passive.

The majority of the individuals selected for BT and turnkey positions were the physically and mentally superior inmates who appeared to be natural leaders. Generally, BTs and turnkeys were more violent and criminally sophisticated than the regular inmates. For example, of the eighteen head BTs at Eastham, eight were in prison for armed robbery, five for murder (one was an enforcer and contract-style killer), one for attempted murder, one for rape, one for drug trafficking, and two for burglary. Their average age was thirty-nine and their average prison sentence was thirty-two years. Of the seventeen turnkeys, there were three murderers, three armed robbers, six burglars, two drug traffickers, one rapist, one car thief, and one person in for aggravated assault. Their average age was thirty-one and their average sentence was twenty-two years. In contrast, the average TDC inmate in 1981 had a twenty-one-year sentence, with a modal age category between twenty-two and twenty-seven. These data clearly show that the BTs and turnkeys were older than most inmates and more likely to be violent recidivists. This is consistent with the patterns noted by others who have described inmate leaders (for example, Clemmer 1940; Schrag 1954).

Race Most of the regular BTs/turnkeys came from the black and white inmate populations. Only a handful of Hispanic inmates were ever recruited for these positions. The staff distrusted most Hispanic inmates, perceiving them as dangerous, clannish, and above all "sneaky." Hispanic inmates, primarily for cultural reasons, were tight-lipped and generally avoided any voluntary interaction with the staff or other inmates. They feared being labeled as pro-staff because physical reprisals from other Hispanics for snitching were common inside as well as outside the prison world. Moreover, Hispanic inmates were generally not as imposing physically as inmates of other races.

Although black and white inmates both served as BTs, power was not equally distributed between the races. The predominantly rural, white, ranking guards kept the "real" power in the hands of the white BTs. That is, of the eighteen head BTs, there were fourteen whites, three blacks, and one Hispanic. The ranking staff members were prejudiced and "trusted" the white BTs more than members of the other two races. In short, with the help of the staff, a "white con" power structure similar to a caste system dominated the inmate society in the same way the "old con" power structure ruled Stateville (Joliet, Illinois) in the 1930s through the 1950s (see Jacobs 1977).

THE STAFF AND UNOFFICIAL CONTROL

The staff at Eastham did not leave control of the prison totally in the hands of their inmate agents. In addition, the guards actively enforced "unofficial" order through intimidation and the routine use of physical force. Rules were quickly and severely enforced, providing inmates with clear-cut information about where they stood, what they could and could not do, and who was boss (see McCleery 1960). The unification or symbiotic relationships of these two groups -- that is, guards as inside outsiders and inmate agents as elite outside insiders -- precluded revolt at practically every level.

Intimidation

Inmates who challenged a guard's authority (for example, by insubordination, cursing at him, or "giving him a hard time") were yelled at by guards or supervisors (sergeants, lieutenants, and captains). Racial epithets, name-calling, derogation, threats of force, and other scare tactics were common. These methods though physically harmless, ridiculed, frightened, or destroyed the "face" of the offending inmate. The following remarks by one ranking officer are an example. "You stupid nigger, if you ever lie to me or to any other officer about what you're doing, I'll knock your teeth in." On another occasion, a supervisor made this typical threat: "Say, big boy, you're some kind of motherfucker, aren't you? I oughta just go ahead and whip your ass here and now."

Verbal remarks such as these were routine. In some cases, inmates were threatened with extreme physical force (for example, "You'll leave here [the prison] in an ambulance") or even death ("Nobody cares if a convict dies in here we'll beat you to death"). Such threats of physical force were scare tactics meant to deter inmates from future transgressions.

Physical Force

Coercive force is an important means of controlling people in any situation or setting. At Eastham, the unofficial use of physical force was a consistent method of prisoner control. Inmates were roughed up daily as matter of course. Within a two-month period, the first author observed over thirty separate incidents of guards using physical force against inmates. Key informants told the observer that this number of instances was not surprising. Indeed, as Marquart (1984) notes, fighting inmates was an important value in the guard subculture. Guards who demonstrated their willingness to fight inmates who challenged their authority were often rewarded by their supervisors with promotions, improved duty assignments, and prestigious labels such as "having nuts" or being a "good" officer. The willingness to use force was a rite of passage for new officers, and those who failed this test were relegated to unpleasant jobs such as cell block and gun tower duty. Those who refused to fight were rarely promoted, and many of these "deviant" officers eventually quit or transferred to other TDC prisons.

Generally, the physical force employed by ranking officers was of two kinds. First, some inmates received "tune-ups" or "attitude adjustments." These inmates were usually slapped across the face or head, kicked in the buttocks, or even punched in the stomach. The intent of a "tune-up" was to terrorize the inmate without doing physical damage. More serious, but still a "tune-up," was the "ass whipping" in which the guards employed their fists, boots, blackjacks, riot batons, or aluminum flashlights. These were meant to hurt the inmate without causing severe physical damage. Like simple "tune-ups," "ass whippings" were a common and almost daily form of unofficial control. Both were "hidden" in that they were conducted in private settings free from inmate witnesses.

The second form of force was beatings. Beatings occurred infrequently and were reserved for inmates who violated certain "sacred" rules by, for instance, attacking an officer verbally or physically, inflicting physical harm on other inmates, destroying prison property, or attempting to lead work strikes, to escape, or to foment rebellion against the rules or officers. Inmates who broke these rules were defined as "resisting" the system and were severely injured -- often suffering concussions, loss of consciousness, cuts, and broken bones. Although beatings were rare, many were conducted in front of other inmates (always in the name of "self-defense") and served to make examples of those inmates who dared to break important norms.

The threat and use of force were an everyday reality under the old order, and the guards routinely used force to subdue "unruly" inmates (see Ninth Monitor's Report 1983). Although rewards and privileges served as important official means of control, the prison order was ultimately maintained through the "unofficial" use of fear and terror. The staff ruled the penitentiary with an iron hand and defined most situations for the inmates. Those inmates who presented a serious challenge (for example, threatening or attacking officers, fomenting work strikes) to the system were harassed, placed in solitary confinement, and sometimes beaten into submission. To the outsider, it might seem that this control structure would create enormous tension and foster mass revolt, but, as we have seen, the small number of guards did not face the inmates alone. The BTs and turnkeys with whom the guards shared power served as a first line of control and functioned as a buffer group between the staff and ordinary inmates.

This type of prisoner control can be referred to as internal because of the important official role given to insiders. It was proactive in nature since the elite inmates knew when trouble was likely to arise and could move to forestall it. BTs and turnkeys functioned as the communication link between the officials and ordinary inmates. The BTs dealt with most of the inmate problems within the living areas and thereby insulated the staff from the multitude of petty squabbles arising in the course of prison life. Riots and mob action was obviated by this relentless BT surveillance and control. Problem situations were passed upward to the guards. In this old order, the staff, BTs, and turnkeys maintained an alliance that ensured social order, peace, the status quo, and stability. But the institutional arrangement that made for such a "well-working" prison fostered an atomistic inmate community fraught with fear and paranoia.

EASTHAM IN TRANSITION

Although there were some efforts to ease overcrowding and to reform prison operations such as medical services, the dominant posture of TDC in 1981 and most of 1982, at all levels, was to resist the court order both through legal action and by noncompliance. Prison officials rejected the intrusion of the court as a matter of principle and particularly feared the consequences of relinquishing such traditional control measures as the BT system. Initially, TDC fought the BT issue. However, additional court hearings in February 1982 made public numerous examples of BT/ turnkey perversion and brutality. (3) In late May 1982, attorneys for the state signed a consent decree agreeing to dismantle the decades-old inmate-guard system by January 1, 1983.

COMPLIANCE

To comply with the decree, the staff in September 1982 reassigned the majority of the BTs to ordinary jobs (for example, laundry, gym, showers) and stripped them of all their former power, status, and duties. Even BTs reassigned as orderlies or janitors in the living areas were not permitted to perform any of their old BT duties. Court-appointed investigators, called monitors, oversaw the selection of orderlies and kept close tabs on their behavior. These outside agents periodically visited Eastham and asked their own inmate informants to make written statements about any orderly misbehavior. Consequently, several inmate orderlies lost their jobs for fighting with and giving orders to the ordinary inmates they were replaced by less quarrelsome ordinary inmates.

To reduce the chances of violence against the former BTs, the staff moved many of them into several blocks and dormitories for mutual protection. While some former BTs were indeed fearful, most did not fear retaliation. As one former BT stated:

> Man, I've been doing this [prison] for a long time and I know how to survive. I know how to do it. I'm not going to stab nobody, I'm going to cut his fucking head off I'm doing seventy years and it doesn't make a bit of difference and I'm not going to put up with any of that shit.

These inmates all spoke of their willingness to use force, even deadly force, in the event of attacks from the ordinary inmates. The ordinary inmates were well aware of the BTs reputations and propensity for violence. They did not seek revenge. In short, the ordinary inmates were glad to be "free" from the BT system and stayed away from the BTs, whom they still feared. As a general rule, when an inmate exemplifies his courage and willingness to fight and stand up for his rights under adverse conditions, he is left alone. Turnkeys were formally removed from their jobs and reassigned elsewhere during the last week of December 1982. These inmates were moved in with their BT counterparts and did not experience any retaliation from the ordinary inmates.

In addition to removing the BTs and turnkeys, TDC was ordered to hire more officers to replace the former inmate-guards. Eastham received 141 new recruits during November and December 1982. The guard force was almost doubled. Guards were assigned to the barricades and had to learn from the former turnkeys how to operate them (for example, how to lock and unlock the doors, what to do when fights broke out). More important, a guard was assigned to every block and dormitory. For the first time in Easthams history (since 1917), guards had assignments within the living areas. Also for the first time, the guards maintained the security counts. (4)

Compliance with the court order also required the TDC to quit using physical force as an unofficial means of punishment and social control. At Eastham, in early 1983, ranking guards were instructed to "keep their hands in their pockets" and refrain from "tuning up" inmates. In fact, guards were told that anyone using unnecessary force -- more force than was needed to subdue an unruly inmate -- would be fired. The staff at first believed this rule would be "overlooked" and that the TDC administration would continue to support a guards use of force against an inmate. But in this they were disappointed. In March 1983, a ranking guard was fired and two others were placed on six months probation for beating up an inmate. Another incident in April 1983 led to the demotions and transfers of three other ranking guards. These incidents were investigated by TDCs Internal Affairs, which was organized in November 1982 to investigate and monitor all inmate complaints about guards use of force. The termination and demotions had their intended effect, for they spelled the end of the guards unofficial use of force (see Houston Chronicle, January 28, 1984). This series of events sent a message to the guards and inmates at Eastham (as well as throughout the TDC) that noncompliance with the court order would be dealt with harshly.

In sum, within six months the staff (aided by the BTs) changed the prisoner control system by abolishing the decades-old building tender/turnkey system without incident. Although the guards initially attempted to resist complying with the decrees restrictions on the use of force, a firing and several demotions broke their will to resist. These changes in response to the reform effort were substantial, and they set in motion a series of further changes that fundamentally altered the guard and inmate societies.

THE NEW ORDER

Once the BTs/turnkeys were removed from their jobs and the guards finally quit using unofficial force, the highly ordered prison social structure began to show signs of strain. The balance of power and hierarchical structure within the prisoner society were leveled, and the traditional rules governing inmate behavior, especially in the living areas, were discarded. That is, the ordinary inmates no longer had to act according to the BTs rules or fear physical reprisals from BTs. The guards use of physical force as a means of punishment was abolished, and a new system of prisoner discipline/control was established that emphasized due process, fairness, and prisoners rights. The implementation of these reforms resulted in three major changes within the prison community.

TABLE 1 / Selected Disciplinary Cases Resulting in Solitary Confinement: Direct Challenges to Authority from 1981 to 1984[a]

	1981	1982	1983	1984
Striking an officer	4	21	38	129
	(1.3)	(6.5)	(12.0)	(49.4)
Attempting to strike an officer	7	9	18	21
	(2.3)	(2.7)	(5.7)	(8.0)
Threatening an officer	4	5	38	109
	(1.3)	(1.5)	(12.0)	(41.8)
Refusing or failing to obey an order	90	65	72	213
	(30.6)	(20.1)	(22.8)	(81.7)
Use of indecent/vulgar language (cursing an officer)	11	14	89	94
	(3.7)	(4.3)	(28.2)	(36.0)
Total	116	114	255	566
Population levels	2,938	3,224	3,150	2,607

[a] Numbers in parentheses indicate the rate per 1,000 inmates. The population figures are based on the average monthly population at Eastham.

CHANGES IN INTERPERSONAL RELATIONS BETWEEN THE GUARDS AND INMATES

The initial and most obvious impact of the *Ruiz* ruling has been on the relations between the keepers and the kept. Formerly, inmates were controlled through relentless surveillance and by a totalitarian system that created a docile and passive ordinary inmate population. In all interactions and encounters, the guards and their agents defined the situation for the ordinary inmates. The penitentiary's social structure was in effect a caste system, whereby those in the lowest stratum (the ordinary inmates) were dictated to, exploited, and kept in submission.

Now, however, with the abolition of the BT/turnkey system and the disappearance of "tune-ups" and "beatings," a new relationship between keepers and kept has emerged. It is characterized by ambiguity, belligerence, confrontation, enmity, and the prisoners overt resentment of the staffs authority (see, for example, Carroll 1974). Inmates today no longer accept "things as they are." They argue with the guards and constantly challenge their authority. Moreover, the guards now find themselves in the position of having to explain and justify the rules to the inmates. The guards no longer totally define situations for the inmates.

Disciplinary reports show the contrast between the new (1983 and 1984) and old (1981 and 1982) orders. (5) We see from Table 1 that reported inmate threats toward and attacks on the guards increased by 500 percent and more over two years. The data do not precisely mirror behavior since some challenges to authority that would have been dealt with by unofficial coercion under the old order had to be reported or ignored under the new one. Nevertheless, it is clear from these data, as well as from interviews and observations, that the behavior of inmates toward the staff became increasingly hostile and confrontational. Simple orders to inmates (for example, "tuck your shirt in," "get a haircut," "turn your radio down") were often followed by protracted arguments, noncompliance, and such blistering verbal attacks from inmates as "Fuck all you whores, you can't tell me what to do anymore," "Get a haircut yourself, bitch," "Quit harassing me, you old country punk," or "Get your bitchy ass out of my face. This is my radio not yours." Not surprisingly, the number of cases for using indecent and vulgar language also steadily rose from 1981 to 1984. Indeed, the experience of verbal abuse became so commonplace that many officers overlooked this rule violation. On one occasion, for example, one author observed an officer ask an inmate why he was leaving his living area. The inmate walked past the officer and gruffly responded, "I'm going to work, so what the hell are you fucking with me for? If you got any other questions, call the kitchen." The officer turned around and walked away.

There are several reasons for this drastic change in interpersonal relations between guards and prisoners. First, there are simply more guards, which translates into more targets for assaults, verbal abuse, and disciplinary reports. Second, the guards are restricted from physically punishing "agitators," so fear of immediate physical reprisals by the guards has been eliminated. Third, the guards no longer have their inmate-agents to protect them from physical and verbal abuse or challenges to their authority by the ordinary inmates. By and large, the inmates feared the BTs more than the security staff. Purging the BT system eliminated this buffer group between the guards and ordinary inmates. Today the guards are "alone" in dealing with the prisoners, and the inmates no longer fear physical retaliation from the officials.

In addition to, and perhaps as important as, these changes in the control structure, the social distance between the guards and prisoners has diminished. The "inmates-as-nonpersons" who once inhabited our prisons have become citizens with civil rights (see Jacobs 1980). In the past, inmates at Eastham, subjected to derogation and physical force and ignored by extramural society, saw little to gain from challenging the system. Recent court reforms, however, have introduced the rule of law into the disciplinary process. Inmates now have many due process privileges. They can present documentary evidence, call witnesses, secure representation or counsel, and even cross-examine the reporting guard. They are in an adversarial position vis `a vis their guards, which at least in some procedural senses entails a kind of equality. Moreover, the inmates moral status has been improved because the guards can no longer flagrantly abuse them without fear of retaliation -- verbal, physical, and/or legal. Although the guards ultimately control the prison, they must now negotiate, compromise, or overlook many difficulties with inmates within the everyday control system (see for example, Sykes 1958; Thomas 1984).

REORGANIZATION WITHIN THE INMATE SOCIETY

The second major change concerns a restructuring of the inmate social system. The purging of the BT/turnkey system and the elimination of the old caste system created a power vacuum. The demise of the old informal or unofficial rules, controls, and status differentials led to uncertainty and ambiguity. In such situations, as Jacobs (1977) and Irwin (1980) suggest, realignments of power in prison often mean the heightened possibility of violence.

TABLE 2 / Selected Inmate-Inmate Offenses Resulting in Solitary Confinement: Weapons Offenses 1981-1984

	1981	1982	1983	1984
Fighting with a weapon	25	31	46	31
	(8.5)	(9.6)	(14.6)	(11.8)
Striking an inmate with a weapon	21	25	40	57
	(7.1)	(7.7)	(12.6)	(21.8)
Possession of a weapon	40	25	59	134
	(13.6)	(7.7)	(18.7)	(51.4)
Homicide	0	1	0	3
	(0)	(.3)	(0)	(1.1)
Total	86	82	145	225
Population levels	2,938	3,224	3,150	2,607

The Rise of Inmate—Inmate Violence

Prior to *Ruiz* and the compliance that followed, inmate-inmate violence at Eastham was relatively low, considering the types of inmates incarcerated there and the average daily inmate population. Table 2 illustrates the trends in inmate-inmate violence at Eastham The data in this table clearly document a rise in serious violence between inmates The most remarkable point here is that the incidence of violence increased while the prison population decreased by over 300 inmates.

Prison overcrowding raises constitutional problems, but it is extremely difficult for a judge to decide when population levels constitute cruel and unusual punishment barred by due process or the Eighth Amendment. To make this decision, judges attempt to link population levels with various major forms of institutional violence (that is, assaults, homicides, suicides). Cox and colleagues (1984) maintain that high degrees of overcrowding (especially in large institutions) have a variety of negative psychological and physical side effects, including higher death and disciplinary infraction rates. However, Ekland-Olson (1985; 32) tested the overcrowding- tension-violence model and concluded, among other things, that "there is no suitable evidence that institutional size or spatial density is related to natural death, homicide, suicide, or psychiatric commitment rates in prison. There is evidence to support the idea that crowding is not uniformly related to all forms of prison violence." While the Eastham data do not allow us to choose between these views, they are consistent with Ekland-Olsons position and suggest that there is no simple relationship between crowding and violence. They also suggest that the socialization of a prison is a more important predictor of violence than crowding.

When the BTs were in power, one of their unofficial roles was to settle disagreements and petty squabbles among the inmates in the living areas. Inmates came to the BTs not only for counsel but to avoid discussing a problem with the guards. The disputes often involved feuding cell partners, love affairs, petty stealing or unpaid debts. The BTs usually looked into the matter and made a decision, thereby playing an arbitrator role. Sometimes the quarrelers were allowed to "fight-it-out" under the supervision of the BTs and without the staffs knowledge. Inmates rarely took these matters into their own hands by attacking another inmate, in a living or work area. To do so would invite a serious and usually injurious confrontation with the BTs.

Fistfights were the primary means for settling personal disputes or grudges. Weapons were rarely used because the BTs information network was so extensive that it was difficult for an inmate to keep a weapon for any length of time. Furthermore, any inmate who attacked another inmate with a weapon was usually severely beaten by the BTs and/or the guard staff. Although the BTs ruled through fear and terror, their presence helped restrain serious violence among the inmates. To avoid the labels of punk, rat, or being weak, inmates involved in personal disputes shy away from telling guards about their problems. With the BTs gone, this leaves the inmates on their "own" to settle their differences. The inmates' sense of justice-- a revenge and machismo-oriented system with characteristics of blood feuds -- is given full sway (see Ekland-Olson 1985). The system means that inmates are virtually "cornered" and forced to use serious violence as a problem-solving mechanism. Physical threats, sexual come-ons, stealing, and unpaid debts are perceived as similarly disrespectful and as threats to one's "manhood." For example, not paying a gambling debt is a form of disrespect, and in a maximum security prison being "disrespectful" can lead to physical confrontations. Not collecting a gambling debt or submitting in the face of threats is also seen as weak or unmanly behavior. Inmates who are labeled weak are often preyed upon by inmates anxious to maintain or establish their reputations as "strong." Fistfights, the "traditional" dispute-settling mechanism in the old order, are no longer an effective means of settling a problem. One inmate, whose response was typical, described the transition from fistfights to serious violence:

> Used to, you could fight on the tank [block] or in the field. You know, they'd [BTs and/or staff] let you settle it right then and there. After a fight, they'd make you shake hands. Yeah, grown men shaking hands after a fight. But it was over, you didn't have to worry about the dude creeping [sneak attack] on you. Now, oh man, there's more knifings and less fistfights. If somebody has trouble, they're gonna try to stick the other guy. Whoever beats the other to the draw wins. See, their attitude has changed. They don't believe in fistfights anymore, its kidstuff to them. If you got a problem with a dude today, you better stick him. It wasn't like that when I was here in the sixties and seventies.

To the inmates, using a weapon proves more effective because if a "tormentor" is seriously wounded he will be transferred to another prison hospital and, when recovered, to another Texas prison. Furthermore, an inmate who uses serious violence for self-protection obtains a reputation for being "crazy" or dangerous, which reduces the possibility of other personal disputes.

To many inmates, killing or seriously wounding a tormentor in response to a threat is justifiable behavior. At Eastham, violent self-help has become a social necessity as well as a method of revenge. Rather than lose face in the eyes of ones peers and risk being labeled weak, which is an open invitation to further victimization, many inmates see assaultive behavior as a legitimate way to protect their "manhood" and self-respect. This is a dangerous situation for all, and especially for genuinely "weak" inmates who feel trapped and may use extreme violence as a last resort.

The Emergence of Inmate Gangs As personal violence escalated, inmate gangs developed, partly as a response to the violence but chiefly to fill the void left by the BTs. Prior to 1982, only one inmate gang, the Texas Syndicate, or TS, existed at Eastham. This group, which evolved in California prisons (see Davidson 1974), consisted of Hispanic inmates primarily from San Antonio and El Paso. It was estimated to have had about fifty full-fledged members and is reputed to have carried out "hits" or contracts on other prisoners at other TDC prisons.

Since 1983 a number of cliques or gangs have appeared at Eastham. Several white groups (Aryan Brotherhood or AB, Aryan Nations or AN, Texas Mafia or TM) and several black groups (Mandingo Warriors, Interaction Organization, Seeds of Idi Amin) have gained a foothold within the inmate society. All of these groups have a leadership structure and recruitment procedures, such as "kill to get in and die to get out" for the AB. Like the TS, these are system-wide organizations. Top-ranking guards at Eastham estimate the number of prisoners who are members at between 8 and 10 percent of the prison population. Of the various groups, the TS and AB are the largest and best organized groups at Eastham.

The presence of the gangs was not really felt or perceived as a security problem until late 1984. Prior to this time, the staff had identified and kept tabs on the gang leaders as well as on recruiting trends. The staff also uncovered several "hits," but violence did not erupt. Then, in November 1984, two ABs stabbed two other ABs one victim was the AB leader. Early December saw four TS members stab another TS in a cellblock. Shortly thereafter, several members of the Texas Mafia murdered another TM in an administrative segregation block, a high-security area housing inmates with violent prison records, known gang leaders, and many gang members. In the final incident a TS leader at Eastham murdered a fellow TS member, in the same segregation block as the previous murder, on January 1, 1985. Thus, gang related violence has emerged at the prison, but within the gangs themselves. In short, the gangs are locked in internal power struggles.

The rise of inmate-inmate violence has created a "crisis" in self-protection. Some inmates have sought safety in gangs, as we have seen. The staff is perceived -- with justification -- as unable to maintain control. Interviews with inmates reveal that gang membership offers identity, a sense of belonging, and a support system for the member. Revenge is also a powerful drawing card (see Jacobs 1974a). Gang members know that if they are threatened, assaulted, or stolen from, they will have assistance in retaliating against the offender. On the other hand, nonmembers who fear for their personal safety feel they must rely on themselves. These inmates have felt it increasingly important to obtain weapons (see Table 2). In short, violence has almost become an expectation, both as a threat and as a means of survival.

REACTIONS OF THE GUARDS

The reforms have upset the very foundations of the guard subculture and work role. Their work world is no longer smooth, well ordered, predictable, or rewarding. Loyalty to superiors, especially the warden, the job, and/or organization -- once the hallmark of the guard staff at Eastham -- is quickly fading. The officers are disgruntled and embittered over the reform measures that have "turned the place over to the convicts."

Fear of the Inmates Part of the *Ruiz* ruling ordered TDC to hire hundreds of guards to replace the BTs. Eastham received 150 new guards between November 1982 and January 1983. For the first time guards were assigned to work in the living areas. It was hoped this increase in uniformed personnel would increase order and control within the institution. Contrary to expectations, the increase in inexperienced personnel and the closer guard-inmate relationships resulted in more violence and less prisoner control. As indicated earlier, assaults on the staff skyrocketed between 1981[4] and 1984 (129). In addition, one officer was taken hostage and three guards were stabbed by inmates at Eastham in 1984. Fear of the inmates is greatest among the rank and file guards, most of whom are assigned to cell block duty and have close contact with the inmates. These personnel bear the brunt of the verbal abuse, assaults, and intimidation that have increased since the new system was implemented. The new guards are hesitant to enforce order, and this is evidenced in the officers less authoritative posture toward the inmates. One guard put it this way: "Look, these guys [prisoners] are crazy, you know, fools, so you gotta back off and let them do their thing now. It's too dangerous around here to enforce all these rules." Previously, guards were not subjected to verbal abuse, threats, and derogation. Compliance was effected through fear and physical force. Today, the guards cannot physically punish "troublemakers" and must informally bargain with the inmates for control. Many officers have stated that they try to enforce the rules but to no avail, since their supervisors overlook most petty rule violations to avoid clogging the prisons disciplinary court docket. (6)

The traditional authoritarian guarding style at Eastham has been replaced with a tolerant, permissive, or "lets get along" pattern of interaction. Furthermore, the guards, especially new officers, (7) fear retaliation from inmates and officials to the point of not enforcing the rules at all. The attitude currently prevailing among the guards is summed up by the following guards statement: "I don't give a damn about what they do, as long as they leave me alone. I'm here to do my eight hours and collect a pay check, and that's it."

"We've Lost Control" The rise in inmate-inmate violence, the emergence of violent gangs, the loss of traditional control methods, the combative nature of guard-inmate interactions, the derogation of guards, and the influx of inexperienced guards have contributed to a "crisis in control" for the guards (Alpert et al. 1985). Many of the guards, especially the veterans, perceive the changes wrought in the wake of *Ruiz* as unjustified and undermining their authority. They feel they can no longer maintain control and order within the penitentiary. This is not because they have not tried the new disciplinary system. Indeed, as we see in Table 3, the total number of solitary-confinement cases has skyrocketed since 1981.

These data reveal that the rate of serious disciplinary infractions (violence and challenges to guards authority) rapidly increased after the reforms in 1983 despite a decrease in the inmate population. The rapid increase in rule violations has demoralized the guard staff to the point of frustration and resignation. Interviews with guards and inmates revealed that most inmates are no longer afraid of "being written up," losing good time, and spending time in solitary confinement. (8)

TABLE 3 / **Inmates Sentenced to Solitary Confinement from 1981 to 1984**

	1981	1982	1983	1984
All offenses	487 (165.7)	404 (175.3)	889 (282.2)	1,182 (453.0)
Population levels	2,938	3,224	3,150	2,607

The traditional means of dealing with "unruly" prisoners have been abolished and replaced with more official, due process methods. Standards and guidelines for the guards use of force have been implemented. Whenever a guard uses force to control an inmate for whatever reason (for example, breaking up fights, taking an inmate into custody), the officer must submit a written report detailing all phases of the incident. When a use of force involves a scuffle, all parties are brought to the prisons hospital to photograph any injuries or abrasions. Forced cell moves are also videotaped. Documentation and accountability are musts for the guard force today. Furthermore, whenever physical force is used against inmates, Internal Affairs investigates the incident. Their investigation of a guard taken hostage on October 15, 1984, involved interviews with thirty-eight prison officials and twenty-one inmates. Twenty-four polygraph tests were also administered (Houston Chronicle, February 14, 1984). This investigation revealed that unnecessary force was used to quell the disturbance. Eleven guards and two wardens were reprimanded, and two guards were demoted and transferred to other prisons. Thus, the disciplinary process itself frustrates the line officers -- so much so that they often "look the other way" or simply fail to "see" most inmate rule violations. Moreover, the implementation of the new disciplinary process has strained the once cohesive relations between the guards and their superior officers. Not only do the latter sometimes fail to back up the guards disciplinary initiatives because of the pressures of crowded dockets, but they may also initiate investigations that result in guards being sanctioned.

SOME CONCLUSIONS ON COURT REFORMS AND PRISONER CONTROL

The *Ruiz* ruling sounded the death knell for the old prison order in Texas. Legal maneuverings and a new prison administration have given increasing substance to the new order that *Ruiz* initiated. Table 4 summarizes the distinctions between the old, or inmate-dependent, order and the new, bureaucratic-legal order. We have included only those elements of each order that are directly relevant to prisoner control.

We do not mean by our headings to suggest that prior to the court ruling Eastham was not bureaucratically organized. Indeed, all of the trappings (for example, rules, records, accountability) were present under the old order, however, those trappings rarely penetrated the daily operations of the prison. Eastham officials enjoyed considerable autonomy from the central prison administration. Guards, particularly those in the midranks, exercised much discretion in their dealings with inmates. The inmate-dependent order openly recognized the importance of informal relations between officers and inmates and the manipulation by staff of a subrosa reward system. The old regime fostered particularistic relations (the "majors boy," BTs, and other institutionalized snitches), which were important to control and kept the inmate community fractured and atomistic. The elite inmates were a reliable source of information about inmate activities that could threaten order. Finally, the control mechanisms consistent with this regime were ends-oriented. That is, order and the dominance of staff over the inmates were maintained by pragmatic means selected over time to achieve these ends. Where force and other sanctions were used by BTs and guards, they were employed immediately following a transgression. This strategy engendered fear among both the offenders and those who observed the punishment.

TABLE 4 / A Summary Depiction of Eastham Before and After *Ruiz*

	Inmate-dependent order Pre-Ruiz era	Bureaucratic-legal order Post-Ruiz era
Decision-making power	Decentralized. Warden establishes many policies and procedures at the prison. Prison administrators enjoy a high degree of autonomy.	Centralized. Warden carries out directives established in central TDC office. Less unit flexibility; prison officials allowed little autonomy.
Staff/inmate relations	Based on paternalism, coercion, dominance, and fear. The majority of the inmates are viewed and treated as nonpersons. Guards define the situation for the inmates.	Based on combative relations wherein guards have less discretion and inmates challenge the staff's authority. Guards fear the inmates.
Prisoner control apparatus	Internal-proactive control system based on information. Guards penetrate the inmate society through a system of surrogate guards. Organized violence, riots, mob action, and general dissent are obviated. Punishment is swift, severe, certain, and often corporal. Control is an end in itself.	External-reactive control system in which the guard staff operates on the perimeter of the inmate society. Loss of information prevents staff from penetrating inmate society; thus they must contain violence. Punishment is based on hearings and due process considerations. Control mechanisms are means-oriented.
Inmate society	Fractured and atomistic due to the presence of BTs—official snitches.	Racially oriented with the emergence of violent cliques and gangs.

The transition toward a bureaucratic-legal order at Eastham permits much less autonomy. To increase central office control over TDCs many prisons, the new TDC administration (under Raymond Procunier) established, in 1984, regional directors to supervise more closely the wardens of individual units. As elsewhere, new policies to carry out court-ordered reforms have also reduced the discretion of all unit officials (Glazer 1978). Written directives regarding disciplinary or supervisory procedures emphasize legal standards more than the traditional, cultural values that once defined prison objectives. The precedence of legal standards is especially evident in the "use of force" policy. Each time some physical means of control is used, a "use of force" report (a series of statements and photographs) must be completed and filed with the central office. Whenever a physical confrontation is anticipated (for example, forced cell moves), the action is videotaped. The watchword is documentation. The bureaucratic-legal order also discourages informal relations between officers and inmates. Yet fewer staff-inmate links limit organizational intelligence and thus the ability to anticipate trouble. Officers regularly complain, "We don't know what's going on back there [in the tanks]." At the same time, prison relations are universalistic all inmates are to be treated alike, and unless they are officially found to have violated some prison rule, they are due equal benefits and freedom regardless of demeanor or attitude. Last, control mechanisms are more means-oriented. The focus is as much on how the control is effected as it is on whether or to what extent it is effective. The legality of the means appears to many staff members to take precedence over the deterrent effect of the control effort. One consequence of this focus is a disciplinary procedure that effectively distances the punishment from the offense in both time and place. Thus, the staffs authority rests not on threat of force or other informal means of domination but on explicit rules.

Although court intervention has made Eastham's operations more consistent with constitutional requirements of fairness and due process, the fact remains that life for the inmates and guards at Eastham is far less orderly than it was before. Authority has eroded, and the cellblocks and halls are clearly more dangerous. Our observations and the data presented in Tables 1 through 3 suggest that the push toward the bureaucratic-legal order, at least in the first few years after the decree, lessened control to the point that many are increasingly at risk behind the walls.

The court-prompted reforms have created for prison officials a dilemma analogous to that experienced by police (Skolnick 1966). Guards, like police, must balance two fundamental values: order and rule by law. Clearly, order can be maintained in a totalitarian, lawless manner. In a democratic society, order must be maintained under rules of law. Having been mandated to maintain control by constitutional means, Eastham prison officials face a problem that pervades our criminal justice system today. Specifically, as Jacobs and Zimmer (1983: 158) note: "[T]he great challenge for corrections is to develop an administrative style that can maintain control in the context of the legal and humane reforms of the last decade."

Officials at Eastham certainly feel this challenge. They feel pressure to comply with the court and the central office directives designed to operationalize that compliance. Yet the unanticipated consequences of today's reforms have jeopardized the staff's ability to maintain and enforce order. While prisoners in many institutions now have enhanced civil rights and are protected by many of the same constitutional safeguards as people in the free society, they live in a lawless society at the mercy of aggressive inmates and cliques. The dilemma apparently facing society and prison administrators revolves around the issues of rights versus control. Should prisons be managed through an authoritarian structure based on strict regimentation, fear, few civil rights, and controlled exploitation, in which inmates and guards are relatively safe? Or should prisons be managed with a bureaucratic-due process structure espousing fairness, humane treatment, and civil rights, in which inmate and guard safety is problematic and where uncontrolled exploitation is likely? One would like to believe that civil rights and personal safety goals within prison settings are not incompatible, but we may ultimately have to confront the fact that to some extent they are. At the very least, the experience at Eastham suggests that reforms, especially in maximum security prisons, should be: (1) phased in gradually rather than established by rigid timetables, (2) implemented with a fundamental appreciation of the entire network of relationships and behaviors involved, and (3) undertaken with a healthy sensitivity to the unanticipated negative consequences that have often surrounded attempts to "do good" (Glazer 1978 Rothman 1980)

Notes

1. The order also called for an end to double celling, but this element was later vacated by the Fifth Circuit Court of Appeals.

2. For a more detailed analysis of the BT system, see Marquart and Crouch (1984).

3. The news media extensively covered these hearings, and press releases provided grisly examples of BT/turnkey brutality and perversions (see the numerous Houston Post and Houston Chronicle articles between February 16 1982, and July 1, 1982).

4. The former BTs had to show the guards how to keep the living area counts. Thus, the staff adopted a system of counting that the BTs had developed.

5. The data presented in the three tables reflect only disciplinary infractions resulting in solitary confinement. We recognize the limitations here and know our data are quite conservative. The TDCs record keeping on all disciplinary cases (minor and major) was nonsystematic, and we had to rely on Easthams disciplinary logbooks. However, our interviews and observations are consistent with the rise in violent and other behavior reflected in the tables.

6. This is like the situation in many large cities, where police and prosecutors have relationships of accommodation with minor criminals. Some crimes must be prosecuted, whatever the cost to the system. Other crimes are not worth the trouble, so agents of justice ignore them or find ways to handle them simply.

7. Interviews with ranking guards indicated that the rise of inmate-guard and inmate-inmate violence has contributed to the turnover of new guards. Of the 246 guards assigned inside the building, 125, or 51 percent, have less than one year of experience, and these numbers include ranking guards.

8. A guard's threat to seek solitary confinement has also become less intimidating since *Ruiz* because of the due process protections imposed and limitations on the good time that can be forfeited. Also, the guard who seeks solitary confinement for an inmate knows he is triggering a hearing in which his own actions may be questioned. The increase in solitary confinement cases should be read in light of these disincentives.

References

ADAM, H. L. (n.d.). *Oriental Crime*. Clifford's Inn, London: T. Werner Laurie.

ALPERT, G., B. M. CROUCH, AND C. R. HUFF (1985). "Prison Reform by Judicial Decree: The Unintended Consequences of *Ruiz v. Estelle*." *Justice System Journal* 291.

BETTELHEIM, BRUNO (1943). "Individual and Mass Behavior in Extreme Situations." 38 *Journal of Abnormal and Social Psychology* 417.

BLASSINGAME, JOHN W. (1979). *The Slave Community*. New York: Oxford University Press.

CALHOUN, EMILY (1978). "The Supreme Court and the Institutional Rights of Prisoners: A Reappraisal." 4 *Hastings Constitutional Law Quarterly* 219.

CARROLL, LEO (1974). *Hacks, Blacks, and Cons*. Lexington, Mass.: Lexington Books.

CHAMPAGNE, ANTHONY, AND K. C. HAAS (1976). "Impact of *Johnson v. Avery* on Prison Administration." 43 *Tennessee Law Review* 275.

CHARRIERE, HENRI (1970). *Papillon*. New York: Basic Books.

CLEMMER, DONALD C. (1940). *The Prison Community*. Boston: Christopher Publishing House.

COLVIN, MARK (1982). "The 1980 New Mexico Prison Riot." 29 *Social Problems* 449.

COX, V. C., P. B. PAULUS, AND G. McCAIN (1984). "Prison Crowding Research: The Relevance for Prison Housing Standards and a General Approach Regarding Crowding Phenomena." 39 *American Psychologist* 1148.

CROUCH, BEN M. (1980). "The Guard in a Changing Prison World." In B. M. Crouch, ed., *The Keepers: Prison Guards and Contemporary Corrections*. Springfield, Ill.: C. H. Thomas.

DAVIDSON, R. T. (1974). *Chicano Prisoners: Key to San Quentin*. New York: Holt, Rinehart & Winston.

EKLAND-OLSON, SHELDON (1985). "Judicial Decisions and the Social Order of Prison Violence: Evidence from the Post-*Ruiz* Years in Texas." Unpublished manuscript.

GLAZER, NATHAN (1978). "Should Judges Administer Social Services?" 50 *Public Interest* 64.

IRWIN, JOHN (1980). *Prisons in Turmoil*. Boston: Little, Brown.

JACOBS, JAMES B. (1974a). "Street Gangs, Behind Bars." 21 *Social Problems* 395.

―――― (1974b). "Participant Observations in Prison." 3 *Urban Life and Culture* 221.

―――― (1977). *Stateville: The Penitentiary in Mass Society*. Chicago: University of Chicago Press.

―――― (1980). "The Prisoners' Rights Movement and Its Impact, 1960–1980." 2 *Crime and Justice: An Annual Review of Research* 429.

JACOBS, JAMES B., AND L. ZIMMER (1983). "Collective Bargaining and Labor Unrest." In J. Jacobs, ed., *New Perspectives in Prisons and Imprisonment*. Ithaca, N.Y.: Cornell University Press.

KIMBALL, EDWARD L., AND DONALD J. NEWMAN (1968). "Judicial Intervention in Correctional Decisions: Threat and Response." 14 *Crime and Delinquency* 1.

KOGON, E. (1958). *The Theory and Practice of Hell*. New York: Berkley Publishing.

MARQUART, JAMES W. (1984). "Outsiders as Insiders: Participant Observation in the Role of a Prison Guard." Unpublished manuscript.

―――― (1985). "Prison Guards and the Use of Physical Coercion as a Mechanism of Prisoner Control." Unpublished manuscript.

MARQUART, JAMES W., AND BEN M. CROUCH (1984). "Co-opting the Kept: Using Inmates for Social Control in a Southern Prison." 1 *Justice Quarterly* 491.

MCCLEERY, RICHARD H. (1960). "Communication Patterns as Bases of Systems of Authority and Power." In R. A. Cloward et al., *Theoretical Studies in Social Organization of the Prison*. New York: Social Science Research Council.

MCWHORTER, WILLIAM L. (1981). *Inmate Society: Legs, Halfpants, and Gunmen: A Study of Inmate Guards*. Saratoga, Calif.: Century Twenty-One Publishing.

MOULEDOUS, J. C. (1962). "Sociological Perspectives on a Prison Social System." Master's thesis, Department of Sociology, Louisiana State University.

MURTON, TOM, AND JOE HYAMS (1969). *Accomplices to the Crime: The Arkansas Prison Scandal*. New York: Grove Press.

NINTH MONITOR'S REPORT OF FACTUAL OBSERVATIONS TO THE SPECIAL MASTER (1983).

ROTHMAN, DAVID (1980). *Conscience and Convenience*. Boston: Little, Brown.

SCHRAG, CLARENCE (1954). "Leadership among Prison Inmates." 19 *American Sociological Review* 37.

SHAW, ALAN G. L. (1966). *Convicts and the Colonies*. London: Faber & Faber.

SHILS, EDWARD A. (1975). *Center and Periphery: Essays in Macrosociology*. Chicago: University of Chicago Press.

SKOLNICK, JEROME H. (1966). *Justice without Trial*. New York: John Wiley.

SOLZHENITSYN, ALEKSANDR I. (1974). *The Gulag Archipelago*. New York: Harper & Row.

——— (1975). *The Gulag Archipelago II*. New York: Harper & Row.

PRIVATE PRISONS IN TEXAS:
THE NEW PENOLOGY FOR PROFIT*

Faced with rising prison populations and limited funds, many state governments have contracted with private companies for the construction, management, and operation of correctional facilities. This paper examines the historical and contemporary role of private sector involvement in Texas during the 1860s and 1980s. First, we briefly describe privatization efforts in nineteenth-century American prisons and discuss the Texas experience. Second, we analyze the political and economic conditions that facilitated a recent second attempt at privatization. Third, we discuss how privatization was implemented and describe the current status of these facilities. Finally, we discuss how this experience may apply to other jurisdictions.

James M. Marquart, Sam Houston State University
Phillip A. Etheridge, The University of Texas - Pan American

ACCORDING TO MANY CORRECTIONAL ADMINISTRATORS and scholars, the nation's correctional system is in a "state of crisis" (Gottfredson and McConville 1987; Ring 1987; Stewart 1986). One proposed solution was to give the private sector a significant role in the administration, finance, and construction of correctional facilities and programs (Logan 1990; Matthews 1989; McDonald, 1989a). Various countries have experimented with private prisons, including Great Britain, Australia, and France (Brakal 1988; Hutto 1990; Rutherford 1989). Despite these international examples, the United States leads in experimenting with this "new" form of correctional management (Hanson 1991; Johnson and Ross 1990; Logan 1990).

During the 1980s, correctional policy makers and scholars acknowledged that the private sector was involved in all aspects of the nation's correctional system, especially by providing specific services on a contractual basis (Garoogian 1987; Immarigeon 1987; Logan 1986). Steinberg (1981) found that many services were provided to correctional facilities by private companies. In an extensive study, Camp and Camp (1984) discovered that private companies provided more than 30 separate services which totaled more than $300 million annually (e.g., food services, medical services, counseling services, educational and vocational training, recreation, maintenance, security). In addition, private-sector entrepreneurs constructed and operated high-security institutions under contract to states (Camp and Camp 1985; Logan and Rausch 1985; Mullen 1985).

To fully understand why prison privatization emerged in the United States during the 1980s we must examine privatization in the context of the conservative movement (Durham 1989a; Press 1989). President Ronald Reagan, elected in 1980, began the drive to increase private-sector involvement in enterprises traditionally operated by the government, including jails and prisons (Jones 1988, Savas 1982). The Reagan administration persuaded state and local governments to turn many services over to private contractors by asserting that in many instances the private sector would be more efficient and more cost-effective than the public sector (AFSCME 1985). Privatization gained additional endorsement in 1987, when the President's

---

* An earlier version of this paper was presented at the annual meetings of the Academy of Criminal Justice Sciences, held in Washington in 1989. The authors gratefully acknowledge George J. Beto for his comments and suggestions on an earlier draft.

Commission on Privatization concluded in its final report: "Privatization . . . may well be seen by future historians as one of the most important developments in American political and economic life of the 20th century" (President's Commission on Privatization 1988:251). Although prison and jail privatization was not a direct product of the Reagan administration, it resulted from a resurgence of conservatism, coupled with local and state governments' concern about an ever-expanding correctional population (Goodstein and McKenzie 1987).

Private-sector involvement included three primary areas: construction, financing, and operation of correctional facilities (Logan 1990). During the 1980s private companies pursued contracts to design and construct state correctional facilities (Dewitt 1986; Sechrest and Price 1985. These companies maintained that they could construct a facility faster and at less cost than could the state (Fenton 1985; Hutto and Vick 1984).

The private sector also has been involved with financing new construction (Weiss 1989). Traditionally, prisons and jails have been owned by the government and financed by tax revenues. Yet because of constraints on state and local budgets during the 1980s, private companies offered to finance construction of facilities. They also agreed to rent them under a contract to the government or to enter a lease-purchase agreement (Leonard 1989). By using these innovative financing schemes, the government is relieved of the need to pay for initial construction costs; nor does it need voters' approval for prison expansion in a bond referendum (Logan 1990; McDonald 1989b).

In the third and most controversial aspect of privatization, private operation of correctional facilities is substituted for public operation, including staffing, management, and day-to-day activities (Logan 1990). In the 1980s, for example, the federal government employed private contractors to operate detention centers for the Immigration and Naturalization Service (INS). In addition, the Federal Bureau of Prisons and the U.S. Marshals Service used private facilities to hold detainees. At the state level, as of May 1990, California, Kentucky, Louisiana, New Mexico, and Texas were contracting with private companies to operate correctional facilities (Thomas 1990). The number of adult inmates in privately operated facilities increased from zero in 1984 (Camp and Camp 1984) to more than 14,000 by January 1989 (Johnson and Ross 1990).

The proponents of privatization presented strong arguments to support their views, but correctional privatization had its critics (AFSCME 1985). Even though some critics conceded that some economic advantages might be associated with privatization, they insisted that the more important questions pertained to the legality and the propriety of private punishment (DiIulio 1986).

Robbins (1986, 1988), a staunch opponent of correctional privatization, raises two critical questions: 1) Is it constitutional to delegate the incarceration function to a private entity? and 2) Do the acts of a private entity operating a correctional facility constitute "state action," thus allowing states to sue the private entity and the government for violations of their civil rights? Concerning the question of constitutionality, McDonald (1989a) and Logan (1990) conclude that neither the federal constitution nor state constitutions legally ban the delegation of correctional authority to private entities. Although this debate continues, a number of states have passed legislation authorizing the delegation of correctional authority to private companies (Hanson 1991). Robbins's second question concerns the liability of the private company and the government in a civil rights lawsuit brought by inmates held in privately operated correctional facilities. The most pertinent case is Medina v. O'Neall (1984), which concerned the INS's contract with a private firm to house undocumented aliens. In this case, several detainees attempted to escape, and a private guard accidentally killed one of them. The Federal District Court ruled that the actions of the private guard constituted "state action" under 42 U.S.C. Section 1983. Thus the detainees were permitted to sue either the government or the private company.

As a result of the *Medina* ruling, there seems to be little doubt that contracting out correctional facilities cannot immunize government against legal responsibility (Logan 1990). As the notion of private operation of correctional facilities expanded, questions also arose, such as "Why has the idea of privatization of prisons drawn so much attention in the 1980s?" Texas experimented with privatization in the 1860s and the 1980s. Both eras contain lessons for correctional policy makers in the 1990s. In this paper we examine the historical and contemporary role of private-sector involvement in one state, Texas. First, we briefly describe privatization efforts in nineteenth-century American prisons and discuss the Texas experience. Second, we analyze the political and economic conditions that facilitated a recent second attempt at privatization. Third, we discuss how privatization was implemented and describe the current status of these facilities. Finally, we discuss how this experience may apply to other jurisdictions.

HISTORICAL BACKGROUND

The private sector historically has been involved with the operations of prisons in the United States (Feeley 1991; McKelvey 1977). Lewis (1967) found that from the beginnings of the earliest penitentiaries in Pennsylvania and New York, prisoners labored to meet their expenses. According to Walker, "The desirability of working prisoners at some form of profitable employment so fixed itself in the minds of public officials that it became the hallmark of nineteenth-century prison management in the United States" (1988:8). The most popular type of inmate prison labor during the early 1800s was the contract system (Lewis 1967). For a fixed fee, states allowed private contractors to supervise prisoners inside the prison walls.

Prison historian Blake McKelvey (1977) uncovered several other forms of private inmate labor, including the piece-rate, the public account, and the lease system. Under the piece-rate system, inmates worked inside prison walls for a private contractor under the supervision of state employees. In public account systems, prisoners worked under state supervision and produced goods for state institutions. The lease system was the most profitable, most brutal, and most corrupt type of inmate labor (Walker 1988). Under this system, prison officials yielded control of the state's prisons, including all equipment, buildings, and inmates, to the highest bidder.

Northern and eastern states primarily contracted out inmate labor (Lewis 1967). After the Civil War many southern states were confronted with inadequate facilities, growing prison populations, money shortages, and public pressure to improve prison conditions. Accordingly, Louisiana, Mississippi, Georgia, Alabama, Florida, and Texas adopted some method of contracting or leasing inmate labor (McKelvey 1977). Leasing became the most popular system in the south (Feeley 1991). The war had devastated southern states economically, and lawmakers chose to lease entire prison systems to turn a profit. By 1880 all 11 states of the former Confederacy had adopted some system of leasing inmate labor (McKelvey 1977). The desire for profits from this labor became the main focus of southern lawmakers, to the exclusion of inmates' welfare (Walker 1988).

Privatization in Nineteenth-Century Texas The Texas experience with inmate labor during the late 1800s paralleled that of other southern states. The notion that hard work reforms prisoners, as well as the belief that inmates should work to defray the cost of their incarceration and even should turn a profit for the state, has been fixed in the minds of Texas public and correctional officials since the prison system opened in 1849 (Walker 1988). According to the Penitentiary Act, which created the Texas penitentiary system, inmates were to be kept busy at whatever labor state officials "deemed most profitable and useful to the State" (Gammel 1898:80). The first scheme employed by prison officials to make the penitentiary self-sustaining involved the installation of a cotton mill in 1854 (Crow 1964; Nowlin 1962). Cloth products were sold to the public; eventually the mill made products for the Confederacy during the Civil War. The end of the Civil War, however, ended the prison-made textile market.

At the end of the Civil War, the Texas state treasury consisted almost totally of worthless Confederate money. The state government was weakened, partly because the U.S. Army was in control. As a result, the state suffered a general breakdown of law and order (Walker 1988). Now that more criminals were being convicted and sent to prison, the prison system was a top priority. Faced with these dismal conditions, lawmakers searched for new methods of prisoner management (Crouch and Marquart 1989). One such method was contracting out inmate labor. In 1866 the Texas Legislature established the Board of Public Labor to regulate this type of labor.

The first contracts for inmate labor were signed in 1866 with two railroad companies. These contracts, however, were terminated in late 1867 because state officials were not convinced that the welfare and safekeeping of its prisoners would be adhered to by the private companies who employed prisoners for private gain" (Walker 1988:21). Despite the failure of this first attempt, state officials were convinced that they had found the path to prison profits.

In April 1871 the state signed a lease with a private company, which gave the company full use of all prison property, including land, buildings, tools, and machinery, for 15 years (Parrish 1976; Sullenberg 1974; Walker 1988). The lessees were required to cover all costs associated with the prison, including food, clothing, and medical care for the prisoners as well as the salaries of guards and prison officials. In return for the inmate labor the lessees paid the state a set yearly fee (Walker 1988). State and prison officials hailed the lease as a profitable solution to the prison problems in Texas.

From the outset there were allegations of inmate neglect and abuse by the lessees and the guards. The earliest criticism of the Texas lease system was made in 1874 by a group of U.S. Army prisoners who were transferred from Texas to Kansas. When the prisoners arrived, Kansas prison authorities contacted Texas officials to complain about the abuses the inmates stated they had incurred under the lessees (Texas Penitentiary Report 1875). A legislative committee was appointed to investigate these allegations; it concluded that inmates were overcrowded, received insufficient clothing in the winter, and were not provided with a sufficient diet or adequate medical treatment. The committee condemned the lessees' disciplinary practices as abusive and brutal (Texas Penitentiary Report 1875). Yet despite these findings, mistreatment of inmates continued; in 1877 the state ended the lease and regained possession of the penitentiary.

In order to relieve taxpayers of the prison burden, the state entered a number of lease agreements between 1878 and 1883 (Nowlin 1962; Parrish 1976; Sullenberg 1974). Prisoners, however, continued to complain of abuse and mistreatment by the lessees. Finally, in 1883, the legislature voted to abolish leasing, succumbing to public pressure regarding the mistreatment of inmates by lessees as well as to the public's resentment that inmates were taking jobs from law-abiding citizens.

Still, state officials maintained that the cost of operating the state's prisons should come from the profits generated from inmate labor, not from tax revenues. This attitude "led to a modification of the leasing system, wherein the state maintained control of the penitentiary and convicts but continued contracting arrangement with private interests" (Martin and Ekland-Olson 1987:7). In the contract-lease system, used between 1883 and 1912, the state hired out inmate labor to private companies, and all the profits went to the state.

In 1909 the Legislature, responding to numerous complaints of mistreatment of inmates, investigated prison conditions and found many of the same conditions that had been reported in 1875: overcrowding, mistreatment and brutality by guards, lack of medical treatment and adequate food, and filthy living conditions (Penitentiary Investigating Committee 1910). When the findings were published, there was a public outcry to improve prison conditions and to eliminate the contracting out of inmate labor. In late 1912 the contract labor system ceased to exist in Texas. Several decades later, however, Texans would witness a new era of prison privatization.

THE ROAD TO MODERN PRISON PRIVATIZATION IN TEXAS

When the 70th Legislature convened in January 1987, political interest in privatization was heightened by five critical problems: 1) total admissions to the prison system had risen by 112.8 percent between 1980 and 1986, from 14,176 to 30,471; 2) the May 1985 settlement in the *Ruiz v. Estelle* (1980) lawsuit limited the number of inmates the Texas Department of Corrections (TDC) could legally house, and called for a two-stage "depopulation" of TDC capacity; 3) the federal court found the state in contempt for failing to comply with the *Ruiz* ruling and threatened to impose massive fines; 4) the Criminal Justice Policy Council predicted a need for new prison construction to prevent a shortage of beds; and 5) a tight state economy prohibited the use of general revenue funds for constructing new prisons.

The biggest problem facing lawmakers was a burgeoning prisoner population, which outpaced the system's capacity. While total prison admissions rose by 112.8 percent between 1980 and 1986, the system's capacity increased by only 51.5 percent, from 26,576 in 1980 to 40,227 in 1986 (Texas Department of Corrections 1987). The dramatic increase in total prison admissions, without an equivalent increase in capacity, demonstrated that demand for prison beds outstripped supply. This situation was heightened on January 16, 1987, when the prisoner population exceeded the court-mandated limit and TDC was forced to "temporarily close its doors to new admissions" (Freelancer and Sanders 1987). Closure of the prison system brought TDC's problems to public attention and pressured legislators to increase capacity.

In addition, legislators had to deal with the federal court's ruling in *Ruiz v. Estelle*. This case can be traced back to June 29, 1972, when David Ruiz, an inmate in the TDC, filed a suit alleging numerous unconstitutional conditions and practices. In December 1980, after a lengthy trial, Judge William Wayne Justice found the "totality of conditions" in the TDC to be unconstitutional (Crouch and Marquart 1989). Overcrowding became the "centerpiece of his opinion due to its aggravating impact on other issues in the case" (Martin and Ekland-Olson 1987:1781). On May 16, 1985, after years of negotiations, a settlement agreement was signed.

The agreement, *Stipulation Modifying Crowding Provisions of Amended Decree* (the "crowding stipulation"), established deadlines by which TDC would effectively reduce the maximum capacity of each prison and of the entire prison system. The crowding stipulation set a system-wide maximum capacity: TDC's population could not exceed 95 percent of the total available beds. Further, the settlement reduced the capacity of TDC in two scheduled depopulations.[1] The first depopulation, which occurred on September 1, 1987, resulted in a loss of 4,241 prison beds. The second depopulation occurred on September 1, 1989 and resulted in a loss of an additional 2,272 beds (Texas Department of Corrections 1987). Legislators were forced either to release thousands of inmates to meet the depopulation figures, to develop a prison construction plan, or to devise alternatives to incarceration.

The third critical problem faced by lawmakers in early 1987 was Judge William Wayne Justice's finding that the state was in contempt of court (*Ruiz v. McCotter* Memorandum Opinion and Order 1986.) Justice condemned the state for failing to comply with specific court orders in *Ruiz v. Estelle*. His opinion was accompanied by a set of remedial orders, setting deadlines for compliance and charging a series of fines that could run as high as $800,500 a day for every day the state did not comply. With the threat of huge fines facing the state, lawmakers scrambled to find solutions.

A fourth problem facing lawmakers was the prediction that the demand for prison beds would continue to increase. The Criminal Justice Policy Council (CJPC) showed a 22.0 percent increase in TDC admissions from 1987 to 1991. Total admissions were projected to increase from 35,134 in 1987 to 42,875 in 1991 (Texas Department of Corrections 1987). The CJPC projected that the increase in the TDC population would lead inevitably to a massive shortage of prison beds if TDC's capacity was not drastically expanded.

If TDC's capacity remained static, the CJPC projected a shortage of 18,378 beds by 1991 (Texas Department of Corrections 1987).

Finally, legislators were confronted with a tight state economy that prohibited the financing of new prison construction. The financial constraints were the direct result of plummeting crude oil prices; in less than six months in 1986, prices fell from $26 per barrel to less than $12 per barrel. For each dollar loss in oil prices, the state lost an estimated $100 million in revenue from oil and natural gas severance taxes (Evans 1986). Lawmakers realized that innovative forms of funding were needed for new prison construction.

LEGISLATION OF PRIVATIZATION

In January 1987, various bills were introduced in the Texas House of Representatives and Senate, which proposed that "[T]he Texas Board of Corrections may contract with private vendors or with commissioners courts of counties for the financing, construction, operation, maintenance, or management of secure correctional facilities."[2] Lawmakers who introduced this legislation stressed that it was needed so the state could respond quickly and inexpensively to the prison crisis.

The original legislation outlined specific requirements for the private vendors. First, each private vendor had to comply with federal court orders and to receive accreditation as an individual facility from the American Correctional Association. Second, the legislation allowed a maximum of 2,000 medium- or minimum-security inmates to be housed in units each holding not more than 500 inmates. Third, vendors had to offer a level of services equal to those provided by the state, with a saving to the state of not less than 10 percent in comparison with the cost of a similar state-operated facility. Fourth, the initial contract would last not more than three years, with an option to renew for additional two-year periods. Fifth, the private vendors would have no authority over setting release and parole dates, awarding good conduct time, approving furloughs or transfers, or classifying inmates. Sixth, an inmate in the private facility would remain in legal custody of TDC. Finally, the primary purpose of the private prison units was to provide prerelease program for inmates, including employment counseling, drug and alcohol counseling, and family counseling. In addition, private vendors were required to provide for regular on-site monitoring by the TDC and for an adequate plan of insurance to protect the state against all claims arising from the services performed under contract by the vendor.

In response to concerns raised by lobbyists representing correctional employees' organizations and the Texas Employees Union, the original legislation was amended to include a clause that prohibited the Board of Corrections from converting any existing state correctional facility into a privately operated facility. In addition, the legislation was amended to allow private correctional facilities to hold more than 500 inmates if the facility was under construction or completed before the enactment of the bill.

Despite general approval from lawmakers, the bills were the subject of intense lobbying. In fact, when legislative committees discussed the privatization bills, representatives from private corrections firms and financial institutions, as well as city and county officials, besieged the capitol. Those who testified in favor of the privatization legislation and who represented private correctional firms included a former speaker of the Texas House of Representatives, a former chief counsel to TDC, and a former legislator (Kilday 1987).

A representative from the Texas State Employees Union offered the only testimony opposing the legislation:

> It is morally wrong for the state to delegate to a corporation the degradation of an individual's liberty .... There is a conflict of interest between corporations and prisons. Profit motives may not be necessarily consistent with the best interest of the prisoners, prison employees or the public .... Cost savings for corporations are often taken by trimming wages and benefits, staff training, vocational and educational programs for prisoners (testimony of Wakie Martin, Senate Criminal Justice Committee, February 10, 1987).

This limited opposition to prison privatization contrasted strongly to the situation in other states, where privatization had been debated (Cody and Bennett 1987; Folz and Scheb 1989). In Texas, legislators hardly discussed the moral or philosophical issues of privatizing state prison facilities. Such issues were overshadowed by the deteriorating conditions in the TDC.

On February 10, 1987 Senate Bill (SB) 251 was approved unanimously by the Senate Criminal Justice Committee and was sent to the full Senate for approval. On February 19 the Senate approved SB 251 by a vote of 23 to 2. The two opposing senators expressed concerns that "the housing of inmates is among the duties of the state and should not be delegated to the private sector" (Toohey 1987a). SB 251 then was sent to the House of Representatives, which approved it by a vote of 122-19 on March 10. Those who voted against the bill said they were concerned about the "state's control and responsibility of prisoners held in private correctional facilities" (Toohey 1987b).

On April 4, 1987, Senate Bill 251 was signed by Governor Bill Clements. Senator Ray Farabee, the author of SB 251, said, "It's not an answer, but it is an alternative and one of the tools that I think will be helpful to meet the increasing need for corrections facilities in the State of Texas" (Robison 1987). Texas Board of Corrections Chairman Al Hughes said that the legislation was 'an important step to begin us on the long road to getting our population problems in hand" (Bunting 1987). With the passage of SB 251, the State of Texas embarked on the most ambitious plan in the United States to use private companies to finance, construct, and manage state prison facilities.

IMPLEMENTATION OF PRISON PRIVATIZATION

The first step toward implementing SB 251 was taken on May 11, 1987, when the Texas Board of Corrections ("the board") unanimously voted to issue a request for proposals for the location, construction, and operation of four 500-man pre-release centers (PRCs). Nineteen proposals were received; two private vendors, Becon-Wackenhut, a partnership of Becon Construction Co. and Wackenhut Services Inc., (Wackenhut) and Corrections Corporation of America, Inc. (CCA), were selected to construct and operate two facilities each. The board's rationale for dividing the award was to allow TDC to compare the two firms' performance, while diluting the risk to the state if one of the two firms should be unable to fulfill its obligation.

After negotiations between the board and the vendors, four sites (two for each company) were chosen. Strong community opposition to the PRCs arose in all four locations, however. Because of this opposition, all four initial locations were changed to locales where the PRCs had public support.

Immediately after the board approved the four locations, contract negotiations began between TDC and the vendors. Several major obstacles developed as negotiations progressed. First, CCA was unable to obtain a construction bond, as required by TDC, that provided 100 percent coverage of payment for services and performance. CCA officials then approached Becon Construction Company and contracted with Becon to build their two PRCs. The second problem pertained to the method of financing the construction and operation of the PRCs. State officials originally had allowed the companies to independently determine the appropriate financing scheme. CCA had planned to own the facilities and to finance its two prisons with 60 percent equity. Wackenhut proposed using long-term, tax-exempt leases backed by appropriations every two years by the state legislature to finance its two facilities.

As negotiations proceeded, two serious problems became apparent. First, state officials realized that if the private companies financed and owned the PRCs and if the state decided not to renew the contract, the state would lose the bed space provided by the facilities. Second, it became evident that the most beneficial financing mechanism for the state was to combine all four prerelease centers into one financing package. These problems forced state officials to develop a new method to finance the PRCs. In the plan to which state officials finally agreed, ownership and financing of the PRCs were separated from construction and operation. This "modified privatization" scheme was based on two legislative bills passed during the 70th Legislature: Senate Bill (SB) 245, which authorized the Texas Board of Corrections to enter into lease-purchase contracts with county commissioners' courts to acquire correctional facilities, and House Bill (HB) 146, which authorized counties, home-rule cities, and nonprofit corporations acting on their behalf to issue revenue bonds to finance the acquisition, construction, and equipping of new facilities for the TDC.

On the basis of HB 146, Liberty County (near Houston) was chosen by the TDC and was authorized by the State Bond Review Board to create a nonprofit financing corporation to float tax-exempt revenue bonds. Accordingly the Liberty County Commissioners' Court created the Texas Correctional Facilities Financing Corporation. The State Bond Review Board approved two bond issues totaling $50 million to finance construction. One bond issue would finance the facilities constructed by Becon and operated by Wackenhut; the second would finance the facilities constructed by Becon and operated by CCA. To pay off the bonds, TDC entered two lease-purchase agreements, authorized under SB 245, with the Texas Correctional Facilities Financing Corporation, whereby it would deposit semiannual payments directly to the trustee to cover the principal and the interest on the bonds.

One of the last aspects of the contract negotiations pertained to the operating contract and the per diem rate that the private companies would receive to house inmates. SB 251 required that private vendors operate the PRCs at a cost saving to the state of at least 10 percent. Thus the TDC used a per diem rate calculated as follows by the accounting firm of Arthur Anderson:

> **The estimated cost per inmate per day of state operated prerelease center facilities totals $38.66 for 1988, $39.09 for 1989, and $39.24 for 1990. Under terms of Senate Bill 251, contracted services must be at least 10 percent below the estimate. Consequently, the maximum cost would be $34.79 in 1988, $35.18 in 1989, and $35.32 in 1990 (Arthur Anderson 1987:2).**

TDC officials concluded that the private companies were to be paid a per diem rate of $34.79 for the first year, less the per diem amount necessary for TDC to pay off the bonds, or $5.81 per inmate. The state would pay $35.25 per diem for the following two years, minus the $5.81. Establishment of the per diem rate was the final hurdle in the negotiation process.

On June 30, 1989, more than two years after SB 251 had been signed by Governor Clements, the first inmates arrived at the four PRCs. By the end of September 1989, all four PRCs were operational and were filled to capacity. Texas now leads the nation in the number of state inmates housed in private prisons.

THE STATUS OF PRISON PRIVATIZATION IN TEXAS

On December 12, 1989, to ensure that private vendors complied with all relevant court orders, Judge Justice drafted the *Stipulation and Order Regarding Private Pre-Release Centers* ("Stipulation"). The Stipulation required the staff of the Texas Department of Criminal Justice-Institutional Division (TDCJ-ID, formerly TDC) to prepare a comprehensive compliance report on each of the PRCs, covering all topics listed in the August 1983 *Report of the Special Master Recommending Certain Reports by the Defendants Relating to TDC Units to be Constructed in the Future*.[3] The Stipulation also provided that a Special Master would verify the accuracy of the compliance reports, and would submit his findings to the private vendors by March 1, 1990. Despite the mandate in the Stipulation, neither CCA nor Wackenhut was added as defendants in the *Ruiz* lawsuit.

Prison staff monitors gathered information from September to December 1989, the PRCs' first months of operation.[4] In December 1989 the monitors completed their reports; on May 15, 1990 the Texas Board of Criminal Justice (formerly the Texas Board of Corrections) released the results of the monitor's internal audit (Arnold 1989). Although the monitors reported many areas of compliance, the board specifically criticized both companies for 1) inadequate health services; 2) insufficient programs to keep prisoners occupied; 3) attributing abusive treatment of inmates to guards' inexperience; 4) filling staff positions slowly or not at all; 5) lack of educational programs for Spanish-speaking prisoners; 6) minimal participation of inmates in substance abuse programs; and 7) absence of self-monitoring (Fair 1990a). In response to the report, board chairman Charles Terrell stated, "I'm frustrated and angry. These findings are very troubling" (Ward 1990).

Representatives from both companies criticized the report and pointed out that the audits were conducted during the "shakedown period" of the PRCs' operation.

In spite of the board's initial reaction to the audit, many of the deficiencies had been resolved by July 9, 1990, the date of the next board meeting, as a result of ongoing negotiations: staff vacancies had been filled, programs had been changed, and new policies to ensure that contracts were followed were in place (Fair 1990b; Hoppe 1990). Responding to the changes, board chairman Terrel stated, "It's apparent . . . that both private vendors have done major program changes . . . and they should be given the opportunity to carry through," (Gonzalez 1990).

In a continuing process of overseeing strict adherence to contractual agreements, a series of comprehensive audits of each PRC was conducted in August 1990.[5] The audits were intended to determine compliance with the terms of the agreement and to assess each of the facilities' compliance with contractual obligations, including all TDCJ-ID policies and procedures, court orders, and applicable state and federal law. In September 1990 TDCJ-ID issued the results of the audits to the companies.

The summary concerning CCA's Cleveland PRC counted 68 findings of noncompliance. Of these findings, 65 were verified as corrected by the monitor. The summary concerning CCA's PRC at Venus contained 93 such findings, of which 81 were verified as corrected (TDCJ-ID 1990d:1). The Wackenhut PRC at Bridgeport produced 67 findings of noncompliance; 56 were verified as corrected. The Wackenhut PRC at Kyle produced 71 findings of noncompliance, of which 58 were corrected (TDCJ-ID 1990b:14. By fall 1991 almost all areas of noncompliance had been corrected.

Prison privatization in Texas was on the agenda of the 72nd Legislature, which convened in January 1991. Legislators received the Sunset Advisory Commission report titled "Contracts for Correctional Facilities and Seances." This report, which is required by SB 251, analyzed the costs and quality of the private prison services as compared to the costs and quality of similar state services. The Texas Sunset Advisory Commission (1990) reached the following conclusions:

1. As of August 31, 1990, the private prisons were operating at close to 10 percent below the cost of a hypothetical equivalent unit run by the state.
2. The TDCJ does not have a state-run equivalent of a private prison unit. Therefore no conclusions could be drawn as to whether the private prisons currently provide services that are equal to or higher in quality than the state's.

Using the findings of the Sunset Commission and the reports of the contract monitors, TDCJ-ID officials entered new contracts with both private vendors commencing September 1, 1991. The new contracts will run for two years, and the per diem rate will remain the same: $32.25 minus the debt retirement. The renewed contracts contain more specific language about the quality of service, educational and vocational programs, and the type of prerelease programming.

DISCUSSION AND CONCLUSION

The present privatization initiative in Texas is neither identical to nor wholly unlike the past practices of inmate leasing. Today's version of privatization does not lease out inmate labor or force inmates to pay for their upkeep. Yet many of the same issues and conditions that existed in the 1860s (e.g., increasing prisoner populations, the political pressure to "do something" about prison conditions, and economic turndown) led to privatization in 1980s (Durham 1989b; McConville 1987). In addition, many of the problems associated with prison privatization in the 1860s (e.g., contractors' failure to abide by the contracts, costs associated with contracts, and quality of contractors' services) have emerged in the 1980s (McAfee 1987). Despite these similarities, the current privatization movement is not a recreation of previous historical events but a phase of innovation for the nation's correctional system (McConville 1987). Although the two movements share the goals of reducing the cost of incarceration and relieving overcrowding, the major difference is that today governmental entities acknowledge that they are ultimately responsible for the care of inmates.

The reemergence of the private sector's involvement with the Texas prison system signaled a new era in Texas corrections, an era distinguished by progressive methods for aiding the thousands of Texas inmates. The most important aspect of this privatization experiment pertains to the type of facility that is operated by the private companies. By using small, (500-man) facilities that offer prerelease programs, lawmakers are taking major steps toward preparing inmates to live outside prison walls.

The operation and management of small, specialized facilities that house low-risk inmates has been touted as a possible role for the private sector in the nation's correctional system (Folz and Scheb 1989; Johnson and Ross 1990). Other states might follow the example of Texas. According to Logan (1990), this already may be a trend: most of the privately operated state prison units in the United States house fewer than 500 low-risk inmates.

A second feature of the Texas privatization experiment is the financing scheme devised to pay for constructing and operating the PRCs. Lawmakers devised a bonding mechanism that did not need voters' approval. By using lease revenue bonds, the state does not technically create a debt. Although the use of such bonds proved successful in Texas, the issuance of bonds that do not need voters' approval to pay for prison construction has been criticized because the government can expand prison construction without public input (Leonard 1989; McDonald 1989b).

A third aspect of the Texas privatization experience pertains to the contract negotiations between the state and the private companies. On the basis of the original contracts, the contract monitors' reports, and the companies' responses to the reports, it appears that some portions of the contracts were ambiguous (e.g., educational programs, vocational programs, prerelease programs). As a result, the companies and the TDCJ-ID spent a great amount of time and money in reaching agreements on how to carry out the contracts properly. State policy makers contemplating prison privatization would do well to study the current situation in Texas.

During the 1980s a unique set of circumstances existed in Texas, which gave rise to the reemergence of prison privatization. Although the private prisons have been operating for several years, it is not yet known whether privatization is the panacea for state prison systems. It is still too early to tell whether privatization is a remedy or just another correctional fad.

ENDNOTES

[1] The state entered a court-approved settlement of *Ruiz v. Estelle* (1980), which established a maximum capacity for each prison unit and a maximum capacity for the entire prison system. The settlement required TDC to reduce the population in the existing 26 units to fit the prescribed limits. The reduction from approximately 37,500 inmates to 32,500 inmates was to occur by depopulating the existing units in two stages over four years.

[2] On December 3, 1986, House Bill 100 was pre-filed by Representatives Clint Hackney (D). On February 2, 1987, Senate Bill 251 was filed by Senator Ray Farabee (D). Senate Bill 251 was approved by the Senate Criminal Justice Committee on February 10, 1987 and was sent to the full Senate for approval. The Senate approved Senate Bill 251 on February 19, 1987. House Bill 100 was approved by the House Committee on Corrections on February 11, 1987 and was referred to a sub committee for further discussion. House Bill 100 was brought up in a subcommittee meeting on February 25, 1987. No further action was taken because Senate Bill 251 had been approved by the Senate on February 19, 1987.

[3] The areas included all health services, classification, staffing, inmate support services, disciplinary system, solitary confinement, administrative segregation, work safety, use of force, access to courts, maintenance, repairs and renovations, out-of-cell activities, necessities, visiting, dining, capacity, single celling, medical care, dental care, and psychiatric care.

[4] The audits of the PRCs were conducted by TDC monitors, who visited the Venus and Bridgeport units after reviewing all TDCJ-ID reports on all four PRCs. At each PRC the monitor toured the physical plant, generally observed the operation of the unit, interviewed appropriate staff members, reviewed selected inmate files, reviewed relevant logs and other documents, and interviewed randomly selected prisoners on a variety of topics. The monitor also noted specifically whether the compliance concerns of the TDCJ-ID monitoring team had been corrected. He noted whether his findings generally were consistent with those of TDCJ-ID reports, described areas of disagreement with or concern about the TDCJ-ID observations, reported whether the deficiencies identified by the TDCJ-ID staff had been corrected by time of the monitor's on-site audit, and listed compliance concerns he observed in addition to the those identified by the TDCJ-ID monitoring team.

[5] The audits of all four PRCs were conducted by selected departments of the TDCJ-ID. These "audit team" reports covered the following areas: classification, Spanish-language assistance, inmate absentee tracking, inmate disciplinary process, inmate grievance procedure, education, mailroom operations, use of force, maintenance, safety, recreation, necessities, access to courts, food service, staffing, administrative segregation, programmatic/non-programmatic activities, support service to inmates, personnel, training and background investigations, commissary, craft sales, inmates' personal property, and health service. The audit teams relied on a wide variety of methods to complete their reports, including reviewing all appropriate documentation and records, interviews with staff and inmates, observations of daily routine, inspections of the physical plant.

REFERENCES

American Federation of State, County and Municipal Employees (AFSCME) (1985) *Does Crime Pay?: An Examination of Prisons for Profit.* Washington, DC: AFSCME.

Arnold, D.D. (1989) *Eighty-Fourth Monitor's Report—Report on the Private Pre-Release Centers.* Austin: Office of Special Master.

Anderson, A. (1987) Personal communication to TDC Executive Director James Lynaugh, December 7.

Brakal, S.J. (1988) "'Privatization' in Corrections: Radical Prison Chic or Mainstream Americana?" *Criminal and Civil Confinement* 14:1-38.

Bunting, K. (1987) "Private Prisons Get Go-Ahead—One Answer to Overcrowding." *Fort-Worth Star-Telegram*, April 15, p. A1.

Camp, C. and G. Camp (1984) *Private Sector Involvement in Prison Services and Operations.* Washington, DC: National Institute of Corrections.

——— (1985) "Correctional Privatization in Perspective." *The Prison Journal* 65:14-31.

Cody, W.J. and A. Bennett (1987) "The Privatization of Correctional Institutions: The Tennessee Experience." *Vanderbilt Law Review* 40:829-49.

Crouch, B.W. and J.W. Marquart (1989) *An Appeal to Justice: Litigated Reforms of the Texas Prisons.* Austin: University of Texas Press.

Crow, H. (1964) "A Political History of the Texas Penal System, 1829-1951." Unpublished doctoral dissertation, University of Texas.

Dewitt, C.B. (1986) "New Construction Methods for Correctional Facilities." *National Institute of Justice Research in Brief*, date, March 1986 pp. 1-8.

DiIulio, J. Jr. (1986) "Prisons, Profits and the Public Good: The Privatization of Corrections." *Research Bulletin* 4. Sam Houston State University Press.

Durham, A.M., III (1989a) "Origins of Interest in the Privatization of Punishment: The Nineteenth and Twentieth Century American Experience." *Criminology* 27:107-39.

——— (1989b) "The Privatization of Punishment: Justification, Expectation, and Experience." *Criminal Justice Policy Review* 3:48-73.

Evans, J., Ed. (1986) "Texas a Net Loser from Falling Oil Prices: Economist Reports." *Energy Studies*, 11. Austin: University of Texas, Center for Energy Studies.

Fair, K. (1990a) "State Board Fires Broadside at Privately Run Prisons." *Houston Chronicle*, May 16, p. 2A.

——— (1990b) "Turnaround in Private Prisons." *Houston Chronicle*, July 10, p. 1A.

Feeley, M. (1991) "The Privatization of Prisons in Historical Perspective." *Research Bulletin* 6. San Houston State University Press.

Fenton, J. (1985) "A Private Alternative to Public Prisons." *The Prison Journal* 65:48-62.

Folz, D.H. and J.M. Scheb (1989) "Prisons, Profits and Politics: The Tennessee Privatization Experiment." *Judicature* 73:98-102.

Freelander, D. and M. Sanders (1987) "TDC Prisons Closed for Weekend." *Houston Post*, January 17, p. A1.

Gammel, H. (1989) *The Laws of Texas, 1822-1897.* Austin: Gammel Book Company.

Garoogian, A. (1987) "Prisons for Profit: A Select Bibliography on Privatization." *Vance Bibliographies* 2132:1-15.

Gonzalez, J. (1990) "Private Prisons Make the Grade in State Review." *Fort Worth Telegram*, July 10, p. A1.

Goodstein, L. and D. MacKenzie, Eds. (1987) *The American Prison: Issues in Research and Policy.* New York: Plenum.

Gottfredson, S. and S. McConville, Eds. (1987) *America's Correctional Crisis*. New York: Greenwood.

Hanson, L.S.C. (1991) "The Privatization of Corrections Movement: A Decade of Change." *Journal of Contemporary Criminal Justice* 7:1-28.

Hoppe, C. (1990) "State Says Prison Firms Making Progress." *Dallas Morning News*, July 10, p. 1A.

Hutto, T. (1990) "Privatization of Prisons." In J. W. Murphy and J. E. Dison (eds.), *Are Prisons Any Better? Twenty Years of Reform*, pp. 111-27. Newbury Park, CA: Sage.

Hutto, T. and G.E. Vick (1984) "Designing the Private Correctional Facility." *Corrections Today* 23:85-90.

Immarigeon, R. (1987) "Privatizing Adult Imprisonment in the U.S.: A Bibliography." *Criminal Justice Abstracts* 3:123-39.

Johnson, B.R. and P.P. Ross (1990) "The Privatization of Correctional Management: A Review." *Journal of Criminal Justice* 18:351-58.

Jones, C.O. (1988) *The Reagan Legacy: Promise and Performance*. Chatham, NJ: Chatham House.

Kilday, P. (1987) "Lobbyists Make Push for Private Prisons." *Dallas Times Herald*, February 10, p. A1.

Leonard, H. (1989) "Private Time: The Political Economy of Private Prison Financing." In D. McDonald (ed.), *Private Prisons and the Public Interest*, pp. 66-85. New Brunswick, NJ: Rutgers University Press.

Lewis, O. (1967) *The Development of American Prisons and Prison Customs*. Montclair, NJ: Patterson Smith.

Logan, C.H. (1986) *Privatization and Corrections: A Bibliography*. Storrs: University of Connecticut Press.

―――― C. (1990) *Private Prisons: Cons and Pros*. Oxford: Oxford University Press.

Logan, C.H. and S.P. Rausch (1985) "Punish and Profit: The Emergence of Private Enterprise Prisons." *Justice Quarterly* 2:303-18.

Martin, S.J. and S. Ekland-Olson (1987) *Texas Prisons: The Walls Came Tumbling Down*. Austin: Texas Monthly Press.

Matthews, R. Ed. (1989) *Privatizing Criminal Justice*. London: Sage.

McAfee, W.M. (1987) "Tennessee's Private Prison Act of 1986: An Historical Perspective with Special Attention to California's Experience." *Vanderbilt Law Review* 40:851-65.

McConville, S. (1987) "Aid from Industry: Private Corrections and Prison Crowding." In S. D. Gottfredson and S. McConville (eds.), *America's Correctional Crisis*, pp. 221-41. New York: Greenwood.

McDonald, D., Ed. (1989a) *Private Prisons and the Public Interest*. New Brunswick, NJ: Rutgers University Press.

―――― (1989b) "Introduction." In D. McDonald (ed.), *Private Prisons and the Public Interest*, pp. 1-19. New Brunswick, NJ: Rutgers University Press.

McKelvey, B. (1977) *American Prisons*. 2nd ed. Montclair, NJ: Patterson Smith.

Mullen, J. (1985) "Corrections and the Private Sector." *Prison Journal* 65(2): 1-14.

Nowlin, J.R. (1962) "A Political History of the Texas Prison System, 1847-1957." Unpublished master's thesis, Trinity University.

Parrish, T.M. (1976) "This Species of Slave Labor: The Convict Lease System in Texas, 1871-1912." Unpublished master's thesis, Baylor University.

Penitentiary Investigating Committee. (1910) *Report to the Penitentiary Investigative Committee*. Austin: Publisher?

President's Commission on Privatization (1988). *Privatization toward More Effective Government*. Washington, DC: U.S. Government Printing Office.

Press, A. (1989) "The Good, the Bad, and the Ugly: Private Prisons in the 1980s." In D. McDonald (ed.), *Private Prisons and the Public Interest*, pp. 19-41. New Brunswick, NJ: Rutgers University Press.

Ring, C.R. (1987) *Contracting for the Operation of Private Prisons*. College Park, MD: AMERICAN CORRECTIONAL ASSOCIATION

Robbins, I.P. (1986) "Privatization of Corrections: Defining the Issues." *Judicature* 69:325-31.

Robbins, I.P. (1988) *The Legal Dimensions of Private Incarceration*. Washington, DC: American Bar Association.

Robison, C. (1987) "Bill on Private Prisons Signed." *Houston Chronicle*, April 15, p. 1A.

Rutherford, A. (1989) "British Penal Policy and the Idea of Prison Privatization." In D. McDonald (ed.), *Private Prisons and the Public Interest*, pp. 42-65. New Brunswick, NJ: Rutgers University Press.

Savas, E.S. (1982) *Privatizing the Public Sector: How to Shrink Government*. Chatham, NJ: Chatham House.

Sechrest, D.K. and S. Price (1985) *Correctional Facility Design* and Construction. Washington, DC: National Institute of justice.

Stewart, J.K. (1986) "Costly Comparisons: Should the Monopoly be Ended?" In P.B. McGuigan and J.S. Paxcale (Eds.), *Crime and Punishment in Modern America*, pp. 365-87. Washington, DC: Institute for Government and Politics.

Steinberg, S. (1981) *Potential for Contracted Management in Local Correctional Facilities*. Washington, DC: National Institute of Corrections.

Sullenberg, T. (1974) "An Interpretive History of the Texas Convict Lease System, 1871-1914." Unpublished master's thesis, Sam Houston State University.

Texas Department of Corrections (1987) *Four Year Construction Plan*. Huntsville: Author.

Texas Department of Criminal Justice-Institutional Division (1990a) *Summary of Operational Review of Corrections Corporation of America Private Pre-Release Centers*. Austin: Author.

——— (1990b). *Summary of Operational Review of Wackenhut Corrections Corporation Private Pre-Release Centers*. Austin, TX: Author.

Texas Penitentiary Report of the Commission Appointed by the Governor. (1875) Houston: State Printer.

"Texas Prison Privatization Nudged Down on Day Rates" (1988). *Public Works Financing*, January, p. 6.

Texas Sunset Advisory Commission (1990) *Contracts for Correctional Facilities and Services*. Austin: Author.

Thomas, C.W. (1990) *Private Corrections Adult Secure Facility Census, May, 1990*. Gainesville: University of Florida, Center for Studies in Criminology and Law.

Toohey, M. (1987a) "Bill Would Allow Contracts for Private Prisons." *Houston Chronicle*, February 20, p. 20A.

——— (1987b) "Bill on Private Prisons Is Approved by House." *Houston Chronicle*, March 11, p. 1A.

Walker, D. (1988) *Penology for Profit: A History of the Texas Prison System 1861-1912*. College Station: Texas A&M University Press.

Ward, M. (1990) "Private Prisons Faulted on Services, Discipline." *Austin-American Statesman*, May 16, p. A1.

Weiss, R.P. (1989) "Private Prisons and the State." In R. Matthews (Ed.), *Privatizing Criminal Justice*, pp. 24-51. London: Sage.

CASES CITED

Medina v. O'Neill 589 F. Supp. 1028 (1984)
Ruiz v. Estelle 503 F. Supp. 1265 (1980)

THE GREAT TEXAS PRISON MESS

*During The Gargantuan Buildup Of The Texas Prison System,
Everyone Wanted In On The Action -- Even Andy Collins, The Boss Himself.
Here's How Greed, Fear, And Vitapro Produced The State's Costliest Scandal.*

By Robert Draper

IT WAS THE STUPIDEST THING THE STATE of Texas has ever done," Andy Collins said about his crowning achievement, his oversight of the greatest expansion of prison beds in the history of the free world. "The public was absolutely, hoodwinked into thinking that the only way the crime problem could ever be solved was prosecution and incarceration. We should've been interceding at an earlier age, dealing with these kids before they ever became crooks. But instead, we are just taking juveniles and feeding them directly into the system. I mean, look who was behind it all. Prosecutors, cops, politicians -- all of them with a self-serving agenda.

"And the media," Collins declared as he leaned over the patio table at his suburban home just north of Houston delivering the accusation with martyr's relish. "The goddam media did as much as anyone to build all those prisons because they farmed the flames of public hysteria. The issue of crime has become entertainment. Turn on the TV, *Cops, Rescue 911*. That kind of crap."

As recently as last December, Collins had been the most powerful bureaucrat in Texas, the executive director of the Texas Department of Criminal Justice (TDCJ). Now it was March, and with news of scandal breaking all around him, his brief second career as a prison consultant was in shambles. By all rights he should have been a basket case -- but here he was, wearing the standard yuppie regalia of khakis, loafers, and tortoiseshell glasses, puffing appreciatively on a cigar, and sipping at a single-malt Scotch while his dachshund yapped away in the back yard and two of his daughters appeared on the patio to hit up their dad for movie money. The tableau was eerily serene; the 45-year-old Midland native with the well padded cheeks and preadolescent grin was one hell of a lot tougher than he looked. He was placing calls to headhunters about job opportunities that had little to do with the way he had spent the past 23 years of his life, and former subordinates in Huntsville were now trashing him in the papers. And yet Andy Collins had not lost an ounce of his old charm and could still downshift from scholarly correctional minutiae to Bubba banter with the ease of a bona fide political master.

"And now," he said, his laughter both sour and triumphant, "now we're worried about the aftertaste of VitaPro! People were willing to feed these sumbitches dog food! And now they're worried about an inmate's aftertaste."

But VitaPro, the soybean-based powder that Texas prisons have been using as a meat substitute, had nothing on the bitter aftertaste of irony that so bedevils Collins nowadays. He stood center stage as the state carried out a frantic buildup that transformed a once-provincial agency centered in rural East Texas into a mighty bureaucracy with outposts in 72 towns -- the biggest prison system concocted by any free society in history. From 1990 to 1995, the TDCJ's annual operating budget ballooned from $700 million to 82.2 billion. All of a sudden, the gloomy prison business was the hottest thing going, and money grabbers poured in from all over North America to get in on the action. Private-prison operators reaped more profits in Texas than anywhere else in the nation. Construction firms and subcontractors raked in hundreds of millions of dollars. Vendors great and small, proffering a myriad of esoteric wares -- state-of-the-art mousetraps, law journals for prison libraries, grease trap-cleaning systems, taut-wire intrusion-detector fences, and, yes, VitaPro -- paid handsome fees to self-styled "corrections consultants" or to lobbyists who would dispense campaign contributions wherever influence could be peddled. Even cities got in on the act by competing for the new state jails that might bring jobs and economic salvation; among the winners were Bonham, Dalhart, Raymondville, and Henderson -- towns so removed from major crime centers that the goal of keeping inmates near their communities was negated. The Texas prison expansion became a feeding frenzy, and the unenviable task of overseeing it fell to Andy Collins. Eventually it began to dawn on him that there had to be a better way to make a living -- and that way, of course, was all around him.

The story of how Andy Collins set himself up to make money as a consultant for VitaPro and other businesses to which he had doled out lucrative contracts began to unravel in early January, just four days after Collins officially left the TDCJ to become a consultant. Law enforcement officials had arrested a man named Patrick Graham for allegedly accepting money in exchange for trying to use his influence to spring a TDCJ inmate. In Graham's wallet was a business card identifying him as a broker for VitaPro, a company that had been awarded a $33.7 million contract by Collins six months earlier. But Graham had a more ominous link to the former TDCJ director: He was Collins' brand-new business partner. In the ensuing weeks, reporters found other contracts Collins had tendered without the approval of the appointed board that oversees the TDCJ. What has emerged is the tawdriest government spectacle since the Sharpstown scandal 25 years ago. Governor George W. Bush has enlisted the services of the Texas Rangers and the FBI to investigate what he has described as "sweetheart contracts" -- implying that Collins may have benefited illegally from such deals. Though Collins has not yet been formally accused of breaking any laws, that may say more about the wording of the laws than the integrity of the ex-director.

But in the rush to judge Andy Collins, the media and the politicians have failed to judge his accomplices in the great prison scandal: themselves. So eager were they to sate the public's bloodlust for locking up criminals and throwing away the key that they helped create a climate of hysteria in which corruption could flourish. The dust from the prison expansion has now settled, and we are left with a sorry mess indeed. The state prison system, which before the buildup was so overcrowded that it had to turn inmates loose after only a few months behind bars, now has 146,000 prison beds but only 129,000 inmates. Eight new prisons have been built but remain closed, for the simple reason that we have no use for them. For that matter, the agency has a warehouse full of VitaPro that it cannot sell and a state-of-the-art meat-packing facility in Amarillo that sat dormant for half a year. To fill empty classrooms, it has "pre-release" classes for inmates who are on their way in as well as on their way out and substance-abuse courses for inmates who have already taken such courses. The TDCJ steadfastly maintains that the empty prisons will be full within a year, but its past record of predicting its future needs has been poor and, anyway, the TDCJ's argument misses the larger problem: While our public schools have gone to seed and state programs for the elderly have dwindled to near-nothingness, the prison system has accumulated a wasteful embarrassment of riches. Is this what Texans wanted?

Exploiting the cloud cover of "urgency," prisons were built poorly and at an exorbitant cost. Some 12,000 "emergency beds" were thrown together in 180 days at the height of the hysteria in late 1994. Those particular prison units have a life expectancy of about twenty years, as opposed to the fifty-to-seventy-year life expectancy of the standard TDCJ prison; they are nothing more than minimum-security warehouses, and yet they carry the price tag of maximum-security prisons.

Construction of the $10.3 million Amarillo meat-packing plant was also deemed for some strange reason an "emergency" back in 1994, a decision that cost the taxpayers probably an extra $1 million even though the facility was built partly using free inmate labor, even though it still lacks essential (and expensive) items; grease traps and bar screens. The TDCJ, according to its own internal figures, also spent $3.3 million more than was to build facilities containing thousands of beds for substance abuse treatment, which state officials had decided was an urgent need -- only to be told later that many of these beds weren't needed after all. (The TDCJ is now spending even more reconfiguring those beds into something it can actually use.) And let us not forget the six Mode II (county-run) private prisons that TDCJ awarded to *high* bidders in early 1994, an expenses-be-damned approach then justified by the belief that the treatment programs offered by the private companies were urgently needed. Two of those prisons sit vacant today, and the prison system may ultimately convert all six into standard facilities which of course will cost more money to accomplish. Beneath this statewide fiasco lurks not merely Collins, but an entire culture of loose money and looser ethics -- a culture, in other words, whose most enthusiastic participants exhibited a moral compass not unlike that of the state's sleaziest inmates.

THE EAST TEXAS TOWN OF HUNTSVILLE is not much different today than it was when James Anthum "Andy" Collins, a dough-faced college kid of nineteen, transferred from the University of Mississippi to Sam Houston State University in the fall of 1970. Huntsville remains the company town of the Texas prison system, which provides more than twice as many jobs (5,219) to Walker County as Sam Houston State, the next biggest employer and itself a participant in the field of criminology. Thanks to the Texas Department of Criminal Justice, the town of 27,142 (not including the 7,450 inmates housed in Huntsville) is recession-proof and demographically blessed by East Texas standards, its restaurants and bars packed nightly with accountants, lawyers, and other well-educated administrative officials on the TDCJ payroll. It's hard to find a person in Huntsville who doesn't have at least an indirect affiliation with the prison system, as local attorneys are reminded whenever they ferret through a jury pool. Walker County farmers, hardware store retailers, and gas station operators owe their livelihoods to the TDCJ -- all for the small price of seeing busloads of men in white rumble through their streets and enduring the harsh lights of the Walls, Wynne, and Holliday units that pierce the blanket of evening.

Isolated from the media and the Legislature, the prison system carries on its activities with regal insularity, satisfied with the arrangement that in this airtight community, everything gets around but nothing gets out. The agency's most renowned autocrats of the past -- prison board chairman-for-life H. H. Coffield, haughty director-dictator George Beto, and his discredited successor, W. J. Estelle -- are immortalized by prison units that bear their names, The new executive director, Wayne Scott, resides, as predecessors did, in the two-story colonial brick affair built for reformist prison boss O.B. Ellis in 1949 -- a mansion not quite as grand as the governors and situated directly across the street from the Walls Unit -- but a mansion nonetheless. Inmates tend Scott's gardens, wash his car, and serve him food, just as they did for Ellis.

The prison system has its own culture and its own esoteric language. To watch the Texas Board of Criminal Justice (the prison oversight board consisting of nine unpaid citizens appointed in staggered six-year terms by the governor) attempt to even make sense of the prison system, much less to regulate it, is an embarrassing spectacle. Over the years board members have variously been indifferent, bewildered, or ethically challenged -- or all of the above, in the case of the present board. Embattled though the TDCJ may be, the board remains utterly at its mercy. "We've had to wait for the media to tell us the things that we're supposed to know," complains new member John David Franz.

Yet the formidable power of the prison system has always been of the austere kind. The assorted middle managers of the TDCJ toil in a poorly lit converted warehouse. The prisons themselves are, with a few recently built exceptions, singularly wretched in appearance. The wardens greet guests in dumpy offices carpeted with institutional fabric the colors of which do not exist in nature. Even today, a prison visitor must identify himself by dropping his drivers license into a tin can that the tower guard lowers by means of a rope. For Texans who like to see their state's prisons bleak and antiquated, the TDCJ does not disappoint.

Dismal trappings notwithstanding, the prison system in the Andy Collins era became the biggest agency in the state. As the executive director of the Texas Department of Criminal Justice, Collins oversaw not only the prisons bill also the parole division and state jail systems. At the time he took over the job in 1994, the TDCJ had 65 prison units. By the time Collins resigned twenty months later, the state boosted 108 prisons. The system housed 72,000 inmates in 1994; by 1996 that number would almost double.

His improbable ascent from summer intern to executive director makes sense only in retrospect. He went to work for the prison system in 1972, while still a student at Sam Houston State, spending a summer vacation as a prison guard in pursuit of his criminal justice degree. His first day on the job at Ellis I was made memorable when an inmate was dragged out of the shoe shop sporting a slashed throat. "I was so goddamned naive," Collins says. "The day I showed up to prison, I didn't know anyone in my family who'd had a divorce, much less been to jail."

He was as one colleague remembered him, "more glib than the average correctional officers," a pudgy and fun-loving frat boy who could intimidate a can of Budweiser but not much else. He advanced through the ranks without making much of an impression, first as an unimposing prison guard and eventually as the warden of Beto I Unit, where even his friends say he was a failure. But he possessed both an acute internal weather vane and a gift for excellent timing. Collins' rise coincided with the landmark *Ruiz v. Estelle* lawsuit, which cited injustices ranging from overcrowding to brutality against inmates and which compelled the ruffians who had been running the show (using thug inmates known as building tenders to keep order) to flee the prison system in droves. "Andy wasn't from the same school as the old bad-ass wardens like Billy McMillan and Beartracks McAdams and Wildcat Anderson," says one former associate from Collins' days at Beto I. "He was post-*Ruiz* through and through."

Collins' knack for good timing has never more apparent than in 1985, when as a beleaguered warden he gave notice and took a job with the Texas Youth Commission. It happened that the new prison board chairman, Al Hughes, insisted that the governor provide him with an executive assistant in Austin. I need some who had institutional knowledge whom I could call at one in the morning and ask, 'What the hell does *ad-seg* mean, anyway?' Or 'How many inmates per shower head does *Ruiz* require?'"

Hughes hired Collins, who thus became acquainted with the more rarefied side of the system, a world peopled by legislators and lobbyists rather than prison gangs. "Oh, man, I thought it was great," Collins says today. Colleagues remember how well the 36-year-old ex-warden took to schmoozing in the Capitol and over pitchers of beer at the Texas Chili Parlor. Collins became a bureaucratic star, using well his gift for gab and his ability to spew out esoteric data he had just recently learned.

The event that placed Collins firmly on the fast track was the prison board's decision at the end of 1986 to install TDCJ financial whiz Jim Lynaugh as director. Lynaugh in turn made Collins his deputy. The new director had worked under state comptroller Bo Bullock for nine years; "He understood money and was an absolute master at the political process," Collins says. But Lynaugh delegated to Collins enormous authority over the prison operations. "Jim didn't talk the lingo of corrections," Collins says of his former "We'd get to talking about putting an air fan in a flytrap at the Retrieve Unit, and his eyes would glaze over." In 1990 to the chagrin of many wardens who remembered Andy Collins as one of their least competent peers -- he was made the director of the TDCJ's institutional division, the overseer of all prison operations.

As Collins' star rose, Lynaugh's began to fall. The board members appointed by new governor Ann Richards in 1991 were more interested in drug treatment than maximum-security confinement, and they regarded Lynaugh as cagey and arrogant. When in 1992 the news leaked that the TDCJ's internal affairs division had been investigating a Richards-appointed board member, it became clear that Lynaugh's days were numbered. But Collins remained the Artful Dodger. As he told a friend, "I got one of Ann's people to let me see her, and I got on her drug-treatment bandwagon real quick."

Lynaugh's departure in September 1993 left a clear path to the top job for Collins. His claim today that "I didn't want the job initially" draws laughter even from his supporters. From the start, Collins campaigned rigorously for the job, soliciting letters of recommendation from politicians all over Texas and Washington, DC. His support was boosted when Lynaugh told Bullock, who had been elected lieutenant governor, that Collins was the best man for the job and Bullock in turn announced that Collins was his man. On April 10, 1994, the board made it official -- but only after six and a half hours of deliberation, during which they resorted to desperate measure of asking interim director Jim Riley to reconsider taking the job. One board member said during the closed-door meeting, "I just don't believe that Andy Collins, as good as he is logistically, has the character to be executive director."

The board member's warning would prove grimly prescient, but Collins began his tenure with a determination to win over his doubters. It worked. "He succeeded beyond our wildest expectations," recalls one opposition board member. The new director was everything Lynaugh wasn't: open-minded, inclusive, seemingly eager to solicit the opinions of the board. He alone had the institutional knowledge and political savvy to cope with events that would engulf the state's criminal justice landscape. "The day I walked into that job," Collins says, "there were decisions that had to be made *that* day. And it would've taken anyone two months minimum to get up to speed. There's no other job in the country that would've prepared a person for this one."

Among his many duties loomed a paramount mission: build more prisons -- *now*. For earlier directors, prison building had not been a central focus because there wasn't any money available. As a result of the *Ruiz* lawsuit's decision that Texas prisons were overcrowded, parole officials started letting out as many as 79 percent of the state's eligible inmates by the early nineties. When the public wouldn't stand for this, the unspoken policy became to let the TDCJ inmates spend the bulk of their sentences in county jails because there was no room at the prisons. But the counties foiled this strategy by filing suit against the state in 1990. With Texas judges, juries, and politicians determined to send most nonviolent criminals to prison, Texans dug deep and approved two state bond issues for prison construction totaling $2 billion.

Collins had to produce beds, tens of thousands of them all at once, and such a task was like nothing any previous director had experienced. Every new prison unit brought with it new travel demands, new contract squabbles, new personnel headaches, new inmate conflicts, and new litigation. Turf wars cropped up everywhere -- between the new privately run prisons and the old prison bureaucracy, between bickering board members, between Senate Criminal Justice Committee Chairman John Whitmire and Huntsville-based House Corrections Committee chairman Allen Hightower -- and Collins was caught in the middle. Appeasement was more Collins' specialty, but there were just too many people to accommodate. Legislators wanted prisons built in their districts and, preferably named after them, new vendors wanted their slice pie. And these requests came on top of the usual ones, such as state officials wanting to hunt quail and deer on prison property and influential Texans wanting some favored inmate to be transferred to a facility closer to home.

Collins' tendency to accommodate important people rankled his underlings. He ramroded the hirings of less-qualified individuals who happened to be recommended by influential legislators and let board members circumvent the TDCJ's construction staff. The director's tenure would eventually be marked by numerous floutings of established procedures, by himself and by board members whose meddling he did nothing to discourage, all of which profoundly demoralized TDCJ staffers.

But Collins himself wasn't exactly having a gay time of it, "I was the first guy in the office and the last to leave," he says. "I worked seven days a week, twenty hours a day on call. Thousand of hours I lost, not compensated for." Prison life became suffocating for the TDCJ lifer, the Huntsville mansion offered no solice. The sound of the Walls Unit inmates pounding their basketballs was like a hammer in his head. The phone rang all night long, with each caller conveying some new mini-crisis for Collins to lose sleep over. One of the inmate house servants had swiped some of Collin's money and a couple of pairs of his jeans. The claustrophobic lifestyle in Huntsville had taken its toll on his personal life, especially when several female prison employees scurrilously charged in a lawsuit that Collins had allowed a prison captain to sexually harass them because the captain knew something about Collins' alleged sexual alliances.

Who needed this kind of grief? All around him, prison entrepreneurs with one tenth of his experience were effortlessly raking it in. Private prison companies like Wackenhut and the Corrections Corporation of America counted Texas as their number one client. The firms were paying hundreds of thousands of dollars to veteran Capitol lobbyists like former Speaker Billy Clayton and Ed Wendler to represent them, and the lobbyists in turn were enriching the campaign coffers of politicians across the state. Topped-out TDCJ wardens and bureaucrats were crossing over to become well-paid private-prison employees. Among those were a number of tough old wardens from the pre-*Ruiz* days. If those dinosaurs could make it in the new world, why couldn't Andy Collins?

Even a prominent former critic of private prisons, Collins' old friend Charles Terrell, the chairman of the prison board from 1987 to 1990, had gone over to the other side. Fully six months before he resigned from the board, Terrell had quietly formed his own company, Corrections Solutions. By 1994 the former prison overseer was hitting up the TDCJ for business. But Terrell -- who had made millions selling insurance in Dallas -- would fare poorly as a prison profiteer. Three times he was thwarted in bids to build and operate a private prison, and in one case he was outright outpoliticked by State Senator Bill Ratliff and State Representative Paul Sadler, who arm-twisted the board to award a contract to a group operating out of Henderson.

But Charlie Terrell would keep turning up, a former public servant dancing in and out of a world gone ethically ablur. He would do business with director Andy Collins before all was said and done. Their fates, in fact, would be bound by a man who would come to epitomize the dark, degenerative side of the great prison boom: Patrick Harold Graham.

CREATURE OF DESTINY THAT HE WAS, Pat Graham slithered into the weed-choked garden of the prison business with the greatest of ease. Graham started out straight, selling Johnny Carson-style blazers at his fathers clothing store in Houston. Later he established his own haberdashery in Humble, but beyond the racks of polyester lay treasures for the taking, and Graham was nothing if not a taker at heart.

Truth be told, he was a likable devil and had "the greatest bullshit of anyone I've ever heard," according to one of his future prosecutors. The early ventures of Graham and his brother and business partner, Mike, involved a forklift business, a natural-gas-pipeline operation, and an alcohol-free teen discotheque. Later would come the attempts to clone cattle, build offices out of recycled garbage, and bring pro basketball to New Orleans. But along the way, Pat Graham made a brief pit stop in the early eighties as an employee for a modest private detention company out of Victoria -- and there he saw gold.

The smell of money must have made his nostrils flare like hoop skirts in a hurricane. Texas was dying for prison beds. In 1987 Graham pronounced himself a jail builder, formed N-Group Securities with Mike, and spent the next three years trying to persuade counties to let him build their jails on spec financed with revenue bonds. The revenues that would pay off the bonds would come from contracts with TDCJ and other entities to house overflow prisoners. And Graham gathered an impressive collection of business associates ex-governor Mark White, former state senator Ray Hutchison (the spouse of eventual U.S. senator Kay Bailey Hutchison), the highbrow private prison company Wackenhut, and a host of county officials who were assured by Graham that a Texas jail would never want for inmates -- that if you built one, TDCJ would come.

Graham's associates became his victims. He charged six counties a total of $73 million, financed with bond issues, for six jails that were worth about $50 million. He demanded, and received, at least $6 million in kickbacks from secret arrangements with underwriters and construction associates, according to court documents. When in 1988 then-director Jim Lynaugh saw the N-Group facility plans for what they were -- minimum-security prison dorms that did not comply with *Ruiz* standards -- he informed Graham that the TDCJ would not be doing business with N-Group. But Graham wasn't going to let a little federal court order spoil the deal. The jails were completed in 1991, and thereafter Graham unleashed a political blitzkrieg urging the TDCJ to contract with counties to house prisoners there: speeches by Mark White (to whom N-Group contributed $225,000 for his failed 1990 bid for governor), angry letters by county judges and local legislators, and indignant newspaper editorials. Lynaugh didn't budge. As he would later testify dryly. "I did not wish to incur the wrath of a federal judge."

When it dawned on the bondholders that they had been sold a bill of goods, they glumly sold the six N-Group facilities to the TDCJ for 50 cents on the dollar and sued Pat and Mike Graham. The N-Group civil lawsuit took place in the fall of 1994, five months after Andy Collins had become the TDCJ's executive director. Collins and Lynaugh both testified at the trial, by which time it was common knowledge that, as Allen Hightower puts it, "You were putting your reputation at one hell of a risk by having any association with Pat Graham." Everyone knew that Graham had been indicted in Pecos County for various jail-building malfeasances. Everyone knew he had snookered the bondholders and pocketed unheard of sums of kickbacks. And as the trial transcript shows, Graham changed his Fifth Amendment plea and agreed to testify following a payment of $50,000 by co-defendant Lott Construction.

Yet Collins turned a deaf ear to the denunciations. Though he had toured the N-Group jails with then prison board chairman Selden Hale and, according to Hale, "didn't have anything particularly nice to say about the facilities," from the witness stand he sounded like N-Group' biggest fan. Rebutting the testimony of his former boss Jim Lynbaugh, Collins testified not only that the six jails *were* suitable for maximum-security purposes but that in fact he saw no reason why the facilities couldn't be used for death row inmates. Long after the jury had declared a $37 million judgment against N-group, observers remain stunned by Collins' Graham-friendly testimony. Perhaps, they speculated, the executive director was simply trying to brown-nose the new prison board chairman, Carol Vance, whose law firm represented one of the several defendants in the N-Group case.

That would have been characteristic of the ingratiating Collins. But a theory does not preclude a more disturbing possibility -- namely, that as the prison boom festered into an avaricious free-for-all, Andy Collins had lost the ability to differentiate between the merely audacious and the downright sleazy. Even the classiest of the private prison companies seemed hopelessly greed-stricken: They variously hired teachers who weren't certified, paid them salaries with Pell Grants until the feds got wind that the required matching funds were never provided, and in the meantime padded company profits by short-staffing the facilities and overcharging inmates on long-distance phone calls. A few legislators brazenly applied their lips to the correctional teat – notably Mark Stiles, of Beaumont, who was riding the prison-building wave as a concrete subcontractor, and Senate Criminal Justice Committee chairman John Whitmire, who took a $4,000-per-month gig with the Harris County probation department while the county was vying for a new Mode II prison to be run by the probation department. Even the self-proclaimed do-gooders, Collins must have figured, had a little bit of Pat Graham in them.

Overseeing Collins was a prison board that at times seemed entranced, if not thoroughly compromised, by the prison boom. Board member Ellen Halbert had gone positively giddy when the mayor of Burnet, hoping to land a proposed substance-abuse facility, offered to name it after her. Halbert's feisty new ally on the board, John David Franz, of Hidalgo, immediately began to lobby other members to bring one of those lucrative prisons to South Texas. John Ward, the former mayor of the prison town of Gatesville and the husband of a teacher in the Windham prison school system, was an outright booster. Josh Allen, a Beaumont construction executive, had been seen huddling with Brown and Root executives just before voting on construction issues (though a TDCJ investigation did not reveal any improprieties). Rufus Duncan, of Lufkin, who had openly bragged to Texas construction companies that he had been "one of the instigators" of the TDCJ's new prison-building scheme, intervened on at least two prison projects and pushed general contractors to hire his friend Hoople Jordan as the dirt-paving subcontractor, even though Jordan's paving material was less durable and would have to be hauled to the sites from a considerable distance, although nearer material was available.

But none of the board members had anything on autocratic chairman Allan Polunsky, whose defiance of procedure Collins often witnessed firsthand. It was the chairman who directed Wackenhut to spend thousands of dollars erecting a fence in front of its Kyle facility so that motorists on Interstate 35 wouldn't see the facilities' inmates playing basketball outside. It was Polunsky who ordered that existing private-prison contracts be re-bid without consulting the other board members. And it was Polunsky who used Collins and other TDCJ officials to clear a path so that Polunsky's old college roommate could claim a share of the TDCJ's grease trap-cleaning business. At Polunsky's request, Andy Collins lunched with Sanitech president David Collins (no relation) and thereafter joined Polunsky in badgering prison staffers into giving the ex-roommate special treatment: canceling contracts with existing vendors, rewriting contract specifications in a way that favored Sanitech, and even letting David Collins pick up his checks at the state treasurer's office in Austin rather than waiting for them to be sent out of Huntsville. By the time the Sanitech president sold his company to a rival in 1995, he had grossed more than half a million dollars doing business with the TDCJ.

If Polunsky and other board members didn't care about ethics, why should Andy Collins? And why, therefore, should anyone rattle his sword at Pat Graham? Besides, Graham wasn't going away. Despite his testimony during the N-Group lawsuit that "I would never build another jail again," Graham was then conceiving a juvenile lock-up facility in Jena, Louisiana. Once again he had solicited some impressive backing: Louisiana governor Edwin Edwards had awarded the project to Graham, the investment group behind it was led by former Houston mayor Fred Hofheinz, and Graham's development partner was none other than Collins' old friend Charlie Terrell. These men saw Graham as a rainmaker. Leave it to the N-Group jury to pass judgment. There was still money to be made.

In June 1995 -- nine months after Collin's friendly testimony in the N-Group lawsuit -- Graham's proposal for the Jena juvenile facility landed on the director's desk. With the proposal came a job offer: Collins could form a company to operate the facility. Other potential private operators had passed on the deal, and Terrell himself had pulled out, but as Collins studied the numbers, he concluded that it was their loss. By his calculations, he stood to clear well in excess of $150,000 annually. Coupled with the $50,000 retirement package he would be receiving, Andy Collins didn't see how he could say no. So he didn't.

On July 12, 1995, without notifying the TDCJ board, Collins quietly formed a Louisiana corporation called Professional Care of America, naming himself, Hofheinz, and former N-Group treasurer James Brunson as the officers. (Four months later, Collins would also incorporate a Texas business he called Certified Technology Consultants and list as his registered agent Lori Lero -- an attorney who happened to be Pat Graham's daughter.) Collins' explanation for not notifying the board is that he didn't want to spook the New York-based bondholders who would be financing the construction of the Jena facility. But he must have known that the potential for a conflict of interest could have made it difficult him to hold both jobs, if word got out. Inevitably, word did get out and in early September Collins was informed by Governor Bush, through Polunsky, that he would have to choose between his two jobs – now.

Collins chose Jena. At the September board meeting, Collins announced his resignation from the Texas Department of Criminal Justice. Aside from briefing Polunsky and his other friend on the board, Gatesville's John Ward, Collins declined to tell the other seven members what his specific plans were. He simply said he was going into private business that he had faced a "reality check" when he recently paid tuition to send his eldest daughter off to Texas A&M.

A number of the board members didn't know what to make of Collins' announcement. The director was making $120,000, living rent-free, and driving a company car -- and he still couldn't afford to send his daughter to a state school? A reporter for the *Austin American-Statesman* met privately with Collins. "You've got to tell me who you're going to work for," Collins says the reporter demanded.

"No," said Collins. "I really don't have to." And that was that. The veteran public servant was now going private all the way.

BUT ANDY COLLINS BEGAN GOING PRIVATE at least six months too soon. For between the time he first read Graham's Jena proposal last June and the time he left office on December 31, three prison vendors benefited from extraordinary contracts with the Texas Department of Criminal Justice -- and all three vendors, Collins admitted to me without hesitation, were companies he in fact had hoped to do business with once he left office at the close of 1995. The evidence can be read to suggest that Collins viewed his last six months in office as a window of opportunity to ingratiate himself with potential employers by awarding them fat contracts that they perhaps did not deserve, with the hope that the favor would be returned.

Collins' first beneficiary was a Houston-based construction company, 3D/Multinational. The TDCJ's records show that on June 27, Collins and a few of his lieutenants met with 3D/I officials in Houston and agreed to award the company a $932,000 contract to design a high-security prototype prison unit without subjecting 3D/I to a qualifications process. Less than seven months later, in January 1996, the just-retired Collins would fly to Oregon with 3D/I officials on a trial run as the company's consultant. The prototype contract was icing on the cake for 3D/l, which had benefited greatly from the prison-building scheme utilized by the TDCJs deputy director of construction, J. B. Cole (who retired last February). Using "construction managers" like 3D/I to oversee all the general contractors and subcontractors would, according to Cole, result in quicker, less expensive prison building. But an analysis of TDCJ figures suggests otherwise: The 12,000 warehouse-like "emergency beds" built using 3D/I as a construction manager turned out to be more expensive per square foot than the average maximum-security facility, and later construction-manager projects cost the state at least $17.2 million more than what it cost to build comparable facilities without construction managers. A main reason for the scheme's excessive cost was the hefty up-front fee paid to "managers" like 3D/I (which pocketed $1.7 million for the emergency-bed program). As a construction manager, 3D/I was never required to prove that it was the best-qualified company. Its hundreds of thousands of dollars' worth of reimbursable expenses were never audited. And in August 1994, 3D/I was even paid $80,000 to write a TDCJ construction-procedures manual, even though the agency already had an updated manual. (Twenty months later, 3D/I had yet to complete the manual.)

Another beneficiary of Collins' largesse was Safeguard Technology, a Hackensack, New Jersey, company that designed fences for the Israeli government. On August 29, 1995, Collins circulated an interoffice memo ordering the purchase of high-security motion-detector fences on an emergency basis. "The immediate porch of the improved security system is a life/safety issue," Collins wrote. "But the recent change in demographic population, we have been required to place inmates in a less secure environment absolutely required. The installation of these systems is required to be accomplished within the next ninety days."

TDCJ staffers couldn't believe what were reading. After all, it had not much more than a year ago that Collins had been heard scoffing at state comptroller John Sharp's recommendation that TDCJ replace its guard towers, or pickets, with motion-detector fences. "Sharp doesn't know what the hell he's talking about," Collins said to staffers more than once "No fence is going to see better than a good pair of eyes." Now Collins was a fence convert, and in short order a $9.2 million contract was awarded to Safeguard without competitive bidding. It turned out that about $6 million of the contract involved the "less secure environment" used to justify the emergency purchase. The rest of the money went to buy fences for five new higher-security units -- units that in fact are set on large compounds that are completely secure, hardly requiring taut-wire intrusion-detection fences being manufactured by Safeguard. In the case of the "less secure" units, those fences were not installed "within the next ninety days"; in fact, three of the ten fences weren't scheduled for completion until December of this year. What this means, of course, is that there was plenty of time to submit the project to a non-emergency competitive bidding process. The fences for the high security units have yet to be erected; they currently reside in a TDCJ warehouse.

So just what was the emergency? Perhaps that Andy Collins was looking for business clients. Four months after awarding the contract, Collins flew to New York and dropped by the Safeguard offices while he was in the neighborhood. Though he admitted to me that he and Safeguard president Moshe Levy had been discussing Collins' doing work for Safeguard on a commission basis, Collins said they didn't sign any deals during his visit: "Actually, I went up there for the Jena deal, because I wanted them to look at the plans of doing something for that particular facility."

In other words, Collins, while still serving as the TDCJ's executive director, was negotiating with a TDCJ vendor to do business with Collins' own private enterprise -- textbook case of conflicted interests.

Collins saved his best act of generosity for VitaPro. In February 1994, well before Collins decided to leave the TDCJ, he was visited in his Huntsville office by former board chairman Charlie Terrell and a Montreal entrepreneur named Yank Barry who was the president of VitaPro. Terrell and Barry wanted to know if the prison system might have a use for VitaPro -- not only for its own inmates, but as a commodity it could sell to other markets throughout the U.S., much as the TDCJ does with the cattle it raises.

A year later, on January 30, 1995, a TDCJ press release trumpeted "an innovative agreement with VitaPro to nationally market, package, and distribute the new soy-based chicken and beef supplement." The release neglected to mention that the $6.7 million contract was awarded without competitive bidding and that Terrell would be paid a commission to help market the product. Terrell was in fact so taken with VitaPro that he became a worldwide broker for the company, services for which Yank Barry paid him more than $40,000 in 1995. One of the markets Terrell advised Barry to target was Louisiana, and in February, at the Ritz-Carlton Hotel in Houston, the former prison board chairman introduced Barry to a stand-up guy who knew the Louisiana market inside out: Pat Graham.

Graham had been busy with the Jena juvenile facility deal, but with the $37 million judgment hanging over his head from the N-Group lawsuit, he also began selling VitaPro -- first in Louisiana and later (though without Barry's permission) in Texas. He even printed up business cards advertising himself as a VitaPro distributor, though his correspondence with Barry makes it clear that Graham was to be considered merely a broker.

VitaPro's merits have been much derided in Texas newspapers of late, perhaps unfairly. The company has dozens of corporate clients, and as an extender -- a way of stretching ten hamburger patties into fifteen, for example -- and as a meat replacement, the soybean product has a proven track record. Other reporters have made sport of the fast-talking ex-felon Barry, but the sins of VitaPro have little to do with him or his brainchild. Instead, they have to do with the way Collins crammed VitaPro down the TDCJ's throat -- particularly beginning in July 1995, when the soon-to-be-retired director extended VitaPro's initial contract to a $33.7 million, five-year deal, without telling the board, his food-service managers, or his second-in-command, Wayne Scott. While staffers were wondering what to do with TDCJs new meat-packing facility in Amarillo and the hog farm it had just acquired from Texas A&M, Collins pressured his subordinates to market VitaPro to Texas schools, and when a market for the product failed to materialize, Collins ordered workers to rewrite prison menus so that they incorporated VitaPro as a meat substitute on a daily basis -- an overusage Barry himself had never promoted and which food-services manager Janie Thomas fought until Collins ordered her to be "a team player."

Upon retirement from the, Texas prison system, Collins immediately began traveling all over America on VitaPro's behalf. Yank Barry, was thrilled with his new spokesman: "He was opening doors everywhere, doing unbelievable work for us," Barry gushes. For the first two months of 1996, VitaPro issued a total of $30,000 in checks to Collins' consulting company or to Collins himself. By Barry's estimates Collins stood to make as much as $80,000 from VitaPro by year's end – and surely would have, just as he would have opened the Jena facility, were it not for his partner Pat Graham.

WHILE A 35-YEAR-OLD HOUSTON huckster named Rocky Harmon was sitting in the Harris County jail in June 1995, awaiting transfer to prison for being popped in a fraudulent basketball ticket scam, his mother called Pat Graham and chewed him out. "You've taken all my husband's money. You've been a terrible influence on my son," she yelled tearfully into the phone. "The least you can do, with all your big connections, is see to it that my boy, Rocky, doesn't get mistreated in prison!"

Harmon's mother had a point: The father *had* been taken to the cleaners in a couple of muffed ventures with Graham, the son had been something of a protégé. "I'll do what I can to help the boy," Graham pledged.

For once, Graham proved true to his word. At his behest, Collins arranged to have Harmon transferred to the Diagnostic Unit in Huntsville, where he was assigned a low-stress job. On July 29, 1995, Harmon's parents and Graham paid him a visit. Collins showed up as well and, according to Collins, chatted with the parents for about five minutes, gave the new inmate "the standard keep-your-nose-clean speech," and departed with Graham. But to the other inmates in the visitation room, a visit by the executive director of the TDCJ, for whatever length of time, was something out of the ordinary. They began to look at inmate 714443 a bit differently after that. Rocky Harmon took note of this and affected a certain swagger.

One day on the volleyball court Harmon approached Dana McIntosh, an inmate serving 75 years for murdering his wife despite his claims of innocence. McIntosh was a special case, a brilliant computer specialist whose data-processing skills were much in demand at the TDCJ, and the staff handled him with uncharacteristic deference. Harmon began his first conversation with McIntosh by saying, "You know, you and I aren't like the others here. We're white, we're educated" McIntosh, who had seen Harmon with Collins but wasn't particularly impressed, cut him off. "We're not alike at all," McIntosh said.

But Harmon persisted. Later, in November, he approached the fifty-year-old inmate with a proposition. "I know you want out of here," Harmon said, "and I know seventy-five years is a long time. I'll bet you could buy your way out of prison." Harmon then got more specific: The friend who had visited him in July was Andy Collins' business partner. For a fee and here -- Harmon discreetly indicated that some of the fee would properly come his way -- Collins and his partner could spring McIntosh.

The older inmate was left with much to consider. Yes, McIntosh wanted out. But not this way, and besides, any arrangement involving a clown like Rocky Harmon was bound to be botched -- most likely Harmon's friend would just take Mcintosh's money and skate with it. On the other hand, what if the executive director of the TDCJ was involved. What would happen to an inmate like McIntosh if he didn't take Collins up on such an offer? How many days would he last in prison? In the middle of November, Mcintosh told his girlfriend, Karyn about the proposition during a Sunday prison visit. She agreed to contact the FBI, and by the beginning of December, the sting was on.

On December 19, Karyn says, she agreed to meet a man who identified himself on the telephone as Harold Robert -- the first and middle names of Pat Graham's father, as it turned out. At a Houston Galleria restaurant, a jowly man in a nice suit sat at her table. According to Karyn, he was without a doubt the man investigators had shown her in photographs -- that is to say, Pat Graham. "He said he was the deputy director of the TDCJ," she says. "He said there were a certain number of inmates who shouldn't be in the system, and this was a service they provided. For $250,000, they would change Dana's inmate status and transfer him to the John Sealy hospital unit in Galveston and put him on a detail where he would be alone and could walk about freely. After giving another $250,000, I could then pick up Dana at the unit and drive off to the airport. Then they would fly us to Louisiana. After that we would catch a plane to Miami, then another plane to the American Virgin Islands, and then take a boat over to the British Virgin Islands. Then we'd fly to Costa Rica and wait six or eight months. And then, for another $250,000, Dana would receive a pardon from the governor and we could go wherever we liked.

"He was about the creepiest man I've ever met."

During the month, Karyn had several other conversations with "Harold Robert," most of which were taped by investigators. On January 3, the FBI provided her with $150,000 in cash. The following morning, she says, Graham called and told her to bring the down payment to a Mexican restaurant on the northeast side of the city. In the parking lot next to the restaurant, Graham climbed inside Karyn's car, whereupon she handed him the box stuffed with fifteen $10,000 bundles. He was just putting the third bundle into his briefcase when law enforcement agents swarmed the car.

Even as the investigators handcuffed Graham and read him his rights, he seemed to mutate before Karyn's eyes. "He looked like this perfect citizen," she remembers. "The countenance on his face was that of a guy who was only trying to help."

IT WAS THE KIND OF HELP COLLINS didn't need. Five days after Graham's arrest, on January 9, the police questioned the just-retired prison director about his role in the escape ploy. He told them the same thing he told me a few weeks later: "I didn't know a thing about it. Graham was just using my name. The guy duped me."

Apparently lost on Collins was how easy a dupe he had become. He had chosen to view Graham as a the vehicle for his own metaphorical jailbreak and was unable or unwilling to see that Graham could only drag him down. Sure enough, Graham's association with both VitaPro and Collins added to emerging questions about the soybean product's contract with the TDCJ, and before long, Collins had become a liability to VitaPiro, necessitating Yank Barry's request on February 26 that Collins resign. And now here was Andy Collins in self-imposed exile north of Houston, pondering the folly of it all while others determined his fate. In a similar limbo reposed a nearby resident, Pat Graham -- who Collins now insisted had been scarcely more than an acquaintance: "I could probably count the times I dealt with Pat on one hand. And the conversations we had were never more than five minutes."

The ex-director was cutting and running from Graham, defending each and every one of the alleged sweetheart contracts, and above all, proclaiming his right to go to work for the recipients of said contracts. "If I can't do business with the people I know," he declared, "who *am* I supposed to do business with?" The question legal investigators will be contemplating, however, is not who Collins did business with, but how and when and why he did business. For now, no evidence exists that Collins committed any crimes -- that he took money or was promised employment in exchange for awarding contracts, or even that he violated some obscure purchasing law. But his actions, legal or not, raise character questions about Collins that have no doubt cast a pall over his consulting career.

"I had a whole list of companies to contact," he told me at the first sign of evening, just before he broke out the Scotch and the cigars. "I could've gone to work for anybody -- because I knew everybody. And I knew how these places worked. I knew how to build stuff. I privatized more prisons than anyone." The name of a prominent private-prison operator who had apparently been interested in Collins, services came up. "The guy's an idiot -- he knows nothing about prisons," said Collins. "I could've helped him. I could've made millions for him."

But Collins' fatal flaw was the same as his business partner's. Over and over, sources had told me that Graham, for all his sleaziness, had possessed more than a few good ideas -- if only he had played them on the up and up. And now the same could be said of Collins. If only he had played it straight with the state. If only he had waited to set up shop until after he resigned. If only he had held out against the greed of the prison expansion instead of becoming its facilitator, its victim, and at last, its ignominious poster boy.

CAPITAL PUNISHMENT 1995

By Tracy L. Snell
Bureau of Justice Statistics Bulletin
U.S. Department of Justice

Sixteen States executed 56 prisoners during 1995. The number of persons executed was 25 greater than in 1994 and was the largest annual number since the 56 executed during 1960 and the 65 in 1957. The prisoners executed during 1995 had been under sentence of death an average of 11 years and 2 months, about 12 months more than the average for inmates executed the previous year.

At yearend 1995, 3,054 prisoners were under sentence of death. California held the largest number of death row inmates (420), followed by Texas (404), Florida (362), and Pennsylvania (196). Eight prisoners were in Federal custody under a death sentence on December 31, 1995.

Between January 1 and December 31, 1995, 26 State prison systems and the Federal prison system received 310 prisoners under sentence of death. Texas (40 admissions), California (36), North Carolina (34), and Florida (31) accounted for 45% of the inmates entering prison under a death sentence in 1995.

During 1995, 56 persons in 16 States were executed — 19 in Texas; 6 in Missouri; 5 each in Illinois and Virginia; 3 each in Florida and Oklahoma; 2 each in Alabama, Arkansas, Georgia, North Carolina, and Pennsylvania; and 1 each in Arizona, Delaware, Louisiana, Montana, and

Highlights

Status of the death penalty, December 31, 1995

Executions during 1995		Number of prisoners under sentence of death		Jurisdictions without a death penalty
Texas	19	California	420	Alaska
Missouri	6	Texas	404	District of Columbia
Illinois	5	Florida	362	Hawaii
Virginia	5	Pennsylvania	196	Iowa
Florida	3	Ohio	155	Maine
Oklahoma	3	Illinois	154	Massachusetts
Alabama	2	Alabama	143	Michigan
Arkansas	2	North Carolina	139	Minnesota
Georgia	2	Oklahoma	129	North Dakota
North Carolina	2	Arizona	117	Rhode Island
Pennsylvania	2	Georgia	98	Vermont
Arizona	1	Tennessee	96	West Virginia
Delaware	1	Missouri	92	Wisconsin
Louisiana	1	22 other jurisdictions	549	
Montana	1			
South Carolina	1			
Total	56	Total	3,054	

- In 1995, 56 men were executed:
  33 were white
  22 were black
  1 was Asian.

- The persons executed in 1995 were under sentence of death an average of 11 years and 2 months.

- At yearend 1995, 34 States and the Federal prison system held 3,054 prisoners under sentence of death, 5.1% more than at yearend 1994. All had committed murder.

- Of persons under sentence of death —
  1,730 were white
  1,275 were black
     22 were Native American
     19 were Asian
      8 were classified as "other race."

- Forty-eight women were under a sentence of death.

- The 237 Hispanic inmates under sentence of death accounted for 8.5% of inmates with a known ethnicity.

- Among inmates under sentence of death and with available criminal histories, 2 in 3 had a prior felony conviction; 1 in 12 had a prior homicide conviction.

- Among persons for whom arrest information was available, the average age at time of arrest was 28; about 2% of inmates were age 17 or younger.

- At yearend, the youngest inmate was 18; the oldest was 80.

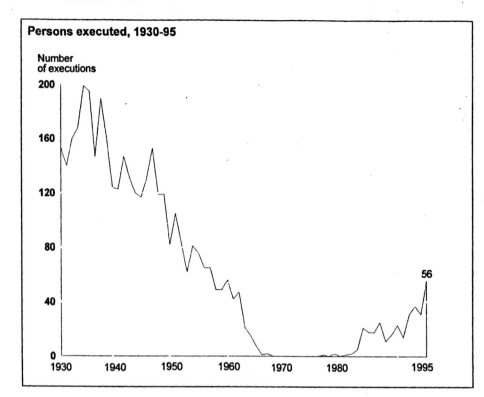

Persons executed, 1930-95

South Carolina. All were men. Thirty of the executed prisoners were non-Hispanic whites; 22 were non-Hispanic blacks; 2, white Hispanics; 1, Asian; and 1, white with unknown Hispanic origin. Forty-nine of the executions were carried out by lethal injection and 7 by electrocution.

From January 1, 1977, to December 31, 1995, a total of 4,857 persons entered State and Federal prisons under sentences of death, among whom 51% were white, 41% were black, 7% were Hispanic, and 1% were of other races.

During this 19-year period, a total of 313 executions took place in 26 States. Of the inmates executed, 171 were white, 120 were black, 19 were Hispanic, 2 were Native American, and 1 was Asian.

Also during 1977-95, 1,870 prisoners were removed from a death sentence as a result of dispositions other than execution (resentencing, retrial, commutation, or death while awaiting execution). Of all persons removed from under a death sentence, 52% were white, 41% were black, 1% were Native American, 0.5% were Asian, and 5% were Hispanic.

Statutory changes

During 1995, 19 States revised statutory provisions relating to the death penalty (table 1). Most of the changes involved additional aggravating circumstances, procedural amendments addressing the rights of victims and their families, and changes in methods of execution.

By State, these statutory changes were as follows:

Arkansas — Added to its definition of capital murder purposely discharging a firearm from a vehicle resulting in the death of another person (Ark. Code Ann. § 51-10-101(a)(10)), effective 7/27/95.

Colorado — Amended its code of criminal procedure establishing appellate review at the sentencing phase of a capital case. Upon conviction of a defendant, a sentencing hearing will be conducted by a three-judge panel; previously, a jury considered evidence and recommended punishment. The amendment also outlines the process by which panel members will be selected (CRS 16-11-103(1)(a)). These revisions became effective 7/1/95.

Connecticut — Revised its penal code to change the method of execution from electrocution to lethal injection; to remove the requirement that the State supreme court review the proportionality of a death sentence compared to penalties imposed in similar cases; and to add to its list of capital felonies murder of a person under age 16 (See P.A. 95-16). These changes became effective 10/1/95.

Delaware — Revised a statute limiting the number of witnesses at the execution to 10 and allowing one adult, either an immediate family member of the victim or the "victim's designee", to be present as one of those witnesses (11 Del. c. § 4209(f)), effective 5/15/95.

Delaware lawmakers also added as an aggravating circumstance murder committed to interfere with the victim's First Amendment rights or as a response to the victim's exercise of those rights or to the victim's race, religion, color, disability, national origin or ancestry (11 Del. c. § 4209(e)(1)(v)), effective 7/6/95.

Idaho — Revised and added sections to its penal code relating to the death penalty. These changes became effective 7/1/95.

Idaho amended its code of criminal procedure to require that, upon conviction of a defendant, the court hold a hearing to weigh aggravating and mitigating factors in the case to determine the appropriateness of a death sentence (19-2515, Idaho Code).

Another procedural amendment set guidelines regarding requests for stays of execution based on petitions to hear new evidence that was not known prior to the deadline for filing of an appeal on such grounds. The statute narrowed the availability of successive post-conviction proceedings (19-2719, Idaho Code).

The Idaho legislature also added new sections to its code of criminal procedure in capital cases: one providing for an inquiry into a convicted defendant's need for a new attorney upon showing of ineffectiveness of the trial lawyer (19-2719A, Idaho Code); another providing for review of a case by the Idaho supreme court, upon remand from a Federal court, to decide whether legal or factual errors can be addressed without remanding the case back to the State district court (19-2818, Idaho Code).

Illinois — Added to its penal code as an aggravating factor murder by discharging a firearm from a motor vehicle when the victim was outside of the motor vehicle (720-ILCS 5/9-1(b)(15)), effective 1/1/95.

Indiana — Amended the code of criminal procedure to specify time limits within which the execution must be carried out, time limits and procedures for addressing petitions for post-conviction relief, and issues for consideration by Indiana's supreme court in conducting automatic review of death sentences (Indiana Code § 35-50-2-9(h), (i), and (j)). Indiana also changed the method of execution from electrocution to lethal injection (Indiana Code § 35-38-6-1). These changes became effective 7/1/95.

Maryland — Amended its code of criminal procedure to modify when an execution can be stayed by a trial judge; to change the time limit for filing an initial post-conviction appeal from 240 days to 180 days; to impose time limits on holding a hearing upon filing of a post-conviction petition; and to allow a convicted inmate to waive the statutory stay of execution imposed during the 180-day period set aside for filing of any post-conviction petitions (1995 Md. Laws ch. 110). These changes became effective 10/1/95.

Montana — Revised the code of criminal procedure to allow evidence to be presented during the sentencing hearing in regard to the harm the offense caused to the victim and his family (46-18-302 MCA), applicable to crimes committed on or after 10/1/95.

Nevada — Added to its penal code as aggravating factors murder of a department of prisons employee who doesn't exercise control over but comes into regular contact with the offender; murder of a person under age 14; and murder of a person because of their race, religion, national origin, physical or mental disability, or sexual orientation (NRS 200.033), effective 10/1/95.

New Jersey — Amended its penal code to allow evidence during the sentencing proceeding pertaining to the victim's character and impact of the

Table 1. Capital offenses, by State, 1995

Alabama. Intentional murder with 18 aggravating factors (13A-5-40).

Arizona. First-degree murder accompanied by at least 1 of 10 aggravating factors.

Arkansas. Capital murder with a finding of at least 1 of 9 aggravating circumstances (Ark. Code Ann. 5-10-101); treason.

California. First-degree murder with special circumstances; train-wrecking; treason; perjury causing execution.

Colorado. First-degree murder with at least 1 of 13 aggravating factors; treason. Capital sentencing excludes persons determined to be mentally retarded.

Connecticut. Capital felony with 9 categories of aggravated homicide (C.G.S. 53a-54b).

Delaware. First-degree murder with aggravating circumstances.

Florida. First-degree murder; felony murder; capital drug-trafficking.

Georgia. Murder; kidnaping with bodily injury or ransom where the victim dies; aircraft hijacking; treason.

Idaho. First-degree murder; aggravated kidnaping.

Illinois. First-degree murder with 1 of 15 aggravating circumstances.

Indiana. Murder with 14 aggravating circumstances. Capital sentencing excludes persons determined to be mentally retarded.

Kansas. Capital murder with 7 aggravating circumstances. Capital sentencing excludes persons determined to be mentally retarded.

Kentucky. Murder with aggravating factors; kidnaping with aggravating factors.

Louisiana. First-degree murder; aggravated rape of victim under age 12; treason (La. R.S. 14:30, 14:42, and 14:113).

Maryland. First-degree murder, either premeditated or during the commission of a felony, provided that certain death eligibility requirements are satisfied.

Mississippi. Capital murder; capital rape; aircraft piracy.

Missouri. First-degree murder (565.020 RSMO).

Montana. Capital murder with aggravating circumstances.

Nebraska. First-degree murder.

Nevada. First-degree murder with 10 aggravating circumstances.

New Hampshire. Capital murder.

New Jersey. Purposeful or knowing murder; contract murder; murder or solicitation thereof by a leader of a narcotics trafficking network.

New Mexico. First-degree murder (Section 30-2-1 A, NMSA).

New York. First-degree murder with 1 of 10 aggravating factors. Capital sentencing excludes persons determined to be mentally retarded.

North Carolina. First-degree murder (N.C.G.S. 14-17).

Ohio. Aggravated murder with 1 of 8 aggravating circumstances. (O.R.C. secs. 2929.01, 2903.01, and 2929.04).

Oklahoma. First-degree murder in conjunction with a finding of at least 1 of 8 statutorily defined aggravating circumstances.

Oregon. Aggravated murder (ORS 163.095).

Pennsylvania. First-degree murder with 16 aggravating circumstances.

South Carolina. Murder with 1 of 10 aggravating circumstances.

South Dakota. First-degree murder with 1 of 10 aggravating circumstances.

Tennessee. First-degree murder.

Texas. Criminal homicide with 1 of 8 aggravating circumstances.

Utah. Aggravated murder; aggravated assault by a prisoner serving a life sentence if serious bodily injury is intentionally caused (76-5-202, Utah Code annotated).

Virginia. First-degree murder with 1 of 9 aggravating circumstances.

Washington. Aggravated first-degree murder.

Wyoming. First-degree murder.

crime on the victim's family (NJSA 2C:11-3c(6)), effective 6/19/95.

New York — Enacted a law creating the crime of capital murder and providing for a sentence of death for persons over age 18 if any of 10 aggravating circumstances exists. The new law prohibits sentencing mentally retarded persons to death (Ch. 1, 1995 session), effective 9/1/95.

Ohio — Amended its code of criminal procedure to establish responsibility of the Ohio supreme court for automatic review of all death sentences and guidelines to be followed in the course of such review. The review includes weighing of all facts and evidence submitted in the case, deciding if aggravating factors outweighed mitigating factors in the case, and consideration of the proportionality of the death sentence compared to similar cases (O.R.C. § 2929.05), effective 9/21/95.

Oregon — Amended its penal code to allow evidence regarding the victim's personal characteristics and the impact of the offense on the victim's family to be entered during the sentencing phase of capital proceedings (ORS 163.150), effective 7/7/95.

Pennsylvania — Added new sections to its capital statute relating to sentencing and execution procedures. One amendment permitted evidence concerning the victim and the effect of the crime on the victim's family to be heard and considered during the sentencing hearing (42 Pa.C.S. § 9711(a)(2), (b), and (c)(2)), effective 3/16/95.

Pennsylvania lawmakers also added provisions which specified time limits for transmission of court records to the governor and issuance of death warrants, terms of confinement upon receipt of the warrant, persons allowed to witness the execution, and certification and postmortem examination procedures following the execution (42 Pa.C.S. § 9711(i), (j), (k), (l), (m), (n), and (o)), effective 12/11/95.

South Carolina — Revised its penal code to allow persons sentenced to death to elect as their method of execution either electrocution or lethal injection. Election of method by the inmate must be made in writing 14 days before the date of execution; if this right is waived, persons will be executed by lethal injection (§ 24-3-540), effective 6/8/95.

South Dakota — Amended an aggravating circumstance allowing for prosecution as a capital offense, stipulating that a crime is considered to be "wantonly vile" if the victim is under age 13 (SDCL 23A-27A-1(6)), effective 7/1/95.

Tennessee — Revised an aggravating circumstance from simple involvement in the commission of certain felony offenses to participating "knowingly" (Tenn. Code Ann. § 39-13-204(i)(7)), effective 5/30/95; and added as an aggravating circumstance intentional mutilation of the victim's body after death (Tenn. Code Ann. § 39-13-204(i)(13)), effective 7/1/95.

Tennessee lawmakers also added to its definition of first degree murder killing during the commission of aggravated child abuse as defined by § 39-15-402 (Tenn. Code Ann. § 39-13-202), effective 7/1/95.

Virginia — Revised its penal code to allow persons sentenced to death to elect as their method of execution either electrocution or lethal injection. The inmate must choose a method at least 15 days before the scheduled date of execution; if this option is waived, persons will be executed by lethal injection (Va. Code § 53.1-233, 234), effective 1/1/95.

Virginia legislators also amended the definition of capital murder to include among enumerated sexual offenses "object sexual penetration" (Va. Code § 18.2-31(5)), effective 7/1/95.

Method of execution

As of December 31, 1995, lethal injection was the predominant method of execution (32 States) (table 2). Eleven States authorized electrocution; 7 States, lethal gas; 4 States, hanging; and 3 States, a firing squad.

Sixteen States authorized more than one method — lethal injection and an alternative method — generally at the election of the condemned prisoner; however, 5 of these 16 stipulated which method must be used, depending on the date of sentencing; 1 authorized hanging only if lethal injection could not be given; and, if lethal injection is ever ruled unconstitutional, 1 authorized lethal gas and 1 authorized electrocution.

Automatic review

Of the 38 States with capital punishment statutes at yearend 1995, 37 provided for review of all death sentences regardless of the defendant's wishes.

Arkansas had no specific provisions for automatic review. The Federal death penalty procedures did not provide for automatic review after a sentence of death had been imposed. While most of the 37 States authorized an automatic review of both the conviction and sentence, Idaho, Indiana, Oklahoma, and Tennessee required review of the sentence only. In Idaho, review of the conviction had to be filed through appeal or forfeited. In Indiana, a defendant could waive review of the conviction.

The review is usually conducted by the State's highest appellate court regardless of the defendant's wishes. In South Carolina, the defendant's right to waive appeal was in litigation; in Mississippi the question of whether a defendant could waive the right to automatic review of the sentence had not been addressed; and in Wyoming neither statute nor case law clearly precluded a waiver of appeal. If either the conviction or the sentence was vacated, the case could be remanded to the trial court for additional proceedings or for retrial. As a result of retrial or resentencing, the death sentence could be reimposed.

Table 2. Method of execution, by State, 1995

Lethal injection		Electrocution	Lethal gas	Hanging	Firing squad
Arizona[a,b]	New Hampshire[a]	Alabama	Arizona[a,b]	Delaware[a,c]	Idaho[a]
Arkansas[a,d]	New Jersey	Arkansas[a,d]	California[a,e]	Montana[a]	Oklahoma[f]
California[a,e]	New Mexico	Florida	Maryland[g]	New Hampshire[a,h]	Utah[a]
Colorado	New York	Georgia	Mississippi[a,i]	Washington[a]	
Connecticut	North Carolina[a]	Kentucky	Missouri[a]		
Delaware[a,c]	Ohio[a]	Nebraska	North Carolina[a]		
Idaho[a]	Oklahoma	Ohio[a]	Wyoming[a,j]		
Illinois	Oregon	Oklahoma[f]			
Indiana	Pennsylvania	South Carolina[a]			
Kansas	South Carolina[a]	Tennessee			
Louisiana	South Dakota	Virginia			
Maryland[g]	Texas				
Mississippi[a,i]	Utah[a]				
Missouri[a]	Virginia[a]				
Montana	Washington[a]				
Nevada	Wyoming[a]				

Note: The method of execution of Federal prisoners is lethal injection, pursuant to 28 CFR, Part 26. For offenses under the Violent Crime Control and Law Enforcement Act of 1994, the method is that of the State in which the conviction took place, pursuant to 18 USC 3596.

[a] Authorizes 2 methods of execution.
[b] Arizona authorizes lethal injection for persons sentenced after 11/15/92; those sentenced before that date may select lethal injection or lethal gas.
[c] Delaware authorizes lethal injection for those whose capital offense occurred after 6/13/86; those who committed the offense before that date may select lethal injection or hanging.
[d] Arkansas authorizes lethal injection for persons committing a capital offense after 7/4/83; those who committed the offense before that date may select lethal injection or electrocution.
[e] Use of lethal gas is currently prohibited in California pending a legal challenge in Federal court.
[f] Oklahoma authorizes electrocution if lethal injection is ever held to be unconstitutional and firing squad if both lethal injection and electrocution are held unconstitutional.
[g] Maryland authorizes lethal injection for all inmates, as of 3/25/94. One inmate, convicted prior to that date, has selected lethal gas for method of execution.
[h] New Hampshire authorizes hanging only if lethal injection cannot be given.
[i] Mississippi authorizes lethal injection for those convicted after 7/1/84 and lethal gas for those convicted earlier.
[j] Wyoming authorizes lethal gas if lethal injection is ever held to be unconstitutional.

Table 3. Minimum age authorized for capital punishment, 1995

Age 16 or less	Age 17	Age 18	Age 19	None specified
Alabama (16)	Georgia	California	New York	Arizona
Arkansas (14)[a]	New Hampshire	Colorado		Idaho
Delaware (16)	North Carolina[b]	Connecticut[c]		Montana
Indiana (16)	Texas	Federal system		Louisiana
Kentucky (16)		Illinois		Pennsylvania
Mississippi (16)[d]		Kansas		South Carolina
Missouri (16)		Maryland		South Dakota[e]
Nevada (16)		Nebraska		Utah
Oklahoma (16)		New Jersey		
Virginia (14)[f]		New Mexico		
Wyoming (16)		Ohio		
Florida (16)		Oregon		
		Tennessee		
		Washington		

Note: Reporting by States reflects interpretations by State attorney general offices and may differ from previously reported ages.
[a] See Arkansas Code Ann.9-27-318(b)(1)(Repl. 1991).
[b] The age required is 17 unless the murderer was incarcerated for murder when a subsequent murder occurred; then the age may be 14.
[c] See Conn. Gen. Stat. 53a-46a(g)(1).
[d] The minimum age defined by statute is 13, but the effective age is 16 based on interpretation of a U.S. Supreme Court decision by the State attorney general's office.
[e] Juveniles may be transferred to adult court. Age can be a mitigating factor.
[f] The minimum age for transfer to adult court is 14 by statute, but the effective age for a capital sentence is 16 based on interpretation of a U.S. Supreme Court decision by the State attorney general's office.

Minimum age

In 1995 eight jurisdictions did not specify a minimum age for which the death penalty could be imposed (table 3). In some States the minimum age was set forth in the statutory provisions that determine the age at which a juvenile may be transferred to criminal court for trial as an adult. Thirteen States and the Federal system required a minimum age of 18; one State age 19. Sixteen States indicated an age of eligibility between 14 and 17.

Characteristics of prisoners under sentence of death at yearend 1995

Thirty-four States and the Federal prison system held a total of 3,054 prisoners under sentence of death on December 31, 1995, a gain of 149 or 5.1% more than at the end of 1994 (table 4). The Federal prison system count rose from 6 at yearend 1994 to 8

Table 4. Prisoners under sentence of death, by region, State, and race, 1994 and 1995

Region and State	Prisoners under sentence of death, 12/31/94			Received under sentence of death			Removed from death row (excluding executions)[a]			Executed			Prisoners under sentence of death, 12/31/95		
	Total[b]	White[c]	Black[c]	Total[b]	White	Black	Total[b]	White	Black	Total[b]	White	Black	Total[b]	White	Black
U.S. total	2,905	1,653	1,203	310	168	138	105	58	44	56	33	22	3,054	1,730	1,275
Federal[d]	6	3	3	2	0	2	0	0	0	0	0	0	8	3	5
State	2,899	1,650	1,200	308	168	136	105	58	44	56	33	22	3,046	1,727	1,270
Northeast	194	71	116	23	6	17	4	2	2	2	2	0	211	73	131
Connecticut	4	2	2	1	0	1	0	0	0	0	0	0	5	2	3
New Hampshire	0	0	0	0	0	0	0	0	0	0	0	0	0	0	0
New Jersey	9	4	5	2	1	1	1	1	0	0	0	0	10	4	6
Pennsylvania	181	65	109	20	5	15	3	1	2	2	2	0	196	67	122
Midwest	443	217	224	43	21	22	16	9	7	11	6	5	459	223	234
Illinois	155	57	98	13	6	7	9	4	5	5	3	2	154	56	98
Indiana	47	31	16	3	3	0	4	3	1	0	0	0	46	31	15
Kansas	0	0	0	0	0	0	0	0	0	0	0	0	0	0	0
Missouri	88	51	37	10	3	7	0	0	0	6	3	3	92	51	41
Nebraska	10	7	2	0	0	0	0	0	0	0	0	0	10	7	2
Ohio	141	69	71	17	9	8	3	2	1	0	0	0	155	76	78
South Dakota	2	2	0	0	0	0	0	0	0	0	0	0	2	2	0
South	1,621	926	672	184	105	78	71	37	33	41	23	17	1,693	971	700
Alabama	136	74	60	17	10	7	8	2	6	2	0	2	143	82	59
Arkansas	37	21	16	4	3	1	1	0	1	2	1	1	38	23	15
Delaware	14	7	7	1	1	0	0	0	0	1	1	0	14	7	7
Florida	353	223	130	31	19	12	19	12	7	3	2	1	362	228	134
Georgia	96	53	43	7	5	2	3	1	2	2	2	0	98	55	43
Kentucky	29	23	6	0	0	0	1	1	0	0	0	0	28	22	6
Louisiana	47	16	31	12	4	8	1	0	1	1	0	1	57	20	37
Maryland	13	2	11	0	0	0	0	0	0	0	0	0	13	2	11
Mississippi	50	20	30	3	0	3	4	0	4	0	0	0	49	20	29
North Carolina	111	55	54	34	19	15	4	4	0	2	2	0	139	68	69
Oklahoma	130	79	40	15	10	4	13	8	4	3	3	0	129	78	40
South Carolina	59	31	28	10	2	8	1	0	1	1	0	1	67	33	34
Tennessee	100	66	32	4	1	3	8	3	5	0	0	0	96	64	30
Texas	391	230	155	40	27	13	8	6	2	19	10	8	404	241	158
Virginia	55	26	29	6	4	2	0	0	0	5	2	3	56	28	28
West	641	436	188	58	36	19	14	10	2	2	2	0	683	460	205
Arizona	121	101	14	5	5	0	8	8	0	1	1	0	117	97	14
California[e]	386	230	148	36	22	13	2	1	1	0	0	0	420	251	160
Colorado	3	3	0	1	0	1	0	0	0	0	0	0	4	3	1
Idaho	20	20	0	0	0	0	1	1	0	0	0	0	19	19	0
Montana	8	6	0	0	0	0	1	1	0	1	1	0	6	5	0
Nevada[e]	65	44	21	11	4	5	1	0	0	0	0	0	75	48	26
New Mexico	1	1	0	2	2	0	0	0	0	0	0	0	3	3	0
Oregon	18	16	1	2	2	0	0	0	0	0	0	0	20	18	1
Utah	10	8	2	0	0	0	0	0	0	0	0	0	10	8	2
Washington	9	7	2	1	1	0	1	0	1	0	0	0	9	8	1
Wyoming	0	0	0	0	0	0	0	0	0	0	0	0	0	0	0

Note: States not listed and the District of Columbia did not authorize the death penalty as of 12/31/94. New York enacted a death penalty statue during 1995 and reported no one under sentence of death as of 12/31/95. Some figures shown for yearend 1994 are revised from those reported in Capital Punishment 1994 NCJ-158023. The revised figures include 26 inmates who were either reported late to the National Prisoner Statistics Program or were not in custody of State correctional authorities on 12/31/94 (12 in California; 4 in Florida; 2 in Texas; and 1 each in Alabama, Arizona, Arkansas, Idaho, Ohio, Oklahoma, Oregon, and Tennessee), and exclude 18 inmates who were relieved of the death sentence on or before 12/31/94 (8 in California; 5 in Texas; and 1 each in Arizona, New Mexico, Pennsylvania, Tennessee, and Washington). The data for 12/31/94 also include 7 inmates in Florida who were listed erroneously as being removed from death row.

[a]Includes 9 deaths from natural causes (3 in Alabama, and 1 each in Arizona, Illinois, Kentucky, North Carolina, Oklahoma, and Texas) 2 suicides (in California and Nevada), and 2 inmates murdered by other inmates (in Florida and Texas).
[b]Totals include persons of other races.
[c]The accounting of race and Hispanic origin differs from that presented in tables 8, 9, and 11. In this table white and black inmates include Hispanics.
[d]Excludes persons held under Armed Forces jurisdiction with a military death sentence for murder.
[e]One inmate who was previously in the custody of Nevada has been transferred to California where he is being held under a separate sentence of death.

at yearend 1995. Three States reported 39% of the Nation's death row population: California (420), Texas (404), and Florida (362). Of the 38 jurisdictions with statutes authorizing the death penalty during 1995, New Hampshire, Kansas, and Wyoming had no one under a capital sentence, and South Dakota, New Mexico, and Colorado had 4 or fewer. New York enacted a new death penalty statute, effective September 1, 1995, and report no one under sentence of death as of December 1, 1995.

Among the 35 jurisdictions with prisoners under sentence of death at yearend 1995, 20 had more inmates than a year earlier, 9 had fewer inmates, and 6 had the same number. California had an increase of 34, followed by North Carolina (28), Pennsylvania (15), Ohio (14), Texas (13), and Louisiana and Nevada (10 each). Arizona and Tennessee had the largest decrease (4 each).

During 1995 the number of black inmates under sentence of death increased by 72; the number of whites increased by 77; and the number of persons of other races (American Indians, Alaska Natives, Asians, or Pacific Islanders) remained constant at 49.

The number of Hispanics sentenced to death rose from 224 to 237 during 1995 (table 5). Twenty-six Hispanics were received under sentence of death, 11 were removed from death row, and 2 were executed. Three-fourths of the Hispanics were incarcerated in 4 States: Texas (68), California (61), Florida (35), and Arizona (18).

During 1995 the number of women sentenced to be executed increased from 43 to 48. Six women were received under sentence of death, one was removed from death row, and none were executed. Women were under sentence of death in 14 States. Almost two-thirds of all women on death row at yearend were in California, Florida, Texas, Oklahoma, and Illinois.

Table 5. Hispanics and women under sentence of death, by State, 1994 and 1995

Region and State	Under sentence of death, 12/31/94		Received under sentence of death		Death sentence removed*	Under sentence of death, 12/31/95	
	Hispanics	Women	Hispanics	Women	Hispanics	Hispanics	Women
U.S. total	224	43	26	6	11	237	48
Alabama	0	5	0	0	0	0	4
Arizona	20	1	1	0	3	18	1
Arkansas	1	0	1	0	0	2	0
California	57	6	4	2	0	61	8
Colorado	1	0	0	0	0	1	0
Florida	33	6	4	0	2	35	6
Georgia	1	0	0	0	0	1	0
Idaho	2	1	0	0	1	1	1
Illinois	8	5	0	0	1	7	5
Indiana	2	0	0	0	0	2	0
Louisiana	0	0	1	0	0	1	0
Mississippi	1	1	0	1	0	1	2
Missouri	0	2	0	0	0	0	2
Nevada	8	1	2	0	0	10	1
New Jersey	1	0	0	0	1	0	0
New Mexico	1	0	1	0	0	2	0
North Carolina	0	2	1	0	0	1	2
Ohio	5	0	0	0	0	5	0
Oklahoma	6	4	0	1	2	4	5
Oregon	1	0	0	0	0	1	0
Pennsylvania	11	4	0	0	0	11	4
Tennessee	1	1	0	0	0	1	1
Texas	60	4	11	2	1	68	6
Utah	2	0	0	0	0	2	0
Virginia	2	0	0	0	0	2	0

*One woman was removed from under sentence of death in Alabama, and no women were executed during 1995. Two Hispanic men were executed in Texas in 1995.

State	Women under sentence of death, 12/31/95		
	Total	White	Black
Total	48	32	16
California	8	6	2
Florida	6	4	2
Texas	6	4	2
Oklahoma	5	4	1
Illinois	5	2	3
Alabama	4	3	1
Pennsylvania	4	1	3
Missouri	2	2	0
North Carolina	2	2	0
Mississippi	2	1	1
Arizona	1	1	0
Idaho	1	1	0
Tennessee	1	1	0
Nevada	1	0	1

Men were 98% (3,006) of all prisoners under sentence of death (table 6). Whites predominated (57%); blacks comprised 42%; and other races (1.6%) included 22 Native Americans, 19 Asians, and 8 persons of unknown race. Among those for whom ethnicity was known, 8% were Hispanic.

The sex, race, and Hispanic origin of those under sentence of death at yearend 1995 were as follows:

State	Persons under sentence of death, by sex, race, and Hispanic origin, 12/31/95		
	White	Black	Other
Male	1,698	1,259	49
Hispanic	215	12	7
Female	32	16	0
Hispanic	2	1	0

Among inmates under sentence of death on December 31, 1995, for whom information on education was available, three-fourths had either completed high school (38%) or finished 9th, 10th, or 11th grade (37%). The percentage who had not gone beyond eighth grade (15%) was over 40% larger than that of inmates who had attended some college (10%). The median level of education was the 11th grade.

Of inmates under a capital sentence and with reported marital status, half had never married; a fourth were married at the time of sentencing; and nearly a fourth were divorced, separated, or widowed.

Among all inmates under sentence of death for whom date of arrest information was available, more than half were age 20 to 29 at the time of arrest for their capital offense; 12% were age 19 or younger; and less than 1% were age 55 or older (table 7). The average age at time of arrest was 28 years. On December 31, 1995, 43% of these inmates were age 30 to 39 and 71% were age 25 to 44. The youngest offender under sentence of death was age 18; the oldest was 80.

Entries and removals of persons under sentence of death

Between January 1 and December 31, 1995, 27 State prison systems reported receiving 308 prisoners under sentence of death; the Federal Bureau of Prisons received 2 inmates. Forty-five percent of the inmates were received in 4 States: Texas (40), California (36), North Carolina (34), and Florida (31).

All 310 prisoners who had been received under sentence of death had been convicted of murder. By sex and race, 164 were white men, 136 were black men, 4 were Asian men, 4 were white women, and 2 were black women. Of the 310 new admissions, 26 were Hispanic men. No Hispanic women were admitted under sentence of death in 1995.

Table 6. Demographic characteristics of prisoners under sentence of death, 1995

Characteristic	Prisoners under sentence of death, 1995		
	Yearend	Admissions	Removals
Number of prisoners	3,054	310	161
Sex			
Male	98.4%	98.1%	99.4%
Female	1.6	1.9	.6
Race			
White	56.6%	54.2%	56.5%
Black	41.7	44.5	41
Other*	1.6	1.3	2.5
Hispanic origin			
Hispanic	8.5%	9.3%	8.6%
Non-Hispanic	91.5	90.7	91.4
Education			
8th grade or less	14.7%	12.1%	21.8%
9th-11th	37.2	41.5	42.3
High school graduate/GED	37.8	35.5	26.8
Any college	10.3	10.9	9.2
Median	11th grade	11th grade	11th grade
Marital status			
Married	25.6%	20.4%	31.5%
Divorced/separated	21.6	22.6	19.2
Widowed	2.5	2.6	2.1
Never married	50.3	54.4	47.3

Note: Calculations are based on those cases for which data were reported. Missing data by category were as follows:

	Yearend	Admissions	Removals
Hispanic origin	257	29	10
Education	422	62	19
Marital status	247	36	15

*At yearend 1994 "other" consisted of 24 Native Americans, 17 Asians, and 8 self-identified Hispanics. During 1995, 4 Asians were admitted; 2 Native Americans and 2 Asians were removed.

Table 7. Age at time of arrest for capital offense and age of prisoners under sentence of death at yearend 1995

	Prisoners under sentence of death			
	At time of arrest		On December 31, 1995	
Age	Number*	Percent	Number*	Percent
Number of prisoners	2,661	100.0%	2,661	100.0%
17 or younger	51	1.9	0	
18-19	262	9.8	20	.8
20-24	741	27.8	257	9.7
25-29	626	23.5	428	16.1
30-34	441	16.6	556	20.9
35-39	272	10.2	575	21.6
40-44	137	5.1	343	12.9
45-49	77	2.9	261	9.8
50-54	34	1.3	125	4.7
55-59	13	.5	56	2.1
60 or older	7	.3	40	1.5
Mean age	28 yrs		36 yrs	
Median age	27 yrs		35 yrs	

Note: The youngest person under sentence of death was a white male in Nevada, born in January 1977 and sentenced to death in November 1994. The oldest person under sentence of death was a white male in Arizona, born in September 1915 and sentenced to death in June 1983.
*Excludes 393 inmates for whom the date of arrest for the capital offense was not available.

Twenty-one States reported a total of 92 persons whose sentence of death was overturned or removed. Appeals courts vacated 55 sentences while upholding the convictions and vacated 30 sentences while overturning the convictions. Florida (18 exits) had the largest number of vacated capital sentences. Arizona reported three commutations of a death sentence; Idaho, Oklahoma, and Pennsylvania each reported one. Mississippi removed 1 inmate when an appellate court struck the capital sentence due to a violation of the inmate's constitutional right to a speedy trial.

As of December 31, 1995, 56 of the 92 persons who were formerly under sentence of death were serving a reduced sentence, 14 were awaiting a new trial, 17 were awaiting resentencing, 2 had all capital charges dropped, and 1 had no action taken after being removed from under sentence of death. No information was available on the current status of 2 inmates.

In addition, 13 persons died while under sentence of death in 1995. Nine of these deaths were from natural causes — three in Alabama, and one each in Arizona, Illinois, Kentucky, North Carolina, Oklahoma, and Texas. Two suicides occurred — one each in California and Nevada. Two inmates were killed by other inmates — one in Florida and one in Texas.

From 1977, the year after the Supreme Court upheld the constitutionality of revised State capital punishment laws, to 1995, a total of 4,857 persons entered prison under sentence of death. During these 19 years, 313 persons were executed, and 1,870 were removed from under a death sentence by appellate court decisions and reviews, commutations, or death.[1]

Among individuals who received a death sentence between 1977 and 1995, 2,468 (51%) were white, 1,975 (41%) were black, 342 (7%) were Hispanic, and 72 (1%) were of other races. The distribution by race and Hispanic origin of the 1,870 inmates who were removed from death row between 1977 and 1995 was as follows: 969 whites (52%), 773 blacks (41%), 101 Hispanics (5%), and 27 persons of other races (2%). Of the 313 who were executed, 171 (55%) were white, 120 (38%) were black, 19 (6%) were Hispanic, and 3 (1%) were other races.

Criminal history of inmates under sentence of death in 1995

Among inmates under a death sentence on December 31, 1995, for whom criminal history information was available, 66% had past felony convictions, including 8% with at least one previous homicide conviction (table 8).

Among those for whom legal status at the time of the capital offense was reported, 42% had an active criminal justice status. Nearly half of these were on parole and about a fourth were on probation. The others had charges pending, were in prison, had escaped from incarceration, or had some other criminal justice status.

Criminal history patterns differed by race and Hispanic origin. More blacks (70%) than whites (65%) or Hispanics (59%) had a prior felony conviction. About the same percentage of blacks (9%), whites (8%), or Hispanics (7%) had a prior homicide conviction. A slightly higher percentage of Hispanics (25%) or blacks (24%) than whites (17%) were on parole when arrested for their capital offense.

Since 1988 data have been collected on the number of death sentences imposed on entering inmates. Among the 2,299 individuals received under

Table 8. Criminal history profile of prisoners under sentence of death, by race and Hispanic origin, 1995

	Prisoners under sentence of death							
	Number				Percent[a]			
	All[b]	White	Black	Hispanic	All[b]	White	Black	Hispanic
U.S. total	3,054	1,513	1,262	237	100.0%	100.0%	100.0%	100.0%
Prior felony convictions								
Yes	1,887	914	826	130	66.3%	64.9%	70.1%	58.6%
No	959	494	352	92	33.7	35.1	29.9	41.4
Not reported	208	105	84	15				
Prior homicide convictions								
Yes	254	125	110	17	8.5%	8.4%	8.9%	7.4%
No	2,728	1,357	1,120	212	91.5	91.6	91.1	92.6
Not reported	72	31	32	8				
Legal status at time of capital offense								
Charges pending	189	106	68	13	6.9%	7.8%	6.0%	6.1%
Probation	275	134	117	21	10	9.8	10.4	9.9
Parole	558	235	266	53	20.4	17.2	23.6	24.9
Prison escapee	44	26	14	3	1.6	1.9	1.2	1.4
Prison inmate	66	32	31	3	2.4	2.3	2.8	1.4
Other status	33	17	14	1	1.2	1.2	1.2	0.5
None	1,575	813	616	119	57.5	59.6	54.7	55.9
Not reported	314	150	136	24				

[a]Percentages are based on those offenders for whom data were reported.
[b]Includes whites, blacks, Hispanics, and persons of other races.

---
[1]An individual may have received and been removed from under a sentence of death more than once. Data are based on the most recent sentence.

sentence of death during that time, about 1 in every 7 entered with two or more death sentences.

Number of death sentences received	Inmates
Total	100 %
1	85.3
2	10.3
3 or more	4.4
Number admitted under sentence of death, 1988-95	2,299

The proportions of whites, blacks, and Hispanics with two or more death sentences were nearly identical.

Executions

According to data collected by the Federal Government, from 1930 to 1995, 4,172 persons were executed under civil authority (table 9).[2]

After the Supreme Court reinstated the death penalty in 1976, 26 States executed 313 prisoners:

Year	Number
1977	1
1979	2
1981	1
1982	2
1983	5
1984	21
1985	18
1986	18
1987	25
1988	11
1989	16
1990	23
1991	14
1992	31
1993	38
1994	31
1995	56

During this 19-year period, 5 States executed 211 prisoners: Texas (104), Florida (36), Virginia (29), Louisiana (22), and Georgia (20). These States accounted for two-thirds of all executions. Between 1977 and 1995, 170 white non-Hispanic men, 120 black non-Hispanic men, 19 Hispanic men, 2 Native American men, 1 Asian man, and 1 white non-Hispanic woman were executed.

During 1995 Texas carried out 19 executions; Missouri executed 6 persons; Illinois and Virginia, 5 each;

[2] Military authorities carried out an additional 160 executions, 1930-95.

Florida and Oklahoma, 3 each; Pennsylvania, Alabama, Arkansas, Georgia, and North Carolina, 2 each; and Delaware, Louisiana, South Carolina, Arizona, and Montana, 1 each. All persons executed in 1995 were male. Thirty-one were non-Hispanic whites; 22 were non-Hispanic blacks; 1 was Asian; and 2 were Hispanic.

Table 9. Number of persons executed, by jurisdiction, 1930-95

State	Since 1930	Since 1977
U.S. total	4,172	313
Texas	401	104
Georgia	386	20
New York	329	
California	294	2
North Carolina	271	8
Florida	206	36
Ohio	172	
South Carolina	167	5
Mississippi	158	4
Louisiana	155	22
Pennsylvania	154	2
Alabama	147	12
Arkansas	129	11
Virginia	121	29
Kentucky	103	
Illinois	97	7
Tennessee	93	
Missouri	79	17
New Jersey	74	
Maryland	69	1
Oklahoma	66	6
Washington	49	2
Colorado	47	
Indiana	44	3
Arizona	42	4
District of Columbia	40	
West Virginia	40	
Nevada	34	5
Federal system	33	
Massachusetts	27	
Connecticut	21	
Oregon	19	
Iowa	18	
Utah	17	4
Delaware	17	5
Kansas	15	
New Mexico	8	
Wyoming	8	1
Montana	7	1
Nebraska	5	1
Idaho	4	1
Vermont	4	
New Hampshire	1	
South Dakota	1	
Minnesota	0	
Rhode Island	0	
North Dakota	0	
Hawaii	0	
Michigan	0	
Maine	0	
Alaska	0	
Wisconsin	0	

From 1977 to 1995, 5,237 prisoners were under death sentences for varying lengths of time (table 10). The 313 executions accounted for 6% of those at risk. A total of 1,870 prisoners (36% of those at risk) received other dispositions. About the same percentage of whites (6%), blacks (6%), and Hispanics (5%) were executed. Somewhat larger percentages of whites (36%) and blacks (36%) than Hispanics (28%) were removed from under a death sentence by means other than execution.

Among prisoners executed between 1977 and 1995, the average time spent between the imposition of the most recent sentence received and execution was more than 8 years (table 11). White prisoners had spent an average of 8 years and 2 months, and black prisoners, 9 years and 5 months. The 56 prisoners executed in 1995 were under sentence of death an average of 11 years and 2 months.

For the 313 prisoners executed between 1977 and 1995, the most common method of execution was lethal injection (180). Other methods were electrocution (121), lethal gas (9), hanging (2), and firing squad (1).

Method of execution	Executions, 1977-95				
	White	Black	Hispanic	American Indian	Asian
Total	171	120	19	2	1
Lethal injection	100	59	18	2	1
Electrocution	62	58	1	0	0
Lethal gas	6	3	0	0	0
Hanging	2	0	0	0	0
Firing squad	1	0	0	0	0

Among prisoners under sentence of death at yearend 1995, the average time spent in prison was 6 years and 6 months.

The median time between the imposition of a death sentence and yearend 1995 was 69 months. Overall, the average time for women was 4.8 years — about three-fourths as long as for men (6.5 years). On average, whites, blacks, and Hispanics had spent from 75 to 80 months under a sentence of death.

	Elapsed time since sentencing	
	Mean	Median
Total	78 mos	69 mos
Male	78	70
Female	58	46
White	80	73
Black	75	64
Hispanic	76	69

Table 10. Prisoners under sentence of death who were executed or received other dispositions, by race and Hispanic origin, 1977-95

Race/Hispanic origin[b]	Total under sentence of death, 1977-95[c]	Prisoners executed		Prisoners who received other dispositions[a]	
		Number	Percent of total	Number	Percent of total
Total	5,237	313	6.0%	1,870	35.7%
White	2,653	171	6.4%	969	36.5%
Black	2,155	120	5.6	773	35.9
Hispanic	357	19	5.3	101	28.3
Other	72	3	4.2	27	37.5

[a]Includes persons removed from a sentence of death because of statutes struck down on appeal, sentences or convictions vacated, commutations, or death other than by execution.
[b]White, black, and other categories exclude Hispanics.
[c]Includes persons sentenced to death prior to 1977 who were still under sentence of death 12/31/95 (14), persons sentenced to death prior to 1977 whose death sentence was removed between 1977 and 12/31/95 (366), and persons sentenced to death between 1977 and 12/31/95 (4,857).

Table 11. Time under sentence of death sentence and execution, by race, 1977-95

Year of execution	Number executed			Average elapsed time from sentence to execution for:		
	All*	White	Black	All*	White	Black
Total	313	189	121	104 mos	98 mos	113 mos
1977-83	11	9	2	51 mos	49 mos	58 mos
1984	21	13	8	74	76	71
1985	18	11	7	71	65	80
1986	18	11	7	87	78	102
1987	25	13	12	86	78	96
1888	11	6	5	80	72	89
1989	16	8	8	95	78	112
1990	23	16	7	95	97	91
1991	14	7	7	116	124	107
1992	31	19	11	114	104	135
1993	38	23	14	113	112	121
1994	31	20	11	122	117	132
1995	56	33	22	134	128	144

Note: Average time was calculated from the most recent sentencing date. Some numbers have been revised from those previously reported.
*Includes Native Americans and Asians.

Appendix. Federal laws providing for the death penalty

8 U.S.C. 1342 - Murder related to the smuggling of aliens.

18 U.S.C. 32-34 - Destruction of aircraft, motor vehicles, or related facilities resulting in death.

18 U.S.C. 36 - Murder committed during a drug-related drive-by shooting.

18 U.S.C. 37 - Murder committed at an airport serving international civil aviation.

18 U.S.C. 115(b)(3)[by cross-reference to 18 U.S.C. 1111] - Retaliatory murder of a member of the immediate family of law enforcement officials.

18 U.S.C. 241, 242, 245, 247 - Civil rights offenses resulting in death.

18 U.S.C. 351 [by cross-reference to 18 U.S.C. 1111] - Murder of a member of Congress, an important executive official, or a Supreme Court Justice.

18 U.S.C. 794 - Espionage

18 U.S.C. 844(d), (f), (i) - Death resulting from offenses involving transportation of explosives, destruction of government property, or destruction of property related to foreign or interstate commerce.

18 U.S.C. 924(i) - Murder committed by the use of a firearm during a crime of violence or a drug trafficking crime.

18 U.S.C 930 - Murder committed in a Federal Government facility.

18 U.S.C. 1091 - Genocide.

18 U.S.C. 1111 - First-degree murder.

18 U.S.C. 1114 - Murder of a Federal judge or law enforcement official.

18 U.S.C. 1116 - Murder of a foreign official.

18 U.S.C. 1118 - Murder by a Federal prisoner.

18 U.S.C. 1119 - Murder of a U.S. national in a foreign country.

18 U.S.C. 1120 - Murder by an escaped Federal prisoner already sentenced to life imprisonment.

18 U.S.C. 1121 - Murder of a State or local law enforcement official or other person aiding in a Federal investigation; murder of a State correctional officer.

18 U.S.C. 1201 - Murder during a kidnaping.

18 U.S.C. 1203 - Murder during a hostage-taking.

18 U.S.C. 1503 - Murder of a court officer or juror.

18 U.S.C. 1512 - Murder with the intent of preventing testimony by a witness, victim, or informant.

18 U.S.C. 1513 - Retaliatory murder of a witness, victim or informant.

18 U.S.C. 1716 - Mailing of injurious articles with intent to kill or resulting in death.

18 U.S.C. 1751 [by cross-reference to 18 U.S.C. 1111] - Assassination or kidnaping resulting in the death of the President or Vice President.

18 U.S.C. 1958 - Murder for hire.

18 U.S.C. 1959 - Murder involved in a racketeering offense.

18 U.S.C. 1992 - Willful wrecking of a train resulting in death.

18 U.S.C. 2113 - Bank-robbery-related murder or kidnaping.

18 U.S.C. 2119 - Murder related to a carjacking.

18 U.S.C. 2245 - Murder related to rape or child molestation.

18 U.S.C. 2251 - Murder related to sexual exploitation of children.

18 U.S.C. 2280 - Murder committed during an offense against maritime navigation.

18 U.S.C. 2281 - Murder committed during an offense against a maritime fixed platform.

18 U.S.C. 2332 - Terrorist murder of a U.S. national in another country.

18 U.S.C. 2332a - Murder by the use of a weapon of mass destruction.

18 U.S.C. 2340 - Murder involving torture.

18 U.S.C. 2381 - Treason.

21 U.S.C. 848(e) - Murder related to a continuing criminal enterprise or related murder of a Federal, State, or local law enforcement officer.

49 U.S.C. 1472-1473 - Death resulting from aircraft hijacking.

Methodological note

The statistics reported in this Bulletin may differ from data collected by other organizations for a variety of reasons: (1) National Prisoner Statistics (NPS) adds inmates to the number under sentence of death not at sentencing but at the time they are admitted to a State or Federal correctional facility. (2) If in one year inmates entered prison under a death sentence or were reported as being relieved of a death sentence but the court had acted in the previous year, the counts are adjusted to reflect the dates of court decisions. (See the note on table 4 for the affected jurisdictions.) (3) NPS counts for capital punishment are always for the last day of the calendar year and will differ from counts for more recent periods.

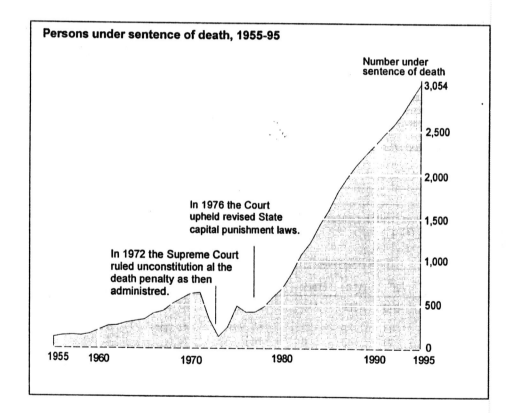

Appendix table 1. Prisoners sentenced to death, and the outcome of their sentence, by year of sentencing, 1973-95

Year of sentence	Number sentenced to death	Number of prisoners removed from under sentence of death							Under sentence of death, 12/31/95
		Execution	Other death	Appeal or higher courts overturned			Sentence commuted	Other or unknown reasons	
				Death penalty statute	Conviction	Sentence			
1973	42	2	0	14	9	8	9	0	0
1974	149	9	4	65	15	30	22	1	3
1975	298	6	4	171	24	66	21	2	4
1976	234	11	5	137	16	43	15	0	7
1977	138	16	2	40	26	33	7	0	14
1978	186	31	4	21	34	60	8	0	28
1979	154	19	9	2	28	58	6	1	31
1980	175	27	11	3	27	46	7	0	54
1981	229	37	12	0	39	71	4	1	65
1982	269	39	13	0	29	63	6	0	119
1983	254	31	12	1	22	54	4	2	128
1984	287	25	10	2	33	57	6	8	146
1985	271	10	3	1	37	63	3	3	151
1986	305	12	13	0	39	49	4	5	183
1987	290	8	8	3	33	54	1	6	177
1988	295	10	6	0	28	44	2	0	205
1989	264	3	6	0	25	47	3	0	180
1990	252	4	4	0	28	27	0	0	189
1991	271	2	5	0	22	16	3	0	223
1992	293	5	1	0	14	19	2	0	252
1993	295	4	4	0	4	8	1	0	274
1994	319	2	1	0	0	3	1	0	312
1995	310	0	1	0	0	0	0	0	309
Total, 1973-95	5,580	313	138	460	532	919	135	29	3,054

Note: Table based upon most recent death sentence received.

Appendix table 2. Prisoners under sentence of death on December 31, 1995, by State and year of sentencing

State	1974-79	1980-81	1982-83	1984-85	1986-87	1988	1989	1990	1991	1992	1993	1994	1995	Under sentence of death 12/31/95	Average number of years under sentence of death as of 12/31/95
Florida	26	14	24	34	34	25	17	19	36	31	30	41	31	362	6.9
Texas	16	16	20	34	58	28	28	24	27	37	31	45	40	404	6.5
California	10	18	50	38	48	34	33	32	24	41	33	23	36	420	7.0
Georgia	9	3	6	6	18	4	8	9	6	7	7	8	7	98	7.6
Arizona	6	8	12	11	7	10	4	10	10	9	14	11	5	117	7.2
Tennessee	6	7	9	14	17	6	3	7	9	7	2	5	4	96	8.5
Nebraska	3	2		2	1	1						1		10	12.2
Arkansas	2	1	1		4	1	4	3		4	7	7	4	38	5.1
Nevada	2	4	10	9	5	5	8	7	4	1	2	8	10	75	7.1
South Carolina	2	3	7	7	7	2	4	2	7	2	7	7	10	67	6.6
Alabama	1	4	18	14	16	7	13	7	4	9	8	25	17	143	6.3
Illinois	1	14	16	14	18	11	8	16	7	14	12	10	13	154	7.1
Kentucky	1	2	8	2	4	1			2	3	2	3		28	8.8
North Carolina	1	3	5	5	1	1		6	10	16	31	26	34	139	3.3
Oklahoma	1	1	8	17	24	10	11	7	11	4	8	12	15	129	6.4
Indiana		5	6	10	6	4		3	2	3	2	2	3	46	8.4
Mississippi		4	4	1	3	3		7	5	2	12	5	3	49	5.7
Pennsylvania		4	16	20	26	20	15	6	17	16	15	21	20	196	6.1
Delaware		2	1			1				4	5		1	14	5.6
Missouri		2	4	12	14	12	2	4	11	6	6	9	10	92	6.1
Idaho		1	3	4	1	3	2	1	1	1	1	1		19	8.5
Maryland		1	1	2	1	1	3	1	1	1	1			13	8.0
Ohio			11	30	21	9	9	9	12	14	10	13	17	155	6.3
Louisiana			4	8	8	1		1	4	6	7	6	12	57	5.0
Montana			1		1	1	1			2				6	*
Utah			1	2	1	2	2		1		1			10	7.6
Washington			1		1			1	1	1	1	2	1	9	*
Virginia				1	12	2	3	5	5	6	6	10	6	56	4.5
Colorado					2				1				1	4	*
New Jersey					1			2			2	3	2	10	3.0
Connecticut							1		2		1		1	5	*
Oregon							1		2	4	4	7	2	20	2.5
Federal									1		5		2	8	*
South Dakota										1	1			2	*
New Mexico												1	2	3	*
Total	87	119	247	297	360	205	180	189	223	252	274	312	309	3,054	6.5

Note: For those persons sentenced to death more than once, the numbers are based on the most recent sentence to death.
*Averages not calculated for fewer that 10 inmates.

Appendix table 3. Number sentenced to death and number of removals, by jurisdiction and reason for removal, 1973-95

State	Total sentenced to death, 1973-95	Number of removals, 1973-95					Under sentence of death, 12/31/95
		Executed	Died	Sentence or conviction overturned	Sentence commuted	Other removals	
U.S. total	5,580	313	138	1,911	135	30	3,054
Federal	9	0	0	1	0	0	8
Alabama	245	12	7	82	1	0	143
Arizona	196	4	6	63	5	1	117
Arkansas	77	11	1	27	0	0	38
California	573	2	22	113	15	1	420
Colorado	15	0	1	9	1	0	4
Connecticut	6	0	0	1	0	0	5
Delaware	32	5	0	13	0	0	14
Florida	734	36	19	297	18	2	362
Georgia	252	20	7	121	5	1	98
Idaho	33	1	1	11	1	0	19
Illinois	234	7	7	59	0	7	154
Indiana	83	3	1	31	0	2	46
Kentucky	58	0	2	27	1	0	28
Louisiana	153	22	3	64	6	1	57
Maryland	37	1	1	20	2	0	13
Massachusetts	4	0	0	2	2	0	0
Mississippi	135	4	1	78	0	3	49
Missouri	126	17	4	12	1	0	92
Montana	13	1	0	5	1	0	6
Nebraska	21	1	2	6	2	0	10
Nevada	105	5	4	18	3	0	75
New Jersey	40	0	1	21	0	8	10
New Mexico	25	0	0	17	5	0	3
New York	3	0	0	3	0	0	0
North Carolina	389	8	5	233	4	0	139
Ohio	298	0	5	129	9	0	155
Oklahoma	251	6	5	110	1	0	129
Oregon	37	0	0	17	0	0	20
Pennsylvania	262	2	7	55	2	0	196
Rhode Island	2	0	0	2	0	0	0
South Carolina	138	5	3	63	0	0	67
South Dakota	2	0	0	0	0	0	2
Tennessee	167	0	4	65	0	2	96
Texas	665	104	14	100	43	0	404
Utah	23	4	0	8	1	0	10
Virginia	102	29	3	7	6	1	56
Washington	26	2	1	14	0	0	9
Wyoming	9	1	1	7	0	0	0
Percent	100%	5.6	2.5	34.2	2.4	0.5	54.7

Note: For those persons sentenced to death more than once, the numbers are based on the most recent sentence to death.

Appendix table 4. Executions, by State and method, 1977-95

State	Number executed	Lethal injection	Electro-cution	Lethal gas	Firing squad	Hanging
Total	313	180	121	9	1	2
Texas	104	104	0	0	0	0
Florida	36	0	36	0	0	0
Virginia	29	5	24	0	0	0
Louisiana	22	2	20	0	0	0
Georgia	20	0	20	0	0	0
Missouri	17	17	0	0	0	0
Alabama	12	0	12	0	0	0
Arkansas	11	10	1	0	0	0
North Carolina	8	7	0	1	0	0
Illinois	7	7	0	0	0	0
Oklahoma	6	6	0	0	0	0
Delaware	5	5	0	0	0	0
Nevada	5	4	0	1	0	0
South Carolina	5	1	4	0	0	0
Arizona	4	3	0	1	0	0
Mississippi	4	0	0	4	0	0
Utah	4	3	0	0	1	0
Indiana	3	0	3	0	0	0
California	2	0	0	2	0	0
Pennsylvania	2	2	0	0	0	0
Washington	2	0	0	0	0	2
Idaho	1	1	0	0	0	0
Maryland	1	1	0	0	0	0
Montana	1	1	0	0	0	0
Nebraska	1	0	1	0	0	0
Wyoming	1	1	0	0	0	0

Note: Data are based on execution methods used since 1977. Lethal injection was used in 58% of the executions carried out.

Eight States — Arizona, Arkansas, Louisiana, Nevada, North Carolina, South Carolina, Virginia, and Utah — have employed two methods.

The Bureau of Justice Statistics is the statistical agency of the U.S. Department of Justice. Jan M. Chaiken, Ph.D., is director. BJS Bulletins present the first release of findings from permanent data collection programs.

This Bulletin was written by Tracy L. Snell under the supervision of Allen J. Beck. James J. Stephan and Jodi M. Brown provided statistical review. Tom Hester and Tina Dorsey edited the report. Marilyn Marbrook administered production. At the Bureau of the Census, Patricia A. Clark collected the data under the supervision of Gertrude Odom.

December 1996, NCJ-162043

Data may be obtained from the National Archive of Criminal Justice Data at the University of Michigan, 1-800-999-0960. The data sets are archived as Capital Punishment, 1973-95.

The data and the report, as well as others from the Bureau of Justice Statistics, are also available through the Internet:

http://www.ojp.usdoj.gov/bjs/

CRITICAL THOUGHT AND ANALYSIS WORKSHEET

Corrections and Punishment

1) Describe the type of punishment issues that are involved in this case:

    a) When and where did it happen?

    b) Were the defendant and the victim treated fairly?

    c) What was good and bad about the punishment?

    d) What would you do to improve the fairness of this situation?

List at least two ethical issues involved in this investigation.

Issues in Criminal Justice

MARKET OF DEATH, MARKET OF FUN: ANATOMY AND ANALYSIS OF A GUN SHOW

by Keith Haley and Tammy Kimball

TEXAS AND THE GUN PHENOMENON

Texas has made a reputation out of "big." The expanse of unoccupied land in some parts of the state seems as vast as the ocean itself. Road signs identify cities ahead that are farther away than crossing several states. Restaurant orders often exceed the size of the average helping in other parts of the country. The extended cab pick-up truck is at home in Texas. Texas is the largest truck sales market in the nation. Then there is Billy Bob's. We guess you know about it.

Texas is also "big" on guns, going far back in its history. Sixty percent of Texas homes have guns, 12 percent higher than the national average for the number firearms in residences (Wilson, 1993). Fifty percent of Texas homes contain more than one gun. It is not surprising that deaths from firearms in the state and assaults on the police also rank high.

Crime and Death in American Society

The current discussion about violence and firearms deaths has reached a crescendo. The rhetoric from new and strange allies pervades all of our media sources and political chambers of the nation. We have apparently concluded that "enough is enough" and the nation is poised for dramatic action. Today seems to be the time to begin chipping away at a national homicide rate which approaches 25,000 deaths annually. Approximately 15,000 of those deaths are by firearm, a percentage that has varied between 55% and 67% for nearly the last three decades (Maguire, Pastore, and Flanagan, 1992). About 19,000 people commit suicide each year using a firearm. Another 1,400 die unintentionally by firearm over the course of a year.

In Texas the shootings are as senseless as anywhere. Wielders of guns kill every day in the big cities of the state. Short tempers, mean spirits, and readily available guns, we suppose, are at the base of virtually all of these killings. Some Texans have pushed to allow all citizens to carry concealed weapons. Such a bill was narrowly defeated this past year and will probably be reintroduced in the legislature. Gun control legislation of one kind or another is up for discussion in nearly all states that have ineffective laws or no laws at all. Finally, the Brady Bill at last conquered the Congress. But with this belated backdrop of concern, do people <u>really</u> understand how "big" and lucrative the firearms business is in America? Do they know how easily and inexpensively they can attend a gun show and obtain one or more of a near infinite variety of firearms and other weapons which have the potential for mass destruction in the wrong hands?

The gun show is a "market of death" or a "market of fun" depending on your perspective. The first-time visitor to a gun show will be astounded at the tens of thousands of firearms available, at the low purchase prices for high caliber handguns and assault rifles, and the size and variety of the crowd which will pass through the turnstiles on any given weekend. The discussion which follows will attempt to present an accurate description of the gun show phenomenon.

The Gun in American Culture

We should not be surprised that America is infatuated with guns. They have served us well in so many respects. Without question, the gun has served as a means of protection for people, their homes, and their property throughout our history. Each year tens of thousands of felons are warded-off, arrested, and even killed by people who have firearms for protection. Unfortunately, many of those who own guns for protection have inadvertently become victims of these same weapons in the hands of family members or others who gain possession of them. This was a conclusion of a study of 388 homicides funded by the National Centers for

Disease Control (Wilson, 1993). Seventy-six percent of the victims studied were murdered by a friend or family member and not by home intruders or strangers carrying guns.

Guns have also been both a symbol and means of power. It isn't only the revolutionaries of the world who see power emanating from the barrel of a gun as Mao Tse-Tung was fond of saying (Schram, 1967). Criminals know that the gun can fix many of their perceived problems almost instantly, particularly the elimination of their competitors and those who double-cross them. Supported by the music genre of "gangsta" rap, children now see the gun as a major source of power in seemingly solving their problems with others who disrespect or offend them (Haley, 1993). Guns are also being used by juveniles to commit an increasing larger share of major crime. Juvenile arrests for murder, robbery, and assault increased 50% between 1988 and 1992 (U.S. Department of Justice, 1992).

Guns in the hands of our leading men and ladies in entertainment have been symbols of sexual prowess. Armed men and women in provocative poses have been standard fare in the entertainment media. The gun as a metaphor and symbol of sexual themes is prolific in Hollywood films. In the October issue of *Texas Monthly*, pictures included, an article by Anne Dingus (1993) discusses the decorative and deadly heroines of Hollywood's past and present western movies.

All were pictured with guns.

From the sophistication and rigor of Olympic competition to the simple enjoyment of family target shooting, millions of Americans own firearms for sport. Hundreds of organizations exist nationwide which promote the sporting side of firearms ownership. The National Rifle Association, Ducks Unlimited, and the National Varmint Hunters' Association are examples of these organizations. While it would be foolish to contend that some of the firearms belonging to the sportsmen and sportswomen of the nation don't result in a number of deaths each year, these gun owners are not the source of the nation's problem with firearms violence.

But perhaps as convincing as anything else in seeing the extent of our cultural ties to firearms is our language. It is "loaded" with such gun metaphors as "square shooter," "shot down," "shoots from the hip," "on target," "quick-draw," "loaded for bear," "gun shy," and "shot his wad." Guns are as American as apple pie.

DESIGN OF THE STUDY

Objectives

By means of the participant-observer method the authors intended to accomplish the following objectives in this study:
1. Describe the gun show phenomenon in North Central Texas.
2. Discuss the organization, administration, and operations of a gun show.
3. Identify the range of legal and illegal weapons available at a gun show.
4. Discuss the implications of the gun show in relation to the nation's struggle to prevent firearms deaths.

Method

The authors attended seven gun shows in the Dallas/Fort Worth metropolitan area beginning September 26, 1993 and ending on January 8, 1994. At each gun show the authors participated as interested shoppers, stopping at many of the several hundred tables at each show and talking with the vendors of all kinds of merchandise. On several occasions purchases were made. Other times the vendors were presented with opportunities to bend the rules and procedures of the show. The authors took field notes during their rounds at the show and expanded and edited their notes after they left the gun show sites.

Specifically, the following gun shows were attended and studied:

1. Dallas Market Hall Arena, Dallas, Texas, September 26, 1993
2. Dallas Convention Center, Dallas, Texas, October 31, 1993
3. Big Town Exhibition Hall, Mesquite, Texas, November 13, 1993
4. State Fairgrounds, Modern Living Building, Oklahoma City, Oklahoma, November 27, 1993
5. Big Town Exhibition Hall, Mesquite, Texas, December 4, 1993
6. Richardson Civic Center, Richardson, Texas, December 11, 1993
7. Dallas Convention Center, Dallas, Texas, January 8, 1994.

Our account of the gun show phenomenon which follows is a composite of our findings at each of the seven gun shows observed. No one show had all of the characteristics we describe in the paper, but all of the gun shows in the study had a large majority of them. Unique features of particular shows are identified.

PRELUDE TO A GUN SHOW

It's like anything else, most of us know little about what really is going on around us until we focus our attention on the specifics. As first author of this paper, I had been away from guns since being a police officer 25 years ago. I did my four-year stint in the Marines and grew up in a family that did lots of hunting and target shooting of one kind or another. By the time I was 14, I was weary of sport shooting, preferring to spend my recreational time playing basketball and running track. My father understood.

My most recent encounter with firearms issues was as the Executive Director of Ohio's peace officer standards and training commission from 1986-1992 where I assisted in drafting firearms legislation concerning the training of police officers and private security personnel. With access to elaborate indoor and outdoor firing ranges at the beautiful Ohio Peace Officer Training Academy, I never took the time to crank off even a single round.

I owned one firearm in the last 20 years, a palmable 22 caliber, five shot pistol which I believed would be useful in home protection. That was before Tech 9's and Mac 10's. What I am saying is that I, like many Americans, was outside of the firearms scene.

In the several weeks before attending the first gun show of my life I began to notice, naturally, the presence of guns and the gun culture much more often than I had before. The heated debate in Congress over the Crime Bill and the Brady Bill, the talk show barrage on violence issues, and President Bill Clinton's and Attorney General Janet Reno's focus on youth violence and the media's depiction of crime and death all began to help me "set my sights"(another gun metaphor) on the issues to be addressed in this paper. One day in the midst of all this backdrop to my first gun show visit, I saw a bumper sticker on the back of a Nissan which read, "Happiness is a warm machine gun." If that's bad, later I learned that you could buy a videotape entitled, "Rock and Roll Machine Gun, " featuring all of the popular assault weapons in action. The person driving this Nissan was a diminutive young woman with her child in a restraining seat. No sign was on the back window which read, "Child on Board." Whatever happened to those things I wondered and is the machine gun to become the latest fad?

I began to anticipate my first show both cautiously and enthusiastically. Questions surged in my mind. Who goes to these things? Would "gang-bangers" be there? Would it be safe with all of those guns, ammunition, and people in one place? How many cops would it take to provide security? What would be for sale and how cheap are the prices? Would I be able to get the information I need to write an interesting descriptive paper? To put it simply, what the authors found at gun shows was absolutely astounding! Now, the story of our findings.

ORGANIZATION AND ADMINISTRATION OF GUN SHOWS

The Gun Show Loophole

Somewhere near the end of the clamor over the Brady Bill in Congress, some of the media discovered the loopholes in the legislation that was supposed to require a background check and a cooling-off or waiting period before obtaining possession of the purchase. Private gun owners can sell their weapons legally to anybody, no questions asked, no waiting period, no background check, and no forms to fill out. This can be done through classified advertisements or much more efficiently for seller and buyer is to do business at a gun show. Bureau of Alcohol, Tobacco, and Firearms spokesman Jack Killorin says: "Easily millions of gun sales can be transacted at gun shows"(Big Loophole in Gun Control Law, 1993). No law prevents a private citizen from selling a gun(s) to a person who walks into a gun show. Frankly, there is no accurate means available to tally how many firearms are sold each year at gun shows. Licensed gun shops sold 7.5 million guns last year, but even that figure depends on the integrity of the dealer in making every sale "official." Strong incentives exist not to do so.

One more problem in relation to the gun show is the fact that no clear-cut definition exists which separates private sellers from licensed dealers, such as the number of guns sold or amount of earnings. At a gun show a private seller can buy a table for approximately $40, setting up right next to a licensed dealer, or merely walk around the show carrying a gun(s) with a "for sale" sign attached. The ATF's Jack Killorin says Texas and Florida are particularly worrisome states because of the frequency of the shows, lax laws, and ease of transit for out-of-state buyers. How did Congress miss the boat on regulation of private sales from classifieds or at gun shows? Or was their intense, but restrained, interest in regulating gun sales a calculated charade?

Structure and Layout

From your first visit to a gun show you will be able to see that they are moneymaking ventures, commerce in its purest form. Thousands of firearms, new and used, change hands at just one gun show. Any activity with that much commercial power is bound to have some organization and rules governing participation and attendance.

First of all, gun shows have to take place in large arenas with access to lots of parking because tens of thousands of people attend them on just one weekend in the Dallas/Fort Worth area and, we would suppose, in other parts of the nation also. Only one of the shows, the Dallas Convention Center, charged for parking. It is interesting that the only other event at the Dallas Convention Center the weekend of October 31, 1993, was the International Beauty Show and it also drew a big crowd. Cosmetics and firearms are both big business in Texas. The combination of these two events resulted in some unlikely companions as each group of attendees walked from the parking lots to the arena. Admission to the arena itself is usually $5.00 at a big show with more than 700 sellers' tables. One of the shows, at the Richardson Civic Center, charged only $4.00 admission, but probably had less than the 400 tables on display, a fact which the show had advertised on a brochure. The admission price, by the way, does not include the right to go in and out of the show. Too many people attend these events on a weekend to permit such liberal passage. The number of tables in a show was determined from advertising brochures and from a reasonably accurate count by the authors. The big weekend shows are likely to have 1,000 display tables or more, most of which are tables of gun sellers.

Since all of the shows occur at large arenas the amenities of crowds need to be attended to. Consequently, food services serving breakfasts and lunches are available at all shows and rest room facilities are, of course, open. All of the shows had tables and chairs available at the concessions and these places seemed to serve as the locus for various groups to sit and discuss firearms issues and other subjects.

Surprisingly, the menus contained a variety of foods beyond sandwiches and beverages. Most of the time a full meal was available for breakfast and lunch.

Once inside the show arenas, a person's itinerary is solely up to them so long as they shop or sell within the prescribed hours of the show, usually from 9:00 A.M. to 5:00 P.M. Some people systematically would cover each row of tables, one-by-one while others randomly selected displays with items they were particularly interested in. Still others sought out a particular dealer they were familiar with. We saw and spoke to numerous people who came to find a particular gun, accessory, or type of ammunition and they often went directly to the sellers who had those items first since there is always the chance that a good deal will be lost if they delay. The prices are very competitive and good deals abound resulting in some vendors selling out of their stock of many popular items.

Rules and Procedures

A number of rules have been established which govern the displays, the items for sale, the sellers, and the customers. Most of these rules were evident at all of the shows observed in this study, including the gun show in Oklahoma City. Sponsors of the shows included the North Texas Gun Club, the Dallas Gun Collectors, and the Oklahoma Gun and Knife Collectors' Association.

Displays. All of the rules which govern sellers' displays can be found on the advertising flyers/brochures which announce each show. The flyers announcing future shows are readily available at the entrance to any current one. Six or eight foot display tables can be purchased in advance of the show for $40-$45. You can get a discount of $5 if you apply early. Since all of the shows begin on Saturday and end on Sunday, all of the show managers require that set-up of displays be completed on Fridays from 3 - 9 P.M. In that some of the vendors are bringing in literally tons of firearms for sale, it would be virtually impossible to do the unloading and set-up on the day of the show. It is also important that parking be near the arena since unloading and setting-up the displays is indeed hard work. Some vendors need electricity for the show in order to show videotapes of their wares in action or to operate other equipment. Once the displays are set-up they are protected by 24-hour security services. Finally, typical of a statement the vendors are required to sign reads as follows:

If it is judged that I have misrepresented the category of items on my table, I hereby agree to forfeit my tables to the sponsor. I also agree to abide by the show rules. I understand that I am responsible for all of the tables in my name and I do not hold the sponsor responsible for my property.

Items for Sale. Gun show rules insure that customers will come to a show and find that firearms and related accessories are indeed the majority of items for sale. Advertising brochures state that "all tables must contain 100% guns, knives, or gun related items." Specific restrictions prohibit martial arts items such as throwing stars and flea market wares which obviously leaves the door open to exclude a variety of things if so desired. All of the shows we attended included displays of militaria, old military weapons, uniforms, tools, vehicles, medals, and flags. A Nazi flag can be found if you look. The shows at the Dallas Convention Center do not permit the sale of ammunition as a result of a city ordinance, but other shows permitted ammo in the arena as long as it was sealed. "Sealed" could be as simple as being in a box. As discussed below, we will see that very loose interpretations were made as to what sale items were permitted at gun shows.

Those who reserve and pay for a display table(s) in advance are required to quantify the percentage of merchandise they will have at the show according to several categories: guns; gun parts; sporting supplies; hunting equipment; ammo; knives; Civil War items; Indian artifacts; old Western items; other(please describe).

Customers. Customers also had certain restrictions placed on them. They were not allowed to go in and out of the show for one admission price. They were permitted to bring firearms to the show for sale, but they had to be checked at the door by security personnel, usually off-duty police officers in uniform, and the guns had to be tied, meaning a plastic ribbon was attached in such a way that the gun could not be fired. Children under 12 years of age were admitted free and all of the shows had substantial amounts of male children present accompanied by their parents or other adults. Customers were free to go up to vendors and offer their firearms for sale or for trade. Additional rules restricted the carrying of cameras into the arena. Finally, customers and vendors alike are warned that all laws must be observed which undoubtedly covers a multitude of sins.

SELLERS AND THEIR WARES

Firearms and Vendors

Unless you have been to a gun show, you cannot begin to imagine the volume and variety of firearms available for sale. Literally, a gun is on display to match every conceivable motive of a shopper whether he is the competitive shooter (trap shooter, skeet shooter, varmint shooter, or tin-can shooter), the collector of old police weapons, war weapons, limited-issue weapons, hunters of virtually anything that moves, and street thugs who are interested in expanding their arsenals.

From conversations with dealers and frequent customers and from an actual estimate based on counting tables we believe that at least 100,000 guns were on hand at the large shows held at the Dallas Convention Center and the Dallas Market Hall Arena. That estimate does not include, by the way, the number of firearms brought to the shows by shoppers who are wanting to sell or trade, a legitimate activity at the shows. Some vendors had as many as 300 pistols displayed on just two tables. Rifles and shotguns were often available from the same vendors. Beneath the display tables were often hundreds of additional weapons secured in boxes or metal cases. As firearms were sold off of the tables, the display was replenished from the cache under the tables or from trucks and trailers parked outside the arena.

It would be impossible to enumerate the near infinite variety of firearms available at the gun shows in this study. Books such as the *Shooter's Bible* and *Gun Digest* are good sources to see the entire list. If it exists, more than likely it was available for sale at a gun show. In general, however, the weapons should fall into the categories you would imagine: rifles, pistols, and shotguns. But it isn't that simple. There are hunting rifles and assault rifles, pistols which fire shotgun shells and high caliber cartridges, sophisticated rifles and pistols for competitive shooting, and hunting weapons designed for very specific purposes such as firing from bench rests, tripods, boats, and other vehicles, or for killing a particular animal or bird. We even saw crank-operated automatic weapons which are legal as a result of a clever design. We also saw machine guns.

To the untrained eye, the first experience at looking at gun show displays is a visual blur. There is simply too much to see. After getting a show or two under your belt, however, you begin to get a feel for the types of vendors and their specialties, the categories of weapons which are sold, and the hot items in the market place to include the firearms whose prices are rising rapidly largely as a result of the specter of the U.S. Congress banning additional weapons. Some of these weapons, many of them imports, are going as fast as the vendors can put them up on the display tables.

We began to think of dealers according to several categories. First, there are the "conventionals" who most often operate real gun shops outside of their homes and have a federal firearms license to do so. Their motive is essentially to make a living. They are extremely knowledgeable concerning their wares and are often armorers. They sell rifles, shotguns, and handguns of the reputable manufacturers such as Remington, Winchester, Browning, Mossberg, Colt, Smith and Wesson, and Glock. None of their items are cheap, but you will also be able to find them next week if something goes wrong with your purchase.

A second type of dealer we called the "specialist." They dealt only in a particular kind of weapon or sport. Some sold hunting rifles and shotguns, for example. Some specialized in assault rifles and survivalist gear, a type that was not present in large numbers at the shows, contrary to what you might think. The volume of sales for the "specialist" was smaller than several of the other type vendors, but many of their items were expensive and appealed only to the select shopper.

"Collectors" were another category of vendor. They bought and sold antique weapons of one type or another. Their interests were black powder guns, war weapons, old West guns, women's guns, or other specialty firearms.

We also saw many of what we referred to as "citizens." These people were similar to the flea market sellers who make a few extra dollars on the weekends. They rented a table or two and displayed an often scanty and disorganized array of used weapons, no doubt acquired cheaply at previous shows.

The last group in our taxonomy of sellers we called "wheeler-dealers." They sold anything that was "hot." They were not interested in much conversation about their wares and one we met was downright discourteous when asked for information about firearms for sale. They were interested in moving stock and in most cases they were doing precisely that.

"Wheeler-dealers" were selling lots of assault rifles. The most popular ones are the Chinese Norinco AK-47, the Chinese Norinco SKS, and various versions of the M-14 and the M-16. Any semi-automatic rifle, however, with a magazine capacity of more than 10 rounds is selling rapidly. The Chinese SKS rifle (7.62 mm) can be purchased as inexpensively as $60 used and for $120 new. The Chinese AK-47 rifle (7.62 mm) can be bought for as little as $150 new. Both of these assault rifles come in either a standard issue length or in a paratrooper's shorter version. The weapons were standard issue to the soldiers of the People's Republic of China and were often encountered by American troops during the Vietnam War.

Similarly, the "wheeler-dealers" had attractive prices on high caliber pistols and they were selling big as personal protection weapons. These pistols were the Chinese Norinco, 7.62 mm or 9 mm; the MAC 11, 9 mm; the Tech 9, 9mm, and the Tech 22, 22 caliber. The Norinco 9 mm can be purchased for less than $100 and is comparable in many ways to the Colt and Glock weapons costing four to five times as much.

Various dealers also sold what might be termed "fad weapons," the cool thing to own at the present. All of these weapons, new or used, are expensive, often costing more than $300. Business remains brisk for "fad guns" such as: the Glock 9 mm; the Colt 45 M1911A1; the Beretta M-9; the Taurus PT-99; and the Browning Hi Power.

Finally, the "wheeler dealers" and the "citizens" were not against making a profit from "Saturday night specials." From $25 to $60 these 25 or 22 caliber pistols were being bought up as personal protection items. The popular models were: Raven; Davis; Llama, Star, Rossi; Harrington and Richardson; and Iver Johnson. One of the "wheeler-dealers" actually had a grab box crammed full of pistols that a customer could sort through and have his choice for $25 or three for $60.

Firearms and Other Accessories for Sale

Published restrictions of the gun show sponsors notwithstanding, a myriad of other items are for sale at gun shows. Some are related to firearms, such as holsters and storage cases, some are not, such as blow guns and beef jerky. All of the shows we attended had large knife displays, many of the knives were hand crafted by the exhibitors themselves and were quite attractive and ornate.

** Technical assistance for the section of the paper describing specific firearms was provided by Nicholas Valcik. The authors are indeed grateful.

Table 1 below contains a short list of other items for sale at the gun shows in this study.

ITEMS

Blow guns of various sizes
Holsters, carrying cases, and gun safes
Magazines and clips
Stocks, barrels and pistol grips
Pistol purses for women
Ammunition of every variety
Hunting and military clothing
Pistol and rifle style crossbows
Firearms manuals
Intricate firearms parts
Bayonets and other military tools
Hairbrushes which double as knives
Hair dryers shaped as pistols
Guitar cases for carrying assault rifles and machine guns
T-shirts, sweat shirts, propaganda books and bumper stickers
German SS and Luftwaffe music tapes
Nazi flags and portraits of General Rommel
Mace and stun guns
Jeeps and other military vehicles
Reloading equipment
BB gun pistols and rifles
Toy models of real weapons such as the Uzi or Thompson submachine gun

Table 1 MERCHANDISE FOR SALE AT GUN SHOWS

In short, if the vendor cleared the initial screening via his application for a table(s), he could sell just about anything he wanted to, although the restrictions against martial arts items were generally upheld. If items had anything to do with hunting, sport shooting, personal protection, or propaganda related to same, they could be sold.

Illegal and Quasi-Legal Sales

A number of items for sale at the shows were illegal to possess under the Texas Penal Code and were specifically supposed to be restricted according to the sponsors. These items were available at all of the shows except the one in Oklahoma City. Switch blade knives, butterfly knives, brass knuckles, and martial arts throwing stars were available at a couple of the shows although not conspicuous. One large knife we saw had a 12" blade and a "brass knuckles" handle giving the wielder, we suppose, the option of either stabbing his opponent or breaking his jaw. We were told that the sale of such items at the shows was ignored since they passed as collectibles and not the weapons they really are.

Novel Accommodations to the Federal Firearms Laws

The fact that the federal firearms laws are loaded with loopholes will probably be no surprise to most people. The Federal Firearms Act of 1934 forbids the purchase of an automatic weapon such as a machine gun without a special license reserved for collectors. Weapons experts will tell you there are several ways to circumvent this law if you want a weapon which fires automatically. Apparently there are a number of ways to modify the sear of a firearm and cause it to fire automatically. One inexpensive and legal adaptation, however, is the Hellfire Switch available for the low price of $24.95.

While carrying out our participant observer roles at the Dallas Market Hall Arena, we noticed a video playing at one of the display tables depicting a man firing what appeared to be a machine gun or other automatic weapon. It turns out that he was demonstrating the Hellfire Switch. This device can be installed on the trigger guard of a semi-automatic rifle, assault type or other model, and it converts the weapon to fully automatic, meaning that once you pull the trigger to the rear and hold it there, the weapon will keep firing until it runs out of ammunition. This weapon, of course, is now the equivalent of a machine gun.

How can guns be legally converted to fully automatic weapons by the Hellfire Switch? It is simple and you receive a card that explains the legality of the conversion when you purchase a Hellfire Switch. Federal law requires that a semi-automatic weapon fire only once for each time you pull the trigger. The Hellfire Switch makes your trigger finger vibrate back and forth several hundred times a minute from the weapon's recoil as the rifle fires at precisely the speed of your vibrating finger. Since your finger is "pulling the trigger," (although the trigger is really pulling your finger) the conversion to fully automatic is legal and extremely deadly.

Another interesting circumvention of the law has to do with the length of the barrel of a shotgun. The National Firearms Act of 1934 prevents the ownership of a shotgun with a barrel shorter than 18 inches. Obviously a short barreled shot-gun would be handy in the commission of a robbery or in conducting gang activity. But why worry about being caught with a "sawed-off shotgun" when you can buy a perfectly legal pistol which fires both shotgun ammunition and powerful pistol loads. The rifling in the barrel makes this weapon legal, unlike the shotgun which has a smooth bore.

The gun shows even provide you with a choice of a pistol which fires one shotgun shell or the "grand daddy" of them all which fires five shotgun shells from a rotating cylinder. This unusual and deadly "pocket cannon" is the Thunder 5 .410/.45 Revolver(1993) manufactured by MIL, Inc., Piney Flats, Tennessee. The price of a new Thunder 5 is $599.00.

Another example of getting around the intent of the law has to do with the restriction on selling a bayonet. Apparently it is illegal to sell a bayonet attached to a military rifle. If the bayonet is sold, however, as a "tent stake" and is not attached to the rifle, it is legal. One of the authors purchased a new Chinese SKS assault rifle for $79.00 along with a $9.95 "tent stake" bought separately from the same vendor.

Other Rule-Bending and Breaking

While it was not the intent of our study to discredit show sponsors or vendors as to how closely they adhered, or not, to the rules of governance at the shows or state and federal laws, we did have the opportunity to see that both the rules and the laws were occasionally ignored. One 18 year old University of Texas at Dallas student who we knew as a member of our college pistol team purchased 500 rounds of 22 LR ammunition from a vendor at the gun show in Mesquite on November 13, 1993. Texas law requires that you be 21 years of age to purchase ammunition. She was not asked for identification. Neither was another member of the pistol team who purchased 1,000 bullets, 200 grain SWC, for reloading. While this student is 22 years old, he looks much younger than 21 and was not asked for identification as required by Texas law.

On September 26, 1993, at the Dallas Market Hall arena one of the authors of this paper was shown by a vendor how to load a high caliber pistol using live ammunition when no ammunition or loaded guns were permitted according to the rules of the show. This same vendor told her that three young men had pulled loaded guns from their belts earlier that same day and attempted to sell them to the vendor. We surmise that a number of vendors would also bend the rules in the interest of promoting a sale.

Propaganda and Paraphernalia

Gun shows have a political soul and as you might imagine it is staunch conservative and clearly protectionist in terms of Second Amendment rights. Aside from our conversations with vendors and customers, nothing could possibly give a more accurate depiction of this conservatism than the slogans found on shirts and bumper stickers for sale at the gun shows. A sample of the ideology can be found in Table 2 below:

SLOGANS

"Buy a gun and piss off the Clintons"
"China has gun control"
"Clinton sucks and Gore swallows"
"An armed society is a polite society"
"Politicians love unarmed peasants"
"Is your church ATF approved?"
"Ted Kennedy's car has killed more people than my gun"
"For personal 24 hour protection - Dial 9 mm"
"I'll give you my gun when Hell freezes over"
"Take a bite out of crime. Shoot the bastard!"
"When the going gets tough, I get a machine gun"
"Happiness is a warm machine gun"

Table 2 Propaganda Shirts, Bumper Stickers, and Posters on Sale at Gun Shows

The shows at the Dallas Convention Center and at the Dallas Market Hall Arena also had dealers which sold books along with the shirts and bumper stickers. Revenge was clearly the theme of several titles available: Up Yours, Get Even, and Screw the Bitch (the bitch being an ex-wife). We might add that the tactics prescribed often involved violence with details on how to effect it. One of the standards of this genre was also present, William Powell's Anarchist's Cookbook. These titles certainly ran counter to the Ken Harris knife display whose sign read "Jesus is Lord."

The end of the Cold War has also had an impact on the gun show. Apparently a large surplus of Russian and Soviet militaria is available. One vendor we spoke to at the Dallas Market Hall arena sold Soviet military medals, hats, and books describing elite units of the Soviet and Russian armies. For $100, a person could buy a barrette worn by an elite Russian fighting force which selects its recruits from only orphans, according to the vendor who spoke with a Russian accent, in order that they would be willing to kill on command with no loyalties to anybody except the state. For an additional $10 you could by the book that told the story of the unique barrette and those who wore it.

We also found the North Texas Arms Rights Coalition (its motto being "Protecting your right to bear arms") soliciting signatures on petitions at two of the shows demanding guarantees from Congress and the state legislature that the right to own firearms will not be curtailed. At the Oklahoma City gun show, signatures were being solicited on petitions to limit the terms of service of members of Congress. In short, politically conservative bent is evident at gun shows in the Dallas/Fort Worth area and in Oklahoma City.

THE PARTICIPANTS

Customers

All things considered, the gun show is a very civil proceeding. Generally, people come to the show looking for a good deal on guns or other items or to sell or trade a firearm. It is the best possible place to see the variety and volume of firearms in existence. You would have to travel hundreds of miles and visit dozens of gun shops to see anything approaching the variety of firearms available at gun shows. Likewise, you would have to run hundreds of classifieds to reach anything near the number of potential buyers for a weapon who come to a gun show. We found that people attending the shows go about their business in an orderly fashion, spending two hours or more at each show, and leaving the show with some type of purchase. We should note that you need to watch your bridgework and your posterior as you walk around the show because lots of people will be carrying rifles and shotguns they have just purchased or are trying to sell and occasionally they are not particularly careful about where they point the barrels.

Our methodology would not allow for an accurate taxonomy of gun show attendees. We should also point out that we were warned to be unobtrusive in our study since it is not unheard of that protesters and others seeming to have anti-gun philosophies have been asked, on occasion, to leave the arenas. We did no surveying or extended interviews with participants. Consequently, our notetaking was done as inconspicuously as possible. We did find the attendees at gun shows, however, to be an interesting mix of people, philosophies, and motives. Below we comment on some of the more perceptible types who go to gun shows.

The variety of people attending shows ranges from what might be termed "rednecks" wearing spurs and shoulder holsters with a matching belt that reads "Billy" to middle-aged couples in formal attire who just came from Sunday church services. One apparent group at all of the shows are the hunters, often dressed as if they just came out of the fields or off of the mountain. The show in Oklahoma City had a majority of attendees in this category.

The survivalist types were also present at all of the shows but not in large numbers. They were dressed in camouflaged uniforms adorned with all of the paraphernalia that would be permissible inside the arena. One conversation we overheard in Mesquite at a vendor's table, immediately after the passage of the Brady Bill, dealt with this theme: "It's all over now," the bearded vendor in bib overalls said, "Communism is here and you better buy them while you can." This vendor was selling custom made guitar and banjo cases to fit your machine guns and assault rifles. He was selling a 22 caliber semi-automatic rifle for $600 that was a replica of a Thompson submachine gun, banjo case included.

Women represented only about 10-15% of all attendees. At several of the shows the women of Harley Davidson were present with their male counterparts, appropriately adorned. Any woman who expressed even the slightest interest in an item for sale was readily attended to by the vendors, primarily out of courtesy often afforded women, we suspect, however, the attention paid the female seemed excessive at times. A small number of the vendors brought wives or women friends and they could be seen often stirring around the arenas.

The vast majority of these attendees looked like the same crowd you would see in a busy shopping mall, mostly middle class in their appearance and generally polite and friendly to all who encountered them. Only a small number of African-Americans or Hispanics attended the shows. Most of the attendees, no doubt, had the money or credit to purchase firearms. Finally, it was also noticeable that fathers often brought their sons to the gun shows.

Officials and Security

The tightest security we saw in the shows we studied was at the Dallas Convention Center. Security officers, many of which were off-duty Dallas police officers, conducted interrogations at the door relative to what you had on your person and did pat down searches for weapons that might be concealed. They also looked in some of the women's purses, a procedure we saw at no other show. If you were bringing a weapon to sell at the show, you were sent to a table where another police officer in uniform checked to see that the weapon was unloaded and then a tie was place on the gun which rendered it safe and inoperable. We imagine that sworn peace officers are used at the security tables in the event that some attendee wanted to be uncooperative.

It is important to point out, however, that at all of the other shows it was the honor system in effect. If you had weapons, you voluntarily went to the security table to have them checked out. You could walk right past the security table and not be stopped. No metal detectors were used at any of the shows. During the many hours we spent in attendance at gun shows, there seemed to be no problems resulting from the lax security measures.

Inside the arenas we seldom saw uniformed police or security officers on patrol. We also noticed that not all of the entrances would have the same degree of security. At one show, we even saw doors with no security other than the person selling the ticket for admission.

Keeping in mind that some of the vendors displayed hundreds of firearms, how is it possible to keep them from being stolen with so many people looking at the weapons and passing by? The tables loaded with weapons were watched closely by the vendors, but many of them also had an electronic security wire with alarm attached through the trigger housing of each firearm, similar to the alarm systems used to prevent clothing from being shoplifted. Those who sold the cheap pistols didn't bother. One striking contrast to the use of this electronic security system, however, was the show in Oklahoma City. No vendors used an alarm system, but displayed just as many firearms as the Texas shows did. We believe that kindness and trust are such a part of the Oklahoma way of life that an electronic security system would be an insult to the Oklahoma residents. The Oklahoma City show was also the only one which permitted customers to go in and out of the show after having their hands stamped. This state has a small population and the business people in Oklahoma know they have to make things as convenient as possible for their clients and customers in order to make a profit. They will even carry items to your vehicle for you.

DISCUSSION

Firearms Purchases at Gun Shows

The "jackpot" for purchasing firearms in the United States is the gun show. If 7.5 million guns are sold through licensed gun shops each year (Big Loophole in Gun Control Law. 1993), millions more are available through gun show sales to and by private citizens. While politically correct legislators clamor over laws to keep handguns out of the minds and hands of children, debate the appropriate waiting period for a gun purchase, and try to identify what is an assault weapon, millions of firearms continue to be traded at gun shows throughout the nation. The United States records approximately 15,000 handgun deaths each year and firearms accidents claim an additional 1,400 lives (Accidental Deaths Decrease, 1993). Thousands more are wounded and maimed for life as a result of firearms. If legislation is needed to control gun shows, what precisely would it be beyond the laws which govern the sale and purchase of firearms in other venues. Would new legislation translate directly into lives saved? California has a 15 day waiting period for purchase while background checks are conducted and it applies to purchases at gun shows also. Such legislation does not seem to have had much impact on homicide and firearms assault statistics in that state.

At the gun shows in this study we saw thousands of people enjoying themselves in a civil manner while they shopped for firearms and accessories needed for various gun sports and for home protection. To these people the gun show was a "market of fun." Nevertheless, should that much firepower be so readily available to the American public? To others, the gun show is a "market of death." A case against the gun show can certainly be made when you consider that David Koresh's Branch Davidians cult built up its arsenal from gun show purchases. Still what infringements should be placed on law abiding citizens and their commerce in order to restrict sales to the relatively small number who will use the firearms they purchase unlawfully or carelessly? The answers to such questions are not easy and legislation probably needs to be levied on the side of moderation in order that the firearms business is not driven underground and that the prices of guns soar, making firearms themselves the object of deadly assaults as is the case with illegal narcotics.

The Legislative Solution

Fever-pitch efforts concerning gun control legislation in legislatures at all levels of government lean toward passing laws which have both symbolic and real value. Some want to ban certain categories of weapons, disqualify a number of potential buyers, and restrict others from possession. Others want to tax guns and ammunition out of existence for all intents and purposes. Any new legislative action will add to the 20,000 gun laws and ordinances already in effect in the United States. Much of the tragedy of homicide in the nation has to do with guns in the hands of children at school. Unfortunately, we already have the federal Gun Free School Zones Act of 1990 which barred the possession of guns in or near a school. We would suspect that state laws would have outlawed this same behavior long before passage of the federal legislation. The violence continues, however.

Colorado, Florida, and Utah held special sessions of their legislatures in 1993 to outlaw the possession and ownership of handguns for anyone under age 18. Exceptions to the legislation are for hunting, target practice, and shooting competition. Again, we would suspect that all of the states had laws which forbade young people and children from carrying firearms in inappropriate places. By the close of 1993, eighteen states had laws which specifically outlawed gun possession by juveniles (Toch, 1993).

A softer approach to denying guns to youth has been tried in several parts of the nation. In Dallas, youths who turn in guns of any kind (no questions asked) will be given two pre-season football tickets for a Dallas Cowboys football game. The advertising theme has been "Real cowboys don't need guns." What the police department got for their efforts was a meager response and several dozen inoperable weapons along with a few firearms that actually had some value. Apparently some law abiding citizens, who are also football fans, cleaned out their drawers and trunks and recognized a good deal when they saw it.

For more than 200 years the firearm has been a staple in American society. We are not the only people fascinated with guns. Check the local movie guide if you have any doubts about it being real fascination to us. A case in point. A new chain of upscale, indoor firearms ranges have opened in Los Angeles and one category of frequent customers is the Japanese tourist who comes in for a quick training course and some target shooting. Many Japanese say, however, after firing a gun they never want to do it again. It is even more amazing that Japanese visitors to the United States would choose such recreation after the furor in Japan over the tragic death of Yoshi Hattori in Baton Rouge in 1992 (Golen, 1993). With so many guns in circulation, so much violence, so many laws, and so much heated controversy about what to do, our nation seems in a quandary as to the next logical steps. Legislation such as the Brady Bill is one response although no one seriously believes it will substantially reduce the firearms violence in the United States. One of the skeptics is Professor James Q. Wilson who has stated:

> The Brady Bill, which I support, may affect the probability that one or two lunatics will get guns and go off on a killing spree, but the chances that the Brady Bill or any feasible gun control measure will really take guns out of the hands of criminals, I think, is quite farfetched (Baker, 1993).

We have done the equivalent of "leaving the barn door open" for more than two centuries concerning firearms regulation and now we are trying to locate and round-up the horses. If effective gun control were even possible, what other costs would it now realize in our society which has become so accustomed to the idea of an armed citizenry? Perhaps there is credence to the position that guns don't kill, people do. Severe and unmitigated penalties for unauthorized gun possession and firearms violence (something we have not really tried) is at least, on paper, a manageable public policy, unlike the thought of trying to regulate the ownership of more than 200 million firearms, the actual figure we should become more aware of as the new "death clock" in New York City's Times Square now records the number of guns added to the nation's arsenal each day.

Peacemaking

The popular musical West Side Story portrays gang rivalry and violence in New York City in the 1950s. While artistic renditions of gang violence are depicted in the movie, no guns appear in the hands of the youth. Today youth gangs thrive on firearms violence and some music, such as Cop Killer, even seems to advocate it. What kind of society have we created for ourselves which allows so many young people to acquire values and form attitudes which legitimate killing another person, for example, for calling them a name or frowning at them? What regulation we implement for controlling the ownership of firearms or their sale at gun shows or any other location would seem to have little import until we face up to some more fundamental issues.

When families, schools, churches, and the vast entertainment industry with all its influence come together and re-establish the sanctity of human life and respect for one's fellow man, we are likely to begin seeing significant reductions in violence in American society. Like contending with other social ills, we may have to live through a couple or more bad patches before things improve. "Make peace, not war," to parody a familiar saying, is probably the answer. In a fractured and factionalized society we have not worked hard at making peace. When we have pushed and "marketed" peace (made a profit out of it), guns and their sale will have little significance in our society.

SUMMARY AND CONCLUSIONS

The gun show is a popular, convenient, and prevalent means of purchasing, selling, and trading firearms for millions of Americans. Texas is one of several states which hosts many gun shows annually. Dozens of gun shows are held in the Dallas/Fort Worth area during the year.

With the highest rates of homicide and firearms violence in the world, the gun remains an important part of American culture. Guns can provide us with power, status, protection, entertainment, sport, symbols of sexual prowess, and a host of popular metaphors replete in our language.

The gun shows described in this study were well organized and operated according to a minimum set of rules which provide for orderly and predictable displays, necessary security, and the accommodation of large crowds of shoppers and vendors. Along with firearms and their accessories, shooting and hunting supplies, militaria, gun collectibles, and propaganda literature are sold at gun shows.

Vendors at the gun shows in this study seemed to fall into several categories: Conventionals; specialists; collectors; citizens; and wheeler-dealers. Those who attend gun shows have specific motives or business to conduct and seem to enjoy the experience. Large crowds of a variety of people pay admission and spend several hours at a gun show. To them the gun show is a "market of fun."

Occasionally, security is lax at gun shows and rules concerning the sale of firearms and ammunition are either bent or broken. Weapons were on sale at the shows in this study which were specifically designed to get around federal and state laws and still perform functions of outlawed weapons. Pistols which fired shotgun shells and knives with brass knuckle handles are examples of such weapons.

Notwithstanding the bonanza of firearms available at gun shows and more than 20,000 gun laws on the books already in the United States, it seems unlikely that more legislation will help to curb firearms violence. Restoring the sanctity of human life and the proliferation of a mutual respect for one's fellow man seems more promising in reducing violence than the control of gun manufacturing, sales, ownership, and possession. As always, families, schools, and churches will need to carry the lion's share of the burden if any improvement is to be realized.

REFERENCES

"Accidental Deaths Decrease." (1993) The Dallas Morning News, September 29.

"America's Vigilante Values." (1992) The Economist. June 20.

Baker, J. (1993) "Gun Control?" The Dallas Morning News, October 3.

"Big Loophole in Gun Control Law." (1993) Prodigy Interactive Personal Service. AP, December 19.

Dingus, A. (1993) "Tex Shooters." Texas Monthly, October.

Golen, J. (1993) "Gun Control Groups Say Slain Japan Student Is But a Statistic." The Dallas Morning News, October 17.

Haley, K. (1993) "Ice-T, No Sugar: Law Enforcement and Political Reactions to the Gangster Rap 'Cop Killer.'" A paper presented at the 1993 Annual Meeting of the Academy of Criminal Justice Sciences, March 15-21, Kansas City.

Kates, D., Jr. and P. Harris. (1991) "How to Make Their Day." National Review, October 21.

Maguire K., A. Pastore, and T. Flanagan. (1992) Sourcebook of Criminal Justice Statistics. Washington, D.C.: U. S. Government Printing Office.

Metcalf, D. (1993) "...And a Cartridge in A Pear Tree." Harper's Magazine. January.

Persinos, J. (1g89) "On Gun Control, Both Sides Win Some, Lose Some." Governing, September.

Marich, J., M. Rand, and J. Robinson. (1990) "Right to Bear Corpses." The New Republic, April 9.

Schram, S. ed. (1967) Quotations from Chairman Mao Tse-Tung. New York: Bantam Books.

"The Battle Over Gun Control: The Black Community Has the Greatest Stake in the Outcome of the Debate." (1993) Black Enterprise, July.

"Thunder Five .410/.45 Revolver." (1993) American Rifleman, October.

Toch, T. (1993) "Violence in Schools." U.S. News and World Report, November 8.

Underwood, N. (1990) "Up in Arms: Proposed Gun Laws Face Massive Opposition." Maclean's, December 10.

U.S. Department of Justice, Federal Bureau of Investigation. (1992) FBI Uniform Crime Reports. Washington, D.C.

Wilson, Laurie. (1993) "Keeping Guns in House Raises Risk of Homicide." The Dallas Morning News, October

ICE-T, NO SUGAR:
LAW ENFORCEMENT AND POLITICAL REACTIONS TO THE GANGSTER RAP "COP KILLER"

by Keith N. Haley, Professor of Criminal Justice
Collin County Community College, Plano, Texas

INTRODUCTION

I got my black shirt on/I got my black gloves on/I got my ski mask on/This shit's been too long/I got my 12 gauge sawed off/I got my headlights turned off/I'm 'bout to bust some shots off/I'm 'bout to dust some cops off (automatic weapons fire....)

Chorus: I'm a Cop Killer/It's better you than me/Cop Killer/Fuck police brutality/Cop Killer/I know your family's grievin'/Fuck 'em/Cop Killer/But tonight we get even/Ha Ha I got my brain on hype/tonigt'll be your night/I got this long-assed knife/And your neck looks just right/My adrenaline's pumpin'/I got my stereo bumpin'/I'm out to kill me somethin'/A pig stopped me for nothin'

(Automatic weapons fire....)
Die, Die, Die Pig, Die!
Chorus....
Fuck the police/Fuck the police/Fuck the police/Fuck the police/Fuck the police/Fuck the police/Fuck the police/ Fuck the police
Chorus....
Break it down/Fuck the police/yeah
Fuck the police/For Daryl Gates
Fuck the police/For Rodney King
Fuck the police/For my dead homies
Fuck the police/For your freedom
Fuck the police/Don't be a pussy
Fuck the police/Have some motherfuckin' courage
Sing along/Cop Killer/Cop Killer/Cop Killer/Cop Killer/
Cop Killer/Wha' do you want to be when you grow up/
Cop Killer/Good choice/Cop Killer/I'm a motherfuckin' Cop
Killer/oocha

So go the lyrics of the song "Cop Killer" which have triggered comments and reactions from the stately, the lowly, the powerful, and the pristine. So what's all of the controversy about? Rapper Ice-T and his supporters say he is simply portraying a fictional character who is voicing frustration and anger with police brutality. Most of America's law enforcement officers and a lot of other people think differently. Then there are some who aren't sure what to make of the song.

Since March of 1992, when the "Body Count" album which contains the controversial number was released, approximately 100,000 copies of the album have been sold each month until Time Warner withdrew "Cop Killer" from the album in July at the request of Ice-T himself. His justification for the decision was that threats had been directed toward Time Warner and its executives. In the meantime, fiery discussions and commentary as well as protests continued over the song "Cop Killer" well into 1993. The year long battle over the legitimacy and interpretation of "Cop Killer" is a story of big money, corporate irresponsibility, national values, political power, free speech, and racial disharmony.

The battle lines concerning the controversial song were drawn early after its release. Most of the nation's police officers and their leadership were outraged by the lyrics of the song and the irresponsibility of Time Warner for making and distributing the "Body Count" album. They called for the withdrawal of the recording. Other demands, including an apology from Time Warner to the law enforcement community, were also made. The nature, volume, and diversity of responses to "Cop Killer" may indeed be unique in the history of the recording industry.

The ability of the police to mobilize and act successfully on their rage concerning "Cop Killer," which many perceived to be a "call to arms" or an "open season" on cops, is itself worthy of study. Other questions are raised by the event. What forces were the police able to bring to bear on Time Warner? What social responsibility do music producers have in selecting artists' work? What issues are raised in the publication of songs such as "Cop Killer" and those of related genre such as "gangster rap" which contain malicious, sexist, inflammatory, and vile material? What effects do such vicious lyrics have on their subjects, whether it be police officers or others? Finally, will the police now be a filter through which all new controversial material concerning them will have to pass? Will there be a "police correctness?"

OBJECTIVES OF THE PAPER

The paper will examine the law enforcement and political reactions to rap singer Ice-T's song "Cop Killer" while focusing on the following objectives:

1. Discuss the controversial lyrics of "Cop Killer."
2. Examine the issues related to the lyrics of gangster rap and related genre.
3. Analyze the leadership and power exerted by the law enforcement community in Texas and the nation in influencing Time Warner to drop "Cop Killer" from future editions of the "Body Count" album.
4. Describe the feelings of law enforcement officers concerning "Cop Killer," Ice-T, and Time Warner.

METHODOLOGY

Popular, social science, and select law enforcement journals and employee association literature were reviewed in order to ascertain the political and law enforcement reactions to Ice-T's "Cop Killer" throughout the nation. The lyrics of the controversial song were analyzed to determine their meaning within the gangster rap genre and to identify the particular words and phrases most offensive to police officers.

Texas law enforcement officers who were instrumental in effecting the "Cop Killer" protest and proposed boycott were interviewed. Moreover, two questions were posted on a national electronic bulletin board, one of which investigated the willingness of police officers nationwide to participate in the proposed boycott against the Time Warner enterprises and products. The second question asked officers to describe their feelings when they first became aware of the lyrics to "Cop Killer."

"COP KILLER" LYRICS AND INTERPRETATIONS

It is only once in a great while that an artist's work is able to simultaneously attract attention from virtually every quarter of the nation. Ice-T, whose real name is Tracy Marrow, managed to accomplish precisely that. "Cop Killer" was a blockbuster which riveted out an indictment and deadly assault on America's police to the background of zinging heavy metal music and simulated automatic weapons fire.

The police should indeed be troubled if the lyrics found on page one of this paper are to be taken at face value and that itself became a central question in the "Cop Killer" episode. If a reader or listener takes the lyrics of the song literally, and tens of thousands have done so, s/he is listening in on a well conceived ambush of police officers. The assailants dress the part with black shirts, gloves, and ski masks and are armed with a 12 gauge shotgun and big knife.

They intend to kill cops tonight because they are fed up with police brutality. Their redress is immediate and fatal for the police. You hear the shots. In the chorus the killer then proclaims his success, his anger over police brutality, and his glee over the fact that the police officer's family is grieving. We know because he laughs.

Later the listener hears how pumped-up the assailant is. His brain is cranked and his stereo is blasting. He needs to kill something in apparent response to being illegitimately stopped by a police officer, a "pig." One more cop dies as you hear the gunfire.

A string of "Fuck the police" ensues. Then the same phrase precedes several specific instigations for murdering police officers: " Daryl Gates," "Rodney King," "Ice-T's dead homies," and certainly not the least inspirational if you are so inclined, "freedom."

Then, should the intended audience be timid or hesitant, there is the encouragement "Don't be a pussy, have some motherfuckin' courage." The anthem blares on to another strand of "Cop Killer."

Finally, there is something for the children to aspire to. Ice-T poses the question, "What do you want to be when you grow-up?" The reply is "Cop Killer" to which Ice-T responds "Good choice." The final line is "I'm a motherfuckin Cop Killer." So why would the police be angry over this song?

THE POLICE WORKING ENVIRONMENT

American police officers spend a substantial portion of their time trying to resolve conflict in an environment that is more than occasionally hostile (Skolnick, 1966). It's not surprising that the police would oppose anything that might exacerbate the level of hostility they already experience. Even police officers suffer fear on the job and far too many officers don't come home from work because they have been assaulted or killed. Table 1 below identifies dangerous circumstances for police officers.

CIRCUMSTANCES AT SCENE OF INCIDENT	TOTAL	PERCENT OF TOTAL
TOTAL	71,794	100.0%
Disturbance calls (family quarrels, man with a gun, etc.)	23,535	32.8%
Burglaries in progress or pursuing burglary suspects	1,112	1.5%
Robberies in progress or pursuing robbery suspects	1,149	1.6%
Attempting other arrests	14,741	20.5%
Civil disorders	1,112	1.5%
Handling, transporting, custody of prisoners	8,323	11.6%
Investigating suspicious persons and circumstances	5,941	8.3%
Ambush (no warning)	350	0.5%
Mentally deranged	937	1.3%
Traffics pursuits and stops	6,754	9.4%
All other	7,840	10.9%

Table 1	**LAW ENFORCEMENT OFFICERS ASSAULTED**
Source:	U.S. Department of Justice, Federal Bureau of Investigation, Law Enforcement Officers Killed and Assaulted, 1990, FBI Uniform Crime Reports (Washington, D.C., 1991), p. 45

The data reveal that disturbance calls, arresting suspects, and managing prisoners are indeed dangerous circumstances for police officers. They frequently result in assaults on the officers.

But assaults on officers aren't the whole story. Some are killed. Fathers, mothers, sons, daughters, sisters, and brothers are lost to their families forever. The community and the nation lose trained and talented officers. In 1992, 136 officers were killed in the line of duty. Texas lead the nation with a total of 13 officers killed (Dallas Morning News, January 22, 1993). This was the fifth straight year Texas had the most officers killed. Perhaps it is more than a coincidence that Texas peace officers were particularly bothered by the song and initiated the national protest movement against Time Warner. They may have had the most to lose if the song served as even the slightest motivation to challenge the police.

LAW ENFORCEMENT INTERPRETATIONS OF "COP KILLER'S" LYRICS

Mainstream American law enforcement was appalled at the lyrics of "Cop Killer." Clearly many officers, their leadership, and their employee organizations interpreted the lyrics as a real threat to their personal safety. Mark Clark of the Combined Law Enforcement Associations of Texas (CLEAT), an organization of 12,000 peace officers, confirmed the perceived threat saying, "What we can't believe is that people who are in the business of entertaining the public would enter into a business relationship that would jeopardize the lives of the men and women that police our communities" (Jet, June 29, 1992).

Police in Houston, Texas had a similar interpretation according to Doug Elder, President of the Houston Police Officer's Association. He stated, "You mix this with the summer, the violence, and a little drugs, and they are going to unleash a reign of terror on communities all across the country" (Donnely, June 22, 1992).

What many consider the triggering event for the nationwide protest and proposed boycott was the May 29, 1992, publication of the "Cop Killer" lyrics in the Dallas Police Association's newsletter in an article entitled "New Rap Song Encourages Killing of Police Officers." Had there been any doubt as to what the majority of police officers in America believed the lyrics meant, the subsequent firestorm of protest would not have ensued.

The plethora of law enforcement and political responses to the song notwithstanding, not all law enforcement officers and their leadership accepted the view that "Cop Killer" advocated violence against the police. There was evidence of a far different interpretation which seemed to break along racial lines. Some African-American officers and their employee associations believed the song's depiction was precisely what Ice-T himself said it was, a fictional character voicing frustration and anger over police brutality.

The National Black Police Association based in Washington D.C. and the African- American Peace Officer Association in Los Angeles opposed any actions against the album and Time Warner. According to the National Black Police Association, "Ice-T is entitled to voice his anger and frustrations with conditions facing oppressed people" (Pareles, 1992). Likewise, Dallas Senior Corporal James Allen of the predominantly African-American Texas Peace Officers' Association said of Ice-T and the song, "He's just a brother expressing himself about the attitude of police across the nation. It's true and we have to deal with it" (St. Pierre, 1992).

Corporal Allen and the Texas Peace Officers' Association Chapter in Dallas, in fact, volunteered to provide security for Ice-T and his band at a 1992 New Year's Eve concert in the city. Ice-T did not respond to the offer but Glenn White of the Dallas Police Association did saying, "It would be in pretty poor taste to work for a band that talks about killing police officers" (St. Pierre, 1992).

Ice-T defends the song and its lyrics by saying it is no different than other fictional works where police are assaulted and killed, the Terminator II movie as case in point. In the song Ice-T said he represents a fictional character "who is fed up with police brutality" (Rule, 1992). This is a commonly given explanation for much of the violence, hate, and obscenity found in the genre of thrash, gangster rap, and other like categories of music.

If that is all there is to it, what's the worry over? But on the other hand, Ice-T said in an interview with Time magazine, "My raps aim to give people courage. Listening to me gives you the ability to say screw the system if it's doing you wrong" (Donnely, 1992). Does that mean the words are meant to cause action or simply to inspire a person to speak-up? It takes some sorting out to find the meaning and the young people who may, in fact, be frustrated might not be able to make the subtle distinctions in interpretation that Ice-T and Time Warner have made.

Ice-T's own life experiences are brought to bare on the issue of the lyrics when asked how the police should feel about the song. Ice-T said," 'Cop Killer' should make cops nervous. I think they should feel threatened. They know they can't take a life without retaliation. I do not say go out and do it." One particularly aggravating circumstance in his own life was when Ice-T was pulled out of a car by the police and laid down on the street. The police left the scene without even saying "Get up" (The New York Times, June 19, 1992).

Time Warner, as might be expected, interpreted the lyrics exactly as Ice-T did. The corporation took the view that the song is fiction but not without a factual base. Time Warner President and CEO Gerald Levin said, "The song is rooted in the reality of the streets," but points out that 'Cop Killer' is no more a call for gunning down the police than Frankie and Johnny is a summons for jilted lovers to shoot one another" (The Wall Street Journal, June 22, 1992). For Time Warner "Cop Killer" was simply a classic case of free expression of an artist protected by the First Amendment. With this almost matter of fact stance the corporation had no plans to alter its course in distribution and sale of the album. In fact, a TW spokesman said, "What guardians of respectability find vile is considered compelling and clever to hundreds of thousands of fans" (*The Wall Street Journal*, June 22, 1992).

OTHER INTERPRETATIONS OF "COP KILLER'S" LYRICS

Some of the many journalists who commented on the song would seem to be having it both ways. They feel the lyrics should sound an alarm because of its reality base in places such as South Central L.A., yet claim the song is hyperbole, boast, and gesture emanating from the black traditions of street life (Editorial, New Republic, August 10, 1992). Are the situations depicted real or not, and if they are not, why the alarm?

Other journalists were as offended as the police. Michael Kinsley (1992) of CNN and Time magazine renown said, "Killing policeman is a good thing. That is the meaning of the words and no larger understanding of black culture, the rage of the streets, or anything else can explain it away." Similarly, the Parents' Music Resource Center was struck by the "vileness of the message" (Donnely, 1992).

POLITICAL REACTIONS TO "COP KILLER"

If the police were feeling neglected and abused coming off the deluge of negative publicity from the Rodney King incident and the Los Angeles riot, their hopes were lifted by support they received from many quarters concerning "Cop Killer," including attention from the very top. It was an election year for the President, the Vice President, and Congress and there were numerous platforms from which they could speak their minds on an issue that connected to violence and crime.

President Bush was quick to react stating that "he is against those who use films and records or television or video games to glorify killing police officers. I don't care how noble the name of the company, it is wrong for any company to issue records that approve of killing police officers" (The Wall Street Journal, June 30, 1992). Vice President Quayle urged Time Warner to reexamine its sponsorship of "Cop Killer," realizing that the government could not act because of First Amendment Rights (The Wall Street Journal, June 22, 1992). Time Warner had no reply.

Then presidential candidate Bill Clinton raised an issue in the Sister Souljah case that was mentioned by more than one critic of Time Warner. Known as the "Clinton Test," Mr. Clinton asked the question, "What if the roles were reversed in Sister Souljah's rap that suggested that blacks take a day off from killing each other and kill only whites for a day?" He said that would make them sound like a speech from David Duke (The Wall Street Journal, June 22, 1992). The logic was persuasive and used by many in expressing their displeasure over the controversial song "Cop Killer."

There were other reactions from political quarters. Several dozen members of Congress angrily protested the record in a letter and urged Time Warner to withdraw the record from production and distribution. State legislator Will Harnett of Texas wrote a letter of protest to Time Warner on May 29, 1992, well before any of the of the other politicians. The Los Angeles Police Commission also called for Time Warner to stop selling the record and said their action was "in concern for all of the police officers throughout the country, ...we have to take a position that we oppose this kind of music" (The New York Times, July 16, 1992).

Oliver North and the Freedom Alliance put pressure on the nation's 50 governors to bring criminal charges against Time Warner in violation of sedition and anti-anarchy statutes (Zimmerman, 1992). The pressure on Time Warner was mounting.

As if the explosive law enforcement and political reactions to "Cop Killer" were not enough, corporate America began to raise a critical issue. Editor-in-Chief Charles Day (1992) of Industry Week believed the Ice-T song struck deeper than the current issue over the lyrics. He believed that American corporations had not identified what their values were not what kinds of behavior they wanted to either encourage or discourage among their workers. The "Cop Killer" song "is hardly a solitary example of corporate indifference to the public interest," according to Mr. Day. Perhaps a lesson might be learned concerning the need to define the values management should hold dear and ask their employees to embrace.

A SAMPLE OF OPINION FROM A NATIONAL COMPUTER BULLETIN BOARD

On January 17, 1993, two questions were posted on the interactive personal service board of Prodigy, a national computer information service. The questions to police officers were:

1. How did you feel when you first read the lyrics of "Cop Killer?"
2. Would you have participated in a boycott against Time Warner if the corporation had not pulled the song from the market?

Only seven responses were received, one from a police widow whose husband was killed in 1989. The responses to question # 1 were examined for common themes. Table 2 below summarizes the results of the inquiry on Prodigy.

RESPONDENT	FEELINGS	BOYCOTT ACTIVITY
A	"anger and grief"	Would boycott
B	"infuriated"	Already boycotting
C	"should know feelings"	Already boycotting
D	"lyrics are trash"	Would boycott
E	"outraged"	Already boycotting
F	"outraged"	Already boycotting
G	"lyrics are free speech"	No response

Table 1 RESPONSES TO PRODIGY BULLETIN BOARD SURVEY

Only one of the respondents to the Prodigy survey failed to react negatively to the lyrics and in most cases the respondents were angered, outraged, and infuriated. The lone dissenter saw the issue of the lyrics in terms of free speech. Relative to the boycott, again all but one would have participated and some of them had started and were continuing to take some boycott action against Time Warner. In sum, six of the seven (85.7%) were both angered by the lyrics of the song and were in favor of boycotting Time Warner had it been necessary to get the song removed from distribution.

THE GANGSTER RAP GENRE

Poetic depictions of crime, violence, racial hatred, sexual assault, and conflict with the police on the streets are a major source of profit in today's music industry, maybe reaping as much as $700 million each year. Ice-T, who is credited with the founding of the particular genre known as "crime rhyme" or "gangster rap", is reported to have 400,000 hard-core fans across the nation. The "Body Count" album which contained "Cop Killer" sold 100,000 copies a month until the song was deleted. It should be noted that this amount of sales was accomplished with virtually no air time for the song on radio or television since the lyrics were considered too offensive to be aired.

Who buys the music? Ice-T claims that 70% of the sales are to middle class white young people who also can afford the T-shirt, hat, and perhaps the jacket. Urban blacks are more likely to hear the tape on pirated copies. Nevertheless business is booming.

Ice-T, who grew up in middle class Los Angeles and did a four year stint in the Army, has had four gold albums beginning with "Rhyme Pays" and including "OG: Original Gangster" which many critics and commentators consider to be his best work. Ice-T, raised as Tracy Marrow, has been successful enough to branch out into other ventures such as his roles in the movies "New Jack City" and "Trespass." "Trespass" was originally intended to be entitled "The Looters," but the L.A. riot changed the movie producer's mind.

To droning yet captivating hip-hop beats rappers such as Ice-T, Ice Cube, and NWA (Niggas With Attitude) pipe out a profitable onslaught of sexism, hatred, homophobia, violence, and crime. But some say there are messages in the music which are truly compelling and can give all Americans an ear to the desperation and hopelessness that reside in the nation's urban centers. So buried within the titles such as "Fuck the Police," "KKK Bitch," "Momma's Gonna Die Tonight," "Home of the Body Bag," "Street Killer," "100 Miles and Runnin," and many others there is, for the most part some injustice or inequity which is supposed to have fueled the rage and hatred that emits from the music. Other titles are more direct in portraying the plight of urban black life. "911 Is a Joke," "Escape from the Killing Fields," "Mind Over Matter," and "Ed," a song which warns of the fast life and drunk driving, point out the futility of much of life in the ghetto. There is something here that needs to be heard and may not be available for most Americans any other way. An understanding of Ice Cube's "Black Korea," some say, might very well have given us a portend of the poor state of relations between Korean merchants and their black customers in L.A. prior to the 1992 riot had anyone been listening.

Because the music is offensive to so many Americans of all creeds and color, the gems of truth which may be found in the vile, profane, and exaggerated language of the gangster rappers and others will more than likely be heard by only a small segment of the American population. Perhaps knowing that the messages are there could spur some other means of finding the truths amidst the hyperbole. For many African-Americans rap is no more attractive, sometimes driving a wedge between people of the same race. L.A.'s new African-American police chief, Willie Williams, claims to have "major problems with rap music as an American, as a parent, and as a 30 year police officer" (Zimmerman, 1992).

One Chicago radio station, whose listening audience is predominantly black, advertises as the station that plays no rap, apparently capitalizing on the widespread distaste for the genre among blacks with higher demographic profiles and incomes (Muwakkil, 1990).

But there are other views on this music of the African-American underclass. Dr. Charles V. Willie, Professor of Education and Urban Studies at Harvard University comments that entertainment through depictions of violence is not new and points out that "the elite in their finery have for years attended opera as form of entertainment and some operas are known to be violent...like Wagner's "Das Rheinhold'" (Jet, April 1, 1991). The language of rap, which conveys the street themes to the underclass and the youth, is simply considered vile and vulgar by the majority of Americans and that fact alone will prevent the messages from ever being heard unless delivered in some other medium.

Poetry by its very definition is to evoke the highest and lowest emotions in human beings. Gangster rap does that indeed and Ice-T would appear to be at the head of the class in this genre. Quincy Jones believes "Ice-T has the best poetic quality of any rapper, and the strongest narrative" he has ever heard (Donnely, 1992). Ice-T has evolved since he first began spinning records in the Army and when the renowned gangster rapper stepped in to the heavy metal world with the controversial "Body Count" album, he evoked some emotions and a whale of a controversy.

THE APPLICATION OF POLICE LEADERSHIP AND POWER

A number of perspectives might logically be taken to tell the story of what happened in the police protest and boycott against Time Warner. It was in many respects a moral victory of sorts against vile and obscene lyrics, with many victories left to be won in that arena in many people's minds. It was no less a media blitzkrieg with scores of journalists around the nation offering their "two columns" or so on the matter. But the perspective on the fight and its accomplishments that is perhaps most plausible is that of a righteous movement orchestrated by an enraged law enforcement community who seldom exercise the real power they possess. That exercise of power and influence on a national scale was accomplished by the contributions of scores of police labor and agency leaders. But several law enforcement officials in Texas made it happen through their moral courage and leadership directed against Time Warner. What odds would anyone have given to American law enforcement officers in this age, thought to be loosely organized nationwide and incessantly pummeled in the media over alleged police brutality and racism, in taking on a multi-billion dollar corporation and winning any concessions? They believe they won and the victory came in slightly more than one month from the call to arms. The story of the "Six Week War" is intriguing.

THE POLICE POWER-UP FOR A FIGHT

Perhaps no different than a lot of other nights Glenn White, Senior Corporal of the Dallas Police Department and Vice President of the Dallas Police Association, was at the Northeast Police Substation doing business as usual when his Sergeant asked him if he had seen the words to a new rap song that was out about killing cops. He had not. But when he did read and reflect on the lyrics of "Cop Killer," his anger began to build and he wanted to do something about it. Out of this one officer's outrage and commitment to change things came a lesson that the recording industry, law enforcement, and lots of other people are not likely to forget. A brief chronology of the events and developments that followed Glenn White's initial steps to fight back are detailed below in an attempt to assist the reader in grasping the essential developments in a well orchestrated, albeit fortuitous, sequence of events and circumstances that allowed the police of the nation to accomplish a feat that heretofore was clearly deemed unassailable.

An analysis and discussion of key leadership issues and the results of interviews with the two most important law enforcement actors in the challenge to Time Warner's might will follow. The concentration and application of power exercised by the police will also be considered.

CHRONOLOGY OF EVENTS

March 1992 - Time Warner releases the "Body Count" album which contained the song "Cop Killer" performed by rapper Ice-T and a new heavy metal band. Before the album's release, against the wishes of Ice-T, the title was changed from "Cop Killer" to "Body Count," the name of one of the songs on the new release and the name of Ice-T's heavy metal band. Early promotion copies of the album were delivered to radio and television stations in miniature "body bags."

May 29, 1992 - Glenn White published the lyrics of the song "Cop Killer" in the May 29 issue of "The Shield," the Dallas Police Association's newspaper. White was astounded that Time Warner, a respectable company in his eyes, could be making money off of a song that suggested the killing of police officers. He urged the readers and their families to write Time Warner in protest and to boycott all their products and movies until the company removed the song. The address of Lenny Waronker, President of Time/Warner Bros. Records was provided in the article.

June 4, 1992 - Eric Wramp, President of the Corpus Christi Police Officers' Association, read White's article and called a press conference to express his anger over the song. That same day Wramp sent a scathing letter to Time Warner.

Dan Calderon, staff writer of the Corpus Christi Caller Times, published the first media article about the police anger and threatened boycott. The story is picked up off of the Associated Press wire service and the nation began to read about "Cop Killer" and the police movement against it.

June 8, 1992 - Ron Delord, President of the 12,000 member Combined Law Enforcement Associations of Texas (CLEAT), held a meeting in Austin to decide strategy and tactics to fight Time Warner.

An Austin resident who holds stock in Time Warner provided CLEAT with a shareholder's packet that delineated Time Warner financial holdings and included the news of a shareholders' meeting in Beverly Hills, California on July 16.

June 9, 1992 - CLEAT staff under the direction of Ron Delord and Mark Clark mobilized a national campaign by mailing out protest packets to hundreds of police associations and other groups across the United States and Canada. The packets contained a CLEAT press release, a copy of Glenn White's article, a copy of the letter sent to Time Warner by a police survivors' organization, Concerns of Police Survivors (COPS), Time Warner stockholders' information, and other items useful in combating Time Warner.

June 11, 1992 - Approximately 75 uniformed police officers and others held a press conference in Arlington, Texas across from Six Flags Over Texas, an enormous amusement park, of which Time Warner holds 50% of the stock. At the press conference, chaired by Ron Delord and Glenn White, the police announced they would attend the stockholders' meeting in Beverly Hills, California on July 16, and encouraged law enforcement officers from across the nation to attend. They would withhold a boycott decision until after the stockholders' meeting in California, but wanted the record pulled, an apology made to law enforcement and police survivors, and a large monetary contribution from "Cop Killer" profits donated to the National Law Enforcement Memorial Fund.

June 11, 1992 to July 15, 1992 - Opposition to "Cop Killer" swelled across the nation despite Time Warner's and Ice-T's stand on the fictional nature of the song and an artist's right of free expression. The police attracted support from diverse quarters: politicians, record store owners, nite club owners, journalists, corporate leaders, the black community, religious leaders, Time Warner stockholders, a vast majority of the public, and celebrities. The more publicity, the stronger the condemnation of Time Warner.

July 15, 1992 - Law enforcement officers and family members held a strategy meeting in Beverly Hills, the night before the stockholders' annual meeting, and invited two Time Warner executives who left the meeting surprised at the level of anger and the strength of the opposition.

July 16, 1992 - The police protested outside the Beverly Hills Wilshire Hotel where the stockholders' meeting was being held. Later inside the hotel Time Warner CEO Gerald Levin was repeatedly interrupted by stockholders who wanted to deal with the "Cop Killer" issue before regular business was attended to. Charlton Heston read the Cop Killer words to a stunned crowd of investors. Many others gave emotion-laden speeches and pleas, most of which were police labor leaders in the United States and Canada, police survivors of assaults, and family to officers.

July 28, 1992 - Ice-T "voluntarily" removed "Cop Killer" from distribution because of alleged death and bomb threats made toward Time Warner executives and him. Ice-T would continue to issue single copies to those who request them but the song would not be produced by Time Warner. Time Warner offered no apology.

July 31, 1992 - CLEAT and several other police associations across the nation declared an end to the verbal assaults on Time Warner and divested from any further boycott activity. Other police associations vowed to fight on to achieve somewhat nebulous objectives.

December 31 1992 - Ice-T played a New Year's Eve concert in Dallas where the crowd measured less than 300. The Dallas Police Association offered no protest, not wanting to promote racial disharmony in the city.

January 28, 1993 - Warner Bros. Records dropped Ice-T from its list of performers as a result of a disagreement over the artwork on the cover of his new album "Home Invasion." Both claim the release from his contract was by mutual agreement. TW said it was the best way to resolve their "creative differences."

February 1993 - Ice-T found an independent distributor, Priority Records, to release his "Home Invasion" album. Record is scheduled to be out by mid-March with apparently no changes in the album's cover art, which depicts a white youth listening to the album while imagining violent images.

LEADERSHIP EMERGES

It didn't take long after Glenn White's publication of the lyrics to "Cop Killer" and the AP wire service story on a proposed police boycott of Time Warner for a momentum to build against the publishing and entertainment giant. But the momentum lacked a clear direction and it needed leadership if it were to accomplish anything. Fortunately for the law enforcement community Glenn White and Ron Delord were willing to step forward, an action that would require great personal sacrifice from both men. Other leaders eventually took up the cause nationwide. From the written coverage available on this event and from interviews with Delord and White, it became evident that their roles could not be minimized in this battle. It is unlikely that anything of significance would have been accomplished without them.

Leadership has many definitions, but virtually all of them contain several key ingredients that played a big part in the campaign against Time Warner. President Eisenhower's definition was "getting someone else to do something you want done because they want to do it." Historian James McGregor Burns (1980) describes transforming leadership as "when one or more persons engage with others in such a way that leaders and followers raise one another to higher levels of motivation and morality." The world is replete with examples of this kind of leadership where the moral high ground belonged to the movement: Gandhi in India, William

Lloyd Garrison on slavery, and King on civil rights. A shared set of motives is at the heart of transforming leadership.

It became clear from the beginning that the police had an issue that the vast majority of the nation would support them on if they could mobilize and manage this attack. Glenn White's article in the Dallas Police Association's newsletter and his call for a boycott against Time Warner was an act of courageously doing something first, also a credible definition of leadership. No less courageous was Eric Wramp's news conference in Corpus Christi, before he had read the political climate . Others might have waited to get a reading of reactions to the song before stepping forward to protest. When the calls began to come in to the offices of the Dallas Police Association and CLEAT in Austin, the police knew they had to get organized. On June 8, 1992, Ron Delord of CLEAT held a strategy meeting in Austin with key staff to discuss the growing media coverage of the "Cop Killer" issue. It was there that a decision was made to expand the fight against the corporation.

Two decisions were made that were critical to the effectiveness of the campaign. First, CLEAT decided to move immediately before the story got old and secondly, a press conference was scheduled for June 11 at Six Flags Over Texas, a "family" amusement park in Arlington, Texas where large numbers of officers could be mobilized from many different agencies in the Dallas/Fort Worth Metroplex. The show of combined law enforcement strength at the press conference in a location that would allow the police to make the striking contrast between the atrocious lyrics of "Cop Killer" and the financially rewarding Six Flags Amusement Park with its family image was a media bonanza. Both attractions of the press conference were Time Warner financed enterprises. In the meantime, both CLEAT and the Dallas Police Association began to mail out packets of information to interested and outraged police officers, survivor organizations, police employee associations, politicians, and the public across the nation. The DPA was asking recipients of the packages, among other things, to boycott Time Warner.

What would be the law enforcement position on "Cop Killer" beyond the fact they were shocked and angered at the song? The decision was made to focus on the greed and immorality of Time Warner for publishing such an offensive work of art and not to become embroiled in a futile controversy over Ice-T's right to perform the song according to the First Amendment which might result in the police being tagged with a position that advocated censorship. This approach allowed the police to bring in an even greater number of supporters, some of which might have flinched if a call for censorship was made.

Next the decision was made by Ron Delord and the CLEAT organization to withhold their call for a boycott, realizing how often this approach proves fruitless. But the threat of a boycott loomed large and Time Warner was left to think about that possibility for awhile.

But as luck would have it, a Time Warner shareholder in Austin gave CLEAT a shareholder's packet that contained an array of financial and investment information about TW, including an announcement of the July 16 annual shareholders' meeting in Beverly Hills, California. CLEAT hoped to bring the protest to a successful conclusion at the July meeting and would be able to keep the story alive in the media for a month and have the time to mobilize a national campaign against Time Warner. In the meantime, the DPA under the leadership of Glenn White and CLEAT, directed by Ron Delord, mailed out nearly 2,000 information packets to law enforcement organizations and other groups across the nation. The CLEAT package contained the following: a CLEAT press release; Glenn White's article; a copy of the Concerns of Police Survivors' letter to Time Warner; an announcement of the July 16 stockholders' meeting; a list of all TW directors and major holdings; and a copy of a visual that was used at the July 11 press conference which simulated a movie poster announcement reading "Time Warner...Now Proudly Presents...Cop Killer."

The press conference on June 11 was an unqualified success. Dozens of police in uniform were there and it was chaired by Delord and White, no doubt both slightly stunned by the amount of media attention given the event. They played opening lines to "Cop Killer" and distributed the lyrics. The media covering the story were clearly struck and went back to their offices and studios to write about it and broadcast the story. The police also announced that they would be at the shareholders' meeting in Beverly Hills on July 16 to demonstrate and promised that lots of other police from across the nation would join them.

The next five weeks prior to the July 16 meeting in Beverly Hills saw public condemnation swell. TW sent two public relations executives to Texas to feel out the strength of the police opposition. They were not impressed, apparently, because TW continued to stand by their artist's right to record and perform the song. Glenn White was drafted into a nationwide schedule of media appearances and he told the "Cop Killer" story to Newsweek, People Magazine, CBS This Morning, and to many others as well on a litany of radio talk and news shows, many of which were in Canada. Keep in mind he was still a working Dallas police officer, but could not escape the movement he started even on vacation in Florida where a magazine descended upon him and his family because they needed photos for an upcoming edition. Glenn White spent a lot of his own money in this campaign and he all but drained his accumulated vacation time in making appearances for this cause he dearly believed in.

Things were coming to a head by the time of a strategy meeting that was held in Beverly Hills on July 15, 1992. Police officers, family members, and representatives from Concerns of Police Survivors attended as well as two TW executives who came to defend the corporation's position on the song. Delord had invited the TW executives and he chaired the meeting. The crowd was angry and emotional. After a couple of hours of listening to the furor over the song, the TW representatives left with no doubt as to what they were confronting. They now knew the opposition was formidable.

On Thursday, July 16, the police protested outside the Beverly Hills Wilshire Hotel. To their surprise, the media personnel outnumbered the police available to demonstrate. Police leaders quickly characterized it as a representative group of the rank and file of law enforcement. Before the shareholders' meeting began a couple of notable incidents occurred. Several youths attempted to aggravate the police by playing "Cop Killer" on their "boom boxes." To avoid a confrontation, the police moved their protest to another location. Next, no other than Ice-T himself makes a cameo appearance by driving by in his Rolls Royce and giving the police protesters the "finger." But the real action was to take place inside.

Now more than 1,200 shareholders were inside the hotel and had been given copies of the lyrics to "Cop Killer" by Glenn White and others. CEO Gerald Levin tried to hold the regular business meeting first and then deal with the controversy with the police. The shareholders demanded addressing the "Cop Killer" issue first.

By now the shareholders had read the lyrics and were virtually "dropped" by the emotion-laden reading of the words to the song by Charlton Heston. Numerous police leaders and others made persuasive presentations. Some of the organizations who had representatives speak at the meeting were the Fraternal Order of Police, the New York City Patrolmen's Benevolent Association, the New York City Detectives' Endowment Association, the Metropolitan Toronto Police Association. Police widow Kathleen Young from Kansas City and Houston minister James Dixon also spoke.

One particularly heart-wrenching speaker was a Suffolk County, New York deputy sheriff who had suffered having his face blown off by a shot gun blast while he was writing the young perpetrator a traffic citation. He described the pain and agony of facial reconstruction and the long emotional struggle back. The words of "Cop Killer" reached a heightened relevance. Opera star Beverly Sills, seated in the front row, was reported to have wept like a baby. The meeting adjourned.

On July 28, 1992, Ice-T held a press conference and said he was voluntarily withdrawing the "Cop Killer" song from the "Body Count" album because of death threats made to Time Warner executives. Still today there is no real evidence that Ice-T was pressured by Time Warner to drop the song, but can there be any doubt that they did since the corporation's stock had dropped significantly in just several weeks and their reputation was soured during the period of the protest. There was no apology for the song by either Ice-T or Time Warner. In fact, Ice-T maintained that he would continue to give out singles of the song at his expense to anybody who wanted a copy. Undoubtedly surprised, the police, who had wanted an apology and the song pulled from the market, expected perhaps they would get an apology and no action on the song. The opposite transpired.

Most of the law enforcement organizations involved in the protest have dropped their call for a boycott and seem reasonably satisfied that the song is no longer being distributed. Some officers and organizations are holding out for the apology from Time Warner. That does not seem likely. CLEAT and other Texas police groups are generally satisfied with the results. It seems that the general mood nationwide is to claim the victory and move on.

BASES OF POWER

Producing intended results and having the capacity to gain compliance are both popular definitions and manifestations of power. American law enforcement was able to accumulate, coordinate, and exercise power in the "Cop Killer" protest in ways they had never done before. What power bases did they operate from in order to arrive at the point of whipping a giant? A number can be identified.

1. The Moral High Ground. Anger and disgust had been brewing in America for several years over the violent and obscene material coming out of the entertainment media, but few were willing to risk their reputations and political capital over a matter that traditionally had been cast as a censorship issue. Now gangster rap had made it something different when the artists' depictions called for killing police officers. The police were able to mobilize support across age, racial, ethnic, religious, and political lines. Who would try to defend a song that advocated killing police officers? Strange allies came together in this movement. In Dallas, for example, the strident and diverse Police Civilian Review Board, not known to see eye to eye on much of anything, all signed a protest letter against the song.
2. Police Labor and Police Management. The two groups have had their differences as of late over working conditions and the management of law enforcement agencies. But "Cop Killer" staked out common turf to be defended if there was ever anything to come together on. Police management, for the most part, contributed their moral and vocal support and stood back while the labor organizations took the lead on this one. It should be pointed out also that losing would have had adverse consequences for whoever led the fight. The rank and file were willing to take the risk. Perhaps they discovered just how strong they can be when the battle is carefully chosen and how much muscle they can flex if needed.
3. The Power of the Buck. It has been reported that the police were considering as the ultimate weapon to use in the fight against Time Warner the withdrawal of police pension funds out of Time Warner stock. The dollar value would have been in the billions with one report suggesting in New York City alone the figure would have reached seven billion dollars. As Time Warner watched its price of shares drop during the controversy, the thought of serious financial hardship had to loom large with the corporation's leadership.
4. Media Support. Virtually all of the media, even while attempting to cover both sides of the issue, in the end came down on the side of the police. Those who put up a defense for Ice-T and Time Warner often seemed unsure about it. Media personnel, like most Americans, were offended by the song and exercised some trepidation over the thought of allowing something of this nature to go unchecked. The police needed to exercise no manipulation in this case, the media punched away as fervently as anybody.
5. Politicians and the Crime Problem. While no politician got into the particulars of gangster rap, there was the issue of shielding the nation's crime fighters from such attack which politicians quickly noticed fit in well with their campaign rhetoric about crime control. Violence in the

media and escalating crime rates did affect voters and the presidential candidates as well as many others commented on the "Cop Killer" controversy. This was a strong component of the broad-based campaign against Time Warner and the growing anti-violence phenomenon in our society.

6. Latent Support for the Police. At last the police saw large and diverse segments of the population support them. In the aftermath of the Rodney King incident and subsequent cases, the media and others seemed to "pile on" law enforcement. "Cop Killer" became a lightning rod for attracting sympathy and support from thousands of people and many organizations who had rarely come forward to defend the police. "Cop Killer" vividly told them what an evening of law enforcement duty might be like and they were touched.

7. Personal Courage and Will. Sometimes things happen as a result of the personal courage and will of an individual or small group of leaders. The half-dozen or so Texas law enforcement officers and officials who took it on their own to speak out against "Cop Killer" are precisely of that ilk. Their actions were not without risk and one would suspect that more than once they did the equivalent of "turning around to see if anybody was still behind them" Fortunately their leadership induced a massive following. In Glenn White's June 9 article in the "The Shield" he exhorted his readers by saying, "WE CAN DO IT!" He made them believe.

RESULTS AND AFTERMATH OF THE "COP KILLER" CONTROVERSY

In slightly more than six months from the height of the "Cop Killer" controversy a lot of things have happened which were the results of the police protest. A number of the salient results are:

1. "Cop Killer" is off the market.
2. A major corporation yielded to police and public pressure.
3. Warner Bros. Records has promised to be more careful in the review of what they publish.
4. Warner Bros. Records dropped Ice-T as one of its recording artists, allegedly over the cover art on his new album "Home Invasion."
5. Rappers who use vile and offensive language in their lyrics are having trouble getting their albums produced.
6. The nation has been awakened on the issue of violence in the media and even television has developed a set of standards concerning violence that it intends to employ in the Fall 1993 season.
7. Ice-T has found a new independent producer and distributor, Priority Records.
8. Ice-T can claim he had a song so bad it had to be dropped from distribution.
9. The police of the nation have discovered that someone out there does care about them.
10. Time Warner has yet to offer a word of apology to American law enforcement.

CONCLUSIONS

Glenn White is back to his normal routine of working patrol until midnight and spending a good portion of his spare time, as usual, being the Vice President of the Dallas Police Association. Ron Delord is spending a lot of time over at the Texas Legislature which just went into session in January of 1993, something it does only every two years. There are always issues affecting the police to be discussed and he is in the throes of it.

Ice-T is about to release his "Home Invasion" album, the target date being March of 1993. No doubt he continues to make money with gangster rap music and has derived some notoriety from the controversy with the police and Time Warner. But when it comes to "Cop Killer" and all that it meant to the police and the public and its ultimate effect on Ice-T, there is perhaps no better way to put it, than to quote a lyric of one of Ice-T's own raps on the album "OG, The Original Gangster", "HOW DID HE GO OUT? HE WENT OUT LIKE A BITCH!"

REFERENCES

Burns, James MacGregor. (1978) Leadership. New York: Harper and Row Publishers.

"Bush Assails Performers on Violence Against the Police," The Wall Street Journal, June 30, 1992.

Calderon, Dan. (1992) "Police Protest 'Cop Killer' Recording." Corpus Christi Caller Times, June 4.

Chumley, Darrell. (1992) "The Police vs. Time Warner: The Story of David Taking Goliath Out to the Woodshed for a Good Whippin.'" The Police Labor Leader, Vol. 2 No. 8, August.

Day, Charles. (1992) "Just What Are Our Values?" Industry Week, August 17.

Donnely, Sally B. (1992) "The Fire Around the Ice." Time, June 22.

Ehrenreich, Barbara. (1992) "...Or Is It Creative Freedom?" Time, July 20.

Ferguson, Tim W. (1992) "Will Sunlight Improve the Taste of Ice-T's Distributor?" The Wall Street Journal, July 21.

"Ice-T's Controversial Record Triggers Boycott." (1992) Jet, June 29.

"Ice-T Defends Song Against Spreading Boycott." The New York Times, June 19, 1992.

"Ice-T Talks Back: You Got a Problem with That?" Rolling Stone Magazine, August 20, 1992.

Interview with Glenn White, February 2, 1993

Interview with Ron Delord, February 5, 1993

Kinsley, Michael. (1992) "Ice-T: Is the Issue Social Responsibility?" Time, July 20.

Kinsley, Michael. (1992) "Speaking in Tongues." The New Republic, July 13.

Leo, John. (1992) "A Model of Corporate Morality." U.S. News and World Report, August 10.

"Momma Dearest." (1992) The New Republic, August 10.

Muwakkil, Salim. (1990) "The Rap Gap: Class Divisions Divide the Black Community." Utne Reader, January - February.

Pareles, Jon. (1992) "Ice-T, Mr. Nice Guy, Cuts the Controversy." The New York Times, August 2.

Pareles, Jon. (1992) "The Disappearance of Ice-T's Cop Killer." The New York Times, August 2.

"Police Group Protests 'Cop Killer' Rap Song." (1992) Associated Press, June 5.

"Rapper Ice-T Defends Song Against Spreading Boycott." (1992) The New York Times, June 19.

"Rapping with Time Warner." (1992) The Wall Street Journal, June 22.

Reilly, Patrick. (1992) "Time Warner is Trying to Ease Anger Over Rap Song." The Wall Street Journal, June 23.

Responses to Prodigy Bulletin Board Survey, January 17, 1993.

Roberts, Johnnie L. (1992) "Time Warner to Cut Controversial Song." The Wall Street Journal, July 29.

Rule, Sheila . (1992) "Rapping Time Warner's Knuckles." The New York Times, July 8.

Skolnick, Jerome. (1966) Justice Without Trial. New York: Wiley.

St. Pierre, Nancy. (1992) "Breaking Rank." The Dallas Morning News, December 31.

"T'd Off: Ice-T Agrees to Stop Promoting His Song, 'Cop Killer'." Economist, August 1, 1992.

"Texas Reports Most Officers Killed in '92." The Dallas Morning News, January 22, 1993.

"Time Warner Gets Protest on Its 'Cop Killer' Album." (1992) The New York Times, July 16.

U.S. Department of Justice, Federal Bureau of Investigation. (1991) "Law Enforcement Officers Killed and Assaulted, 1990, FBI Uniform Crime Reports. Washington D.C.

Walker, Samuel. (1983) The Police in America: An Introduction. New York: McGraw-Hill.

Warner Bros. Records (1992) "Body Count."

Warner Bros. Records (1991) "O.G.: Original Gangster."

White, Glenn. (1992) "New Rap Song Encourages Killing Police Officers." The Shield, May 29.

"Who Should Be Blamed for the Violence at Movie Theaters?" (1991) Jet, April 1.

Zimmerman, Kevin. (1992) "All Claiming Victory in 'Cop Killer' Battle." Variety, August 3.

Zimmerman, Kevin. (1992) "Hip-hop Hub Hewn by Recent Racial Uproar." Variety, June 22.

BLACK BEFORE BLUE

by Dusty Rhodes

IN THE COUNCIL CHAMBERS AT DALLAS CITY HALL, a prominent black leader steps to the podium to demand racial reform in the Dallas Police Department. Reading a statement signed by leaders of 28 civic groups, the man asks the council to establish a civilian police review board with subpoena powers; to have the chief of police promote more black officers; and to ensure that blacks comprise 25 percent of the police force within the next two years.

Newspaper accounts the following day will note that these are the same demands being touted by hundreds of black protesters. So who is this black leader appearing before city council? Is this the controversial county commissioner John Wiley Price stirring up trouble again? Is it Roy Williams? Or Marvin Crenshaw? Perhaps M.T. Avant?

No. It was A. Maceo Smith the late A. Maceo Smith -- and the time was November 1972.

But this scene could have been on the evening news last week. Or yesterday. Because now, 20 years later, black citizens are still protesting, and black leaders are still pressing virtually the same demands. Now, 20 years later, the police force still hasn't gotten to that 25 percent mark that A. Maceo Smith thought could be accomplished by 1974.

Now, 20 years later, almost nothing has changed except the names of the city council members and the faces of the protesters and the fortunate fact that today's protests, unlike the '72 demonstrations, weren't sparked by a series of police shootings of blacks.

For the past three months, the grievances of a few hundred black cops -- members of the Texas Peace Officers Association have threatened to throw the city of Dallas into a racial crisis.

As the result of TPOA-inspired protests at the southeast police substation, county commissioner and city councilman were charged with assault and resisting arrest; at a tense emergency meeting of the city council, a packed chamber of citizens traded horror stories about racial abuse; and separate groups of white cops and black cops have marched on City Hall and police headquarters, both voicing contempt for their superiors — but from diametrically opposed perspectives.

In the flurry of headlines and fracases, the issues that sparked such bitter conflict -- allegations of racial disparity in hiring, promotion, and discipline within the Dallas Police Department -- have been obscured. But even without the sideshows, these issues wouldn't have gotten much press. They don't come packaged in handy bite-size anecdotes; they suffer from the lack of a single startling case or poster child to illustrate the cause.

Until now, the racial conflict within the department has displayed itself publicly only in the courts, where officers have filed a dozen lawsuits against the city, separately alleging both racial discrimination and reverse discrimination. Some of these cases date back 15 years. All remain open and unfinished.

As with most such allegations these days, there is no smoking gun, no overt, blatant policy that reeks of racism. Civil-rights legislation has abolished such evils. Yet there is evidence that racism continues to plague the Dallas Police Department it's just taken on a subtler, more sophisticated form. It is tempting to lay all the blame for the trouble roiling the department at the feet of the Dallas chapter of the Texas Peace Officers Association, a predominantly black organization whose 350 members represent about 60 percent of the 564 African-Americans in the Dallas force.

TPOA is one of four DPD associations. Founded in 1975, it is older and more established than either the Dallas Police Patrolman's Union or the Latino Peace Officers Association. But like those two groups, it is dwarfed by the Dallas Police Association or DPA -- the department's oldest, largest, most powerful, and best known group. Some black officers join only DPA, which offers an attractive legal representation plan in exchange for dues; others hold membership in both organizations. A few belong only to TPOA.

TPOA has always been different in large part because, unlike most employee unions, its primary agenda extends so conspicuously beyond the immediate self-interest of its members. Notes former Dallas chief Mack Vines, now teaching criminal justice at a Florida college, "Minorities really represent their community. There's a culture and lifestyle connection there that is not always present for white officers." The group's formal credo spells this out: "Bridging the gap between the African-American community and the law-enforcement establishment through mutual respect, trust, cooperation and positive interaction."

This slogan has translated into a series of actions quite unlikely for a police association, such as TPOA's public support of a stronger citizen review board and its members' inclination to file internal grievances against fellow officers alleging unprofessional or abusive behavior with citizens.

In the close-knit police culture, these actions are uncommon. Says Vines, "it's expected and preferred that if there is any wrongdoing or violations of policy committed by an officer, that they'll be appropriately reported. But it isn't easy for a complaint to be made against another officer. There's a tendency for that person (the complainant] to be ostracized. There's a real ripple effect."

Now, TPOA is doing something even more extreme. Having first prompted commissioner John Wiley Price to lead his "warriors" in regular protests at the southeast substation since Labor Day, TPOA members are now trying to turn up the heat by marching every morning, rain or shine, on the sidewalk outside downtown police headquarters.

Their determination to force change is fueled by a potent combination of ugly history and bitter personal experience combination that leads many African-American officers to reject the traditional brotherhood of police in favor of the brotherhood of their race.

It is what makes this group of Dallas cops so troublesome: they're black before they're blue.

It's still early on a weekday morning, but TPOA president James Allen has already spent two hours at the gym. Back home in Oak Cliff -- in a den so tidy that there are visible vacuum tracks in the carpet he juggles his ever-beeping pager, his ever-ringing phone, and a reporter's questions.

Considering all the ruckus he's kicked up, Allen's not a particularly intimidating physical presence: in fact, he's almost tiny not quite 5 ft 7 inches and under 145 pounds, with an easy smile and calm, matter of fact manner that softens his more strident statements. His words often sound more radical on paper than they do in person.

Now in his second term as TPOA president Allen lacks the charisma and rhetorical skills that some of his predecessors possess; flashiness runs counter to his nature.

A 38-year-old senior corporal with almost 15 years on the force, Allen says he got into police work because of a lifetime desire "to do something for my people." At first, he thought that meant becoming a minister. But during college, he decided police officers could have a more practical influence. Once he enrolled in a criminal justice course, he was convinced. "It fascinated me -- the power that a police officer has," Allen recalls. "And I said, "This right here, this is how you bring about changes in the system.'"

As for what motivates whites to become police officers, Allen doesn't offer any theory until asked. But it's clearly a topic he's thought about: "Pay, job security, and tradition," he ticks off. "It's been passed down from generation to generation in some families."

"And then I wouldn't dare overlook the fact that some white guys tend to look at police work as another method to keep black people in line. It's almost like well, ain't no almost about it -- it's a different kind of Klan movement. It's crazy, and people don't want to hear it. But in reality, if you look at it...it has always been used for that. [During the civil rights movement] law-enforcement personnel became very instrumental in keeping black folks in line. And I can't overlook that that attitude still exists to a degree, and some people get into it for that purpose."

Acutely sensitive to the gulf between white cops and African-Americans, Allen spoke to dozens of minority community groups while assigned to a beat in West Dallas. "I told them up front, 'I know your attitude about police officers, and I agree half of them aren't worth a darn. But give me the chance to show you that I want to make a difference!"

Allen's harsh views have similarly shaped his relationships within the DPD. "I started talking about blackness in the academy," Allen recalls "I didn't accept the terminology that we're all the same in blue." Once graduated, he and other TPOA members earned a reputation for criticizing other officers' actions.

This kind of outspokenness was bound to cause him trouble. And now, looking over his resume, Allen says it has.

A "resume," in DPD lingo, is the document that lists an officer's record of discipline and commendations. Allen has 25 commendations, including a Life Saving Award. He also has three reprimands and a termination (he was later reinstated). He believes the termination, two of the three reprimands, and even the Life Saving Award were all the result of his vigilante reputation.

The two reprimands, both early in his career, were relatively trivial. The first involved Allen's arrest of a marijuana peddler who turned out to be passing off parsley as pot. A jail sergeant filed a "false arrest" complaint against Allen -- even though DPD had no field-testing equipment at the time. Allen suspects that complaint may have been in retaliation for an abuse complaint he had lodged around the same time against a white officer.

The second was even pickier: Allen's boss wrote him up for "failure to follow established procedures" after Allen's parked squad car got bumped by a citizen motorist. Allen had been parked on the wrong side of the street at the time.

But by 1987, the environment was ripe for a collision between Allen and DPD. By this time, Allen had become a leader in TPOA. DPD, for its part, was in turmoil over the shooting of an elderly African American who had called to report a burglary. A congressional subcommittee was headed for Dallas to conduct a hearing into problems between DPD and the black community and Allen was slated to speak before the panel.

But just before he could do so, his supervisor sent him off to a two-week crime-prevention training school in New Braunfels. At the end of the first week, Allen's instructor agreed to let him leave early on Friday, and Allen returned to Dallas for TPOA's presentation to the sub-committee. Nonetheless, DPD officials charged him with being AWOL from the training school. After the instructor confirmed Allen's claim that he had permission to be absent, he says, the administration took another tack.

When he submitted his expense report from the two-week school, Allen turned in two receipts from a Steak and Ale restaurant -- one for $22.36 and one for $32.85. He says he told a Fiscal Affairs Department clerk that the $32.85 receipt wasn't accurate, that it was meant to substitute for several meal receipts he had lost. The clerk reimbursed Allen for the full amount.

Days later, however, Allen repaid DPD for the $32.85 receipt on the advice of his sergeant and his attorney. Nevertheless, DPD launched an investigation into the matter, eventually firing Allen for filing a "false report." An assistant city manager subsequently reinstated Allen, noting that $32.85 was not a sum "sufficiently significant to warrant termination."

Three times, Allen has been transferred against his will -- always, he says, after lodging some sort of complaint. He now works the white neighborhoods of North Dallas, a beat that frustrates his desire to work in an African-American neighborhood. Allen also claims that he was in line for a promotion to sergeant, when his supervisor "forgot" he had the required seniority and passed over him, promoting another black officer instead.

One final incident offers further evidence of Allen's persecution -- or paranoia. In the mid-1980s, Allen and his wife invested in a laundromat and a beauty salon. During renovation of one of the businesses, a plumber on the job called Allen, panicked by the constant presence of an unmarked police car. About the same time, a black colleague tipped Allen that the department was watching him. "I think they were wondering where I got all the money from," Allen says.

Although he's willing to explain these incidents in detail, Allen has little to say about the other highlight of his resume — his Life Saving Award. He brushes it aside, muttering something about pulling a family out of a burning house. "I appreciate whoever wrote it up," he says. "But it just looked at it as an appeasement-type thing, because about that time, we were complaining that blacks were not being recognized."

AMONG TPOA MEMBERS, COLORFUL RESUMES like Allen aren't the exception -- they're the rule. For example, Senior Corporal Calvin Howard, founder of the" Dallas chapter, has 33 commendations, five reprimands, and a one-day suspension. He was also terminated for defrauding the government -- a charge for which he stood trial and was subsequently acquitted. Nevertheless, when he finally won reinstatement, DPD docked him a year's pay.

Another TPOA member, Senior Corporal Harold Cornish has 24 commendations, 11 reprimands, and two suspensions totaling 13 days. He was also fired twice: once for sexual harassment (a white officer claimed Cornish touched himself in the crotch area in front of a white jail nurse) and once for a whole list of impolite actions — insubordination, discourtesy to a fellow employee, "conduct subversive to good order and discipline," and disobeying a direct order -- committed when Cornish asked pointed questions of a superior during roll call. Both times, Cornish won reinstatement from the city manager.

All these officers attribute at least some of their problems to departmental attempts to silence — or at least punish — them for their activism.

No police chief wants to see dissent in the ranks, and Dallas Chief Bill Rathburn is no different: He doesn't like TPOA's pickets. "I'd prefer they didn't protest at all," he says. "I think it's very unprofessional, and it doesn't produce any results."

However, that doesn't mean Rathburn's at odds with TPOA's substantive agenda. On the contrary, he believes that he and the group have the same goal in mind "a police department that's truly representative of the community at all levels," the chief says. "When you clear away all the dust, I don't think they have any strong disagreement with me," Rathburn says.

Indeed, when Rathburn appeared recently before the city council's public safety committee, he distributed charts depicting racial statistics of his department and pointed out all the weakest spots for council members.

According to these charts, DPD has made some progress in minority hiring: almost 37 percent of the recruits hired in the past year and a half are black. Yet the department still doesn't come close to reflecting the racial makeup of the city. Where Dallas is about 48 percent white, DPD is 71 percent white. Where Dallas is about 29 percent black, DPD is only 19.5 percent black.

But the biggest racial disparity, from a statistical standpoint, occurs in the punishment of officers. From the smallest official reprimand all the way up to termination, blacks consistently get disciplined in disproportionate numbers. For example, black officers get 34.5 percent of disciplinary actions rendered exclusively by sergeants, even though they comprise only 19.5 percent of the force; 54 percent of demotions and terminations have targeted blacks.

In his book *In the Line of Duty*, Dallas policeman Steve Elwonger describes the short, ill-fated career of Dallas' first black policeman. His name was William McDuff, and he was 63 years old when he was hired, in October 1896, to patrol the black Springtown area. That December, McDuff arrested two youths for fighting at a church. A few nights later, at 7:30 on Christmas Eve, the two youngsters stood in McDuff's front yard yelling. When the elderly officer came out to ask the boys to pipe down, one of them pulled out a gun and fatally shot McDuff in the head.

It would be 50 years before Dallas would hire another full-fledged black policeman.

THROUGHOUT THE SOUTH, BLACKS FIRST RECEIVED POLICE jobs during Reconstruction. But they had only token status, writes W. Marvin Dulaney, a University of Texas at Arlington professor who serves as history curator at the Dallas Museum of African-American Life and Culture: assigned to black neighborhoods, they were forbidden to wear uniforms, banned from promotion, and often barred from arresting whites. When Reconstruction ended, most departments purged blacks from their ranks.

A 1947 Dallas Times Herald article alludes to a single black "deputy policeman" hired in 1906. And Dulaney writes of two black men who, in 1936, became Dallas officers — for a day. It was "Negro Day" at the Texas State Fair, and a group of black officers from Houston, Galveston, Beaumont, and San Antonio — known as the Texas Negro Peace Officers Association -- was scheduled to march in a parade at the fair. When the Dallas Negro Chamber of Commerce pointed out that the city wouldn't be represented, Dallas' police chief assigned two station orderlies to don uniforms. Once the parade was over, they returned the blue suits and returned to their previous work.

Ten years later, the notion of hiring black police on even a trial-basis was still novel enough to embroil Dallas' city council in a dispute "considered by observers to be charged with political dynamite," according to a 1946 *Dallas Times Herald* article. The council eventually did vote unanimously to allow DPD to hire 14 black officers. More than 90 blacks applied; of these, DPD hired two. Newspaper accounts reassured readers that several other cities had black officers, that the pair in Dallas would always be supervised by white commanders, and that they would be assigned only to black neighborhoods.

On February 10, 1947, these two black officers hit the streets -- literally, assigned to foot patrol near the intersection of Thomas Avenue and Hall Street, then a bustling black section of town. Reporting for work in plain clothes, they changed into uniforms in a nearby housing project (DPD's locker room would not be integrated until 1955). Trained apart from white recruits, they patrolled without a squad car (no black would be given a car until 1961). Each time they arrested a lawbreaker, they had to walk their prisoner to the nearest pay phone and call the station to dispatch a white officer to take the suspect downtown.

Although there was no written policy saying black officers couldn't arrest whites, this awkward arrangement made it virtually impossible, since any whites in the area were driving through in cars.

By the mid-1950s, black leaders were clamoring for more black police to help reduce crime in their areas. One of the handful of blacks hired as a result of this outcry was Mackeroy Tuck.

Tuck, who retired in 1984 and is now running for president of the local National Association for the Advancement of Colored People, has a knack for phrasing his opinions diplomatically. This skill helped him survive 29 years with DPD with no disciplinary action — a feat he finds hard to fathom to this day.

As the only African-American in his academy class, Tuck was the target of occasional racial "jokes." One day, while the class was studying gaming laws, the instructor called on Tuck to explain the rules of shooting dice. "I told him I didn't know the rules because I had never shot dice," Tuck recalls. Yet the next day, the instructor asked him again.

Tuck chose to ignore the prejudice he encountered. To do otherwise would have required too much time -- because not a day went by without a slur, he says.

It would be years before Tuck donned a uniform. In the '50s, all of DPD's black officers -- all six of them were working undercover, usually in vice, where they were assigned to break up gambling operations in the backrooms of black bars.

This tactic would haunt DPD in later years, when federal agencies would force the city to hire black cops. The city attorney would constantly fall back on the excuse that blacks didn't want to be police because they'd lose the respect of their own community. But any truth to that statement could be traced back to DPD's own policies, as Tuck attests: "People in my community saw me as a glorified snitch."

Tuck eventually rose to detective. When the department phased out that out by converting detectives to sergeants, Tuck got stripes. He can't remember exactly when this occurred (he constantly apologizes for his faulty memory of dates), but he is proud enough of it that the house he today uses as a real estate office has blue shutters with cutouts that are, unmistakably, sergeant stripes.

As a sergeant Tuck supervised a predominantly white division where, he says without elaboration, he encountered "resistance." Again, he chose to ignore it. "All I wanted was eight hours of respect," Tuck says. "I'd get my loving somewhere else."

In 1968, when Bill Cosby and Robert Culp were playing crime-fighting partners in a sitcom called "I Spy," the Dallas Police Department launched a recruiting drive explicitly including "Negroes." At the time, blacks comprised 19% of the city but only 1-percent of the police force. So on March 17, the *Dallas Morning News* ran a feature story announcing this incredible "opportunity" for blacks.

In the seventh paragraph of this fullpage story, the writer reassures readers that African-Americans were actually qualified for police work: "The Negro officers as a group have proved to be as capable as white officers. Some are outstanding."

As proof, the article cited a letter written to the chief by a white businessman who had been given a traffic citation by a black: "Many times in the back of my mind I have thought that if a Negro ever tried to give me a ticket for anything, hell would break loose then and there. Well, after today, I guess I am a poor liar. I was stopped for going straight ahead instead of 'left lane must turn left' and given a ticket by the most well trained, well-behaved man I have ever met. And he was right, too, darn it! In the past 16 years, this is ticket No. 2 for me, and if I get one tomorrow, I hope it is from a man as nice about it as this [officer] was, regardless of color."

The reporter apparently conducted anonymous interviews with many of the 15 blacks then on the force. Most reported rosy relationships with both white citizens and white officers, but a few noted, "We weren't accepted at first...In the beginning some of the officers wouldn't even speak to us." According to the story, black recruits were simply hard to find due to the negative feeling that this race generally has toward the police."

A year later, in an Associated Press story headlined "Texas Negroes Cool to Police Jobs," DPD's lone black recruiting officer, Emmett Hill, reported that the biggest obstacle to recruiting blacks remained hostility toward police: "White officers must learn to approach Negroes without using provocative terms like 'boy.'"

Calvin Howard, now a senior corporal with almost 20 years on the force, began organizing the local chapter of TPOA in 1974. He had joined DPD in 1972, after working two years for the Tarrant County sheriff's office, where he was a member of a local TPOA chapter.

At the time, DPD had about 35 black officers on a force of more than 1,700. The fledgling TPOA chapter organized in secret, meeting every Sunday for a year in a black fraternity house, chosen because it had bars on all the doors and windows. They felt that if the department found out we were trying to organize an association, that we'd probably get fired," Howard recalls.

The fears weren't completely groundless. Once they received their charter and announced their organization, the dozen or so black officers in the group began to notice they were being written up for minor infractions such as being late to roll call or being seen without a hat. "All kinds of nit-picking stuff," Howard says. "All the sudden, everything you do, they find something wrong with it."

The strongest reaction, though, came from the Dallas Police Association. All the charter members of TPOA had been members of DPA; all but one dropped out of DPA once TPOA went public.

In a way, DPA served as the catalyst for the information of TPOA, Howard says. "We had met with members of DPA about problems we were having as far as transfers, getting job assignments, hiring more minority applicants, and the president of the organization at the time told me that 'that was not a [DPA] association concern; that was a personal concern.' So we were paying dues into an association that was not addressing African-American officers' concerns."

The biggest issue, of course, was full integration of the police department. TPOA wanted more blacks and Hispanics hired and the association's board members were about to get their chance to make it happen.

By the mid-1970s, there was a persistent rumor consistently denied by police administrators that DPA had set a "magic number" of 100 for black officers; that once the 2,000 member force reached that figure, no more blacks would be recruited. By the summer of 1978, there were 96 blacks on the force.

TPOA board members met several times with then Chief Don Byrd to push for more. Finally, they sent Byrd a letter complaining about the lack of black hires and hinting that some DPD recruiters might be discouraging black applicants. Byrd responded by summarily transferring all seven TPOA board members who had signed the letter to DPD's personnel division, where they became known as the "Sudden Seven." Later that summer, Sergeant Mackeroy Tuck joined the group.

It was a temporary assignment; Byrd gave the Sudden Seven only 120 days to put up or shut up — to prove they could recruit blacks. And he made the transfer in June, when the most fertile recruiting grounds — black colleges — were mostly closed for the summer.

The Sudden Seven set out to try to sell a job with built-in barriers to entry against those from the lower rungs of the economic ladder. For one thing, applicants who met all the requirements had to come to Dallas at their own expense twice first for three days for civil-service, physical-fitness, and polygraph tests, then two months later, after a thorough background check, for an interview. To overcome that problem, TPOA helped applicants arrange transportation and offered them lodging.

But the preliminary requirements themselves contained a list of other "cut factors," as they were known. Applicants could be disqualified for having a flawed credit history or a relative with a police record. Experimentation with marijuana was grounds for rejection. Female applicants could be rejected for having had a child out of wedlock or a venereal disease. Mexican-American applicants were rejected if anyone in their family was living in the U.S. illegally.

Other "cut factors" were purely subjective; an applicant could be disqualified for being "immature." The Sudden Seven, TPOA, and later a friendly lawyer all worked together to get such disqualifiers removed, but some, like the credit-rating cut factor, fell only after the Sudden Seven's 120 days had elapsed.

Another conspicuous Dallas disqualifier — the requirement for 45 hours of college credit — was often viewed as a handicap to minority hiring. Before transferring the Sudden Seven, Byrd had considered a 13-point plan called "Specific Program for the Recruitment of Black Males" that called for dropping the college requirement. But TPOA lobbied against dropping the education requirement; in fact, city statistics have shown that blacks hired by DPD tend to have more college hours than whites.

The Sudden Seven spent weeks on the road, meeting with applicants in college lounges and motel rooms. During their first 30 days, 43 blacks applied. DPD administrators claimed the Sudden Seven's efforts were a failure — that only three blacks had been hired during the 120-day experiment. But Tuck points out that the hiring process usually takes a minimum of three months --and says dozens of minority applicants recruited by the Sudden Seven found their way onto the force after the 120-day deadline.

No one disputes one of the Sudden Seven's finds: a young Jackson State College student named James Allen. About the same time, TPOA's fundamental claim that DPD discriminated against blacks gained credibility, thanks to two federal rulings.

The first resulted from complaints TPOA had filed in 1976 with the Justice Department and the federal Office of Revenue Sharing.

On September 1, 1978, the revenue sharing office sent city officials a letter threatening to take away $15 million in federal funds because of two substantiated allegations: that DPD did not reflect the racial makeup of the city and therefore discriminated in hiring, and that DPD's promotional practices discriminated against blacks.

The city adopted an attitude of limited cooperation. Then city manager George Schrader submitted a report proposing that DPD attract more minority recruits by expanding the age range of the police cadet corps to 30 (cadets could attend college full-time and be reimbursed for half their tuition). As for upward mobility, Schrader noted that fewer than one-third of the blacks eligible to take the sergeant's exam did so. "Some minorities are not motivated to compete on the examinations as they felt they had little chance of promotion even if successfully scoring high on the examination," he wrote.

Less than a year later, DPD statistics indicated that relatively few black applicants were hired, that those who were hired often failed to make it through the academy, and that no black officers had been promoted.

This, the federal agency concluded, was "quite disturbing."

The second validation black officers received came in a federal class-action suit filed by Brenda Davis, a black woman who had applied to DPD. On December 18, 1979, U.S. District Judge Patrick Higginbotham handed down an order ruling that DPD's hiring practices were discriminatory.

The suit had been filed three years earlier by two young lawyers: Martin Frost and Kenneth Molberg. Frost, of course, has gone on to become a Dallas congressman; Molberg is currently county chairman of the county Democratic Party.

In these heady days after Bill Clinton's victory, it might seem that Molberg would have to search his memory for the details of such an old case. On the contrary; "I talked to Brenda just the other day," Molberg says. Not only was it his first lawsuit — "I had that case the first day I got out of Law school," he says but the suit is still open and active today. "I've had four children since I took this case," Molberg says, "and one or them is now 13."

Public reaction to his first round of success in the case -- endless appeals have followed made another indelible mark on his memory. "It was a very unpleasant time," he says. "I remember all the hate mail I got after the *Morning News'* lead story on the Higginbotham ruling."

To decide whether or not DPD had discriminated, the judge cited DPD's own statistics: that between 1973 to 1977, 22 percent of applicants to DPD were black, but only 14 percent of DPD hires were black.

The city argued that blacks have a conditioned aversion to police that makes them reluctant to seek such jobs, that the black-applicant flow was so high only because of DPD's strong minority-recruitment efforts. But "for the city's argument to be valid," Higginbotham concluded, "it would have to show that the strong recruitment efforts were directed at an applicant pool less well qualified than the applicant pool it would have had without strong recruitment...

"It then passes to the city to show that the disparity is the result of some force other than unlawful discrimination. The city offered no such explanations except generalized statements about blacks' reluctance to engage in police work because of their attitude 'toward the man.'...

"Apart from its typecasting bias, that argument blinks at the reality of the numbers of blacks that did apply. The question of why blacks have been disparately failed has not been answered."

TPOA members and Molberg struggled to come up with, proposals to improve the hiring process. One recommendation led to a change in the racial composition of the three-man interview boards who are the final hurdle applicants' face (Brenda Davis had made it through the entire screening process before being rejected by a panel of three white males).

At one point, there were 273 claimants in this class-action suit. By then, Ronald Reagan had appointed Higginbotham to a higher court, and Judge Robert Porter took over the case. Over the next few years, he rendered decisions that reduced the effect of Higginbotham's order and whittled the class of claimants down to about 100. Higginbotham's fundamental finding, however, withstood all subsequent appeals.

In January 1981, DPD had 1,971 cops -- and only 118, or 6 percent, were black. With these bleak statistics and two federal rulings against it, city officials finally adopted an affirmative-action plan calling for an 85 percent increase in the number of black police officers by 1984, and for black recruits to comprise 20 percent of each DPD academy class.

Molberg takes some pride in the knowledge that his ongoing lawsuit has affected DPD's hiring practices. "We did see an upswing in the number of blacks hired by DPD," he says. "It has not been enough, but I shudder to think what it would've been had some of those things not been done back then."

In 1987, the city began developing yet another affirmative-action plan. This one, slightly stronger than the '81 version, called for an aggressive program of promoting minorities.

The Dallas Police Association responded by staging a press conference to attack the plan. DPA president Monica Smith claimed the scheme wasn't feasible and, besides, minority officers wouldn't want to be promoted that way.

Sergeant Linda Patterson, then president of TPOA, responded by assuring the media that her group would welcome the plan. "Anyone that's career-oriented certainly is not going to turn down an opportunity to be promoted," she said.

On February 10, 1988, after months of debate, the city council was set to approve the plan. That day, several hundred police wives and supporters marched from DPA headquarters to city hall "to show support for officers," according to a *News* story.

Nevertheless, the city council adopted the plan, designed to last through 1992. It gave DPD specific hiring targets: 33.3 percent black and 11 percent Hispanic for each of the next five years without lowering standards. The idea was to have DPD reflect the racial composition of the city by 1992, with 29 percent blacks and 12 percent Hispanics.

In truth, it was a grandiose goal; at the time DPD's ranks were 12.9 percent black and 6.1 percent Hispanic. Ten days later, the affirmative-action plan was met with embarrassing high-level resistance. In announcing the promotions of 10 new sergeants -- six white, two black, and one Hispanic -- Chief of Police Billy Prince issued a written statement apologizing for having "passed over" three white officers to promote one of the black cops, Leroy Griffin, number 13 on the list of eligible officers. "I regret this was necessary," Prince declared "I understand and sympathize with those who were passed over. I hope it is understood, however, that we must carry out the policies of the city council.

Indeed, Prince's decision to promote Griffin seemed calculated to make mockery of affirmative action. Within days, the *Times Herald* was showcasing Griffin's tarnished work history: he had been disciplined 11 times and suspended once for violations ranging from repeated tardiness to public intoxication (off duty) to failure to carry a gun (also off duty). Griffin would eventually be fired for an off-duty incident that occurred when he was again intoxicated.

By comparison, the three would be sergeants passed over in favor of Griffin had stellar records. None had received any disciplinary actions or complaints; on the contrary, one had received the Medal of Honor, DPD's third highest honor. DPA subsequently filed a reverse-discrimination lawsuit on behalf of the three white officers, asking for $13.5 million.

All of this began a pattern. Over the next few years, as various police chiefs made affirmative-action promotions, sometimes skipping over white officers, sometimes making executive appointments that allowed black officers to skip up a rank or two, DPA filed more lawsuits alleging reverse discrimination.

The conflict between the two unions, one mostly black, one mostly white, has delayed progress, Allen believes. "If they would get behind us," he says, "things could be accomplished much faster."

DPA president Smith says she isn't against affirmative action; she's just against the way the DPD has tried to carry it out. Her idea of a good affirmative action program offers no special efforts on behalf of minorities; instead, she would improve officer's benefits package to compete better with private industry for a diversified pool of recruits. After that, she suggests DPA improve its internal training programs to assure all officers a equal shot at upward mobility.

But affirmative action is just one of whole pile of bones the two groups have in contention. TPOA has publicly lobbied for an empowered citizen review board, drug testing for officers, and the addition of homosexuals onto the force. Recently, TPOA has proposed that the police department phase in a requirement that all officers live in Dallas.

DPA opposes all these notions.

The two groups are at odds even at seemingly basic concerns, such as pay and benefits. White DPA takes out radio ads accusing the city council of wasting money on parking lots and recommends targeting such funds to boost the pay of crime fighters, TPOA opposes special treatment for cops, insisting that all city employees need a raise. Where DPA was founded on the principles of unity, esprit de corps, and a patented "We're all blue" attitude, TPOA publicly denounces one of the cornerstones of that concept— the "code of silence," the tradition dictating that police officers never rat on or another.

Then there are the conspiracy theories each group harbors about the other. Allen says officers have, in the past, tipped him that DPA was plotting to "bust" TPOA by having several hundred white officers join. Allen says a few whites did show up at one meeting, but their plan, if there was one, was thwarted by TPOA's membership rules — every new member has to be sponsored by a current member. Adds Allen, "If Monica wants to join, though, I will personally sponsor her."

Smith, for her part, has an even longer list of allegations about TPOA — an organization she claims to have no access to and little knowledge of, aside from the impress in that "they have only one issue"— affirmative action— "in mind."

Eager to dismiss her smaller rival, she attributes TPOA's creation not to black officers themselves, but to Levi Davis, an African-American assistant city manager. "Management has created these divisions in order to divide and conquer" the department, Smith says. Under city manager Charles Anderson, Davis' assignment was "to form the black fire fighters association [and] the black police officers association," Smith declares; "TPOA has some beginnings prior to that, but they really weren't organized or formed until Mr. Levi Davis did it."

In fact, TPOA was chartered more than a decade before Davis even became Assistant City manger. And Davis denies Smith's story, dismissing it as "nonsense." Says Davis, "I spent a lot more time working with DPA than TPOA."

Last month, TPOA won a preliminary round in one of its racial-discrimination suits. The ruling, handed down by visiting Judge Robert G. Moss, declares DPD's sergeants' test discriminatory.

James Allen is not surprised that the city council, at DPD's urging, is planning an appeal. "Whites don't want to give up power," he says. "When you talk about relinquishing power to a black man, that's more frightening than anything else, because now you're on the same level that he is, even though history has always dictated that white is right.

"But nobody's trying to knock anybody out of power. We're just saying, 'Give us a piece of the pie. Give us what's ours."

In short, last month's ruling amounts to no more than a modest victory in the middle stages of the Dallas Police Department's bitter — and protracted — civil war.

THE ROOKIE

by Dusty Rhodes

VINCENT A. REETZ DIDN'T FEEL LIKE GOING TO WORK. He was suffering from a case of diarrhea so severe he was afraid he'd have to find a bathroom every five minutes — which wouldn't be easy, considering that he was a Dallas police officer about to head out on patrol. His fiancée Leslie, a registered nurse, urged him to stay home. But Reetz had never called in sick before, and he wasn't about to let a little upset stomach ruin that record.

R. L. "Gunny" Rose also ignored his instincts that night. Around 1:30 a.m., Protection Network called to notify him that the alarm at his South Oak Cliff floral shop had been tripped — again. Veterans Florist had been burglarized regularly over the past few weeks by crooks who stole everything from the photocopier to potted plants. Rose had tried several tactics to stymie the thieves — boarding up some of the windows, storing plants in his van. On this night, he dressed and got all the way out to his driveway before he stopped, went back inside, and strapped on his shoulder holster and gun.

Both men would have been better off following their initial instincts. For Reetz, December 15, 1990, would be his last shift on a job he loved, and possibly the end of his law-enforcement career. For Rose, the consequences were disastrous: he would die before the next dawn.

Shortly after he arrived at his floral shop, Rose waved down an approaching police car, which Reetz was driving. Reetz's partner, Senior Corporal Michael Epple, stepped out of the car, spoke briefly with Rose, and then set off around the west side of the building, searching for the burglar.

Reetz stayed in the squad car a moment longer to punch a computer code telling the dispatch center they had arrived at the call. He looked up just in time to see a man holding a handgun bolt south across the parking lot toward a chainlink fence. Reetz drew his pistol and ordered the man to drop his gun.

Instead, the stranger turned, and as he did, his weapon swung toward the officer. Reetz fired a single shot. He later found out the man he'd killed was Rose.

Over the next few months, this tragedy would be recounted dozens of times in newspapers and on television. The story quickly took on racial overtones — Reetz is white, Rose was black — and the florist's death marked the third time in four years that a white DPD officer had killed an innocent black at a crime scene.

Leaders of the black community were outraged. County Commissioner John Wiley Price called for a U.S. Department of Justice probe, claiming that Rose had been unarmed. Roy Williams, a 14-1 plaintiff planning to run for public office, asked for a congressional investigation of the incident. And local attorney James Belt was quoted in the *Dallas Times Herald* as saying Rose's death "looks like Etta Collins revisited," referring to a 1986 incident in which an unarmed 70-year-old black woman who'd reported a burglary at her neighbor's house was shot through her own glass door when Dallas police officers mistook her metal cane for a gun.

Unlike Etta Collins, Rose had indeed been armed. But to many blacks, his death seemed no more logical than hers. Rose wasn't merely innocent, he was a model citizen — a retired Marine, a veteran of the Vietnam conflict, a respected businessman, a devoted grandfather. For a man such as this to die from a policeman's bullet seemed so absurd, there could be only one explanation: Rose's death must be yet another example of white cops all too eager to kill blacks.

In an attempt to quell the public outcry, the Dallas Police Department treated Rose almost as it would a fallen officer. A deputy Chief was assigned to assist the Rose family. The department helped plan Rose's funeral and the city paid for it. Sam Gonzales, acting police Chief at the time, attended the service, along with the mayor and several other high-ranking officers.

However, no legal action was taken against Vincent Reetz. A grand jury declined to indict him. DPD's internal affairs division ruled his use of deadly force justified, and Reetz's supervisors recommended that he not be disciplined. Nevertheless, on February 28, 1991, Reetz resigned from the police force.

Now, almost two years after the incident, Reetz has agreed to speak publicly about the shooting for the first time. His telling adds color and shape to a catastrophe that has long been viewed as yet another black-and-white blunder. Reetz, too, places racial overtones on the story, although in his view, the racism was introduced in the aftermath of the shooting. Reetz claims then-acting police Chief Gonzales forced him to resign, primarily for political reasons — because he was a white man who killed a black man. Reetz recently filed suit against the city of Dallas, asking for reinstatement and back pay. He is charging reverse discrimination.

The two principals in this tragedy — Rose and Reetz — were promptly reduced to one-dimensional roles: noble victim and careless cop. The media routinely described the 53-year-old florist in terms of his military career and business accomplishments. Reetz was routinely defined as a 25-year-old rookie, still in the probationary stages of police training.

Both descriptions were true, but the quick sketch of Reetz was not the whole truth. Reetz wasn't your average rookie; he graduated at the top of what was then the largest academy class in the history of the Dallas Police Department, and he was widely regarded by his peers and superiors as the most promising recruit.

Reetz, a compact man with a receding hairline and a boxer's nose, still hopes to continue his police career. These days, he makes a living as a sales representative for a police-supply company. To keep his law enforcement certification current, he spends 16 hours a week working as an unpaid patrolman for a small community near Dallas.

Reetz claims he always wanted to be a policeman. When he was 17, he joined a Boy Scout Explorer post and began volunteering at the county sheriff's department in his small hometown near Denver. He and a buddy made the local newspaper when they chased down a pair of robbers after seeing an elderly woman get her purse snatched. He was so zealous he snitched on a few high-school classmates for buying and selling pot and helped arrest a few friends for drunken driving.

"Now don't get me wrong. I had friends and I went out and had a good time," Reetz says. "But I knew that to be a policeman, you could never break the law, you had to stand for something, you had to set a good example, and that's what I did."

At 21, he became a reserve officer and dispatcher for another small Colorado town. A year later, he took a dispatch job with the police department of a Denver suburb. He was biding his time there, sending out applications to various police departments, when he heard Dallas was hiring. When the Dallas Police Academy notified him he had been accepted, he was exuberant. His lifelong dream was about to come true.

His friends in Colorado, though, tried to slow him down. "Everybody up in dispatch told me, 'You're crazy to go to Dallas. They treat their cops like shit.' They said, 'Hey man, they *shoot* the police down there. They have no respect for the police.' They told me about racial problems down here ... but I just didn't believe it was that bad. I really, honestly didn't," Reetz says. "So I gave my two weeks notice the day Dallas called, and I was gone."

Reginald Hubbard taught police work at the academy, and he recalls being impressed by the student he knew as Vini. Says former Senior Corporal Hubbard: "I rated him as the number one recruit."

One of his academy classmates says Reetz was "the best in our academy — academic-wise, athletic-wise, everything else."

Take marksmanship, for example. On every shooting test — day fire shotgun, low light shotgun, day fire pistol, low light pistol — Reetz scored 100 percent. He was the only member of the class to do so.

"Unfortunately," he says now, thinking grimly of the deadly skill with which he shot the florist, Rose.

But marksmanship wasn't the only academy training that came into play that night.

The academy placed an understandably high emphasis on officer safety. One strategy for officer safety involved identifying anybody at a fresh crime scene. Hubbard taught the recruits to ask for identification and check for weapons.

"It has happened where somebody has robbed a 7-Eleven, put the clerk in the back, and assumed the identity of the clerk," Hubbard says. "Any time you go to a situation where a person there is potentially part of the problem, get an ID."

To drive home the concept of officer safety, academy instructors used some pretty melodramatic devices. One was a shooting scenario in which Reetz, as the best shot in the class, held his gun on a "suspect," who held a gun dangling at his side. Reetz couldn't fire until the "suspect" moved his gun. And even though Reetz had the advantage of being in the ready position, he never "won." The best he could do was "tie."

The lesson was, according to one of Reetz's classmates, "If you wait for somebody to point a gun at you, you're already dead."

An even more dramatic lesson came in officer survival training. One day, veteran officers stormed into the classroom carrying graphic color photos of police officers who had died in the line of duty — officers in full uniform lying dead at crime scenes. As the veterans held these pictures aloft, they yelled at the recruits, *"You want this to fucking happen to you? You want this to happen to your partner? You get lackadaisical, you make one wrong move out there, and you're fuckin' DEAD!"*

"That class had a huge impact on me," Reetz says.

Another concept, taught more subtly at the academy, also played a part in Rose's death. It's the concept that when the police issue a command, it *will* be obeyed, that something's wrong if it's *not* obeyed.

Although this notion is foreign to most civilians, it is ingrained in police. At the academy, it's taught from virtually the first day, when recruits are instructed to pronounce the word "police" Texas-style. They are taught to put heavy emphasis on the first syllable, to say "POH-leece" instead of "puh-LEECE," since the conventional pronunciation of the word is too likely to be misunderstood as a drawled version of "please."

DPD's academy lasts 25 weeks. By the end of that time, the instructors come to know their students fairly well. Reginald Hubbard is no longer on the Dallas police force (he was fired after passing numerous bad checks) and is therefore free to speak plainly about his memories of Reetz. (Because of Reetz's suit, all police department personnel are prohibited from speaking of Reetz or the Rose killing.) When asked if Reetz seemed zealous and itching for action, Hubbard says yes — every student was.

"Most every recruit is pretty much gung ho and happy and excited. That's typical. At the academy, they hear veteran cops tell their war stories, and they want to go out and make stories of their own.

"But I don't think Vini was any more overzealous than anybody else," Hubbard says. "I didn't have any concerns that he would get out there and shoot somebody for no reason. I don't think he would purposely want to hurt anybody. He did not show any signs of that; he's a quite sensitive guy."

Hubbard happens to be black.

Reetz graduated on August 20, 1990, and it didn't take him long to realize the job wasn't quite what he'd fantasized. For starters, the civilian population didn't seem to appreciate his presence. After years of idolizing cops, Reetz was stunned to discover that other people not only didn't respect his uniform and his badge, they sometimes abused him because of it. Hearing himself called "pig" was practically painless compared to the night he and his partner watched a boulder bounce off their squad car, narrowly missing Reetz's head, as they walked into a restaurant for dinner.

But Reetz's biggest shock was how busy and violent the job was. He was assigned to South Dallas, and the stress was constant and intense. Reetz, who had asked for an assignment in North Dallas, felt the tension in his gut, frequently suffering stomach cramps and diarrhea. If he had known as a child what police work was really like, "I probably would have been a fireman," Reetz says.

He spent a good deal of his time pulling over "occupied stolens." Or rather, *chasing* stolen vehicles. Their drivers usually don't just pull over.

His first week on the job, Reetz was involved in a chase in which the occupants bailed out and left the car in gear and headed toward a busy intersection. Reetz jumped out of his squad car, sprinted to the stolen vehicle, slammed it into park and then ran after the driver. After chasing the man a block down the street, he ended up face-to-face with the suspect in someone's backyard, surrounded by a tall wooden fence. When he radioed for assistance, Reetz couldn't tell the dispatcher his location. He yelled into his handset, "I am one block either north, south, east or west of where I started from!" Reetz used his flashlight to signal a police helicopter. Backup soon arrived and arrested the suspect.

Another time, he and his partner turned on their lights to stop a stolen car the computer showed had been used in an armed robbery. When the occupants of that vehicle hit a parked car and jumped out, a Mac 10 machine gun tumbled from the driver's lap.

Reetz, because he was a rookie, always rode with a field training officer, or FTO. FTOs are veteran cops who take a special 40-hour course to learn how to train fresh recruits on the street. Each rookie goes through a four-phase probationary period, taking more and more initiative as he or she progresses. In each phase, the rookie is paired with a different FTO.

Reetz's third FTO was Senior Corporal Michael Epple, then 30 years old, with about five years experience. He had just completed his FTO course April 27, 1990, while Reetz was still in the academy. (Epple, speaking through another officer, declined to comment for this story.)

According to Reetz, during their first week as partners, he and Epple responded to a burglary-in-progress call and arrived to find a man standing outside the house. When Reetz shined his flashlight on the man and requested ID, the man had a ready answer: "Hey, I'm the one that called you!" But as Reetz turned to tell Epple the situation, the self-professed "complainant" took off running.

This ruse is common enough that cops have a name for it — they call it "cool breezin'."

"I chased that man for eight blocks, over fences, around pools, through backyards, with dogs who bit him" Reetz says, "We finally caught him and who was he? He was the *bad* guy. He was the ex-boyfriend of the lady who lived in the house. I think he had been stalking her."

Reetz says this episode was still fresh in his mind a few nights later when he and Epple pulled up to a burglary call at Veterans Florist and found a man already there — a man who also took off running.

VINCENT A. REETZ, AND R. L. "GUNNY" ROSE had a lot in common. Had they met under different circumstances, they might even have been friends.

Rose, nicknamed "Gunny" because he had been a gunnery sergeant in the Marine Corps, shared Reetz's profound respect for the law. Rose was the sort of man who would scold his wife for parking over a white line; "Somebody else may want to park next to you," he'd say.

Like Reetz, Rose had won awards for his marksmanship. And like Reetz, who dotes on Leslie, who is now his wife, Rose was devoted to his family. After more than 20 years of marriage, he and his wife Evelyn not only worked together in their floral shop, they enjoyed each other's company enough that they went to lunch together almost every day.

They met after Rose returned from Vietnam to run a Marine recruiting office in Dallas. By the time he retired in 1976, Rose had 20 years of military service. He and a Navy recruiter opened a used-car lot called Nama Auto Sales (for Navy and Marine), but the business folded after six months.

Rose had plenty of other occupations to keep him busy. He had his own janitorial business, he was an insurance agent, and he was the landlord of a rental property. He was, according to his wife, a workaholic.

"He never did really break the regimen of the military," she says. "He'd get up in the morning and he'd exercise, lift weights and things, he'd run, come back and ride his exercise bike, get in this thing for a while" — she gestures toward a portable sauna — "sit right over there and shine his shoes, and he would be ready for the day."

He was known in the neighborhood as the man who refused to use an edger to trim around the circular driveway in front of his large home. He preferred to chop the stray grass with a shovel instead, insisting that he needed the exercise.

He was also known for his generosity. "He was the man in the community who always helped the seniors," his wife says.

When their youngest daughter, Nicole, reached preschool age, Evelyn had time to take up a hobby — flower arranging. She enrolled in classes at Mountain View Community College, where she heard about a floral shop for sale.

Called Veterans Florist, it was on South Lancaster Road, near the Veterans Affairs Medical Center. The owners, a couple of veterans, hoped to sell to another veteran. They wanted a $5,000 down payment, and after looking at the shop, Rose told Evelyn that if she came up with half the money, he would pay the rest. They bought the shop in 1979. Evelyn did most of the flower arranging; R. L. made the deliveries.

Over the years, they had a burglary now and again, but in November 1990, the shop's alarm started going off almost weekly. The crooks took typewriters, an adding machine, a television, even the little credit card processing machines. Mostly, however, they stole plants.

The Roses discussed how to deal with the break-ins. "I had told him, "Why don't you just close off all the windows?" Evelyn recalls. "He said, 'Nobody's gonna make me close up the shop.' I said, 'Why don't we just sell it? We can take the money and pay off the house.' He said 'Nah, I'm not gonna let nobody make me do that.'"

Every time the alarm went off, Rose would get dressed and drive to the shop, often arriving there ahead of the police. On the night of December 14, though, a pair of officers were on the scene before the alarm company had even notified the police.

Officers Michael J. Smith and Rene Dominguez heard an alarm go off as they were driving down South Lancaster. They lowered their windows to pinpoint the source, and zeroed in on Veterans Florist. Via radio, they asked the dispatch center if they'd been notified of a burglar alarm at 4819 South Lancaster. While the dispatcher was checking, Smith and Dominguez heard another officer asking for assistance in stopping an occupied stolen vehicle.

The call for assistance was just a block and a half away. By the time the dispatch center radioed back to confirm the burglary alarm, Smith and Dominguez were on their way to back up their fellow officer.

It was just one of a series of small coincidences that would add up to tragedy that night.

THIRTY-NINE SECONDS. That's the time that elapsed between Reetz and Epple's arrival at the scene and Epple's call for an ambulance. That's how much time it took to end one man's life and another man's career.

The following account is compiled from recent interviews with Reetz, along with documents from DPD's internal affairs division investigation, which includes sworn statements taken from Reetz, Epple, and all backup officers, both on the scene and in subsequent follow-up inquiries.

Around 1:40 a.m., Reetz and Epple were helping another team of officers near Tyler and Davis streets search for suspects who had bailed out of a stolen vehicle, when a dispatcher broadcast the call of a burglary alarm at 4819 South Lancaster. Even though they were a good 10 minutes away from the location, Epple punched the Code 5 key on the car's computer, signaling dispatch that he and Reetz were en route to the call.

Reetz drove to South Lancaster, but by the time they arrived, the alarm had reset and was no longer audible. In the dark, and without the sound to guide him, Reetz drove past the address by a block or two. When he realized his mistake, he made a U-turn. As he did so, Epple punched a Code 6 into the computer to indicate they had arrived at the call. It was a busy Thursday night, though, and the computer jammed and never beeped an acceptance of the signal.

Still searching for the address, Reetz noticed a brown van parked in front of a one-story business. Beside the open driver's door stood a man — a man who he would later learn was Gunny Rose — waving both hands in a circular motion, indicating he wanted the police car to stop. Although he was unsure whether they were at the correct address, Reetz pulled in and parked several feet behind and to the left of the van. Before he got his car into park, Reetz says, Epple got out and began walking toward the van.

Reetz turned off the squad car, grabbed his flashlight, and had one foot out of the car when he remembered the computer hadn't taken Epple's Code 6. Reetz leaned across the car, punched the button again, and watched to make certain the computer accepted the signal.

Epple, meanwhile, approached Rose and asked, "Are you the owner?" Rose nodded and told the officer he thought he had just seen the burglar stick his head out a window on the right side of the building. Epple drew his gun and walked toward that side of the building.

Reetz was 22 feet away from Rose, in a car with the radio chattering. He heard none of the brief conversation between Epple and Rose. By the time he looked up from the car computer, all Reetz saw was Epple with his weapon drawn, walking to the right, disappearing around the corner of the building.

Just then, according to Reetz, Rose leaned into the van and emerged with a gun in his right hand. He held the gun behind his right leg momentarily with his gaze still focused toward the right side of the building, where Epple had gone. This pose sent a chill through Reetz, who, at this point, knew only two things for sure: Epple had not had time to thoroughly ID this man and Epple was unaware that this man had a gun.

The only other information Reetz had was in his subconscious:

"Anytime you go to a situation where a person there is potentially part of the problem get an ID..."

"Hey, I'm the one that called you ..."

"You want this to fuckin' happen to you? You want this to happen to your partner?"

Suddenly, for reasons no one will ever know, Rose bolted to his left across the parking lot. Reetz felt relief; maybe this man was the thief — or perhaps a lookout trying to get away. Reetz would simply do what he had done in similar situations before — draw his pistol and order the man to drop his gun. In his short law-enforcement career, he had done this maybe 70 times before, and it had always worked. Always, always, always.

So Reetz drew his 9mm Sig Sauer and started dropping to the ground. As he did so, he yelled, *"POH-leece! Drop your gun!"*

But according to Reetz, Rose didn't. Instead, he turned quickly, his left arm nipple-height across his chest, like an honor guardsman carrying a flag, the gun in his right hand pointed toward Reetz.

BOOM!

Reetz heard a shot and saw the man fall backward before he even realized the sound had come from his own gun. The bullet ripped through the man's left wrist, through his shirt pocket, into his chest.

Reetz panicked. His mind was full of the kind of obscenities people use to try to express unutterable shock. *"Shit. Oh man. Shit. I can't believe this is happening."* Gun still drawn, he approached the man, who was lying on this back with his hands above his head and the gun still within reach. The man was mumbling, trying to say something, moving his arms. Reetz screamed at him: "Don't do that! Don't go for that fuckin' gun! Don't make me shoot you again!" Reetz stepped closer and pushed the man's gun a few inches away. Epple, about 30 feet down the side of the building, heard the shot and headed back to the parking lot to see what had happened. Before he even rounded the corner he heard Reetz screaming: "Why did you do that?! Why'd ya make me fuckin' do that?! Why'd ya point a gun at me?!" When Epple got close enough to see the man on the ground, he told Reetz, "I think you just shot the owner."

Epple found Rose's pulse and radioed for an ambulance. Then he picked up the gun, put it on the back floorboard of the squad car, and went back around the building to continue searching for the burglar, leaving Reetz standing over Rose.

The first two backup officers to arrive where H. A. Brown and Brenita Dunn. They found Reetz on his knees, about eight feet from Rose, with his gun still drawn, saying over and over, "Why did he point the gun at me?" Brown noted that Reetz "got up and started crying and waving his arms in the air." After checking on Rose, the two officers reminded Reetz to reholster his gun, and then guided him to their squad car.

"I think I shot the owner," Reetz told Dunn.

According to her sworn statement, Dunn, who is black, responded, "Until we find out what's going on, be thankful you're alive and not on the ground. Think about your training from the academy."

Dunn's words, Reetz says now, snapped him out of his hysteria.

Evelyn Rose's first clue that something had gone wrong came when her oldest daughter, Donna, called. Donna had just gotten a call from the alarm company, requesting that someone with a key go to the floral shop.

About the same time, Evelyn got a call from Methodist Medical Center, informing her that her husband had been involved in "an accident." She assumed he had been in a wreck. She woke her younger daughter, Nicole, then 14, and together they went to the hospital. For what seemed like a long while, they were kept waiting. They noticed that there were many police personnel in the waiting area too. Someone brought Evelyn her husband's wallet. Then, a little later, they took her into a room and, without explaining how, told her that her husband had died.

She drove herself and Nicole home and called her son-in-law. He took her to the floral shop — or as close as he could. Police wouldn't let Mrs. Rose near her own property. Finally, someone told her that her husband had been shot by an officer.

The scene was swarming with people. Eight backup officers and a canine unit had been called to make sure a burglar wasn't still present. Smith and Dominguez, the patrolmen who first heard the alarm, had stopped by to see what all the commotion was. But most of the people on the scene, 19 in fact, were there to investigate the shooting: two sergeants, six investigators from the physical evidence section, five from crimes against persons, three from internal affairs, one lawyer from the city attorney's office, another from the Dallas Police Association, and a doctor from the medical examiner's office.

While they collected evidence, Reetz sat sequestered in a squad car a half-block down the street with two other officers, talking about anything but the shooting.

At 3:50 a.m., about two hours after the shooting, Reetz was brought back to the scene to do a "walk-through." As he described the shooting, the 19 investigators followed him around the scene asking questions. Only then did he finally see the address, the sign saying Veterans Florist, and realize he had actually been at the burglary call.

The session was tape-recorded, and the transcript of his statement is the same account Reetz gives today. The most significant detail, though, doesn't come in his telling of what happened. It's the thing that didn't happen — Reetz never made a conscious decision to fire his gun.

That night almost two years ago, he told investigators, "... I don't even remember firing it, it just went off, boom, and he went down real hard."

He tells it exactly the same way today: "I don't even remember firing, because I thought he fired at me. When I shot, I didn't even know I shot. It was just training. It was instinct, that I'm about to get killed."

Epple also did a walk-through that night. His account dovetailed with Reetz's with a few exceptions. Epple says he took an indirect route to Rose, walking all the way to the passenger side of the van, and talking to him across the vehicle, and that he assumed Reetz was standing near Rose on the driver's side of the van. Reetz recalls Epple standing in front of the van. Epple also says Reetz had the car's spotlight on but not the headlights; Reetz says he left the headlights on but didn't use the spotlight.

It was almost noon — 10 hours after the shooting — by the time Reetz finished answering questions and signing statements at the station. An officer drove him to Leslie's apartment, where she prepared breakfast for them. Then the other officer left and Reetz broke down.

"He was, god, every emotion you could think of," Leslie says. "He was like, 'I can't believe this has happened. I never thought it would happen to me.' It was just incredibly traumatic. We did a lot of crying."

She took him to her parents' home, where her mother gave him a tranquilizer. When he finally dozed off, he slept for 24 hours.

WHEN SHE WAS A CHILD, EVELYN ROSE'S FATHER ran a funeral home, and she grew up with a pragmatic attitude about death. "Death is a part of life," she says. She recalls reacting to her husband's death with a sort of "cold, hard, numb" feeling. Her greatest concern seems to have been its effect on Nicole.

Evelyn Rose is practical, unsentimental, slightly cynical but not bitter.

But she's not buying Reetz's story.

She doesn't believe Reetz was driving; she believes it was "his night to sleep," that he was dozing in the passenger seat and therefore groggy when he and Epple arrived at Veterans Florist.

She doesn't believe her husband answered Epple's question, "Are you the owner?" with a mere nod of his head. "He was not the type of man that would nod his head," she says. "He would talk to you. He would say yes, I am the owner."

She doesn't believe that the squad car and the van were parked in the positions shown on police diagrams. She believes they were closer together, close enough for Reetz to have heard Epple's conversation with her husband.

She doesn't believe her husband ever took his gun out of his holster. Or if he did, she doesn't believe he would hide it behind his leg. "He was not that type of person," she says.

She doesn't believe her husband was running that night, because, she says, he couldn't, that he was hurt, that he had had surgery earlier that week. He had a wart removed from the sole of his left foot.

She believes that Reetz could have taken cover behind the squad car before pulling his gun, and therefore wouldn't have felt threatened if her husband actually did turn with his gun. And she believes that her husband was shot with his hands up gesturing to say "I'm not the one."

She also believes Reetz and Epple rehearsed their story together before backup units arrived.

Another person who has some doubts about Reetz's story is James Allen. Allen is a corporal in the Dallas Police Department and a 14-year veteran on the force. He is better known, though, as president of the Texas Peace Officers Association, an organization of African-American law-enforcement professionals.

Allen believes Reetz did fear for his life, but part of that fear was based on Rose's race. He blames DPD for not addressing the natural fear almost everyone has for different races. "People don't want to look at the possibility that white people are afraid of black people," he says. "You're talking about putting a white kid in a predominantly black environment late at night. His level of fear in general tends to escalate. And I don't think that fear level has been explored enough, at least not here in Dallas."

Allen believes Reetz probably wouldn't have fired if the man pointing the gun at him had been white. He bases this belief on his experience participating in simulated scenarios at the academy. In one burglary-in-progress scenario, he has a man emerge from behind a building holding a gun at his side. Allen says white recruits tend to fire faster if the man with the gun is black than if he is white.

Allen places part of the blame on Epple, for failing to find out whether Rose had a gun. "I've been doing this a long time," he says, "and I still, when I get to a call and the owner's there, the first thing out of my mouth, almost, is: Do you have a weapon? Where is it? And I unload it. They may even get pissed off because I didn't search the building fast enough, and the burglar got away. But I'm concerned about my safety."

Allen also places part of the blame on Rose, for getting out his gun. Allen says that every time he is a guest on a radio talk show, which is quite often, he reminds citizens that they should put away any weapon once police are called. He blames DPD for not making such community education a priority.

Within six hours of the shooting — while investigators were still taking statements and gathering evidence — deputy Chief Ray Hawkins surprised reporters by revealing details about Rose's wounds and particulars from officers' statements, apparently breaking department policy in doing so. DPD's official response to the shooting was so candidly apologetic that, days later, *The Dallas Morning News* ran a front page story hailing the police department's "new attitude."

According to that story, Hawkins avoided blaming anyone other than his officers for the tragedy: "When [Hawkins] described what actions by Mr. Rose precipitated the shooting, he quickly noted that the store owner's actions were reasonable."

A few weeks later, a memo went out to all DPD patrol division commanders instituting a policy designed to ensure that police would clearly identify and protect any "complainant or witness" at a crime scene.

But Reetz didn't mind the department apologizing for his mistake. He wanted to apologize himself. He told other officers of his overwhelming urge to attend Roses's funeral, but no one seemed to think it was a good idea. "I guess it just wasn't proper," Reetz says, "but I wanted to pay my respects because he was a good guy."

He waited a few weeks, until he thought he wouldn't interrupt any of Roses's family members or friends, then went to the cemetery to look for the grave. It was so new, it had no tombstone yet; he had to get a map from the office in order to find it.

"I know this may sound stupid and ludicrous and insane, but my main mission was to find out *why*," Reetz says. "I was hoping a voice would come out and say ... just a reason why he turned and pointed the gun."

Six months later, he visited the grave again. "He knows," Reetz says. "He knows what happened that night."

Reetz knows what happened that night, too. And he has finished second-guessing himself.

"I am really sorry it happened the way it did," Reetz says, "but I feel I did what I was trained to do."

When the Dallas Police Department concluded its investigation of the shooting, Senior Corporal Epple faced two allegations: That he failed in his responsibility as an FTO to communicate 'pertinent information' to Reetz, and that he violated standard operating procedure by searching the florist's shop alone, without his partner. He received a letter of reprimand and was demoted to patrolman for five months.

Reetz also faced two allegations: failure to Code 6, and failure to render aid to Rose. Both allegations are minor and in Reetz's mind, specious. Most of his superiors apparently agreed.

On February 25, 1991, Sergeant R. C. Dillon, who was in charge of the on-scene investigation, sent acting Chief Sam Gonzales a three-page memo disagreeing with both allegations against Reetz.

Concerning the Code 6 allegation, Dillon wrote: "It is normally the passenger's responsibility to operate the MDT [the squad car's computer] in a two-man element ... Because operating the MDT was not Officer Reetz's primary responsibility ... and [because of] the fact that the officers had tried unsuccessfully to send the arrival code prior to pulling into the drive of the business ... I recommend that this allegation be unfounded and therefore no disciplinary action be instituted against Officer Reetz for this allegation."

Dillon also objected to the second allegation: "According to testimony from Senior Corporal Epple, Mr. Rose was still breathing and was not bleeding profusely from his wound. As CPR can only be given to persons who have stopped breathing and whose heart has stopped, there was no reason to begin any CPR. As there was no major external loss of blood evident from Mr. Rose, there was no need for direct pressure to stop bleeding. An ambulance had already been ordered and there was absolutely no other medical care that Officer Reetz could have given Mr. Rose."

Lieutenant E. G. Silva sent a shorter memo suggesting the Code 6 allegation be sustained, but also disagreed with the second allegation. "I also do not believe that Apprentice Officer Reetz was in any condition after the shooting to be held accountable for his actions in respect for giving first aid."

Deputy Chief Terrell Bolton and assistant Chief Greg Holliday concurred with Sergeant Dillon's memo. And neither internal affairs nor any of Reetz's superiors suggested Reetz be terminated from the force.

So it came as a shock to Reetz when, on February 27, a Wednesday, he received a call from his attorney, Bob Baskett, saying he would be fired unless he resigned by 9 o'clock the following morning.

Basket says he had gotten a call from acting Chief Gonzales. Gonzales, now Chief of police in Oklahoma City, declined to comment for this story, citing Reetz's current lawsuit. But Baskett remembers the gist of his conversation with Gonzales. "I don't remember his exact language," Baskett says, "but it was clear to me that the message being conveyed was simply if Vince [Reetz] didn't resign, he was going to be terminated."

Since this action had not been recommended by the chain of command, Baskett believes two other factors motivated Gonzales. "The situation here was a little different because of Reetz's probationary status. The truth of the matter is, they didn't have to find any misconduct. A nonprobationary employee would not have been terminated for the conduct that was found wanting here.

"But then, we had a terrible political environment at the time, too ... And I think the environment contributed," Baskett says. "It was like, if we don't do something to him, if we don't get rid of him, we'll have people running around screaming and yelling."

There was, perhaps, one additional factor. In the three months that had elapsed since the shooting, the city had hired William Rathburn as the new Chief of police. He was due to arrive on Monday, March 4. In a letter to Reetz, Dallas Police Association president Monica Smith wrote that she believed the city wanted Reetz's case closed before Rathburn's arrival.

"It is my opinion that Chief Gonzales agreed to take the heat of the decision for Chief Rathburn," Smith wrote. "Then, the new Chief could start with a noncontroversial slate. The city manager [Jan Hart] certainly did not want Chief Rathburn to make a decision in this case which would either create friction between the new Chief and Ms. Hart or between the new Chief and the community."

Reetz, though, wasn't thinking about city or department politics. Given less than 24 hours to make his decision, he was just a rookie watching his childhood dream dissolve. Desperate for advice, he talked to everyone he could — his lawyers, his parents, and Monica Smith. He even tried to get hold of Rathburn. But Rathburn was on his honeymoon.

FINALLY, REETZ AND HIS FIANCÉE, LESLIE, REALIZED HE HAD TO RESIGN.

"Our decision was based on him being able to get another job," she says. "We knew if he got fired, no one would hire him. Really, it was me pushing him to do it, because I was thinking of the future."

The next morning, Reetz met with Gonzales and handed him a letter of resignation. The meeting lasted five, maybe 10 minutes, and Reetz used part of that time to make a final request, which Gonzales denied.

"I told him I wanted to meet with Mrs. Rose," Reetz says. "I wanted to tell her what happened out there. I wanted to tell her that, God knows, I did *not* want to hurt Mr. Rose. And I wanted to tell her it was not because he was black; it was because I was in genuine fear for my life."

For about a year, Reetz tried to get on with his life. He applied for jobs at several suburban police departments, but was turned down at every one once his history was uncovered. Finally, convinced he had been unfairly treated, Reetz decided to take legal action. He consulted some lawyers he knew and was directed to a 30-year-old civil rights attorney named Noemi Collie.

Collie lives and works in a garage apartment hung with beaded curtains in every doorway and folk art on every wall. She shares this space with her poet boyfriend and a menagerie of animals. It's hard to picture a square like Reetz sitting on the rattan sofa of Collie's hippie pad.

"I do not have a good impression of police officers," she says, adding that all of her other lawsuits involving police are brutality cases. "I had to think really hard about this case. It scared me a little bit. But in the long run, that's what made me take it."

Over and over, she reiterates that this case shouldn't detract from the claim that Evelyn Rose still might file against the city if she does not receive an acceptable settlement. (Mrs. Rose is still negotiating with the city.) "I think the city should compensate the Rose family," Collie says. "But two wrongs don't make a right."

Part of the reason Collie decided to represent Reetz was that she'd come to like him as a person. "He has a conservative edge, for sure ... But he's not a power-monger; he's not out there to get off on showing off his gun. That's not who he is," she says.

When Reetz came to her, he didn't know the term "reverse discrimination." That was Collie's idea. "This is the only claim he has available to him," she says. "I believe the facts that I can prove are circumstantial evidence of racial discrimination. The only reason he lost that job is because the city was feeling racial pressure."

Collie seems to have more confidence in the case — for which a trial date has not been scheduled — than her client.

Still seeking a police job, Reetz left recently to look for work back in Colorado.

REGULATION OF SEXUALLY ORIENTED BUSINESSES

By Texas Law Enforcement Management And Administrative Statistics Program

Introduction

Sexually Oriented Businesses (SOBs) were at one time considered enterprises relegated to the back alleys and sleazier parts of major urban centers. This, however, is no longer the case. In fact, the past 25 years have witnessed an explosion of SOBs in and around many major suburban and urban areas.

Sexually oriented businesses that were once housed in rundown, smoke-filled store fronts have taken on a new look. In particular, establishments that house topless or totally nude entertainment are in many areas glistening up-scale palaces of glass and chrome designed to appeal to the young and middle-aged upwardly-mobile male.

Owners of these businesses are also no longer content with word-of-mouth advertising as they appear to have embarked on advertising campaigns by way of billboard, print, and the television media, to name a few. Similar movement has been observed in SOBs offering modeling, escort, and massage services. Some even openly advertise bondage and domination (B&D) and sadomasochism (S&M) services. Most mainline video and magazine stores now carry some level of sexually oriented videotapes and/or magazines.

Until recently, agencies responsible for the regulation of SOBs have been in a reactive mode partially due to departmental and legal guidance as well as the evolving position of the United States Supreme Court with court challenges to legislation on First and Fourteenth Amendment grounds. For the most part, the Texas legislature, through the Texas Local Government Codes, has given the power of regulation of SOBs to local governments. As such, each jurisdiction has the opportunity to regulate their operation on the basis of local community standards.

> The prohibition against pornography in the United States is fast becoming unenforceable. It has been estimated that the nation's pornographers conduct a $4 billion-a-year business. The ten leading men's "skin" magazines were expected to generate close to $475 million in revenues . . .The adult film business was expected to gross over $365 million. . . .The biggest component of the United States sex business is the thousands of adult bookstores and peep shows around the country. Large adult bookstores and peep shows in New York's Times Square area can gross $10,000 a day. Thirty percent of all newsstand sales comes from periodicals that only 20 years ago might not lawfully have been at a newsstand at all. The hottest item in the movie business is the videotape, and the hottest thing in videotape is X-rated movies. There are now unmistakable signs of organized crime's growing interest in the pornography business in the United States

Background

During the 1970s, many jurisdictions in Texas experienced rapid growth in the Sexually Oriented Businesses industry. In Harris County alone, over 40 SOBs were in operation fronting for prostitution. Because competition was intense between establishments, some owners sought to eliminate the competition by arson, physical assaults, and threats to female employees (Griffin 1995). Control and regulation of SOBs has been a challenge to regulating agencies because of the victimless nature of the offense, most infractions must be witnessed, and the low-priority and/or lack of human resources in many jurisdictions.

Bill Blackwood Law Enforcement Management Institute of Texas

Attitudinal Determinates

Residents' attitudes at a particular locale often have a direct bearing on whether or not certain businesses will be allowed to operate. This syndrome has been given the acronym N.I.M.B.Y., or "Not In My Backyard." For example, residents of Texarkana exerted pressure on local government to stop the opening of a club which was to include a restaurant and a "topless" bar. Thirty minutes before the business was scheduled to open, the license to operate was revoked. This was accomplished through an ordinance prohibiting sexually oriented businesses from operating within 1,000 feet of a residential neighborhood, school, public park, licensed day-care center, or church. Inside the Bowie County Correctional Center was a meeting place used for counseling, meals, recreation, library services, and church services. Because the room was used intermittently for church services, the court ruled against the club. Although the ruling was later overturned by a federal court judge, pressure exerted by a local citizen's group in conjunction with the Texarkana Police Department were eventually successful in closing the business.

Citing the Texas Local Government Code, the city of Texarkana, in local ordinance No. 202-94 regulating the operation of sexually oriented businesses, pointed to the following:

(1) Texas Local Government Code, Section 215.074 which authorizes home-rule cities to regulate the location and control of conduct of, among other things, theaters, movie theaters, and all public places.
(2) Texas Local Government Code, Section 215.075 which authorizes home-rule cities to license any lawful business, occupation or calling that is susceptible to the control of police power.
(3) Texas Local Government Code, Sections 54.004 and 217.042 which authorizes cities with home-rule to enforce all ordinances necessary to protect health, life and property, and to preserve and enforce the good government, order and security of such cities and inhabitants.
(4) Texas Local Government Code, Section 243.003 which authorizes home-rule cities to adopt, by ordinance, regulations regarding sexually oriented businesses as the municipality considers necessary to promote the public health, safety and welfare.

Other examples of jurisdictions that have used the Texas Local Government Code as a basis for regulating the operation of SOBs include:

Amarillo Municipal Ordinance No. 5862
Dallas County Sexually Oriented Business Proposed Ordinance dated 6-7-95
Fort Worth City Code Section 21-18
Harris County Sexually Oriented Business Ordinance Draft dated 1/96
Randall Country Sexually Oriented Business Order No. 93-31
San Antonio Ordinance No. 82135

Laws Applicable to SOBs

Statewide laws available to all Texas agencies regulating SOBs include, but are not limited to the following:

V.C.T.A. Penal Code, Sec. 21.06. Homosexual conduct
V.C.T.A. Penal Code, Sec. 21.07. Public lewdness
V.C.T.A. Penal Code, Sec. 21.08. Indecent exposure
V.C.T.A. Penal Code, Sec. 21.11. Indecency with a child
V.C.T.A. Penal Code, Sec. 42.01. Disorderly conduct
V.C.T.A. Penal Code, Sec. 43.02. Prostitution
V.C.T.A. Penal Code, Sec. 43.03. Promotion of prostitution
V.C.T.A. Penal Code, Sec. 43.04 Aggravated promotion of prostitution
V.C.T.A. Penal Code, Sec. 43.05. Compelling prostitution
V.C.T.A. Penal Code, Sec. 43.22. Obscene display or distribution
V.C.T.A. Penal Code, Sec. 43.23. Obscenity
V.C.T.A. Penal Code, Sec. 43.24. Sale, distribution, or display of harmful material to minor
V.C.T.A. Penal Code, Sec. 43.25. Sexual performance by a child
V.C.T.A. Penal Code, Sec. 43.26. Possession or promotion of child pornography
V.C.T.A. Penal Code, Sec. 43.251. Employment harmful to children
V.C.T.A Texas Alcoholic Beverage Code, Sec. 101.62. Offensive noise on premises
V.C.T.A Texas Alcoholic Beverage Code, Sec. 101.63. Sale to certain persons
V.C.T.A Texas Alcoholic Beverage Code, Sec. 101.64. Indecent graphic material [on premises]
V.C.T.A Texas Alcoholic Beverage Code, Sec. 101.70. Common nuisance
V.C.T.A. Health and Safety Code, Sec. 343.011. Permitting a public nuisance

Nuisance Abatement in SOB Regulation

The United States Supreme Court added nuisance abatement statutes to the arsenal of SOB regulators in *Arcara v. Cloud Books*, 106 S. Ct. 3172, 1986. In *Arcara*, a New York City X-rated bookstore fronting for prostitution claimed First Amendment protection against closing by local authorities. In denying First Amendment protection, the Supreme Court made available to local governments nuisance abatement statutes which could be utilized to regulate difficult establishments (Potier 1987). These statutes permit any resident of the state of Texas, whether a private citizen or public official, to enter into a suit against a public nuisance. For example, the Texas Civil Practice and Remedies Code, Section 125 states in part that "any district, county, or city attorney, the attorney general or a citizen of the state may sue to enjoin the use of a place for the purposes of constituting a nuisance" (Vernon's Texas Codes Annotated 1995:605). Section 101.70 of the Texas Alcoholic Beverage Code also permits the same action as in Section 125 of the Texas Civil Practice and Remedies Code as a public nuisance, and public nuisance relief can also be found under the Texas Health and Safety Code, Sanitation and Environmental Quality, Section 343.011 which states that "a person may not cause, permit, or allow a public nuisance under this section on any premises."

Method

This bulletin is based on the responses of 18 Texas SOB regulating agencies that reported current or prior existing SOBs within their jurisdictions. Of the 18 agencies, 16 reported that SOBs are currently operating in their jurisdiction, and two reported their prior existence. For purposes of analysis, only 16 agencies will be listed as reporting due to the lack of data from two agencies that no longer have SOBs in their jurisdiction.

Adult Clubs Fight On

EL PASO—The U.S. Supreme Court's decision not to hear them out apparently won't dissuade the owners of adult businesses from continuing efforts to topple an El Paso ordinance they say is intended to shut them down. The high court refused to hear an appeal of a lower court's ruling upholding a 1987 law prohibiting sexually oriented clubs from operating within 1,000 feet of a church, school, residential neighborhood or other adult businesses. Attorney Michael Gibson said club owners aren't ready to give up their efforts to continue operating in locations prohibited by the ordinance. "Quite frankly, my people are ready to fight to the death," said Gibson, who represents Naked Harem, a nude club (*Houston Chronicle*, Nov. 29, 1995, p. 42A).

Sexually Oriented Businesses reported. All of the responding agencies indicated that one or more of the SOBs listed in Table 1 was either presently or had at one time operated within their jurisdiction.

Table 1

Type of Sexually Oriented Business

	Agencies Reporting	
Sale of sexually explicit books or magazines	14	(77.7%)
Partially nude female dancing	13	(72.2%)
Massage services	11	(61.1%)
Lingerie modeling	11	(61.1%)
Nude modeling	10	(55.5%)
Escort services	10	(55.5%)
Sexually related novelties	9	(49.9%)
Partially nude male dancing	8	(44.4%)
Theater presenting sexually explicit movies	8	(44.4%)
Selling or renting X-rated videos	8	(44.4%)
Totally nude female dancing	7	(38.8%)
Totally nude male dancing	4	(22.2%)
Bathhouses	2	(11.1%)

Selling sexually explicit books and magazines was the most common SOB reported. The prevalence and popularity of X-rated bookstores appears to dominate the SOB industry perhaps because most have expanded their stock to also include X-rated videotapes and sexually related novelties. Nine agencies (49.9%) indicated that they have SOBs vending sexually related novelties. However, it is uncertain if these were independent establishments or part of a larger business. Eight agencies (44.4%) reported X-rated movie theaters and businesses selling or renting X-rated videotapes. Five SOB establishments reported are overwhelmingly directed toward the male consumer. These include 13 agencies (72.2%) reporting partially nude female dancing, 11 (61.1%) reporting massage and lingerie modeling services, and 10 agencies (55.5%) reporting nude modeling and escort services. Seven agencies (38.8%) reported totally nude female dancing.

Eight agencies (44.4%) reported partially nude male dancing establishments. It is interesting to note that half as many nude and partially nude male dancing establishments are in operation as compared to female nude and partially nude establishments. Four (22.2%) respondents indicated that they have totally nude male SOBs in their jurisdiction.

Only two agencies (11.1%) reported the existence of bathhouses. Since these establishments cater almost exclusively to bisexual and homosexual males, this finding comes as no surprise. These establishments are usually located in major urban centers with a substantial male bisexual/homosexual population. The two agencies reporting bathhouses are located in major urban centers.

SOB Unit Personnel and Procedures

Of the 18 responding agencies, 16 (88.8%) indicated they had a unit dedicated to the regulation of SOBs. Later responses revealed that most of these units shared other duties such as general investigations, narcotics, or other special assignments. Twelve (66.6%) respondents said that they had departmental procedures regarding the regulation of SOBs, and six (33.3%) said that they did not.

Captains command two (11.1%) of the units, lieutenants command 11 (61.1%), sergeants command three (16.6%), and two (11.1%) agencies listed no commanding officer (see Figure 1).

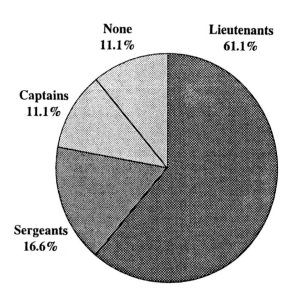

Figure 1

SOB Commanding Officers

Of the total amount of ranking officers assigned to SOBs, eight agencies (44.4%) had only one ranking officer, four agencies (22.2%) reported two, two agencies (11.1%) reported three, two agencies (11.1%) reported four, and two agencies (11.1%) reported none. One agency (5.5%) reported having the ability to utilize officers from other jurisdictions, two (11.1%) have attorneys assigned, and one agency (5.5%) had Alcoholic Beverage Commission personnel assigned.

The number of line-level officers varied dramatically. One agency (5.5%) reported 21 officers assigned, one agency reported 20 officers assigned, followed by 13, six, and two officers. Finally, four agencies (22.2%) claimed five officers assigned, five agencies (27.7%) had three, and three (16.6%) had no officers assigned to the SOB unit.

SOB Training

The respondents were asked to indicate the level of training regarding ordinances and statutes received by officers assigned to SOBs. Ten agencies (55.5%) indicated that their officers do not receive any training, and eight agencies (44.4%) reported training in ordinances and statutes. When asked how many hours of training SOB unit officers received, 12 agencies (66.6%) reported zero. It should be noted that agencies reporting zero indicated that their training was "on-the-job." Three agencies (16.6%) reported two hours of annual training, one (5.5%) reported four hours, one (5.5%) reported 20 hours, and one agency (5.5%) reported 40 hours of annual training (see Figure 2).

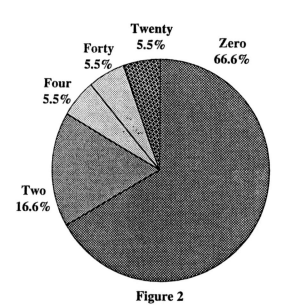

Figure 2

Hours of Annual Training

Crime and Regulation Problems Emanating from SOBs

It has been reported, often without substantiating empirical support, that SOBs are sources of serious crime and that they generate serious crime problems in their immediate vicinity. When asked what percentage of serious crime occurred in or close to SOBs, seven agencies (44.4%) reported zero. Two agencies (11.1%) attributed one percent, three percent, and 10 percent, respectively. One agency (5.5%) attributed five percent and four agencies (22.2%) listed "unknown." This finding is significant in that it disputes the common belief that SOBs generate serious crime within the business and in the neighboring community.

When asked what percent of time is spent regulating SOBs, two agencies (11.1%) indicated zero, one percent, two percent, five percent, 15 percent, 90 percent, and 100 percent, respectively. One agency (5.5%) reported 30 percent and three agencies (16.6%) reported 50 percent. As previously mentioned, a vast majority of these agencies are multi-tasked, and as indicated by the responses, only three could be considered as having regulation of SOBs as their primary task. This finding appears to indicate that, in general, the operation of SOBs do not present a serious crime problem to the majority of the agencies reporting. If they did, considerably more personnel and resources would be directed toward their regulation.

Respondents were asked to indicate the problem areas by percentage of time spent. Table 2 displays the responses in rank order according to the number of agencies reporting each element as a problem area. Table 3 ranks each element by total percentage points indicating the total amount of SOB regulation time expended.

Table 2

Problem Area by Percentage of Time Spent

	Agencies	Percentage(s) Indicated	Total %
Prostitution	11 (61.1%)	1, 5, 10, 10, 10, 15, 15, 15, 20, 30, 50	171
Obscenity	11 (61.1%)	1, 1, 10, 10, 15, 15, 15, 30, 30, 40	167
Drug sales	10 (55.5%)	1, 1, 2, 5, 5, 10, 15, 15, 20, 20	94
Contributing to delinquency of minor	10 (55.5%)	2, 2, 4, 5, 5, 5, 10, 10, 20, 30	93
Gambling	10 (55.5%)	1, 1, 1, 2, 5, 5, 5, 7, 10, 25	62
B-drinking	9 (49.9%)	1, 5, 5, 5, 10, 10, 10, 20, 20	86
Soliciting for prostitution	7 (38.8%)	1, 2, 5, 10, 16, 20, 30	84
Sex acts on premises	7 (38.8%)	2, 3, 5, 10, 15, 20, 50	105
Escort services	7 (38.8%)	1, 2, 5, 9, 10, 25, 40	92
Drug use	7 (38.8%)	1, 1, 1, 5, 10, 15, 20	53
Nude modeling	6 (33.3%)	1, 5, 10, 20, 25, 80	181
Rental & sale of X-rated videos	5 (27.7%)	1, 2, 5, 10, 20	38
Lingerie modeling	5 (27.7%)	1, 2, 3, 10, 25	41
Partially nude female dancers	4 (22.2%)	5, 10, 20, 70	105
Totally nude female dancers	4 (22.2%)	1, 2, 5, 20	28
Sexually explicit books and magazines	4 (22.2%)	1, 2, 5, 10	18
Massage services	4 (22.2%)	1, 3, 5, 10	20
Sexually oriented novelties	3 (16.6%)	1, 5, 10	16
Partially nude male dancers	3 (16.6%)	1, 2, 5	7
X-rated movie theaters	2 (11.1)	2, 10	12
Robbery	2 (11.1%)	1, 5	6
Bathhouses	1 (5.5%)	5	5
Rape	1 (5.5%)	1	1
Totally nude male dancers	1 (5.5%)	15	15

Table 3

Problem Area by Amount of SOB Regulation Time Spent

Violation	Agencies	Percentage(s) Indicated	Total %
Nude modeling	6 (33.3%)	1, 5, 10, 20, 25, 80	181
Prostitution	11 (61.1%)	1, 5, 10, 10, 10, 15, 15, 15, 20, 30, 50	171
Obscenity	11 (61.1%)	1, 1, 10, 10, 15, 15, 15, 30, 30, 40	167
Sex acts on premises	7 (38.8%)	2, 3, 5, 10, 15, 20, 50	105
Partially nude female dancers	4 (22.2%)	5, 10, 20, 70	105
Drug sales	10 (55.5%)	1, 1, 2, 5, 5, 10, 15, 15, 20, 20	94
Contributing to delinquency of minor	10 (55.5%)	2, 2, 4, 5, 5, 5, 10, 10, 20, 30	93
Escort services	7 (38.8%)	1, 2, 5, 9, 10, 25, 40	92
B-drinking	9 (49.9%)	1, 5, 5, 5, 10, 10, 10, 20, 20	86
Soliciting for prostitution	7 (38.8%)	1, 2, 5, 10, 16, 20, 30	84
Gambling	10 (55.5%)	1, 1, 1, 2, 5, 5, 5, 7, 10, 25	62
Drug use	7 (38.8%)	1, 1, 1, 5, 10, 15, 20	53
Lingerie modeling	5 (27.7%)	1, 2, 3, 10, 25	41
Rental & sale of X-rated videos	5 (27.7%)	1, 2, 5, 10, 20	38
Totally nude female dancers	4 (22.2%)	1, 2, 5, 20	28
Massage services	4 (22.2%)	1, 3, 5, 10	20
Sexually explicit books and magazines	4 (22.2%)	1, 2, 5, 10	18
Sexually oriented novelties	3 (16.6%)	1, 5, 10	16
Totally nude male dancers	1 (5.5%)	15	15
X-rated movie theaters	2 (11.1%)	2, 10	12
Partially nude male dancers	3 (16.6%)	1, 2, 5	7
Robbery	2 (11.1%)	1, 5	6
Bathhouses	1 (5.5%)	5	5
Rape	1 (5.5%)	1	1

Referral Capabilities and Assistance Availability

Fourteen (77.7%) agencies reported that they could refer SOB cases to other divisions within their department for further investigation. Of the divisions mentioned, 11 agencies (61.1%) could refer cases to the narcotics division, 9 agencies (49.9%) indicated general investigations, seven agencies (38.8%) used the patrol division, and one agency (5.5%) used the tactical division.

Fifteen (83.3%) of the respondents indicated that they could pull personnel from other divisions with regard to SOB regulation. Of the divisions mentioned, 10 agencies (55.5%) reported that they could draw personnel from general investigations, nine (49.9%) indicated the patrol division, eight (44.4%) indicated the narcotics division, and seven (38.8%) indicated the tactical division.

The respondents were asked from what outside agencies—local, state or federal—was assistance received. Fifteen agencies (83.3%) regularly receive assistance from the Alcoholic Beverage Commission and state and local licensing and permit agencies. Twelve agencies (66.6%) reported that they regularly receive assistance from fire code inspectors, and one agency (5.5%) received assistance from the state attorney general.

When queried about close working relationships with other local, state, and federal agencies, 14 agencies (77.7%) reported that they work closely with the local district attorney, and four agencies (22.2%) did not. Twelve agencies (66.6%) did not work closely with the U.S. attorney, while five agencies (27.7%) reported that they did. Twelve agencies (66.6%) did not refer cases to other federal agencies, but five agencies (27.7%) reported that they did.

Year SOB Unit Formed

The respondents were asked to indicate the year that their SOB unit was formed. Table 4 gives a breakdown of the year and number of SOB units established.

Table 4

Year SOB Formed

Year	Number
1970	1
1974	1
1978	1
1985	2
1986	1
1987	1
1988	2
1990	1
1992	1
1993	2
1994	1
1995	1
No unit	2
Unknown	1

SOB Unit Goals

The respondents indicated that the goals of their respective SOB units are manifold. Fourteen (77.7%) agencies reported that a portion of their goal is regulation of totally or partially nude dancing establishments. Fourteen (77.7%) agencies also reported that a portion of their goal is improving the community through regulation of SOBs, and thirteen (72.2%) reported uncovering prostitution in totally or partially nude dancing establishments. Twelve agencies (66.6%) listed reducing crime emanating from SOBs, 11 (61.1%) reported uncovering drug violations in totally or partially nude dancing establishments, regulation of prostitution in massage parlors and escort services, and uncovering gambling violations. Eleven agencies (61.1%) also reported that a portion of their goal is the regulation of Alcoholic Beverage Commission violations in totally or partially nude dancing establishments and uncovering violations regarding minors in SOBs. Eight agencies (44.4%) reported that a portion of their goal is improving the community through the elimination of SOBs, and five (27.7%) reported uncovering homosexuality in X-rated theaters and peep shows.

How SOBs Are Targeted

The survey queried respondents as to what SOB activities are targeted for enforcement. Sixteen (88.8%) responded that they target prostitution and soliciting for prostitution. Thirteen (72.2%) target sex acts and drug use on the premises. Eleven (61.1%) target obscenity violations, drug sales on the premises, and contributing to the delinquency of minor violations. Nine (49.9%) target gambling on the premises. Eight (44.4%) target B-drinking, and two (11.1%) target robbery and rape on the premises.

Violations Occurring in SOBs Which Receive the Most Attention

Respondents were asked to indicate which violations related to the operation of SOBs receive attention "very often," "often," "occasionally," "rarely," or "never." Table 5 contains the responses.

Table 5

SOB Violations Which Receive the Most Attention*

	Very Often	Often	Occ.	Rare.	Never
Prostitution	4	5	4	3	0
Obscenity	3	1	7	5	0
Sex acts on premises	3	3	6	3	0
Soliciting for prostitution	3	3	5	5	0
B-drinking	1	4	4	4	3
Sale of drugs	2	3	6	5	0
Contributing to the delinquency of a minor	2	2	5	6	2
Drug use	1	3	5	6	1
Gambling	0	1	4	10	1
Robbery	0	0	1	11	4
Rape	0	0	1	9	6

*Two agencies did not complete this portion because they were not actively involved in regulation efforts.

Origin of Complaints

When respondents were asked to identify the origin of the complaints from which regulatory action occurs, 14 (77.7%) reported that 20 percent or less came from police officers in the field, and 12 agencies (66.6%) reported that 50 percent or less originated from neighborhood groups. Nine (49.9%) indicated that 20 percent or less of the complaints came from citizens, except for one agency (5.5%) that reported 80 percent. Nine agencies (49.9%) also reported that 30 percent or less came from other city departments. Seven agencies (38.8%) reported that between 35 to 100 percent of their activity is initiated by officers assigned to the SOB unit. Five agencies (27.7%) reported that 20 percent or less of the complaints received came through calls for services, and four agencies (22.2%) reported that 20 percent or less of the complaints they received arose from data analysis.

Apparently, the vast majority of regulatory action taken against SOBs comes first from observed violations by members of SOB regulatory units and second from neighborhood groups and organizations. Complaints from customers of SOBs would most probably be found among citizen's calls for service. Thus, this would seem to support the victimless nature of the vast majority of action taken against SOBs.

Analysis of complaints handled by SOB units. Ten agencies (55.5%) indicated that they handled 20 or less complaints during the past year concerning SOBs. One agency (5.5%) handled 118, another 45, and another 150 complaints. Five (27.7%) agencies indicated that they did not know the number of complaints that were handled by their respective SOB unit. Of the complaints reported, the respondents were asked how many arrests were made during 1995 by the SOB unit. Seven agencies (38.8%) indicated that no arrests had been made. One agency each (5.5%) indicated 1, 7, 8, 15, 50, 103, 190, and 200 arrests, respectively. Three agencies (16.6%) did not know how many arrests had been made during the previous year (see Table 6). It should be noted that 11 (61.1%) agencies reported that they made 15 or less arrests during the entire year of 1995. When viewed over a period of one year, the arrest data reported do not appear to be high for SOB units with 20 or more personnel assigned. That would indicate that SOB units with 20 or more personnel assigned make approximately 17 arrests per month.

Of those arrests, respondents were asked how they were divided by percentage. Table 7 contains a listing by violation, the number of agencies reporting arrests for the violations, percentage of arrests per violation, and total percentage of the agencies reporting. Table 8 compares the arrest data presented in Table 7 with the problem areas reported in Table 2.

Table 6

Number of Arrests in 1995

Agencies	Arrests
7	0
1	1
1	7
1	8
1	15
1	50
1	103
1	190
1	200
3	Unknown

Injunction Against City Sought by Topless Club

Developers of a Memorial-area topless club said in a lawsuit Tuesday that the city of Houston stripped them of previously approved building permits, apparently because of their sexually oriented business. Town & Country Way Ltd. wants a state district court injunction against the city so remodeling can be completed on the building to house the club at 911 Town & Country Blvd. The City Attorney's Office declined to discuss the pending litigation, although the lawsuit says the contention that property adjacent to the club—land planned to be used for club patron parking—had a deed restriction that would not allow the (club) property to be used as a sexually oriented business. It would be unlawful, the lawsuit said, to apply that restriction to the club property, which has no such deed restrictions against adult clubs. State Judge Joseph "Tad" Halbach set a hearing on the request for an injunction against the city. The lawsuit was filed by Fort Worth attorney John Gamboa on behalf of Town & Country Way and its president, David Selmon. Gamboa said in the lawsuit that the company gained a lease agreement last November to develop a "gentlemen's cabaret" at the location. Company representatives paid the appropriate redevelopment fees to the city in February, and received approval of plans by all designated departments of the city March 13. The proposed parking lot, at 909 Town & Country Blvd., was leased by the company from Highland Management Co. last December, the lawsuit said. Gamboa wants the city barred from blocking construction or occupation of the premises or from having city employees harass the company or its workers. It also seeks unspecified damages and attorney fees (Flynn 1996).

Table 7

Arrests by Violation

Violation	Agencies	Percentage(s) Indicated	Total %
Prostitution	10 (55.5%)	5, 5, 10, 15 30, 30, 33, 35, 90, 100	323
Sex acts on premises	8 (44.4%)	3, 5, 10, 17, 50, 60, 100	235
B-drinking	6 (33.3%)	1, 5, 10, 10, 20, 30	76
Obscenity	5 (27.7%)	2, 5, 7, 30, 50	94
Soliciting for prostitution	6 (33.3%)	5, 9, 10, 10, 15, 60	49
Gambling	5 (27.7%)	1, 2, 10, 10, 15	38
Sale of drugs on premises	4 (22.2%)	2, 4, 10, 20	36
Contributing to delinquency of a minor	3 (16.6%)	2, 5, 50	57
Drug use on premises	2 (11.1%)	1, 10	11
Robbery	0		
Rape	0		

Table 8

Comparison of Arrest Data to Reported Problem Areas

Problem Area	Agencies Reporting A Problem	Agencies Reporting Arrests	Difference
Prostitution	11 (61.1%)	10 (55.5%)	1 (5.5%)
Sex acts on premises	7 (38.8%)	8 (44.4%)	1 (5.5%)
B-drinking	9 (49.9%)	6 (33.3%)	3 (16.6%)*
Obscenity	11 (61.1%)	5 (27.7%)	6 (33.3%)*
Soliciting for prostitution	7 (38.3%)	6 (33.3%)	1 (5.5%)
Gambling	10 (55.5%)	5 (27.7%)	5 (27.7%)*
Sale of drugs on premises	10 (55.5%)	4 (22.2%)	6 (33.3%)*
Contributing to delinquency of a minor	10 (55.5%)	3 (16.6%)	7 (38.8%)*
Drug use on premises	7 (38.8%)	2 (11.1%)	5 (27.7%)*
Robbery	0	0	0
Rape	0	0	0

*Indicates a substantial disparity between the reported problem and the corresponding report of arrests for the same violation

Laws Used in SOB Regulation

The respondents were asked to identify the various laws and codes utilized by their agency in SOB regulation. Eleven agencies (61.1%) used the Texas Code of Criminal Procedure, and five agencies (27.7%) indicated that they use these codes 100 percent of the time.

To determine which sections of the code are most utilized, the respondents were asked to identify those referred to most often. Eleven agencies (61.1%) use Section 101 of the Texas Alcoholic Beverage Code, and seven agencies (38.8%) indicated use of Section 125 of the Texas Civil Practices and Remedies Code, Common and Public Nuisances.

The survey asked the respondents if they believed more stringent laws would aid in regulating SOBs. Eleven agencies (61.1%) indicated that more stringent laws would not be helpful, and seven agencies (38.8%) desired more stringent laws.

Level of Success Achieved

The agencies were asked to characterize their success with regard to their chosen methods of regulating SOBs. The methods consisted of "Strict Code Enforcement," "Selective Enforcement of Certain Laws," "Enforcing Violations on a Complaint Basis," and "Encourage the Owners to Police their Own Businesses." They were ask to characterize their efforts using the following: "Very Successful," "Successful," "Somewhat Successful," and "Rarely Successful" (see Table 9).

Table 9

Methods of Regulation

Methods	Agencies
Strict Enforcement	
Very Successful	6 (33.3%)
Successful	5 (27.7%)
Somewhat Successful	4 (22.2%)
Rarely Successful	1 (5.5%)
Selective Enforcement	
Very Successful	4 (22.2%)
Successful	7 (38.8%)
Somewhat Successful	5 (27.7%)
Rarely Successful	0
Complaint Basis	
Very Successful	1 (5.5%)
Successful	4 (22.2%)
Somewhat Successful	5 (27.7%)
Rarely Successful	6 (33.3%)
Owners Police Their Own	
Very Successful	1 (5.5%)
Successful	5 (27.7%)
Somewhat Successful	2 (11.1%)
Rarely Successful	6 (33.3%)

Executive Room's SOB License Revoked

TEXARKANA, TEXAS—Police Chief Gary Adams has revoked the Executive Room's sexually oriented business license because an underaged female was allowed to enter on Aug. 4. A letter dated Sept. 15 was mailed by certified mail to Diana Goldman at the Executive Room, detailing the reason for the revocation and her appeal options. Though the controversial business has not opened its doors since Aug. 6, a federal lawsuit is pending and a Nov. 7 trial date stands. Dallas-based attorney Steven H. Swander, who represents Ms. Goldman, received a copy of the letter via fax Monday and a hard copy Tuesday. "I have not yet been able to get a hold of her. She calls occasionally," he said. "I don't really know if it will be appealed. I would advise her to appeal because I was told that the girl lied about her age and presented a false ID." According to the city's ordinance concerning the revocation of the SOB license, Ms. Goldman has 10 calendar days after she received the letter to appeal by filing a written appeal with the city secretary. If the letter is returned by the postal service, it will be posted on the door of the business and considered received on the day it is posted. The city's Permit and License Appeal Board makes a final decision on the matter. The city council updated that board at a meeting last month, appointing four people including Texarkana Citizens Against Pornography Co-Chairman Richard Walker. TCAP picketed the club nightly until its recent closure. If Ms. Goldman is displeased with the decision, she may appeal to the State District Court, the letter reads. If Ms. Goldman does not appeal or if the revocation is upheld, the business will not have a license and "there really would be no reason for the lawsuit any longer," said city Attorney Mary Kay Fisher. "There would be no issue to decide." An attorney whose firm was hired to represent the city in the case agrees. "If they don't appeal or if they appeal and it is upheld then they no longer have a license, so I think that would moot most of the issues in the case," Randall Goodwin said. The suit was filed against the city on May 10 by Ms. Goldman. It claims the business owners' 1st and 14th Amendment rights were violated by the May 8 suspension of its license. Adams suspended the license claiming it was within 1,000 feet of a church and school which are housed in the Bowie County Correctional Center. The business opened June 2 when a federal judge signed a temporary order against the city. It remained in operation offering nude dancing to male members until Aug. 6. A poster was taped on the front door Aug. 7 stating the business would reopen Aug. 10. It never did. Swander says other issues affect the business' closed doors. "I think a major issue is the definition of the codes to preclude people from bringing in their own alcohol," he said. Numerous times the Executive Room was raided and customers arrested because they brought liquor into the club. "Advertisements encouraged patrons to bring their own alcohol because Ms. Goldman understood the law to read BYOB was OK," Swander said. "In normal circumstances, if they had more financial backing, the city would have had another lawsuit filed against them," Swander said. He blames the protesting group [TCAP Texarkana Citizens Against Pornography], the lack of capital to fight the BYOB controversy and a dispute with the city over sales tax for the extended closure of the business (Brazile 1995).

Respondents were asked to indicate their future plans for their SOB unit. Fourteen agencies (77.7%) did not wish to expand but rather keep the unit at its present level. Two agencies (11.1%) indicated that they would like to expand, and two agencies (11.1%) did not respond.

Conclusion

Research has shown that pressure to regulate SOBs has been noted to originate from "... a small minority [which] is extremely adverse to the availability..." of such enterprises. Research also indicates that although the general public is concerned over the availability of sexually oriented material and businesses, "... it is sharply divided over the extent to which such materials should be regulated" (Wu & McCaghy 1993:13). A survey was conducted on residents of the Clinton neighborhood of New York City which borders on Times Square, an area notorious for SOBs. Among the findings was the common consensus among respondents that the demand for adult entertainment should be tolerated. However, the residents agreed that such enterprises should operate without constituting a nuisance to the neighborhood (Shaughnessy & Trebbi 1980).

As pointed out by the above research, ambivalence exists in various communities concerning the operation of SOBs. Perhaps one of the more effective methods of gauging community sentiment would be to heighten publicity when applications for SOB permits are submitted. Because the ultimate obligation of issuing permits has been given to county sheriffs and chiefs of police, public exposure may have a tendency to generate interest and subsequent action by concerned individuals or organizations. Their objections could be made known to the issuing authority either individually or through open public hearings.

As indicted by survey results, the vast majority of the regulatory action taken against SOBs does not emanate from public complaints or any other agency. Rather, arrests occur because of independent action taken by SOB unit officers monitoring the operation of the establishments. Oftentimes arrests are not effected at the time of the violation. Rather, warrants are secured for mainly misdemeanor violations that are usually executed simultaneously in raids on a number of SOBs.

References

Adult Clubs Fight On. (1995, Nov. 29). *Houston Chronicle*, p. 42A.

Aracra V. Cloud Books, 106 S. Ctr. 3172 (1986).

Brazile, S.W. (1995, Sept. 20). Executive Room's SOB License Revoked. *Texarkana Gazette*, p. 1D.

Cook, J. (1978, Sept 18). The X-rated Economy. *Forbes*, pp. 81-92.

Flynn, G. (1996, April, 10). Injunction Against City Sought by Topless Club. *Houston Chronicle*, p. A18.

Griffin, N.W. A Case History and Reevaluation of the Harris County Sexually Oriented Business Regulations. Paper presented to the Bill Blackwood Law Enforcement Management Institute of Texas.

Potier, I.L. (1987). Aracra v. Cloud Books, Inc.: Locking Out Prostitution. Hastings. *Constitutional Law Quarterly* 15(1):181-192.

Shaughnessy, E.J., and Trebbi, D. (1980). *Standard for Miller—A Community Response to Pornography*. Landham, MD: University Press of America.

Vernon's Texas Codes Annotated, Civil Practice and Remedies Code, Sec. 125 (1995).

Wu, B., and McCaghy, C. (1993). Attitudinal Determinates of Public Opinions toward Legalized Pornography. *Journal of Criminal Justice* 21:13-27.

Thank you to the following agencies for participating in this month's bulletin.

Arlington Police Department
Amarillo Police Department
Austin Police Department
Dallas Police Department
El Paso Police Department
Fort Worth Police Department
Harris County Sheriff's Department
Houston Police Department
Irving Police Department
North Richland Hills Police Department
Odessa Police Department
Pasadena Police Department
Plano Police Department
Randall County Sheriff's Department
Richardson Police Department
San Antonio Police Department
Texarkana Police Department
Travis County Sheriff's Department

CRIME ANALYSIS: THE ADMINISTRATIVE FUNCTION

Mark Stallo
Dallas Police Department

While listening to the radio on the way to work, you learn about a crime spree from the newscaster. When you arrive at work, you are anxious to begin examining the crime to narrow in on potential suspects and perhaps supply names or other leads to the detectives working the case. However, once you reach your office you are brought back to the reality of your assignment priorities. A council person, city official, or high-ranking police official has an important speech that afternoon, and his assistant forgot to ask ahead of time for vital speech material on crime statistics. As you are accustomed to hearing, they don't need the crime statistics you collected yesterday for a similar crisis; they need data from a different area, for a different time frame, for a different crime. You get to work, reluctantly putting aside your ideas about analyzing the crime spree.

The scenario just described probably occurs in cities across the country all too regularly. Despite frustration created for the ambitious crime analyst who may want to spend more time solving crimes, this type of work represents a very important function of any crime analysis unit: administrative crime analysis and reporting. This involves providing descriptive information about crime to department administrators, command staff, and officers, as well as to other city government personnel and the public. Such reports provide support to administrators as they determine and allocate resources or help citizens have a better understanding of the community. This chapter will discuss these consumers and goals in greater detail. It begins with a brief description of the crime analysis unit of the Dallas Police Department.

Administrative Analysis in Dallas

The Dallas Police Department crime analysis unit incorporates both centralized and decentralized approaches to analyzing crime and related information. The centralized portion of the crime analysis unit employs programmers who access information from the mainframe, network administrators who distribute data, and crime analysts who prepare the data for reports and analyze them for trends and patterns. This central office handles requests for information from the public, city hall, police administrators, civic groups, other police departments, and other city agencies that need assistance analyzing data.

The centralized office is also responsible for preventing overlap in job functions between their office and the decentralized units. Most of the information that is collected and delivered to the citizens, politicians, and others is not pertinent to the operation of the police department. Nevertheless, when there is a project related to analyzing the status of a particular type of crime (such as robberies, aggravated assaults, theft, etc.) over time, or of a specific group of people, such as juveniles or repeat offenders, the information is quickly shared with units throughout the department where it would be useful.

The responsibilities of the decentralized portion of the crime analysis unit are quite diverse. Analysts are scattered throughout the city, reporting to a number of different supervisors, each with varying needs. Each of the six patrol divisions has an analyst. Although they have similar responsibilities, analysts in each geographical area also have unique responsibilities. Within each division, the analyst is responsible for providing information to the leadership, patrol officers, and division-level detectives who generally handle burglary and theft offenses.

In addition to the six patrol analysts, there are a number of other analysts assigned to specific units. For example, analysts are assigned to the Crimes Against Persons Division, the Narcotics Unit, the Auto Theft Unit, and the Youth and Family Crimes Unit. These individuals have responsibility for preparing reports, collating and analyzing their specific crime responsibilities, and coordinating with the patrol analyst to provide the proper information for officers to intercede in potential problems within the city.

For these decentralized analysts to do their jobs effectively, a great deal of information is required. Since the early 1970s, the Dallas Police Department has collected much of that information through an automated data entry system. In its original incarnation, officers collected information in the field and subsequently called it in to a clerk for direct entry. This saved a great deal of time over the alternative of writing out the report and having it entered into the computer system later. Throughout the years the system has been refined to become even more efficient. Today, the information can be collected in three ways. The officer can gather the information at the scene and call a clerk to enter the report into the computer, the officer can enter the offense report directly into a mobile digital terminal (MDT), or, for non-emergency calls, a clerk can take the report directly over the phone from citizens. For the offenses of burglary, robbery, or rape, additional information related to method of operation (MO) is required that is not included on the MDT screens. The officer must therefore call these offenses in to a clerk.

These procedures greatly enhance the speed at which data is available for analysis. A typical offense can be entered and viewed by an analyst, detective, or patrol officer at a remote site within one to two hours. Before dissemination of the offense reports, arrest reports, and other paperwork, the information is reviewed by non-sworn employees called staff reviewers, who determine if the facts described in the various reports fit the proper offense or arrest categories. The information becomes available for supervisors' review or crime analysis functions depending on how quickly and accurately the staff reviewers complete their task. This is the only opportunity provided for reviewing a report before it is printed up at the investigative office and the affected patrol station.

The offense, arrest, and call (911) information can be accessed in raw form from mainframe terminals or personal computers with 3270 emulation. However, this large amount of raw information only demonstrates the volume of the problem and does not reflect patterns or trends. To obtain this kind of information in the past, officers had to ask a programmer who had the ability to write a program. This process became congested because the number of requests far exceeded the capabilities of the few staff programmers. To ameliorate this problem, the police department automated the information exchange and moved from the mainframe computer, where processing time was expensive and the programming function was cumbersome, to a personal computer environment, where data are more accessible and the costs are greatly reduced.

Currently, each night a batch program takes the crime, call, and arrest data for the previous day and creates a text file that is sent via modem from the city Information Services Department to the police department, located in another building. These data can then be disseminated and analyzed in customized ways. For example, the data can be obtained according to geographical location, specific crime type, premises location, or other variables. This allows a decentralized crime analyst to concentrate on his or her assigned crime problems, while allowing a crime analyst in the robbery section to specifically look at robberies, and officers assigned to the gang unit to review only gang-related crime. The central crime analysts receive information on all crimes that have occurred citywide. These crime analysts are responsible for developing crime patterns that cross division boundaries. This information is then distributed to the appropriate units for use in solving crime problems.

As information is updated, old files are overwritten. This enables analysts to see changes in the status of incidents under investigation (e.g., was the incident unfounded or was it deemed a crime and coded as such). In addition, new suspect or arrest information is added. This dynamic information structure gives the analyst an up-to-date picture of crime within the city. If the patrol detectives personally revise the investigative reports when new information is received, the likelihood that he or she will discover patterns and trends is greatly improved.

Administrative Crime Analysis -- General Concepts

The administrative function of crime analysis involves analyzing data in a number of areas to produce multiple reports. Most of the tasks are not related to life-threatening crime problems; even the term "administrative" implies that this type of analysis is routine and quite mundane. However, this type of analysis can lay the groundwork for future police actions, such as tactical action plans, and serves the information needs of many people. Administrative analysis communicates the status of crime to police personnel, city government officials, politicians, the press, and the public, to name a few. If administrative crime analysis is conducted correctly, the police department and the citizens it serves will be able to develop and execute effective plans to reduce crime.

As is true with all crime analysis, whether administrative or tactical, the timeliness of available data is paramount. Powerful computers and elegant software are not very effective if the data being analyzed are old. If your data are a week or a month old before being analyzed, the pattern may have changed, the criminal may have moved to another area or city, or the problem may have shifted in some other way. Therefore, it is imperative that an analyst find a way to get this data entered in a timely manner.

Requests for administrative crime analysis are usually initiated by outside agencies or individuals and involve comparing crime based on a number of factors. The heart of administrative crime analysis involves comparisons of one geographic area of a city to another, one time frame to another (e.g., this month compared to the last three months, this year compared to last year, first shift compared to second shift), or the number of different crimes per 1,000 residents. These requests can be broad in scope, such as how the largest 20 cities in the country compare by crime category per 1,000 inhabitants; or narrow, such as how many convenience store robberies occurred on the second shift, in June of this year, compared to June of last year. Another typical request is to analyze crimes in a certain area before and after a particular police program or action is implemented. These types of comparative analyses involve a great deal of effort and time and are potentially very valuable.

Caution must be exercised, however, when conducting these comparisons. While looking at crime before and after a police action seems like a logical approach to determining if that action effected a change, many police agencies fail to consider the many other factors that may have influenced a fluctuation in crime. For instance, if there has been a 5 percent reduction in burglaries in a certain area after a saturated patrol effort, this drop may or may not reflect the impact of saturated patrol on crime. For example, this 5 percent drop becomes insignificant if the citywide crime statistics have dropped by

10 percent. Alternately, saturated patrol may be only one of many efforts and environmental factors in the target area. Therefore, to avoid errors when making conclusions based on an analysis, a police department needs to look at several additional factors. These can include an overall measure of citywide change in crime, change in the crime of interest in other areas of the city, the weather, community programs, or concurrent police actions. This level of analysis will help the department to better understand what is working to effect change and what is not.

Geographic Information Systems and Mapping

Previous chapters have discussed another important area of administrative analysis: geographic mapping of crimes to conduct comparisons. For many consumers of administrative crime analysis, "a picture is worth a thousand words." They can look at a map that illustrates different sets of data and determine whether a crime pattern exists or if previously undiscovered relationships are revealed.

Mapping software has many uses, for administrative analysis, the best use of this software involves providing information about crime and police services based on numerous community boundaries. In today's community policing environment, analysts must provide information specific to neighborhood associations or crime watch groups rather than only by police-recognized beats or divisions. Mapping software allows the analyst to be flexible and to update crime and other police information within any geographic boundary.

Maps will vary depending on the types of information being conveyed. A spot map indicating where vacant houses, liquor stores, or suspected drug houses are located will often show a correlation to violent crime. This kind of map overlays symbols, representing the different types of buildings and crime that is occurring within certain geographic boundaries, on a street grid. Figures 6.1 and 6.2 are examples of spot maps.

Another very useful type of map, called a thematic or shaded map, can represent an analysis of one or more sets of data. This type of map can be used for a quick look at such factors as the number of crimes in a geographic area or the amount of income in the same area. Figures 6.3 and 6.4 are examples of thematic maps. By combining the symbol information with the thematic map, you can visualize certain relationships.

Geographic crime analysis has become much easier and more widespread than it once was. It is quite evident that this type of analysis will continue to grow and should be an integral part of any crime analysis function.

CENTRAL DIVISION

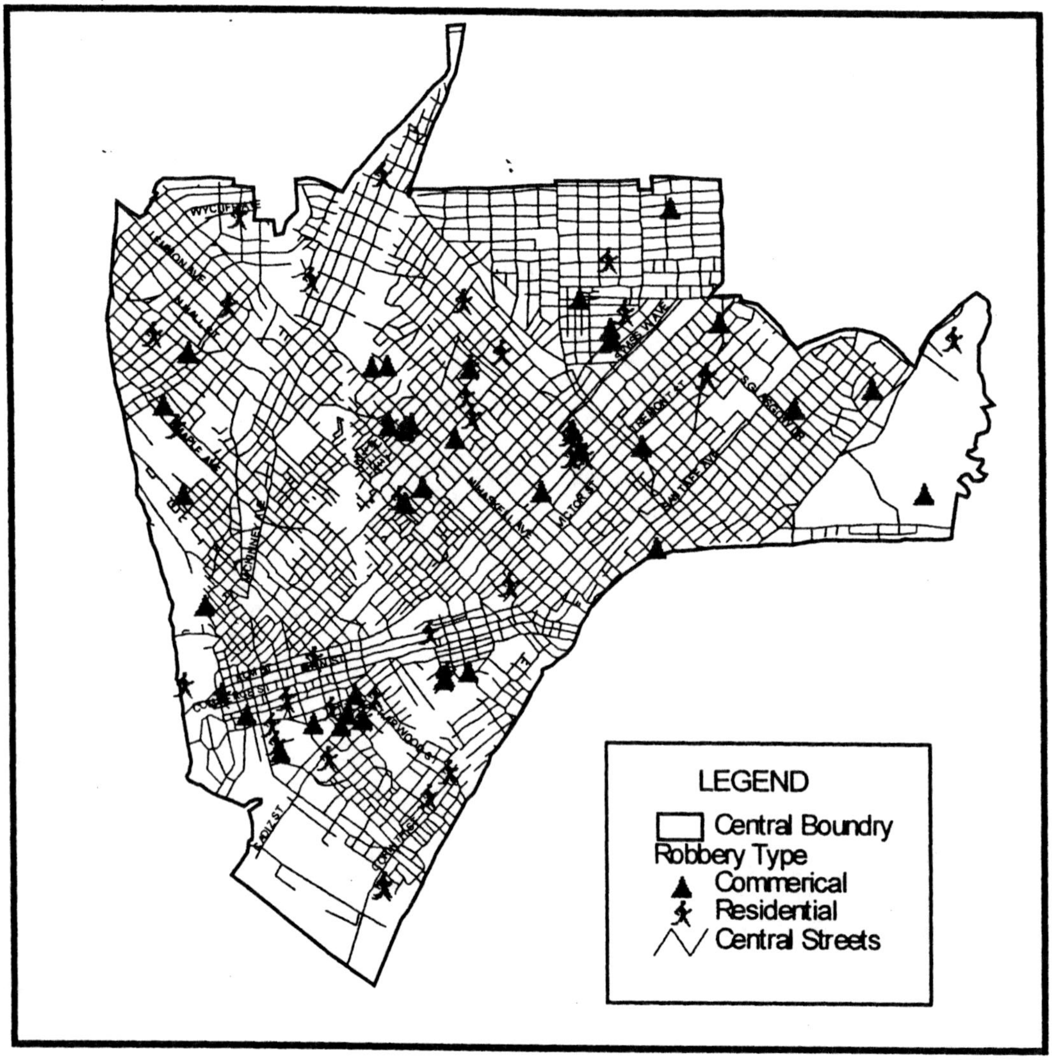

LEGEND
- Central Boundry
- Robbery Type
  - ▲ Commerical
  - 🏃 Residential
  - ∕\∕ Central Streets

INDIVIDUAL ROBBERY	
APRIL '91	139
MARCH '91	158
TOTAL	297
DIFFERENCE	-19

BUSINESS ROBBERY	
APRIL '91	30
MARCH '91	46
TOTAL	76
DIFFERENCE	-16

Provided By: Dallas Police

Figure 6.1

Information Management and Crime Analysis

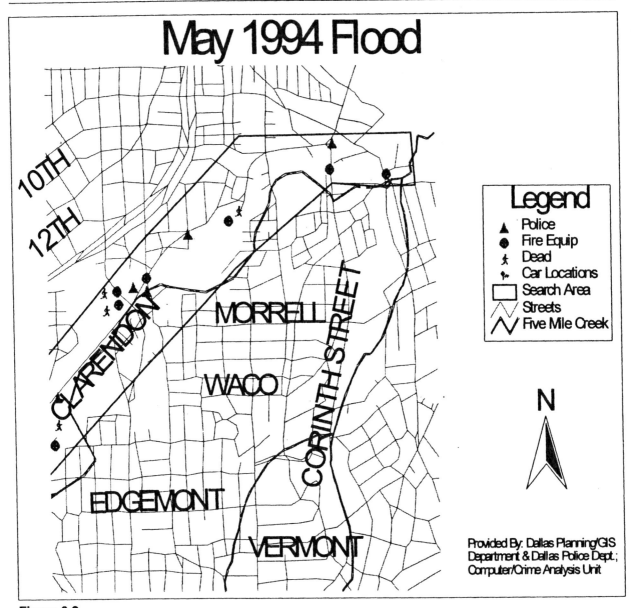

Figure 6.2

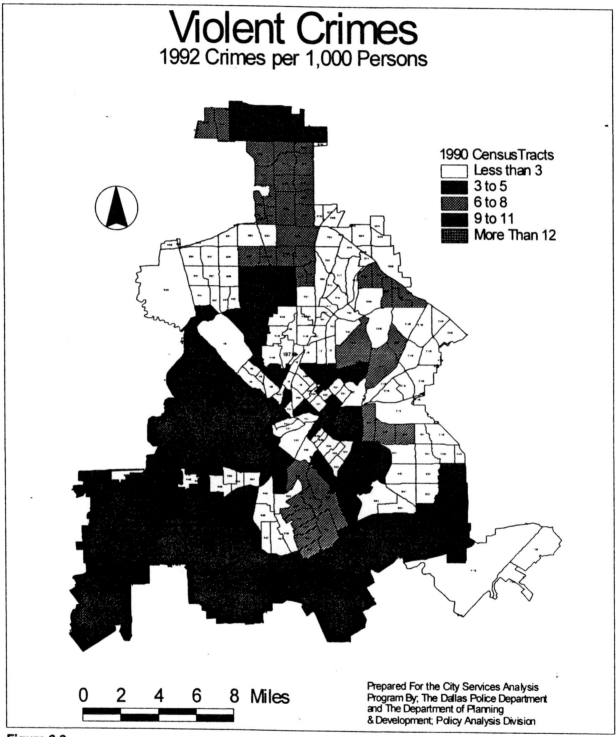

Figure 6.3

Crime Analysis

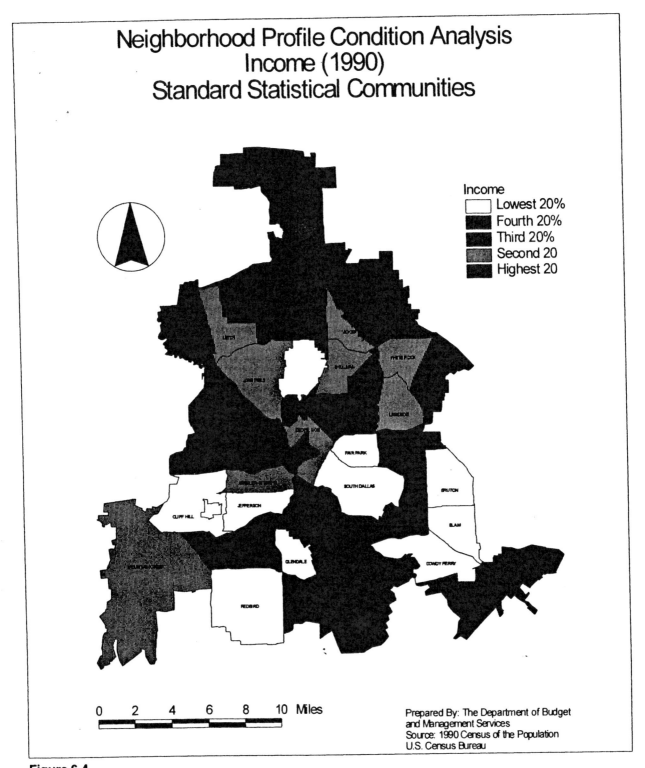

Figure 6.4

Linking Data

The ability to link data from various sources has also gained popularity among those in the political arena. For example, community leaders often request statistics that relate directly to their districts. These politicians may want to know how an area is split among various police leaders so they can know who is responsible for delivering service to constituents. In addition to crime and related data, politicians often want to know how the police department plans to address the crime problems identified. Although this exchange of information is important, it may create conflicts between individual political leaders and other city government officials. These conflicts can occur when politicians attempt to influence city operations that are generally the responsibility of city agency managers, such as the police chief, director of public works, etc.

Successful integration of community data and police activity depends on including census and other community data. Inclusion of demographic data ensures that community quality-of-life policy-making decisions will be based on a full understanding of community characteristics. The most recent reliable census data can tell an analyst how many individuals have lived in an area. In addition, analysts can capture median income, education level, and other valuable information. Analysts can also include the number of buildings that are occupied and vacant and the value of the property in a tract or block group, prove 'ding a clearer picture of the type of neighborhoods that exist within a city. This type of information is extremely important for police personnel or managers to consider when making decisions about how to address crime problems in a neighborhood.

Requests for Statistics from Community Members

Administrative analysis also provides crime statistics to community members, most often based on specific citizen requests. Police agencies do provide unsolicited information to the public if they believe the community should be aware of particular crime trends or problems. Community dissemination/education can absorb a great deal of police resources because the needs for this information are often quite diverse. Requests for information frequently come from citizens inquiring about an area in which they are considering purchasing a home, or from real estate agents who need to know about crime at 20 or 30 different addresses. Requests also arise from legal disputes between individuals and the business community, where both sides need information for a lawsuit.

Individuals or university students and professors conducting research also ask for police statistics in various formats. The press is another regular consumer of crime and related police information. Other police departments may request information for an investigation if they do not have access to the same information sources. These are just a few examples of the possible information requests the police department may receive. The source of requests is limited only by the imaginations of potential consumers of the information.

There are a number of options for police departments when trying to meet these information needs. Some departments have chosen to have analysts staff telephone request lines, but this is probably the most disruptive and expensive method for handling requests. When there are a large number of interruptions, the analytical function is impossible to maintain. As an alternative, police departments might benefit from placing crime statistics in the public library, on the Internet (as has been done in

Dallas), or in other public areas. This approach allows citizens to receive crime information at no cost and at their own convenience.

The Internet can also be used to anticipate the crime information needs of citizens. Many organizations and individuals need crime statistics based on geographic areas, and it is easy enough to post these types of statistics on a weekly or monthly basis. This approach could reduce some of the problems associated with press reporters or real estate companies who need information quickly. In addition, communicating with the public through the Internet gives the police department a progressive and responsive image. People can post inquires and review answers to their questions at their leisure. The Internet can be a very effective communication tool when used properly.

To enhance positive police/community relations, it may be necessary to automate these information dissemination processes. Without automation, a police department can quickly become overwhelmed by the number of requests for information from many sources.

Command Staff Reports

Analysts must provide crime information to field-level and executive staff on a timely and regular basis. The format of such reports can be simple, such as a small chart showing the status of crime for the previous week or month, or more complex, involving elaborate maps and statistical analysis indicating possible future trends. As for the content of these reports, they may include comparisons of each geographic area over time, both with itself and with other areas. This information can also be compared with a similar time frame from the previous year. This type of report indicates what percentage of different crimes have been committed and which are likely to continue unless some other variable causes change. It can also help determine if police-related activity may have caused the changes observed. Reports can also help identify where long-term and new crime hot spots are located. Table 6.1 contains examples of these types of basic reports.

When crime or a few components of crime are on an upswing, analysts should look at the reasons for the increase. This analysis is not for tactical deployment; the purpose is to identify why the increase is occurring. Once the causes of the increase have been identified, the department can address the upward crime trend. When conducting this type of analysis, analysts should compare recent crime statistics with a similar time frame in the past. This comparison should not only include the number of crimes but also where they occurred, who committed them, the victims, the MO, etc. The analysis could also include maps and charts to make the comparisons more user-friendly.

Another common type of administrative report involves analyzing groups of individuals to get a better understanding of the group and its probable impact on the future of crime. An example of this type of analysis involves looking at juvenile offender characteristics. A goal of this type of analysis might be to determine the size of the juvenile criminal population, how many repeat offenders are in the community, and what plans a department has implemented or needs to implement to reduce juvenile participation in crime. This approach could be used to examine family violence, gang-related crime, hate crimes, and many other offenses.

Recently, the Dallas Police Department examined the effect that juvenile offenders will have on future crime and the prime offending age. The Dallas Independent School District provided information on where student growth was estimated to be occurring and where after-school programs had been implemented, as well as planned future sites for such programs. One study revealed that there will be increases in elementary school attendance throughout the city; however, the northern section of Dallas will see more of an increase in middle and high school students. Furthermore, based on current plans, there might not be enough after-school activities in the northern section of town to keep these young people occupied. This type of information is very valuable in long-term planning for both the school system and the police agency.

Table 6.1

Staff Crime Briefing

I. INDEX CRIMES YEAR TO DATE   Thru 03-07-95

UCR Category	This Month	Last Month	% Change	This Year	Last Year	% Change	This Month	This Month Last Year	% Change
Murder	1	2	-50	4	7	-43	1	1	0
Rape	1	5	-80	15	21	-29	1	3	-67
Agg. Assault	37	42	-12	193	168	15	37	51	-27
Robbery									
Business	6	11	-45	31	26	19	6	3	100
Individual	26	21	24	130	176	-26	26	32	-19
Total Violent	71	81	-12	373	398	-6	71	90	-21
Burglary									
Business	27	30	-10	154	105	47	27	24	13
Residential	32	31	3	171	176	-3	32	46	-30
Theft	336	381	-12	1641	1549	6	336	387	-13
Auto Theft	66	89	-26	374	368	2	66	85	-22
Total	532	612	-13	2713	2596	5	532	632	-16

II. DIVISION REVIEW YEAR TO DATE VERSUS LAST YEAR TO DATE BY PERCENT   Thru 03-17-95

	Central	Northeast	Southeast	Southwest	Northwest	North Central
Murder	-43	-71	-21	-48	9	150
Rape	-29	9	-12	-27	-11	25
Agg. Assault	15	24	1	13	16	38
Robbery						
Business	19	-6	-11	3	-40	-21
Individual	-26	-2	2	-12	-12	-13
Total Violent	-6	9	-1	0	1	15
Business Burg	47	7	25	-4	13	10
Residential Burg	-3	-17	21	-3	14	13
Theft	6	1	-7	3	-5	10
Auto Theft	2	9	11	0	13	2
Total	5	1	3	1	2	10

Special Situations

Each community has special events that take place regularly, such as parades, fairs, sporting events, or other community affairs. These situations involve a great deal of planning by many city resources. Analysts may assist in planning by preparing a report that projects the types of crimes that may need to be addressed, or simply providing maps to the planning committee that can be used to organize a parade route or parking. It does not matter what type of event will be occurring; the crime analysis unit can give ample support to make event planning successful.

The type of analysis used for event planning parallels that used for other similar projects. For example, preparing a map for a parade or other event could include landmarks and community information. The same or very similar data could be used to work with citizens in making community policing decisions. Therefore, an analyst should maintain information on locations such as vacant buildings, liquor stores, businesses, suspected drug houses, and other places that can affect an event. This community information will greatly assist a department in properly staffing an event.

Staffing Allocation

The purpose of personnel allocation analysis is to optimize the use of resources. In other words, have appropriate numbers of officers been assigned to the proper geographic areas during the optimum hours? Usually, analytic software is used to calculate the consequences of personnel allocation changes. For example, analyses can estimate the response time to service requests for any specified time period. Once breaks, vacations, and other leaves are included, the necessary staffing can be calculated to accomplish stated goals.

Staffing allocation analysis is also used to configure beat realignments. This involves creating boundaries based on the type of workload in the area, while factoring in the specific geographic barriers of the region such as rivers, railroad tracks, expressways, bureau or division boundaries, and other types of restrictions. With the advent of community-based policing, traditional police boundaries are becoming less and less important.

Analysts as Trainers

Crime analysts are excellent resources for training front-line officers. They can convey the value of useful and timely information in making the police officer more productive. This training should involve a two-pronged approach: First, it is important to stress to the officers that placing accurate information in computer files, in their proper fields, is vital. For instance, in Dallas, officers and clerks have for many years placed important information about suspects' tattoos, scars, associates, and nicknames in the narrative section of the report instead of in fields designed to capture this information. Searching the "tattoo" field for thousands of offenses would not be very difficult, while searching the narratives of these same reports, looking for key phrases, is an impossible task. Second, once the officers realize the importance of properly capturing and updating information, they can be trained in the best methods of retrieving and using information to improve their abilities to serve the community.

Uniform Crime Reporting (UCR)

Almost all police departments participate in the UCR program through reports provided to a state planning agency that, in turn, delivers the information to the FBI. The crime analysts are often responsible for this reporting. In addition to requiring the crime data in its raw form, many state governments require other routine reports. These reports may be about hate crimes, gang-related crimes, forms of victimization, or virtually any other matter of community concern. Although these reports do not require a great deal of analysis or large amounts of time to prepare or update them, they may become quite time-consuming unless they are automated.

Conclusion

The administrative function is one of the most demanding and varied responsibilities for any crime analyst. This responsibility includes providing a range of services, including UCR reports, comparison reports, presentations, maps, staffing allocations, training, and many more not mentioned in this chapter, to a range of consumers, from police department personnel to citizens and politicians. The key to providing such a wide range of information, while maintaining efficiency and performing other duties, is to automate as many functions as possible. By automating reports and keeping regular formats, analysts can maintain other responsibilities and still find time to become a more efficient crime analyst.

MAPPING SOFTWARE AND ITS VALUE TO LAW ENFORCEMENT

Mark Stallo
Dallas Police Department

Across the country, many police departments are moving toward community-based or problem-oriented policing. Community-based policing is predicated on the concept that the police department should interact more closely with a community to solve problems and improve the quality of life. In order for this to work effectively, police departments and citizens need to share crime and police-related information. Unfortunately, many police departments only track or plot crime as it relates to traditional police boundaries. Some police departments have transformed their boundaries to accommodate the use of census or other demographic data. In other words, many police departments must evaluate crime statistics on a citywide basis or by artificial beats or reporting areas. A solution to this problem can come from a variety of mapping software programs. This software can be adapted to customize neighborhoods, crime watch groups and other more community-oriented boundaries.

Many benefits can be derived by using mapping software. Mapping provides the ability to display data in a variety of geographical forms, which makes identifying trends and patterns much easier. The data can be displayed by points in relation to boundaries, thematically and so on. Simply stated, it makes use of the old adage "a picture is worth a thousand words." The type of data is limited only by one's imagination. Today, data can be transferred from many sources into a database-compatible format, which can be read into most mapping software. The greatest expense with most mapping software involves the time required by personnel to become knowledgeable with the program. This process can range from a few weeks for basic usage to several months for more advanced applications. Nevertheless, the underlying assumption is that individuals will use the software on a regular basis to keep their skills at an optimal level.

The emphasis of this article is to demonstrate how to combine police-related information with other data, such as census tracts, for more effective decision making. As police departments and the citizens they serve become more familiar with each other and the specific problems related to individual neighborhoods, community-based policing will become more effective. Many times, information related to community activities and potential community problems (drug houses, bootleg houses and so on) is not analyzed together by the police department and citizens. This analysis can be most effective when the police accept and use current community input to analyze ongoing community problems. Examining all information related to the community (number of churches, schools and hospitals) can be directly linked with criminal activity, including crime, vice information and demography data.

By working with crime watch groups and neighborhood associations, the police department and the citizens can make informed decisions. All relative information about a neighborhood can be analyzed before a plan of action is developed. This article will explain that, by linking relationships within a community and using computer mapping software, a neighborhood can improve its access to information and increase its capability to improve the quality of life. Nevertheless, it is critical that the data related to this neighborhood be timely. Analysis is useless if the data being evaluated are several weeks old.

Initially, most would conclude that a mapping software package is useful for displaying dots or squares on a map, showing various occurrences of crime, calls for service or arrests. Often, the map covers a small neighborhood, showing these crimes or calls in close proximity to each other. Although this can be useful, there are many more procedures for analyzing and displaying the data. For example, Dallas police officers have always suspected that violent crimes resulted near drug-trafficking areas. Yet this was difficult to demonstrate until the violent crimes were mapped over suspected drug house locations. A very strong correlation was shown (see map 1). This type of information, in conjunction with other intelligence information such as bootleg houses, vacant buildings and so on, assists the police command staff in deciding where to deploy police personnel and conduct covert operations.

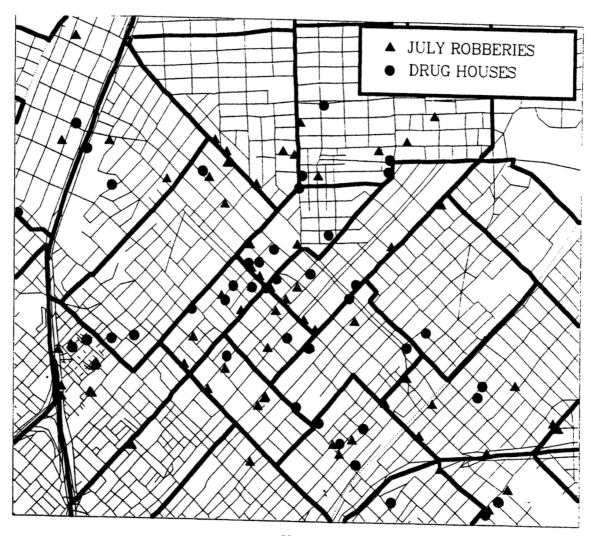

Map 1
Correlation between crime and drug house locations

Mapping software enables all of the neighborhood problems to be observed at one time. Furthermore, as these community problems are resolved, the impact of this action can be measured by reviewing recent occurrences of crimes or calls on a neighborhood map. This opens a dialogue with the citizens about their insight into the police department's approach to making their community a better place. The need for open communication with citizens and increased community involvement is paramount to community policing. Mapping specific calls, crimes or arrest data brings the message home, thus motivating local citizens to get involved.

There is a wide variety of information that has already been developed and that can assist police agencies in better serving their communities. For example, the Census Bureau has published extensive information related to populations in every community across the country. This information is at the census-block level, which is a very small geographical boundary. There are 310 census tracts and approximately 20,000 census blocks within the city of Dallas. Also, there is significant information on the tract level, which is a conglomerate of census blocks. This information can assist police departments with understanding the population by race, income, occupancy information, and the value of housing in neighborhoods. This can be invaluable in customizing a plan to improve a neighborhood. Crime and other related police functions are the major components missing when an analysis of a neighborhood is conducted. This problem can be corrected by associating as much data as possible with neighborhood boundaries. The integration of police data, demographic data and other information can improve the planning process.

The boundary function of most mapping software is equally important for analysis purposes. For years, police departments have divided their cities by reporting areas (districts), beats, sectors, and divisions (bureaus or precincts). These boundaries are assigned a number, and the entire police operation is driven by these boundary names. Beats and car assignments are designed by these boundaries; however, very few people know where the boundaries are located without seeing them mapped and displayed on paper. Often, police boundaries are ranked by crime volume, without regard for how close each boundary is located to another. Today, a computerized map provides a means for displaying a variety of layers of boundaries, from the smallest to the largest, as they relate to the city. For example, other frequently used boundaries, such as census blocks and tracts, crime watch boundaries, council districts, and public housing, can be layered to show a specific correlation. The data displayed can be linked to existing data about geographical areas, such as crime to census data.

A variety of significant factors makes these boundaries extremely useful. For instance, by using a boundary, the map contained within it can be developed into a separate map. Data within a boundary can be counted, singled out for display or analyzed in several ways. In addition, many police departments are only able to report crime by designated police boundaries. This occurs because many departments have not perceived a need to produce statistics by communities or other non-police boundaries. A mapping package provides the ability to report crime in a flexible manner.

Data read by mapping systems can be in a variety of formats. Police-related information ranges from crimes, calls for service, arrests, known offenders, and suspected drug house locations, to several other categories. By using base boundary data, such as the name of a boundary, data can be collected into one database, as it relates to any specific boundary. The police data can also be added to other list data, such as population, property value and other census data. Furthermore, it can be determined if a crime victim and/or suspect(s) fit the general profile of the inhabitants of the neighborhood. Did the complainant come to shop, buy drugs or attend an event? In addition, any data with an address can be associated to a boundary.

Once the data have been added to the system, several options exist for using the data. Data can be searched in multiple ways. The data that are displayed on the computer screen can also be counted and interpreted. If a crime pattern is visually observed, the computer can provide a report of the incidents that are displayed on the screen. There are numerous types of data searches. A typical search might be to find a certain type of crime that occurred in a particular time frame, with a similar method of operation and similar suspect descriptions. This analysis can be handled outside of a mapping program or within. Either method will create the search. Distance searches can be more efficiently covered within mapping software. Diameter searches or what you see is what you get (WYSIWYG) on the computer screen can also be conducted within mapping software.

Throughout the previous paragraphs, several concepts have been covered. Sample uses of a mapping system can be used to explain these concepts. The use of tabular data that is related to a boundary, such as the number of murders or the number of disturbance calls by reporting area or beat, is a basic but important function. Tabular data can be related to the boundary within the mapping program. The data are then displayed by a colored or shaded thematic map, which gives a quick overview of the density of crimes or calls within any type of geographic area as compared to other similar geographic areas (map 2). Another key factor in examining boundary data is the use of population data. For example, if a black male is the victim of a crime in a predominantly white or Hispanic neighborhood, what brought the black complainant to the neighborhood? This type of analysis helps to pinpoint community problems.

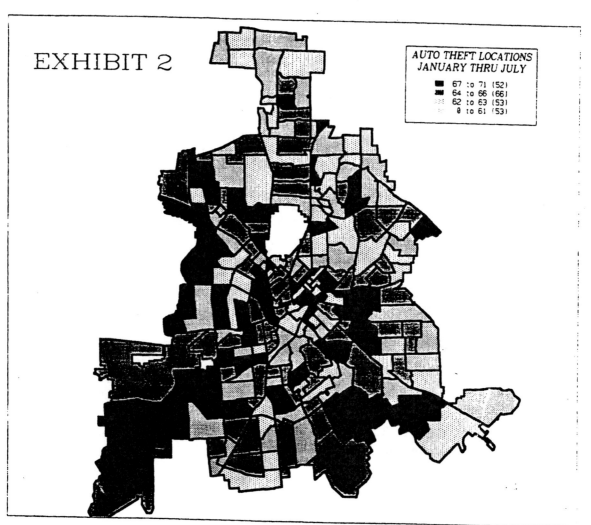

Mapping software can be a very useful tool within the law enforcement field. Many useful mapping software packages are on the market today. The prices and functions of these packages vary widely. Prices range from $1,000 to many times this amount. Some packages can perform very exact engineering functions, while others are designed for the purpose of displaying information. Many of the mapping software can interact with a variety of other software, such as spreadsheets and databases, which broaden their function. Some software can read data only from within a standard programming environment, while others can read data from unlimited sources. Use of this technology provides versatility and produces the capability to perform a wide variety of studies. Therefore, it is important to consider a police department's current and future needs before purchasing mapping software. Many times, it may be practical to purchase a relatively inexpensive program while the more complicated package is being developed.

Mapping software operates on several platforms, including the mainframe environment, UNIX, Macintosh, Windows and DOS. These software have a wide array of uses, but all contain three basic components: maps, boundaries and data. One other very important distinction must be made. Maps can be displayed in multiple formats; however, this article has been limited to vector (line map) and raster (pictorial map) capabilities. Mapping brings about tremendous opportunities for observing data. The most effective method of explaining how data can be displayed is to outline a few examples of the major functions of typical mapping software.

There are other more general uses of mapping software, such as designing parade routes or drawing landmarks inside of the map for a special event. It is also possible to import building designs and display building plans, floor by floor. This is useful for tactical operations or when evaluating offenses inside multilevel buildings. In some areas of the country, agencies have the ability to link the streets (vector images) to a map of the underlying terrain (raster images), which opens a wide variety of applications, such as crime scene search, auto accident reconstruction and emergency preparedness. The future of mapping in law enforcement is wide open and bounded only by one's imagination.

CRITICAL THOUGHT AND ANALYSIS WORKSHEET

Issues in Criminal Justice

1) What are three major points made in the article you just read about crime or justice administration in Texas?

2) Do you agree or disagree with the three major points you identified in Question #1 above? Explain why you agree or disagree with the major points? What evidence exists to support your positions?

Acknowledgments

"The Killer Cadets" written by Skip Hollandsworth. Reprinted with permission from the December, 1996 edition of *Texas Monthly*.

"Crime in Texas: 1996" from the Texas Department of Public Safety, April 1997.

"Crossing" written by Robert Draper. Reprinted with permission from the December, 1995 edition of *Texas Monthly*.

"McDuff was Free to Kill" written by Gary Cartwright. Reprinted with permission from the August, 1992 edition of *Texas Monthly*.

"The Public Hell of Bob Carreiro" written by Mimi Swartz. Reprinted with permission from the January, 1996 edition of *Texas Monthly*.

"Family Violence Intervention: Attitudes of Texas Officers" written by Sylvia Stainaker, Pat Shields & Daniel Bell. Reprinted with permission from the October, 1993 edition of *Police Chief*. Copyright © 1993 by International Association of Chiefs of Police.

"Merchant of Death" written by Robert Bryce. Reprinted with permission from the June, 1996 edition of *Texas Monthly*.

"See No Evil" written by Skip Hollandsworth. Reprinted with permission from the May, 1993 edition of *Texas Monthly*.

"The Sweet Song of Justice" written by Joe Nick Patoski. Reprinted with permission from the March, 1997 edition of *Texas Monthly*.

"The Last Ride of the Polo Shirt Bandit" written by Helen Thorpe. Reprinted with permission from the March, 1997 edition of *Texas Monthly*.

"Gang Rape" written by Bill Minutaglio. Reprinted with permission from the May 31, 1992 edition of *Dallas Morning News*.

"Texas Rangers Revisited: Old Themes and New Viewpoints" written by Harold Weiss, Jr. Reprinted with permission from the April, 1994 edition of *Southwestern Historical Quarterly*. Copyright © 1994 by Texas State Historical Association.

"The Twilight of the Texas Rangers" written by Robert Draper. Reprinted with permission from the February, 1994 edition of *Texas Monthly*.

"The Death Beat" written by Christine Wicker. Reprinted with permission from the February 8, 1994 edition of the *Dallas Morning News*.

"Rush to Justice" written by Keith Kachtick. Reprinted with permission from the January, 1996 edition of *Texas Monthly*.

"The High Times of Gerry Goldstein" written by Mimi Swartz. Reprinted with permission from the April, 1996 edition of *Texas Monthly*.

"Does DaRoyce Mosely Deserve to Die?" written by Skip Hollandsworth. Reprinted with permission from the February, 1996 edition of *Texas Monthly*.

"Crime and Punishment in Dallas" written by Richard Fricker. Reprinted with permission from the July, 1989 edition of ABA Journal. Copyright © 1989 by Richard Fricker.

"Who Determines Who will die" written by Tamar Lewin. Reprinted with permission from the February 23, 1995 edition of *New York Times*. Copyright © 1995 by New York Times.

"Death Row Granny" by Glenna Whitley. Reprinted with permission from the Jan/Feb, 1995 edition of the *Dallas Observer*. Copyright © 1995 by Glenna Whitley.

"Prison Guards and Snitches" written by James Marquardt, editor. Reprinted with permission from The Dilemmas of Corrections: Contemporary Readings, 3ed. Copyright © 1986 by Waveland Press.

"A Guard in Gangland" written by Robert Draper. Reprinted with permission from the August, 1991 edition of *Texas Monthly*.

"Judicial Refrom and Prison Control" written by James Marquardt. Reprinted with permission from Vol 19, 1985 of *Law and Society Review*. Copyright © 1985 by Law & Society Association;.

"Private Prisons in Texas: The Penology for Profit" written by Philip Ethridge and James Marquart. Reprinted with permission from the March, 1993 edition of *Justice Quarterly*. Copyright © 1993 by the Academy of Criminal Justice Sciences.

"The Great Texas Prison Mess" written by Robert Draper. Reprinted with permission from the May, 1996 edition of *Texas Monthly*.

"Black Before Blue" written by Dusty Rhodes. Reprinted with permission from the September 17, 1992 edition of the *Dallas Observer*.

"The Rookie" written by Dusty Rhodes. Reprinted with permission from the September 17, 1992 edition of the *Dallas Observer*.

"Regulation of Sexually Oriented Businesses" written by Jim Ruiz. Reprinted with permission from the TELEMASP Bulletin, Vol 3. No. 4.